MindTap
QUICK START GUIDE

1. To get started, navigate to www.cengagebrain.com and select "Register a Product."

A new screen will appear prompting you to add a Course Key. A Course Key is a code given to you by your instructor — this is the first of two codes you will need to access MindTap. Every student in your course section should have the same Course Key.

2. Enter the Course Key and click "Register."

If you are accessing MindTap through your school's Learning Management System, such as BlackBoard or Desire2Learn, you may be redirected to use your Course Key/Access Code there. Follow the prompts you are given and feel free to contact support if you need assistance.

3. Confirm your course information above and proceed to the log in portion below.

If you have a CengageBrain username and password, enter it under "Returning Students" and click "Login." If this is your first time, register under "New Students" and click "Create a New Account."

4. Now that you are logged in, you can access the course for free by selecting "Start Free Trial" for 20 days or enter in your Access Code.

Your Access Code is unique to you and acts as payment for MindTap. You may have received it with your book or purchased separately in the bookstore or at www.cengagebrain.com. Enter it and click "Register."

NEED HELP?

VOYAGES
in World History

VOYAGES
in World History

Volume 2: Since 1500

Third Edition

Valerie Hansen
YALE UNIVERSITY

Kenneth R. Curtis
CALIFORNIA STATE UNIVERSITY LONG BEACH

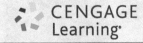

CENGAGE
Learning·

Australia · Brazil · Mexico · Singapore · United Kingdom · United States

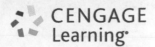

Voyages in World History **Volume 2: Since 1500, Third Edition**
Valerie Hansen/Kenneth R. Curtis

Product Director: Paul R. Banks

Product Manager: Scott A. Greenan

Development Editor: Jan Fitter

Media Editor: Kate MacLean

Product Assistant: Andrew Newton

Marketing Manager: Kyle Zimmerman

Senior Content Project Manager: Carol Newman

Senior Art Director: Cate Rickard Barr

Manufacturing Planner: Fola Orekoya

IP Analyst: Alexandra Ricciardi

IP Project Manager: Betsy Hathaway

Production Service and Compositor: Cenveo® Publisher Services

Text and Cover Designer: Melissa Welch, Studio Montage

Cover Image: Chinese Artist Ai Weiwei holds some seeds from his Unilever Installation 'Sunflower Seeds' at the Tate Modern on October 11, 2010 in London, England. The sculptural installation comprised 100 million handmade porcelain replica sunflower seeds. Visitors to the Turbine Hall were able to walk on the work, which opened on October 12, 2010 and ran through May 2, 2011. (Photo by Peter Macdiarmid/ Getty Images)

Library of Congress Control Number: 2015942983

Student Edition:
ISBN: 978-1-305-58341-2

Loose-leaf Edition:
ISBN: 978-1-305-86535-8

Cengage Learning
20 Channel Center Street
Boston, MA 02210
USA

Cengage Learning is a leading provider of customized learning solutions with employees residing in nearly 40 different countries and sales in more than 125 countries around the world. Find your local representative at **www.cengage.com**.

Cengage Learning products are represented in Canada by Nelson Education, Ltd.

To learn more about Cengage Learning Solutions, visit **www.cengage.com**.

Purchase any of our products at your local college store or at our preferred online store **www.cengagebrain.com**.

Printed in Canada
Print Number: 01   Print Year: 2017

Brief Contents

Contents

CHAPTER 15

Maritime Expansion in the Atlantic World, 1400–1600   434

Traveler: *Bernardino de Sahagún*

CHAPTER 16

Maritime Expansion in Afro-Eurasia, 1500–1700   468

Traveler: *Matteo Ricci*

Photo credits: Clipart courtesy FCIT, from *Narrative and Critical History of America* (New York: Houghton, Mifflin, and Company, 1886)I:156 // Courtesy of the Ricci Institute for Chinese-Western Cultural History at the University of San Francisco Center for Asia Pacific Studies

CHAPTER **17**

Religion, Politics, and the Balance of Power in Western Eurasia, 1500–1750 *498*

Traveler: *Evliya Çelebi*

CHAPTER **18**

Empires, Colonies, and Peoples of the Americas, 1600–1750 *530*

Traveler: *Catalina de Erauso*

Photo credits: Portrait of an African, c.1757–60 (oil on canvas), Ramsay, Allan (1713–84) (attr. to)/Royal Albert Memorial Museum, Exeter, Devon, UK/Bridgeman Images // Portrait of Rammohun Roy (1774–1833) 1832 (oil on canvas), Briggs, Henry Perronet (1792–1844)/© Bristol Museum and Art Gallery, UK/Bridgeman Images

Photo credits: Mikhail Alexandrovitch Bakounine, c.1865 (photogravure), Nadar, (Gaspard Felix Tournachon) (1820–1910)/Private Collection/The Stapleton Collection/Bridgeman Images // Portrait of a Japanese man named Fukuzawa Yukichi, a samurai and officer on the 1862 Takenouchi mission to Europe, employed as an interpreter of Dutch and English, 1862 (albumen print), Potteau, Jacques-Philippe (1807–76)/Pitt Rivers Museum, Oxford, UK/Bridgeman Images

CHAPTER **27**

War, Revolution, and Global Uncertainty, 1905–1928

Traveler: *Emma Goldman*

806

CHAPTER **28**

Responses to Global Crisis, 1920–1939

Traveler: *Halide Edib*

840

Photo credits: Library of Congress Prints and Photographs Division[C-USZ62-48793] // From *Memoirs of Halide Adviar* Edib (N.J.: Gorgias Press). Reprinted by permission of Gorgias Press.

CHAPTER 29
The Second World War and the Origins of the Cold War, 1939–1949
872

Traveler: *Nancy Wake*

CHAPTER 30
The Cold War and Decolonization, 1949–1975
900

Traveler: *Ernesto ("Che") Guevara, 1960*

CHAPTER 31
Toward a New World Order, 1975–2000   *932*
Traveler: *Nelson Mandela*

CHAPTER 32
Voyage into the Twenty-First Century   *966*

Traveler: *Ai Weiwei*

Photo credits: Peter Macdiarmid/Getty Images

MAPS

VISUAL EVIDENCE IN PRIMARY SOURCES

MOVEMENT OF IDEAS THROUGH PRIMARY SOURCES

WORLD HISTORY IN TODAY'S WORLD

Preface

What makes this book different from other world history textbooks?

- Each chapter opens with a narrative about a traveler, whose real-life story is woven throughout the chapter. The *interactive map activity*, available through MindTap™, continues the story of the traveler online, allowing students to click on each important location the traveler visited to learn more about the historical, cultural, and political significance of the journey.
- Shorter than most world history textbooks, this survey still covers all of the major topics required in a world history course, as well as others we have found to be of interest to our students.
- The book's theme of movement highlights cultural contact and discovery and is reinforced in each chapter through the opening map, highlighting a specific traveler's journey, as well as through the unique chapter features, including *Movement of Ideas Through Primary Sources* and *Visual Evidence in Primary Sources*, which teach analytical skills and provoke critical thinking by inviting students to compare viewpoints.
- Brief *Context & Connections* inserts within the chapter text provide specific linkages and comparisons with other regions and periods, and the broader chapter-ending *Context and Connections* essay helps students understand the connections among different regions and periods, as well as global effects and trends.
- A robust digital support package includes numerous ways for students to further engage with the main themes of the text. The interactive environment of MindTap™ helps students exercise their critical thinking skills through a variety of activities and in a variety of formats.
- A beautiful, engaging design features an on-page glossary, a pronunciation guide, and chapter-opening focus questions. These tools help students grasp and retain the main ideas of the chapters.

This world history textbook will, we hope, be enjoyable for students to read and for instructors to teach. We have focused on thirty-two different people and the journeys they took, starting forty thousand years ago with Mungo Man in Australia (Chapter 1) and concluding in the twenty-first century with Chinese artist Ai Weiwei. Each of the thirty-two chapters introduces multiple focus points. First, the traveler's narrative introduces the home society and the civilizations visited, demonstrating our theme of the movement of people, ideas, trade goods, and artistic motifs and the results of these contacts. We introduce other evidence, often drawn from primary sources (marked in the running text with italics), to help students reason like historians. Each chapter also covers changes in political structure, the spread of world religions, and prevailing social structure and gender relations. Other important topics include cultural components and the effects of technology and environment.

The chapter-opening narratives enhance the scope and depth of the topics covered. The travelers take us to Tang China with the Japanese Buddhist monk Ennin, to Africa and South Asia with the hajj pilgrim Ibn Battuta, to Peru with the cross-dressing soldier and adventurer Catalina de Erauso, across the Atlantic with the African Olaudah Equiano, and to Europe during the Industrial Revolution with the Russian anarchist Mikhail Bakunin. Their vivid accounts are important sources about these long-ago events that shaped our world. Almost all of these travel accounts are available in English translation, listed in the suggested readings at the end of each chapter. Students new to world history, or to history in general, will find it easier, we hope, to focus on the experience of thirty-two individuals before focusing on the broader trends in their societies and their place in world history.

Instead of presenting a canned list of dates, each chapter covers the important topics at a sensible and careful pace, without compromising coverage or historical rigor. Students compare the traveler's perceptions with alternative sources, and so awaken their interest in the larger developments. Our goal was to select the most compelling topics and engaging illustrations from the entire record of human civilization and to present them in a clear flowing narrative in order to counter the view of history as an interminable compendium of geographical place, names, and facts.

We have chosen a range of travelers, both male and female, from all over the world. These individuals help cast our world history in a truly global format, avoiding the Eurocentrism that prompted the introduction of world history courses in the first place. Some travelers were well born and well educated, while others were not.

Our goal in focusing on the experience of individual travelers is to help make students enthusiastic about world history, while achieving the right balance between the traveler's experience and the course material. We measure our success by all the encouragement we have received both from instructors who teach the course and from students.

We aspire to answer many of the unmet needs of professors and students in world history. Because our book is not encyclopedic, and because each chapter begins with a narrative of a trip, our book is more readable than its competitors, which strain for all-inclusive coverage. They pack so many names and facts into their text that they leave little time to introduce beginning students to historical method, which we do explicitly at the start of Chapter 2 and continue to do in subsequent chapters. Because our book gives students a chance to read primary sources in depth, particularly in the Movement of Ideas Through Primary Sources feature, instructors can spend class time teaching students how to reason historically—not just imparting the details of a given national history. Each chapter includes focus questions that make it easier for instructors new to world history to facilitate interactive learning.

Our approach particularly suits the needs of young professors who have been trained in only one geographic area of history. Our book does not presuppose that instructors already have broad familiarity with the history of each important world civilization.

Theme and Approach

Our theme of movement and contact is key to world history because world historians focus on connections among the different societies of the past. The movement of people, whether in voluntary migrations or forced slavery, has been one of the most fruitful topics for world historians, as are the experiences of individual travelers. Their reactions to the people they met on their journeys reveal much about their home societies as well as about the societies they visited.

Our focus on individual travelers illustrates the increasing ease of contact among different civilizations with the passage of time. This theme highlights the developments that resulted from improved communications, travel among different places, the movement of trade goods, and the mixing of peoples. Such developments include the movement of world religions, mass migrations, and the spread of diseases like the plague. *Voyages* shows how travel has changed over time—how the distance covered by travelers has increased at the same time that the duration of trips has decreased. As a result, more and more people have been able to go to societies distant from their own.

Voyages and its integrated online components examine the different reasons for travel over the centuries. While some people were captured in battle and forced to go to new places, others visited different societies to teach or to learn the beliefs of a new religion like Buddhism, Christianity, or Islam. This theme, of necessity, addresses questions about the environment: How far and over what terrain did early man travel? How did sailors learn to use monsoon winds to their advantage? What were the effects of technological breakthroughs like steamships, trains, and airplanes—and the use of fossil fuels to power them? Because students can link the experiences of individual travelers to this theme, movement provides the memorable organizing principle for the book, a principle reinforced in the interactive online journeys offered by the *interactive map activity* on MindTap.

Having a single theme allows us to provide broad coverage of the most important topics in world history. Students who use this book will learn how empires and nations grew in power or influence, and how their ways of organizing their governments differed. Students need not commit long lists of rulers' names to memory; instead they focus on those leaders who created innovative political structures. This focus fits well with travel, since the different travelers were able to make certain journeys because of the political situation at the time. For example, William of Rubruck was able to travel across all of Eurasia because of the unification brought by the Mongol empire, while the size and strength of the Ottoman empire facilitated Evliya

Çelebi's travels to Vienna and Egypt and across Southwest Asia.

Many rulers patronized religions to increase their control over the people they ruled, allowing a smooth introduction to the teachings of the major world religions. Volume 1 introduces the major religions and explains how originally regional religions moved across political borders to become world religions. Volume 2 provides context for today's complex interplay of religion and politics and the complex cultural outcomes that occurred when religions expanded into new world regions. The final two chapters analyze the renewed contemporary focus on religion, as seen in the rise of fundamentalist movements in various parts of the world. Our focus on travelers offers an opportunity to explore their involvement with religion, and *Voyages'* close attention to the religious traditions of diverse societies, often related through the travelers' tales, will give students a familiarity with the primary religious traditions of the world.

The topic of gender is an important one in world history, and throughout, *Voyages* devotes extensive space to the experience of women. Although in many societies literacy among women was severely limited, especially in the premodern era, we have included as many women travelers as possible. In addition, extensive coverage of gender and comparison across chapters of women's experiences in different societies allow students to grasp the experience of ordinary women.

Features

We see the features of this book as an opportunity to help students better understand the main text and to expand that understanding as they explore the integrated online features. Here, we describe the features in the printed book. Details about online features are found in the Ancillaries section on the next page.

Chapter Opening Introduction and Map

The beginning of each chapter should capture the student's attention at the outset. The opening section provides a biographical sketch for the chapter's traveler, a portrait, and a passage from his or her writings (or, if not available, a passage about the individual). A map illustrates the route of the traveler using imaginative graphics.

Movement of Ideas Through Primary Sources

This feature offers an introduction, an extensive excerpt from one or more primary sources, and discussion questions. The chosen passages emphasize the movement of ideas, often by contrasting different perspectives on an idea or a religious teaching. The feature aims to develop the core historical skill of analyzing original sources. Topics include "*The Analects* and the Qin Emperor's Stone Texts," "The Five Pillars of Islam," as described in the Hadith of Gabriel and by a contemporary Chinese encyclopedia, and an Iranian narrative of political and commercial competition in early modern Southeast Asia, "Iranians and Europeans at the Court of Siam."

Visual Evidence in Primary Sources

The goal of this feature is to train students to examine an artifact, a work of art, or a photograph and to glean historical information from the find or artwork. A close-up photograph of a recently discovered Chinese terracotta wrestler, for example, shows students how the figure differs from the famous terracotta warriors, and they are asked as well to compare the Chinese wrestler with a Greek example in a later chapter. Portraits of George Washington and Napoleon Bonaparte lead students to analyze the symbolism they contain and how the portraits serve as representations of political power. Discussion questions help students analyze the evidence as they examine the source.

World History in Today's World

This brief feature picks an element of modern life with roots in the period under study. We chose topics interesting to students (for example, "Recreating the World's Oldest Beer" and "From 'Shell Shock' to Post-Traumatic Stress Disorder"), and we highlight their relationship to the past. This feature should provide material to trigger discussion and help instructors explain why world history matters, since students often have little sense that the past has anything to do with their own lives.

Changes in the Third Edition

Every chapter of this new edition has been carefully checked and revised for readability and clarity of language. In every chapter, topics and subtopics have been added or elaborated on, and recent scholarship has been incorporated throughout the text. Some highlights of specific changes in the second edition follow.

- A new feature has been added: roughly eight to ten Context & Connections inserts within the running text of each chapter. These inserts relate to the surrounding text and describe developments or comparisons that link to other regions and periods to help show students how world history interrelates across time and space. The Context & Connections inserts often include key terms from other chapters, which are highlighted in color with their chapter reference to help emphasize recurring themes and ideas. These inserts complement, but are distinct from, the end-of-chapter Context and Connections essays.
- A total of ten Visual Evidence in Primary Sources and seven Movement of Ideas Through Primary Sources features have been replaced or significantly changed.
- Approximately 30 percent of the illustrations have been replaced with new images, with an eye toward visual interest and engagement.
- A new section at the start of Chapter 2—"Complex Societies and the Discipline of History"— introduces students to historical method and the nature of sources.
- Chapter 4's new traveler, China's Grand Historian Sima Qian, lived during the Han dynasty and wrote a record from the legendary past to 100 B.C.E., after the Qin dynasty (221–207 B.C.E.) unified the empire for the first time.
- Chapter 7 has a new traveler, Egeria, a Spanish pilgrim who from 381 to 384 traveled from the Roman empire's western edge to Jerusalem, Egypt, and Constantinople. Chapter 8 explicitly compares her experience with that of the Japanese Buddhist pilgrim Ennin, and Chapter 9 contrasts their pilgrimages with the hajj of Islam.
- Chapter 12 includes a new section, "The Changing Lives of Women in China's Commercial Revolution," which further illustrates the life of women in Song China.
- In Chapter 14, a new historical analysis of the fall of Constantinople will help students understand the global nature of world history.
- Chapter 15's new traveler is Bernardino de Sahagún, a Franciscan friar who compiled the *General History of the Things of New Spain*, also

known as the Florentine Codex, by interviewing the native Nahua people of central Mexico in their own language and recording their answers in Nahuatl with a Spanish summary.

- In Chapter 17, the first main section has been refocused to concentrate on the Ottoman and Safavid empires and their relations. In addition, the chapter's concluding Context and Connections essay now analyzes early modern developments in light of recent scholarship on the role of climate change.
- The new traveler in Chapter 20, Rammohun Roy, a prominent Indian reformer and figure in the Bengal Renaissance, offers an Indian's perspective on the transition from Mughal to British rule.
- Coverage of Mexico from 1910 through Carranza has been moved from Chapter 27 to Chapter 25, providing enhanced continuity in the coverage of Mexican history.
- Chapter 27 has a new traveler, the anarchist and feminist Emma Goldman, who brings to the narrative a broader critique of the Bolshevik system in Russia and an in-depth look at a radical view of women's issues in the early twentieth century.
- The survey of contemporary global affairs in Chapter 32 has been thoroughly updated and also includes greater emphasis on women's leadership.

Ancillaries

Instructor Resources

MindTap™
MindTap for *Voyages in World History*, Third Edition is a personalized, online digital learning platform providing students with an immersive learning experience that builds critical thinking skills. Through a carefully designed chapter-based learning path, MindTap allows students to easily identify the chapter's learning objectives, improve their writing skills by completing unit-level essay assessments, read short and manageable sections from the e-book, and test their content knowledge with a chapter test that employs Aplia™ questions (see Chapter Test description on the next page).

- *Setting the Scene:* Each chapter of the MindTap begins with a brief video that introduces the chapter's major themes in a compelling, visual way that encourages students to think critically about the subject matter.

- *Interactive Traveler Map:* A unique interactive map activity expands upon each chapter's story of the traveler, allowing students to follow along the journey and click on each stop to learn more about where the traveler went and why it was historically significant. Opening learning objectives, posed as questions, help students focus on what to take away from each unique traveler experience, and place the journey in the context of the chapter's overarching lesson.
- *Review Activities:* Reading comprehension assignments were designed to cover the content of each major heading within the chapter.
- *Chapter Test:* Each chapter within MindTap ends with a summative chapter test. It covers each chapter's learning objectives and is built using Aplia critical thinking questions. All chapter tests include at least one map-based activity. Aplia provides automatically graded critical thinking assignments with detailed, immediate explanations on every question. Students can also choose to see another set of related questions if they did not earn all available points in their first attempt and want more practice.
- *Reflection Activity:* Every chapter ends with an assignable, gradable reflection activity, intended as a brief writing assignment through which students can apply a theme or idea they've just studied.
- *Unit Activities:* Chapters in MindTap are organized into multi-chapter units. Each unit includes a brief set of higher-stakes activities for instructors to assign, designed to assess students on their writing and critical thinking skills and their ability to engage larger themes, concepts, and material across multiple chapters.
- *Classroom Activities:* MindTap includes a brief list of in-class activity ideas for instructors. These are designed to increase student collaboration, engagement, and understanding of selected topics or themes. These activities, including class debate scenarios and primary source discussion guides, can enrich the classroom experience for both instructors and students.

MindTap also includes a variety of other tools that will make history more engaging for students:

- *The Instructor's Resource Center* provides a large collection of searchable, curated readings intended for use in World History. Individual readings may be assigned to students along with a brief assessment to enhance their learning experience.
- *ReadSpeaker* reads the text out loud to students in a voice they can customize.
- *Note-taking and highlighting* are organized in a central location that can be synced with Ever-Note on any mobile device a student may have access to.
- *Questia* allows professors to search a database of thousands of peer-reviewed journals, newspapers, magazines, and full-length books—all assets can be added to any relevant chapter in MindTap.
- *Kaltura* allows instructors to insert inline video and audio into the MindTap platform.
- *ConnectYard* allows instructors to create digital "yards" and communicate with students based upon their preferred social media sites—without "friending" students.

Instructor Companion Website

This website is an all-in-one resource for class preparation, presentation, and testing for instructors. Accessible through Cengage.com/login with your faculty account, you will find an Instructor's Manual, PowerPoint presentations (descriptions below), and test bank files (please see the Cognero® description below).

Instructor's Manual: For each chapter, this manual contains: chapter outlines and summaries, lecture suggestions, suggested research topics, map exercises, discussion questions for primary source documents, and suggested readings and resources.

PowerPoint® Lecture Tools: These presentations are ready-to-use, visual outlines of each chapter. They are easily customized for your lectures. There are presentations of only lectures or only images, as well as combined lecture and image presentations. Also available is a per-chapter JPEG library of images and maps.

Cengage Learning Testing, Powered by Cognero®: The test bank for *Voyages in World History*, Third Edition is accessible through Cengage.com/login with your faculty account. This test bank contains multiple-choice and essay questions for each chapter.

Cognero® is a flexible, online system that allows you to author, edit, and manage test bank content for *Voyages in World History*, Third Edition. Create multiple test versions instantly and deliver through your LMS from your classroom, or wherever you may be, with no special installs or downloads required.

The following format types are available for download from the Instructor Companion Website: Blackboard, Angel, Moodle, Canvas, and Desire-2Learn. You can import these files directly into your LMS to edit, manage questions, and create tests. The test bank is also available in PDF format from the Instructor Companion Website.

Cengagebrain.com

Save your students time and money. Direct them to www.cengagebrain.com for choice in formats and savings and a better chance to succeed in your class. Cengagebrain.com, Cengage Learning's online store, is a single destination for more than 10,000 new textbooks, eTextbooks, eChapters, study tools, and audio supplements. Students have the freedom to purchase à la carte exactly what they need when they need it. Students can save 50 percent on the electronic textbook and can pay as little as $1.99 for an individual eChapter.

Custom Options

Nobody knows your students like you, so why not give them a text that is tailor-fit to their needs? Cengage Learning offers custom solutions for your course—whether it's making a small modification to *Voyages in World History*, Third Edition to match your syllabus or combining multiple sources to create something truly unique. You can pick and choose chapters, include your own material, and add additional map exercises along with the Rand McNally Atlas to create a text that fits the way you teach. Ensure that your students get the most out of their textbook dollar by giving them exactly what they need. Contact your Cengage Learning representative to explore custom solutions for your course.

Student Resources

MindTap™

The learning path for *Voyages in World History*, Third Edition MindTap incorporates a set of resources designed to help students develop their own historical skills. These include interactive, auto-gradable tutorials for map skills, essay writing, and critical thinking. They also include a set of resources developed to aid students with their research skills, primary and secondary source analysis, and knowledge and confidence around proper citations.

Cengagebrain.com

Save time and money! Go to www.cengagebrain.com for choice in formats and savings and a better chance to succeed in your class. Cengagebrain.com, Cengage Learning's online store, is a single destination for more than 10,000 new textbooks, eTextbooks, eChapters, study tools, and audio supplements. Students have the freedom to purchase à la carte exactly what they need when they need it. Students can save 50 percent on the electronic textbook and can pay as little as $1.99 for an individual eChapter.

Writing for College History, 1e [ISBN: 9780618306039] Prepared by Robert M. Frakes, Clarion University. This brief handbook for survey courses in American history, Western civilization/European history, and world civilization guides students through the various types of writing assignments they encounter in a history class. Providing examples of student writing and candid assessments of student work, this text focuses on the rules and conventions of writing for the college history course.

The History Handbook, 2e [ISBN: 9780495906766] Prepared by Carol Berkin of Baruch College, City University of New York and Betty Anderson of Boston University. This book teaches students both basic and history-specific study skills such as how to read primary sources, research historical topics, and correctly cite sources. Substantially less expensive than comparable skill-building texts, *The History Handbook* also offers tips for Internet research and evaluating online sources.

Doing History: Research and Writing in the Digital Age, 2e [ISBN: 9781133587880] Prepared by Michael J. Galgano, J. Chris Arndt, and Raymond M. Hyser of James Madison University. Whether you're starting down the path as a history major or simply looking for a straightforward and systematic guide to writing a successful paper, you'll find this text to be an indispensable handbook to historical research. This text's "soup to nuts" approach to researching and writing about history addresses every step of the process, from locating your sources and gathering information, to writing clearly and making proper use of various citation styles to avoid plagiarism.

You'll also learn how to make the most of every tool available to you—especially the technology that helps you conduct the process efficiently and effectively.

The Modern Researcher, 6e [ISBN: 9780495318705]
Prepared by Jacques Barzun and Henry F. Graff of Columbia University. This classic introduction to the techniques of research and the art of expression is used widely in history courses but is also appropriate for writing and research methods courses in other departments. Barzun and Graff thoroughly cover every aspect of research, from the selection of a topic through the gathering, analysis, writing, revision, and publication of findings, presenting the process not as a set of rules but through actual cases that put the subtleties of research in a useful context. Part One covers the principles and methods of research; Part Two covers writing, speaking, and getting one's work published.

Acknowledgments

It is a pleasure to thank the many instructors who read and critiqued the manuscript through its development in this and previous editions, as well as those who reviewed and class-tested MindTap and our other digital offerings:

Zachary Alexander, Snead State Community College
Barbara Allen, La Salle University
Mark Baker, California State University Bakersfield
Jessica Weaver Baron, Saint Mary's College
Albert Bauman, Hawai'i Pacific University
Natalie Bayer, Drake University
Christopher Bellito, Kean University
Robert Bond, Cuyamaca College
Marjan Boogert, Manchester College
Timothy Boyd, University of Buffalo
Maryann Brink, University of Massachusetts-Boston
Paul Buckingham, Morrisville State College
Jochen Burgtorf, California State University Fullerton
Celeste Chamberland, Roosevelt University
Annette Chamberlin, Virginia Western Community College
Patty Colman, Moorpark College
Tracey-Anne Cooper, St. John's University
Marcie Cowley, Grand Valley State University
Matthew Crawford, Kent State University
Brian Daugherity, Virginia Commonwealth University
Courtney DeMayo, Heidelberg University
Katie Desmond, Feather River College
Salvador Diaz, Santa Rosa Junior College
Audra Diptee, Carleton University
Kimberly Dowdle, Jackson State University
Jeffrey Dym, Sacramento State University
Don Eberle, Bowling Green State University
Jayme Feagin, Georgia Highlands College
Angela Feres, Grossmont College
Christopher Ferguson, Auburn State University
Christina Firpo, California Polytechnic State University
Nancy Fitch, California State University Fullerton
Candace Gregory-Abbott, California State University Sacramento
Eric Gruver, Texas A&M University
Kenneth Hall, Ball State University
Tracy Hoskins, Taylor University
Victor Jagos, Scottsdale Community College
Ellen J. Jenkins, Arkansas Tech University
Phyllis Jestice, University of Southern Mississippi
Gustavo Jimenez, Los Angeles Mission College
Michael Kinney, Calhoun Community College
Mark Lentz, University of Louisiana-Lafayette
Jodie Mader, Thomas More College
Susan Maneck, Jackson State University
Christopher Mauriello, Salem State University
Derek Maxfield, Genesee Community College
Scott Merriman, Troy University
Alexander Mirkovic, Arkansas Tech University
Houston Mount, East Central University
Stephen Neufeld, California State University Fullerton
Mari Nicholson-Preuss, University of Houston
Bill Palmer, Marshall University
Peter Patsouris, Three Rivers Community College
Sean Perrone, Saint Anselm College
Julio Pino, Kent State University
Dave Price, Santa Fe College
Elizabeth Propes, Tennessee Technological University
Carey Roberts, Arkansas Tech University
Anne Rose, Grand Valley State University
LaQuita Saunders, Arkansas State University
Charles Scruggs, Genesee Community College

Scott Seagle, Chattanooga State Community College

Tatiana Seijas, Miami University

Julia Sloan, Cazenovia College

Al Smith, Modesto Junior College

Jeffrey Smith, Lindenwood University

David Stefancic, Saint Mary's College

Pamela Stewart, Arizona State University

Kirk Strawbridge, Mississippi University for Women

Julie Tatlock, Mount Mary College

Philip Theodore, Mississippi Gulf Coast Community College

Lisa Tran, California State University Fullerton

Sarah Trembanis, Immaculata University

Sarah Tucker, Washburn University

Kimberly Vincent, North Carolina State University

Timothy Wesley, Pennsylvania State University

Robert Wilcox, Northern Kentucky University

James Williams, University of Indianapolis

Deborah Wood, Genesee Community College

Kent Wright, Arizona State University

Valerie Hansen would also like to thank the following for their guidance on specific chapters: Haydon Cherry, Yale University; Stephen Colvin, London University; Fabian Drixler, Yale University; Benjamin Foster, Yale University; Karen Foster, Yale University; Paul Freedman, Yale University; Phyllis Granoff, Yale University; Thomas R. H. Havens, Northeastern University; Stanley Insler, Yale University; Mary Miller, Yale University; Frederick S. Paxton, Connecticut College; Stuart Schwartz, Yale University; Koichi Shinohara, Yale University; Francesca Trivellato, Yale University; and Anders Winroth, Yale University.

The study of world history is indeed a voyage, and Kenneth Curtis would like to thank the following for helping identify guideposts along the way. First, thanks to colleagues in the World History Association and the Advanced Placement World History program, especially Omar Ali, University of North Carolina Greensboro; Ross Dunn, San Diego State University; Alan Karras, University of California, Berkeley; Patrick Manning, University of Pittsburgh; Laura Mitchell, University of California, Irvine; Heather Salter-Streets, Washington State University; and Merry Wiesner-Hanks, University of Wisconsin-Milwaukee. Ken would especially like to commemorate the scholarly stimulation, friendship, and generous spirit of the late Jerry Bentley of the University of Hawai'i. He would also like to acknowledge the support of his colleagues in the history department at California State University Long Beach, especially those who aided with sources, translations, or interpretive guidance: Houri Berberian, Craig Hendricks, Ali Igmen, Andrew Jenks, Timothy Keirn, Margaret Kuo, Sharlene Sayegh, and Donald Schwartz.

The authors would also like to thank the many publishing professionals at Cengage Learning who facilitated the publication of this book, in particular: Jan Fitter, whose desire to get it right shaped this and previous editions; our original editor, Nancy Blaine, for guiding us through the entire process from proposal to finished textbook, and her able successor, Cara St. Hilaire, who supervised the revisions; Jean Woy, for the extraordinary historical judgment she brought to bear on the first edition and her continuing guidance; Cate Rickard Barr, for managing another stellar design; Carol Newman, for shepherding the book through the final, chaotic prepublication process; Charlotte Miller, who oversaw creation of the book's distinctive maps; and Kate MacLean, who coordinated the multimedia components that accompanies the MindTap.

In closing, Valerie Hansen would like to thank Brian Vivier for doing so much work on Volume 1; the title of "research assistant" does not convey even a fraction of what he did, always punctually and cheerfully. She dedicates this book to her children, Lydia, Claire, and Bret Hansen Stepanek, and their future educations.

In recognition of his father's precious gift of curiosity, Ken dedicates this book to the memory of James Gavin Curtis.

About the Authors

Valerie Hansen

Valerie Hansen teaches Chinese and world history at Yale University, where she is professor of history. Her main research goal is to draw on nontraditional sources to capture the experience of ordinary people. In particular, she is interested in how sources buried in the ground, whether intentionally or unintentionally, supplement the detailed official record of China's past. Her books include *The Open Empire: A History of China to 1600* (2000) and *The Silk Road: A New History* (2012). In the past decade, she has spent three years in China: 2005–2006 in Shanghai on a Fulbright grant, and 2008–2009 and 2011–2012 teaching at Yale's joint undergraduate program with Peking University. She is currently working on a book about the world in the year 1000 and the many unexpected connections that tied different regions together for the first time.

Kenneth R. Curtis

Kenneth R. Curtis received his Ph.D. from the University of Wisconsin-Madison in African and Comparative World History. His research focuses on colonial to postcolonial transitions in East Africa, with a particular focus on the coffee economy of Tanzania. He is professor of History at California State University Long Beach, where he has taught world history at the introductory level, in special courses designed for future middle and high school teachers, and in graduate seminars. He has worked to advance the teaching of world history at the collegiate and secondary levels in collaboration with the World History Association, the California History/Social Science Project, and the College Board's Advanced Placement World History program.

Note on Spelling

Students taking world history will encounter new names of people, terms, and places from languages that use either different alphabets or no alphabet at all (like Chinese) and that have multiple variant spellings in English. As a rule, we have opted to give names in the native language of whom we are writing about, not in other languages.

Our goal has been to avoid confusing the reader, even if specific decisions may not make sense to expert readers. To help readers, we provide a pronunciation guide on the first appearance of any term or name whose pronunciation is not obvious from the spelling. A few explanations for specific regions follow.

The Americas

Only after 1492 with the arrival of Columbus and his men did outsiders label the original residents of the Americas as a single group. For this reason, any word for the inhabitants of North and South America is inaccurate. We try to refer to individual peoples whenever possible. When speaking in general terms, we use the word *Amerindian* because it has no pejorative overtones and is not confusing.

Many place names in Spanish-speaking regions have a form in both Spanish and in the language of the indigenous peoples; whenever possible we have opted for the indigenous word. For example, we write about the *Tiwanaku* culture in the Andes, not *Tiahuanaco*. In some cases, we choose the more familiar term, such as *Inca* and *Cuzco*, rather than the less familiar spellings *Inka* and *Cusco*. We retain the accents for modern place names.

East Asia

For Chinese, we have used the pinyin system of romanization. However, on the first appearance of a name, we alert readers to nonstandard spellings, such as Chiang Kai-shek and Sun Yat-sen, that have already entered English.

For other Asian languages, we have used the most common romanization systems (McCune-Reischauer for Korean, Hepburn for Japanese). Because we prefer to use the names that people called themselves, we use *Chinggis Khan* for the ruler of the Mongols (not *Genghis Khan*, which is Persian) and the Turkish *Timur the Lame* (rather than *Tamerlane*, his English name).

West Asia and North Africa

Many romanization systems for Arabic and related languages like Ottoman Turkish or Persian use an apostrophe to indicate specific consonants (*ain* and *hamza*). Because it is difficult for a native speaker of English to hear these differences, we have omitted these apostrophes. For this reason, we use *Quran* (not *Qur'an*).

VOYAGES
in World History

Clipart courtesy FCIT, from *Narrative and Critical History of America* (New York: Houghton, Mifflin, and Company, 1886)ii:156

Bernardino de Sahagún

In 1529, at the age of thirty, **Bernardino de Sahagún** (1499–1590) landed in Veracruz, Mexico, only eight years after the Spanish army had conquered Mexico, and only thirty-seven years since Christopher Columbus had arrived in the Americas. On shipboard, Sahagún (sah-hah-GUHN) had already begun to study the local language, Nahuatl (NAH-watt). A university graduate, Sahagún was a Franciscan friar, and starting in 1547, he began to interview the local elders and collect material for a twelve-volume book, *General History of the Things of New Spain*, that he finished fifty years after he arrived in Mexico. In a note to the reader, he explained why he wrote in Nahuatl:

Although many have written of the Conquest of this New Spain [Mexico] in Spanish, according to the account of those who conquered it, I desired to write it in the Mexican language [Nahuatl].... Those who were conquered knew and gave an account of many things which transpired among them during the war of which those who conquered them were unaware. For these reasons, it seems to me, to have written this history, which was at a time when those who took part in the very Conquest were alive, has not been a superfluous task. And those who gave this account were principled persons of good judgment, and it is believed that they told all the truth.*

*Bernardino de Sahagún, *The Florentine Codex*, vol. I, trans. Arthur J. O. Anderson and Charles E. Dibble Santa Fe, N.M.: The School of American Research and the University of Utah, 1950–1982), p. 101.

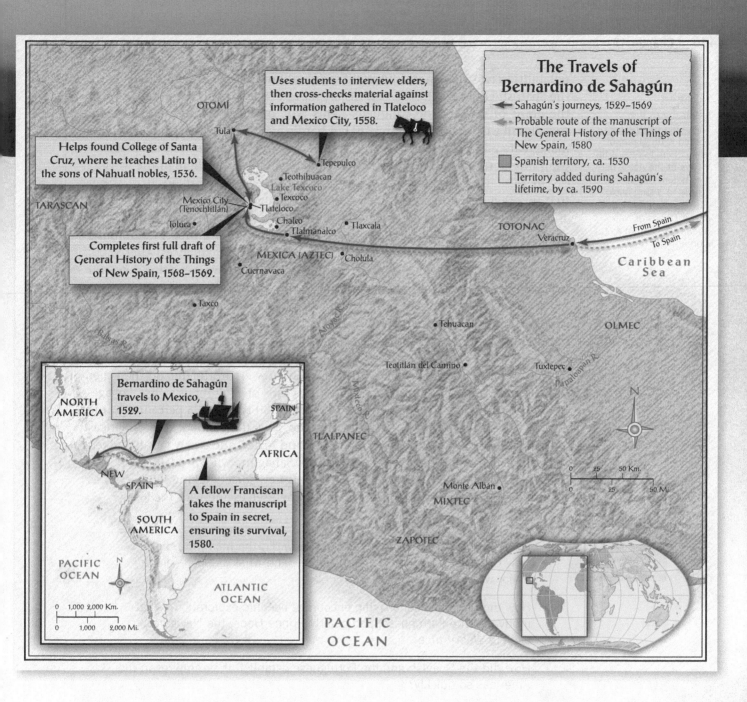

The Travels of Bernardino de Sahagún

← Sahagún's journeys, 1529–1569

⇠ Probable route of the manuscript of The General History of the Things of New Spain, 1580

■ Spanish territory, ca. 1530

□ Territory added during Sahagún's lifetime, by ca. 1590

Uses students to interview elders, then cross-checks material against information gathered in Tlateloco and Mexico City, 1558.

Helps found College of Santa Cruz, where he teaches Latin to the sons of Nahuatl nobles, 1536.

Completes first full draft of General History of the Things of New Spain, 1568–1569.

Bernardino de Sahagún travels to Mexico, 1529.

A fellow Franciscan takes the manuscript to Spain in secret, ensuring its survival, 1580.

Sahagún here displays a remarkably up-to-date understanding of historical method, yet he was writing more than four hundred years ago. Because all the historical accounts of the conquest were in Spanish and reflected the view of the conquerors, Sahagún sought out the local people so that he could find out about what the Spanish had overlooked. Realizing the importance of eyewitness accounts as primary sources, he interviewed people old enough to have observed the conquest. And at a time when most of his contemporaries, even among the Franciscans, looked down on native peoples, Sahagún defended his informants as being both of good character and truthful—crucial measures of

Bernardino de Sahagún

A Franciscan friar, Sahagún (1499–1590) worked with a team of researchers to record the history of the Aztec peoples before the Spanish arrived in a long book entitled *General History of the Things of New Spain*, also known as the Florentine Codex.

reliability. The single most important source about the society in Mexico before the Spanish conquest, his *General History* narrates the arrival of Europeans from the point of view of the conquered. This type of account survives in literate societies like China (see Chapter 16) but hardly ever in illiterate societies, which makes Sahagún's *General History* of significance to anyone curious about European interactions with nonliterate indigenous peoples anywhere in the world.

In 1492, Columbus's voyage connected Europe with the Americas in a way that no previous contact had; the resulting exchange of plants, animals, people, and disease shaped our modern world. Unlike Viking voyages to Newfoundland around 1000 and Ming Chinese voyages to East Africa in the 1400s, Columbus's four voyages between 1492 and 1506 had far-reaching consequences. After 1300, while the Mexica (or Aztec) in Mexico and the Inca in Peru were creating powerful expansionist empires, on the opposite side of the Atlantic, Europeans were learning about geography as part of their humanistic studies. Spanish and Portuguese explorers traveled farther and farther, first to the islands of the Mediterranean and the Atlantic, then to the west coast of Africa, and finally to the Americas, always claiming colonies for their monarchs. The Europeans transported plants, animals, and people (often against their will) to entirely new environments on the other side of the Atlantic. Within one hundred years of Columbus's first voyage, millions of Amerindians had perished (the death toll reached 95 percent in some areas), victims of European diseases that no one understood. The Americas absorbed new populations from both Europe and Africa, and a new racially mixed society formed under Spanish colonial rule. Sahagún, who lived through two major epidemics and died in the third, saw this new society taking shape even as he observed the settlers fighting both among themselves and with the locals.

FOCUS QUESTIONS

> How did the Aztec form their empire? How did the Inca form theirs? How did each hold their empire together, and what was each empire's major weakness?

> How did humanist scholarship encourage oceanic exploration? What motivated the Portuguese, particularly Prince Henry the Navigator, to explore West Africa?

> How did the Spanish and the Portuguese establish their empires in the Americas so quickly?

> What was the Columbian exchange? Which elements of the exchange had the greatest impact on the Americas? On Afro-Eurasia?

The Aztec Empire of Mexico, 1325–1519

Because of the work of Sahagún and other Spanish missionaries, and because of archaeological discoveries, we know the history of the Aztec empire that Cortés and his forces defeated in 1521. Starting sometime around 1325, the Mexica (meh-SHE-kah), a people based in western Mexico, moved into central Mexico to

Tenochtitlan (modern-day Mexico City), which became the Aztec capital. The Mexica were one of many Nahua peoples who spoke the Nahuatl language. Like the Maya, the Nahua peoples had a complex calendrical system, built large stone monuments, and played a ritual ball game. The Mexica believed in a pantheon of gods, headed by the sun, that demanded blood sacrifices from their devotees. To sustain these gods, they continually went to war, gradually conquering many of the city-states in central Mexico to form the **Aztec empire**.

Sahagún's Research Method

The Nahua (NAH-wah) peoples spoke a language called Nahuatl that did not have a written form. Nahuatl texts combine pictures with rebus writing, which uses images to represent something with the same sound; in English, for example, a picture of an eye functions as a rebus for the word *I*. The Nahua's writing served as a trigger to memory; people who had been trained to tell a certain story could look at a Nahua manuscript and be reminded of the details. Because someone who did not know the story could not read it, this was not a full-fledged writing system. When the first Franciscans arrived, some five years before Sahagún, they created a new alphabet for Nahuatl and taught it to their Nahua students, mostly the sons of powerful families, who attended missionary schools and, after 1536, the Jesuit College at Santa Cruz.

The Jesuit College was successful because it unintentionally replicated the traditional Nahua schooling system. Before the Spanish arrived, boys and girls left their families at the age of fifteen to live in separate houses for boys and girls where they studied Nahua traditions. Finished at seventeen or eighteen, the girls returned to their homes to marry; the boys stayed until around twenty-one, when they took up their father's occupations. The Jesuits did not educate the girls, but the college trained boys of exactly the same age as those in the Nahua houses.

Over the course of his long life, Sahagún developed a sophisticated research method to recover the pre-Spanish past. First he made up a long outline for his *General History*. He then drew up long questionnaires detailing the topics he wanted to ask the Nahua about. For example, as he explains, when he wanted to find out in which month the new year began, he *"gathered together many elders, the most competent I could find, and together with the most able of the college students, they decided, saying that the year began on the second day of February."** In reply to Sahagún's questions, the elders drew traditional pictorial narratives on bark paper or deerskin. The young students then wrote notes in Nahuatl in the margins surrounding those drawings. To make sure that he was collecting accurate information, Sahagún conducted all his interviews in three separate cities. Sahagún combined all the information to write his *General History*.

● **CONTEXT&CONNECTIONS** Sahagún's research method was modeled on and expanded that of the Roman Pliny the Elder in his *Natural History*, completed more than one thousand years earlier between 77 and 79 C.E. After writing his long outline, Pliny consulted written sources and interviewed different scholars. He wrote entries on different topics, ranging from technological breakthroughs to the artists of his time, but he did not cross-check his information or use recorded questionnaires as Sahagún did. ●

Aztec empire

An empire based in Tenochtitlan (modern-day Mexico City) that ruled over 4 to 6 million people in modern-day Mexico and Guatemala.

*Luis Nicolau D'Olwer, *Fray Bernardino de Sahagún (1499-1590)*, trans. Mauricio J. Mixco (Salt Lake City: University of Utah Press, 1987), p. 108, n3.

The first versions of Sahagún's *General History*, dating to 1569, were entirely in Nahuatl (for the reasons explained in the opening of the chapter), but Sahagún later decided to add Spanish translation, so that his final product had two columns, one of Nahuatl explanation and a second one in Spanish, which was heavily illustrated with original paintings and sketches done by his informants. Nothing in Sahagún's education at the Spanish university of Salamanca prepared him for this task or introduced such a method; there he had studied the classic curriculum influenced by humanism (discussed later in this chapter). The use of a questionnaire that evolved as he interviewed more people, the conversations with multiple informants, and the cross-checking of information are all hallmarks of modern social science, and indeed Sahagún is often called the world's first anthropologist.

Sahagún was like a modern anthropologist in another way: he did not judge the Nahua. He recorded all their customs, including human sacrifice, because he wanted to understand them and to produce a complete record.

● **CONTEXT&CONNECTIONS** In this way, Sahagún was like the Greek Herodotus (ca. 485–425 B.C.E.), often called the father of history, who wrote about the Scythian practice of making handkerchiefs of human flesh in an equally dispassionate tone. Sahagún and Herodotus alike wanted to understand their subjects and did not pass judgment on their practices, however bloodthirsty they may have seemed. ●

Many of his fellow Spaniards despised the Nahua as utterly uncivilized, and their objections to his work caused Sahagún many problems. His masterwork survives today only because a fellow Franciscan smuggled the full work back into Spain and told no one, including Sahagún, about it. It was preserved in the library of the Medicis in Florence, which is why scholars today refer to the *General History* as the Florentine Codex.

The Mexica Settlement of Tenochtitlan

Sahagún's informants agreed that around the 1200s various groups migrated to central Mexico. The heart of this area is the Valley of Mexico, 10,000 feet (3,000 m) above sea level and surrounded by volcanoes. The Valley of Mexico contains many shallow lakes and much fertile land. The last Nahua groups to arrive referred to themselves as "Mexica" (meh-SHE-kah), the origin of the word *Mexico*, but many historians call them by the modern word *Aztec*. Although *Aztec* is a term that no one at the time used, this text uses it to refer to the empire the Mexica built. Linguistic analysis of the Nahuatl language indicates that its speakers originated somewhere in the southwest United States or northern Mexico.

By the 1300s, some fifty city-states, called **altepetl** (al-TEH-peh-tuhl), occupied central Mexico, each with its own leader, or "speaker," and its own government. Each altepetl had a palace for its ruler, a pyramid-shaped temple, and a market. The Mexica migrated to the region around the historic urban center of Teotihuacan, a large city with many lakes. Since this region was already home to several rival altepetl, the Mexica were forced to settle in a swampland called **Tenochtitlan** (teh-noch-TIT-lan). The Mexica gradually reclaimed large areas of the swamps and on the drier, more stable areas erected stone buildings held together with mortar. They planted flowers everywhere and walked on planks or traveled by canoe from one reclaimed area to another. Much of what they built lies under the massive cathedral of Mexico City, but even today, archaeologists use Sahagún's information to locate different temples; of the seventy-eight different temples whose existence he recorded, archaeologists have located more than forty.

altepetl
The 450 city-states of the Aztec empire that each had its own leader and government, a palace for its ruler, a pyramid-shaped temple, and a market.

Tenochtitlan
Capital city of the Aztec empire, which the Mexica reclaimed from swampland, with a population of some two hundred thousand people.

Traditional accounts say the Mexica people arrived at Tenochtitlan in 1325, a date confirmed by archaeological excavation. At its height, Tenochtitlan contained sixty thousand dwellings, home to perhaps two hundred thousand people in an area of 5 square miles (13 sq km). The central marketplace offered cooked and uncooked food, slaves, tobacco products, and luxury goods made from gold, silver, and feathers. Consumers used cotton cloaks, cacao beans, and feather quills filled with gold dust as media of exchange, since the Mexica had no coins.

Nahua Religion

The Mexica believed that their patron god was Huitzilopochtli (wheat-zeel-oh-POSHT-lee), whose name meant "the hummingbird of the south." Also the warrior god of the sun, Huitzilopochtli played a key role in the Mexica origin legend. On the long migration from their original homeland in Aztlan, the Mexica arrived at a mountain where an elderly priestess guarded a temple. A ball of feathers fell from the sky, and she became pregnant with a young male fetus, the future Huitzilopochtli. Ashamed by the news of her mother's pregnancy, her daughter organized an army to kill her mother. Huitzilopochtli, still in the womb, emerged as a full-grown warrior, killed the priestess's daughter, and rolled her body parts down the hill as his army defeated the attackers.

This legend provides a rationale for the massive Mexica blood sacrifices, many of which occurred in the Great Temple in Tenochtitlan. The Nahuatl term for human blood was "precious water." The most important Nahua deity, the sun, controlled agriculture and crops, primarily the corn, beans, and peppers that were the main source of food. The sun was so important that Sahagún collected multiple sayings just about the sun. For example, if a young woman said, *"I discover my sun, I set out my sun,"** she meant that she was married. Because of the sun's importance, eclipses terrified the Nahua, and Sahagún recorded their reactions: *"The common folk raised a cry, lifting their voices, making a great din, calling out, shrieking. There was shouting everywhere. People of light complexion were slain as sacrifices; captives were killed. All offered their blood; they drew straws through the lobes of their ears."**

Every 260 days, after twelve months had passed, the Nahua celebrated the festival of the sun, first by fasting for four days, and then blowing conch shells. As during eclipses, *"Straws were drawn through the flesh. And they cut the ear lobes of small children lying in cradles. Everyone drew blood. There were then no greetings. There was only the drawing of blood."**

Ranking just under the sun-god were the gods of rain and agriculture. The deities, the Mexica believed, needed to drink much human blood, usually of prisoners of war, so that they would keep the soil fertile, the harvest plentiful, and the succession of seasons regular; this is the kind of belief, utterly different from the Spaniards, that Sahagún hoped to understand and recorded for future generations.

While many societies engaged in human sacrifice, the Mexica apparently killed unusually high numbers of people at one time; scholars continue to debate how many. Spanish sources may have exaggerated the death toll to discredit their predecessors, but they gave much lower numbers of sacrificial victims for other

*Bernardino de Sahagún, *The Florentine Codex*, vol. I, trans. Arthur J. O. Anderson and Charles E. Dibble (Santa Fe, N.M.: The School of American Research and the University of Utah, 1950–1982), pp. 181, 2; vol. III, p. 216.

Mexica Skull-Mask Worshipers used deerskin straps to tie this skull-mask around their waists in a display of fearsomeness. The mask was made by applying small fragments of turquoise, black lignite coal, and white conch to the front half of a skull (the human teeth are original). The highly polished pyrite eyes glisten in the light, and the red mollusk shell nose inlays replicate the color of flayed human tissue. The mask vividly captures the importance of human offerings to the Mexica deities.

Amerindian peoples, suggesting that the Mexica indeed performed more sacrifices.

Nahua Society The Nahua peoples treated certain human beings like gods. The leader of the Mexica, their Great Speaker, was carried in a feathered chair. His advisers never looked at the Great Speaker or addressed him directly: a screen always separated them from him. Sahagún's informants described his clothing, hats, and throne on different holidays in great detail. The Great Speaker was in charge of all external matters, including war, the receipt of gifts, and relations with other altepetl. A group of nobles, priests, and successful warriors chose the new Great Speaker, and although they treated him as their ritual superior, they could depose him if they did not approve of his rule. All the top officials came from the royal family and had large private estates.

Most of the Nahua were commoners, each of whom belonged to a "big house," a group who believed they were descended from a common ancestor. The lowest-ranking people in Nahua society were slaves, often the original residents of the Valley of Mexico. Ordinary people and slaves farmed the land and generated the surplus that underpinned the expansion of the Mexica altepetl. Because they had no draft animals, metal tools, or wheels, everything had to be carried and cultivated by hand.

Corn ripened in only fifty days, providing sufficient food for a family as well as a surplus. Grinding corn was exclusively women's work; for fear that they might antagonize the gods, men were forbidden to help. Ordinary people were required to pay tribute to their Mexica overlords by contributing a share of the crop, performing labor service, paying other goods, and most onerous of all, providing victims for human sacrifice.

The Military and the Conquests of the Mexica If successful in battle, warriors could rise in Mexica society to a high position. They then received lands of their own and were not required to pay taxes on them. Conversely, the best human sacrifice one could offer to the gods, the Nahua believed, was a warrior taken captive in battle. In their system of thirteen heavens and eight underworlds, the highest heaven, the Paradise of the Sun-God, was for men who had killed the enemy in battle and for women who had died in childbirth, a type of battle in its own right. The elders told Sahagún about that heaven: it was like a desert, and the dead, armed with shields to protect them from the sun, could see the sun only through holes in their shields. After four years, the dead changed into hummingbirds and other beautiful birds who drank honey from flowers both in heaven and on earth itself.

Map 15.1 **The Aztec Empire** Starting from their capital at Tenochtitlan (modern Mexico City), the Mexica conquered neighboring peoples living between the Gulf of Mexico and the Pacific Ocean, who were required to pay taxes and submit tribute, but received few benefits in return. When Cortés landed on the coast of Mexico, he quickly found allies among the conquered peoples, particularly the Tlaxcalans.

The Mexica troops fitted their clubs, spears, and darts with blades made from obsidian, a volcanic glass. They protected themselves with thick cotton armor. Hand-to-hand combat was considered the most honorable form of warfare.

In 1428, the Mexica launched a series of conquests that led to the creation of an empire. By 1500, they had conquered 450 altepetl in modern Mexico, extending all the way to Guatemala, and ruled over a subject population estimated at between 4 and 6 million (see Map 15.1).

The Aztec empire, though large and with a beautiful capital, had one major weakness. Once the Mexica conquered a given people, they demanded tribute and took sacrificial victims from them, yet they did nothing to incorporate them further into their empire.

● **CONTEXT&CONNECTIONS** This Mexica policy was similar to that of the Mongols, who also conquered other peoples to get tribute and did little to foster loyalty to their new overlords. The Mexica also allowed the peoples they had conquered to speak their own language. ●

The Inca Empire, 1400–1532

The **Inca empire**, 2,500 miles (4,000 km) to the south in the Andes, differed significantly from the Aztec. Because no one like Sahagún collected information there just after the conquest, historians must weigh Spanish testimony against archaeological remains. Each time the Inca conquered a new group, they have

Inca empire

Andean empire founded in 1438 by Pachakuti (d. 1471), which ruled over a peak population of 10 to 12 million.

ayllu

Andean kin groups of the Inca empire that worked the land in several adjacent ecological zones as a hedge against crop failure in any one zone.

found, they integrated them into the empire, requiring them to perform labor and military service and resettling some groups to minimize the chances of revolt. Like the Mexica, the Inca worshiped deities that demanded human sacrifices, but never as many as in Mexico. Although the Inca successfully integrated subject peoples, they did not have an orderly system of succession, resulting in conflict each time their ruler died.

Inca Religion and Andean Society

The ordinary people of the Andes lived in kin groups called **ayllu** (aye-YOU) that worked the land in several adjacent ecological zones so they could backup yields should the crops in one zone fail.

Most ayllu were divided into smaller subgroups, and men tended to marry women from another subgroup. All the people in a given ayllu recognized one common ancestor. Ordinary people believed that, in addition to their ancestors, hundreds of spirits (*wak'a*) inhabited places in the landscape such as streams, caves, rocks, and hills.

The most important Inca deities, ranking far above these local spirits, were the Creator, the Creator's child the Sun, and the Thunder gods. By 1500, the sun-god had become the most important deity, probably because the Inca ruler, the Sapa Inca, or "Unique Inca," claimed descent from the sun-god. The priest of the sun-god was the highest-ranking priest in Inca society and the second most powerful person in the Inca empire.

Both the Sapa Inca and the sun-god priest belonged to the aristocracy, which was divided into three tiers: the close relatives of the ruler and previous rulers, more distant relatives, and then the leaders of the groups the Inca had conquered. Although most Inca traced their ancestry through their father's line, the ruler's mother's family played a central role in court politics because the ruler took his wives from his mother's family.

● **CONTEXT&CONNECTIONS** The Inca had no orderly system of succession. In a practice much like the tanistry prevalent among the Mongols, each time the Inca ruler died, all those of his male kin who hoped to succeed him launched an all-out war until a single man emerged victorious. ●

During his reign, the Sapa Inca lived as a deity among his subjects. Even so, he had to keep the support of the aristocracy, which could easily overthrow him at any time.

Like the ayllu ancestors, the ruler was believed to continue to live even after death. The Inca mummified the bodies of deceased rulers and other high-ranking family members. They placed the mummies in houses around the main square of Cuzco, their capital city high in the Andes at an elevation of 11,300 feet (3,450 m). One Spanish observer described their interaction with these mummies:

Most of the people of Cuzco served the dead, I have heard it said, who they daily brought out to the main square, setting them down in a ring, each one according to his age, and there the male and female attendants ate and drank....The mummies toasted each other and the living, and the living toasted the dead.*

---

*Terence d'Altroy, *The Incas* (Malden, Mass.: Blackwell, 2002), p. 97 (citing Pedro Pizarro).

The Marvels of Incan Engineering at Machu Picchu The settlement at Machu Picchu, which stands 8,000 feet (2,400 m) above sea level, embodies the Incan talent for engineering in its even stone houses arrayed on multiple levels, connected by manmade waterways and more than one hundred stairways. Built around 1450 as a summer palace for the ruler Pachakuti, the site was abandoned after the collapse of the Inca empire and rediscovered by outsiders only in the early 1900s. Today it is one of the world's most visited sites and the most famous of all the Inca ruins. (©Kelsey Green/Shutterstock.com)

He did not explain how the living communicated with the dead, but it seems likely that priests intervened.

The Inca organized the worship of local spirits who inhabited places in the landscape, ancestors of the rulers, and deities into a complex ritual calendar specifying which one was to be worshiped on a given day. Of 332 shrines in Cuzco, 31 received human sacrifices, in many cases a young boy and a young girl, a symbolic married couple. These usually occurred in times of hardship, like an epidemic, or during unusual astronomical events, like eclipses. Occasionally, larger sacrifices occurred, such as when a ruler died, and one source gives the largest number of sacrificial victims killed at a single time as four thousand.

The Inca Expansion

As the Aztec believed their history began with their occupation of Tenochtitlan, the Incas traced their beginnings to their settlement in Cuzco. Archaeological evidence suggests that the Inca moved to Cuzco sometime around 1400.

443

Map 15.2 **The Inca Empire** In 1438, the Inca ruler Pachakuti took power in the capital at Cuzco and led his armies to conquer large chunks of territory along the Andes. Two north-south trunk routes, with subsidiary east-west routes, formed a system of over 18,000 miles (30,000 km) of roads. By 1532, the Inca ruled an empire of 1,500 square miles (4,000 sq km).

Although oral accounts conflict, most accept the date of 1438 as the year Pachakuti (patch-ah-KOO-tee) (d. 1471), the first great Inca ruler, seized the throne from his brother in a coup and launched the military campaigns outward from Cuzco. The Inca conquered neighboring lands because they desired the goods produced in each ecological zone: the herds of llamas and alpaca, crops like grain and potatoes, and the gold, feathers, shells, and minerals from the jungle lowlands and the shore.

Much of Inca warfare consisted of storming enemy forts with a large infantry, often after cutting off access to food and water. For several days enemy forces traded insults and sang hostile songs such as this: *"We will drink from the skull of the traitor, we will adorn ourselves with a necklace of his teeth, … we play the melody of the pinkullu [a musical instrument resembling a flute] with flutes made from his bones, we will beat the drum made from his skin, and thus we will dance."** Attackers in quilted cotton launched arrows, stones from slingshots, and stone spears, and in hand-to-hand combat used spears and clubs, some topped with stone or with bronze stars.

Like other Andean peoples, the Inca knew how to extract metallic ore from rocks and how to heat different metals to form alloys. They made bronze and copper, but they did not develop their metallurgical expertise beyond making club heads, decorative masks, and ear spools for the nobility.

At its height, the Inca army could field as many as one hundred thousand men in a single battle, most of the rank-and-file drawn from subject peoples who were required to serve in the army. The rate of Inca expansion was breathtaking. Starting from a single location, Cuzco, the Inca conquered large chunks of southern, central, and coastal Peru, Ecuador, the eastern lowlands of Peru and Bolivia, and the mountains of Argentina and Chile. By 1532, they ruled over a population estimated at 10 to 12 million (see Map 15.2).

One major legacy of the Inca empire was its magnificent road system. While some routes predated the Inca conquest and were built as early as 1000 B.C.E., the Inca linked them together into an overall system. Since the Inca did not have the wheel, most of the traffic was by foot, and llamas could carry small loads. With no surveying instruments, the Inca constructed these roads across deserts, yawning chasms, and

*Terence d'Altroy, *The Incas* (Malden, Mass.: Blackwell, 2002), pp. 226–227.

The Great Road Reunites Six Nations

In June 2014, the World Heritage Committee of UNESCO recognized the Incan road network, Qhapaq-Ñan (kah-pahk ni-ahn), or the Great Road, as a World Heritage site. The application was unusual for several reasons: Qhapaq-Ñan is not a single location but 273 individual temples, towers, forts, and hostels in 137 locations on a section of the road 435 miles (700 km) long. This is the World Heritage site.

Although only a fraction of the original network, the road crosses six different Latin American countries—Peru, Colombia, Ecuador, Bolivia, Chile, and Argentina—that have warred in the past and even recently over contested borders. (Peru and Ecuador fought intermittently for over 150 years before they agreed to a new border in 1995.) Attracted by the potential increase in tourists that World Heritage sites bring, the six nations came together to make a joint application some twelve years in the making. "We are all very happy," said Luis Jaime Castillo Butters, an archaeologist and a deputy culture minister in Peru, on hearing of the UNESCO approval.

A marvel of engineering, the original network's roads run up and down rain forests, deserts, and high mountains. They reached maximum use under the Inca empire in the 1400s, when the network extended across and along the full extent of the Andes Mountains. The transportation system played a key role in holding the Inca empire together, because it linked the capital at Cuzco with all outlying towns. Supplies could reach the remote site of Machu Picchu only because of the Qhapaq-Ñan road network.

Although one Inca bridge made of braided grass survives even today (a drive about four hours away from Cuzco), the road network is badly damaged in many areas. Tractor farming and cellphone towers pose the greatest threat to the existing sections of the original road. Other sections have already been paved over and converted into highways. The participating governments hope that the granting of World Heritage status will make it possible to raise the funds for necessary repairs and conservation measures.

Sources: Ralph Blumenthal, "Incas' Road Among Additions to World Heritage List," *New York Times,* June 23, 2014.

mountains over 16,000 feet (5,000 m) high. Individual messengers working in shifts could move at an estimated rate of 150 miles (240 km) per day. (See the feature "World History in Today's World: The Great Road Reunites Six Nations.")

- **CONTEXT&CONNECTIONS** These rates for the Inca messengers as recorded by the Spanish are far faster than Persian messengers' 90 miles (145 km) per day or the Mongols' 60 miles (97 km) per day, both traveling on horseback. The Inca messengers ran on excellent, but steep roads, and they must have switched off often. As fast as the Inca messengers were, the Inca armies moved much more slowly, covering perhaps 7–9 miles (12–15 km) per day. Armies throughout the ancient world traveled at a rate of 10–20 miles (16–32 km) per day. Other empires—the Persians, the Romans, and the Chinese—devoted considerable resources to building roads. But as extensive as these road systems were, they did not match the Incas in their engineering ingenuity because they used the wheel and the Inca did not. ●

. . . .

Inca Rule of Subject Populations

Unique among the Andean peoples, the Inca incorporated each conquered land and its occupants into their kingdom. They brought many images of subjects' ancestral deities to Cuzco, holding the images hostage so that their devotees would not rise up against their Inca overlords.

quipu

Inca system of record keeping that used knots on strings to record the population.

● **CONTEXT&CONNECTIONS** Like the Assyrians, the Inca resettled thousands of people, forcing them to move to regions far from their original homes. They also, like the Assyrians and the Mongols, encouraged different peoples to submit to them by treating those who surrendered much more gently than the peoples they had to fight in combat. ●

The Inca allowed local leaders to continue to serve but required everyone to swear loyalty to the Inca ruler, to grant him all rights to their lands, and to perform labor service as the Inca state required. Inca officials also allowed indigenous leaders a place in the central government at the lower level. Those of high birth could serve in the Inca government as long as they learned Quechua (KETCH-wah), the language of the Inca.

Each year Inca officials counted the population, not with a written script but by using a system of knotted strings, called **quipu** (key-POOH). Since no one can understand the quipu records, the population of the Inca empire remains unknown. Each town had a knot keeper who maintained and interpreted the knot records, which were updated annually. Some 850 examples survive today. With different knots, thicknesses, composition (of llama and alpaca fiber or cotton), and dyed hue, the strings of the quipus contain much information. Some nineteenth-century written translations of quipus have been found, but no one has managed to link a translation with a surviving example. Scholars are creating computer databases in the hope that they will provide a modern equivalent of the Rosetta Stone for understanding these still-undeciphered records.

Keeping Records with Knots The Inca kept all their records by using knotted strings, called quipu, attaching subsidiary cords, sometimes in several tiers, to a main cord. Different types of knots represented different numeric units; skipped knots indicated a zero; the color of the string indicated the item being counted.

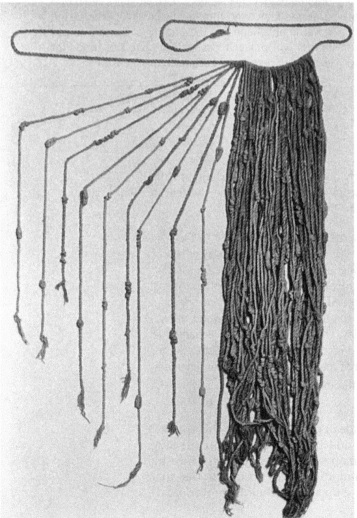

The Granger Collection, NYC

To fulfill the Inca's main service tax, male household heads between twenty-five and fifty had to perform two to three months' labor each year. However, the Inca did not treat all subject peoples alike. From some resettled peoples they exacted extra months of labor, and many subject groups who possessed a specific skill, such as carving stones or making spears, performed that skill for the state. Others did far less. For example, many Inca looked down on a people they called Uru, literally meaning "worm," who lived on the southern edge of Lake Titicaca, because their only labor service was to catch fish, gather grasses, and weave textiles. An even more despised group was required each year to submit a single basket filled with lice, not because the Inca wanted the lice, but because they wanted to teach this group the nature of their tax obligations.

Each household also contributed certain goods, such as food, blankets, textiles, and tools, that were kept in thousands of storehouses throughout the empire. One Spaniard described a storehouse in Cuzco that particularly impressed him: "*There is a house in which are kept more than 100,000 dried birds, for from their feathers articles of clothing are made.*"* This storehouse system functioned so well that the corn and potatoes in the storehouses could support an army for months.

Despite its size, the Inca empire appeared stronger than it was. Many of the subject peoples resented their heavy labor obligations, and each time an Inca ruler died, the ensuing succession disputes threatened to tear the empire apart.

Intellectual and Geographic Exploration in Europe, 1300–1500

Between 1300 and 1500, as the Mexica and Inca were expanding their empires overland in the Americas, European scholars extended their fields of study to include many new topics. Meanwhile, new printing technology made books more available and affordable, enabling university students like Sahagún to read and compare many more books than in earlier centuries. Portuguese and Spanish ships colonized lands farther and farther away, as the pace of European exploration hastened, especially after 1450, when many different explorers, of whom Christopher Columbus is only the most famous, crossed the Atlantic.

The Rise of Humanism

Since the founding of universities in Europe around 1200, students had read Greek and Latin texts and the Bible. Instructors used an approach called scholasticism, in which the main goal was to reconcile the many differences among ancient authorities to form a logical system of thought. Often instructors taught a single book, or part of a book, over the course of a year. Around 1350, a group of Italian scholars pioneered a new intellectual movement called **humanism**. Humanists studied many of the same texts as before, but they tried to impart a more general understanding of them to their students in the hope that students would improve morally and be able to help others do the same.

One of the earliest humanist writers was the Italian poet Petrarch (1304–1374). Scholasticism, Petrarch felt, was too abstract. It did not teach people how to live and how to obtain salvation. Although he composed much poetry in Latin, he is remembered for the poetry he composed in Italian, one of several European vernacular languages that came into written use in the fourteenth and fifteenth centuries.

In 1487, a Venetian woman named Cassandra Fedele (fay-DAY-lay) (1465–1558) set out her own understanding of humanism in a public address. Having

humanism

Intellectual movement begun around 1350 in Italy by scholars who opposed scholasticism. Emphasized the study of the humanities, which included traditional fields like logic, grammar, arithmetic, and music and newer fields like language, history, literature, and philosophy.

*Terence d'Altroy, *The Incas* (Malden, Mass.: Blackwell, 2002), p. 281.

Mariotto Albertinelli (Italian, 1474–1515). Sacrifice of Isaac, ca. 1509–13 Oil on panel (oak), 9 5/16 x 6 15/16 x 3/16 in. (23.6 x 17.6 x 0.48 cm) Gift of Hannah D. and Louis M. Rabinowitz 1959.15.13b/Yale University Art Gallery

The Art of Humanism Just as Abraham is about to sacrifice the naked Isaac, the angel of God appears and stops him. The painter Mariotto Albertinelli (1474–1515) painted this scene on a thin piece of walnut wood, 10 by 7 inches (24 by 18 cm), most likely intended as decoration for a cabinet. The story of Abraham's averted sacrifice, immensely popular throughout Europe, was also the subject of a play written by Spanish missionaries in Mexico that taught the evils of human sacrifice.

studied Greek and Latin with a tutor, Fedele urged her audience to study Cicero, Plato, and Aristotle because, she maintained, while wealth and physical strength cannot last, *"those things which are produced by virtue and intelligence are useful to those who follow."* She continued: *"And how much more humane, praiseworthy and noble do those states and princes become who support and cultivate these studies! Certainly for this reason this part of philosophy has laid claim for itself to the name of 'humanity,' since those who are rough by nature become by these studies more civil and mild-mannered."** She eloquently expressed the major tenet of humanism: studying the humanities made students, whether from noble or low-born families, more refined and better people. Humanists believed that citizens should have a good grasp of rhetoric, history, and ethics and use the accounting they studied to manage their household finances. With such a citizenry, the state was bound to prosper.

Rather than treat Latin translations as flawless, the humanists checked them against texts in the original languages, including the Greek of the Bible. When they did, they found that many of the most difficult-to-understand passages were corrupted by translation errors. One product of humanist scholarship was multilingual editions of the Bible that printed the Latin, Greek, Hebrew, and Aramaic texts on the same page so that scholars could compare them. This type of book provided a prototype for Sahagún when he handwrote the manuscript of his *General History* with columns in Nahuatl and Spanish on the same page.

Historians call this period of humanist revival the **Renaissance**, which means "rebirth," to contrast it with the earlier centuries. Most historians no longer see the Renaissance as a sharp departure from earlier periods; they recognize that the intellectual advances of the twelfth and thirteenth centuries underpinned those of the humanist era.

---

*Cassandra Fedele, "Oration to the University of Padua (1487)," in *The Renaissance in Europe: An Anthology*, ed. Peter Elmer et al. New Haven: Yale University Press, in association with the Open University, 2000), pp. 52–56.

Europe's First Movable Type

The introduction of printing in Europe contributed greatly to the humanist movement because movable type made books cheaper. Johannes Gutenberg (ca. 1400–1468) printed the first European book, a Bible, using movable type sometime before 1454.

● **CONTEXT&CONNECTIONS** This was not the first book in the world made using movable type; the Chinese knew about movable type as early as the eleventh century, and the world's earliest surviving book using movable type was made in Korea in about 1377. Moreover, Gutenberg printed most of his copies of the Bible on paper, a Chinese invention. ●

Movable type, however cumbersome for Chinese with its thousands of characters, functioned beautifully for alphabetic languages like Latin. Close analysis of Gutenberg's earliest books shows variation among individual letters, suggesting that he may have made hundreds of the same letter by hand, maybe even from wood, and did not cast them from a metal mold as is often supposed.

Within fifty years of its introduction, printing had transformed the European book. Although European readers had once prized illuminated manuscripts prepared by hand, with beautiful illustrations and exquisite lettering, now typesetters streamlined texts so that they could be printed more easily. Some of the most popular books described marvels from around the world.

● **CONTEXT&CONNECTIONS** The Latin translation of the Greek geographer Ptolemy (ca. 100–170) and the travel account of Marco Polo (1254–1324), a Venetian who traveled in Asia, were both in Christopher Columbus's personal library, and he carefully wrote long notes in the margins of the passages that interested him. ●

Early European Exploration in the Mediterranean and the Atlantic, 1350–1440

Widely read travel accounts like Marco Polo's whetted the appetite for trade and exploration. European merchants, primarily from the Italian city-states of Venice and Genoa, maintained settlements in certain locations far from Europe, such as Constantinople and the island of Cyprus (see Map 15.3). These communities had walled enclosures called *factories* that held warehouses, a place for ships to refit, and houses for short- and long-term stays. The Ottoman conquest of Constantinople in 1453 encouraged many of these merchants to go west rather than east through the Islamic world.

Starting around 1350, European navigators began to sail past the Strait of Gibraltar into the Atlantic Ocean. In 1350, two Italian explorers wrote the first book about the Canary Islands and their non-Christian inhabitants. The Europeans captured some of these Canary Islanders and sold them in the slave markets of Europe, where they were much in demand. After 1350, cartographers began to show the various Atlantic islands off the coast of Africa on their maps.

One motivation for exploring these unknown islands was religious. As the Catholic rulers of Spain and Portugal regained different Islamic cities in Iberia during the thirteenth and fourteenth centuries in a campaign called the *Reconquista*, they hoped to expand Christian territory into North Africa. At the time, Spain itself contained several distinct kingdoms. In 1415, a Portuguese prince named Henry, now known as **Henry the Navigator** (1394–1460), captured the Moroccan fortress of Ceuta (say-OO-tuh). Using the rhetoric of the Crusades and armed with an order from the pope, his goal was to convert the inhabitants to

Renaissance

Literally "rebirth." Term used to refer to the period of humanist revival in Europe. Most historians now play down this term, recognizing that the intellectual advances of the twelfth and thirteenth centuries underpinned those of the humanist era.

Henry the Navigator

(1394–1460) Portuguese prince who supported Portuguese explorations in the Mediterranean, Atlantic, and along the West African coast.

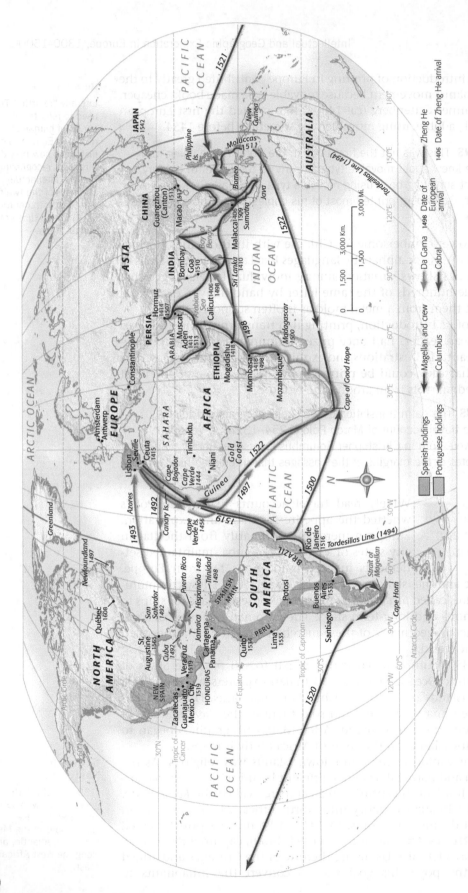

Map 15.3 The Age of Maritime Expansion, 1400–1600 Between 1400 and 1600, maritime explorers pioneered three major new routes: (1) across the Atlantic Ocean from Europe to the Americas, (2) across the Pacific from the Americas to Asia, and (3) south along the west coast of Africa to the Cape of Good Hope. Once the Portuguese explorer Vasco da Gama rounded the Cape in 1498, he connected with the well-traveled hajj route linking East Africa with China that Zheng He's ships had taken in the early 1400s (see page 456).

Christianity. Even today, Ceuta is part of Spain, and its population includes Christians, Jews, and Muslims.

Henry tried to take the Canary Islands for Christianity in 1424, but the inhabitants, armed only with stone tools, repelled the invaders; nevertheless, the Portuguese continued to capture and enslave Canary Islanders. Eventually, he Portuguese occupied the island of Madeira, and in 1454 they established plantations there, which soon exported large amounts of sugar.

● **CONTEXT&CONNECTIONS** Many navigators were afraid to venture past the Madeira Islands because of the dreaded torrid zone. Greek and Roman geographers had posited that the northern temperate zone, where people lived, was bordered by an uninhabitable frigid zone to the north and a torrid zone to the south, whose scorching heat made it impossible to cross. ●

Many Europeans had assumed that Cape Bojador, in modern Morocco, marked the beginning of the impenetrable torrid zone (see Map 15.3). But in 1434 the Portuguese sailed past the cape and reported that no torrid zone existed.

The Portuguese Slave Trade After 1444

Since no torrid zone existed, Henry realized, the Portuguese could transport slaves from the west coast of Africa and sell them in Europe. Portuguese vessels had already brought back thirty-eight African slaves from West Africa. In 1444, Henry dispatched six caravels to bring back slaves from the Arguin bank, south of Cape Bojador in modern-day Mauritania. The caravel was a small sailing ship, usually about 75 feet (23 m) long, that had two or three masts with square sails.

In 1444, Henry staged a huge public reception of the slaves for his subjects. The ships' captains presented one slave each to a church and to a Franciscan convent to demonstrate their intention to convert the slaves to Christianity. An eyewitness description captures the scene: *"These people, assembled together on that open space, were an astonishing sight to behold.... Among them were some*

The Varied Lives of African Migrants to Venice Completed in the early 1490s, this painting by Vittore Carpaccio (1460–1526) shows hunters shooting birds on a lagoon. Note the presence of African gondoliers (for example, the man in the right foreground). These men, most likely skilled rowers in their homeland, continued the same profession after their arrival in Europe.

Vittore Carpaccio (Italian, about 1460 - 1526) Hunting on the Lagoon (recto); Letter Rack (verso), about 1490 - 1495, Oil on panel 75.6 x 63.8 cm (29 3/4 x 25 1/8 in.) The J. Paul Getty Museum, Los Angeles

who were quite white-skinned, handsome and of good appearance; others were less white, seeming more like brown men; others still were as black as Ethiopians.... But what heart, however hardened it might be, could not be pierced by a feeling of pity at the sight of that company?"*

This may seem to be an early critique of slavery, but in fact, the author, like many of his contemporaries, saw the trade in slaves as a Christian act: the Africans, as non-Christians, were doomed to suffer in the afterlife, but if they converted to Christianity, they could attain salvation. From its very beginnings, the European slave trade combined the profit motive with a missionary impulse.

Within ten years the Portuguese slave traders had reached agreements with two rulers in northern Senegal to trade horses for slaves each year. The price of a horse varied from nine to fourteen slaves. Horses did not live long in sub-Saharan Africa's tropical climate, but because rulers liked them as a symbol of power and a war tool, the demand never flagged. By the time of Henry's death in 1460, Portuguese ships had transported about 1,000 slaves a year, fewer than the 4,300 slaves who crossed the Sahara overland in Muslim caravans each year at the time. After 1460, the oceanic trade continued to grow. Many of the African slaves worked on sugar plantations, either in the Canary Islands or on Madeira.

The Portuguese continued their explorations along the African coast, and in 1487, a Portuguese ship commanded by Bartholomew Dias rounded the Cape of Good Hope and the southern end of Africa. The Portuguese became convinced that the quickest way to Asia and the riches of the spice trade was around Africa, as Chapter 16 will show.

The Iberian Conquest of Mexico, Peru, and Brazil, 1492–1580

Christopher Columbus's landfall in the Caribbean had immediate and long-lasting consequences. Representatives of the Spanish and Portuguese crowns conquered most of Mexico and Latin America with breathtaking speed. In 1517, the Spanish landed for the first time on the Aztec mainland; by 1540, they controlled all of Mexico, Central America, and the northern sections of South America. Portugal controlled Brazil by 1550. By 1580, Spain had subdued the peoples of the southern regions of South America. Given that the residents of the Canary Islands, armed only with stone tools, managed to repel all attempts to conquer them for 150 years, how did the Spanish and Portuguese move into the Americas and conquer two sophisticated empires so quickly?

The subject peoples of the Aztec empire, who had not been integrated into the empire, welcomed the Spanish as an ally who might help them overthrow their overlords. Moreover, the Spanish arrived in Peru just after the installation of a new Sapa Inca, from whom his opponents still hoped to wrest power. The Europeans had other advantages, like guns and horses, which the Amerindians lacked, but the newcomers were completely unaware of their most powerful weapon: the disease pools of Europe.

---

*Peter Russell, *Prince Henry "the Navigator": A Life* (New Haven: Yale University Press, 2000), pp. 242–243, n8, citing *Crónica dos Feitos na Conquista de Guiné*, II: 145–148.

Columbus's First Voyage to the Americas, 1492 In 1479, Isabella (1451–1504) ascended the throne of Castile and married Ferdinand of Aragon, unifying the two major kingdoms of Spain. Throughout the 1480s, Columbus approached both the Spanish and the Portuguese monarchs to request funds for a voyage to the Indies by sailing west from the Canary Islands.

● **CONTEXT&CONNECTIONS** Following the revival of interest in Greek and Roman geography in the twelfth century, all informed people realized, as the ancients had, that the globe was round. The American writer Washington Irving (1783–1859) invented the myth that everyone before Columbus thought the world was flat. ●

In keeping with the scholastic and humanist traditions, Columbus cited several authorities in support of the new route he proposed. One passage in the Bible (II Esdras 6:42) stated that the world was six parts land, one part water. Columbus interpreted this to mean that the distance from the Iberian Peninsula to the western edge of Asia in Japan was only 2,700 miles (4,445 km). In actuality, the distance is over 6,000 miles (10,000 km), and the world is about 70 percent water and 30 percent land, but no one at the time knew this.

In rejecting his proposal, the scholars advising the Portuguese and Spanish monarchs held that the distance from Spain to Japan was far greater than Columbus realized. The men on board a ship, they reasoned, would die of starvation before reaching Asia. Although right about the distance from Iberia to Japan, these advisers did not realize that the Americas lay in between.

Several developments in 1492 prompted Isabella and Ferdinand to overturn their earlier decision. Granada, the last Muslim outpost in Spain, fell in 1492. In that same year the rulers expelled all Jews from Spain, a measure that had been enacted by France and England centuries earlier.

● **CONTEXT&CONNECTIONS** In 2014, the Spanish government offered citizenship to the descendants of the Jews expelled in 1492, but because the new law requires them to renounce their current citizenship, few are expected to apply. ●

Delighted by the conquest of Granada, Ferdinand and Isabella decided to fund Columbus, primarily because they did not want the Portuguese to do so, and also because he was asking for only a small amount of money, enough to host a foreign prince for a week. The monarchs gave Columbus two titles: *admiral of the ocean sea* and *viceroy*, a new title indicating he would govern any lands to which he sailed. Columbus was entitled to one-tenth of any precious metals or spices he found, with the remaining nine-tenths going to Isabella and Ferdinand. No provision was made for his men.

Columbus departed with three ships from Granada on August 3, 1492, and on October 12 of the same year arrived in the Bahamas. He soon proceeded to Hispaniola, a Caribbean island occupied by the modern nations of Haiti and the Dominican Republic. Although Europeans knew about Islamic navigational instruments such as the astrolabe, Columbus did not use them. He sailed primarily by dead reckoning: he used a compass to stay on a westerly course. By dropping a float from the ship's bow and counting the seconds until the stern passed the float, he estimated his speed and so the approximate distance he traveled in a day. From his travels to the Canary Islands and the Azores, Columbus knew when the prevailing wind across the Atlantic blew east and when west.

On his first return trip, Columbus wrote a letter to his royal sponsors, Isabella and Ferdinand, about his impressions of the island where he had landed:

> *Hispaniola is a wonder. The mountains and hills, the plains and the meadow lands are both fertile and beautiful.... The harbors are incredibly fine and there are many great rivers with broad channels and the majority contain gold.... The inhabitants of this island, and all the rest that I discovered or heard of, go naked, as their mothers bore them, men and women alike.... I gave them a thousand pretty things that I had brought, in order to gain their love and incline them to become Christians.**

The two sides exchanged gifts and tried to make sense of each other's languages. The island's residents spoke **Arawak**. *"They are the color of Canary Islanders (neither black nor white),"** Columbus noted, an indication that he thought of the Arawak as potential slaves.

In keeping with his humanistic background, Columbus updated Ptolemy to fit with his own experience. He explained to the Spanish monarchs that *"Ptolemy and the other geographers believed that the world was spherical."* Columbus believed this until his third voyage, when he came *"to the following conclusions concerning the world: that it is not round as they describe it, but the shape of a pear, ... or that it is like a round ball on part of which is something like a woman's nipple."** Columbus's eyes were troubling him, so the ocean seemed to tilt upward, and this was the only way he could explain it.

Columbus always thought that he had gone to Japan; he had no idea that he had landed on a continent unknown to the ancients. The first map to use the word *America* on a new continent (much smaller than reality) appeared in 1507; before then everyone assumed that Columbus and all the other explorers immediately after him were somewhere in the Indies.

Arawak

General name for a family of languages spoken in the 1500s over a large region spanning from modern Venezuela to Florida. Also refers to speakers of these languages.

A Comparison of Columbus's and Zheng He's Voyages

Many people have wondered why the Spanish and the Portuguese, and not the Chinese of the Ming dynasty, established the first overseas empires. The Chinese, who first set off in 1405, had almost a century's head start on the Europeans. (See the feature "Visual Evidence in Primary Sources: Comparing Zheng He's and Columbus's Ships.")

China was richer than either Spain or Portugal. It was arguably the most prosperous country in the world in the early fifteenth century, while Spain and Portugal were far smaller. Yet their small size gave both the Portuguese and the Spanish powerful motivation to seek new lands.

Unlike Europeans, the Chinese had no concept of a "colony"—nothing comparable to Madeira or the Canary Islands. The Ming emperor (r. 1403–1424) did not intend to make his huge empire bigger by using the voyages. He simply hoped

---

*J. M. Cohen, trans., *The Four Voyages of Christopher Columbus* (New York: Penguin, 1969), pp. 117–118, 35, 218.

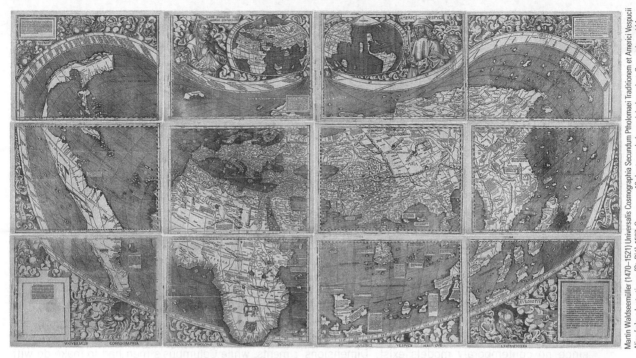

Martin Waldseemüller (1470–1521) Universalis Cosmographia Secundum Ptholomaei Traditionem et Americi Vespucii Alioru[m]que Lustrationes, [St. Dié], 1507. One map on 12 sheets, made from original woodcut, Geography and Map Division, Library of Congress

The First Map to Show the Americas   In 1507, a German mapmaker named Martin Waldseemüller published one hundred copies of this printed map of the world, in twelve sections, each measuring 18 by 24.5 inches (46 by 62 cm). When the Library of Congress purchased this map from a German library in 2001, it paid $10 million for it. This map depicts the Americas as a continent separate from Asia, a fact Columbus never realized. Waldseemüller named the new landmass "America," for Amerigo Vespucci, a navigator whose writings deeply influenced the mapmaker. Although difficult to see here, the word "America" appears halfway down the continent of South America, to the left of Africa.

to be acknowledged as the rightful ruler of the Chinese. Rulers of earlier Chinese dynasties had sometimes conquered other peoples, but in contiguous neighboring lands, never overseas.

The Ming government ordered an end to the voyages in 1433 because they brought no financial benefit to the Chinese. In contrast, the Spanish and Portuguese voyages brought their countries immediate returns in gold and slaves and the promise of long-term profits if settlers could establish enterprises such as sugar plantations.

- **CONTEXT&CONNECTIONS** A critical difference between Columbus's voyages and the Chinese ones was that the navigators on the Chinese treasure ships followed the best-traveled oceanic route in the world before 1500. Muslim pilgrims from East Africa traveled up the East African coast to reach their holy city of Mecca, and Chinese pilgrims sailed around Southeast Asia and India to reach the Arabian peninsula. The Zheng He voyages simply linked the two hajj routes together. In contrast, when Columbus and other European explorers set off, they were consciously exploring, looking for new places to colonize and going where no one else (or at least no one else that anyone remembered) had gone before. ●

Comparing Zheng He's and Columbus's Ships

What did Columbus's and Zheng He's ships look like? Since no drawings of any of their boats survive, nautical historians must compare multiple images of boats from the period to reconstruct what these vessels looked like. Even then, crucial information is still missing: the actual length of Columbus's main ship, the *Santa Maria*, ranged anywhere from 80–120 feet (24–37 m). A small wooden boat left as an offering in a church near Barcelona reveals the most about the construction of the *Santa Maria*. In the 1440s or 1450s, a sailor crafted it to give thanks for surviving a storm. Since he was not a shipbuilder, it may not be entirely accurate. But it has much more information about construction than do many drawings.*

We know even less about the Zheng He ships, since no contemporary models exist. Dimensions written in Chinese units survive, but scholars disagree about what they mean. Earlier studies used one value to arrive at a mind-boggling length of 400 feet (122 m), but a recent study, using a new

*Franceo Gay and Cesare Ciano, *The Ships of Christopher Columbus* (Roma: Libreria dello Stato, 1996).

value, has halved that to 200 feet (61 m), which naval historians agree is the longest possible length for an entirely wooden ship. Otherwise it would simply snap into pieces.

These estimates suggest that the Zheng He vessels were between 166 and 250 percent bigger than Columbus's.

The full fleet of 317 Chinese treasure ships, led by Admiral Zheng He, carried 28,000 men; the doctors on board outnumbered Columbus's entire crew. The Chinese ships were technologically more advanced, too. The ships had watertight compartments that could contain a leak. If Columbus's sailors could not plug a leak, the entire ship would fill with water and sink. The Chinese sailors feasted on fresh fish that thrived in their watertight compartments, while Columbus's men had to make do with hardtack, or dried biscuits.

Yet the size of the treasure ships was also a drawback. At 200 feet (61 m), they were simply too big to sail into unknown waters. One of Columbus's original three ships ran aground during the first voyage, and he complained that his ships were too large for successful exploration.

Comparison of Columbus's and Zheng He's Fleets

	Distance Traveled	Length of Ships	Number of Ships	Size of Crew	Number of Voyages
Columbus's ships	4,000 miles (6,400 km)	80–120 feet (24–37 m)	3	87	4
Zheng He's ships	7,000 miles (11,000 km)	200 feet (61 m)	317	28,000	7

These sails were made with bamboo slats so that they could be shortened during storms and let out when the winds were lighter.

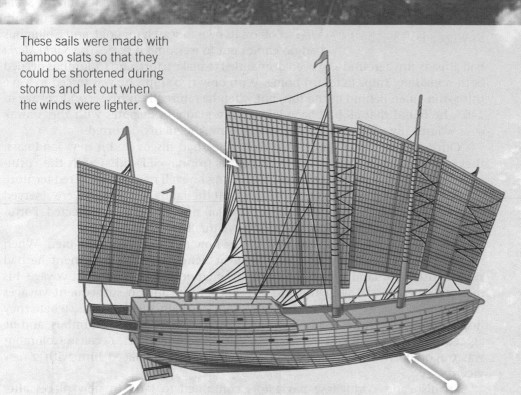

The rudder could be raised and lowered depending on the depth of the water. (After Bjorn Landstrom, *The Ship: An Illustrated History*)

The Chinese ships all had separate watertight compartments that significantly reduced the risk of sinking because of a single leak. *If you were a Spanish shipbuilder, would you adopt this feature from the Chinese ships, or is some other feature more important? Why?*

The cloth sails had only one size. If it was too windy to use them, the sailors could pull some of them down.

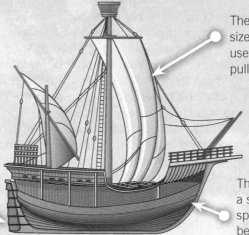

This rudder was attached to the boat's stern and could not be moved up and down.

The base of this ship forms a single compartment. If it sprang a leak that could not be repaired, it would sink. (After Bjorn Landstrom, *The Ship: An Illustrated History*)

Spanish Exploration After Columbus's First Voyage, 1493–1517

From the beginning Columbus did not exercise tight control over his ships, the *Niña*, the *Pinta*, and the *Santa Maria*. When he first reached the Americas, the ship *Niña* set off on its own to search for gold, and Columbus had no choice but to welcome it back. The *Santa Maria* had already run aground and been dismantled to make a fort, and Columbus needed both remaining ships to return home. With only two ships, he was forced to leave thirty-nine men behind in the fort, but when he returned on his second voyage in 1493, he found that all had been killed, presumably in disputes with the Arawak over women. By then skirmishes with the Arawak regularly occurred.

Once the Spanish realized that Columbus had discovered a new landmass, they negotiated the **Treaty of Tordesillas** (tor-day-SEE-yuhs) with the Portuguese in 1494. The treaty established a dividing line: all newly discovered territory west of the line belonged to Castile, while all the lands to the east were reserved for Portugal. Lands already ruled by a Christian monarch were unaffected. Portugal gained Africa, the route to India, and eventually Brazil.

Columbus never solved the problem of how to compensate his men. When recruiting sailors in Spain he spoke of great riches, but the agreement he had signed with Ferdinand and Isabella gave his men nothing. On his first voyage, his men expected to sail with him to Asia and return, but on subsequent voyages many joined him expressly so that they could settle in the Americas, where they hoped to make fortunes. In 1497, the settlers revolted against Columbus, and he agreed to allow them to use Indians as agricultural laborers. Because Columbus was unpopular with the settlers, in 1499 the Crown replaced him with a new viceroy.

Spanish and Portuguese navigators continued to land in new places after 1503. The Spanish crossed 120 miles (193 km) from Cuba to the Yucatán Peninsula in 1508–1509 and reached Florida in 1510. In 1513, Vasco Núñez de Balboa (bal-BOH-uh) crossed through Panama to see the Pacific, and by 1522 the Portuguese navigator Magellan had circumnavigated the globe, although he died before his ship returned home.

Treaty of Tordesillas

Treaty signed by the Portuguese and the Spanish in 1494 that established a dividing line: all newly discovered territory west of the line belonged to Castile, while all of the islands to the east were reserved for Portugal.

The Conquest of Mexico, 1517–1540

One of the early Spanish **conquistadors**, Hernán Cortés (hare-NAN kor-TES; 1485–1587), who led the conquest of Mexico, came first to Hispaniola in 1506 and moved to Cuba in 1509. Like many of the other Spanish conquistadors, he came from a family of middling social influence and made his fortune in the Americas. Cortés, in Cuba, learned that the Maya peoples of the Yucatán spoke of a larger, richer empire to the north. In two weeks he recruited 530 men to launch an expedition.

When Cortés landed on the coast of Mexico in early 1519, he immediately met a woman who helped him penetrate the Spanish-Nahuatl language barrier: a Nahua noblewoman named **Malinche** (mah-LEEN-chay) who had grown up among the Maya and could speak both Nahuatl and Mayan. Given to Cortés as a gift, Malinche learned Spanish quickly. The Spaniards called her Doña Marina. As adviser to Cortés, she played a crucial role in the Spanish conquest of Mexico, partly because she commanded the respect of the Nahua peoples.

Cortés landed on April 20, 1519, and slightly over two years later the Aztec had surrendered their capital and their empire to him (see Map 15.1). Yet this outcome was far from certain. After all, the Spanish had only 1,500 men.

conquistadors

Literally "conquerors," the term for the Spaniards who conquered Mexico, Peru, and Central America in the 1500s.

Malinche

A Nahua noblewoman, trilingual in Spanish, Nahuatl, and Mayan, who served as translator for and adviser to Cortés.

Cortés's Interpreter, Malinche This image, created by a local artist, dates to the 1500s and shows what Cortés's army, a mixed force, looked like. The Spaniards, with their heavy armor and a single horse, contrast sharply with the local peoples, who use bands tied around their foreheads to bear the weight of food in containers as well as to carry a small child (*far left*). Malinche, who was Cortés's mistress and interpreter, stands at the far right, with the bearded Cortés on her left. (Snark/Art Resource, NY)

The encounter between the Nahua and the Spaniards is unusual because we have surviving sources from both sides—the European colonizers and the indigenous peoples. One of Cortés's foot soldiers, Bernal Díaz del Castillo, wrote the most detailed account from the Spanish point of view. Sahagún's *General History* is not the same as a contemporary Nahua eyewitness account, yet since Sahagún and his team systematically crosschecked what their informants reported, it is the best Nahuatl-language account we have.

Sahagún records the response of the reigning Great Speaker Moctezuma (also spelled Montezuma) to the first envoy from the Spanish:

> It especially made him faint when he heard how the guns went off at the Spaniards' command, sounding like thunder.... And when it went off, something like a ball came out from inside, and fire went showering and spitting out.... And if they shot at a hill, it seemed to crumble and come apart.... Their war

gear was all iron. They clothed their bodies in iron, they put iron on their heads, their swords were iron....

And their deer that carried them were as tall as the roof.

The Spaniards' "deer" were horses, an animal not native to the Americas, whose size greatly impressed the Mexica.

On their way to Tenochtitlan, the Spaniards fought a major battle lasting nearly three weeks with the people of Tlaxcala (tlash-CAH-lah). After their defeat, the Tlaxcalans became the Spaniards' most important allies against the hated Mexica overlords. When, in November 1519, the Spaniards first arrived at the capital city of Tenochtitlan, the Great Speaker Moctezuma allowed them to come in unharmed. The Spaniards could not believe how beautiful the city was. Bernal Díaz, described this event: *"Gazing on such wonderful sights, we did not know what to say, or whether what appeared before us was real, for on one side, on the land, there were great cities, and in the lake ever so many more, and the lake itself was crowded with canoes, and in the Causeway were many bridges at intervals...."*

For one week the Spaniards and the Mexica coexisted uneasily, until the Spanish placed Moctezuma under house arrest. Then, in the spring of 1520, while Cortés was away, one of his subordinates ordered his men to massacre the city's inhabitants, and prolonged battles resulted. The Spaniards killed Moctezuma and, after suffering hundreds of casualties, retreated to Tlaxcala, the city of their allies. At this point, it seemed that the Mexica would win.

But by then smallpox had reached the Americas. The native peoples of America had little or no resistance to European smallpox, measles, malaria, sexually transmitted diseases, or even the common cold. Beginning in December 1518, disease ravaged Hispaniola and then Puerto Rico, Jamaica, and Cuba, and in the spring of 1520, smallpox crossed into the Yucatán and arrived in Tenochtitlan. Moctezuma's successor died of smallpox in early December, and the mass deaths threw the entire city into disarray.

Even so, the Spaniards had great difficulty conquering the Aztec empire. It took eighty days of sustained fighting before Tenochtitlan surrendered in August of 1521. Spanish guns and cannon were not decisive. Some one hundred thousand troops and a portable fleet of boats supplied by the Tlaxcalans enabled the Spaniards to win.

In 1524, the first Franciscan friars arrived in Mexico. The Franciscans became the most important missionary order among the Nahuatl speakers. They searched for parallels between native beliefs and Christian teachings; at the same time they suppressed practices, like human sacrifice and polygamy, that they saw as un-Christian. (See the feature "Movement of Ideas Through Primary Sources: *The Sacrifice of Isaac*: A Sixteenth-Century Nahuatl Play.") The Spanish gradually imposed a more regular administration over Mexico under the governance of a viceroy.

The Spanish Conquest of Peru, 1532–1550

The order of events in the Spanish conquest of Peru differed from that in Mexico, where Cortés had arrived before smallpox. In a smallpox epidemic in 1528 many Inca, including the Sapa Inca, died. War among the contenders to the throne broke out. In November 1532 the Spanish forces arrived, led by Francisco Pizarro (pih-ZAHR-oh) (1475–1541), at the moment of greatest

*Stuart B. Schwartz, *Victors and Vanquished: Spanish and Nahua Views of the Conquest of Mexico* (New York: Bedford/St. Martin's, 2000), pp. 97, 133.

instability in the Inca kingdom: when the newly enthroned Sapa Inca had not yet completely subdued his main rival. Atahualpa (ah-tuh-WAHL-puh; also spelled Atawallpa) had become ruler only after defeating his older half-brother, whom he still held in captivity. Atahualpa had taken severe countermeasures against his brother's supporters, many who sided immediately with the Spaniards.

When Pizarro and his 168 men arrived at the important city where Atahualpa was living, Atahualpa initially received the Spanish peacefully. Then, on their second day in the city, the Spanish attacked unexpectedly. Their guns, armor, and horses gave them an initial advantage. An estimated seven thousand Inca, yet not a single Spaniard, died in the carnage.

Pizarro himself captured Atahualpa, who offered to pay an enormous ransom for his release: the Inca filled a room 2,600 cubic feet (74 cubic m) half with gold and half with silver, which the Spaniards melted down and divided among Pizarro's troops. Those with horses received 90 pounds (41 kg), equivalent today to perhaps $500,000, and those on foot half that amount. Then the Spanish reneged on their agreement and killed Atahualpa.

It took twenty more years for the Spanish to gain control of Peru. In 1551, they named the first viceroy for Peru and gradually established a more stable administration. The first Spanish census, taken in the 1570s, showed that half the population had died from European disease, with the toll in some places reaching as high as 95 percent. The Amerindians who lived at high altitudes suffered much fewer losses than those living on the coast.

The Portuguese Settlement of Brazil, 1500–1580

In 1500, Pedro Álvares Cabral (kah-BRAHL) (1467/68–1520) landed in Brazil. Although the Portuguese claimed Brazil following Cabral's voyage, few of them came to this resource-poor country. Most Portuguese sought their wealth in Asia, as discussed in the next chapter. In 1533 the Portuguese monarch John III (r. 1521–1557) made a systematic effort to encourage the settlement of Brazil by dividing it into fifteen slices, each occupying 160 miles (260 km) of the coastline and extending inland indefinitely. He granted these territories to Portuguese nobles, many of them his courtiers.

John III also authorized the Jesuits, or Society of Jesus, a new order of Catholic priests founded in 1540, to preach in Brazil. Many Jesuits traveled to the interior, converted the indigenous peoples, and then resettled them in villages. (The Jesuits were also active and influential in Asia, as Chapter 16 explains.) The settlers searched for gold throughout the sixteenth century but never found significant amounts.

Instead, the Portuguese began to build sugar plantations, with the guidance of technicians brought from the Canary Islands. Since so many of the indigenous Amerindians had died, the plantation owners imported slaves from Africa.

The Structure of Empire and the Encomienda System

In 1580 Philip II succeeded to the throne of both Spain and Portugal, and the two countries remained under a single king until 1640. The Portuguese and Spanish empires had evolved parallel structures independently. The highest colonial official, the viceroy, presided over a royal colony and governed in concert with an advisory council who could appeal any decisions to the king.

Both empires had the **encomienda system**, first established by the Spanish in 1503. Life under the Aztec and the Inca empires had accustomed the peoples of

encomienda system
(Literally "entrusted") System established in 1503 by the Spanish in the hope of clarifying arrangements with the colonists and of ending the abuse of indigenous peoples of the Americas.

The Sacrifice of Isaac: A Sixteenth-Century Nahuatl Play

The members of the Catholic orders who lived in Mexico used different approaches to teach the Nahua peoples about Christianity. In addition to printing bilingual catechisms in Spanish and Nahuatl, they sponsored the composition of plays in Nahuatl on religious themes. Since these plays were not published but only circulated in handwritten manuscripts, very few survive. The short play *The Sacrifice of Isaac* recounts the story from the Hebrew Bible of Abraham and Isaac, which addresses a topic of great interest to the Nahua peoples: human sacrifice. The playwright chose the most important story in the Hebrew Bible. The ancient Hebrews believed that God tested Abraham, the chosen leader of their people. This story was also important to Muslims, who believed that Abraham almost sacrificed a different son, Ishmael (who makes an appearance in the play as an evil character). The lively quality of the Nahuatl language suggests that it was written sometime after the Spanish conquest, probably by a native speaker who converted to Christianity, and not by a Spanish missionary who learned Nahuatl as a second language.

As in the Bible, God the Father appears in the play to ask Abraham to sacrifice his son Isaac, but he later sends an angel to instruct Abraham to offer a lamb instead. Abraham, his first wife, and Isaac all embody obedience, a virtue prized both by the ancient Hebrews and the Nahua peoples. Abraham's slave Hagar and her son Ishmael urge Isaac to disobey his father, and both still worship the sun (not God), two sure clues to the audience that they are evil. Corresponding faithfully to the version in the Hebrew Bible, the play shows an obedient Isaac offering himself for sacrifice until the moment the angel intervenes.

> **What does the text propose as a substitute for human sacrifice?**

Source: The Sacrifice of Isaac, translated by Barry D. Sell, with the assistance of Louise M. Burkhart, in *Nahuatl Theater, Volume 1, Death and Life in Colonial Nahua Mexico*, ed. Barry D. Sell and Louise M. Burkhart, with the assistance of Gregory Spira (Norman: University of Oklahoma Press, 2004), pp. 149–153, 159–161.

The Devil, Ishmael, and Hagar Trick Isaac

(Demon enters dressed as an angel or an old man.)

Demon: O young man, what are you doing? You appear to me to have very great cares.

Ishmael: Yes, there is much that worries me. But how do you know if I have some cares? Who told you?

Demon: Do you not see that I am a resident of heaven? I was sent here from there in order to tell you what you are to do here on earth.

Ishmael: Let me hear your commands.

Demon: Listen, here is what has you so occupied today. It concerns the high-born noble Isaac, who is of such good life. He always gives credence to the commands of his father. But you have been thinking that you want him to no longer obey his father and his mother. I will tell you how to do it.

Ishmael: How very content I am to hear your words. Let me enjoy your help since you are a resident of heaven and you are a helper of people.

Demon: Take right to heart my commands. Look. Today his father and his mother have invited people to a banquet. There will be great contentment and enjoyment. But you are to oblige him to abandon his father and his mother by you and him going somewhere to play. And if he so ruinously obeys you they will despise their child for it even though they greatly love him.

Ishmael: I will carry out your command in that fashion.

Demon: As for me, I am going into heaven for I came to console you and to tell you what you are to do....

(Hagar the slave enters along with her child Ishmael.)

Hagar: Today the great ruler Abraham has yet again invited people to a banquet because of the great esteem he has for his child. But as for us, since we are lowly servants, we are held in no regard. And as for you, my child, you are doubly luckless. Would that I could find relief in you, that you could give relief to all my earthly torments, for in truth your birth and your lot are eternal weeping.

(At that point she and her child weep together.)

Ishmael: You, sun, who are very high up, warm us with your very great radiance everywhere in the world, with which you are able to please all the people of the earth. But as for us, the two of us are suffering. We are doubly luckless. But now know, O my mother, what I will do today when all are eating. Perhaps I can sneak [Isaac] out so that we will go play somewhere. Thus he will violate the orders of his father so that he will no longer love him with his heart.

Hagar: What you are thinking is very good. Do it so.

Abraham and Isaac on the Mountain

Abraham: Now listen, O my beloved child. The All-powerful, God, has strictly ordered me to [make sure] that his precious sacred commands are realized so that he will see if we people of the earth love him and if we carry out his sacred commands, for he is the ruler of the living and the dead. Now receive death with great humility, for he speaks thusly: I will be able to raise the dead for I am eternal life everywhere in the world. May his will be done.

(At that point Abraham weeps and the Misericordia is played on wind instruments.)

Isaac: Do not cry, O my beloved honored father, for it is with very great happiness that I receive death. May the precious sacred commands of God be done as he has ordered you [to do them].…

Angel: Abraham! Abraham!

(He seizes his hand.)

Abraham: Who are you that calls me?

Angel: Now listen up! By the power of God and by his orders, he has thus seen how you love him and carry out his sacred commands so that you do not violate them. For today you brought your beloved child, whom you greatly love, to the top of the mountain here in order to make an offering of him to the All-powerful, God the Father. Now it is by his precious will that I have come to tell you to leave him alone so that your beloved child, Isaac, will not die.

Abraham: May his precious commands be done as is his will. Come, O my beloved child, for you have now been saved from the hands of death.

(At that point he loosens the cloth with which the eyes are wrapped and he undoes the rope with which the hands are bound.)

Angel: Now know that the substitute for your beloved child will be a little lamb you are to make ready. Such is the will of God. Let us be on our way, for I am going to leave you at your home.

Mexico and Peru to shipping large quantities of goods, especially precious metals, to their rulers, and the encomienda system continued to collect resources and send them on to the center. Under this system, the monarchs "entrusted" (the literal meaning of *encomienda*) a specified number of Amerindians to a settler, who gained the right to extract labor, gold, or other goods from them in exchange for teaching them about Christianity. The monarchs took as their model the governmental structure used to administer lands newly recovered from Muslim kingdoms in the Reconquista.

At first the Spaniards who received encomienda grants had much more power than the immigrants who had not, but over time their advantage lessened. The encomienda recipients had easy access to unskilled labor and could collect tribute from the locals, but ordinary Spaniards could obtain a land grant and hire labor to build estates of their own. Although designed to protect the indigenous peoples, the encomienda system often resulted in even greater exploitation.

The social structure in the colonies was basically the same throughout Latin America. At the top of society were those born in Europe, who served as military leaders, royal officials, or high church figures. Below them were creoles, those with two European parents but born in the Americas. Those of mixed descent (mestizos in Spanish-speaking regions, memlucos in Brazil) ranked even lower, with only Amerindians and African slaves below them. By 1600, one hundred thousand Africans lived in Brazil, many working in the hundreds of sugar mills all over the colony.

The Columbian Exchange

Columbian exchange

All the plants, animals, goods, and diseases that crossed the Atlantic, and sometimes the Pacific, after 1492.

At the same time that European diseases like smallpox devastated the peoples living in America, European animals like the horse, cow, and sheep came to the Americas and flourished. In the other direction came plant foods indigenous to the Americas like tomatoes, potatoes, peanuts, and chili peppers. This transfer is referred to as the **Columbian exchange**.

Of all the European imports, smallpox had the most devastating effect on the Americas. Only someone suffering an outbreak can transmit smallpox, which is contagious for about a month: after two weeks of incubation, fever and vomiting strike; the ill person's skin then breaks out with the pox, small pustules that dry up after about ten days. Either the victim dies during those ten days or survives, typically with a pock-marked face and body.

One Nahuatl description captures the extent of the suffering:

> *Sores erupted on our faces, our breasts, our bellies…. The sick were so utterly helpless that they could only lie on their beds like corpses, unable to move their limbs or even their heads…. If they did move their bodies, they screamed with pain.**

Although no plants or animals had an effect as immediate as smallpox, the long-term effects of the Columbian exchange in plants and animals indelibly altered the landscape, diets, and population histories of both the Americas and Afro-Eurasia. When Columbus landed on Hispaniola, he immediately realized how different the plants were: "*All the trees were as different from ours as day from*

---

*Michael Wood, *Conquistadors* (Berkeley: University of California Press, 2000), p. 81, citing the *Florentine Codex*.

night, and so the fruits, the herbage, the rocks, and all things." He also remarked on the absence of livestock: *"I saw neither sheep nor goats nor any other beast."**

On his second voyage in 1493, Columbus carried cuttings of European plants, including wheat, melons, sugar cane, and other fruits and vegetables. He also brought pigs, horses, sheep, goats, and cattle. More like wild boars than modern hogs, pigs were the first to adapt to the Americas, eating wild grasses, reproducing in large numbers, and moving into many areas emptied of humans by the depredations of smallpox.

While smallpox traveled from Europe to the Americas, there is evidence that syphilis traveled in the other direction. The first well-documented outbreaks of syphilis in Europe occurred around 1495, and one physician claimed that Columbus's men brought it to Madrid soon after 1492. No European skeletons with signs of syphilis before 1500 have been found, but an Amerindian skeleton with syphilis has, suggesting that the disease did indeed move from the Americas to Europe. Causing severe pain, syphilis could be passed to the next generation and was fatal for about one-quarter of those who contracted it, but it did not cause mass deaths.

Assessing the loss of Amerindian life from smallpox and the other European diseases has caused much debate among historians because no population statistics exist for the Americas before 1492. Different historians have come up with estimates for the regions with the heaviest populations—Mexico, between 4 and 6 million, and Peru, between 10 and 12 million—but even these numbers are controversial. Figures for the precontact population can be little more than guesswork. The first reliable figures for Amerindian populations came with Spanish colonization. In 1568, Spanish authorities counted 970,000 non-Spanish living in Mexico and 1.2 million living in Peru. For the entire period of European colonization in all parts of the Americas, guesses at the total death toll from European diseases, based on controversial estimates of precontact populations, range from a low of 10 million to a high of over 100 million.

By 1600, two extremely successful agricultural enterprises had spread through the Americas. One was sugar, and the other was cattle raising, which took advantage of huge expanses of grasslands in Venezuela and Colombia, from Mexico north to Canada, and in Argentina and Uruguay. In each case the Spaniards began on the coastal edge of a grassland and followed their rapidly multiplying herds of cattle to the interior.

As European food crops transformed the diet of those living in the Americas, so too did American food crops transform the eating habits of people in Afro-Eurasia. American food crops moved into West Africa, particularly modern Nigeria, where even today people eat corn, peanuts, squash, manioc (cassava), and sweet potatoes.

● **CONTEXT&CONNECTIONS** Two crops in particular played an important role throughout Afro-Eurasia: corn (maize) and potatoes (including sweet potatoes). Both produced higher yields than wheat and grew in less desirable fields, such as on the slopes of hills. Although few people anywhere in the world preferred corn or potatoes to their original wheat-based or rice-based diet, hungry people gratefully ate the American transplants when their primary crop failed. By the eighteenth century corn and potatoes had reached as far as India and China, and the population in both places increased markedly. ●

---

*Alfred W. Crosby, *The Columbian Exchange: Biological and Cultural Consequences of 1492* (Westport, Conn.: Greenwood Press, 1972), p. 4, n2, citing Christopher Columbus, *Journals and Other Documents on the Life and Voyages of Christopher Columbus*, trans. Samuel Eliot Morison (New York: The Heritage Press, 1963), pp. 72–73, 84.

1492: The Break Between the Premodern and Modern Worlds

History departments offer many yearlong survey classes, and individual instructors often choose midway points for their classes. Not so for world history, which almost always breaks at 1500 (or 1492).

Christopher Columbus's landing on the island of Hispaniola changed the world permanently, and we know as much as we do about precolonial Mexico because of the work of Sahagún, his informants among the Nahua elders, and his young trilingual research assistants.

Many claims have been made about voyagers who reached the Americas before Columbus. Some of these voyages have left convincing evidence, like the Viking settlement at L'Anse aux Meadows on Canada's Atlantic coast in about 1000 or the chicken bones showing contact between Polynesia and the west coast of South America in the 1350s. Some of the claims are utterly baseless: absolutely no evidence suggests that Zheng He's ships reached the Americas, as has been proposed. Some theories are possible without being certain: English fishing

boats that sailed from Bristol to Iceland in 1480 and 1481 to seek new fishing grounds for cod might have made it all the way to the Americas, but they left no traces there. Whatever the credibility of these claims—and new evidence is emerging all the time—none of these voyages did more than touch down in the Americas, and they had no lasting impact. Columbus's voyages were utterly different.

After Columbus's landfall in 1492, the pace of events accelerated. Spain conquered Mexico in 1521 and Peru in 1551. The once-powerful Aztec and Inca empires collapsed quickly. They both had internal weaknesses; the many subject peoples of the Mexica resented their overlords, and the Inca were right in the middle of a protracted succession struggle.

The Europeans also had superior weapons made from metal. The Mexica and the Inca knew how to work different metals, including gold and silver, but they could not work iron, and they had no metal weapons. Theirs were

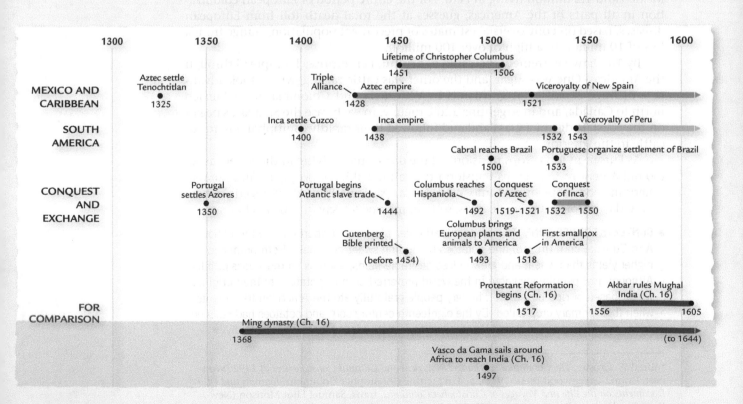

all made from stone and wood. Recall the eyewitness description from the *General History*, or Florentine Codex, of the Spanish army: their guns produced "thunder," they were clothed head to toe in iron, and their "deer" (read: horses) "were as tall as the roof."

European horses were only one example of the unfamiliar plants and animals that flowed from Europe to the Americas and from the Americas to Africa and Eurasia in the Columbian exchange. Cows, sheep, and pigs came to the Americas and altered the American landscape; tomatoes, potatoes, corn, and chili peppers traveled the other way, transforming first the European and then the African and Asian diets.

As discussed in Chapter 16, silver from Spanish mines in the Americas had an equally dramatic effect on the European economy. After 1550, when the Spanish mastered the technique of using mercury to separate silver from ore, they began to ship large quantities of silver home via the Philippines. The silver brought great prosperity to the Spanish empire and financed European purchases in Asia.

The diseases that came to the Americas from Europe devastated native peoples: smallpox progressed on its deadly route from Hispaniola to Puerto Rico, Jamaica, and Cuba and then on to Mexico and Peru. Because no population figures predate Columbus, it is impossible to know how many perished, but estimates range between 10 and 100 million. In 1568, the Spanish counted 2,170,000 non-Spanish survivors in Mexico and Peru, the two areas with the heaviest indigenous populations. Everyone else had died.

The mass deaths of the Amerindians preceded the large-scale movement of Europeans and Africans to the Americas. The migrations in the first hundred years after Columbus's arrival in Hispaniola produced the mixed population of the Americas today.

Before 1492 world history often concerns individual regions and the intermittent contacts among them. After 1492, Europe, the Americas, and Africa were so tightly connected that events in one place always affected the others. In the next chapter we will learn what happened when Europeans traveled to Asia.

Key Terms

Bernardino de Sahagún (436)
Aztec empire (437)
altepetl (438)
Tenochtitlan (438)
Inca empire (442)
ayllu (442)

quipu (446)
humanism (447)
Renaissance (449)
Henry the Navigator (449)
Arawak (454)
Treaty of Tordesillas (458)

conquistadors (458)
Malinche (458)
encomienda system (461)
Columbian exchange (464)

For Further Reference

Coe, Michael, and Rex Koontz. *Mexico: From Olmecs to the Aztecs*. London: Thames and Hudson, 2013.

Cook, David Noble. *Demographic Collapse: Indian Peru, 1520–1620*. Cambridge: Cambridge University Press, 1981.

D'Altroy, Terence. *The Incas*. Malden, Mass.: Blackwell Publishing, 2002.

D'Olwer, Luis Nicolau. *Fray Bernardino de Sahagún (1499–1590)*, trans. Mauricio J. Mixco. Salt Lake City: University of Utah Press, 1987.

Flint, Valerie I. J. *The Imaginative Landscape of Christopher Columbus*. Princeton: Princeton University Press, 1992.

Grafton, Anthony, et al. *New Worlds, Ancient Texts: The Power of Tradition and the Shock of Discovery*. Cambridge, Mass.: The Belknap Press of Harvard University Press, 1992.

Lockhart, James. *The Nahuas After the Conquest: A Social and Cultural History of the Indians of Central Mexico, Sixteenth Through Eighteenth Centuries*. Stanford: Stanford University Press, 1992.

McEwan, Colin, and Leonardo López Luján. *Moctezuma Aztec Ruler*. London: British Museum Press, 2009.

Quinn, David B. "Columbus and the North: England, Iceland, and Ireland." *William and Mary Quarterly*, 3d series, 49, no. 2 (1992): 278–297.

Schwartz, Stuart B. *The Iberian Mediterranean and Atlantic Traditions in the Formation of Columbus as a Colonizer*. Minneapolis: The Associates of the James Ford Bell Library, University of Minnesota, 1986.

Smith, Michael E. *The Aztecs*. Malden, Mass.: Blackwell Publishing, 2003.

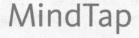 **MindTap** is a fully online, highly personalized learning experience built upon Cengage Learning content. MindTap combines student learning tools—readings, multimedia, activities, and assessments—into a singular Learning Path that guides students through the course.

16 Maritime Expansion in Afro-Eurasia, 1500–1700

Matteo Ricci

Courtesy of the Ricci Institute for Chinese-Western Cultural History at the University of San Francisco Center for Asia Pacific Studies

The Italian priest **Matteo Ricci** (1552–1610) knew as much about China as any European of his time. Though frustrated by the small number of converts he made to Christianity during his two decades as a missionary, Ricci (REE-chee) described Chinese political and social life in positive terms. In reading the passage below, we should be aware of the implicit criticism that Ricci, as an intellectual, makes of his own society, where men of war, he thought, had too much power and influence. Still, Ricci was correct in his assessment that China was more populous, more prosperous, and more stable than Europe in the first decade of the seventeenth century:

It seems to be quite remarkable... that in a kingdom of almost limitless expanse and innumerable population, and abounding in copious supplies of every description, though they have a well-equipped army and navy that could easily conquer the neighboring nations, neither the King nor his people ever think of waging a war of aggression.... In this respect they are much different from the people of Europe, who are frequently discontent with their own governments and covetous of what others enjoy.... Another remarkable fact and... marking a difference from the West, is that the entire kingdom is administered by... Philosophers. The responsibility for orderly management of the entire realm is wholly and completely committed to their charge and care.... Fighting and

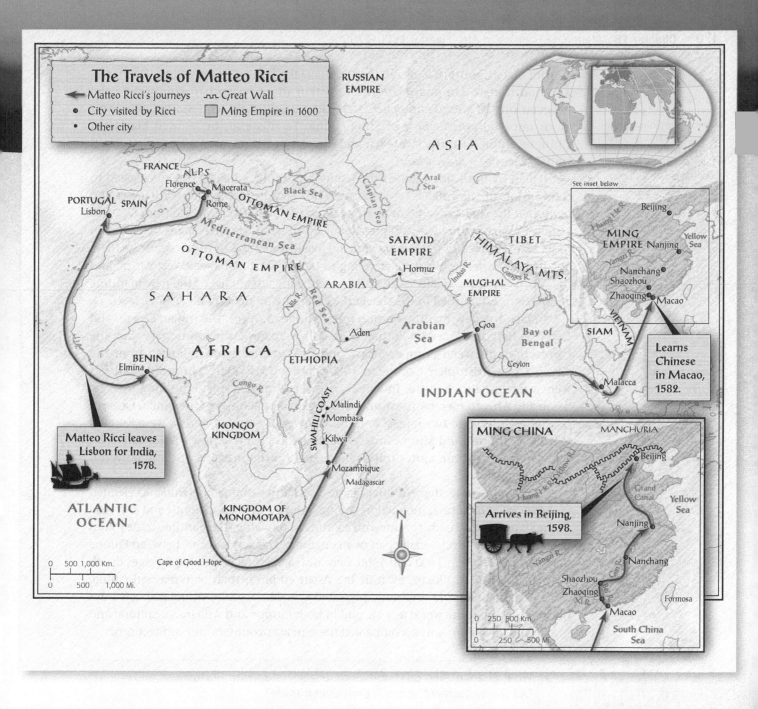

The Travels of Matteo Ricci

- → Matteo Ricci's journeys
- • City visited by Ricci
- • Other city
- ⌐⌐ Great Wall
- ☐ Ming Empire in 1600

RUSSIAN EMPIRE

ASIA

See inset below

MING EMPIRE

Beijing
Huang He R.
Yellow Sea
Nanjing
Yangzi R.
Nanchang
Shaozhou
Zhaoqing
Macao

FRANCE
ALPS
Florence
Macerata
Rome
OTTOMAN EMPIRE
Black Sea
Aral Sea
Caspian Sea

PORTUGAL SPAIN
Lisbon
Mediterranean Sea

TIBET
HIMALAYA MTS.

OTTOMAN EMPIRE

SAFAVID EMPIRE
Hormuz

SAHARA

Nile R.
Red Sea

ARABIA

MUGHAL EMPIRE

Indus R.
Ganges R.

Goa

Learns Chinese in Macao, 1582.

VIETNAM

AFRICA

ETHIOPIA

Aden

Arabian Sea

Bay of Bengal

SIAM

Congo R.

KONGO KINGDOM

SWAHILI COAST
Malindi
Mombasa
Kilwa

Ceylon

INDIAN OCEAN

Malacca

BENIN
Elmina

Matteo Ricci leaves Lisbon for India, 1578.

Mozambique
Madagascar

MING CHINA

MANCHURIA

Huang He R. (Yellow R.)

Beijing

ATLANTIC OCEAN

KINGDOM OF MONOMOTAPA

Arrives in Beijing, 1598.

Grand Canal

Yellow Sea

Nanjing

N

Yangzi R.

Nanchang

Shaozhou
Zhaoqing
Xi R.

Gan R.

0 500 1,000 Km.
0 500 1,000 Mi.

Cape of Good Hope

Macao

Formosa

0 250 500 Km.
0 250 500 Mi.

South China Sea

violence among the people are practically unheard of.... On the contrary, one who will not fight and restrains himself from returning a blow is praised for his prudence and bravery.*

*"The Diary of Matthew Ricci," in *Matthew Ricci, China in the Sixteenth Century*, trans. Louis Gallagher (New York: Random House, 1942, 1970), pp. 54–55.

Matteo Ricci

(1552–1610) Italian Jesuit missionary who traveled to China in the sixteenth century. Tried unsuccessfully to reconcile Christianity with Confucianism and convert Ming scholar-officials.

From Ricci's point of view, all that China lacked was religious truth. He understood that to communicate his Christian ideas he had to conform to the expectations of the *"Philosophers,"* the scholar-officials who staffed the enormous imperial bureaucracy of Ming China. To this end, he learned Mandarin Chinese, studied Confucian texts, and dressed in silk garments to show a social status *"equal of a Magistrate."*

Italian by birth, Ricci joined the Jesuits, a Catholic religious order dedicated to "conversion of the Infidels" (see Chapter 15). Because it was the Portuguese who pioneered the direct oceanic route from Europe to Asia, Ricci traveled from Rome to Lisbon to learn Portuguese and prepare for his mission. He then spent four years in India before traveling to China, where he lived from 1582 until his death in 1610. Meanwhile, other Jesuits were traveling to Japan, Brazil, Quebec, West Africa, and the Mississippi River Valley. The Jesuits were taking advantage of the new maritime connections established in the sixteenth century by pioneering navigators.

In fact, the new maritime routes from Europe to Africa, the Indian Ocean, and East Asia first developed by Portuguese sailors were far less revolutionary than the connections between Europe, Africa, and the Americas that followed from the voyages of Christopher Columbus (see Chapter 15). While European mariners were a new presence in the Indian Ocean, they traveled on routes long used by Asian and African merchants, connecting the diverse peoples of the Indian Ocean's coastal regions. The two largest and most powerful empires of Asia were Mughal (MOO-gahl) India and Ming China. As Matteo Ricci's story shows, Europeans who traveled the maritime routes initially operated on the margins of these powerful Asian empires.

At the same time, the creation of more direct and sustained networks accelerated commercial and cultural interaction among Europe, Africa, and South and East Asia in the sixteenth and early seventeenth centuries. Following the maritime trade routes to China, Matteo Ricci became part of an ongoing "great encounter" between Europe and China.* Between 1400 and 1600, new and deepening economic linkages developed in the Indian Ocean, even as the Asian empires, such as India and China, became larger and more ambitious. Increased global interaction stimulated new ways of thinking about the world as well, and in both Europe and Asia major cultural and intellectual developments accompanied these new encounters and connections.

FOCUS QUESTIONS

> What changes and continuities were associated with Portuguese and Dutch involvement in the Indian Ocean trade?

> What were the main political characteristics of the major South Asian and East Asian states? How was their development influenced by the new maritime connections of the sixteenth and early seventeenth centuries?

> How did the religious and intellectual traditions of Eurasia change during this period, and what were the effects of encounters between them?

---

*E. Mungello, *The Great Encounter of China and the West, 1500–1800*, 2d ed. (Lanham, Md.: Rowman and Littlefield, 2005).

Maritime Trade Connections: Europe, the Indian Ocean, and Africa, 1500–1660

Unlike the Atlantic, the Indian Ocean had long served to connect rather than divide, facilitating trade among East Africa, the Persian Gulf, India, Southeast Asia, and China along maritime routes complementing the Silk Road that had long bridged eastern and western Eurasia by land. The Portuguese added a new element to these networks in the early 1500s. Though their intention was to create an empire like that being constructed by Spain in the Americas, their political and military ambitions went largely unmet. The Dutch followed the Portuguese and had a greater economic impact, bringing with them innovations in naval technology and business organization that stimulated older oceanic trade networks while also building new ones.

Africa was connected to both the Atlantic and Indian Ocean systems. In East Africa, the Portuguese encountered an existing commercial network. In West Africa, however, an entirely new oceanic trade began: the Atlantic slave trade.

Portugal's Entry into the Indian Ocean, 1498–1600

Henry the Navigator's exploration of the Atlantic Ocean culminated in 1488 when Bartholomew Dias and his crew rounded the southern tip of Africa at the Cape of Good Hope (see Map 15.3, page 450). The Portuguese journeys had both economic and religious motives: in seeking an oceanic trade link with Asia, the Portuguese sought to outflank Muslim intermediaries who controlled the land routes through western Asia and North Africa. They were also keenly aware of the West African gold that was enriching their Muslim enemies in Morocco, and by sailing south they hoped to divert those riches to their own treasuries.

In 1497 the Portuguese explorer **Vasco da Gama** (1460–1524) sailed for India. Arriving in East Africa after rounding the Cape of Good Hope, da Gama hired a local pilot who used Arabic-language charts and navigational guides to lead the Portuguese from Africa to western India. One of these books boasted of the superiority of Arab knowledge: *"We possess scientific books that give stellar altitudes.... [Europeans] have no science and no books, only the compass.... They admit we have a better knowledge of the sea and navigation and the wisdom of the stars."* * The Portuguese were sailing into the same well-charted waters visited by Zheng He one hundred years earlier (see Chapter 15).

When they reached India, the Portuguese anchored their ships in cosmopolitan ports that were part of the world's most extensive maritime trading system. In the western Indian Ocean, merchants transported East African gold, ivory, slaves, and timber to markets in southern Arabia, the Persian Gulf, and western India. Among the many goods exported from India along the same routes was highly valuable cotton cloth, often dyed by Indian craftsmen specifically to appeal to customers in distant markets across the ocean. On the east coast of India, another set of maritime networks connected the Bay of Bengal and the markets of Southeast Asia with Ming China. Here silk and sugar joined the long list of traded commodities. Cinnamon from the fabled "spice islands" was particularly precious.

Vasco da Gama

(1460–1524) Portuguese explorer who in 1497–1498 led the first European naval expedition to reach India by sailing around the Cape of Good Hope, laying the foundation for the Portuguese presence in the Indian Ocean in the sixteenth century.

---

*Ahmad ibn Majid, *Book of Useful Information on the Principles and Rules of Navigation*, cited in *Saudi Aramco World*, July/August 2005, p. 46.

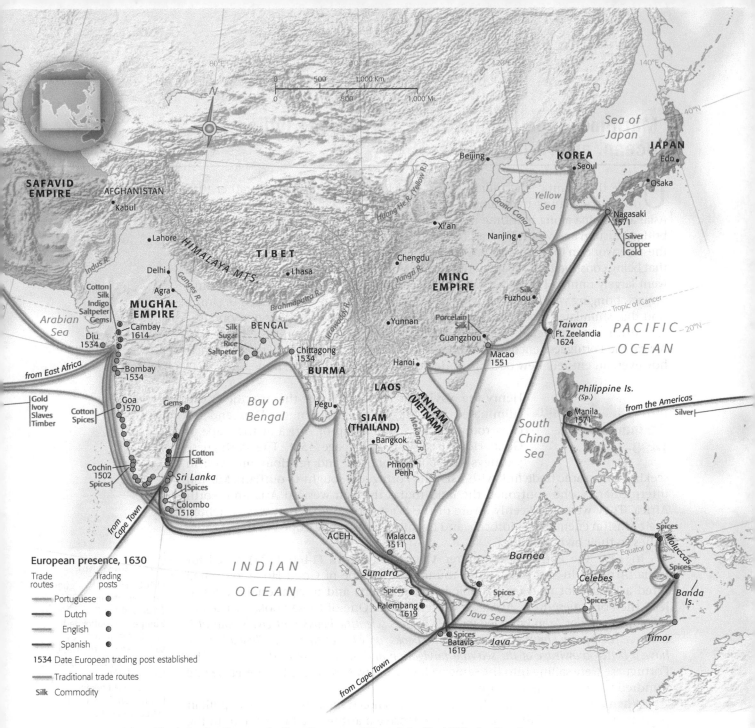

Map 16.1 Maritime Trade in the Eastern Indian Ocean and East Asia By 1630, the Dutch had overtaken the Portuguese in Indian Ocean trade, the French and English were becoming more active, and Spanish silver from American mines was stimulating trade across South, Southeast, and East Asia. Dutch ships passed through Cape Town in South Africa bearing Asian and African cargo for European markets. Still, the dominant powers in Asia remained land-based empires such as the Mughal empire in India and the Ming empire in China. Traditional trade routes controlled by local sailors and merchants were also growing in volume in the seventeenth century.

Europeans had long coveted Asian goods; the legendary "wealth of the orient" had motivated the voyages of both Columbus and da Gama. Even though the Portuguese now had direct access to these markets, they still faced a significant problem: European economies produced almost nothing that Asians valued. In fact, the first Indian king with whom da Gama negotiated ridiculed the poor quality of his gifts.

Nevertheless, the Portuguese could profit from their superior military technology. A prime example was Malacca, which they captured in 1511. Previously ruled by Muslims, the city was home to over fifteen thousand traders from all over the Indian Ocean world. Now the Portuguese controlled the narrow straits separating Sumatra from the Malay Peninsula, through which spices flowed on their way to India, Iran, and the Mediterranean (see Map 16.1). They profited handsomely. Using their cannon to seize trading centers all the way from East Africa to the South China Sea, the Portuguese earned a reputation as rough, greedy, and uncivilized.

In some cases the Portuguese redirected trade away from existing channels and toward their own coastal fortifications. In East Africa, for example, the gold trade into the Indian Ocean had been dominated for centuries by Swahili (swah-HEE-lee) merchants, coastal African Muslims who lived in cities built of coral stone and sailed to the Persian Gulf and beyond. The Swahili town of Kilwa was ideally situated, close to the gold deposits of the interior and also one of the furthest points south to which mariners from India, Persia, and Arabia could make a safe round trip in the same year harnessing the monsoon winds. Then the Portuguese used their cannon to destroy the sea walls of Kilwa and diverted the gold southward through their settlement in Mozambique (see map on page 469). That they did so while flying militant Crusader crosses on their sails did not endear them to local Muslim merchants and rulers.

But the degree of disruption the Portuguese caused at Kilwa was exceptional. More often, they simply inserted themselves into existing commercial networks and used military force to extort payments from Asian and African rulers and traders. "What they set up was not an empire," argues one historian, "but a vast protection racket."* Portuguese officials required that all ships trading in the ocean purchase a license, and if an Indian Ocean captain was found trading without one he risked Portuguese cannon fire. In effect, "the Portuguese were selling protection from violence which they themselves had created."*

When it came to promoting their religion, there was a large gap between Portuguese ambition and achievement. Initially, they had hoped to ally with "Prester John," a mythical Christian African ruler. Though Prester John was just a legend, the Portuguese *did* form an alliance in Eastern Africa with the Christian kingdom of Ethiopia. In fact, in 1542 Cristovão da Gama, son of the navigator, died while leading Portuguese forces against a Muslim enemy of the Ethiopian king. But the Ethiopians, Christians for over a millennium before the Portuguese arrived, had their own unique liturgy and orthodox beliefs and resented Jesuits attempts to convert them to Roman Catholicism. The alliance did not last, and in eastern Africa and all across the Indian Ocean world, it was Islam rather than Christianity that proved most attractive to new converts.

By the early seventeenth century, other European and Asian powers were adopting ship-based cannon and challenging Portuguese dominance. In 1622, a

---

*Michael Pearson, *The Indian Ocean* (London: Routledge, 2003), p. 121.

Burning of Churches by Muslims and the Death of Cristobal de Gama and the Fall and Death of Ahmed Ibn Ibrahim al-Ghazi (1506–43) Shot by a Portuguese Musketeer, c. 1900 (oil on canvas), Kegneketa Jemileri Hailu of Gondar (fl.1900)/Horniman Museum, London, UK/Bridgeman Images

The Ethiopian-Adal War In 1542–1543, Ahmad ibn Ibrahim al-Ghazi led Somali invaders from Adal in an attack on Ethiopia. Military alliances based on religion gave the conflict a wider regional impact, with Portuguese Catholics aiding Christian Ethiopia, and Ottoman Sunnis supporting Muslim Adal. The Somalis captured Cristóvão da Gama, son of the Portuguese mariner, and executed him after he refused to convert to Islam. In the top frame of this painting (by a later Ethiopian), Ahmad ibn Ibrahim al-Ghazi kills a priest, while his soldiers burn Christian churches. At the bottom, the Christians have their revenge: al-Ghazi falls from his horse, shot by a Portuguese soldier.

British-Iranian alliance drove the Portuguese from the strategic port of Hormuz, at the mouth of the Persian Gulf (see map on page 469). In 1698, an Arab siege drove the Portuguese from Fort Jesus, their principle fortress on the East African coast. But the most potent challenge to Portuguese commercial profit came from Dutch merchants, who were, by the early seventeenth century, developing both more efficient business systems and more advanced shipping technologies.

The Dutch East India Company, 1600–1660

Early Dutch trading ventures in Europe and the Atlantic were often very profitable, but merchants could be financially ruined if violent storms sank their ships or pirates stole their cargo. To spread the risk, they developed **joint-stock companies**, a new form of business enterprise based on the sale of shares to multiple owners. The joint-stock system allowed men and women of small means to buy a few shares and potentially reap a modest profit with little risk, since investors shared losses as well as profits.

These joint-stock companies put the Dutch at the forefront of early modern commercial capitalism. The development of financial institutions such as banks, stock exchanges, and insurance companies increased the efficiency with which capital could be accumulated and invested. Rather than seeking a single big windfall, investors now looked for more modest but regular gain through shrewd

joint-stock companies

Business organizations in which shares are sold to multiple stockholders to raise funds for trading ventures, while spreading both risk and profit; often backed by government charters granting monopolies of trade in particular goods or with specific regions.

reinvestment of their profits. This dynamic was at the core of the new capitalist ethos associated with the **bourgeoisie**, the rising social group in Amsterdam and other urban areas of western Europe in the seventeenth century. The bourgeoisie based their social and economic power, and their political ambitions, on ownership of property rather than inherited titles.

● **CONTEXT&CONNECTIONS** In some places, trading was a low-status activity, beneath the dignity of elite families. Wishing to acquire higher status, successful merchants in cultures as diverse as China and Spain would educate their sons to be "gentlemen" (in Spain) or "scholars" (in China). But in northern Europe, and especially in Holland, commerce came to be seen as a noble calling, a cultural reorientation that accompanied the birth of modern capitalism. ●

The greatest of the joint-stock companies, and the largest commercial enterprise of the seventeenth century, was the **Dutch East India Company**, founded in 1602. The government of the Netherlands granted a charter to the company giving it a monopoly on Dutch trade with Asia, overseen from company headquarters in Batavia in what became the Dutch East Indies (today's Indonesia). In the coming centuries, other European powers would copy the Dutch model and use chartered companies to extend their own national interests.

Though a forerunner of modern corporate capitalism, the Dutch East India Company was a heavily armed corporate entity that paid little heed to free-market principles, often obtaining its profits through force. *"Trade cannot be maintained without war,"* said one governor of the East India Company, *"nor war without trade."** The Dutch thus repeated the Portuguese pattern of using military force in the Indian Ocean to secure commercial profit, while at the same time introducing modern, more efficient business and administrative techniques. In addition to their commercial innovations, the Dutch had made major advances in ship design and construction.

In 1641, they seized Malacca and its profitable straits from the Portuguese. After 1658, the Dutch East India Company commanded Indian Ocean sea lanes from the island of Ceylon (today's Sri Lanka), a central point from which to connect the trade routes of the eastern and western halves of the ocean (see Map 16.1). To facilitate the long journeys from Batavia, Malacca, or Ceylon back to Holland, in 1652 the Company established a fort at Cape Town, at the southernmost tip of Africa. Cape Town became a "refreshment station" where ships could take on fresh water, perhaps some beef, and most importantly some fruit, without which sailors would suffer from scurvy. The Dutch East India Company administered Cape Town not from Amsterdam but from Batavia.

● **CONTEXT&CONNECTIONS** The environs of the Dutch settlement at Cape Town were the only place in sub-Saharan Africa where Europeans could live permanently without being decimated by malaria and other tropical diseases. Soon, a growing community of Dutch-descended settlers, later known as "Boers" ("farmers"), was competing with indigenous peoples for land and resources. Their descendants would dominate South African politics under apartheid and they remain an integral part of the nation today. ●

bourgeoisie

The French term for urban middle-class society—people with education and property but without aristocratic titles.

Dutch East India Company

Founded in 1602 in Amsterdam, a merchant company chartered to exercise a monopoly on all Dutch trade in Asia. The company was the effective ruler of Dutch colonial possessions in the East Indies.

---

*James D. Tracy, *The Political Economy of Merchant Empires* (New York: Cambridge University Press, 1991), p. 1.

Romeyn de Hooghe (attributed to) Joost van den Vondel

The Battle of Makassar In the region that today comprises Malaysia and Indonesia, the efforts of the Dutch East India Company to control strategic trade routes brought conflict with political and religious authorities. In 1693, they had arrested an influential Muslim preacher, Sheikh Yusuf al-Makassar, and sent him into exile in Cape Town (thus introducing Islam into South Africa). Then in 1699, the Company launched a full-scale war and successfully added Makassar to their Southeast Asian empire.

Apart from carrying spices and other goods back to Europe, the Dutch made substantial profits by plugging into existing Afro-Asian trade routes. For example, they sold Indian cottons in Africa and Southeast Asia, and transported spices from the Moluccas to India and the Persian Gulf. This inter-Asian trade was a partial answer to the old question of what the Europeans might offer to trade in Asian markets. However, the main solution to that problem was silver.

The Dutch were lucky that at this time the entire Indian Ocean economy was being stimulated by large quantities of silver mined by the Spanish in South America and shipped across the Pacific. In the seventeenth century, increased access to silver finally gave European traders bargaining power in Asia. The Spanish city of Manila in the Philippines became the destination for the Manila Galleons, an annual shipment of silver from Mexico, with additional supplies flowing eastward from Europe through the Mediterranean. Thus, the flow of silver between the Americas and Asia was helping to lay the foundation of a global economy connecting the Atlantic and Pacific economies with that of the Indian Ocean. The Dutch were perfectly positioned to benefit.

The Dutch East India Company made huge profits, especially from the spice trade. To do so, they sometimes violently intervened in local affairs to increase production. On the Bandas Islands, the Dutch were unhappy with the low level of nutmeg production. Their answer was to kill or exile the local farmers, turn their lands into nutmeg plantations, and replace the local population with slaves drawn from East Africa, Japan, and India.

Dutch investors were delighted with a rate of profit that ranged from several hundred to several thousand percent, as were European consumers who, thanks to the efficiency of Dutch methods, could now enjoy Asian spices at much cheaper prices. According to one historian, seventeenth-century Holland was so prosperous the country enjoyed an "embarrassment of riches."*

Africa and the Atlantic Ocean, 1483–1660

While the East African coast had oceanic links connecting the Swahili city-states with India, the Persian Gulf, and the wider world, West Africa's international networks were traditionally land-based, across the Sahara. When the Portuguese sailed down the West African coast in the fifteenth century, therefore, these were the first significant coastal contacts that West Africans had experienced. (See the feature "Visual Evidence in Primary Sources: An Ivory Mask from Benin, West Africa.")

Portugal's initial goals were the discovery of gold and transit to the East, as well as trade in commodities such as pepper and ivory. A new source of profit developed after they settled Madeira in 1454 and began growing sugar, already part of the Mediterranean economy, on Atlantic islands (see Chapter 15).

● **CONTEXT&CONNECTIONS** Sugar and slaves were fundamental to the Atlantic plantation system (covered in Chapter 19 of Volume 2). Cane sugar, originally from India, spread to the Mediterranean, where enslaved Europeans ("Slavs") worked on Arab plantations. The Portuguese brought this system to islands in the Atlantic, then to coastal Brazil. In the seventeenth century, sugar production, and demand for slaves, boomed when the Dutch, British, and French established plantations in Brazil and the Caribbean, which by the eighteenth century accounted for the vast majority of African slave imports in the Americas. ●

The **Kongo kingdom** (see map on page 469) was one of the earliest African societies to be destabilized by the new Atlantic slave trade. When the Portuguese arrived at the capital city of Mbanza Kongo in 1483, they found a prosperous, well-organized kingdom with extensive markets in domestically produced cloth and iron goods. King Afonso Mvemba a Nzinga (uh-fahn-so mm-VEM-bah ah nn-ZING-ah) (r. 1506–1543) converted to Christianity, renamed his capital San Salvador, sent his son Enrique to study in Lisbon, and exchanged diplomatic envoys with both Portugal and the Vatican.

Aided by the Portuguese, Afonso undertook wars of conquest that added territory to the Kongo kingdom. In West Africa, as in many parts of the world, captives taken during war might simply be killed, but more often they were exchanged, redeemed for a ransom, or kept as dependent workers. Slaves were a byproduct of the fighting, not its purpose. Now, into this traditional system came the new labor demands of the Atlantic plantation system. Portuguese merchants were anxious to purchase war captives, and Afonoso's battles had the side effect of further stimulating the market for slaves. As demand for slaves increased, tragically so did the supply.

Kongo kingdom

West-central African kingdom whose king converted to Christianity in the early sixteenth century and established diplomatic relations with the Portuguese. Became an early source of slaves for the new Atlantic slave trade.

---

*Simon Schama, *An Embarrassment of Riches: An Interpretation of Dutch Culture in the Golden Age* (New York: Vintage, 1997).

An Ivory Mask from Benin, West Africa

The kingdom of Benin (see map on page 469) already had a long history of political and cultural achievement before the arrival of the first Europeans in the sixteenth century. Believed to be descendants of Oduduwa (oh-doo-doo-wah), ancestor of all Yoruba kings, Benin's rulers, the *obas*, were associated with great spiritual powers. Starting in the fourteenth century, Beninese artists, organized into a guild by the king, began producing magnificent brass sculptures of royalty. Using a sophisticated "lost-wax" technique, they made a beeswax model, covered it with clay, fired the sculpture to melt the wax inside, poured molten bronze into the clay form, and then broke off the outer clay layer. Their achievement was not only technical but also artistic. The Benin bronzes are known for their naturalism, a quality that made them highly attractive to European collectors. In fact, in 1897, the British colonial government looted over a thousand of these invaluable pieces, and the fight to return them to West Africa continues.

The bronze used in these sculptures, however, was imported from the Mediterranean and was therefore extremely expensive. Beninese artists more often carved masks and wall decorations directly from wood and ivory, sometimes incorporating cowrie shells imported from the Indian Ocean. This ivory mask, made around 1520, depicts Idia (ee-DEE-ah), the Queen Mother of Oba Esigie (eh-see-GEE-ay). Like the Benin bronzes, it conveys a powerful sense of the individuality of its subject. The Portuguese were present in West Africa by this time and had allied with King Esigie and helped him fight off an enemy invasion. Their role in West African politics was still quite marginal, however, as indicated by the minor representation of European figures at the top.

A century and a half after this mask was made, a Dutch visitor in 1688 was impressed with the capital city:

The houses in this town stand in good order, one close and evenly placed with its neighbor, just as the houses in Holland stand. . . . The king's court is very great. It is built around many square-shaped yards. These yards have surrounding galleries where guards are always placed. I myself went into the court far enough to pass through four great yards like this, and yet wherever I looked I could still see gate after gate which opened into other yards. *

Though pepper was the main item of trade with Europeans when Oba Esigie ruled, by the time this Dutch observer described Benin, the market in slaves had become dominant. Here, as elsewhere in West Africa, a painful era had begun.

---

*Olfert Dapper, *Description of Benin* (Madison: University of Wisconsin Press, 1998), p. 40.

In Benin, as in many African societies, the Queen Mother was a pivotal figure in the king's council, and he often relied on her to gain a consensus of opinion among clan leaders.

The Queen Mother had a special role in representing the interests and opinions of women.

The oba of Benin, King Esigie, is said to have worn this mask on his hip at a commemoration ceremony for Queen Idia.

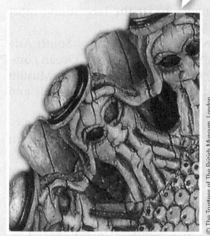

The figures on top represent the Portuguese who allied with King Esigie and helped him thwart an enemy invasion. These Portuguese figures resemble the mudfish often found in Beninese sculptures. Like mudfish, the Portuguese could travel both in the water and on land. *From the way they are represented on this mask, what might we infer about the extent of Portuguese influence on life in Benin?*

Alarmed at the escalating market for slaves driven by Portuguese demand, King Afonso complained to his *"brother king"* in Portugal: *"Many of our people, keenly desirous as they are of the wares and things of your Kingdoms,...seize many of our people, freed and exempt men....That is why we beg of your Highness to help and assist us in this matter...because it is our will that in these Kingdoms there should not be any trade of slaves nor outlet for them."** Foreign goods and foreign traders had distorted the traditional market in slaves, which had previously been an incidental byproduct of warfare, into an economic activity in its own right. Afonso's alliance with the Portuguese had led to rising violence, but his complaint fell on deaf ears.

As other European nations became involved in slave trading and sugar production, the demand for slaves increased decade by decade. At first, only those African societies closest to the western coasts were affected, yet by the eighteenth century the rise of the Atlantic slave trade would fundamentally alter the terms of Africans' interactions with the wider world.

Empires of Southern and Eastern Asia, 1500–1660

In the course of Matteo Ricci's long journey, he came in contact with a great variety of peoples, cultures, and political systems. By far the largest and most powerful of these societies were Mughal India and Ming China.

Mughal India was a young and rising state in sixteenth-century South Asia with an economy stimulated by internal trade and expanding Indian Ocean commerce. Keeping the vast Mughal realms at peace, however, required India's Muslim rulers to maintain a stable political structure in the midst of great religious and ethnic diversity.

In the sixteenth century, Ming China was the most populous and most productive society in the world. We have seen that Matteo Ricci was impressed with its order and good governance. But even while the Ming dynasty earned Ricci's admiration, it was beginning a downward spiral that would end in a change of dynasty in 1644.

Since political leaders in the neighboring East Asian states of Vietnam and Korea had long emulated Chinese systems and philosophies of statecraft, Ming officials recognized these states as "civilized." Japan, while also influenced by China in many ways, was by Ming standards disordered and militaristic in this period, though it did achieve a more stable political system in the seventeenth century. While Japanese rulers excluded European merchants and missionaries in the seventeenth century, the kingdom of Siam in Southeast Asia was far more influenced by rising maritime trade and the increasing European presence.

Mughal dynasty

(1526–1857) Mughal emperors who controlled most of the Indian subcontinent from their capital at Delhi during the height of their power in the sixteenth and seventeenth centuries.

Emperor Akbar

(r. 1556–1605) The most powerful of the Mughal emperors, who pursued a policy of toleration toward the Hindu majority and presided over a cosmopolitan court.

The Rise of Mughal India, 1526–1627

During Matteo Ricci's four-year stay in western India, the **Mughal dynasty**, the dominant power in South Asia, was at the height of its glory under its greatest leader, **Emperor Akbar** (r. 1556–1605), whose armies controlled most of the Indian subcontinent. Ruling 100 million subjects from his northern capital of Delhi, the "Great Mughal" was one of the most powerful men in the world.

---

*Cited in John Reader, *Africa: A Biography of the Continent* (New York: Vintage, 1999), pp. 374–375.

The Mughal state was well positioned to take advantage of expanding Indian Ocean trade. It licensed imperial mints that struck hundreds of millions of gold, silver, and copper coins. Dyed cotton textiles were a major export, along with sugar, pepper, diamonds, and other luxury goods.

State investment in roads helped traders move goods to market. The Mughals also supported movement of populations into previously underutilized lands by granting tax-exempt status to new settlements. Such settlements transformed the eastern half of Bengal (today's Bangladesh) from tropical forest land into a densely populated rice-producing region.

Agriculture was the ultimate basis of Mughal wealth and power, providing 90 percent of the tax income that paid for Mughal armies and the ceremonial pomp of the court at Delhi. The Mughals sent tax clerks out to the provinces, who surveyed the lands and diverted much of the revenue to Delhi. In those parts of India where a pre-Mughal aristocracy was used to collecting and retaining these taxes, the Mughals confirmed the old rulers' rights to 10 percent of the local revenue, and thus ensured their loyalty. This revenue system, controlled from the top but recognizing the prerogatives of local rulers, was part of a broader Mughal attempt to integrate existing Indian authorities into their government.

A principal political challenge the Mughal rulers faced was that their Islamic faith differed from the Hindu beliefs of most of their subjects. Though people may be conquered by the sword, more stable forms of administration are needed to turn conquest into long-term rule. Akbar's policy was one of toleration and inclusion. He canceled the special tax that Islamic law allows Muslim rulers to collect from nonbelievers and granted Hindu communities the right to follow their own social and legal customs. Hindu *maharajahs* and rural aristocrats were incorporated into the Mughal administrative system. Since Hindus were accustomed to a social system in which people paid little attention to matters outside their group, they could view the ruling Muslims as simply another caste with their own rituals and beliefs. Thus, the Mughals achieved a stable social order.

Akbar's policy of religious tolerance was continued by his successor Jahangir (r. 1605–1627) and his remarkable wife **Nur Jahan** (1577–1645). Jahangir himself was a weak ruler, addicted as he was to opium and alcohol. When faced with regional rebellions, therefore, it was Nur Jahan (noor ja-HAN), an intelligent and skilled politician, who took charge and kept Mughal power intact. Since women were secluded in the *zezana*, or women's quarters, she could not appear at court in person. Instead she issued government decrees through trusted family members. Taking a special interest in women's affairs, she donated land and dowries for orphan girls. From an Iranian family, Nur Jahan also patronized Persian-influenced art and architecture, building many of the most beautiful mosques and gardens in north India. So great was his admiration of Nur Jahan that Jahangir had coins struck with her image, a privilege usually reserved for the emperor himself.

Nur Jahan was also interested in commerce and owned a fleet of ships that took religious pilgrims and trade goods to Mecca. Even more than Akbar's, her policies facilitated both domestic and foreign trade and had a strong influence on the wider world. Indian merchants, sailors, bankers, and shipbuilders were important participants in Indian Ocean markets, and the cosmopolitan ports of Mughal India teemed with visitors from Europe, Africa, Arabia, and Southeast Asia (see Map 16.1). But there was little Chinese presence, and no attempt to follow up the fifteenth-century voyages of Zheng He (see Chapter 15). Unlike the Mughal rulers of India, the leaders of Ming China saw maritime trade more as a threat than as an opportunity.

Nur Jahan

(1577–1645) Mughal empress who dominated politics during the reign of her husband Jahangir and had a lasting cultural influence on north India.

Ming dynasty

(1368–1644) Chinese imperial dynasty in power during the travels of Matteo Ricci. It was at its height during the fifteenth century, but by 1610 the Ming dynasty was showing signs of the troubles that would lead to its overthrow.

The Apogee and Decline of Ming China, 1500–1644

By 1500, the **Ming dynasty** in China was at the height of its power and prestige. In 1368, the Ming had replaced the Mongol Yuan dynasty, and the early Ming rulers were highly conscious of the need to restore Confucian virtue after years of what they saw as "barbarian" rule. Like earlier Chinese dynasties, the Ming defined their country as the "Middle Kingdom" and called the emperor the "Son of Heaven." China was at the center of the world, and the emperor ruled with the "Mandate of Heaven."

The emperor's residence in the Forbidden City in Beijing (bay-JING), constructed during the early Ming period and still standing today, was at the center of a Confucian social order based on strict hierarchical relationships. The emperor stood at the top of a social hierarchy in which everyone owed him unquestioning obedience, while the emperor was expected to emulate the benevolent behavior of the greatest Confucian sages, seeking the best interests of those below him. Likewise, junior officials owed obeisance to senior ones, younger brothers to older ones, wives to husbands, and children to parents. Only men of similar age and status were "equal."

Hierarchy governed foreign relations as well. Ming officials respected those societies that had most successfully emulated Chinese models, such as Korea and Vietnam. Japan and the societies of Inner Asia were usually thought of as "inner barbarians," peoples touched by Chinese civilization but still uncouth. All the rest of the world's peoples were regarded as "outer barbarians." From a Ming standpoint, the only proper relationship between any of these other kingdoms and China was a tributary one. Foreign kings were expected to send annual missions bearing tribute in acknowledgment of China's preeminent position.

Confucians believed that if such stable hierarchies of obeisance and benevolence were maintained, then the people would prosper. And in the early sixteenth century, peace and prosperity were indeed the norm in Ming China. The networks of canals and irrigation works on which so much of the empire's trade and agriculture depended were refurbished and extended. Most important for trade and governance was the Grand Canal, connecting the political and military capital Beijing with the productive Yangzi River Valley and fertile rice-producing regions further south. Public granaries were maintained as a hedge against famine. At the height of the Ming, the roads were kept safe and ordinary people could find justice in the courts. New food crops, including maize, peanuts, and potatoes from the Americas, helped improve nutrition. The Columbian exchange, therefore, contributed to significant population growth in Ming China.

The **examination system**, based on the Confucian classics and requiring years of study, helped ensure that the extensive Ming bureaucracy was staffed by competent officials at the local, county, and imperial levels. With a hierarchy of well-educated officials supervised by dynamic emperors, the early Ming efficiently carried out essential tasks of government.

The elaborate and expensive Ming bureaucracy required an efficient system of tax collection. For that purpose, in 1571 Ming officials decided that all tax payments must be made in silver, generating a surge in global demand. Some silver came from Japan, but the rising demand in China was largely met by silver from the Spanish Americas. In East Asia, as in the Indian Ocean, American silver was facilitating both domestic and interregional commerce.

examination system

Chinese system for choosing officials for positions in the Ming imperial bureaucracy. Candidates needed to pass one or more examinations that increased in difficulty for higher positions.

● **CONTEXT&CONNECTIONS** The great global demand for silver would have negative consequences for some Amerindian communities. In South America, for example, the great silver mines of Potosí relied on the heavy toil of Amerindian workers, who often died as they labored to extract the valuable metal. Some of the silver arriving in south China came from Acapulco via the Spanish Philippines, a trans-Pacific axis of early modern international trade. ●

Despite the importance of silver imports, Ming officials strongly distrusted those who engaged in seaborne trade. They saw the ocean as an unpredictable realm, where uncontrollable Japanese pirates (or Chinese pirates disguising themselves as Japanese) had now been joined by European warrior-merchants. In addition, there were real economic trade-offs from the silver-tax system. Inflation accompanied economic growth: rising prices were particularly distressing for the less well-off. And fiscal reliance on silver made the Chinese economy vulnerable to distant economic shocks, as when global silver supplies took a sharp drop after 1620. By that date, economic contraction was contributing to an accelerating crisis in Ming governance.

The decline of the Ming is associated with the **Wanli Emperor** (r. 1573–1620). As a young ruler, he had displayed great energy in turning back an invasion from Japan. As he aged, however, the Wanli Emperor developed an apathetic attitude toward his duties, allowing personalities and petty jealousies to influence the imperial court. Uneducated eunuchs, whose traditional role was limited to caring for the imperial household, rose in influence at the expense of scholar-officials. Without imperial oversight, corruption increased: gifts could determine the outcome of court cases, grain intended for famine relief was sold on the market, and irrigation works went untended. Bandits vexed merchants on the roads, and local peasant uprisings became more common. When Matteo Ricci was finally granted permission to enter the Forbidden City and performed the ritual *kowtow*, prostrating himself with his forehead on the ground, he did so before a vacant Dragon Throne. The Wanli Emperor was inaccessible, remaining deep in the recesses of the Forbidden City.

Matteo Ricci, in his tribute to Ming governance cited in the chapter opening, failed to notice the decay that was setting in below the impressive façade of the Wanli Emperor's court. In 1644, northern invaders from Manchuria, taking advantage of the unrest caused by Chinese peasant rebellions, breached the walls of Beijing and drove the Ming from power.

Wanli Emperor

(r. 1573–1620) Ming emperor at the time of Matteo Ricci's mission to China. Vain and extravagant, he hastened the decline of the Ming dynasty through lack of attention to policy and the promotion of incompetent officials.

Tradition and Innovation: Korea, Vietnam, Japan, and Siam, 1500–1650

The societies most strongly connected to Chinese civilization in the early modern period were Korea, Vietnam, and, more loosely, Japan. The Choson (choh-SAN) dynasty of Korea, which closely followed the Ming imperial model, established one of the world's most stable political systems, ruling the Korean peninsula from 1392 until the early twentieth century. The capital at Seoul (sole) was home to a Confucian academy where young men trained for examinations that led to social prominence and political power.

Early modern Korea benefitted from a remarkable series of innovations undertaken by the **Emperor Sejong** (r. 1418–1450). Earlier, learning to read and write had required years of training in Chinese script. Then in 1446, Sejong (SAY-jung) brought together a group of scholars to devise a new phonetic script based on the Korean language. This distinctive han'gul (HAHN-goor) writing system, still in use today, greatly expanded literacy. Emperor Sejong then supported projects to write

Emperor Sejong

(r. 1418–1450) Korean emperor of the Choson dynasty, credited with the creation of the han'gul script for the Korean language.

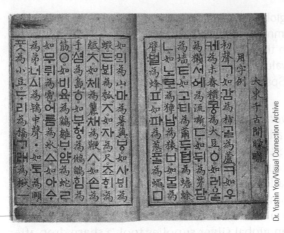

King Sejong and the Korean Alphabet *Hunminjeongeum* ("The Correct Sounds for the Instruction of the People") was a project sponsored by King Sejong to extend literacy by creating an alphabet based on spoken Korean. The text shown here (along with Sejong's statue in Seoul) is from 1446. Written in a mixture of Chinese and han'gul characters, it was used as a primer by those who could already read Chinese characters to learn the new phonetic script.

the history of the country in the new Korean script and to translate key Buddhist texts, using woodblock printing as well as moveable type to produce less expensive books. Korea became one of the world's most literate societies.

Vietnamese leaders copied Chinese imperial models while at the same time jealously guarding their independence. After the Ming had invaded and occupied northern Vietnam, a decade of sustained resistance led to their defeat and the creation, in 1428, of the new **Lê dynasty**. Legend tells us that General Lê (lee) sent a gift of cattle to his retreating Ming counterpart, as if to say that the invasion would not stop Vietnam from pursuing positive relations with China. Indeed, Confucian scholar-officials, literate in Chinese, gained greater influence in this period at the Vietnamese court. Military expeditions expanded the size and strength of the imperial state, and agrarian reforms led to greater equality in landholding and greater productivity in agriculture.

Japan lay further outside the orbit of Chinese civilization than either Korea or Vietnam. Political power was decentralized during Japan's Ashikaga (ah-shee-KAH-gah) shogunate (1336–1568), and the Japanese emperor, unlike his Chinese, Korean, and Vietnamese counterparts, was a ritual figure with no real authority. The greatest political power was the *shogun*, a supreme military ruler who acted independently of the imperial court. But the Ashikaga shoguns themselves had little control over the *daimyo* (DIE-mee-oh), lords who ruled their own rural domains. As each daimyo had an army of *samurai* (SAH-moo-rye) military retainers, incessant warfare spread chaos through the islands.

Ashikaga Japan was a land of contrasts. While the daimyo lords engaged in violent competition for land and power, they also acted as benefactors of Buddhist monasteries that promoted spiritual reflection. The samurai warriors, with their strict *bushido* code of honor and loyalty, were also practitioners of the Zen school of Buddhism, with its emphasis on mental discipline and acute awareness. (Zen practitioners are less interested in scriptural study and ritual observance than in inward contemplation, focusing on *being in the moment*.) Flower arranging and the intricate tea ceremony were peaceful counterpoints to the ceaseless war making.

Lê dynasty

(1428–1788) The longest-ruling Vietnamese dynasty. Drawing on Confucian principles, its rulers increased the size and strength of the Vietnamese state and promoted agricultural productivity.

Himeji Castle Incessant warfare during the Ashikaga period led the Japanese daimyo lords to build well-fortified stone castles. The introduction of cannon in the sixteenth century made the need for such fortifications even greater. Himeji Castle was begun in 1346; Toyotomi Hideyoshi greatly expanded and beautified it in the late sixteenth century. Now a UNESCO World Cultural and Heritage Site, Himeji is the best-preserved castle in all of Japan. (Jon Arnold Images Ltd/Alamy)

In the late sixteenth century, several Japanese lords aspired to replace the Ashikaga family; the most ambitious was **Toyotomi Hideyoshi** (r. 1585–1598), whose plans included not only the consolidation of power on the Japanese islands but also conquest of the Ming empire. In 1592, as Matteo Ricci was journeying in southern China, Hideyoshi's forces attacked the Korean peninsula with an army of two hundred thousand soldiers. A statue of Admiral Yi in central Seoul still commemorates his use of heavily fortified "turtle ships," armed with multiple cannon and with wooden planks shielding their decks, to defend Korea against the Japanese attack.

● **CONTEXT&CONNECTIONS** The East Asian balance of power would later be radically altered when industrialization empowered the Japanese empire after 1868. While Hideyoshi's earlier dream of conquering Ming China may have been a pipe dream, from 1894 to 1895 the Japanese navy did indeed crush the Chinese fleet in the Sino-Japanese War. In the 1930s, the Japanese military began its assault on China on the road to the Second World War. ●

In a power struggle following Hideyoshi's death, the Tokugawa (TOH-koo-GAH-wah) clan emerged victorious. After 1603, the **Tokugawa shogunate**

Toyotomi Hideyoshi

(r. 1585–1598) A daimyo (lord) who aspired to unify Japan under his own rule. His attempts to conquer Korea and China failed.

Tokugawa shogunate

(1603–1868) The dynasty of shoguns, paramount military leaders of Japan. From their capital at Edo (now Tokyo), Tokugawa rulers brought political stability by restraining the power of the daimyo lords.

485

centralized power by restraining the independence of the daimyo, forcing them to spend half the year in the shogun's new capital of Edo (today's Tokyo). Compared with the highly centralized imperial model of Korea, political power in Japan was more diffuse, with many daimyo still controlling their own domains. But the Tokugawa system brought a long-term stability that made possible economic and demographic growth. With peace came economic growth, and in the seventeenth century, as market exchanges became central to the Japanese economy, Japanese cities such as Osaka and Nagasaki emerged as vibrant commercial centers.

When the Tokugawa attempted to tame the power of the daimyo, some sought to protect their independence by forming diplomatic and trade alliances with Jesuit missionaries. Unlike in China, the Jesuits attracted many Japanese converts, but that only increased the shoguns' antagonism to the imported faith. After 1614, Tokugawa edicts outlawed Christianity. Hundreds of Japanese Christians were killed, some by crucifixion, when they refused to recant their beliefs. Apart from an annual Dutch trade mission confined to an island in the port of Nagasaki, no Europeans were allowed to enter the country. Japanese trade with China and Korea, however, continued to flourish.

In contrast to Vietnam, Korea, and Japan, the Southeast Asian kingdom of Siam (overlapping with today's Thailand) was influenced as much or more by Indian Ocean connections as by contact with China. Its Buddhist rulers welcomed merchants from all lands and sent emissaries and splendid gifts, including elephants, to the rulers of Iran, Mughal India, and Ming China. Then in the 1500s, with their rising kingdom struggling to establish independence from Burma, Siamese kings cultivated an alliance with the Portuguese, whose cannon and superior style of military fortification helped the Siamese extend their domains. Later, Siamese leaders also welcomed the Dutch, French, and British, although Asian traders still outnumbered European ones. Buddhism, Islam, and Hinduism were all more common than Christianity.

Siamese officials were usually careful to balance their relationships with the different, often competing, foreign communities. That balance was temporarily broken in the 1680s when one king sided too strongly with the French, much to the irritation of the Iranians and the English. (See the feature "Movement of Ideas Through Primary Sources: Iranians and Europeans at the Court of Siam"). In the longer term, however, Siam's diplomatic strategy was successful: the kingdom has maintained its independence ever since, its culture a rich amalgam of Southeast Asian, Indian, Chinese, Muslim, and European influences.

Eurasian Intellectual and Religious Encounters, 1500–1620

Early modern Eurasian intellectual ferment was often associated with new religious ideas. In western Europe, the Protestant Reformation divided Christians over basic matters of faith. Matteo Ricci himself was a representative of the Catholic Reformation, which sought to re-energize Roman Catholicism. In Mughal India, many people converted to Islam, and the new faith of Sikhism was founded. In China, Matteo Ricci attempted to convince Ming scholar-officials that Christianity was compatible with the oldest and purest versions of Confucianism.

Challenges to Catholicism, 1517–1620

While Renaissance humanism had led to significant artistic and intellectual achievement in western Europe (see Chapter 15), it coincided with increasing corruption in the Catholic Church. Popes and bishops raised money for prestigious building projects, such as the magnificent Saint Peter's Basilica in Rome, by selling "indulgences," which church authorities said could bring forgiveness of sins and entrance into heaven. Thus the cultural richness of the Roman church was underwritten by practices that some European Christians viewed as corrupt and worldly.

An infuriated cleric named **Martin Luther** (1483–1546) argued that salvation could not be purchased; only God could determine the spiritual condition of a human soul. With the availability of new printed versions of the Bible in vernacular languages (Luther himself translated the Bible into German), western European Christians no longer needed priests fluent in Latin to interpret God's will for them: the individual could find God's meaning in his own Gospel reading. Such ideas could be seen as a direct assault on the authority of priests, bishops, and the papacy itself. When Luther refused to recant, he was excommunicated. He then began to lead his own religious services, initiating the Protestant Reformation.

● **CONTEXT&CONNECTIONS** The Protestant Reformation was not the first great rift among Christians. In the eleventh century the "Great Schism" had divided the Eastern Orthodox and Roman Catholic branches of Christendom. Catholics recognized the authority of the pope in Rome and used Latin as the official church language. Orthodox communities, many with Greek as their liturgical language, recognized instead regional patriarchs owing nominal obeisance to the patriarch of Constantinople (even after the city was captured by Muslim Turkish invaders in 1453). ●

Not all the western Europeans who left Catholicism became "Lutherans"; others developed a variety of alternative church structures, rituals, and beliefs. In the seventeenth century, the number of Protestant churches multiplied. With European kings and princes choosing sides, these divisions between Christians would lead to terrible violence (as those reading Volume 2 will learn in the next chapter).

Still, much of Europe, like Matteo Ricci's hometown in central Italy, remained securely Catholic. But the Protestant Reformation shook the Catholic Church out of its complacency, leading to a response known as the **Catholic Reformation**. A major focus of the Catholic Reformation was more rigorous training of priests to avoid the abuses that had left the church open to Protestant criticism. As a member of the Jesuit order, or Society of Jesus, Ricci was especially trained in the debating skills needed to fend off Protestant theological challenges. The Jesuits were one of several new Catholic orders developed to confront the Protestant challenge and to take advantage of the new maritime routes to spread the Catholic faith around the world, thus globalizing the Catholic Reformation. The debating skills Ricci learned to counter Protestant arguments would come in handy when he later tried to convince Chinese thinkers of the validity of his Christian faith.

Another challenge to Catholic belief that developed during Ricci's lifetime was the "new science" associated with his fellow Italian **Galileo Galilei** (1564–1642). Catholic theologians had reconciled faith and reason by incorporating classical Greek thinkers, especially Aristotle, into church teachings. Galileo (gal-uh-LAY-oh) struck at the heart of that intellectual system by challenging both the authority of Aristotle and Catholic assumptions about the natural world. He contradicted

Martin Luther

(1483–1546) German theologian who in 1517 launched the Protestant Reformation in reaction to corruption in the Catholic Church. His followers, called Lutherans, rejected the priestly hierarchy of Catholicism, emphasizing that believers should themselves look for truth in the Bible.

Catholic Reformation

Reform movement in the Catholic Church, also called the Counter-Reformation, that developed in response to the Protestant Reformation. The church clarified church doctrines and instituted a program for better training of priests.

Galileo Galilei

(1564–1642) Italian scientist who provided evidence to support the heliocentric theory, challenging church doctrine and the authority of Aristotle. He was forced to recant his position by the inquisition, but his theories were vindicated during the scientific revolution.

Iranians and Europeans at the Court of Siam

The following description of foreign intrigue at the court of Siam is taken from the account of a diplomatic mission sent by the shah of Iran to the king of Siam in 1686. Written in Farsi (or Persian) by the Iranian envoy's secretary, *The Ship of Sulaimān* details both the longstanding influence of the Iranian merchant community, which had provided Siamese kings with key ministers and advisors, and the more recent favor shown to a French ("Frankish") advisor.

The author, Muhammad Rabī ibn Muhammad Ibrāhīm, emphasizes the cosmopolitan nature of the Siamese court and the extent of King Phra Narai's diplomacy across the Indian Ocean and around the world to Europe. By this time, Portuguese, Dutch, French, and British traders had been added to the existing mix of Indian, Malay, Chinese, and Iranian merchant communities in Siam.

As is so often the case, our source for this history is hardly an objective one: we should consider where and how ibn Muhammad Ibrāhīm brings a specifically Iranian point of view to his narrative. Still, much of what he tells us confirms what other accounts of the time tell us, such as the tendency of the Siamese to absorb diverse cultural influences and merge them into a distinctive blend (a process that continues in Thailand today).

Apart from giving us an inside view of Siamese politics, *The Ship of Sulaimān* also reveals a broader pattern typical of the early modern Indian Ocean: the ways in which Europeans inserted themselves into established Asian patterns of trade and diplomacy.

❭ To what extent does the European presence seem to represent continuity in this account, or have the Europeans changed the rules of the game?

❭ How did the Frenchman's military advice begin to change the diplomatic relations between Siam and other Indian Ocean powers?

Source: Muhammad Rabī ibn Muhammad Ibrāhīm, *The Ship of Sulaimān*, translated by John O'Kane (New York: Columbia University Press, 1972), pp. 94, 99–100, 103–104, 109–111.

From *The Ship of Sulaimān*

Since Siam is close to the ports of India and is situated on the sea route to China and Japan, merchants have always been attracted to settle there....Perhaps the best of these peoples is a group of Hindus who make it a point to refrain from all forms of violence and oppression....They refuse to kill any form of life and abstain from eating meat....But the Siamese themselves...do not adhere to any fixed doctrine but will admit into their creed whatever is convenient.

From the time [Iranian] merchants first arrived... each was honored with the utmost respect, presented with a house, and given a specific position in the Siamese king's administration....

[T]he king of Siam sincerely was interested... to learn about the other kings of the inhabited world...and sent everywhere for pictures depicting the modes of living and the courts of foreign kings [and] grasped the clear fact that perfect kingship,

glory and higher forms of government are the exclusive privilege of Iran. Thus...he abandoned his former style of clothing and started to wear Iranian clothes, our kind of long embroidered tunic, trousers, shorts and shoes and socks....

Since the king first broadened his horizons with education until this present day, he has been secretly devoted to Iran and has cherished hopes of effecting friendly contacts with our royal court....[He has also] often sent gifts to the governor of Hyderabad and different rulers of India, as well as to kings of various other regions....

[After the death of an Iranian who served as prime minister at the Siamese court, Ibrahim tells us, the Iranian community in Siam became divided into two factions, causing a leadership vacuum.]

The group of Iranians which was left was neither worthy nor capable of assuming higher rank....

Two or three persons who were actually offered responsible positions by the king would not accept, fearing the jealousy of their Iranian peers.... Everyone whom the king entrusted with tasks and sent abroad fell into debauchery and never came back to Siam. Soon the situation reached a point of urgency.... The king was not able to find an Iranian to act as prime minister and since the Siamese are not capable of handling the affairs of state, the king never used them in the past and was not prepared to use them now. The only candidate who remained was that one Frank [Frenchman] who had originally worked as a sailor....

Since he is in fact an extremely clever man and full of shrewd tricks, from the beginning he took pains to acquire the appearance of a good character.... [In Siam] the important factor...is to know the language well and to be versed in their protocol. Thus the Frank applied himself to learn the local speech, the laws and customs of the land and he had the luck to be in a position where there were no capable rivals to oppose him.... After a short time he rose to the post of prime minister and he has held that office for three or four years now.

The Frank minister has succeeded in penetrating into the king's affections to such an extent...that there is never a moment in public or in private when he is not at the king's side. To the world at large this Christian minister displays a record of service, integrity, thrift and sincerity and makes every effort to increase the state revenues and cut down expenses. However, it is a fact that every year he sends huge sums of money from the king's treasury abroad to the Frank kingdoms, supposedly for business purposes. Up until now there have been absolutely no visible returns from that money.

In accord with the spirit of hatred which exists between Islam and the infidels, the Christian minister is ever competing with Muslims for the upper hand, and...the Frank has tried to drive the Iranians out. By way of harming their reputation he is always on the lookout to expose their improper deeds and find some sign of their disloyalty to the king....

Despite the fact that the Iranians have long taken the trouble to help the king of Siam and have displayed their generosity and fairness by instructing him about the outside world, that illegitimate-born Frank, that Christian...has caused the king to alter his attitudes and now the king's inner thoughts wander on the path of error. Outwardly as well the king appears beguiled.

The Frank minister exercises a great influence on state policy and is continually provoking the king to injustice by saying, "How long will you continue to squander your benevolence on merchants and travelers who appear from every land and especially from Hyderabad and the states of India?... If you were wise you would hire a group of Franks, build several ships and proceed to capture the merchants and travelers of those parts.... Confiscate all their cargo and supplies. That will give the foreign kings cause to take note of your rank and position...."

The result of this calamity is that lately fewer and fewer travelers and merchants have been coming to Siam. The prime minister's behavior has even caused the English king to open the doors of war and it is a standing order amongst the English to capture Siamese ships wherever they appear. The English king also gave the order that no Englishman was to remain in Siam. If this [French] Christian stays in favor and continues along the same path, the Siamese king's power and kingdom will soon go into serious decline.

Aristotle by showing that a body in motion would stay in motion unless acted upon by an external force, an insight that would later prove essential to new understandings of planetary motion. Pointing his telescope toward the heavens, Galileo discovered spots on the sun, craters on the moon, and other indications that the heavens were not a place of absolute, unchanging perfection as the church had said.

Galileo also affirmed the heliocentric theory, first proposed in 1543 by the Polish astronomer Nicolaus Copernicus, which placed the sun, rather than the earth, at the center of the solar system. Church authorities argued that the heliocentric theory contradicted the book of Genesis by displacing the earth from its central place in God's creation. The inquisition, a church bureaucracy devoted to the suppression of heresy, tried Galileo and forced him to recant his support for the heliocentric theory. But the "scientific revolution" that Galileo had helped to launch could not be so easily suppressed (as those who read Chapter 21 will learn).

The ferment of the new ideas arising from the Protestant Reformation and the "new science" helped sharpen Matteo Ricci's intellectual training and prepare him for his travels. In India he took part in lively religious and philosophical debates that were valuable preparation for his missionary work in China.

Islam, Sikhism, and Akbar's "Divine Faith," 1500–1605

In the Mughal capital of Delhi, Akbar, in addition to bringing Hindus and Muslims together, attracted to his court scholars, artists, and officials from Iran, Afghanistan, and Central Asia. Mughal India proved a fertile environment for artistic growth as Persian, Turkish, and Indian influences flowed together. The best-known example of Persian architectural influence on India is the Taj Mahal, a "love poem in marble" built by Akbar's grief-stricken grandson as a memorial to his wife.

Akbar was keenly interested in religion, and he routinely invited leaders from various religious traditions to debate at his court. In 1579, the year after Ricci arrived at Goa, an embassy arrived from the Great Mughal requesting that Catholic missionaries come to Delhi. *"We hope for nothing less than the conversion of all India,"** wrote Ricci. Two missionaries went to Delhi, bringing a richly produced, lavishly illustrated, and very costly Bible as a gift for the emperor. Although the emperor did not convert, his interest in the Jesuit mission characterized his open-mindedness.

During this time, Sufism was also attracting new converts. In addition to obeying the Muslim laws of submission, Sufis were mystics who used special prayers and rituals, such as rhythmic motion and repetitive chanting of the ninety-nine names of God, to bring them closer to the Divine. They showed great devotion to the spiritual leaders who guided them in these practices, later venerating these teachers' tombs and often treating them as places of pilgrimage. Some Muslim scholars, especially those who stressed the more legalistic aspects of Islam, looked with suspicion on the emotional Sufi forms of religious devotion. Anxious to hear both sides, Akbar brought both the legal scholars and the Sufi mystics to his court and listened intently to their debates. Akbar also brought Jews, Hindus, and representatives of other faiths, such as Sikhs (sicks), to Delhi. Sikhism was a new faith whose monotheistic followers rejected the caste system while striving to reconcile Islamic and Hindu beliefs. Akbar extended to the Sikhs the same tolerance he had

---

*"The Diary of Matthew Ricci," in *Matthew Ricci, China in the Sixteenth Century*, trans. Louis Gallagher (New York: Random House, 1942, 1970), p. 114.

granted more established religions (though a later emperor would reverse that policy).

Having encountered so many different spiritual traditions, Akbar announced his own adherence to a "Divine Faith" that he said both included and transcended them all:

> *O God, in every temple I see people that seek Thee; in every language I hear spoken, people praise Thee; if it be a mosque, people murmur in prayer; if it be a Christian church they ring the bell for love of Thee...it is Thou whom I seek from temple to temple.** *

Akbar's "Divine Faith" never spread beyond the Mughal court and disappeared after his own death.

● **CONTEXT&CONNECTIONS** Centuries later, a Hindu reformer paid tribute to Akbar's open-mindedness, contrasting him with later, more orthodox Mughal sultans. Still *"celebrated for his clemency, for his encouragement of learning, and for granting civil and religious liberty to his subjects,"* he said, Akbar *"reigned happy, extended his power and his dominions, and his memory is still adored."†* ●

Meanwhile, Hinduism itself was undergoing important changes and reforms. The epic story of the *Ramayana*, formerly read only by priests trained in the ancient Sanskrit language, was retold in 1575 by a prominent poet using the commonly spoken Hindi language, making this story of the ancient king, a manifestation of the god Vishnu, more accessible. This development reflected new forms of Hindu devotion that de-emphasized the role of Brahmin priests. Like the translation of the Bible into vernacular languages and the new availability of Buddhist texts in the Korean han'gul script, the Hindi *Ramayana* promoted religious inquiry at all levels of society, not just among kings, priests, and philosophers.

. . . .
Ricci in China: Catholicism Meets Neo-Confucianism, 1582–1610

Ming China was less religiously diverse than Mughal India, with Buddhism as the empire's majority faith. In fact, when Ricci first arrived there, he adopted the beard, flowing robes, and shaved head of a Buddhist priest.

Private Collection/De Agostini Picture Library/Bridgeman Images

Akbar with Representatives of Various Religions at His Court For years, the Mughal emperor Akbar hosted weekly conversations among scholars and priests of numerous religions, including the Jesuits seen here on the left. Akbar sponsored the translation of varied religious texts, including the Christian Bible, into Farsi (the Persian language) even though he himself was illiterate. When criticized by some Muslim scholars for his patronage of Hindu arts and his openness to other religious traditions, including the Jewish faith, Akbar is said to have replied, *"God loves beauty."*

---

*Steven Warshaw and C. David Bromwell with A. J. Tudisco, *India Emerges* (Berkeley: Diablo Press, 1974), p. 60.

†Raja Rammohun Roy, *The English Works*, vol. 1, ed. Jogendra Chunder Ghose (Calcutta: Srikanta Roy, 1901), p. 307.

He soon learned, however, that the Confucian scholar-officials mocked the poorly educated Buddhist clergy. Ricci subsequently changed his appearance to appeal to this more prestigious class of individuals. His plan was to convert China from the top down.

Confucian scholars emphasized education as the main route to self-cultivation. While most of the emperor's subjects remained illiterate peasant cultivators, boys from more privileged households were taught to read from a young age. After they had mastered the basics, they had to memorize the classic texts of Confucianism, collections of poems, and histories of past times that usually focused on the virtues of ancient sages.

In theory, any young man could take the annual examinations and, if successful, become an imperial official. In reality, only the elite could afford the private tutors needed for success. Still, the Ming system was based on merit: wealth and status could not purchase high office, and even the privileged had to undergo years of intensive study.

● **CONTEXT&CONNECTIONS** In the nineteenth century, Chinese reformers hoped to strengthen the empire's position in an industrializing world by balancing tradition with modernization, for example, by adjusting the imperial examinations to include natural sciences, mathematics, and modern languages. Conservatives resisted those changes, and China fell behind its rivals. Even today, though Confucianism is no longer the topic, aspiring university students in China (and Korea and Japan) study intensively for brutally difficult examinations to earn a place at a top university and thus a secure government job. ●

Although women were barred from taking the examinations, the Ming emphasis on education did contribute to the spread of female literacy. Foreign observers noted how many girls were able to read and write. However, while boys read histories of sages and virtuous officials, girls usually read stories about women who submitted to their parents when they were young, obeyed their husbands once they were married, and listened to their sons when they became widowed. Singled out for special praise were widows who demonstrated eternal loyalty to their husbands by declining to be remarried. Chinese girls were thereby indoctrinated into the Confucian ideal of strict gender hierarchy.

Matteo Ricci paid careful attention to debates between advocates of various schools of Confucianism as he built up an argument for the compatibility of Confucianism and Christianity. At this time the Neo-Confucian philosophy of Wang Yangming (1472–1529) was especially influential. While other Confucians had emphasized close observation of the external world, Wang stressed self-reflection, arguing that everyone possesses innate knowledge. Ricci accused Wang's Neo-Confucian followers of distorting Confucianism, arguing that the original ethos of Confucianism was both more pure and more compatible with Christianity. By returning to the original works of the sages, Ricci said, the Chinese literati would discover that one could convert to Christianity while retaining their ancient ethical and philosophical traditions.

Once his language skills were sufficiently developed, Ricci took advantage of a favorite Ming pastime to share his views. Scholar-officials would often invite interesting speakers to a banquet and, after dinner, hold philosophical debates. For many in the audience Ricci's well-known ability to instantly memorize and repeat long lists of information, and even repeat them backward, would have been of greater interest than his views on Confucian philosophy and Christian theology. It was a highly relevant skill in a society where difficult exams were the main path to power and status. While his hosts might have been entertained by his arguments, few were persuaded by them.

Ricci also impressed his hosts with examples of European art and technology, especially printed books, paintings, clocks, and maps. Some Chinese artists experimented with European techniques of landscape painting, and Ming astronomers were impressed by European telescopes and the precision with which the Jesuits could predict such events as eclipses. Late-sixteenth-century European clocks, while not very reliable by later standards, were much more accurate than the water clocks used by the Chinese. Ricci's world map, locating the "western barbarians" for the first time in relation to the "Middle Kingdom," was such a success that Chinese artisans were employed to print reproductions.

For Ricci, however, mnemonic tricks, maps, and clocks were only a means to convert his audience to Christianity. Criticizing both Buddhism and Neo-Confucianism, Ricci emphasized those aspects of the Western tradition that appealed most to Confucian intellectuals: its moral and ethical dimensions rather than its character as a revealed religion. For example, after learning that Chinese scholars were disturbed by accounts of the suffering and death of Jesus, he largely avoided that central aspect of Christianity. (See the feature "World History in Today's World: Christianity in China.")

The most influential work published in Chinese under Ricci's name was *The True Meaning of the Lord of Heaven*. Composed together with Chinese Christian converts, who provided key insights on Confucian thinking and guidance with difficult translation issues, it is a dialogue between a "Chinese Scholar" and a "Western Scholar." In the following passage the text criticizes Buddhism and argues for the compatibility of Confucianism and Christianity:

CHINESE SCHOLAR: *The Buddha taught that the visible world emerges from "voidness" and made "voidness" the end of all effort. The Confucians say: "In the processes of Yi there exists the Supreme Ultimate" and therefore make "existence" the basic principle [of all things] and "sincerity" the subject of the study of self-cultivation. I wonder who, in your revered view, is correct?*

WESTERN SCHOLAR: *The "voidness" taught by the Buddha [is] totally at variance with the doctrine concerning the Lord of Heaven [i.e., Christianity], and it is therefore abundantly clear that [it does] not merit esteem. When it comes to the "existence" and "sincerity" of the Confucians, however...they would seem to be close to the truth.**

---

*Matteo Ricci, *The True Meaning of the Lord of Heaven*, trans. Douglas Lancashire and Peter Hu Kuo-chen, S.J. (Paris: Institut Ricci-Centre d'études chinoises, 1985), p. 99.

Christianity in China

Marxist ideology predicts that religion will fade away as an educated society develops a more scientific outlook. But even after six decades of official atheism, the number of practicing Chinese Christians in the People's Republic of China has increased dramatically.

Exact numbers are difficult to obtain because most Chinese Christians practice their faith outside of the official religious "Patriotic Associations" recognized by the government. Thus, although there are about 12 million Roman Catholics, at least half are members of unregistered congregations, unrecognized (and therefore not counted) by the government. When the communist government set up the National Catholic Patriotic Association in the 1950s, it took over from the Vatican the power to appoint bishops, a role central to church tradition and to papal authority. Many Catholics, still loyal to the papacy, worship with "underground" priests and bishops. Though there has been some diplomacy aimed at reconciliation, tensions between the Vatican and the communist government over appointment of bishops continues, and Chinese Catholics were prevented from traveling to South Korea when Pope Francis I visited Seoul in 2014.

Meanwhile, Protestant growth in China has been even more spectacular, from less than 1 million in 1949 to perhaps 60 million today, with the vast majority practicing in unregistered churches. In the 1950s, the government amalgamated all the different Protestant denominations into one bland, mainstream organization: the National Protestant Patriotic Association. But the official church was never intended to promote or accept the kind of rapid growth we see today, nor are most communist officials tolerant of the more emotional, evangelical forms of worship that now appeal to so many.

"Contain religion" is official policy, and local party bosses often prevent the prominent display of crosses. Occasionally, there are signs of conciliation; perhaps some communist authorities recognize that churches help people to cope with the destabilizing social changes brought on by rapid economic growth. Still, arbitrary oppression can reappear at a moment's notice. In early 2014, for example, officials in Wenzhou ordered the destruction of a large and prominent church they had earlier approved, citing "zoning" violations. "People are stunned," said one local Christian. "They have completely lost faith in the local religious authorities."

Will at least limited government tolerance toward Christianity continue? Perhaps, so longe as unregistered churches lay low and avoid national or international links that challenge communist party supremacy.

Source: "Church-State Clash in China Coalesces Around a Toppled Spire," Ian Johnson, New York Times, May 29, 2014.

Such arguments did not convince many, but at least in China Ming authorities accepted Catholicism as a legitimate school of philosophy (as in Mughal India, and in sharp contrast to the repression faced by Christians in seventeenth-century Japan).

Some European Catholics felt that Ricci's attempt to reconcile Christianity and Confucianism went too far. For example, Ricci argued that veneration of ancestors was compatible with Christianity and the biblical command to "honor your father and your mother." Less flexible church authorities felt that Chinese ancestor rites were pagan and should be rejected. Ricci knew that such a rigid interpretation of cultural practice would limit the appeal of Christianity among potential converts, who would be ostracized by family and friends if they abandoned their household shrines. In fact, after an eighteenth-century pope later declared that ancestor worship was idolatrous, Catholicism lost its status as a legitimate faith in China. Nevertheless, by debating these issues, Ricci had helped to lay the foundation of what became an ongoing "great encounter" between Europe and China.

Empires of Land and Sea

When Christopher Columbus sailed west to reach the "Indies," he greatly underestimated the circumference of the globe. The better-informed Portuguese, whose route Matteo Ricci followed to China, succeeded where Columbus failed by establishing a direct oceanic link to the riches of the Indian Ocean and South China Sea. Nevertheless, the biologic, demographic, political, and economic consequences of Columbus's journeys were more dramatic. The "Columbian encounter," which brought the Eastern and Western Hemispheres into systematic contact for the first time, was in many ways the starting point of modern world history.

Prior to 1500 the Indian Ocean, in contrast to the Atlantic, was already interconnected, although those connections were commercial and cultural rather than political or military, and largely remained so. Ming emperors had proven uninterested in pursuing political dominance across the ocean at the time of Zheng He in the fifteenth century (see Chapter 15), while the Portuguese and other European powers tried but failed. The story of maritime expansion in Asia is therefore as much one of continuity as of change. Massive land-based empires, especially the Mughal dynasty in India and the Ming dynasty in China, remained the dominant powers. Inter-Asian trade remained the key to commercial profit, even as the Portuguese and later the Dutch inserted themselves into these markets. In Africa, the Atlantic slave trade was new and an ominous sign for the future, but at first it affected only a few coastal West African societies; East African city-states continued their traditional orientation toward commerce with India and the Persian Gulf.

However, there were also important changes in the Indian Ocean world in the sixteenth and seventeenth centuries. The destructive power of ship-based cannon allowed the Portuguese to seize crucial transit points such as Malacca, setting an example that would later be followed by the Dutch, British, and French. The innovative ship designs and commercial practices of the Dutch further stimulated trade and made the competition between European chartered companies a new feature of Asian politics. The influx of American silver was

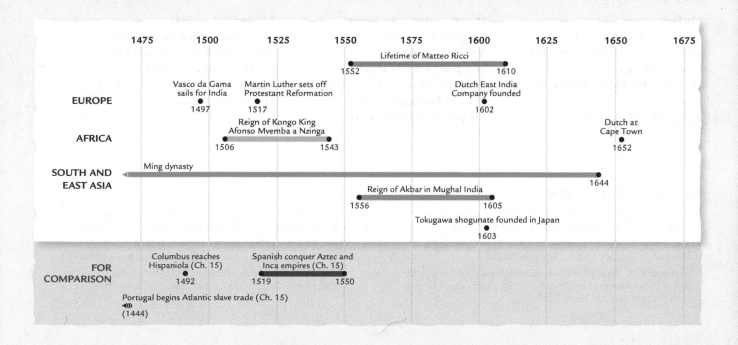

EUROPE
- Lifetime of Matteo Ricci — 1552 to 1610
- Vasco da Gama sails for India — 1497
- Martin Luther sets off Protestant Reformation — 1517
- Dutch East India Company founded — 1602

AFRICA
- Reign of Kongo King Afonso Mvemba a Nzinga — 1506 to 1543
- Dutch at Cape Town — 1652

SOUTH AND EAST ASIA
- Ming dynasty — to 1644
- Reign of Akbar in Mughal India — 1556 to 1605
- Tokugawa shogunate founded in Japan — 1603

FOR COMPARISON
- Columbus reaches Hispaniola (Ch. 15) — 1492
- Spanish conquer Aztec and Inca empires (Ch. 15) — 1519 to 1550
- Portugal begins Atlantic slave trade (Ch. 15) — (1444)

crucial. Increased availability of silver coins facilitated trade and gave European merchants the wherewithal to compete more effectively in Asian markets. The implications were not yet clear to Asian rulers, but the foundations had been laid for a new global market controlled from Europe.

Christian missionaries like Matteo Ricci played only a small part during this time of intellectual ferment across Afro-Eurasia. Whereas in some areas of the Americas, such as the Andes and Mesoamerica, conversions to Catholicism quickly followed Spanish conquest, in Africa and Asia it was Islam that expanded during this period. While the Protestant Reformation played a role in propelling the Jesuits and other Catholic orders out into the world to expand the pope's religious domain, and while "new science" forced the Catholic Church to respond to new intellectual challenges, neither European science nor religious reform had a significant impact in Asia before the end of the seventeenth century. Instead, existing religious and intellectual modes of discourse—between Muslims and Hindus in India, and between Buddhists and Confucians in China—remained the norm. In some places Christian missionaries contributed to the debate, but only in rare cases did they have a significant influence; in this regard, Japan and Kongo were exceptional.

Meanwhile, religious divisions were deepening in western Eurasia, where in both Christian and Muslim lands religion and politics formed a combustible mixture in the seventeenth and eighteenth centuries. The struggle for religious ascendency in western Europe divided the continent between warring Catholic and Protestant powers, while the old rivalry between the Sunni and Shi'ite branches of Islam magnified the struggle between the Iranian Safavid and Turkish Ottoman empires for regional predominance. In the new age of gunpowder weapons, the stakes of such conflicts would prove higher than ever before.

Key Terms

Matteo Ricci (470)
Vasco da Gama (471)
joint-stock companies (474)
bourgeoisie (475)
Dutch East India Company (475)
Kongo kingdom (477)

Mughal dynasty (480)
Emperor Akbar (480)
Nur Jahan (481)
Ming dynasty (482)
examination system (482)
Wanli Emperor (483)
Emperor Sejong (483)

Lê dynasty (484)
Toyotomi Hideyoshi (485)
Tokugawa shogunate (485)
Martin Luther (487)
Catholic Reformation (487)
Galileo Galilei (487)

For Further Reference

Brocky, Liam Matthew. *Journey to the East: The Jesuit Mission to China, 1579–1724*. Cambridge, Mass.: Belknap, 2008.

Brook, Timothy. *The Troubled Empire: China in the Yuan and Ming Dynasties*. Cambridge, Mass.: Belknap, 2010.

Chaudhuri, K. N. *Asia Before Europe: Economy and Civilization of the Indian Ocean from the Rise of Islam to 1750*. Cambridge, England: Cambridge University Press, 1990.

Clulow, Adam. *The Company and the Shogun: The Dutch Encounter with Tokugawa Japan*. New York: Columbia University Press, 2014.

Cook, Harold J. *Matters of Exchange: Commerce, Medicine, and Science in the Dutch Golden Age*. New Haven: Yale University Press, 2008.

Dale, Stephen Frederick. *Indian Merchants and Eurasian Trade, 1600–1750*. Cambridge, England: Cambridge University Press, 1994.

Findly, Ellison Banks. *Nur Jahan: Empress of Mughal India*. New York: Oxford University Press, 1993.

Green, Toby. *The Rise of the Trans-Atlantic Slave Trade in Western Africa, 1300–1589*. New York: Cambridge University Press, 2011.

Laven, Mary. *Mission to China: Matteo Ricci and the Jesuit Encounter with the East*. London: Faber & Faber, 2011.

Pearson, Michael. *The Indian Ocean*. New York: Routledge, 2007.

Sherif, Abdul. *Dhow Cultures and the Indian Ocean: Cosmopolitanism, Commerce, and Islam*. New York: Columbia University Press, 2010.

Spence, Jonathan. *The Memory Palace of Matteo Ricci*. New York: Viking Penguin, 1984.

Subrahmanyam, Sanjay. *The Portuguese Empire in Asia, 1500–1700*. 2d ed. London: Wiley-Blackwell, 2012.

Swope, Kenneth M. *A Dragon's Head and a Serpent's Tail: Ming China and the First Great East Asian War, 1592-1598*. Norman: University of Oklahoma Press, 2012.

MindTap

MindTap is a fully online, highly personalized learning experience built upon Cengage Learning content. MindTap combines student learning tools—readings, multimedia, activities, and assessments—into a singular Learning Path that guides students through the course.

17 Religion, Politics, and the Balance of Power in Western Eurasia, 1500–1750

Public Domain

Evliya Çelebi

The adventures of **Evliya Çelebi** (ev-lee-yah che-LEH-bee; 1610–1683) began with a dream. Son of the chief goldsmith to the powerful sultan of the Ottoman empire, at eighteen years old Çelebi was already highly gifted in the art of religious recitation (he would recite the entire Quran over one thousand times in his lifetime). In 1628, he dreamt of a visit from the Prophet Muhammad himself, who told him, "*You will be a world traveler and unique among men.*"* This nocturnal blessing was welcome, since Çelebi already had a great curiosity about the world around him. "*I longed,*" he wrote, "*to set out for the Holy Land, towards Baghdad and Mecca and Medina and Cairo and Damascus.*"* Visiting those places and many more, he became the greatest of all Ottoman voyagers: even today in the Turkish language, you say of someone who feels a constant urge to travel: "Evliya Çelebi gibi," "He is like Evliya Çelebi."

As recorded in his *Book of Travels*, Çelebi ventured from his birthplace of Constantinople (today's Istanbul) across the vast Ottoman empire. His most memorable journey came when he performed the hajj, visiting the holy sites of Mecca, Medina, and Jerusalem, before settling in Cairo, the great commercial and intellectual center of early modern Islam. He also went beyond the empire, to Europe and Iran. In Europe, he witnessed and participated in the wars fought between the sultan's forces and those of the Holy Roman empire, while in Iran he described the tense relations between its Safavid dynasty and his own Ottoman rulers.

Though both the Ottomans and Safavids were Muslim societies, religious differences amplified their political and military competition. The Ottomans, controlling the most holy sites of Islam in Arabia, were defenders of the dominant Sunni (SOO-nee) branch of Islam, while the Safavids promoted the competing Shi'ite (SHEE-ite) interpretation. Çelebi encapsulated the competition between them in an account where, with characteristic

---

*Robert Dankoff and Sooyong Kim, translation and commentary, *An Ottoman Traveller: Selections from the* Book of Travels *of Evliya Çelebi* (London: Eland Publishing, 2010), pp. 7, 36. Reprinted by permission.

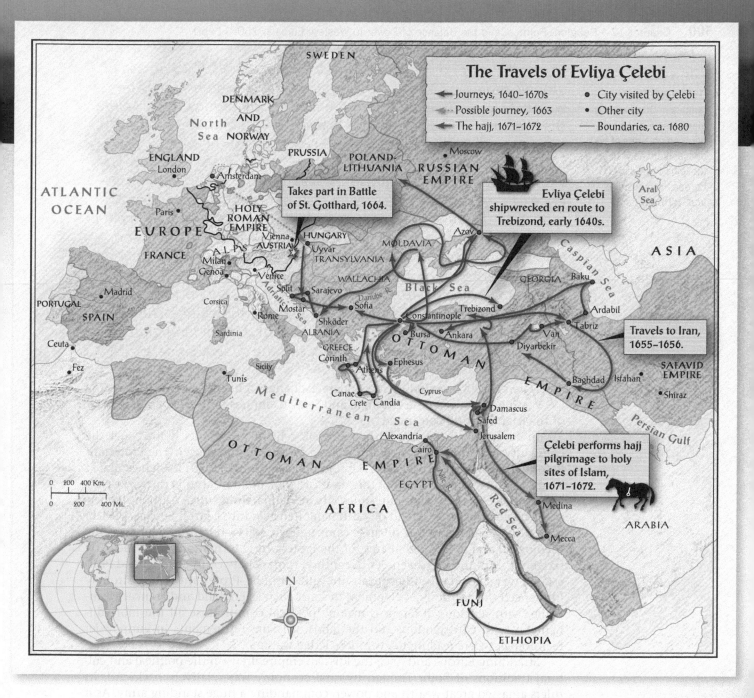

The Travels of Evliya Çelebi

← Journeys, 1640–1670s   ● City visited by Çelebi
← Possible journey, 1663   ● Other city
← The hajj, 1671–1672   — Boundaries, ca. 1680

Takes part in Battle of St. Gotthard, 1664.

Evliya Çelebi shipwrecked en route to Trebizond, early 1640s.

Travels to Iran, 1655–1656.

Çelebi performs hajj pilgrimage to holy sites of Islam, 1671–1672.

humor, he described how a sixteenth-century Ottoman ruler rejected a gift from the Shi'ite Safavid shah while building the extraordinary Sûleymaniye Mosque:

*T*he minaret on the left with the three galleries is called the Jewel Minaret.... The reason is that, in order for the foundation to settle, Sûleyman Khan had the building of this mosque stop for a year.... Shah Thamasp, the King of Persia [Iran] when he heard of the halt

Evliya Çelebi

(1610–1683) The most famous of Ottoman travelers; his writings contain rich portraits of his own society as well as those he visited in Europe, Iran, Arabia, and North Africa.

to construction, dispatched a great embassy with 1000 purses of money and a box of all kinds of valuable jewels. In his letter he wrote, "I heard that you did not have enough money to complete the mosque.... I have sent you this amount of money from the treasury and these jewels. Sell them and spend the money, and take pains to finish the mosque. Let us have a share in your pious works...." Sûleyman Khan was incensed by the letter. In the presence of the [Safavid] emissary he distributed the 1000 purses of money to the Jews in Constantinople ... then he gave the architect Sinan the box of jewels while the emissary was still present and said to him: "The so-called precious stones he sent are worthless beside the stones of my mosque. So put them with the rest and use them in the construction." When the emissary understood the situation, he was dumbstruck.... Meanwhile, the chief architect used the jewels to decorate the grooves of that minaret with artistry of all sorts ... that is why it is called the "Jewel Minaret."*

When Çelebi reported this legendary exchange of insults a century later, the struggle between the Ottoman and Safavid empires for the geographic heart of the Islamic world continued.

In seventeenth-century Europe as well, religious divisions helped fuel the competition of ambitious men and women for wealth and power. The Protestant Reformation was opposed by the Habsburg dynasty, which, with its rich capital at Madrid funded by the wealth of the Americas, took up the Catholic cause. Çelebi's travels took him to the Habsburg-ruled city of Vienna, from which Catholic emperors struggled not only to fend off Ottoman offensives into central Europe—Çelebi himself participated in one of these campaigns in 1664—but also to suppress the theological and political challenge of the Protestant Reformation. From the early sixteenth until the late seventeenth century, warfare between Catholics and Protestants was a constant of European life, and Catholic–Protestant rivalry strongly influenced the political development of states such as England and France. Meanwhile, with religious differences making political compromise all the more difficult in both Christendom and the lands of Islam, refinements in gunpowder technologies were leading to ever more lethal warfare.

Straddling Europe and Asia, the Russian empire drew on the political and cultural traditions of both. Though its rural economy was relatively backward, its rulers amassed great wealth and power, commanding a huge standing army. As it expanded, the Russian empire became home to a wide diversity of peoples, including Jews, Armenians, and Muslims.

Since the interconnected societies of western Eurasia, from England in the northwest to Iran in the southeast, were at the center of emerging world systems of trade and empire, the competition among them had a lasting influence on the global balance of power. By the mid-eighteenth century, the Safavid empire had

---

*Robert Dankoff and Sooyong Kim, translation and commentary, *An Ottoman Traveller: Selections from the* Book of Travels *of Evliya Çelebi* (London: Eland Publishing, 2010), pp. 13–14. Reprinted by permission.

collapsed and Iran would no longer be a major political player. The Ottoman empire, while still a significant presence, had lost the initiative to rising European states, including a newly expansive Russian empire and Prussia, the strongest of numerous German kingdoms. The balance of power in western Eurasia now favored France, Britain, Austria, Prussia, and Russia, and by 1750 national competition had largely replaced religious rivalries. The building blocks for a European-dominated global order were in place.

> What were the main features of the Ottoman and Safavid empires in the seventeenth century, and how did religious competition fuel competition between them?

> How did the Protestant Reformation affect contests for political supremacy within and between seventeenth-century European states? When and why did religion come to play a less prominent political role?

> How did the experiences of Russians, Armenians, and Jews exemplify the early modern connections between Europe and Asia?

> How did the balance of power between the dominant states of western Eurasia shift during this period?

FOCUS QUESTIONS

Ottoman Power and Safavid Challenge

Their seizure of Constantinople in 1453 had magnified the Ottoman empire's Great Power status and facilitated their further expansion into southeastern Europe. The Ottomans were the most successful of the Turkic-speaking peoples who had migrated westward from the central Eurasian steppes to conquer sedentary agricultural societies. Similarly, the Safavids were also Turkic-speaking and nomadic in origin, but they assimilated into Persian culture as they established their capital at the great city of Isfahan (is-fah-HAHN), a cosmopolitan center of trade and culture. Both societies were Islamic, although the Sunni Ottomans and the Shi'ite (SHEE-ite) Safavids embraced conflicting interpretations of their common faith.

Shi'ites believe that when Muhammad died, religious and political authority should have passed through his son-in-law Ali to Ali's son Hussein. Sunni Muslims, in contrast, argue that the Prophet's successors (the *caliphs*) could be chosen freely from among Muhammad's close companions. In the seventh century, the two sides came to blows. First, Ali was killed, and then his son Hussein fell in battle. Shi'ites still visit the tomb of Hussein in Karbala (in today's Iraq), and every year an elaborate festival of mourning is held to commemorate his death.

Educated men and women in both empires learned Arabic for prayer and religious study, but for everyday purposes the Ottomans spoke Turkish and the Safavids spoke Farsi (also known as Persian). In both empires, Sufi brotherhoods developed complex rituals designed to bring their members closer to God.

Ultimately, the Ottoman system of government proved more enduring. Although assaults on Vienna were turned back in both 1529 and 1683, the

Ottomans remained a major power in Europe as well as North Africa and the Arab lands southeast of Anatolia. While the Safavids collapsed in the early eighteenth century, they bequeathed a large swath of Shi'ite population as a permanent legacy of their rule.

The Ottoman Empire, 1500–1650

The splendor of the Sublime Porte, center of Ottoman power in Constantinople, was legendary. The sultan's palace defined the city as a center of political power, while other monumental buildings expressed its religious focus—for example, the Hagia Sophia, an ancient Christian church converted into a mosque after the Ottoman capture of the city, and the sixteenth-century Sûleymaniye Mosque. European visitors of the time were awestruck by the Ottoman capital. Çelebi describes one such group of *"Frankish [European] infidels"*: *"Wherever they looked, they put finger to mouth and bit it in astonishment.... They threw off their Frankish hats and cried out in awe, 'Maria, Maria!'"**

The people of Constantinople fully mirrored the ethnic and religious diversity of the empire. In the neighborhood of Galata, for example, Çelebi found *"eighteen Muslim quarters, seventy quarters of Greek infidels, three of cranky Franks, one of Jews, and two of Armenians."* Çelebi noted that one neighborhood was full of *"grief-stricken* Mudejars *[Muslims] who came from Spain, driven out by the infidels"** after the Christian reconquest of Iberia was completed in 1492 (see Chapter 15). Although this diverse population was residentially segregated, and each community was substantially responsible for its own internal affairs, they shared common public spaces such as markets, gardens, and public baths. Constantinople was one of the world's most cosmopolitan cities, *"famous,"* Çelebi wrote, *"among travelers in Arabia and Persia, India and Yemen and Ethiopia."**

The glories of their capital reflected the successes of Ottoman governments and military elites in effectively administering and taxing the peasants, craftsmen, and merchants of their sprawling and productive domains. From their Anatolian heartland, where Turkish peasants predominated, the Ottomans added Palestine, Syria, Arabia, Iraq, and much of Hungary to the sultan's domains in the sixteenth century.

Though cavalry warfare was the origin and heart of the Ottoman military, after the conquest of Constantinople, with outlets to both the Black Sea and the Mediterranean, a great navy was constructed as well. By the sixteenth century, the Ottoman fleet had become dominant in the Black Sea and on the eastern and southern shores of the Mediterranean, and the Ottoman navy defeated Christian fleets in the Red Sea, Persian Gulf, and Indian Ocean. From southeastern Europe, Ottoman armies marched into the German-speaking lands of central Europe. The Ottomans also ruled Greece and conquered all of the Mediterranean coast of North Africa except Morocco, which remained the only significant Arab-ruled kingdom. In Egypt, Arabia, and Syria, Arabs were ruled by Turkish-speaking Ottoman administrators. Meanwhile, the increasing scale of Ottoman military operations on land and sea and the organization necessary to use gunpowder weapons, such as muskets and cannons, led to greater military professionalism.

---

*Robert Dankoff and Sooyong Kim, translation and commentary, *An Ottoman Traveller: Selections from the* Book of Travels *of Evliya Çelebi* (London: Eland Publishing, 2010), pp. 16, 18–19, 21. Reprinted by permission.

During this period, slaves became more important in the Ottoman military and in the central administration of the empire (after a winning battle in southeastern Europe, Evliya Çelebi casually described his *"share of the booty"* as *"one girl, one boy, and seven horses"**). Indeed, to help meet their ever-increasing military manpower needs, the Ottomans had begun to rely on enslaved soldiers from conquered Christian lands, the **Janissaries**. Janissaries trained year-round and became skilled at using gunpowder weapons. As the need for such soldiers increased, the Ottomans regularly enslaved Christian youth in the Balkan and Caucasus Mountains to meet the demand, leaving a simmering sense of grievance among the communities that were forced to give up their children.

The concept of "elite slaves" may sound strange, but reliance on slaves as soldiers and administrators was an old tradition. A sultan might not be able to trust his own brothers or sons because they were vying for power of their own, but the loyalty of a slave general was absolute. If he disobeyed he could simply be killed: he had no family ties to protect him. By the sixteenth century, Janissaries played a central role in administration as well as in the military. Even the sultan's chief minister was a slave.

After conquering Arabia and Palestine, the Ottomans controlled Mecca, Medina, and Jerusalem, the three holiest cities for Muslims. Mecca was the Prophet's home city and the focal point of the Muslim *hajj*, or pilgrimage; Medina is an Arabian town that gave Muhammad shelter and rallied to his side when the people of Mecca at first rejected his message; Jerusalem is the city from which he is reported to have ascended into heaven after his death.

Since these were the holy pilgrimage sites to which all Muslims aspired to travel, their supervision was a great responsibility. Ottoman sultans therefore emphasized their role as guardians of Islam and claimed to be *caliphs*, successors to the earthly power of the Prophet.

While basing their legitimacy on Islam, however, Ottoman rulers needed to stabilize their rule over dozens of different communities with diverse religious

"Battle of Vienna,SultanMurads with janissaries" by G. Jansoone - own photo of an old document. Licensed under Public domain via Wikimedia Commons - http://commons.wikimedia.org/wiki/File:Battle_of_Vienna,SultanMurads_with_janissaries.jpg#mediaviewer/File:Battle_of_Vienna, SultanMurads_with_janissaries.jpg

Janissaries Taken from Christian villages as boys, converted to Islam, and rigorously trained in the military arts, for centuries Janissaries formed the elite corps of the Ottoman military. They are shown here in 1683 during their siege of the Habsburg capital of Vienna. Notwithstanding their elaborate headgear, colorful uniforms, and curved swords, the muskets at their shoulders indicate the centrality of gunpowder weapons to seventeenth-century warfare in western Eurasia.

Janissaries

An elite corps of slaves trained as professional soldiers in the Ottoman military. Janissary soldiers were Christian youths from the Balkans who were pressed into service and forced to convert to Islam.

---

*Robert Dankoff and Sooyong Kim, translation and commentary, *An Ottoman Traveller: Selections from the* Book of Travels *of Evliya Çelebi* (London: Eland Publishing, 2010), p. 190. Reprinted by permission.

Süleyman

(r. 1520–1566) Credited with the development of literature, art, architecture, and law and for inclusive policies toward religious minorities, Süleyman extended the Ottoman empire while maintaining economic and political stability.

and legal traditions. The master strategist was Sultan **Süleyman** (r. 1520–1566). A strong military leader who greatly expanded the empire, Süleyman (soo-lay-MAHN) also devised an administrative system that reconciled central authority with local autonomy. His court reflected the ethnic diversity of his empire. Turkish was the language of administration and military command, Arabic the language of theology and philosophy, and Persian the language of poetry and the arts. Europeans called him "Süleyman the Magnificent" for the dazzling opulence and splendor of his court. But within the empire he became known as "Süleyman the Lawgiver" for bringing peace and stability to the realm. The sultan's officials gained power through merit rather than family lineage. As an Austrian ambassador reported, *"Those who are dishonest, lazy and slothful never attain to distinction, but remain in obscurity and contempt. That is why they succeed in all they attempt ... and daily extend the bounds of their rule."** *

Süleyman centralized religious authority and sponsored the building of mosques and religious schools, partly to combat the intermixture of pagan practices with Islam. He sent religious experts to rural Anatolia to promote Islamic orthodoxy among peasants who still embraced folk beliefs, deities, and rituals. Nevertheless, the Ottomans did not impose a single legal system on existing cultural and religious traditions. Instead, they allowed local Christian and Jewish populations, for example, to govern their own affairs and maintain their own courts as long as they remained loyal to the sultan and paid their taxes promptly.

● **CONTEXT&CONNECTIONS** Süleyman's achievement in reconciling central authority with the ethnic, linguistic, and religious diversity of his subjects anticipated by half a century *Emperor Akbar's* ability to consolidate *Mughal* power over the equally vast and diverse Indian subcontinent (key terms in Chapter 16). Both were Muslim rulers who waived the *jizya* tax that Islamic law allowed them to impose on nonbelievers. Their legacies of tolerance were not sustained, however. In the late seventeenth century one of Akbar's successors alienated his Hindu subjects by ruling more stringently in the name of Islam (see Chapter 20), while during the First World War the collapsing Ottoman empire undertook brutal suppression of minorities, most clearly in the Armenian Genocide (see Chapter 27). ●

In foreign affairs, Süleyman was aggressively expansionistic, in Europe as well as in northern Africa and western Asia. In 1534, his armies captured the strategic city of Baghdad from their Safavid rivals, restoring Sunni authority over the Arab society of the region. (As a result, since that time, Arabs of that region have been divided into Sunni and Shi'ite communities.) The Ottomans dominated the Red Sea and thus access to Islam's holy pilgrimage sites; swept across North Africa, tapping into the riches of the Nile River; charged across the Balkans to take command of the Hungarian plain; and dominated the rich commerce of the Black Sea (see map on page 499). Within this vast world, Evliya Çelebi could securely travel under his sultan's writ.

The prospect for even greater expansion into Europe was present both in Süleyman's time and a century later when Çelebi traveled to Christian lands. Ottoman assaults threatened the Habsburg empire in central Europe and the Venetian republic in Italy and the Adriatic, but Vienna's defenders turned back the Ottoman siege of the city in 1529, and in the Mediterranean a combined European fleet

---

The Turkish Letters of Ogier Ghiselin de Busbecq, Imperial Ambassador at Constantinople, 1554–1562, trans. Edward S. Foster (New York: Oxford University Press), p. 66.

under Spanish command defeated the Ottoman navy in 1571. Still, the Ottomans stayed on the offensive in southeastern Europe into the later seventeenth century, and in 1683 were once again at the gates of Vienna.

Çelebi was an eyewitness to many of those later campaigns, but his description of an invasion of Muslim Tatar horsemen plundering and pillaging all the way to Amsterdam was pure fantasy (reminding us that we need to assess primary sources critically and seek independent confirmation when possible). Quite realistic, however, was his description of a Habsburg victory over Ottoman forces in Austria in 1664: "*On this side was our bloodthirsty army of Islam. . . . They were tired and weak. For twenty days they had suffered from nonstop rain. Men and horses were sapped of their strength, hungry and starving.... What good were they against the infidel army on the opposite side ... covering the ground like a black cloud?*"* Thus Çelebi paid grudging tribute to the coalition of western armies that had combined their forces to hold off the Ottoman advance.

Still, even as Çelebi joined a diplomatic delegation to Vienna the next year, the Ottomans had great bargaining power. They held firm control over the Balkans, Greece, and much of Hungary. With their large and well-equipped army, the Ottomans were a major player in the European balance of power.

European diplomats thus sought an ally against the persistent Ottoman threat in the shah of Safavid Iran (referred to at the time as Persia). As the Austrian ambassador noted:

> On [the Ottoman] side are the resources of a mighty empire, strength unimpaired, experience and practice in fighting . . . endurance of toil, unity, discipline, frugality and watchfulness. . . . [W]orst of all, the enemy is accustomed to victory, and we to defeat. . . . Persia alone interposes in our favor; for the enemy, as he hastens to attack, must keep an eye on this menace to his rear.†

The Habsburgs and the Safavids found that mutual antipathy to the Ottomans gave them a starting point for cooperation.

The Shi'ite Challenge: Foundations of Safavid Iran, 1500–1629

Iran is a rich and productive land with a long history of influence in western and southern Asia. With Mesopotamia and the Mediterranean to the west and the Indus Valley and India to the south and east, the land called Persia benefited from contacts with other civilizations. Its agricultural wealth and its location as a commercial crossroads also attracted invaders. In the early sixteenth century, some of these invaders founded the **Safavid dynasty** (1501–1722) and challenged the power of the Ottoman empire.

Known as *kizilbash* ("redheads") because of the color of their turbans, the Safavid invaders were members of an unorthodox Islamic sect led by a man named Ismail (r. 1501–1524). The "redheads" swept down from Azerbaijan,

> **Safavid dynasty**
> (1501–1722) Dynasty that established Shi'ite Islam as the state religion in Iran and challenged the powerful Ottoman empire. The Safavids fell to invaders from Central Asia in the early eighteenth century.

---

*Robert Dankoff and Sooyong Kim, translation and commentary, *An Ottoman Traveller: Selections from the* Book of Travels *of Evliya Çelebi* (London: Eland Publishing, 2010), p. 225. Reprinted by permission.

†*The Turkish Letters of Ogier Ghiselin de Busbecq, Imperial Ambassador at Constantinople, 1554–1562*, trans. Edward S. Foster (New York: Oxford University Press), p. 66.

conquered the Persian-speaking lands, and drove west, capturing the important cities of Baghdad and Basra. Ismail then adopted mainstream Shi'ite beliefs and imposed them on his conquered subjects, including both Sunni Muslims and followers of Persia's ancient Zoroastrian faith. Though the Ottomans retook Baghdad, the Shi'ites, long a suppressed minority, now controlled a major Islamic state.

To ensure the religious and political loyalty of their subjects, the Safavids decreed that the names of the early Sunni caliphs should be publicly cursed. That was a problem for Evliya Çelebi: when, on a diplomatic mission, he first heard the public cursing of a leader that he, as a Sunni, venerated, he recounted, *"I nearly went out of my mind. . . . I could easily have killed that accursed curser; because when Ottoman envoys come to Persia they have the liberty of killing up to four Kizilbash cursers for the sake of the Four Companions of the Prophet."** Since he was on a diplomatic mission, he resisted the temptation, and the Safavid governor decreed that there was to be no public cursing of Sunni caliphs, upon pain of death, while the Ottoman officials were present. As they did with the Habsburgs, with the Safavids the Ottomans alternated between warfare and diplomacy.

Although the shift toward Shi'ism in Iran was permanent, over time the religious passions that drove initial Safavid policies died down. The greatest Safavid ruler, Shah **Abbas I** (r. 1587–1629), built the capital at Isfahan, which was a city of half a million residents when a European visitor commented on *"the great number of magnificent palaces, the agreeable and pleasant houses . . . the really fine bazaars, the water channels and the streets of which the sides were covered with tall plane trees."*[†] The gardens of Isfahan were legendary. (See the feature "Movement of Ideas Through Primary Sources: A French View of the Iranians.")

Abbas I

(r. 1587–1629) Safavid ruler who created a long and stable reign, beautified the capital city of Isfahan, promoted foreign trade, and repelled Ottoman invaders.

● **CONTEXT&CONNECTIONS** During the reign of Shah Abbas and his successors, Iranian culture spread both east and west. Persian verse was widely admired, influencing Swahili poets in East Africa (see Chapter 16) as well as Urdu poets in India, who used Arabic script to write lyrical poetry in a Persian-inflected variation of the local Hindi language. Isfahan, a showcase for Persian architecture and engineering, influenced the graceful silhouette of the Taj Mahal in India. In addition to creating beautiful abstract patterns on rich carpets, Persian artists were famous for miniature paintings depicting scenes from everyday life, art forms that influenced artisans and painters from Delhi to Constantinople. ●

The economy also blossomed under Abbas's long and stable rule, with new irrigation works supporting agriculture, extensive markets for handicrafts, and a pilgrim trade servicing visitors to the holy sites of Shi'ite Islam. Iranian silks, carpets, and ceramics were traded overland and by sea to the east and west and also into Indian Ocean circuits, most especially by minority communities of Armenian Christians (see page 525).

In addition, Shah Abbas invited other European merchants and diplomatic representatives to Isfahan. Abbas was anxious to acquire guns and cannon and training for professional soldiers. The antagonism of many Iranian leaders to all things Christian and European was offset by the Safavid need to cultivate European

---

*Robert Dankoff and Sooyong Kim, translation and commentary, *An Ottoman Traveller: Selections from the* Book of Travels *of Evliya Çelebi* (London: Eland Publishing, 2010), p. 56. Reprinted by permission.

†Cited in Ronald W. Ferrier, *A Journey to Persia: Jean Chardin's Portrait of a Seventeenth Century Empire* (London: I. B. Tauris, 1996), p. 44.

Safavid Court This painting shows the court of Shah Süleyman II in the late seventeenth century. The shah is entertained by musicians, while his retainers prepare for an evening hunt, with a European visitor looking on. The style is Iranian, although European influence can be seen in the use of perspective to create a pastoral background. Süleyman II was an ineffective ruler who enjoyed these luxuries as his empire declined in power. (Ms E-14 f.98a Shah Suleyman II (1641–91) and his courtiers (gouache on paper), Persian School, (17th century)/Institute of Oriental Studies, St. Petersburg, Russia/ The Bridgeman Art Library)

allies in their struggle with the Ottomans. The Safavid rulers abided by the old adage that *"the enemy of my enemy is my friend"* in seeking European alliances against Constantinople.

After the death of Shah Abbas in 1629, however, the quality of Iranian leadership declined. Over the next century, with their economy and military weakening, the Safavids became vulnerable to just the sort of invasion from the steppes that had brought them to Iran in the first place.

Safavid Collapse and Ottoman Persistence, 1650–1750

Shah Abbas had neglected to groom a competent successor. The next shah, pampered in the seclusion of the royal harem his whole life, set an example of debauchery and corruption that spread throughout his court. Shi'ite clerics, who had been principal supporters of the Safavid dynasty, were appalled, especially by the monarch's continual drunkenness.

A French View of the Iranians

Jean de Chardin (1643–1713) was a Frenchman who travelled twice to the Safavid empire in Iran (then called Persia), learning the language and forming strong opinions about the inhabitants. His *Travels in Persia* is a valuable primary source on European-Iranian relations in the late seventeenth century.

Still, as with all such travel accounts, we must be cautious about accepting his portrait at face value. It is important to consider the author's own point of view. For one thing, Chardin was a jeweler frustrated by what he saw as Iranian "deceits" and "tricks" in his business dealings, experiences that may have colored his perspective.

Also important to remember is that Chardin was a Protestant member of the bourgeoisie, the emerging French middle class, which stressed ethics based on plain speaking, hard work, foresight, and thrift. Therefore, as much as the following document is a comment on Iranians, it also reveals Chardin's own worldview through the contrasts he draws between his own society and that of his hosts.

> **In Chardin's account, what are the most positive and negative attributes of the Persians?**

> **In which passages and in what terms does Chardin assert superior values for his own society in contrast to those of the Persians?**

Source: Sir John Chardin, *Travels in Persia, 1673–1677*, an abridged English version of *Voyages du chevalier Chardin en Perse, et autres lieux de l'Orient* (London: Argonaut Press, 1927), p. 70. Spelling and usage have been modernized.

From *Travels in Persia*

They [Iranians] are true philosophers on the account of [their] . . . hope and fear of a future state; they are little guilty of covetousness, and are only desirous of getting, that they may spend it; they love to enjoy the present, and deny themselves nothing that they are able to procure, taking no thought for the morrow, and relying wholly on providence, and their own fate; they firmly believe it to be sure and unalterable . . . so when any misfortune happens to them, they are not cast down, as most men are, they only say quietly [so] it is ordained. . . .

The most commendable property of the manners of the Persians, is their kindness to strangers; the reception and protection they afford them, and their universal hospitality, and toleration, in regard to religion, except the clergy of the country, who, as in all other places, hate to a furious degree, all those that differ from their opinions. The Persians are very civil, and very honest in matters of religion; so far that they allow those who have embraced theirs, to recant, and resume their former opinion. . . . They believe that all men's prayers are good and prevalent; therefore, in their illnesses, and in other wants, they admit of, and even desire the prayers of different religions. . . . This is not to be imputed to their religious principles . . . but I impute it to the sweet temper of that nation, who are naturally averse to contest and cruelty. . . .

Two opposite customs are commonly practiced by the Persians; that of praising God continually, and talking of his attributes, and that of uttering curses, and obscene talk. Whether you see them at home, or meet them in the streets, going about business or walking; you still hear them uttering some blessing or prayer. . . . The least thing they set their hand to do, they say, "In the Name of God"; and they never speak of doing anything, without adding, "If it pleases God. . . ." [At] the same time, come out of the same men's mouths a thousand obscene expressions. All ranks of men are infected with this odious vice. Their bawdy talk is taken from Arse, and C——t, which modesty forbids one to name. . . . [W]hen they have spent their Stock of bawdy names, they begin to call one another Atheists, Idolaters, Jews, Christians; and to say to one another, "The Christians Dogs are better than thou. . . ."

The Eastern People are not near so restless, and so uneasy as we; they sit gravely and soberly, make no motion with their body . . . for they don't believe that a man that is in his wits, can be so full of action as we are . . . I'll repeat it once more: The Persians are the most kind people in the world; they have the most moving and the most engaging ways, the most complying tempers, the smoothest and the most flattering tongues, avoiding in their conversation, relations or expressions which may occasion melancholy thoughts. . . .

As civil as that nation is, they never act out of generosity. . . . They do nothing but out of a principle of interest, that is to say, out of hope or fear: And they cannot conceive that there should be such a country where people will do their duty from a motive of virtue only, without any other recompense. It is quite the contrary with them; they are paid for everything, and beforehand too. One can ask nothing of them, but with a present in one's hand. . . . The poorest and most miserable people never appear before a great man, or one from whom they would ask some favor, but at the same time they offer a present, which is never refused, even by the greatest lords of the kingdom. . . .

As for what relates to travelling, those journeys that are made out of pure curiosity are . . . inconceivable to the Persians. . . . They have no taste of the pleasure we enjoy in seeing different manners from ours, and hearing of a language which we do not understand. . . . They asked me if it was possible that there should be such people amongst us, who would travel two or three thousand leagues with so much danger, and inconveniency, only to see how they were made, and what they did in Persia, and upon no other design. These people are of the opinion, as I have observed, that one cannot better attain to virtue, nor have a fuller taste of pleasure than by resting and dwelling at home, and that it is not good to travel, but to acquire riches. . . . It is from this spirit of theirs no doubt, that the Persians are so grossly ignorant of the present state of other nations of the world, and that they do not so much as understand geography, and have no maps; which comes from this, that having no curiosity to see other countries. . . . The Ministers of State generally speaking, know no more what passes in Europe, than in the world of the moon. The greatest part, even have but a confused idea of Europe, which they look upon to be some little island in the North Seas, where there is nothing to be found that is either good or handsome; from whence it comes, say they, that the Europeans go all over the world, in search of fine things, and of those which are necessary, as being destitute of them.

The last Safavid shah attempted to reverse these trends and regain the support of the clergy by imposing harsh conditions of public morality. He banned music, coffee, and public entertainments, restricted women to the home, and even destroyed the imperial wine cellar. People soon tired of such heavy-handed moral impositions, however, and public support for the Safavids slipped even further. The Safavid empire was therefore easy pickings for the Afghan invaders who descended on Isfahan in 1722 and left it in ruins. The deepest and longest-lasting legacy of the Safavid dynasty was the predominance of Shi'ite Islam in Iran and its borderlands.

The Ottomans, in contrast, persisted as a significant political and military power into the mid-eighteenth century without any radical change to their political order and with an empire that still included much of southeastern Europe (see Map 17.2, page 526). Unlike Safavid Iran, where the quality of the shah's character was such a determining factor, Ottoman administrative reforms had created stronger and more reliable institutions for both civilian and military affairs. A clear example came in the year 1648, when both the Ottoman court and the people of Constantinople grew disaffected with a sultan who spent lavishly on luxuries while ignoring matters of state. But his subsequent assassination did not lead to disorder; instead, the smooth transition to more effective leadership showed the underlying strength of Ottoman institutions.

As a sign of continuing vigor on the international scene, Ottoman armies laid siege to Vienna once again in 1683, and as late as 1739 Ottoman forces defeated the Austrians, who ceded Balkan territory to Constantinople. In general, however, the Ottomans' place in the Great Power balance was now defensive rather than expansionistic, with eighteenth-century military leaders defending the empire's borders against rising powers, especially Russia.

As the "gunpowder revolution" continued to make warfare more deadly, it also made defending an empire with expansive frontiers more expensive. While Ottoman agricultural and commercial production was still substantial, economic expansion was no longer keeping up with population growth, making it difficult to find the revenue for further military investment. Despite such longer-term problems, however, the Ottomans persisted, and in the eighteenth century their realm remained large and prosperous.

The Mystical Path: Sufism in Early Modern Islam

The diversity of Muslims should now be clear, considering differences between Sunnis and Shi'ites, as well as the cultural and linguistic diversity of Arabs, Turks, Iranians, Mughal Indians, and many others. We can understand that complexity even further by looking at the mystical **Sufi** forms of Islamic worship.

Although Sufis adhere to a number of different schools, and may be either Sunni or Shi'ite, the core of their faith is to approach divine truth and love by seeking intimate communion with God. While all Muslims hope that living virtuous lives will gain them entry into heaven, Sufis believe that through certain ritual practices they can achieve a mystical union with the divine even in the here and now. Like all Muslims they practice the five "pillars" of the faith: professing that *"there is no God but God and Muhammad is His Prophet"*; praying five times daily; fasting during the month of Ramadan; supporting the poor through charity; and, if possible, making the pilgrimage to Mecca and Medina. To these mandates members of Sufi brotherhoods add additional prayers and rituals, such as the repeated recitation of the ninety-nine names of God.

Sufi

A mystical form of Islam in which adherents follow a set of specified practices, often involving meditation and rhythmic movement, in an attempt to become closer to God. Sufis pay great respect to the leaders of their brotherhoods even after death, often erecting shrines, which they visit as saints' tombs.

Evliya Çelebi himself seems to have been a member of a Sufi order, and in his *Book of Travels*, he sometimes refers to himself as a "dervish." In its original meaning, a dervish was a wandering holy man, an ascetic who had given up all material possessions to devote himself to God (like the wandering monks of medieval Europe or the holy men of India). While Çelebi certainly was a wanderer, he was definitely not an ascetic. During Ottoman times, however, the term dervish came to be applied to whole Sufi communities, most famously to the Mevlevi Order of "whirling dervishes." Through complex rotational dances to music of intensifying rhythm, they sought to become vessels into which God might enter.

Sufism played an exceptionally important role in the spread of Islam beyond its original Arab heartland, facilitating converts' incorporation of local shrines and beliefs into their newly adopted universal religion. For example, Sufis often placed special emphasis on the spiritual power of their teachers and continued to venerate them after death. The tomb of a saintly Sufi teacher, whose *baraka*, or divine grace, continued to aid his disciples, then became a place of veneration and pilgrimage, giving those for whom a pilgrimage to Mecca and Medina was impossible a local point of ritual importance. Emotive Sufi practices, incorporating local music and dance rhythms, were more attractive to rural peoples than more staid and legalistic Islamic practices.

- **CONTEXT&CONNECTIONS** Sufism spread widely in Africa, the Middle East, and across the Indian Ocean world. Sufi brotherhoods encouraged conversions by blending local leadership and cultural practices with Islamic forms, a process known as religious *syncretism* (Chapter 18). For that very reason, Sufis were, and still are today, often looked down upon and even attacked by Muslims who have viewed Sufi practices as impure or even heretical. •

Religion and Politics in Western Europe

The sixteenth century and the first half of the seventeenth century were a time of turmoil in western Europe. As religious strife became entangled with the ambitions of emperors, kings, and princes, warfare became more common. Urbanization and commercialization heightened social tensions, and attempts to expand royal power often met resistance.

The Habsburgs were the most powerful family in Europe at the beginning of this period. Originally from central Europe, the **Habsburg dynasty** aspired to create a pan-European Catholic empire. Conflict with the Ottomans was one check on Habsburg ambitions. Another was the rise of Protestant England and competition from the Catholic kings of France. By the mid-seventeenth century the reach of Habsburg dominance had contracted to a central European empire ruled from Vienna, still a great European power, but no longer a global one.

By the early eighteenth century the religious wars were over and European stability had returned. Catholic France and Protestant England had established stable constitutional orders that allowed their leaders to focus on international expansion. Apart from Habsburg Austria, the strongest military power in central Europe was Prussia, the rising power in the politically fractured German-speaking lands. By 1750 England, France, Austria, and Prussia, along with Russia, were the dominant European powers.

Habsburg dynasty

Powerful ruling house that expanded from Austria to Spain, the Netherlands, and the Spanish empire, as well as throughout the German-speaking world when Charles V (r. 1516–1556) was elected Holy Roman emperor.

Pope Francis, Europe, and the World

Catholics believe that the papacy traces its lineage through 265 previous popes in an unbroken line back to Saint Peter, a disciple of Jesus Christ. By the sixteenth century, in breaking from that lineage, Protestants pointed to the Church's corruption, its focus on worldly matters of wealth and power.

Again in 2013, scandals were rocking the Catholic Church. Jorge Mario Bergoglio was elected to serve as Pope Francis I and, with his emphasis on personal simplicity, pledged broad reforms. Priorities included cleaning up the corrupt Vatican Bank, cooperating with civil authorities in identifying and prosecuting pedophile priests, and bringing greater overall transparency to church affairs.

It is significant that Pope Francis, from the South American nation of Argentina, is the first non-European pope chosen in over 1200 years. From late Roman times through the twentieth century, western Europe was the demographic and cultural center of Roman Catholicism. Today, however, all the growth in Catholic numbers, like growth in Christianity generally, is taking place in Africa, Asia, and Latin America. Pope Francis has acknowledged that trend by appointing more diverse church leaders.

In 1900, 65 percent of the world's 291 million Catholics lived in Europe. Today, just 24 percent of the world's 1.1 billion Catholics are European (and among those are many who no longer practice as faithfully as their great-grandparents did). The percentage of the world's Catholics in North America has stayed relatively flat, going from 5 percent to 8 percent in that same period.

In contrast, in 1910, only 24 percent of Catholics lived in Latin America or the Caribbean; today that percentage is 39 percent. The Asian-Pacific percentage of Catholics, although relatively small, has still more than doubled in that period, from 5 percent to 12 percent. By far the greatest growth of the church has taken place in sub-Saharan Africa, which was home to less than 1 percent of Catholics in 1900 but over 16 percent today.

Although the Catholic Church is notoriously slow to change, it seems inevitable that the worldwide growth in membership outside of Europe will have cultural implications and maybe even theological ones. At a minimum, it seems to be just a matter of time before an African pope joins the long list of successors to Saint Peter.

Source: Pew Research, Religion and Public Life Project, "The Global Catholic Population," February 13, 2013, http://www.pewforum.org/2013/02/13/the-global-catholic-population/.

The Habsburgs: Imperial Ambitions and Political Realities, 1519–1648

The greatest of the Habsburg monarchs was Charles I, who from 1516 to 1556 ruled Spain and the Habsburg domains in central Europe. Charles's Spanish possessions included all the wealth of the Americas, and the Netherlands, rich in trade, was part of his family inheritance, which also made him king of Naples, controlling the southern part of Italy. The central European territories dominated from Vienna were crucial in the European military balance.

In 1520, the pope crowned Charles as Holy Roman Emperor, after he had been elected to that position by seven of the many archbishops and princes who ruled over German-speaking lands. Charles thus became the principal defender of the Catholic faith. (See the feature "World History in Today's World: Pope Francis, Europe, and the World.")

With extensive territorial possessions in Europe and all the wealth of the Americas at their disposal, it seemed that the Habsburgs might be able to create a political unity in western Europe. But the French were a powerful a rival in the west, while the Ottoman Turks challenged Habsburg supremacy in eastern Europe and the Mediterranean. Equally significant were the violent repercussions from the Protestant Reformation that began to appear in the mid-sixteenth century (see Map 17.1).

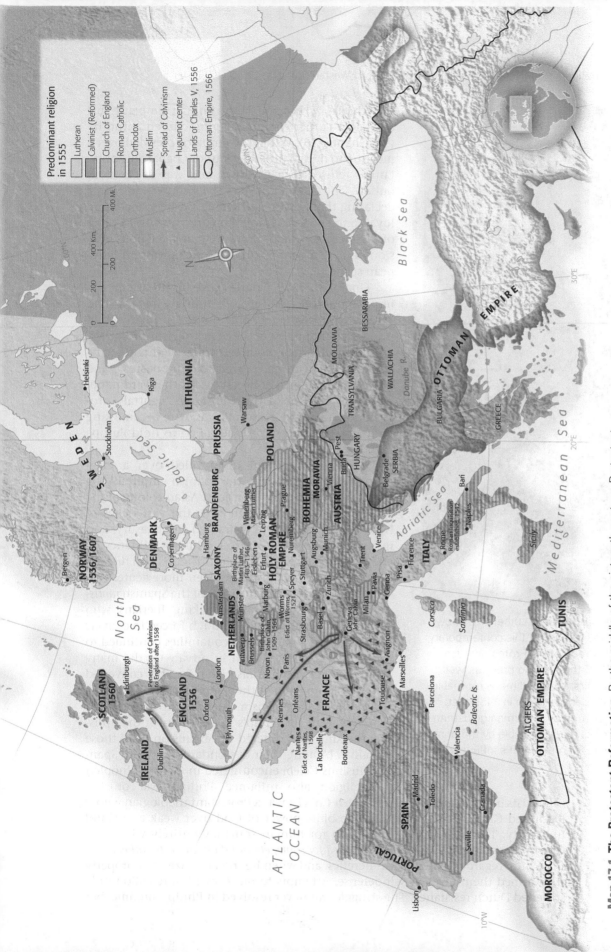

Map 17.1 The Protestant Reformation By the middle of the sixteenth century, Protestant churches were dominant in England, Scotland, the Netherlands, Switzerland, and Scandinavia. German principalities were divided between Protestants and Catholics. Catholicism remained dominant across most of southern Europe, though Protestants formed a significant minority in France. The religious landscape was especially complex in southeastern Europe where, under Ottoman authority, there were substantial communities of Catholics, Protestants, Orthodox Christians, and Muslims.

Predominant religion in 1555

- Lutheran
- Calvinist (Reformed)
- Church of England
- Roman Catholic
- Orthodox
- Muslim
- → Spread of Calvinism
- ▲ Huguenot center
- Lands of Charles V, 1556
- Ottoman Empire, 1566

400 Mi.
400 Km.
0   200
0   200

N

ATLANTIC OCEAN

North Sea

IRELAND
Dublin

SCOTLAND 1560
Edinburgh

Penetration of Calvinism to England after 1558

ENGLAND 1536
London
Oxford
Plymouth

Rennes
Orléans
Nantes
Edict of Nantes, 1598
La Rochelle
Bordeaux
FRANCE
Paris
Noyon
Birthplace of John Calvin, 1509–1564
Toulouse
Marseilles
Avignon

NETHERLANDS
Amsterdam
Antwerp
Brussels
Strasbourg
Worms
Edict of Worms, 1521
Marburg
Birthplace of Martin Luther, 1483–1546
Eisleben
Erfurt
Leipzig
Wittenberg Martin Luther
Hamburg

Baltic Sea

SWEDEN
Stockholm

Helsinki
Riga

LITHUANIA

DENMARK
Copenhagen

NORWAY 1536/1607
Bergen

SAXONY
BRANDENBURG
PRUSSIA
Warsaw
POLAND

HOLY ROMAN EMPIRE
Nuremberg
Speyer
Stuttgart
Augsburg
Munich
Basel
Zurich
Geneva John Calvin
Milan
Pavia
Genoa
Trent
Venice

BOHEMIA
Prague
MORAVIA
AUSTRIA
Vienna
HUNGARY
Pest
Buda

TRANSYLVANIA
MOLDAVIA
WALLACHIA
Danube R.
BESSARABIA

Black Sea

OTTOMAN EMPIRE

BULGARIA
SERBIA
Belgrade

GREECE

Adriatic Sea

ITALY
Florence
Pisa
Rome Roman Inquisition established, 1542
Naples
Bari

Corsica
Sardinia
Sicily

Mediterranean Sea

SPAIN
Madrid
Toledo
Seville
Granada
Valencia
Barcelona
Balearic Is.

PORTUGAL
Lisbon

MOROCCO

OTTOMAN EMPIRE
ALGIERS
TUNIS

10°W   0°   10°E   20°E   30°E
50°N

Martin Luther preaching, c.1517 (engraving), German School, (16th century)/ Private Collection/The Stapleton Collection/Bridgeman Images

Martin Luther Preaching Martin Luther was known as a powerful preacher, as seen in this contemporary depiction. The rapid spread of his Protestant ideas, however, resulted from the printing press as well. Korean craftsmen had first invented metal moveable type in the fourteenth century, then in 1455 that achievement was repeated by a German goldsmith. The lower cost of books made possible by the printing press then allowed Martin Luther's influence to spread far and wide.

Philip II

(r. 1556–1598) Son of Charles V and king of Spain. Considering himself a defender of Catholicism, Philip launched attacks on Protestants in England and the Netherlands.

Charles V became Holy Roman emperor just as Martin Luther was challenging church authority (see Chapter 16). When the emperor presided over a meeting to bring Luther back under papal authority, Luther refused to back down and was declared an outlaw. The German princes then chose sides, some declaring themselves "Lutherans," others remaining loyal to the pope and Holy Roman emperor. Decades of inconclusive warfare followed, and religious division became a permanent part of the western European scene.

Finally, in 1555, Charles gave up his attempt to impose Catholicism through military means, and agreed to a peace recognizing the principle that princes could impose either Catholicism or Lutheranism within their own territories. Exhausted, he abdicated his throne, retired to a monastery, and split his inheritance between his brother Ferdinand, who took control of the Habsburgs' central European domains, and his son Philip, who became king of Spain. The Habsburgs had failed to hold Europe together.

Philip II (r. 1556–1598) ruled over a magnificent court at Madrid, the Spanish empire in the Americas, and the new southeast Asian colony of the Philippines. However, even with the vast riches of New Spain, wars severely strained the treasury, and increased taxes led to unrest. Philip's militancy in attempting to impose Catholic orthodoxy on his subjects made religious divisions even more acute. One example is the rebellion in 1568 of the Spanish *moriscos* (mohr-EES-kos), Arabic-speaking Iberians who stayed in Spain after 1492. Though forced to convert to Christianity, many morisco families continued to practice their original faith in private (as did many Spanish Jews, who had also been forcibly converted to Catholicism). When the church moved to impose strict Roman Catholicism, the moriscos rebelled. It took two years for Philip's forces to crush the uprising; the king then ordered the expulsion of all those left alive. (Among their descendants were the Spanish Muslims Çelebi encountered in Constantinople.)

Religion also inflamed Philip's war on the Calvinists in his Dutch provinces. **John Calvin** was a Protestant theologian whose Reformed Church emphasized the absolute power of God over weak and sinful humanity. The possibility of salvation for human souls lay entirely with God, Calvin argued: *"eternal life is foreordained for some, eternal damnation for others."*

Philip regarded Calvinists as heretics, and when he tried to seize their property they armed themselves in self-defense. Attempts to put down the rebellion only stiffened Dutch resistance. The struggle was never resolved in Philip's lifetime, but

A la fin ces Voleurs infames et perdus ;   Monstrent bien que le crime (horrible et noire engeance)   Et que cest le Destin des hommes vicieux
Comme fruits malheureux a cet arbre pendus   Est luy mesme instrument de honte et de vengeance ,   Desprouuer tost ou tard la iustice des Cieux .

Israel ex. Cum Priuil. Reg.

The Hanging Tree This French engraving from 1633 shows the awful violence that ravaged Europe during the Thirty Years' War. The victims, says the text, *"hang from the tree like unfortunate fruit."* (Erich Lessing/Art Resource, NY)

in 1609 a treaty was signed that led to the effective independence of the Dutch United Provinces. It was in this political context that the Dutch East India Company emerged as a powerful trading enterprise (see Chapter 16).

Protestant England was another constant source of concern to Philip. Its rulers harassed the Spanish at every turn, for example by supporting the privateers who plundered Spanish treasure ships in the Caribbean. In 1588, Philip sent a great naval armada to invade England, but poor weather combined with clever English strategy to defeat the attempt. The English took the defeat of the Spanish Armada as a sign that God was indeed on their side.

By the early seventeenth century, the Spanish Habsburgs were reeling from the expense of fighting on so many fronts, even as silver imports from the New World began to decline. Like the rulers of Ming China, another great empire for which expanding supplies of silver were a necessity (see Chapter 16), the Spanish Habsburgs found themselves in a difficult financial position. In addition, the peace of 1555 had broken down, and warfare continued to rock central Europe.

Unrest between Catholic and Lutheran rulers finally led to the catastrophic **Thirty Years' War** (1618–1648). As armies rampaged through the countryside, up to 30 percent of the rural population died from famine and disease. Finally, the Peace of Westphalia (1648) recognized a permanent division between Catholic and Protestant Germany. The ideal of a single overarching imperial structure was gone, replaced by the concept of separate national states that recognized one another's sovereignty and agreed to abide by rules governing war and diplomacy. After 1648, the era of Habsburg dominance and of religiously inspired warfare came to an end.

John Calvin

(1509–1564) A Protestant leader whose followers emphasized individual scriptural study and the absolute sovereignty of God.

Thirty Years' War

(1618–1648) Series of wars fought by various European powers on German-speaking lands. Began as a competition between Catholic and Lutheran rulers and was complicated by the dynastic and strategic interests of Europe's major powers.

Still, Vienna remained an impressive cosmopolitan capital, drawing on the cultural riches of central Europe. Evliya Çelebi noted the prolific use of religious statues and paintings in Vienna's Catholic churches, which as a Sunni Muslim, he (like many Protestants) viewed as idolatrous. But fair-minded as usual, he goes on to relay to his Ottoman audience the Catholic explanation: *"When the priests harangue the people, just as your sheikhs do, they have difficulty conveying their message with fine words alone. So we convey the message through images of the prophets and saints and paradise, depictions of divine glory.... But we do not worship them in any way."** Çelebi was especially impressed by European painting: *"When one sees the depiction of paradise,"* he wrote of one painting, *"one wishes to die and go to heaven. . . . Truly, when it comes to painting, the Franks prevail over the Indians and Persians."**

He also acknowledged the skills of Vienna's men of learning, comparing Austrian doctors and scholars favorably to ancient Greek and medieval Muslim models. *"In the city of Vienna,"* he wrote, *"there are perfect masters of surgery ... and scholars of such wisdom and skill the equal of Ibn Sina and Pythagoras together."*† He was equally impressed by their libraries, complaining that Muslims did far less to preserve their ancient texts. Vienna's commercial life, too, brought praise from Çelebi. Of the numerous shops, he wrote, *"so prosperous and well stocked are they that each shop is worth an Egyptian treasure."**

On the other hand, he also found fault with Habsburg society, as during a diplomatic mission to Vienna in 1665, where he wondered at the free mixing of men and women in the city: *"The women sit together with us Ottomans, drinking and chatting, and their husbands do not say a word.... The reason is that throughout Christendom women are in charge, and they have behaved in this disreputable fashion ever since the time of the Virgin Mary.** Of course, he exaggerated Austrian women's equality, knowing that his Ottoman readers would be fascinated by reports of the Europeans' transgression of strict social segregation by gender.

● **CONTEXT&CONNECTIONS** Evliya Çelebi's comments on Christian women repeat a stereotype that circulated widely in the Muslim world. In fact, Austrian and Ottoman societies were equally patriarchal; that is, men defined women's lives legally and socially. Muslim societies, though, had adopted the ancient eastern Mediterranean practice of sharply segregating the sexes and veiling women in public. This practice was initially limited to elites, but as with footbinding in China (see Chapter 20), elite practice became popular custom. While European women enjoyed relatively greater liberty of social interaction, fathers and husbands controlled their educations, marriages, property, and housing—their bodies if not their minds—just as in Constantinople. ●

As we might expect given that the Ottomans and Austrians had recently fought a bitter war, Çelebi was particularly critical of Habsburg military affairs. He contrasted the Austrians unfavorably to the Hungarians: *"The Austrians ... have no stomach for a fight and are not swordsmen and horsemen. Their infantry musketeers, to*

---

*Robert Dankoff and Sooyong Kim, translation and commentary, *An Ottoman Traveller: Selections from the* Book of Travels *of Evliya Çelebi* (London: Eland Publishing, 2010), pp. 240–241, 230–232. Reprinted by permission.

†J. W. Livingstone, "Evliya Çelebi on Surgical Procedures in Vienna," *Al-Abath* 23 (1970): 232.

be sure, are real fire-shooters; but ... they can't shoot from the shoulder as Ottoman soldiers do. Also, they shut their eyes and fire at random."* Like the Persians, he said, the
Austrians were guilty of excessively brutal forms of torture, and for this and other
reasons he had a better opinion of the Hungarians, who "though they have lost their
power, still have fine tables, are hospitable to guests, and are . . . true warriors. . . . They
do not torture their prisoners as the Austrians do. . . . In short, though both of them are
unbelievers without faith, the Hungarians are the more honorable and cleaner infidels."*

Çelebi's visit came during a break in the fighting, as the military balance
between Austrians and Ottomans in southeastern Europe seesawed back and forth.
Though horsemanship, as Çelebi indicated, still had strong cultural and military
value in the seventeenth century, it was the effective use of gunpowder weapons
that was fast becoming crucial to success. Mastering that technology, the
Habsburgs, though now limited to central Europe, managed to hold their own and
remain one of the Great Powers of western Eurasia.

Religious Conflict and Political Control in France and England, 1500–1715

In France and England, ambitious kings claimed ever
greater power, though in both countries their plans
were complicated by religious differences as well as
conflicts with noblemen who resented losing some
of their own authority to the king's men. In the end
both countries found paths to political stability but
followed very different formulas: absolute monarchy in France, and a constitutional balance of power between king and parliament in England.

French Protestants, largely Calvinists known as Huguenots (HEW-guh-noh),
were a relatively small but prosperous minority (see Map 17.1). Catholic persecution reached a crescendo in 1572. The Saint Bartholomew's Day massacre began
as an anti-Protestant conspiracy led by the mother of the French king, the assassination of Huguenot leaders followed by riotous assaults on Protestants beginning
in Paris and spreading across the country. Tens of thousands of Huguenots were
butchered, and the Saint Bartholomew's Day massacre permanently crippled the
Protestant communities of France. After a change in dynasty, however, compromise followed. In 1598 the Edict of Nantes granted limited toleration of Protestant
worship within a specified group of cities.

The dominant French political figure of the age was Cardinal Richelieu (1585–
1642). Though Richelieu was a high-ranking Catholic Church official, he formu-
lated his policies wholly in the interests of the French monarchy. For example, to
position France as the leading defender of the Catholic faith, he was willing to ally
France with German Protestants against Spain's Catholic monarch. But tensions
came with Richelieu's attempt to amass greater power for the king and his ministers, which alienated the French nobility, while the common people resented
increased taxes to pay for military campaigns.

Revolts broke out soon after Cardinal Richelieu died, with the child-king
Louis XIV (r. 1643–1715) having just come to the throne. From 1648 to 1653,
France was wracked by civil war. But the French monarchy survived the crisis, and
Louis XIV came of age to become a monarch of legendary power. His court and
Versailles Palace rivaled Constantinople's Sublime Porte in splendor and luxury.

Louis XIV
(r. 1643–1715) Known
as the "Sun King," Louis
epitomized royal absolut-
ism and established firm
control over the French
state. Aggressively pur-
sued military domination
of Europe while patron-
izing French arts from
his court at Versailles.

---

*Robert Dankoff and Sooyong Kim, translation and commentary, *An Ottoman Traveller: Selections
from the* Book of Travels *of Evliya Çelebi* (London: Eland Publishing, 2010), pp. 230–231. Reprinted
by permission.

Banquet Given in Honour of Louis XIV (1638–1715) by the Corps Municipal at the Hotel-de-Ville, c.1680 (oil on canvas), French School (17th century)/Musee Carnavalet, Paris, France/Bridgeman Images

Louis XIV   All French politics orbited around the "Sun King." Louis cultivated the support of the nobility by hosting lush entertainment at his palace of Versailles. Here the setting is urban, as he is honored at a banquet hosted by the leaders of the municipal government of Paris.

When Louis XIV became king, the nobility still dominated the countryside, and they remained jealous of their prerogatives. Both lords and peasants lived in a world where local affiliations and obligations were more important than national ones. As during medieval times, peasants labored on their lords' estates and were subject to manorial courts.

Following Richelieu's example, Louis increased the number of royal officials sent to the countryside and provincial cities, men who depended on royal patronage and owed their loyalty to the king. These officials enforced royal edicts that cut into the power of the landed nobility. By now the nobles had given up the fight; there were benefits to staying on the king's good side. The nobles sought their own royal patronage as they gravitated toward Louis' lavish court at Versailles, enjoying its extravagant banquets, first-rate theater and music, and scandalous gossip.

Louis XIV's motto—"*One King, One Law, One Faith*"—emphasized the Catholic nature of his kingdom. After he revoked the Edict of Nantes in 1685, hundreds of thousands of French Protestants fled to England, Switzerland, the Netherlands, and Cape Town in South Africa. Like Richelieu before him, Louis was determined to weaken Spain and Austria and position France as the world's dominant Catholic power, poised to challenge England in a global competition for empire.

Louis XIV's form of government has been termed "royal absolutism." "*I am the state,*" he said, implying that all of public life should be directed by his own will. The French "Sun King" was the envy of all who aspired to absolute power, including contemporary English monarchs. However, in England the outcome would be entirely different, with parliamentary checks on royal power.

Under Queen Elizabeth, English society had entered the seventeenth century in relative tranquility and with increasing national confidence. In religious matters, Elizabeth followed the Anglican Church of England tradition established by her father, King Henry VIII. Although Catholicism was made illegal, Henry actually retained many Catholic rites and traditions, including a hierarchy of powerful bishops.

Many English Protestants wanted further reform to purge Catholic influences. Among them were the English Calvinists, Protestant reformers known as **Puritans**, who grew discontented with the Stuart kings who came to power after Elizabeth. They scorned the opulence of court life and Anglican bishops' culture of luxury and what they saw as continuing "Roman" elements in Anglican rituals and church organization.

Under the Stuart king Charles I (r. 1625–1649), tensions exploded. Charles pursued war with Spain and supported Huguenot rebels in France, but he could not raise taxes to finance his wars without the approval of Parliament. In 1628, when Parliament presented a petition of protest against the king, he disbanded it for eleven years. By then, Charles was so desperate for money that he had no choice but to reconvene Parliament. Reformers in Parliament tried to use the occasion to compel the abolition of the Anglican ecclesiastical hierarchy. When Charles arrested several parliamentary leaders on charges of treason, the people of London reacted with violence. The king fled London, and the English Civil War (1642–1649) began.

Puritan leader Oliver Cromwell (1599–1658) organized the opposition to the king's forces. Puritan soldiers showed their disdain for residual Catholic influences on the Church of England by stabling their horses inside Anglican cathedrals, smashing statues, and knocking out stained-glass windows. After seven years of fighting, Cromwell prevailed. The king was captured and, in 1649, beheaded. Cromwell became Lord Protector of the English Commonwealth and instituted a series of radical reforms. But the Commonwealth was held together by little other than his own will and his control of the army, and some of his policies were highly unpopular. Puritan suppression of the theaters, for example, while in keeping with strict Calvinist ideals, was resented by many Londoners (just as imposed morality had provoked unrest in late Safavid Iran.)

After Cromwell died, Parliament invited Charles's son home from exile to reestablish the monarchy. But Anglicans saw the last two Stuart kings as too tolerant of Catholicism. So powerful was their prejudice that they even blamed Catholics for the Great Fire that swept through London in 1666, inscribing on the monument commemorating the tragedy: "*But Popish frenzy, which wrought such horrors, is not yet quenched*" (an accusation that was scratched out only in 1831).

In the so-called Glorious Revolution of 1688, Parliament took charge to assure that the English monarch, head of the Church of England, would always be staunchly Protestant. They drove the last Stuart king from the throne and invited a reliably Protestant princess, together with her Dutch husband, to take his place. The accession of Queen Mary and King William made permanent the Protestant character of the English monarchy.

As a result of the Glorious Revolution, William and Mary were required to accept the principle of annual parliamentary meetings. In 1689, they also approved a **Bill of Rights**. While restrictions on individual liberty remained, including

Puritans

Seventeenth-century reformers of the Church of England who attempted to purge the church of all Catholic influences. They were Calvinists who emphasized Bible reading, simplicity and modesty, and the rejection of priestly authority and elaborate rituals.

Bill of Rights

In 1689, King William and Queen Mary of England recognized a Bill of Rights that protected their subjects against arbitrary seizure of person or property and that required annual meetings of Parliament.

substantial disabilities for English Catholics, and while most people had no voice in governance, the Bill of Rights established important precedents—freedom of speech in Parliament, for example, and the right to trial by jury—for England and for the world (see Chapter 22).

By the eighteenth century, the balance between king and Parliament gave a stable foundation to England and to the wider British society that came after union with Scotland in 1707. Commerce thrived both domestically and internationally, where the British navy "ruled the waves." The French and the British, with their very different political cultures and religious foundations, would soon be engaged in a global contest that would bring war to Europe, the Americas, and South Asia (see Chapter 19).

Between East and West: Russians, Jews, and Armenians

The geographic distinction between Europe and Asia is conventional but somewhat misleading. As we have seen, the Ottoman empire had its roots in Central Asia and Anatolia but was a significant European power as well. Likewise, Russia looked both west and east in its early development and its imperial expansion. *"In Europe we are Asiatics,"* a later Russian author commented, *"whereas in Asia we are Europeans."** By the mid-seventeenth century, under the Romanov dynasty, the Russian empire was moving westward toward Sweden and Poland, eastward into Siberia, and southward toward the edges of Ottoman and Safavid power. The influence of the Russian Orthodox Church spread along with the empire.

The Russians and Ottomans were not the only people who straddled both Asia and Europe. Jews and Armenians are two important examples of peoples who lived all across western Eurasia, as well as in North Africa and the Indian Ocean world. Their experiences bring to the fore world history's emphasis on the movement and interaction of peoples.

The Rise of the Russian Empire, 1500–1725

Before the sixteenth century, the Slavic-speaking Russian people had been deeply influenced by Greek-speaking Byzantium. Medieval Russian princes and merchants cultivated relations with Constantinople, and the monastic tradition of Orthodox Christianity took deep root. Thus Russian rulers took the title tsar ("Caesar"), asserting continuity with the Byzantine emperors who, until they lost Constantinople to the Ottomans, had been the standard bearers of the Orthodox faith.

Tsar Ivan IV (r. 1533–1584) centralized power in his own hands while extending Russia's frontiers. His strategy of maintaining a large territorial buffer around the core Russian lands to protect them from invasion would become a perennial element of Russian imperial policy. Ivan's accomplishments, however, came with a price. He earned the nickname "Ivan the Terrible" for the random cruelty of his later years. Following Ivan's death came a "time of troubles" with no

---

*Fyodor Dostoevsky, cited in Tony Judt, *Post-War: A History of Europe since 1945* (New York: Penguin, 2005), p. 749.

clear successor to the title of tsar. Then in 1613 the Russian nobles offered royal power to Mikhail Romanov. The Romanov dynasty (1613–1917) continued Russia's imperial expansion.

● **CONTEXT&CONNECTIONS** The Russian and Ottoman empires endured straight into the twentieth century. The Romanov dynasty came to an end when the Bolsheviks under *Vladimir Lenin* (Chapter 27) seized power in 1917 and brought communism to Russia; the Ottoman empire collapsed in the wake of World War I, its core territories forming the modern Republic of Turkey (see Chapter 28). ●

Profit lured Russian traders to the east, where the quest for animal furs led them across the Ural Mountains to frigid Siberia; state power followed later. Already in the seventeenth century, Russians were trading furs on a substantial scale, meeting demand from England to Iran. In fact, Evliya Çelebi described a specialized Ottoman guild of furriers whose goods included *"furs of sable, ermin, Russian silver fox"* and *"outlandish bearskin caps."**

Agricultural surpluses, however, were the main sources of revenue for the tsars and the Russian nobility. Distinctive about Russia was the long persistence of serfdom. Russian peasants were tightly bound to their villages, and the tsars and aristocracy increasingly saw these "souls," as they called them, as property that could be bought and sold. The oppressive conditions of serfdom in Russia contrasted with developments in western Europe, where serfdom had either disappeared altogether or where peasant obligations were becoming less burdensome. Serfdom would long remain a marker of Russian backwardness (see Chapter 23).

Still, a major reorientation toward the west began under Tsar **Peter the Great** (r. 1685–1725). Peter visited western Europe as a young monarch, and came back urgently aware that his country had fallen behind in technology and science. As tsar, he was determined to put Russia on par with the rising states to his west. To enable rapid transformation, he accumulated greater power for himself by bringing the nobles more tightly under control. In a move that symbolized both Peter's desire to bring the country in line with Western models and his mastery over the nobles, he ordered Russian aristocrats to shave off their luxurious beards, and his courtiers were required to dress in the latest Western fashion. Any Russian man who wanted to keep his old-fashioned Orthodox beard would now have to pay a "beard tax" and carry a metal receipt marked with the motto: *"the beard is a superfluous burden."* As with the imposition of the *queue* hairstyle by the Manchu in China (see Chapter 20), men's heads instantly showed who was in charge. Change in Russia would flow in just one direction: from the top down.

With great expense and immense manpower Peter built the new city of St. Petersburg, situated on the Baltic Sea, to serve as Russia's "window on the West." Its elegant baroque buildings, emulating those of Rome and Vienna, stood in contrast to the churches and palaces of Moscow, which reflected Central Asian architecture. Henceforth, Russia would be a power in both Europe and in Asia. (See the feature "Visual Evidence in Primary Sources: European and Asian Influences in Russian Architecture.")

Peter the Great

(r. 1685–1725) Powerful Romanov tsar who built a new Russian capital at St. Petersburg, emulated Western advances in military technology, and extended the Russian empire further into Asia.

---

*Robert Dankoff and Sooyong Kim, translation and commentary, *An Ottoman Traveller: Selections from the* Book of Travels *of Evliya Çelebi* (London: Eland Publishing, 2010), p. 27. Reprinted by permission.

European and Asian Influences in Russian Architecture

Architecture reflects the diverse cultural influences on a people who straddle the geography of Europe and Asia. Russia's cultural exceptionality within the history of European Christianity traces back to the tenth century, when Prince Vladimir chose to affiliate the Principality of Kiev with the Greek-speaking Byzantine Church, headquartered in Constantinople, rather than with the Latin-speaking Catholic Church centered in Rome (or with the Muslims of the Volga River). Apart from strong Byzantine influence in religion, art, and architecture, early Russians also had long-term cultural exchanges with the nomadic peoples of the Eurasian steppe, a cultural factor that was greatly enhanced when Russia was absorbed into the Mongol empire in the fourteenth century. In the early modern period, as the Russian empire expanded south and east, interactions with Iranian and Turkish peoples also left their cultural mark.

Russia's cultural orientation shifted westward, however, under Peter the Great and his successors. As a young monarch, Peter traveled west to France and the Netherlands hoping, among other goals, to find allies for his wars with the Ottoman empire. In the process he became aware of the great advances

St. Basil's Cathedral was built by Ivan the Terrible in the 1550s to commemorate his conquest of the khanate of Kazan centered on the Volga River, whose rulers were Muslim descendants of Mongolian conquerors. The church's bright colors were added later, in the seventeenth and eighteenth centuries.

Some scholars theorize that the "onion dome" architecture was inspired by the central mosque at Kazan (destroyed by Ivan's army), combined with Greek Byzantine influences and Renaissance styles from Italy.

The official name of the church is the "Cathedral of the Protection of Most Holy Theotokos on the Moat." Theotokos is a Greek title ("God-bearer") for Mary, the mother of Jesus.

The close proximity of St. Basil's to Red Square in Moscow, near the Kremlin, the heart of Russia's political establishment, shows the traditionally close connection between tsarist rule and Russia's Orthodox Christian Church.

Image Source/Superstock

In 1929, under the officially atheistic communist government of the Soviet Union, the church was secularized and turned into a museum. Currently, one church service a year is held at St. Basil's, which has been a UNESCO World Heritage Site since 1990.

taking place in Western shipbuilding and resolved to create a Baltic fleet along modern lines. Similarly, he built the city of St. Petersburg in emulation of the latest architectural styles and employing Western construction techniques. From the eighteenth century onward, then, Russia's cultural legacy has included a broad range of European and Asian features in music, religious life, dance, and architecture. Examples can be found in the images here, with striking architectural and aesthetic differences between St. Basil's Church in Moscow and the Winter Palace in St. Petersburg.

The Winter Palace building was originally planned as the main residence of the Romanov family and as the focal point for the new city of St. Petersburg, begun in 1703 after Peter the Great returned from his tour of western Europe. It took hundreds of thousands of conscripted laborers more than two decades to complete the city.

Later Romanovs moved the capital back to Moscow, though they returned to the milder climate of St. Petersburg during the winter; hence the name "Winter Palace." Continual additions eventually led to a palace with over fifteen hundred rooms.

The palace complex was greatly expanded and thoroughly redecorated in the elaborate Baroque style during the reign of Empress Catherine the Great (r. 1762–1796; see Chapter 20) under a French architect. **_What are the main differences in architectural form between St. Basil's Church and the Winter Palace, and what varying cultural influences do they show?_**

Peter Christopher/Masterfile

Catherine began the art collection that today forms the core of the Hermitage Museum, one of the world's great art galleries. Today, the Hermitage Museum attracts over 3 million visitors each year.

The Winter Palace played a central role in later Russian history. In 1905, revolution erupted when the tsar's guard massacred protesters in its courtyard (see Chapter 27). In 1917, after the abdication of the last tsar, the building was temporarily the seat of the Russian government once again, until the communists moved the capital back to the Kremlin in Moscow.

Peter's ultimate goal was clear when he created a regular standing army larger than any in Europe, bringing in the latest military technology from the West while working toward Russian self-sufficiency in guns and cannon. He also sponsored a new educational system to train more efficient civilian and military bureaucrats. But the situation of the serfs was worse than ever. It was their heavy taxes that paid for the grandeur of St. Petersburg and the power of the Russian military, and it was their sons who fought in Peter's armies, extending Russia's frontiers in wars against Sweden and Poland, and laying the groundwork for later conquests of Muslim steppe societies. For all the elegance of Peter's new capital, the top-down tsarist command structure and the expansionist thrust of his imperial strategy had not changed very much since the days of Ivan the Terrible.

The Jewish and Armenian Diasporas

In his *Book of Travels*, Evliya Çelebi was careful to describe the customs and languages of the many different peoples he met. When describing the "Jewish" language, he started with the numbers "un, dos, tire, korta," describing not Hebrew but Ladino, the language based on medieval Spanish spoken by the Iberian Jews known as the Sephardim. Driven into exile from Catholic Spain in 1492, many Sephardim found refuge in the Ottoman empire, both in North Africa and in Çelebi's own Constantinople.

In Ottoman lands, as in Europe, Jews faced persistent popular prejudice. Çelebi himself referred to them as *"an ancient and accursed people."* Still, the Koran defines Jews as "People of the Book," a status that gives them autonomy from Islamic law and the right to adjudicate their own affairs. As long as they paid their taxes, Ottoman Jews were free to regulate their community following their own laws and customs. As they had in medieval Spain, Ladino-speaking Jews made significant contributions to the intellectual and commercial life of the Ottoman empire, for example by serving as medical doctors. Sephardic Jews could also be found in largely Arab cities like Baghdad and in Iranian Isfahan as well. Some even settled in Jerusalem, from which their ancient Hebrew ancestors had been forcibly expelled in the days of the Roman empire.

The larger branch of the Jewish *diaspora*—from a Greek word meaning "dispersal"—were the **Ashkenazim**, Jews who had settled in central and eastern Europe and spoke Yiddish, a German-derived language mixed with Hebrew and, in the east, with words from Slavic languages. The Ashkenazim were broadly scattered: many were peasant villagers within the Russian empire; further west they were more likely to live in cities and engage in commerce. Partly by their own preference and partly because of their exclusion by Christians, Ashkenazim usually lived not just as religious outsiders but as a community apart, following their own legal traditions and usually marrying within their own group. Thus, while they both contributed to and borrowed from majority communities over a very long period, the European Jews remained culturally distinctive in their music, cuisine, and folktales, as well as in their Yiddish language.

In this setting, the Ashkenazim were vulnerable and insecure, facing deep prejudice, and sometimes theft of property or even violent attacks, from their Christian neighbors. Çelebi witnessed a chilling ceremony in the Balkans during which Christians had marched through the town at night with statues of Jesus and his mother, Mary. They explained to Çelebi that they had been commemorating an

Ashkenazim

The largest group in the Jewish diaspora, speaking the German-derived language of Yiddish and living in central and eastern Europe.

---

*Robert Dankoff and Sooyong Kim, translation and commentary, *An Ottoman Traveller: Selections from the* Book of Travels *of Evliya Çelebi* (London: Eland Publishing, 2010), pp. 93–94. Reprinted by permission.

episode in which, they claimed, Jews had once kidnapped Jesus and Mary. When their forebears supposedly found out about this, Çelebi was told, they *"armed themselves, and began to search for Jesus in the Jews' houses ... with a great hue and cry, just like last evening. Then they found Jesus and Mary in a Jew's house and massacred all the Jews."** All across Europe, Jewish communities faced this kind of terrifying intimidation, often based on similar historical distortions casting their ancestors as killers of the Christian messiah.

The Armenians, followers of an ancient orthodox Christian church, lived across an even wider Eurasian arc, including Russian and Ottoman lands, with distinct Armenian neighborhoods in Constantinople, Jerusalem, and other cities. Their mountainous homeland was dangerous territory, on the borderlands between the Ottoman and Safavid empires. In fact, Shah Abbas I resettled as many as 150,000 Armenians in a separate quarter of Isfahan in a move intended both to secure his border with the Ottomans and to make use of Armenian skills in handicrafts and commerce. Though the move was involuntary, the Armenians of Isfahan were allowed to build churches and look after their own community's affairs. By the seventeenth century, Iranian Armenians were at the center of a commercial network stretching across the Indian Ocean, with business interests all the way from the Mediterranean to the South China Sea.

When Evliya Çelebi visited the Adriatic port of Dubrovnik (in today's Republic of Croatia), he found a city with *"numerous Armenians, Greeks, Jews, Persians, and Franks . . . a place of security and a safe haven of Christendom, a very prosperous entrepôt."** In fact, the city's largely Christian government had sought Ottoman protection against the expanding Venetian republic. Here it seems that safety of travel, security of property, and the right to practice your own religion and regulate your own community made the Ottoman empire a place where diverse peoples might thrive. While it may have been cold comfort to Christian families whose children were taken away for service in the Janissary corps, in Çelebi's time it still seemed possible for diverse Ottoman subjects to live together in relative peace and prosperity.

The Shifting Balance of Power in Western Eurasia by 1750

By the mid-eighteenth century the center of Eurasian power was shifting north and west (see Map 17.2). Britain, France, Austria, and Prussia were ascendant, with the rulers of imperial Russia, whose armies penetrated deeper into Asia, looking west for models of military innovation. This was not yet global hegemony: most African and Asian rulers continued to mind their own affairs with little reference to Europeans; Ottoman sultans remained lords over vast and rich territories; and the great Qing and Mughal dynasties in China and India were still wealthier and more populous than any single European state. But in hindsight, we see the foundations of a Europe-centered world being laid.

Having solved its constitutional crisis, British society took the lead in creating more refined and efficient business methods, building on early Dutch innovations.

---

*Robert Dankoff and Sooyong Kim, translation and commentary, *An Ottoman Traveller: Selections from the* Book of Travels *of Evliya Çelebi* (London: Eland Publishing, 2010), pp. 209, 207. Reprinted by permission.

Map 17.2 Western Eurasia in the Early Eighteenth Century By the early eighteenth century the Habsburg attempt to unify western Europe had failed, and the continent was permanently divided between Catholic and Protestant powers. In 1715 the dominant powers in the west were France, Britain, Austria, and Prussia. The Russian and Ottoman empires to the east were formidable military powers, but the golden age of Spain had ended.

French Bourbon lands
Spanish Bourbon lands
Austrian Habsburg lands
Prussian lands
Great Britain
Boundary of the Holy Roman Empire
Russian Empire
Russian gains, by 1725
Ottoman Empire, 1722

ATLANTIC OCEAN

PORTUGAL
Lisbon

SPAIN
Madrid
Tagus R.
Duero R.
Ebro R.
CATALONIA
GIBRALTAR (Gr. Br.)

Balearic Is.
Minorca (Gr. Br.)

Mediterranean Sea

FRANCE
Paris
Seine R.
Loire R.
Garonne R.
Toulouse
Marseilles
Rhône R.

GREAT BRITAIN
SCOTLAND
Edinburgh
ENGLAND
London
Thames R.
IRELAND
Dublin

North Sea

NORWAY
Oslo

KINGDOM OF DENMARK
DENMARK

SWEDEN

Baltic Sea

St. Petersburg
INGRIA
ESTONIA
LIVONIA
Riga
LITHUANIA

RUSSIAN EMPIRE
Moscow
Smolensk
Don R.
Dnieper R.

POLAND
Warsaw
Vistula R.
EAST PRUSSIA
Kiev
UKRAINE
Dniester R.

UNITED NETHERLANDS
Utrecht.
Rhine R.
HANOVER
BRANDENBURG-PRUSSIA
Berlin
Elbe R.
SAXONY
Oder R.
SILESIA
BOHEMIA
BAVARIA
Danube R.

HOLY ROMAN EMPIRE
PALATINATE
LORRAINE
Strasbourg
SWITZERLAND
SAVOY
MILAN
GENOA
Po R.
AUSTRIA
Vienna
MODENA
TUSCANY
PAPAL STATES
Rome
KINGDOM OF NAPLES
Naples

Corsica (Genoa)
Sardinia (Austria)
Sicily (Savoy)

Tyrrhenian Sea

REPUBLIC OF VENICE
Adriatic Sea

CROATIA
SLAVONIA
HUNGARY
Buda
Pest
BOSNIA
HERZEGOVINA
SERBIA
Belgrade
TRANSYLVANIA
MOLDAVIA
WALLACHIA
BULGARIA
Danube R.

MONTENEGRO
ALBANIA
GREECE

OTTOMAN EMPIRE
Constantinople
Aegean Sea

CRIMEA
Black Sea

0   150   300 Mi.
0   150   300 Km.

10°W   0°   10°E   20°E   40°E

50°N   60°N

In 1694, for example, the founding of the Bank of England made it much easier for the government to raise funds at modest interest rates for the building of infrastructure, especially for naval expansion. Trade was Britain's life blood, its navy essential for global commercial success. The slave-based sugar plantations of the West Indies brought misery to Africans but vast fortunes to Englishmen, providing them with capital that could be used for investment in new techniques of industrial manufacture (see Chapters 19 and 23). Meanwhile, by 1750 Britain had become by far the world's greatest sea power.

The English and French monarchies had been great rivals since the middle ages. By 1750 their competition was going global, with competing colonial and trade interests in North America, the West Indies, and South Asia.

As Paris became Europe's most important center of philosophy (see Chapter 21), King Louis XV built on his father's accomplishments, investing in both a large army and a naval force strong enough to challenge the British. French success at maintaining its central role on the European continent while challenging the British across the oceans was limited, however, by the great expense of having to maintain military forces decade after decade on both land and sea (while their enemy could focus on its navy).

● **CONTEXT&CONNECTIONS** After a series of early-eighteenth-century wars proved inconclusive, the *Seven Years' War* (1756–1763; Chapter 19) swung the imperial balancer of power in favor of Great Britain. Sometimes referred to by historians the first truly "world" war, it was fought simultaneously in the West Indies, North America, India, and continental Europe. British control of India (see Chapter 20) and Canada (see Chapter 25) were important outcomes. ●

In Protestant-dominated northern Germany, **Prussia** was the rising power in the aftermath of the Thirty Years' War. Although the German-speaking lands were still divided into numerous territories, Prussia, from its capital at Berlin, emerged as the strongest German state. King Frederick William I (r. 1713–1740) made his country a pioneer in military technology and organization, using the latest cannon and muskets and developing a professional standing army of well-trained and disciplined troops. Precision marching and constant drilling were the hallmarks of the Prussian military. The middle class had little political influence. Instead, the traditional rural aristocracy, accepting and benefiting from the Prussian kings' innovations, was the bedrock of royal absolutism. Their cooperation in taxing and controlling the peasants gave Frederick William and his successors resources to expand the military and make Prussia a force to be reckoned with.

Prussia

With its capital at Berlin, Prussia was the rising German power of the eighteenth century. Its military prowess set it in competition with Habsburg Austria for influence over the many German-speaking kingdoms and principalities.

Austria, with its traditional leading role among German states, was threatened by Prussia's rise, leading to complex diplomacy and sometimes war. When Habsburg Austria sought to bolster its position through an alliance with France, the Prussians allied themselves with Britain, a tangle of alliances that by the mid-eighteenth century was turning local conflicts into international ones. Similar alliances and entanglements would mark European power politics straight into the twentieth century, when the First World War saw French, Britain, and Russia allied against Germany, Austria, and the Ottoman empire (see Chapter 27).

Evliya Çelebi wrote in a confident, sometimes even arrogant, tone of superiority about the varied Christian and Muslim lands he visited. Indeed, from his mid-seventeenth-century perspective the Ottoman empire was something to boast about: even as he enjoyed his peaceful retirement in Cairo, Ottoman armies were preparing once again to lay siege to Vienna. But the balance of power was changing. Çelebi did not see it coming, but the winds of history were shifting, and the direction of that change was from the west.

Climate Change and the Seventeenth Century

We are apt to read the historical time lines below from left to right, perhaps seeing events like the English Civil War (1642–1649) and the collapse of the Ming dynasty in China (1644) as entirely disconnected. But what happens if we scan our regional time lines vertically, looking for connections between global, regional, and national histories?

A long-standing approach has been to emphasize interactions of large states and empires. As this chapter shows, important lessons can be learned for both northern Europe and western Asia by charting the dynamics of state-building in a period when gunpowder technology raised the stakes of military victory and defeat and when religious conflict fueled imperial competition.

Another obvious global link in early modern times is the increase in maritime networks. Indeed, the previous two chapters have shown the transformative power of new oceanic interchange, though we need to be cautious not to overemphasize European impacts. While the effects of Christopher Columbus's voyages were indeed revolutionary, Matteo Ricci's story indicates that Europeans of his time were relatively marginal to the histories of powerful societies like Mughal India and Ming China.

In the past few decades, quite different sorts of connections across regional histories have been developed by environmental historians exploring the dynamics of the Columbian exchange (see Chapter 15). They have shown the profound effects of multidirectional biological exchanges—flows of plants, animals, seeds, and germs—across the oceans and around the world following the integration of the Eastern and Western Hemispheres. Among other implications of the Columbian exchange, we are now well aware of its impact on the size and distribution of human populations.

Most recently, the study of climate change has offered a radically new approach to integrating early modern global history, as seen in Geoffrey Parker's *Global Crisis: War, Climate Change and Catastrophe in the Seventeenth Century* (2013). European historians have long noted a conjunction between the "little ice age" of the seventeenth century and the century's political crises, religious conflicts, societal mayhem, and violence. Professor Parker has now extrapolated that story and made it global.

Parker argues that in the 1600s "an intense episode of global cooling coincided with an unparalleled spate of revolutions and state breakdowns around the world.... Throughout the Northern Hemisphere, war became the norm for resolving both domestic and international problems."* If participants in the political struggles of western Eurasia used religion to explain their motives and behavior, climate

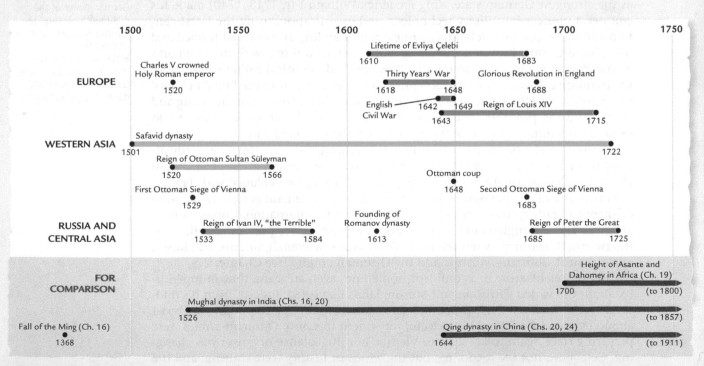

historians looking at the miserable harvests of the 1640s might point to a more basic cause of conflict: hunger.

During the 1640s, we find on our time lines civil wars in England and France; the destruction of the Ming dynasty in China; and rebellion in the Ottoman palace. Amazingly, the suicide of the last Ming emperor, the beheading of the English king, and the assassination of the Ottoman sultan all took place within the space of just five years, between 1644 and 1649. Was that just a coincidence? Of course, a detailed understanding of each of these events requires close attention to particular actors and their specific circumstances. But there was a common context, says Professor Parker. Cooler temperatures caused poor harvests and lower tax revenues in England, France, China, and the Ottoman empire, weakening their rulers, inspiring revolts, and bringing decades of war and violence.

Fortunately, the 1680s brought greater stability. The English had their Glorious Revolution (1688), bringing balance to relations between king and Parliament; Louis XIV asserted royal authority in France (the Versailles Palace was built at this time); and the Ottomans were once again strong enough to lay siege to Vienna (1683). The return of stability, Parker notes, coincided with warmer weather and better harvests.

If the conjunction of climate change and global crisis in the seventeenth century has a message for us today, it is not a reassuring one. If contemporary global warming is more than a short-term weather cycle, and if large climate swings do correlate with widespread outbursts of violence, then we could be in for difficult times.

---

*Geoffrey Parker, *Global Crisis: War, Climate Change and Catastrophe in the Seventeenth Century* (New Haven: Yale University Press, 2013), pp. xvi–xvii.

Key Terms

Evliya Çelebi (500)
Janissaries (503)
Süleyman (504)
Safavid dynasty (505)
Abbas I (506)
Sufi (510)

Habsburg dynasty (511)
Philip II (514)
John Calvin (515)
Thirty Years' War (515)
Louis XIV (517)
Puritans (519)

Bill of Rights (519)
Peter the Great (521)
Ashkenazim (524)
Prussia (527)

For Further Reference

Beik, William. *Louis XIV and Absolutism: A Brief Study with Documents.* New York: Bedford/St. Martin's, 2000.

Bergin, Joseph. *The Seventeenth Century: Europe 1598–1715.* New York: Oxford University Press, 2001.

Braudel, Fernand. *The Mediterranean and the Mediterranean World in the Age of Philip II.* Sian Reynolds, trans. New York: Harper and Row, 1972.

Casale, Giancarlo. *The Ottoman Age of Exploration.* New York: Oxford University Press, 2011.

Chardin, Jean de. *A Journey to Persia: Jean Chardin's Portrait of a Seventeenth Century Empire.* Ronald W. Ferrier, trans. and ed. London: I. B. Tauris, 1996.

Clot, Andre. *Suleiman the Magnificent.* London: Saqi Books, 2004.

Cressy, David, and Lori Anne Farrell, eds. *Religion and Society in Early Modern England: A Sourcebook.* New York: Routledge, 2005.

Dankoff, Robert, and Sooyong Kim. *An Ottoman Traveler: Selections from the Book of Travels of Evliya Çelebi.* London: Eland Publishing, 2010.

Fichtner, Paula Sutter. *Terror and Toleration: The Habsburg Empire Confronts Islam, 1526–1850.* New York: Reaktion Books, 2008.

Friedrich, Karin. *Brandenburg-Prussia, 1466-1806: The Rise of a Composite State.* New York: Palgrave Macmillan, 2011.

Hughes, Lindsay. *Russia in the Age of Peter the Great.* New Haven: Yale University Press, 2000.

Isom-Verhaaren, Christine. *Allies with the Infidel: The Ottoman and French Alliance in the Sixteenth Century.* London: I.B. Tauris, 2013.

Ruderman, David B. *Early Modern Jewry: A New Cultural History.* Princeton: Princeton University Press, 2011.

Şahin, Kaya. *Empire and Power in the Reign of Suleyman.* Cambridge: Cambridge University Press, 2013.

Savory, Roger. *Iran Under the Safavids.* New York: Cambridge University Press, 2007.

Tezcan, Baki. *The Second Ottoman Empire: Political and Social Transformation in the Early Modern World.* New York: Cambridge University Press, 2010.

 **MindTap** is a fully online, highly personalized learning experience built upon Cengage Learning content. MindTap combines student learning tools—readings, multimedia, activities, and assessments—into a singular Learning Path that guides students through the course.

18

Empires, Colonies, and Peoples of the Americas, 1600–1750

Catalina de Erauso

By the early 1600s, the Spanish had conquered the once-mighty Aztec and Inca and secured an American empire. But in some areas that they had not effectively occupied, Amerindian peoples held on to their independence. A battle-hardened young soldier, **Catalina de Erauso** (1585–1650), described an encounter with one such group in South America:

On the third day we discovered a village of Indians who immediately took up arms. We went in and, feeling the [muskets] they scattered leaving some dead…. [A soldier] weary of his helmet, took it off to wipe off the sweat. A demon of a boy about twelve years old, who was blocking our exit up in a tree, fired an arrow which knocked him over. He was so badly hurt, unfortunately, that he died the next day. We cut the boy into ten thousand pieces…. The Indians, meanwhile, were returning to the village, about ten thousand of them. We attacked them with such fury and wreaked such havoc among them that a gutter of blood like a river flowed down through the place…. [I]n the houses of the village more than seventy thousand pesos in gold dust were found. Along the edge of the river, much more was found, and they filled their hats with it.*

---

*Early Americas Digital Archive, *The Autobiography of Doña Catalina de Erauso*, an electronic edition. http://mith.umd.edu/eada/html/display.php?docs=erauso_autobiography. xml&action=show%2522. Original Source: Ferrer, Joaquín María de. *Historia de la Monja Alférez (Doña catalina de Erauso)*. Madrid: Tipo Renovación, 1918. Translation and annotations by Dan Harvey Pedrick. Copyright 2007. This text is freely available provided the text is distributed with the header information provided.

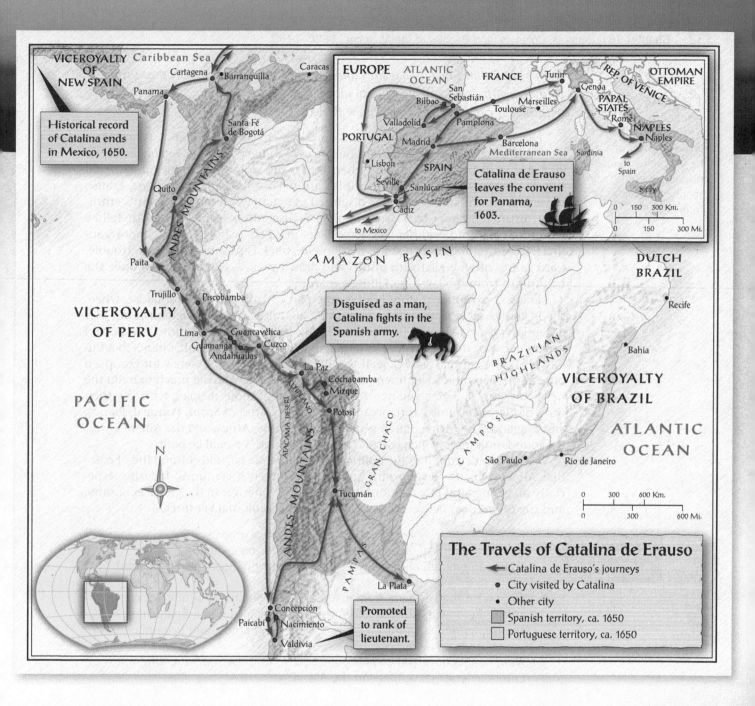

VICEROYALTY OF NEW SPAIN

Caribbean Sea

Cartagena • Barranquilla • Caracas

Panama

Historical record of Catalina ends in Mexico, 1650.

Santa Fé de Bogotá

Quito

ANDES MOUNTAINS

Paita

Trujillo

Piscobamba

VICEROYALTY OF PERU

Lima • Guancavélica • Cuzco
Guamanga • Andahuailas

AMAZON BASIN

EUROPE   ATLANTIC   FRANCE   Turin   REP. OF VENICE   OTTOMAN EMPIRE
          OCEAN
San Sebastián   Genoa   PAPAL STATES
Bilbao   Marseilles   Rome   NAPLES
Valladolid   Pamplona   Toulouse   Naples
PORTUGAL   Madrid   Barcelona   Sardinia   to Spain
          SPAIN   Mediterranean Sea
Lisbon
Seville   Sanlúcar   Sicily
Cádiz

Catalina de Erauso leaves the convent for Panama, 1603.

0   150   300 Km.
0   150   300 Mi.

to Mexico

DUTCH BRAZIL

Recife

Disguised as a man, Catalina fights in the Spanish army.

La Paz
Cochabamba
Mizque
Potosí

BRAZILIAN HIGHLANDS

Bahia

VICEROYALTY OF BRAZIL

PACIFIC OCEAN

ATACAMA DESERT   ALTIPLANO   ANDES MOUNTAINS   GRAN CHACO

CAMPOS

ATLANTIC OCEAN

São Paulo • Rio de Janeiro

N

Tucumán

0   300   600 Km.
0   300   600 Mi.

The Travels of Catalina de Erauso

⟵ Catalina de Erauso's journeys
• City visited by Catalina
• Other city
  Spanish territory, ca. 1650
  Portuguese territory, ca. 1650

PAMPAS

La Plata

Concepción
Paicabí • Nacimiento
Valdivia

Promoted to rank of lieutenant.

Surprisingly, it was a woman who painted this matter-of-fact picture of slaughter. Catalina de Erauso (kat-ah-LEE-nah day eh-rah-OO-so) was born in northeastern Spain and was placed in a convent by her family at age four. At age fifteen, when she was about to take the permanent vows that would confine her for a lifetime, she stole the keys and escaped:

I went out into the street (which I had never seen before) not knowing which way to turn or where to go.... I made myself a pair of trousers from a skirt of

Catalina de Erauso

(1585–1650) Female Basque/Spanish explorer who, dressed as a man, lived the life of a soldier and adventurer in the Spanish colonial Americas.

*blue cloth that I had, and a shirt and leggings from the green shift that I wore underneath. Not knowing what to make of the rest of my [nun's] habit, I left it there. I cut off my hair and threw it away.**

Disguised as a boy, Erauso found employment as a personal assistant for a local nobleman, but she left when he *"insisted to the point of laying his hands on me."* Afraid of being found out by her father, she stole some money, boarded a ship for Panama, and joined the Spanish army. For the next twenty years, Erauso traveled in the Spanish Americas, disguised as a man. A member of Spain's ethnically distinct Basque (bask) community, Erauso often teamed up with fellow Basques as she soldiered her way across Panama, Peru, Chile, Bolivia, and Argentina. According to her own story, her violent streak kept getting her into trouble. Card games often ended with insults and drawn swords, and more than once she had to run from the law after killing a man.

Erauso's exceptional story has become part of Latin American folklore, where she is known as *la monja alférez* (la mon-ha al-FAIR-ez), "the lieutenant nun." Her deception was made easier by frontier conditions, as new arrivals from Europe and Africa increased decade by decade, interacting with indigenous inhabitants in a fluidly changing cultural landscape. It was literally a "new world"—new for European officials, settlers, and adventurers; new for African slaves who did much to build the new American societies; and new for America's indigenous peoples, who saw their ways of life undermined as they came under the control of Spain, Portugal, France, and England. The interaction of peoples from Europe, Africa, and the Americas was the foundation upon which colonial American societies would be built.

This chapter examines the political, economic, social, and cultural life of colonial America in the seventeenth and early eighteenth centuries, focusing especially on gender and race relations, the role of the Americas in the global economy, and the differences between the various European colonial ventures.

FOCUS QUESTIONS

❯ How were political, economic, and social lives organized in Spain's American empire, and how were they linked with global developments?

❯ What were the key demographic and cultural outcomes of interaction among European, African, and Amerindian peoples in the Spanish empire, as well as in the colonies of Portugal, France, and Britain?

❯ What connections and comparisons can we draw between the different European colonial ventures in the Americas?

The Americas in Global Context: The Spanish Empire, 1600–1700

The Spanish laid waste to the Aztec and Inca empires in a remarkably short time (see Chapter 15). To rule their vast new territories, they immediately set up a highly centralized government that relied on close cooperation between crown

*Early Americas Digital Archive, *The Autobiography of Doña Catalina de Erauso,* an electronic edition. Original Source: Ferrer, Joaquín María de. *Historia de la Monja Alférez (Doña catalina de Erauso).* Madrid: Tipo Renovación, 1918. Translation and annotations by Dan Harvey Pedrick. Copyright 2007.

and church. It was a strictly hierarchical power structure, with officials from Spain and locally born Spaniards at the top, the increasing number of people of mixed descent in the middle, and Indians and African slaves at the bottom. As Erauso's story shows, however, the farther one went from centers of authority the more fluid relations of gender and race became, giving at least some people with modest backgrounds new possibilities in life.

From Conquest to Control

When Erauso arrived in Panama in 1603, the Spanish empire was the most powerful European colonial venture in the Americas and a rising maritime force, having established a base of power at Manila in the Philippines. True, a Spanish armada had been repulsed by England in 1588, and the Dutch, still under Spanish rule, were laying the foundations for their own global enterprise. But Philip II of Spain could count on American silver as a foundation for power (see Chapter 17) while the Spanish continued to advance their imperial frontier.

During the sixteenth century, the Spanish Habsburgs asserted increasing authority through a centralized bureaucracy headed by the Council of the Indies. In 1535, they sent the first viceroy to Mexico City, and in 1542 a second was dispatched to Lima. From that time forward, the emperor in Madrid sent officials to America as representatives of royal power. Four **viceroyalties** were eventually created: New Spain (with a capital at Mexico City), Peru (Lima), New Granada (Bogotá), and La Plata (Buenos Aires; see Map 18.1). Below the viceroys were an array of subordinate officials, such as governors and municipal authorities.

viceroyalties

Seats of power of the Spanish officials representing the king in the new world.

• **CONTEXT&CONNECTIONS** Spain's colonial structure was quite centralized compared to other imperial systems in world history. In the Ottoman empire, for example, the sultan's officials were more likely to work through intermediaries representing subject peoples such as Greeks or Armenians (see Chapter 17). In Spanish America, conquered Amerindians had very limited opportunity to secure official representation. •

The other great institution of Spanish rule was the Catholic Church. The pope granted the Spanish crown the right to exercise power over the church in the Americas in all but purely spiritual affairs. Civil authorities appointed and dismissed bishops, while church leaders often served as top government officials. In the early colonial period, bishops sent directly from Spain occupied the higher church positions. In frontier areas, missionaries brought both Catholicism and Spanish rule.

At the same time that their missionary work extended the zone of Spanish control, some priests criticized the appalling conditions that ensued. Many representatives of Catholic religious orders positioned themselves as protectors of indigenous peoples against more rapacious Spanish settlers. The most prominent of these was the Dominican friar **Bartolomé de las Casas**, who argued for humane treatment of Amerindians as he criticized *"the outrageous acts of violence and the bloody tyranny"* of Spaniards who had *"lost all fear of God, all love of their sovereign, and all sense of self-respect."**

Bartolomé de las Casas

(ca. 1484–1566) A Spanish Dominican friar who argued for the humanity of Amerindians and criticized Spanish mistreatment of them.

As more Iberians crossed the ocean, American-born Spaniards grew in number. Known as *criollos* (kree-OY-os) ("creoles" in English), by the seventeenth century they were participating in government. Although officials from Spain continued to hold the top positions, criollos became a social and economic elite,

---

*Bartolomé de las Casas, *A Short Account of the Destruction of the Indies*, trans. Nigel Griffin (London: Penguin, 2004), p. 42.

Map 18.1 The Spanish Empire in the Americas This map of the early-eighteenth-century Americas shows the territorial dominance of the Spanish empire and its four viceroyalties. Though Portuguese Brazil was also large and rich, English and French colonial possessions were small and poor in resources by comparison. We should remember that this map shows European *claims* to territory. Some Amerindian societies remained autonomous and unconquered, especially in more remote regions of mountains, forests, and deserts.

often by seizing Amerindian land and exploiting Amerindian labor. Over time, they would become dissatisfied with the dominance of *peninsulares*, civic and religious officials sent directly from Spain (see Chapter 22).

Although lust for gold had been a principal motive of the early conquistadors, it was silver that filled the Spanish treasury and transformed the world economy. In 1545, the Spanish found a whole mountain of silver high in the Andes at **Potosí** (poh-toh-SEE), the greatest silver discovery in world history. Andean silver enabled European trade with Asia, and much of the silver extracted from Potosí ended up in China, stimulating the development of a more integrated early modern world economy (see Chapter 16).

Silver mining generated huge profits, but not for the workers who dug open the mountain. Conditions were so brutal that force was needed to get workers for the mines. Though the crown had placed restrictions on *encomienda* (in-coh-mee-EN-dah) holders (see Chapter 15), a new legal system called the *repartimiento* (reh-par-TEE-me-en-toh) gave Spaniards the right to coerce Amerindian labor for specific tasks. Although the intent of reforming the encomienda system had been to limit abuses, most Spaniards still casually assumed they retained a right to enslave Amerindians. Erauso, for example, commented that during one of her trading ventures a civic leader *"put me in charge of ten thousand llamas to pack with and about one hundred or so Indian drivers."** Apparently, the Amerindians had no say in the matter.

Although the Spanish called their Andean labor system *mita* (mee-tah)—the same name used by the Inca for their system of labor tribute—the Spanish mita differed greatly from the Inca one. Under the Inca, mita required every household to contribute labor for tasks such as military service, road construction, and the maintenance of irrigation works. Exemptions were granted for families in difficult circumstances, and workers were fed, clothed, and well treated. In contrast, the Spanish paid scant attention to the well-being of local communities or individual laborers. Under the Spanish mita system, every adult male had to spend one full year out of every seven working in the mines at wages that were not sufficient for his own support, let alone for his family.

After 1554, both Spanish profits and Amerindian suffering multiplied with the discovery of the **mercury amalgamation process**, which increased the efficiency of silver extraction from ore but also led to illness and death for many miners. Meanwhile, women, children, and the elderly back in their villages had to work harder to compensate for the absence of adult males. The silver economy predicated the wealth of some on the suffering of many: that was to be a recurring theme in Latin American history.

By 1600, Potosí was a major market, with a population over one hundred thousand when Erauso set off with her llamas and one hundred Indians: *"[The official] gave me a large amount of money to go to the plains of Cochabamba, buy wheat and mill it, and take it to Potosí where it was scarce and valuable."** The llamas were indigenous, but the wheat grew from European seed, an example of the ongoing Columbian exchange (see Chapter 15).

Expanding markets accompanied the growth of administrative centers such as Mexico City, Lima, and Buenos Aires, which stimulated local and regional trade in foodstuffs. In colonial Latin America, market-based agriculture took place on large

Potosí

Location high in the Andes in modern Bolivia where the Spanish found huge quantities of silver. Silver exports from Potosí and other American mines helped finance development of the early modern world economy.

mercury amalgamation process

A process used to increase the efficiency with which silver could be extracted from ore. The use of mercury was highly toxic and led to the death of many Amerindian mine workers.

---

*Early Americas Digital Archive, *The Autobiography of Doña Catalina de Erauso,* an electronic edition. Original Source: Ferrer, Joaquín María de. *Historia de la Monja Alférez (Doña catalina de Erauso).* Madrid: Tipo Renovación, 1918. Translation and annotations by Dan Harvey Pedrick. Copyright 2007.

haciendas

Large estates characteristic of colonial agriculture in Latin America.

estates known as **haciendas** (ha-cee-EN-das). While many Amerindian communities remained largely self-sufficient by farming small village plots, the Spanish hacienda owners focused on meeting the rising demand for agricultural produce. In addition to growing crops for sale, many grazed vast herds of cattle.

Within the boundaries of their own large estates, hacienda owners had almost total control, governing their lands and the people who lived on them without reference to outside authority. They used debt peonage as a means of control, making loans to "their" Indians that were to be repaid in labor. But wages were never enough to repay the debt. Often, descendants of the original borrowers inherited these obligations and became permanently bound to a single estate, unable to seek higher wages or better working conditions elsewhere.

The Silver Mine at Potosí The silver mines of Spanish America, of which Potosí was the greatest, enriched the Spanish treasury and facilitated the expansion of global trade. As this engraving from 1590 shows, however, it was the heavy toil of Amerindian workers on Potosí's mountain of silver that made it all possible. Spanish mine operators used the mercury amalgamation process to increase the yield of silver from ore, resulting in the frequently lethal mercury poisoning of workers such as those seen here. (The Granger Collection, NYC)

● **CONTEXT&CONNECTIONS** The hacienda system would long persist in Latin America, and the inequalities associated with large agricultural estates actually increased after the colonial period, when nineteenth century hacienda owners began to focus on production of commercial crops for international markets. Many previously autonomous villagers in Central America, to give one example, were forced onto plantations to cultivate bananas and other commodities for rock-bottom wages (see Chapter 25). ●

African labor supplemented that of Amerindians in some parts of Spain's American empire, most notably in Peru and Mexico. In the early conquest period, African slaves played a variety of roles, including fighting alongside the Spanish conquerors of the Andes and engaging in skilled crafts they brought with them from Africa, such as goldsmithing. As the mixed Spanish/Amerindian population grew, however, Afro-Peruvians began to lose their status as intermediaries between the Spanish and Amerindians, and by the eighteenth century they had become a despised subclass of manual laborers. Still, Afro-Peruvians made important cultural contributions to colonial society. (In coastal Peru, as in the Mexican coastal state of Guerrero where Africans also lived in large numbers, African musical instruments and rhythms are still found today.)

Spain's main goal was to extract minerals and other raw materials from America. Although it imported from the Americas such goods as dyes, cotton, and livestock hides for the manufacture of leather, no product came close in value to the tons of silver bullion sent in the annual armadas both directly to Spain and via the Manila galleons from Mexico to the Spanish Philippines (see Chapter 16).

Taking much from its American empire but investing little, Spain failed to lay the foundations for long-term economic growth. While other European nations were developing innovative commercial organizations (see Chapter 16), the Spanish crown and nobility were overly reliant on mineral wealth. As a consequence, the Dutch, English, and French effectively challenged stagnant Spain for American preeminence during the seventeenth and eighteenth centuries.

● **CONTEXT&CONNECTIONS** The Spanish crown and Spanish nobility remained largely aloof from commercial life, unlike in the Netherlands, where merchant capitalists dominated (see Chapter 16), or in England, where traders and trading companies were to be patronized by the crown and by the landed gentry (see Chapter 21). ●

Colonial Society: Gender and Race on the Margins of Empire

The basic patterns of life in Spanish-speaking America were set by 1750, and the subjugation of indigenous societies was well advanced. Large-scale haciendas and mining operations were the foundation of commercial economies based on exploitation of the labor of Amerindians and African slaves. Officials from Spain dominated the upper ranks of both church and state, while criollos became local officials, hacienda landowners, and merchants. On the further frontiers, away from vice-regal centers like Mexico City and Lima, the Spanish presence was weaker, often with only a few hacienda owners or missionaries extending colonial networks to otherwise autonomous indigenous communities. (See the feature "World History in Today's World: Indigenous Studies and Indigenous Languages.")

Between the small Spanish elite at the top of the social hierarchy and the Amerindians who continued to practice ancient cultural traditions at the bottom, a complex mix of peoples and cultures emerged. Ingredients of this mix included European immigration, the forced migration of African slaves, and indigenous

Indigenous Studies and Indigenous Languages

In recent years, the world's indigenous peoples have become a focal point of scholarly research. Scholars of Indigenous Studies have focused on issues of persistent poverty: only 5 percent of the world's people are classified as "indigenous," but they make up nearly 15 percent of the global poor. Culture is another major concern. Just as scientists worry that rapid species extinction decreases the planet's biodiversity, so linguists argue that whenever an indigenous language disappears, cultural diversity suffers. When a language is lost, so is all the knowledge embedded within it.

In South America, although many indigenous American languages have faded away in the centuries since conquest, over 600 survive today. The Quechua (KETCH-wah) language is the most prolific, still spoken by over 10 million people in the Andes Mountains (see Chapter 15). The Spanish banned Quechua for official purposes in colonial times and restricted education and religious worship to Spanish and Latin. Nevertheless, Quechua survived and is now recognized as an official national language in Bolivia, Ecuador, and Peru. That cultural persistence has not brought economic benefit, however: Quechua speakers are among the poorest people in the Americas.

In North America as well, some indigenous tongues are spoken by substantial numbers: there are over 1 million speakers of Nahuatl, the language of the Aztecs, in Mexico, nearly 200,000 Navajo speakers in the United States, and about 140,000 people able to communicate in one of the Algonquian languages in Canada. But in some areas, like California and the Pacific Northwest, the situation is dire. California once had ninety indigenous languages. Only fifty survive, and half of those are spoken only by a small number of elders. In a race against time, linguists, cultural anthropologists, and tribal educators are developing programs to help indigenous speakers pass their knowledge on to a new generation.

The issue is also global: *National Geographic* researchers have identified five regions where indigenous languages are in the greatest danger of extinction: eastern Siberia, northern Australia, central South America (including Amazonia), Oklahoma, and the Pacific coastal regions of Canada and the United States. Without accelerated intervention, they predict that "by 2100, more than half of the more than 7,000 languages spoken on Earth—many of them not yet recorded—may disappear, taking with them a wealth of knowledge about history, culture, the natural environment, and the human brain."

Source: National Geographic, "Disappearing Languages," http://travel. nationalgeographic.com/travel/enduring-voices/.

populations that, though weakened by disease and deprivation, began a demographic recovery by the later seventeenth century.

The Spanish elite brought an outlook concerned with enforcing strict hierarchies of caste, gender, and religious and ethnic identity. Men were guided by a code of family honor, responsible for the virginity of their daughters and the fidelity of their wives. At the same time, they did not hold themselves to the same standards, often boasting of their multiple sexual conquests.

● **CONTEXT&CONNECTIONS** The fixation of the Spanish elite with *limpieza de sangre*—"purity of blood"—went back to the period of the Reconquista, when the Spanish reconquered Iberia from Muslim rulers (see Chapter 15). At that time, reserving public office for men of pure Spanish descent was instituted to keep converted Jews and Muslims out of positions of power. This policy was transferred to the Americas: those of non-Spanish and non-Catholic origin were expected to defer to their social superiors. ●

Maintaining elitist hierarchies in the courts, schools, and urban spaces of Mexico City, Lima, and other bastions of Spanish authority was easy enough. Outside the cities, however, conditions were more fluid. Spanish men rarely brought their wives and families to the Americas, and liaisons between Spanish men and indigenous women made "purity of blood" impossible to maintain. In Mexico by the seventeenth century, for example, a distinct *mestizo* (mes-TEE-zoh), or mixed Spanish/Amerindian, category had emerged.

Under frontier conditions, the Catholic Church also had difficulty imposing religious orthodoxy. In Spain itself, the inquisition (the Catholic bureaucracy devoted to suppressing heresy) strictly monitored the beliefs and behavior of the population. Families of *conversos* and *moriscos* (mohr-EES-koz), who had been forcibly converted from Judaism and Islam, were subjected to special scrutiny. On the colonial frontier, however, such groups were sometimes able to retain elements of their old faith, such as by incorporating Jewish rituals into their family traditions.

Converted Amerindians were the largest group of Catholics deviating from church doctrine, especially in Mexico and Peru, where missionaries had baptized many descendants of the Aztec and Inca. Many Amerindians embraced the church as a way to adapt to their new world, perhaps feeling that their old gods had abandoned them. At the same time, these converts adapted Christianity to maintain their own spiritual, ritual, and aesthetic traditions. Unlike in China, where Matteo Ricci had adapted Christianity to the traditions of his intended converts (see Chapter 16), in Spanish America it was not the missionaries but the colonized peoples themselves who blended their cosmologies and ritual traditions into Catholicism.

While some church leaders campaigned against the continuation of "idol worship" among baptized Amerindians, more often Spanish missionaries tolerated such practices. Amerindian populations gradually stabilized after the great losses of the sixteenth century, and where they formed a majority, as in the Andes, missionaries had little choice but to work through indigenous cultures. The result was a blend of existing and imported ideas known to historians as religious **syncretism**.

Unlike the Aztec (and Maya) pantheon of gods, the Christian God was resolutely male. Still, veneration of Mary as the Virgin Mother allowed Catholic Aztecs to retain the female presence in their religious worship previously represented by the fertility goddess Tonantzin. The centrality of the female principle in Mexican worship crystallized in the cult of the **Virgin of Guadalupe**.

In 1531, a peasant named Juan Diego reported to a Spanish bishop that the Virgin Mary had appeared to him. The bishop was initially doubtful but was unwilling to suppress the great popularity of the new cult. Though apparitions of the Virgin Mary were relatively common in Spain, the Virgin of Guadalupe had a special appeal in Mesoamerica, helping to fill the gap left as worship of goddesses like Tonantzin declined. In fact, the seventeenth-century Basilica of Our Lady of Guadalupe was built at the foot of a hill where Tonantzin herself had earlier been worshipped. Represented as dark in complexion, like most of her devotees, the Virgin of Guadalupe remains a symbol of Mexican identity and an embodiment of religious syncretism.

● **CONTEXT&CONNECTIONS** World historians have written about religious syncretism in a wide variety of global contexts, such as the Africanization of Islam and the cultural adaptation of Buddhism in China. The history of Christianity has repeatedly demonstrated how converts to the faith have blended new beliefs with older ones. Indeed, a thousand years before the appearance of the Virgin of Guadalupe, northern European converts to Christianity had adapted many of their pagan rituals to the new faith, as when German converts continued the old custom of bringing evergreen boughs into their homes to mark the winter solstice: today's "Christmas trees" are a legacy of that Germanic Christian syncretism. ●

mestizo
Offspring of an Amerindian and Spanish union. Cultural and biologic blending became characteristic of Mexican society.

syncretism
The fusion of cultural elements from more than one tradition. In colonial Latin America religious syncretism was common, with both Amerindians and Africans blending their existing beliefs and rituals with Catholicism.

Virgin of Guadalupe
An apparition of the Virgin Mary, with a dark complexion, said to have appeared to a Mexican farmer in 1531. The cult of the Virgin of Guadalupe exerted a powerful attraction to Mesoamerica's surviving Amerindians. She remains a symbol of Mexican identity.

In Catalina de Erauso's story, the Catholic Church plays a more practical role. Once, after she had stabbed a man in a fight, she sought refuge in a church, where the civil authorities could not pursue her without the bishop's permission. In tough spots such as these she also relied on fellow members of the Basque-speaking minority for protection. Facing discrimination in Iberia, many Basques joined the Spanish army in the Americas. Erauso was exceptionally proud of her Basque heritage, but when dealing with Italians or Portuguese she was always quick to identify herself with Spain and assert Spanish superiority. Her multiple identities are another example of the fluidity of frontier life.

Erauso's autobiography also gives us fascinating insights into race and gender in frontier Spanish America (though we should bear in mind that she may have been more concerned with dramatic storytelling than the absolute truth). Once in Peru, she tells us, she deserted the army and wandered alone into the mountains, where she nearly died but was rescued by two men who took her to their mistress's ranch:

The lady was a half-breed, the daughter of a Spaniard and an Indian. She was [a] widow and a good woman who, upon seeing me and hearing of my plight and helplessness, pitied me and kindly took me in. She put me in a reasonable bed, fed me well, and allowed me to rest and sleep, with which I restored myself.... Seeing that I was totally lacking, she gave me a decent woolen suit, and went on treating me very well and generously. She was comfortably well-off and had many pack animals and cattle. Few Spaniards passed through there and it seems she wanted me as a spouse for her daughter.*

Erauso never intended to marry the girl: "*The daughter was very dark, and ugly as the devil, very contrary to my taste, which was always the pretty faces.*"* Still, she pretended to go along with the plan while accepting the widow's gifts. Meanwhile, she simultaneously became engaged to the niece of a Spanish official and, once again, accepted gifts from her potential in-law. "*Then came the part where I mounted the horse and disappeared,*"* she writes, never learning whatever became of the two young women she had courted.

What might explain Erauso's success at wooing young women in the guise of a man? Even allowing for embellishments, this incident suggests that Iberian men (as Erauso presented herself to be) were highly desirable marriage partners for families wishing to sustain or improve their social status. Marriage to a Spaniard could "improve" the family blood line, but outside the main cities, Spanish men were in such short supply that Erauso could easily, by her own account, contract multiple engagements. Of course, Spanish women were even less available as marriage partners. Most Spanish men could not afford to "import" wives from Iberia, so they made the best unions they could, usually fathering mixed-race children.

Erauso's narrative shows the complexities of the **casta system** of racial hierarchy, with dozens of terms for various racial mixtures and skin tones. She describes

casta system

The system of racial categorization in the Spanish Americas. Dozens of different "casta" terms were developed for various mixtures of European, African, and Amerindian descent. Though a flexible system that allowed movement "up" or "down" the racial hierarchy, markers of Spanish descent always carried the highest status.

---

*Early Americas Digital Archive, *The Autobiography of Doña Catalina de Erauso*, an electronic edition. Original Source: Ferrer, Joaquín María de. *Historia de la Monja Alférez (Doña catalina de Erauso)*. Madrid: Tipo Renovación, 1918. Translation and annotations by Dan Harvey Pedrick. Copyright 2007.

Mexican Casta Painting A popular artistic tradition in colonial New Spain was the depiction of family groups of mixed heritage. This work by Miguel Cabrera is labeled, "From a Mestizo and an Indian, Coyote." Dozens of combinations are shown in other paintings, for example: *castizo*—one Spanish parent and one *mestizo* parent; *morisco*—one Spanish parent and one *mulatto* parent; *zambo*—one mulatto parent and one Indian parent; and *lobo*—one African parent and one Indian parent. Wealth and social status are clearly linked to racial background in casta paintings, but often, as here, poorer families are depicted quite sympathetically.

De Meſtizo y d India; Coyote

Elisabeth Waldo-Dentzel

the widow as a "half-breed" who is "good" and "well-off," trying to interest a Spaniard in marrying her "black" and "ugly" daughter. Here we see two fundamental racial realities. On the one hand, racial mixing was accepted as a part of life. On the other hand, whiteness always conferred status. So even in the many places where mestizos or mulattos (of mixed Spanish/African descent) formed the majority, social conventions and racial prejudices reinforced the superiority of Spanish descent, even among those of mixed race. Perhaps the widow thought marriage to a white soldier like Erauso could improve the color and status of her "ugly" daughter's children.

Gender relations and the social roles of women varied by social class. As in many societies, including the North African ones that had strongly influenced medieval Iberia, Spanish men demonstrated their wealth and status by keeping women away from the public realm. Elite parents, preoccupied with protecting the family honor, arranged unions for adolescent daughters who would, upon marriage, lead restricted lives. Those for whom no acceptable marriage could be found were sent to convents. Poorer families in which women played vital economic roles as farmers and artisans could not imitate such behavior; darker skin and ruddy complexions resulting from outdoor work marked their lowly status.

At the same time, elite women sometimes had access to education, and those in convents might rise to positions of authority within their all-female communities. **Sor Juana Inés de la Cruz** (1648–1695) was the most famous of such women. Born into a modest family, she was a child prodigy who learned to read Latin before the age of ten. She became a lady-in-waiting for the viceroy's wife in

Sor Juana Inés de la Cruz

One of the great literary figures of colonial New Spain. Wrote poetry, prose, and philosophy despite having been denied a university education. Best known for her defense of the intellectual equality of men and women.

Mexico City and a popular figure at court. But after her application to the University of Mexico was denied, she entered the convent. In contrast to Catalina de Erauso, who saw the convent as a prison, for Sor Juana life in an all-female community allowed her to develop her remarkable literary and intellectual skills.

Sor Juana's writings cover many topics, and her poetry is still taught to Mexican schoolchildren. She is best known for her passionate defense of the spiritual and intellectual equality of women with men: *"There is no obstacle to love / in gender or in absence, / for souls, as you are well aware, / transcend both sex and distance."** After years of correspondence and debate with church leaders who denounced her work, however, she saw the futility of trying to change their minds and stopped publishing altogether. In 1694, church officials forced her to sell her library of four thousand books, and the next year she died of plague.

Sor Juana's story illustrates the degree to which New Spain duplicated the Spanish social order. But Erauso's narrative reminds us that the "new world" could also mean new possibilities. In frontier conditions, the watchfulness of church and state was not as strong as it was in Europe or in Mexico City, giving Erauso a chance to carve out a life appropriate for her personality and ambition.

Brazil, the Dutch, New France, and England's Mainland Colonies

Throughout the sixteenth century and into the seventeenth, Spain remained the dominant imperial force in the Americas. Portugal, though more focused on Asia, did control Brazil, with its vast economic potential. Then, by the mid-seventeenth century, Spain was losing its global lead to up-and-coming Protestant powers, especially England and the Netherlands, and to the competing Catholic monarchy of France (see Chapter 17). Latecomers France and England started their settlements in North America well after the Spanish had created their great empire to the south. In French and British North America as well, the interactions of Europeans, Africans, and indigenous peoples created diverse cultural patterns, and again, the farther one moved toward the frontier, the more fluid those interactions were.

The Portuguese and Brazil

In the sixteenth century, Portugal's overseas efforts focused on the Indian Ocean (see Chapter 16). Brazil, discovered by accident and acquired by treaty, was an afterthought, with no large cities to conquer and no empires to plunder. Portuguese settlement was initially limited to the coast, and apart from a lucrative trade in precious types of wood, Brazil initially offered little promise.

This situation changed dramatically in the later sixteenth century with the expansion of sugar plantations in northeastern Brazil. By the end of the seventeenth century, 150,000 African slaves made up about half of the colony's population. Meanwhile, Portuguese adventurers pushed into the interior seeking slaves, gold, and exotic goods such as brightly colored feathers from the Amazon. In 1695, gold was discovered in the southern interior. European prospectors brought African slaves to exploit the gold deposits, displacing the local Amerindians in the process.

Missionaries were powerful players in Brazil. Jesuits operated large cattle ranches and sugar mills to raise funds for church construction and missions to the interior.

---

*Quoted in Octavio Paz, *Sor Juana*, trans. Margaret Sayers Peden (Cambridge: Harvard University Press, 1988), p. 219.

As in the Spanish and French empires, Catholic missionaries often did their best to protect Indians from more brutal forms of colonial exploitation, but in the process they unwittingly introduced epidemic diseases that devastated the very people they had come to "save." Religious orders thus inevitably extended colonial control to the frontier, undercutting indigenous life. Thus, by the early eighteenth century, profits from sugar and gold had turned Brazil into Portugal's most important overseas colony.

As soon as the sugar plantation economy took hold in northeastern Brazil, slaves began to run away into the interior. Some of the runaways assimilated into Amerindian groups (see Chapter 19). Others formed their own runaway communities known as *quilombos* (key-LOM-boz). Since the members of quilombos were born and raised in different African societies, their political and religious practices combined various African traditions and gods.

The quilombo community of **Palmares** (pal-MAHR-es) was founded in the early seventeenth century, where slave runaways adapted the Central African institution of *kilombo*, a merit-based league of warriors that cut across family ties, ruled by their elected *Ganga Zumba* (Great Lord). Their syncretic religious life combined traditions of the Kongo kingdom (see Chapter 16) with other African traditions and Catholicism. With tens of thousands of residents, Palmares defended itself against decades of Portuguese military assaults until it was finally defeated in 1694. However, the adaptation of African religion and culture to the American environment continued long afterward.

By 1750, Brazil had an exceptionally diverse culture. The Brazilian elite remained white, dominating laborers who were primarily African. As in Spanish

> **Palmares**
>
> The largest and most powerful maroon community (1630–1694) established by escaped slaves in the colonial Americas. Using military and diplomatic means, their leaders retained autonomy from Portuguese Brazil for over half a century.

Africans in Colonial Brazil This watercolor from 1775 depicts a "royal parade" in which African cultural influence is unmistakable. While the "king" seems to wear a European-style crown, the umbrella is a characteristically West African symbol of kingship. The Brazilian penchant for parading in elaborate costumes began in colonial times and still culminates each year in Carnival celebrations infused with African cultural legacies

DEA/G. DAGLI ORTI/Getty Images

America, a large mixed-race group emerged, along with a similarly complex hierarchy. Catholicism served to unite Brazilian society while manifesting its diversity. While membership in religious brotherhoods devoted to specific saints or to the Virgin Mary was common across all social groups, for example, each brotherhood was organized by men from similar social backgrounds as determined by a combination of wealth, color, and place of origin. Across that spectrum, regardless of background, Brazilian Catholicism showed the infusion of African beliefs and rituals, although syncretism was, of course, strongest among the most recent African arrivals.

Though many were condemned to work in the brutal conditions of the sugar cane fields, Africans in colonial Brazil actually played many different roles, some even serving as soldiers. Indeed, the quality of African artisans' work frustrated some Portuguese immigrants who found it difficult to compete, and free blacks, facing no legal restrictions, were sometimes quite successful. A former slave named Cardoso, for example, bought his own freedom, made a fortune in trade, and left his money to his Catholic brotherhood.

As in the Spanish Americas, Brazil's social and racial hierarchy was flexible enough that individuals or families might try to improve their standing. Dress, speech, education, marriage, and above all, economic success were means by which Brazilians of mixed descent might gain higher status. Still, the basic polarities remained: white at the top of society, black at the bottom.

The Dutch in the Americas Like the Portuguese, the Dutch were initially focused on Indian Ocean trade. However, from 1630 to 1654, they seized control of the northeastern coast of Brazil as part of their larger global offensive against the Catholic empires of Spain and Portugal. After an extremely violent conflict, in 1619 the Protestant Dutch had won their independence from Catholic Spain, which at that time also ruled over Portugal and therefore Brazil. Following the model of the successful Dutch East India Company, a group of merchants formed the Dutch West India Company in 1621 to penetrate markets and challenge the Spanish in the Americas. They sought advantage through aggressive capitalism, constantly reinvesting their profits in faster ships and larger ventures. In Brazil, the most important of these were the sugar plantations, to which the Dutch brought more capital investment and a larger supply of slaves.

Ousted from Brazil by the Portuguese in 1654, some Dutch planters transferred their business techniques and more advanced sugar-processing technology to the Caribbean. The resulting explosion of sugar production transformed Spanish-ruled islands like Cuba and Puerto Rico, as well as English ones like Jamaica and Barbados and French ones like Martinique and Saint-Domingue, and had dramatic consequences for Africa and the world economy (see Chapter 19).

Farther north, the Dutch West India Company founded the colony of New Netherland in 1624 and traded up the Hudson River Valley, allying with the powerful Iroquois Confederacy to tap into the lucrative fur trade. A small number of Dutch immigrants came as settlers to farm these rich and well-watered lands. But overall, Dutch commercial goals were still focused on Southeast Asia. In 1664, the Dutch surrendered New Netherland to the English without a fight. Their largest outpost, New Amsterdam, was renamed New York, and henceforth only the French and English would compete for dominance in North America.

New France, 1608–1754

Since the days of Columbus, European navigators had sought a western route to Asia. In the second half of the sixteenth century, French mariners sailed up the St. Lawrence River looking for a "northwest passage" to Chinese markets. What they found instead was the world's largest concentration of freshwater lakes and a land teeming with wildlife. In 1608, Samuel de Champlain founded the colony of New France with its capital at **Québec** (keh-BEC). In the later seventeenth century, French expeditions on the Mississippi and Ohio Rivers added vast territories, although here there were fewer Europeans and less immediate economic impact. The abundance of valuable furs in today's Canada was what most attracted French attention. Their indigenous trading partners did the actual work of trapping beavers and bringing the pelts to French trading posts. The yields of Amerindian trappers increased with the use of iron tools from Europe, driving the quest for fur ever deeper into the interior.

Québec

(est. 1608) Founded by Samuel de Champlain as the capital of New France (in modern Canada); became a hub for the French fur trade and the center from which French settlement in the Americas first began to expand.

● **CONTEXT&CONNECTIONS** Just like the Russians, who were expanding fur gathering into Siberia, French fur traders went far beyond the frontiers of formal colonial control, driven by lucrative European, Ottoman, and *Safavid* markets (Chapter 17). North American and Siberian peoples benefited little from the fur trade, however, and were also vulnerable to newly imported diseases. From a merchant's standpoint, Northern furs were akin to Southeast Asian spices (see Chapter 16): with great value relative to weight, both were cheap to transport and fetched exceptionally high prices. ●

Living far from other Europeans, French fur traders adapted to the customs of the First Nations peoples (as they are called in Canada). For example, tobacco smoking was an important ritual that cemented trade and diplomatic alliances. Sometimes traders assimilated deeply into First Nations communities, and their children were Amerindian in language and culture. More often French trappers and traders visited only seasonally; their mixed-race children, known in French as *métis* (may-TEE), learned both French and indigenous languages such as Cree and served as cultural and commercial intermediaries between First Nations and European societies.

métis

In colonial New France, the offspring of a European and Amerindian union.

Museum of Fine Arts, Boston/Laurie Platt Winfrey/The Art Archive

French Fur Trader French traders ventured far beyond the borders of European colonial society in their quest for valuable furs such as beaver pelts. They frequently adopted the technologies, languages, and customs of Amerindian peoples, and sometimes married into Amerindian societies. At the same time, on the other side of the world, the global fur market was also driving Russian traders deep into the forests of Siberia.

The fur trade had complex environmental and political effects. Once their traditional hunting grounds were exhausted, Amerindians had to venture farther to lay their traps. Bands came into conflict as they competed for beaver pelts, while guns for which they traded furs made skirmishes more lethal. New technologies and the desire for new commodities (iron tools and alcohol, as well as firearms) affected indigenous life well beyond the areas of European colonial control. On the Great Plains, for example, the introduction of firearms from New France and horses from New Spain enabled a new and more efficient style of buffalo hunting and mobile warfare among groups like the Lakota Sioux (see Chapter 25).

In the St. Lawrence region, the French were allied with the **Huron** people, who were receptive to the Jesuit missionaries who came up the river. French traders established residence in Huron country and negotiated with local chiefs to supply them with furs. Division of labor by gender facilitated the process. Since Huron men worked in agriculture only when clearing fields in early spring, they were available for hunting and trading parties during the rest of the year, while the women stayed behind to tend the fields. The political power and economic resources that came from the fur trade therefore went mainly to men, a development that undercut the traditional power of Huron women: male chiefs became more powerful at the expense of the matriarchs chosen by their clans to represent them on the Huron confederacy council.

While some Huron chiefs and hunters benefited from fur trading, the overall effects of contact with the French were disastrous. By 1641, half of the Huron population had been killed by disease. Many Huron sought baptism, praying that the priests' holy water would save them from the smallpox that the missionaries themselves had unknowingly introduced.

Meanwhile, French settlers were attracted to the farmlands surrounding the city of Québec, where some fifty thousand French men and women lived by 1750. These farmers, and the small urban population they supported, represented the beginnings of quite a different European presence in what would later become Canada. While the fur traders and missionaries sought to integrate into indigenous societies in their search for pelts to buy or souls to save, French settlers were driven by the search for cheap land and higher wages. In later years, as their numbers swelled and the frontier advanced, such settlers would increasingly displace First Nations peoples (see Chapter 25).

In the first half of the eighteenth century, however, the most valuable French possessions in the Americas were not vast North American territories but relatively small Caribbean islands. Using African slave labor, French plantations in the West Indies made huge profits producing sugar for European markets. The same was true for England.

Mainland English Colonies in North America

For the English, as for the French, the Caribbean islands and sugar were the economic focal points of their American venture (see Chapter 19). Also like the French, the English were relative newcomers to mainland America in the first half of the seventeenth century, settling initially in Virginia and Massachusetts. Jamestown, founded in 1607 and the first permanent English settlement in **Virginia**, was nearly wiped out in its early years, but by the 1630s the colony was thriving after the colonists discovered a lucrative Atlantic market for tobacco. Long used by Amerindian peoples for social and ritual purposes, tobacco became the foundation of Virginia's prosperity and generated a strong demand for labor.

Huron
A matriarchal, Iroquoian-speaking Amerindian group in the St. Lawrence region that was devastated by the smallpox brought by French fur traders and missionaries in the mid-seventeenth century.

Virginia
(est. 1607) English colony in North America with an export economy based on tobacco production. The use of European indentured servants gave way to dependence on slave labor.

In colonial North America, Amerindians formed a miniscule part of the labor force. Unlike the Spanish, who used Amerindians as miners and as farm labor, the English often drove Amerindians off the land with the goal of replacing them with "civilized" English farmers. Not only were the indigenous peoples weakened by disease, there were also cultural barriers. In eastern North America's woodland societies, women were the principle farmers, while men focused more on hunting. English colonists therefore had little success in recruiting the local men as dependent workers.

● **CONTEXT&CONNECTIONS** Patterns of European global settlement were determined largely by disease environments. In New England, in the southwestern corner of Africa at Cape Town (see Chapter 16), and in Australia (see Chapter 21), Afro-Eurasian diseases like smallpox proved fatal to indigenous peoples, clearing the way for colonies of European settlement. Across most of Africa and Asia, however, it was Europeans who were more vulnerable to local disease. There, Europeans would never constitute more than a tiny percentage of the total population, even following their nineteenth-century conquests (see Chapters 24 and 26). ●

North America's English farmers were in direct competition with indigenous peoples for the land, water, and hunting opportunities they needed to survive. Sir Walter Raleigh, a major investor in Virginia settlement, had set a precedent when, after putting down a late-sixteenth-century Irish rebellion, he created settlements where the "*savage Irish*" were to be replaced by more dependable English farmers. In Virginia, the "savages" were Amerindian rather than Irish, but Raleigh's strategy remained the same. Throughout the English colonies, European settlers generally drove indigenous peoples toward the margins of colonial settlement. (See the feature "Movement of Ideas Through Primary Sources: Prospero and Caliban.")

However, plantations in England's southern colonies required more work than free settlers could provide. One solution was indentured labor. In this system, employers paid for the transportation costs of poor English and Irish peasants in return for four to seven years of work, after which they received either a return passage or a small plot of land. Cheap as this labor was, tobacco planters needed a labor force even cheaper and more servile. In 1619, when the first shipment of captive Africans arrived at Jamestown, they were treated as indentured servants. By the 1650s, however, a racial distinction between white servants and African slaves had become the rule. By the late seventeenth century, planters were buying larger numbers of African slaves in Virginia markets.

Colonial authorities worried about contact between Europeans and Africans; as early as 1630, one Hugh Davis was whipped "*for abusing himself to the dishonor of God and the shame of Christians, by defiling his body in lying with a Negro.*"* By the later seventeenth century, Virginia law prohibited all interracial unions. Though such liaisons continued, of course, the principle that would later be known as the "one drop" rule was being established: any sign of African descent became a badge of inferiority, with both mixed-race Virginians and the small number of free blacks suffering persistent discrimination. Such racial absolutism in the English colonies stood in contrast to the more flexible hierarchies of color and status common in Brazil and the Spanish Americas.

---

*Quoted in George Fredrickson, *White Supremacy: A Comparative Study in American and South African History* (New York: Oxford University Press, 1981), p. 100.

Prospero and Caliban

When Catalina de Erauso arrived in New Spain, William Shakespeare was the leading playwright in the English-speaking world. Shakespeare's imagination, like that of many Europeans in the early seventeenth century, was stimulated by tales of exotic adventure in what one of Shakespeare's characters referred to as "this brave new world." That line comes from *The Tempest* (1611), a drama that reflects European fascination with new discoveries in the Americas. Shakespeare used reports from Virginia settlers who had survived a shipwreck to weave a fantastic tale of magic, revenge, and the triumph of justice.

A great magician named Prospero and his daughter, Miranda, are stranded on an island. In the scene below, Prospero speaks with a misshapen monster named Caliban, the only native inhabitant of the island. From Prospero's perspective, Caliban deserves harsh treatment. In spite of the kindness shown by the magician, the monster attempted to rape Miranda. Things look very different from Caliban's viewpoint. The powers he inherited from his mother, Sycorax, cannot counter Prospero's magic, and he has no choice but to serve as the magician's slave while plotting his vengeance. Their unequal positions are even reflected in their names, which might be translated as "Prosperity" and "Cannibal." Though Shakespeare presents Prospero as having justice on his side, we should look for places where he also allows Caliban to voice his complaints as an abused native imprisoned by a colonial master.

> Does the author encourage us to empathize with Caliban?

> Is Caliban's situation in any way analogous to that of conquered Amerindian peoples?

Source: Excerpt from William Shakespeare, *Tempest.* http://the-tech.mit.edu/Shakespeare/tempest/index.html. The glossary is original.

The Tempest, Act I, Scene 2

Prospero: Thou poisonous slave, got* by the devil himself
Upon thy wicked dam,* come forth!

Caliban: As wicked dew as e'er my mother brush'd
With raven's feather from unwholesome fen
Drop on you! a south-west blow on ye
And blister you all o'er!

Prospero: For this, be sure, tonight thou shalt have cramps,
Side-stitches that shall pen thy breath up; urchins*
Shall, for that vast of night that they may work,
All exercise on thee;* thou shalt be pinch'd
As thick as honeycomb, each pinch more stinging
Than bees that made 'em.

Caliban: This island's mine, by Sycorax my mother,
Which thou takest from me. When thou camest first,
Thou strokedst me and madest much of me, wouldst give me
Water with berries in't, and teach me how
To name the bigger light, and how the less,
That burn by day and night:* and then I loved thee
And show'd thee all the qualities o' the isle,
The fresh springs, brine-pits, barren place and fertile:
Cursed be I that did so! All the charms
Of Sycorax, toads, beetles, bats, light on you!
For I am all the subjects that you have,

*got Begotten.
*dam Mother.
*urchins Goblins.
*exercise on thee Torment you.

*day and night The sun and moon.

548

Which first was mine own king: and here you
sty* me
In this hard rock, whiles you do keep from me
The rest o' the island.

Prospero: Thou most lying slave,
Whom stripes* may move, not kindness! I have
used* thee,
Filth as thou art, with human care, and lodged
thee
In mine own cell, till thou didst seek to violate
The honour of my child.

Caliban: O ho, O ho! would't had been done!
Thou didst prevent me; I had peopled else*
This isle with Calibans.

Prospero: Abhorred slave,
Which any print of goodness wilt not take,
Being capable of all ill! I pitied thee,
Took pains to make thee speak, taught thee each
hour
One thing or other: when thou didst not, savage,
Know thine own meaning, but wouldst gabble like
A thing most brutish, I endow'd thy purposes
With words that made them known. But thy vile
race,

Though thou didst learn, had that in't which good
natures
Could not abide to be with; therefore wast thou
Deservedly confined into this rock,
Who hadst deserved more than a prison.

Caliban: You taught me language; and my profit on't
Is, I know how to curse. The red plague rid you
For learning me your language!

Prospero: Hag-seed,* hence!
Fetch us in fuel; and be quick, thou'rt best,
To answer other business. Shrug'st thou, malice?
If thou neglect'st or dost unwillingly
What I command, I'll rack thee with old cramps,
Fill all thy bones with aches, make thee roar
That beasts shall tremble at thy din.

Caliban: No, pray thee.
Aside
I must obey: his art is of such power,
It would control my dam's god, Setebos, and make
a vassal of him.

Prospero:
So, slave; hence!

*sty Imprison.
*stripes Whippings.
*used Treated.
*else Otherwise.

*hag-seed Child of a witch.

549

● **CONTEXT&CONNECTIONS** The "one drop" rule in the United States has historically meant that even individuals with one black parent and one white parent have been classified as "black." The term *mulatto* exists, but one would hardly refer to a U.S. president as "mulatto." In South Africa, in contrast, people of mixed race call themselves "coloured," a positive label affirming a distinctive social and racial identity. In contrast to both the United States and South Africa, in Brazil and much of Latin America, numerous racial classification are arranged along a scale from white to black, and an individual's placement on that scale may be influenced by markers of wealth, education, and other social factors beyond mere skin color. ●

Even as slave bondage increased, Virginia evolved a system of governance in which free, propertied white men had a voice, and they took more and more matters into their own hands during England's long constitutional crisis in the seventeenth century (see Chapter 17). By the 1660s, Virginia's assembly, the House of Burgesses, was acting as an independent deliberative body. By the eighteenth century, Virginia's ruling class of planters were accustomed to running their own affairs and jealous of any signs of English interference (see Chapter 22).

Slavery was less important in the middle colonies, where New York City and Philadelphia emerged as vibrant political and economic centers. Twenty thousand German settlers had arrived in Pennsylvania by 1700, but the European immigrant population was still primarily English and Scottish. (After 1707, with the union of England and Scotland, we may refer to the two groups together as "British.")

New England

Colony that began with the arrival of English Calvinists in 1620s, and characterized by homogeneous, self-sufficient farming communities.

The settlement of **New England** began with the arrival in the 1620s and 1630s of religious dissenters dissatisfied with the established Church of England. More English settlers soon came for economic reasons: land was cheap, and wages were relatively high. As in French Québec, entire families migrated to New England intending to recreate the best features of the rural life they knew in England and combine them with American economic opportunity. Whereas elsewhere European men outnumbered European immigrant women, in New England their numbers were equally balanced, making cultural and racial mixing much less common. Since families did their own farm work, there was little call for slave labor.

In the seventeenth and early eighteenth centuries, then, England's mainland colonies were of limited economic and strategic importance. The silver of New Spain and the sugar of the West Indies generated profits on a much greater scale. With a hostile alliance of French and Indian societies to the north and west, the potential for expansion beyond the Atlantic seaboard seemed uncertain. However, by 1750, England and France were poised to battle for control of such diverse colonial territories as the Ohio River Valley, plantation colonies in the Caribbean, and trade settlements in South Asia (see Chapters 19 and 20). By that time the significance of Britain's mainland American colonies had grown substantially, and by the eighteenth century they had achieved a degree of self-governance. Not willing to give up the voice in public affairs to which they had become accustomed, colonists would increasingly resist attempts by the English monarchy to impose more central control (see Chapter 22).

Comparisons Across the Colonial Americas

By 1750, Europe's impact on the Americas was profound. While different geographical conditions led to diverse economic and demographic outcomes, the various political, religious, and cultural traditions of the European colonial powers also left deep marks.

● **CONTEXT&CONNECTIONS** Throughout the Americas, one common feature was the continuing effects of the *Columbian exchange* (Chapter 15). First introduced by the Spanish, horses and cattle flourished on wide-open American grasslands. Other domesticated imports, especially sheep and pigs, added to livestock supplies. European grains like wheat and barley were planted along with American crops like maize, potatoes, squash, and tomatoes, creating a richer and more varied diet than was common in Europe. ●

However, few Amerindians shared in the bounty. Contagious disease continued to cause high mortality, even beyond the formal boundaries of European empires. The decimation of Amerindian populations transformed the landscape. In Mexico, Amerindian farmlands were converted to grazing for European livestock; in the Chesapeake area, tobacco plantations replaced the more varied Amerindian agricultural and hunting landscapes.

All European powers harnessed American profits to augment the wealth and power of their monarchs and to advance their place among the contending Great Powers (see Chapter 17). Although they all tried to strictly regulate their colonial economies—for example, by restricting colonial trade to ships bound for the mother country—actual imperial control of commerce was never as great in practice as it was in theory. In the seventeenth century, smuggling and piracy were common, and colonists were frequently able to evade laws that required them to trade only with their home countries. Later in the eighteenth century, when European states attempted to regulate trade more closely, tensions with colonists resulted (see Chapter 22).

Within the various colonies, quite different economic regimes took hold. Some enterprises were merely extractive: mines in Spanish America or furs in New France, for instance. Here indigenous people formed the workforce (usually by compulsion in New Spain and often voluntarily in Canada). In New Spain, large mining operations and expanding urban centers offered growing markets for hacienda owners, exceptionally powerful men whose large estates commanded the labor and obedience of dependent workers, usually Amerindians or mixed-race mestizos.

Lacking minerals to exploit, the economies of the English colonies all relied on agriculture (and, in New England, fishing), though their agricultural regimes and settlement patterns differed. In temperate New England, independent farmers worked small but productive plots, largely with family labor. In contrast, large plantations were the characteristic form of landholding in colonial Carolina, where the coastal settlement resembled the West Indian pattern, exploiting massed African slave labor to produce great quantities of high-value commodities for export. In Virginia, slave labor was central to the economy, but the plantations were smaller than in Carolina, and European settlers generally used relatively fewer slaves to supplement family and indentured labor.

Religious traditions shaped the development of all of the colonial American cultures. Not surprisingly, the religious rivalries of the Reformation were exported to the Americas. The politics of the Reformation magnified territorial and commercial competition between the Catholic Spanish and Protestant English, as well as between the Catholic Portuguese and Protestant Dutch. These politics also affected French settlement. After 1627 the French monarchy, doubtful of Huguenot loyalty, banned Protestant emigration to New France. Among the English colonies, Rhode Island and Pennsylvania were the only colonies that guaranteed freedom of religious worship, accommodating Catholic settlers who were not welcome in New England or Virginia. (See the feature "Visual Evidence in Primary Sources: Catholic and Protestant Churches in the Americas.")

Catholic and Protestant Churches in the Americas

The great diversity of Christian religious beliefs and rituals is clearly demonstrated by church architecture. There is a sharp contrast between the interior of the Spanish colonial church of Santa Maria Tonantzintla (*left*) in Puebla, Mexico, and that of the Old Whaling Church (*right*) in Sag Harbor, New York. The Spanish church embodies the Catholic preference for richly embellished church interiors associated with elaborate rituals, while the colonial English church reflects the asceticism and simplicity of the Calvinist tradition.

The name of the church, *Tonantzintla*, means "place of our little mother" in the Nahuatl (NAH-watt) language. Tonantzintla was the name of the Aztec earth goddess who converts then identified with the Virgin Mary, mother of Jesus.

The term "indigenous baroque" has been used to describe this elaborately decorated form of church architecture. "Indigenous" refers to the use of Amerindian design elements, while "baroque" refers to the florid, expressive style of ornamentation then popular in southern Europe.

One architectural commentator has written of this church: "The fruits, flowers, children, faces, masks, birds, figures of saints and more, together form an extraordinary mosaic—a frank '*horror vacui*,' or fear of empty spaces—that is so typical of the Baroque style and here is interpreted in an indigenous fashion."*

The Catholic mass at that time was held in Latin. Preparing for communion, the priest performed the Eucharistic rite, in which bread is transformed into the body of Christ, facing the altar, which was designed to move the congregation's focus forward and upward, toward the heavens. **How does the function of this church differ from that of the Old Whaling Church?**

akg-images/Gilles Mermet/Newscom

*Ignacio Cabral, *Religious Architecture in San Andrés Cholula, Puebla.* http://www.puebla-mexico.com/tag/santa-maria-tonantzintla/

The name "Old Whaling Church" commemorates the sea captains who sponsored its construction. From colonial times into the nineteenth century, the whaling industry provided income and employment for many New Englanders.

The church was built in the "Greek Revival" style, emphasizing clean, classical lines and an overall emphasis on order and harmony. The parishioners were entirely of European ancestry: there is no trace of Amerindian or African influence.

David Lyons/Alamy

Old Whaling is a Presbyterian church, a branch of Protestantism strongly influenced by the teachings of John Calvin (see Chapter 17). Members of such "reformed" churches emphasized Bible reading, quiet contemplation, hard work, strict discipline, and the avoidance of all forms of excess. *How are those values reflected in this Presbyterian church's architecture?*

The democratic structure of the Presbyterian Church contrasts sharply with the Roman Catholic Church hierarchy. While Catholic bishops are appointed from Rome, Presbyterian "elders" are elected by their own congregations.

Presbyterianism was the dominant faith of seventeenth-century Scotland, and it was largely Scottish immigrants who brought the faith to British North America.

As part of colonial competition and the tensions following the Protestant Reformation, the English developed a strongly negative view of the Spanish and their empire. Associating Spain with religious intolerance and violent treatment of native peoples, the "black legend" of Spanish barbarism and cruelty infused English literature and philosophy. In the twentieth century, the Mexican poet Octavio Paz turned the "black legend" on its head, arguing that it was actually the English who were most harsh, by excluding Amerindians from colonial life altogether. Paz argued that the Spanish church at least allowed indigenous people *"to form a part of one social order and one religion."* That chance to be an accepted part of colonial society, *"even if it was at the bottom of the social pyramid,"* Paz wrote, *"was cruelly denied to the Indians by the Protestants of New England."**

Perhaps Paz underestimated the missionary impulse among Protestants, some of whom did make a strong effort toward converting Amerindians. He was correct, however, in pointing out the difference between the more fluid racial hierarchy of the Spanish empire and the more rigid forms of racial discrimination that developed in English North America. The Spanish system (and the Portuguese one in Brazil), though based on hierarchy and inequality and emphasizing Amerindian and African inferiority, was flexible, allowing for gradations of identification and classification among people of mixed European, African, and Amerindian backgrounds. The English system of racial classification was more sharply segregated. Though substantial intermixing occurred among the main population groups in the early colonial period, English authorities made little accommodation for mixed-race identities.

Gender identities were strongly fixed in every colonial society. However, as we have seen, social realities could be more fluid on the frontier, as when French fur traders interacted with matrilineal First Nations peoples and adopted their customary respect for female authority.

Catalina de Erauso was, of course, most exceptional. Badly wounded in a fight, and thinking she had better confess her sins before she died, Erauso told a priest about her deception. He did not believe her, but the nuns sent to discover the truth confirmed that she was actually a woman. After she recovered, Erauso went to Spain to seek a pension from the king for her service as a soldier, and to Rome to meet the pope. News of her strange story spread across Europe, and as she journeyed by horseback across France on her way to Italy, people came out to the road to see the famous woman warrior in a man's uniform. During her papal audience at the Vatican, the pope chastised Erauso for her violent behavior, but then granted her formal permission to dress as a man for the rest of her life.

While in Rome, Erauso narrated her story to an unknown scribe, ending with the following anecdote:

> *While strolling along the wharf in Naples one day, I perceived the loud laughter of two girls who were chatting with a couple of boys. We stared at each other and one said to me, "Where to, Lady Catalina?" I answered, 'To give*

*Octavio Paz, *The Labyrinth of Solitude* (New York: Grove Press, 1961), pp. 101–102.

*you a hundred whacks on the head, my lady whores, and a hundred slashes
to whoever may wish to defend you!' They shut up and slipped away.**

How did Erauso see herself? Did she resent having to act as a man to live her own life as she pleased? Or was her cross-dressing more than a masquerade? History provides no additional evidence.

It seems that Erauso preferred the life of the colonial frontier. According to legend, she returned to Mexico, disappeared into the mountains with a pack of burros, and was never heard from again. She was one of many European immigrants for whom the Americas represented new possibilities.

---

*Early Americas Digital Archive, *The Autobiography of Doña Catalina de Erauso,* an electronic edition. Original Source: Ferrer, Joaquín María de. *Historia de la Monja Alférez (Doña catalina de Erauso).* Madrid: Tipo Renovación, 1918. Translation and annotations by Dan Harvey Pedrick. Copyright 2007.

CONTEXT AND CONNECTIONS

Spain, the Americas, and the World

That the Habsburg dynasty won the sixteenth-century silver and gold lottery was significant for world history (see Chapter 17). American mineral wealth, combined with extensive Habsburg territorial control in Europe, elevated the court of Madrid to the top rank in an interconnected world where European dynastic rivalries had gone global. The political and military impulses of the *reconquista* (the Christian reconquest of Iberia, completed in 1492) were then transferred to the international stage, as Catalina de Erauso's narrative shows. The Spanish emphasis on "purity of blood" once directed at Jews and Muslims was one such continuity (even as, ironically, racial mixture was common in the Spanish Americas); the admixture of militarism and Catholicism was another.

Spain's leading role would not long endure, however: even the fabulous riches flowing from Potosí and other American mines were not sufficient to enable the Spanish to turn back the challenge of the Protestant Reformation or to maintain their lead in imperial affairs (see Chapter 17). Following the Spanish head start, the English, French, and Dutch were left to vie for what seemed less desirable territories to the north. Though initially less well endowed with resources and population, the colonial economies of the northern Europeans were more dynamic.

The Dutch were pioneers in the development of the tools of merchant capitalism, including joint-stock companies and chartered monopolies to develop new markets (see Chapter 16). The English, who had begun their American venture as little more than pirates, built on and further developed these tools of mercantile capitalism to become the greatest naval force in the world by the eighteenth century, further expanding their empire in both Asia and the Americas. By then, with Spain reduced to a minor power, it was the British and the French who would compete for European supremacy on the global stage (see Chapters 19 and 20).

We should not, however, repeat the common error of overstating the global role of the West in the period from 1500 to 1750. The Americas were unique in the degree to which the Western impact transformed society environmentally, politically, and culturally. Even here, though, some indigenous societies long remained outside the orbit of colonial empires, and through cultural mixing and merging, indigenous traditions continued.

In Afro-Eurasia, European ascendency was less assured in the early eighteenth century. Land-based empires still remained more important in Asia than maritime ones. As we shall see in upcoming chapters,

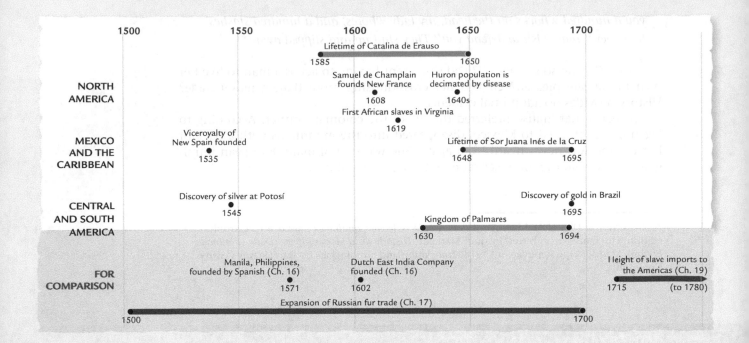

	1500	1550	1600	1650	1700

NORTH AMERICA

Lifetime of Catalina de Erauso
1585 — 1650

Samuel de Champlain founds New France
1608

Huron population is decimated by disease
1640s

First African slaves in Virginia
1619

MEXICO AND THE CARIBBEAN

Viceroyalty of New Spain founded
1535

Lifetime of Sor Juana Inés de la Cruz
1648 — 1695

CENTRAL AND SOUTH AMERICA

Discovery of silver at Potosí
1545

Discovery of gold in Brazil
1695

Kingdom of Palmares
1630 — 1694

FOR COMPARISON

Manila, Philippines, founded by Spanish (Ch. 16)
1571

Dutch East India Company founded (Ch. 16)
1602

Height of slave imports to the Americas (Ch. 19)
1715 — (to 1780)

Expansion of Russian fur trade (Ch. 17)
1500 — 1700

European global dominance was not fully secured until the nineteenth century, in the wake of the Industrial Revolution.

Although Europeans had only a tiny footprint on the African continent by 1750, millions of African lives had been utterly transformed by the Atlantic slave trade. Their experiences in the Americas varied, with some finding opportunities in the new world, much like Catalina de Erauso. The most common new world story for Africans, however, was the hardship of brutal plantation work. On the sugar islands of the West Indies, Africans slaved to harvest the sugar and other crops that enriched and empowered their European masters. The trade in slaves brought untold misery to both those Africans forced into exile and to the continent of Africa itself, as we will see in the next chapter.

Key Terms

Catalina de Erauso (532)
viceroyalties (533)
Bartolomé de las Casas (533)
Potosí (535)
mercury amalgamation process (535)
haciendas (536)

mestizo (539)
syncretism (539)
Virgin of Guadalupe (539)
casta system (540)
Sor Juana Inés de la Cruz (541)
Palmares (543)

Québec (545)
métis (545)
Huron (546)
Virginia (546)
New England (550)

For Further Reference

Benton, Lauren A. *Law and Colonial Cultures: Legal Regimes in World History, 1400–1900.* New York: Cambridge University Press, 2002.

Burns, Kathryn. *Colonial Habits: Convents and the Spiritual Economy of Cuzco, Peru.* Durham: Duke University Press, 1999.

Eccles, William J. *The French in North America, 1500–1783.* Rev. ed. Lansing: Michigan State University Press, 1998.

Fernandez-Armesto, Felipe. *The Americas: The History of a Hemisphere.* London: George Weidenfeld and Nicholson, 2003.

Kamen, Henry. *Empire: How Spain Became a World Power, 1492–1763.* New York: HarperCollins, 2003.

Lavrin, Asunción. *Sexuality and Marriage in Colonial Latin America.* Lincoln: University of Nebraska Press, 1992.

Nash, Gary. *Red, White and Black: The Peoples of Early North America*. 6th ed. New York: Prentice Hall, 2009.

Nellis, Eric. *An Empire of Regions: A Brief History of British Colonial America*. Toronto: University of Toronto Press, 2010.

Paz, Octavio. *Sor Juana*. Margaret Sayers Peden, trans. Cambridge, Mass.: Harvard University Press, 1988.

Restall, Matthew. *Latin America in Colonial Times*. Cambridge: Cambridge University Press, 2011.

Sweet, James H. *Recreating Africa: Culture, Kinship, and Religion in the African-Portuguese World, 1441–1770*. Durham: University of North Carolina Press, 2006.

Taylor, William. *Magistrates of the Sacred: Priests and Parishioners in Eighteenth Century Mexico*. Stanford: Stanford University Press, 1996.

MindTap

MindTap is a fully online, highly personalized learning experience built upon Cengage Learning content. MindTap combines student learning tools—readings, multimedia, activities, and assessments—into a singular Learning Path that guides students through the course.

19

The Atlantic System: Africa, the Americas, and Europe, 1550–1807

Portrait of an African, c.1757–60 (oil on canvas), Ramsay, Allan (1713–84) (attr. to)/ Royal Albert Memorial Museum, Exeter, Devon, UK/Bridgeman Images

Olaudah Equiano

In 1789, members of England's growing abolitionist movement, campaigning against the slave trade, provided an eager audience for a new publication, *The Interesting Narrative of the Life of Olaudah Equiano, or Gustavus Vassa, the African*. For many, it was the first time they heard an African voice narrate the horrors of slavery. The story of **Olaudah Equiano** (ca. 1745–1797) shows how he suffered as a slave, but also how he beat the odds. Equiano's readers learned of the horrors of the infamous Middle Passage across the Atlantic:

The first object which saluted my eyes when I arrived on the coast was the sea, and a slave-ship.... These filled me with astonishment, which was soon converted into terror.... [T]hey made ready with many fearful noises, and we were all put under deck ... now that the whole ship's cargo was confined together [the stench of the hold] was absolutely pestilential. The closeness of the place, and the heat of the climate, added to the number in the ship, which was so crowded that each had scarcely room to turn himself, almost suffocated us.... This wretched situation was again aggravated by the galling of the chains, now become insupportable; and the filth of the [latrines], into which the children often fell, and were almost suffocated. The shrieks of the women, and the groans of the dying, rendered the whole a scene of horror almost inconceivable.*

---

*Olaudah Equiano, *The Interesting Narrative of the Life of Olaudah Equiano, or Gustavus Vassa, the African*, ed. Vincent Carretta, 2d ed. (New York: Penguin, 2003), p. 55.

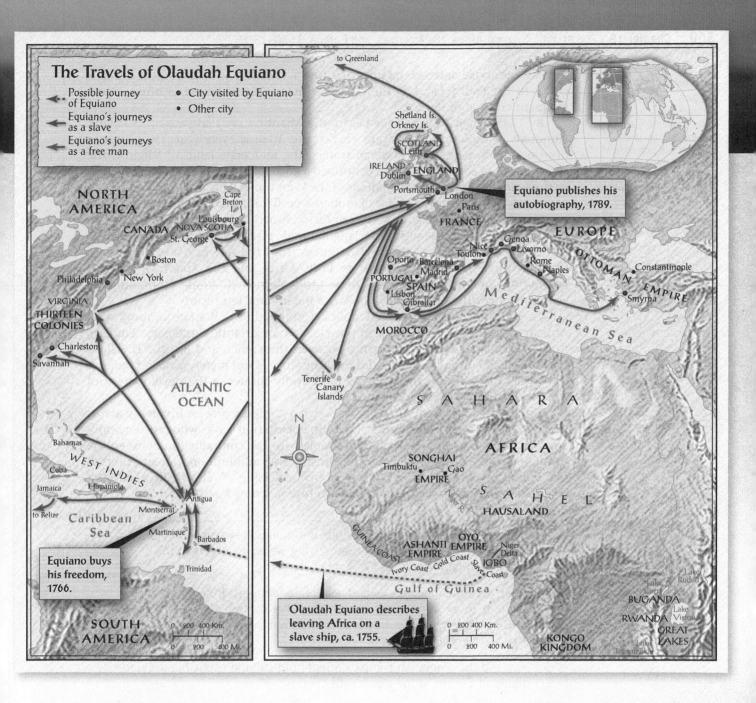

The Travels of Olaudah Equiano

- ← Possible journey of Equiano
- ← Equiano's journeys as a slave
- ← Equiano's journeys as a free man
- • City visited by Equiano
- • Other city

Equiano publishes his autobiography, 1789.

Equiano buys his freedom, 1766.

Olaudah Equiano describes leaving Africa on a slave ship, ca. 1755.

Map labels: to Greenland; Shetland Is.; Orkney Is.; SCOTLAND; Leith; IRELAND; Dublin; ENGLAND; Portsmouth; London; Paris; FRANCE; EUROPE; Nice; Genoa; Toulon; Livorno; Rome; Naples; OTTOMAN EMPIRE; Constantinople; Oporto; Barcelona; Madrid; PORTUGAL; SPAIN; Lisbon; Gibraltar; Smyrna; Mediterranean Sea; MOROCCO; Tenerife; Canary Islands; SAHARA; AFRICA; SONGHAI EMPIRE; Timbuktu; Gao; SAHEL; HAUSALAND; Niger R.; GUINEA COAST; ASHANTI EMPIRE; OYO EMPIRE; Niger Delta; IGBO; Ivory Coast; Gold Coast; Slave Coast; Gulf of Guinea; KONGO KINGDOM; BUGANDA; RWANDA; GREAT LAKES; Lake Rudolf; Lake Albert; Lake Victoria; Lake Tanganyika

NORTH AMERICA; Cape Breton; Louisbourg; NOVA SCOTIA; CANADA; St. George; Boston; Philadelphia; New York; VIRGINIA; THIRTEEN COLONIES; Charleston; Savannah; ATLANTIC OCEAN; Bahamas; WEST INDIES; Cuba; Jamaica; Hispaniola; to Belize; Caribbean Sea; Antigua; Montserrat; Martinique; Barbados; Trinidad; SOUTH AMERICA

0 200 400 Km.
0 200 400 Mi.

At least 12 million Africans had similar experiences between the sixteenth and nineteenth centuries, and an unknown number perished even before they reached the slave ports on the West African coast.

The historical importance of Equiano's *Interesting Narrative* has been established and his adult activities well-documented, though some scholars question the authenticity of its earliest passages. (Some evidence, albeit inconclusive, suggests that the author was born in the Americas and created his account of Africa and the voyage across the Atlantic by retelling other slaves' stories, reminding us to be cautious when using memoirs as history.) Still, whether Olaudah Equiano (oh-lah-OO-dah ek-wee-AHN-oh) personally experienced the terror he reports in

Olaudah Equiano

(1745–1797) Afro-British author and abolitionist who told of his enslavement as a child in Africa, his purchase of his own freedom in the West Indies, his move to England, and his wide travels as a sailor.

the passage above or based the story on other accounts, few other sources bring us closer to the reality faced by millions of Africans in this period or offer a more eloquent critique of slavery.

By 1745, when Equiano's life began, the Atlantic slave trade was at its height. Hundreds of thousands of Africans crossed the Atlantic every year. They lived in diverse environments—the Brazilian tropics, the temperate lands of Virginia, the rocky shores of Nova Scotia—and performed a great variety of tasks. Most, however, were destined for the sugar plantations of the West Indies. Sugar was the foundation of the Atlantic economy, a source of immense profit and great suffering.

Complex interconnections between Africa, America, and Europe characterized the Atlantic system. The so-called triangular trade sent Africans to the Americas as slaves; sugar, tobacco, and natural resources from the Americas to Europe; and manufactured goods from Europe to both Africa and the Americas. Africans labored on American plantations whose profits enriched Europe, stimulating its economic growth, while in much of Africa life became less secure.

The Atlantic system fostered political competition. Warfare among West Africans increased, while European powers vied for Atlantic supremacy; Equiano himself participated in naval clashes between the French and British. The slave trade also had cultural repercussions. Africans arrived not merely as slaves but also as carriers of traditions that were to profoundly influence the development of American societies (see also Chapter 18).

Finally, the abolition of slavery was itself a complex process involving actors from different parts of the Atlantic, including plantation slaves who resisted bondage and Europeans who grew uncomfortable with the contradiction between the inhumanity of plantation slavery and Christianity's admonition to treat others as you would be treated yourself. It was to his readership of fellow Christians that Olaudah Equiano especially appealed with his *Interesting Narrative*.

FOCUS QUESTIONS

> How were existing African economic and political systems integrated into the Atlantic plantation system? What were the effects of this interaction on Africans and African societies?

> What were the major social and economic features of the plantation complex in the West Indies and on the American mainland? What cultural patterns in the Americas showed the influence of forced African migration?

> How did the plantation complex affect political and economic developments in Europe in the eighteenth century?

> What led to the abolition of the British slave trade in the early nineteenth century?

African History and Afro-Eurasian Connections, 1550–1700

Judging the impact of the Atlantic slave trade on African history requires understanding Africa's cultural and geographic context. Contrary to common assumptions, Africa had not been an isolated continent: it had ancient connections to Europe and Asia across the Mediterranean, the Red Sea, and the Indian Ocean.

Africa's diverse deserts, grasslands, and rainforests produced a variety of political systems. Some Africans lived in small bands of hunter-gatherers, while others were subjects of powerful monarchs. Equiano described the Igbo-speaking villages in the Niger Delta region of West Africa as productive communities where yam-based agriculture supported a dense population. Other nearby societies had more centralized and hierarchical political structures, but in Igbo (ee-BWOH) society, men and women accumulated titles and authority on the basis of achievements rather than birth. As was nearly universal in Africa, clan elders played a crucial role in negotiating the consensus needed for community decisions. Even when owing tribute or obeisance to a more distant chief or king, African villages retained their own mechanisms for keeping peace and administering justice.

Much of the cultural and economic energy of the continent came from interaction among African peoples themselves. For example, in the **Great Lakes region** of east-central Africa, migration led to fruitful encounters between Africans of different linguistic and cultural backgrounds. Bantu-speaking migrants from the west brought knowledge of grain agriculture, and invented sophisticated iron technologies. In return, these farmers gained access to cattle from their pastoralist neighbors, descendants of migrants from the upper Nile River Valley. In the societies that resulted, farming provided the bulk of calories and was the focus of work, while cattle represented wealth and prestige. No proper marriage contract could be negotiated unless the groom's family gave cattle to the family of his intended. Agriculture in the Great Lakes region was also stimulated by the introduction of plantains (bananas), a Southeast Asian fruit that traveled across the Indian Ocean with Indonesian voyagers to the island of Madagascar. Supported by agricultural surpluses and dominated by clans wealthy in cattle, a number of powerful kingdoms such as Rwanda and Buganda emerged in the seventeenth-century Great Lakes region.

Many other African societies had formative contacts with external political systems, commercial markets, and religious traditions. For example, Ethiopia, Kongo, and South Africa all had connections to the wider Christian world. The Ethiopian Coptic Church, connected to the Orthodox branch of the faith and with a strong monastic tradition, was already over a thousand years old when the Portuguese attempted a military alliance in the sixteenth century, in the same period when the royal court of Kongo was converting to Roman Catholicism (see Chapter 16).

In the Kongo kingdom, civil war and invasion by outside forces had led to disintegration of the monarchy and the abandonment of the Kongo capital of San Salvador in the seventeenth century. Into this political vacuum stepped **Kimpa Vita** (ca. 1680–1706). In a powerful example of religious syncretism (see Chapter 18), Kimpa Vita declared that she had been visited by Saint Anthony and conversed with God, who told her that the people of Kongo must unite under a new king. She taught that Christ and the apostles were black men who had lived and died in Kongo. Her doctrine was popular, and her followers repopulated the old capital city. But Portuguese missionaries regarded her beliefs as heresy. She was captured by rivals, tried for witchcraft, and burned at the stake. But the Kongo tradition of depicting Jesus as an African endured.

● **CONTEXT&CONNECTIONS** Kimpa Vita's role as a prophetess was in keeping with Kongo traditions of female spiritual leadership. Across Africa, in fact, it was often women who were touched with the gift of communicating with unseen forces, as the story of the *Xhosa Cattle Killing* in South Africa in response to nineteenth-century European intrusions also shows (key term in Chapter 26). In Mesoamerica, the identification of

Great Lakes region
A temperate highland region in and around the Great Rift Valley in east-central Africa, characterized by agriculture and cattle pastoralism, a substantial iron industry, and dense populations.

Kimpa Vita
(ca. 1680–1706) Christian reformer in the Kongo kingdom, also known as Dona Beatriz. She preached that Jesus Christ was an African, blending Kongo beliefs with Catholic ones, before being executed as a heretic by a leader vying for the Kongo throne.

the Aztec fertility goddess Tonantzintla with the Catholic *Virgin of Guadalupe* was yet another example of converts to Christianity retaining a female principle through religious *syncretism* (Chapter 18). ●

Utterly different from both the mysticism of Ethiopia's Coptic faith and the syncretism in the Kongo was the Protestant Christianity brought to seventeenth-century South Africa by Dutch Calvinists and French Huguenots (see Chapter 17) as they expanded at the expense of the indigenous Khoisan (KOI-sahn)-speaking peoples, who lacked both metal weapons and resistance to diseases such as smallpox. It would be another two centuries, however, before significant numbers of southern Africans converted to Christianity (see Chapter 26).

The *Dar-al-Islam*—the domain of Islam—gave Africans an even more significant avenue for early modern global interconnections. From the Indian Ocean coast, Muslim Swahili merchants and sailors had long plied maritime trade routes connecting East Africa with India and the Persian Gulf (see Chapter 16). After the Arab sultans of Oman (oh-MAAN) wrested control of Fort Jesus in Mombasa from the Portuguese in 1696, Swahili princes and aristocrats generally acknowledged their authority while continuing to regulate the affairs of their own city-states. Traditional Swahili arts and crafts—poetry, jewelry, and elaborately carved wooden doors for wealthy houses—continued through such political transitions, combining Islamic and African motifs.

Sahel

Arid region south of the Sahara Desert that played an important historic role as a West African center of trade and urbanization. Islam traveled with the caravans across the Sahara, making the Sahel a diffusion point for Islam in West Africa.

The other center of African Islam was the **Sahel**, the arid region south of the Sahara where Islam had come across the desert with Arab traders from the north. That caravan trade in salt, gold, and slaves had further stimulated an existing African urban civilization based on trade among grain farmers, cattle pastoralists, and producers in the rainforest further south. Kola nuts from the forest, for example, were a mild stimulant highly appreciated by Muslim consumers in the Sahel (and later by "cola" drinkers worldwide).

The great Niger River was an essential concourse for West Africans. Flowing from the mountains of the west, through the savanna to the desert's edge, and on through the rainforests of the coastal Niger Delta—where Equiano placed his childhood home—the river was a highway of trade, with West Africa's most important cities clustered on its banks. Fisherman drew on its natural bounty, and the river's great inland delta, far north at the edge of the Sahara desert, was a highly productive agricultural region.

The cities along the Niger River connected West Africa with Mediterranean economies through the trans-Saharan trade. Cities like Timbuktu were southern destinations for camel caravans from North Africa. (The term "Sahel" shares the same Arabic root as the word "Swahili," both referring to a sea shore. Since crossing the Sahara was like traversing an ocean, to an Arab merchant Timbuktu seemed like a port.)

Songhai empire

(1464–1591) Important Islamic empire with prosperity based on both interregional and trans-Saharan trade. Stretched from the Atlantic into present-day Nigeria, reaching its height in the sixteenth century before being invaded by Morocco.

The **Songhai empire**, with its capital at Gao along the Niger River, arose from a thousand-year-old tradition of large-scale states in this region (see Map 19.1). In addition to leading armies of conquest, the *askias* (emperors) of Songhai (song-GAH-ee) were patrons of Islamic arts and sciences. The Sankore Mosque in Timbuktu, with its impressive library, became a center of intellectual debate, drawing scholars from far and wide. Timbuktu was famous for its gold trade as well as its book market, where Arab and African Muslim scholars eagerly sought finely bound editions. When rulers, traders, and intellectuals from Songhai went on the hajj (pilgrimage) to Arabia, they amplified the empire's connections with the broader world.

Map 19.1 Major African States and Trade Routes, ca. 1500 In the sixteenth century, Africa's primary global connections were across the Sahara Desert, up the Nile, across the Red Sea, and into the Indian Ocean. Large kingdoms and empires such as those of Songhai in the west and Ethiopia in the northeast benefited from participation in world trade, as did the Swahili city-states in the east. The arrival of Europeans added a new set of interconnections along the West African coast, but only in South Africa did Europeans come as settlers. Large states were the exception in Africa; smaller societies populated vast regions of the continent.

563

Entrance of Heinrich Barth's (1821–65) Caravan into Timbuktu in 1853, from "Travels and Discoveries in North and Central Africa" by Barth, engraved by Eberhard Emminger (1808–85) published 1857 (colour engraving), Bernatz, Johann Martin (1802–1878) (after)/Bibliotheque Nationale, Paris, France/Archives Charmet/The Bridgeman Art Library

Caravan Approaching Timbuktu The city of Timbuktu was an important terminus of the trans-Saharan trade dating back to the thirteenth century, its strategic location on the Niger River making it central to the wealth and power of the Songhai empire. Under the patronage of Songhai's rulers, Timbuktu became an important center of Islamic scholarship as well: the library at the Sankore Mosque attracted both African and Arab scholars. Although the site is today protected by its status as a UNESCO World Heritage Site, in 2013 some of Timbuktu's precious manuscripts were destroyed by Muslim extremists who hoped to wipe out records of Afro-Islamic synthesis.

Even within the mighty Songhai empire, however, most Africans lived in small agricultural villages. In the rural societies of the Sahel, Islam spread slowly. Here older gods and ritual practices endured, sometimes incorporated with elements of Islam. Even in cities like Timbuktu and at the court of powerful Songhai kings, syncretism was characteristic of West African Islam, for example, when African customs regarding marriage and inheritance were blended with the influence of Islamic law.

● **CONTEXT&CONNECTIONS** Enduring African cultural practices in the Islamic Sahel, such as a loose attitude toward veiling women, were criticized by Arab visitors and more orthodox African clerics. The goal of purifying Islamic practice would inspire West African religious reformers in the nineteenth century (see Chapter 26). In West Africa, *Sufi* brotherhoods (Chapter 17) played an important role in adapting the imported faith to local traditions, which was also the case in India under the *Mughals* and in the Ottoman empire during the time of *Evliya Çelebi* (Chapters 16 and 17). ●

The success of the askias (AH-skee-as) attracted military as well as commercial attention from Songhai's Moroccan neighbors to the north. Morocco's leaders had remained independent of the Ottoman empire and had successfully driven off the Portuguese. The Moroccan sultan envied Songhai's gold and salt mines, and in 1591 the army he sent out from Marrakesh conquered Songhai, shattering it into smaller kingdoms, chiefdoms, and sultanates. Never again would a large-scale African state rise to such dominance in the Sahel.

Meanwhile, when Songhai was at its height in the sixteenth century, Europeans were constructing fortifications along the West African coast. Though the major centers of population and prosperity still lay in the interior regions of the Sahel, connected to the wider world across the Sahara, European merchants were now striving to redirect West African trade to the coast. Gold was always of interest, but they came over time to focus on another commodity: slaves. By the eighteenth century, African Muslims whose ancestors may have crossed the Sahara to Morocco by camel might instead be enslaved and sent by ship to Jamaica. While connections to the Islamic world across the Sahara Desert and the Indian Ocean continued, by the eighteenth century Africa's international connection was turning toward the Atlantic Ocean and beyond, to the Americas.

Africa and the Americas: The Plantation Complex

European occupation of the Americas, the continuing decline of Amerindian populations, and new trade links with West Africa set the stage for the rise of the **Atlantic plantation system**. The enslavement and forced emigration of millions of Africans to the Americas reaped huge fortunes for the British, French, Dutch, Spanish, and Portuguese who controlled the system. On the islands of the Caribbean, where the plantation complex was centered, landscapes changed dramatically as imported plants and animals replaced indigenous ones and Africans became the predominant population. Sugar planters exploited their slave labor to supply expanding global markets for sugar and related products like molasses and rum.

As Equiano's story illustrates, Africans were more than passive victims of the Atlantic slave trade and plantation system. Many resisted. And though mortality rates among slaves were high and survivors were often deprived of the use of their own languages, many managed to retain much of their culture and contributed it to the new American societies (see also Chapter 18). Meanwhile, in West Africa, integration into the Atlantic system disrupted many indigenous societies.

Atlantic plantation system

The focal point in the new set of interchanges among Africa, Europe, and the Americas that peaked in the eighteenth century. Utilized African slave labor to produce large quantities of agricultural products, particularly sugar, for international markets.

The Economics of Plantation Production

From the very beginning, Africans played a variety of roles in the conquest and settlement of the European New World empires (see Chapter 18). As we saw with the settlement of Brazil, for example, Africans worked as artisans, traders, and soldiers, as well as plantation slaves. The skills that Africans brought with them to the Americas included metalworking, weaving, and agricultural knowledge that contributed to the introduction and spread of crops like rice. In the Spanish empire as well, Africans played multiple roles and were part of evolving patterns of racial and cultural intermixture. Still, in the Caribbean and British North America, the words "black" and "slave" had become nearly synonymous by the eighteenth century.

When the Spanish first conquered the islands of the Caribbean, they were unable to effectively exploit the labor of the indigenous Amerindian inhabitants, who could stand neither the strain of European rule nor the deadly effects of diseases for which they had no immunity. Europeans later imported indentured

Twenty-One Million Slaves

According to the International Labor Organization (an agency of the United Nations), 21 million people in the world were living in slavery in 2012, with the biggest number in central and southeastern Europe, followed by Africa, the Middle East, Asia/Pacific, Latin America, and the Caribbean.

After Great Britain abolished slavery in its empire in 1834, the country began an international campaign to suppress the institution. With the abolition of slavery in Brazil in 1888, three hundred years of slave importation into the Americas finally came to an end. Subsequent national and international laws and treaties banned slavery globally.

Nevertheless, people have used a number of different strategies to enslave their fellow human beings. Some involve the continuation of traditional systems. In Mauritania, for example, descent-based slavery, where some children still inherit their parents' slave status, bonds individuals to particular families for life without compensation or freedom of movement.

Debt peonage (long present in Latin America; see Chapter 18) is another old practice that continues: a desperate man takes a loan on terms that guarantee it can never be repaid and then has to do his creditor's bidding without pay for the rest of his life. His children may even inherit the unpaid debt and find themselves enslaved as well.

Even today, slave owners anxious for profit use confinement as well as physical and emotional abuse to prevent complaints or attempts at escape. Women from India or the Philippines, for example, might sign contracts to work as domestic servants in Persian Gulf countries, only to find that they are trapped within the household, their passports seized and their voices silenced. Some have accused construction companies in Qatar of abusing slaves, mainly from South Asia, in the buildup to the 2022 World Cup.

Perhaps the most horrible crimes in our world take place at the intersection of child slavery, human trafficking, and the global sex trade. The U.S. Department of State has estimated that as many as a million underage kids are exploited sexually for profit every year, often illegally transported across national borders by organized crime syndicates, who also control "sex tourism" in countries like Thailand. The campaign to bring freedom to those crushed by slavery, begun by Olaudah Equiano and other eighteenth-century abolitionists, is still not complete.

Source: International Labor Organization, "21 Million People Are Now Victims of Forced Labour," http://www.ilo.org/global/about-the-ilo/newsroom/news/WCMS_181961/lang–it/index.htm.

---

servants, but they were vulnerable to the tropical diseases such as yellow fever and malaria that had come from Africa. By 1680, when sugar had become virtually the sole focus of West Indian agriculture, neither Europeans nor Amerindians could provide sufficient labor.

Enslaved Africans filled the void. They were expensive, but from a sugar planter's perspective they were worth the investment because they could survive the harsh Caribbean disease environment. West Africans had long been exposed to the same Afro-Eurasian diseases as Europeans; unlike Amerindians, they were therefore resistant to diseases like smallpox. In addition, through genetic adaptation and childhood exposure, Africans were also more likely to survive malaria and yellow fever, which were deadly to Europeans. Tragically, their ability to survive in difficult disease environments, enhanced their value as slaves. (See the feature "World History in Today's World: Twenty-One Million Slaves.")

Slavery had been common before, but the scale and commercial orientation of the sugar industry were something new. Many societies allowed for slavery, but most were "societies with slaves" where slavery existed but was not the main driver of production, and not "slave societies" where slaveholding is at the heart of social and economic life. "Societies with slaves" were common in the Islamic world and in Africa itself. Equiano described a mild form of servitude in the Niger Delta region, where the slaves had a lower place in society but retained legal rights. Genuine "slave societies," in contrast, developed in northeastern Brazil and the Caribbean, where 80 percent of enslaved Africans were sent and where slavery was central to every facet of social and economic life.

● **CONTEXT&CONNECTIONS** As we have seen in Chapter 17, slavery was common in the Ottoman empire. However, that was a "society with slaves" rather than a genuine "slave society." Under the Ottomans, while slaves played a wide variety of roles, including military and administrative leadership, the bulk of production came from free artisans and peasant farmers. Such "societies with slaves" have been fairly common in world history; there are fewer examples of societies, like those of the Roman empire or the early modern Caribbean, fundamentally based on the deployment of massed slave labor in agriculture. ●

Purchasing and provisioning a sugar plantation, and buying the slaves needed to work it, took substantial capital. Sugar planters were men of property, often middle-class businessmen striving to improve their finances and elevate their social standing by, for example, using sugar profits to build impressive country houses, including some of the finest estates and chateaux of eighteenth-century France and Britain. More broadly, the need to provision the sugar islands with food, clothing, and manufactured goods stimulated economic development in eighteenth-century North America and western Europe, providing many Europeans with jobs and markets for their goods.

Absentee ownership of Caribbean plantations became more common, and the work of overseeing slave labor usually went to lower-status European immigrants, legendary for their harshness, or to men of mixed race. Lighter skin did not automatically confer higher status, however: Equiano told of a French sugar planter on Martinique with "*many mulattoes working in the fields [who] were all the produce of his own loins!*"*

Slaves performed all the backbreaking work of planting, weeding, harvesting, and processing. Because raw sugar is bulky, the juice had to be squeezed out of the cane and boiled down for shipment. Sugar production was thus an agro-industrial enterprise, organized like a factory where profitable operation requires that the assembly line is always rolling, with raw materials ready at hand. Sugarcane was processed year round, with full-time use of the crushing machinery and the large copper boiling kettles. The entire process was physically strenuous, and the kettles sometimes exploded, maiming or killing African laborers.

The brutal work lives of slaves on Caribbean sugar plantations thus had much in common with the harshest forms of later factory labor, governed by the relentless grinding of machines rather than by more gentle rhythms of nature. Only Sunday was a day of rest, and even then slaves usually needed to work on their small food plots.

Under such conditions, overseers frequently worked Africans to death. Barbados is representative. In 1680, fifty thousand African slaves toiled on the island. Over the

---

*Olaudah Equiano, *The Interesting Narrative of the Life of Olaudah Equiano, or Gustavus Vassa, the African*, ed. Vincent Carretta, 2d ed. (New York: Penguin, 2003), pp. 105–109.

From William Clark, *Ter. Views in the Islands of Antigua*, 1823, © British Library Board

Caribbean Sugar Mill Sugar production was an industrial as well as agricultural enterprise. Here wind power is used to crush the sugarcane; the rising smoke indicates the intense heat of the furnaces used to boil down the juice. The slaves' work was hard, dangerous, and unceasing: such machinery was usually operated six days a week, year-round.

next forty years, planters imported another fifty thousand slaves, but the total black population actually *dropped* to forty-five thousand because the harsh conditions and poor diet led to high mortality and low birth rates. As Equiano noted, the overseers, *"human butchers, … pay no regard to the situation of pregnant women. The neglect certainly conspires with many others to cause a decrease in the births, as well as in the lives of the grown negroes."** Equiano calculated that Barbados, not the worst island in terms of African mortality, required a thousand fresh imports annually just to maintain a level population (see Table 19.1). One historian has put it with chilling simplicity: "Most of the slaves died early and without progeny."[†]

Equiano himself escaped the harsh fate of working on a Caribbean sugar plantation. While still a boy he was sold to a British naval officer; he spent much of his early life aboard ships and developed a lifelong fondness for London. He was then sold to a Philadelphia merchant with business interests in the West Indies. Aboard ship, Equiano had learned to read and had developed a good head for numbers. He enjoyed good treatment and significant freedom while tending to his master's business, which sometimes included trading in slaves. Of course, he witnessed many cruelties:

It was very common in several of the islands, particularly in St. Kitt's, for the slaves to be branded with the initial letters of their master's name, and a load

---

*Olaudah Equiano, *The Interesting Narrative of the Life of Olaudah Equiano, or Gustavus Vassa, the African*, ed. Vincent Carretta, 2d ed. (New York: Penguin, 2003), pp. 105–109.

[†]Patrick Manning, "Migrations of Africans to the Americas: The Impact on Africans, Africa, and the World," *The History Teacher*, 26 (May, 1993): 295.

Table 19.1 Importation and Black Population Statistics for the British West Indies

Year	Barbados: Slave Imports	Barbados: Total Black Population	Jamaica: Slave Imports	Jamaica: Total Black Population	Leeward Islands: Slave Imports	Leeward Islands: Total Black Population
1640–1650	18,700		?		3,000	
1670		30,000		7,000		3,000
1651–1675	51,100		8,000		10,100	
1680		50,000		15,000		9,000
1676–1700	64,700		77,100		32,000	
1713		45,000		55,000		30,000

Note: The British Leeward Islands consisted of Antigua, Barbuda, Anguilla, the British Virgin Islands, Montserrat, and St. Kitts–Nevis.

Source: From Richard Dunn, *Sugar and Slaves: The Rise of the Plantar Class in the English West Indies, 1624–1713* (New York: Norton, 1972), pp. 230, 312.

of heavy iron hooks hung around their necks…. I have seen a negro beaten till some of his bones were broken, for only letting a pot boil over. It is not uncommon, after a flogging, to make slaves go on their knees and thank their owners and … say "God Bless You."*

While distressed by his own bondage, Equiano was keenly aware of the even worse fate he could have faced as a field slave.

Sugar was not the only slave-produced plantation crop in the Americas. Slaves also labored on the tobacco plantations of Virginia and the rice and indigo plantations of Carolina (see Chapter 18). But in British North America, slave mortality was lower, and a better diet and more equal gender balance led to higher fertility. Unlike in the Caribbean, the slave populations of the British colonies were self-reproducing by 1720, although planters continued to import slaves.

● **CONTEXT&CONNECTIONS** In the United States, slavery is associated with cotton production in the Deep South, which became a genuine "slave society." The extension of cotton, however, was a later, nineteenth-century development. Only in the wake of the *Industrial Revolution* (Chapter 23) did mass production of cotton begin in the Americas. ●

African Culture and Resistance to Slavery

African resistance to slavery was endemic. Slaves everywhere looked for ways to escape their bondage and, failing that, to resist their captivity in large or small ways. Slave traders, owners, and overseers were ever vigilant, and exacted gruesome penalties for open insubordination. Equiano tells of a slave trader who had once cut off the leg of a slave for running away. When Equiano asked how the man could square such an action with his Christian conscience, the trader simply said *"that his scheme had the desired effect—it cured that man and some others of running away."**

---

*Olaudah Equiano, *The Interesting Narrative of the Life of Olaudah Equiano, or Gustavus Vassa, the African*, ed. Vincent Carretta, 2d ed. (New York: Penguin, 2003), pp. 105–109, 59.

Slaves often found safer, more subtle ways to assert their humanity and express their defiance. Songs and stories derived from African cultural traditions might be used to ridicule a master using coded language he could not understand. Religious rites—African, Christian, or a synthesis of multiple belief systems and rituals—might serve as assertions of dignity and spiritual resilience. Music played an important role in maintaining cultural independence, and slaves' songs often ridiculed their masters. Knowing that Africans often use drums to communicate, slave owners banned them from the slave quarters. Still Africans were inventive in using whatever they could find to keep the beat; if all they had was their own bodies, then complex rhythmic clapping and slapping was enough.

Resistance to slavery sometimes began even before the slave ships arrived in America. Equiano describes the nets that were used to keep Africans from jumping overboard and relates that *"one day ... two of my wearied countrymen, who were chained together ... preferring death to such a life of misery, somehow made through the nettings and jumped into the sea."** Insurrections aboard slave ships were also common, as this dramatic description from 1673 attests:

*A master of a ship ... did not, as the manner is, shackle [the slaves] one to another ... and they being double the number of those in the ship found their advantages, got weapons in their hands, and fell upon the sailors, knocking them on the heads, and cutting their throats so fast as the master found they were all lost ... and so went down into the hold and blew up all with himself.**

Even after landing, some Africans managed to escape. Yet if an individual or a small group got away, where would they go, and how would they live? Options for escaped slaves included joining pirate groups in the Caribbean, settling among Amerindian populations, or forming their own autonomous communities.

Already in the sixteenth century, escaped slaves were banding together to form **maroon communities**. Perhaps the best known were the *quilombos* of Brazil, of which Palmares was the largest and best known (see Chapter 18). Palmares was unique in scale, but significant maroon communities also took root in the interior regions of Venezuela, Guyana, and Florida. In some places, runaway slaves assimilated into indigenous societies, occasionally resulting in larger-scale cooperation with Amerindians. In Florida, for example, Africans who escaped from slavery in Carolina and Georgia formed an alliance with Creek Indians, and the cultural interaction between the two groups led the "Black Seminoles" to adopt many elements of Creek culture.

Some Caribbean sugar islands were too small for maroons to escape and avoid recapture, but the interior mountains of Jamaica were perfect for that purpose. When the Spanish fled Jamaica in 1655 during a British attack, they left behind hundreds of African slaves who headed for the hills. Now free, these maroons farmed, fished, and occasionally pillaged British sugar plantations on the coasts. Their threat to the British came not so much from raiding but from the sanctuary they could provide to other escaped slaves. In the early eighteenth century, the British and maroons fought to a stalemate, leading to a treaty that allowed the

maroon communities

Self-governing communities of escaped slaves common in the early modern Caribbean and in coastal areas of Central and South America.

---

*Richard Ligon, *A True and Exact History of the Island of Barbadoes* (London: Parker and Guy, 1673), p. 47.

maroons autonomy in exchange for the promise that they would hunt, capture, and return future runaways.

Even when Africans had to resign themselves to their fate as plantation slaves, covert resistance was possible. Slowing down and subverting the work process was common, even where the risk of the whip was ever present.

Religion is perhaps the area where Africans could best resist the psychological and spiritual torments of enslavement without risking flight or outright rebellion. Where Africans were greatest in number, their religious practices showed the strongest continuity. In both Brazil and Cuba, for example, Africans (like the Amerindians of Mesoamerica) merged their existing beliefs with Christianity. In both colonies the *orisas* (or-EE-shahs), gods of the Yoruba (yaw-roo-bah) people (of present-day western Nigeria), were transformed into Catholic saints. The illustration on this page shows Xàngó (CHAN-go) the Yoruba deity of fire, thunder, and lightning, who was especially venerated. The illustration also shows Naná Buruku (supreme creator and mother of the spirits of the sun and moon) and Oxala Oxalufan (a wizened elder representing peace and tranquility).

In areas where Africans were a smaller percentage of the population, as in most of British North America, European cultural influences were more dominant. But religion allowed self-assertion here as well. While white Christians preached obedience now and rewards in the afterlife, slaves sung hymns of liberation and focused on biblical stories relevant to their plight, such as that of Moses leading his enslaved people to freedom.

Equiano's life story shows us an unusual strategy of escape from slavery: working within the system. His freedom came about through a combination of good fortune and business acumen. He was fortunate that his final owner was a

African Gods in the Americas West African gods still worshiped in the Americas include Naná Buruku, Oxala Oxalufan, and Xàngó invoked for his physical power and bravery. These West African *orisas* appear as *santos*, or saints, in the hybrid Christian-African religions of *Santeria* (from Cuba) and *Candomblé* (originating in Brazil). Santeria and Candomblé follow the African tradition of recognizing the special spiritual qualities of women. Their priestesses are especially attuned to possession by divine spirits and serve as conduits of communication with them.

NANÁ BURUKU

Gil Abelha

OXALÁ - OXALUFAN

Gil Abelha

XÀNGÓ

Gil Abelha

member of the Society of Friends, called Quakers, who had strong doubts about whether Christians should own slaves. This master agreed that if he could repay the money of his purchase, Equiano would have his freedom, and he allowed Equiano to trade on his own account in his spare time to make that possible. In 1767, having surprised his master by saving the required amount, Equiano returned to England, which he regarded as his home. Still, he frequently went back to sea, even joining an unsuccessful voyage to the North Pole. He worked as a hairdresser for the London elite and learned to play the French horn. When they had the chance, free blacks like Equiano explored the many possibilities of the interconnected Atlantic world.

manumission

The voluntary freeing of slaves by their masters.

In some places, the freeing of slaves, or **manumission**, was encouraged as an act of Christian charity. Of course, those most likely to be freed were women, children, and the elderly, though in in colonial Latin America the church did encourage manumission. Moreover, in the Spanish Americas all persons were assumed to be free unless proven otherwise, so black men who escaped their masters and moved far enough away had a good chance of "passing" as free men.

In British North America, in contrast, manumission was rare and legal codes made little distinction between free blacks and slaves. Here the equation between skin color and slave status was so strong that free blacks were in a very uncomfortable situation, as Equiano's story of his arrest in Georgia shows:

> *After our arrival we went up to the town of Savannah; and the same evening I went to a friend's house ... a black man. We were very happy at meeting each other .... [A]fter supper ... the watch or patrol came by, and, discerning a light in the house ... came in and sat down, and drank some punch with us.... A little after this they told me I must go to the watch-house with them; this surprised me a good deal after our kindness to them, and I asked them "Why so?" They said, that all Negroes who had a light in their houses after nine o'clock were to be taken into custody, and either pay some dollars or be flogged.**

This was not an isolated incident: on other occasions Equiano's trade goods were confiscated for no reason other than his vulnerability as a black man, and several times he was nearly re-enslaved in spite of the document he always carried with him attesting to his freedom. Thereafter, Equiano avoided Georgia and Carolina altogether.

Effects of the Atlantic Slave Trade on West Africa

As early as the sixteenth century, the Atlantic slave trade had brought conflict to some West African societies, such as the Kongo kingdom (see Chapter 16). Over the next two centuries, as the Caribbean sugar industry dramatically increased the demand for African slaves, the transformative consequences of the Atlantic plantation system became greater and greater for West African social, economic, and military institutions.

---

*Olaudah Equiano, *The Interesting Narrative of the Life of Olaudah Equiano, or Gustavus Vassa, the African*, ed. Vincent Carretta, 2d ed. (New York: Penguin, 2003), p. 158.

Whether African leaders embraced the slave trade as a means of increasing their own wealth and power or sought only to shield their people from its ravages, few escaped its impact.

One society whose leaders participated in the Atlantic slave trade was the rising **Asante kingdom**. Asante was an expanding power in the forest region of eighteenth-century West Africa, and as its rulers pursued their ambitions, their armies took many prisoners. Before the rise of the Atlantic trade, these war captives would have been sent home through prisoner exchanges, redeemed for ransom, or kept as household servants and farm workers. (Only rarely would they be killed; labor was scarce relative to land in most of Africa, so both the productive and reproductive power of men and women were highly prized.) But where war captives had once been a mere byproduct of wars fought for other purposes, now some African leaders, as in Asante, had an added motive for military expansion, including access to valuable imported goods. British slave traders sailed to Cape Coast Castle, one of many coastal fortifications built to facilitate the slave trade, to pay with currency, rum, cloth, and guns for these unfortunate captives.

The kings of **Dahomey** (dah-HOH-mee) were even more aggressive in using the slave trade to advance state interests, trading slaves for guns to build a military advantage over their neighbors. As the prices for slaves rose during the eighteenth century, more and more guns were imported into West Africa. Faced with aggressive neighbors like Dahomey, other African rulers found they too needed to enter the slaves-for-guns trade for their own self-defense. Thus, protecting your own people could leave little choice other than selling people from neighboring societies.

It was a vicious cycle reinforced by differing European and African gender preferences. Europeans preferred to buy young males, since they were destined for hard physical labor. Males therefore fetched the highest prices on the Atlantic market. West African societies, however, preferred female slaves, valuing both their contribution as agricultural and domestic workers and the added fertility they brought to a village or clan: Africans tended to count their wealth in people. Thus leaders of societies like Asante and Dahomey could doubly benefit from the slave trade, exchanging imprisoned men for imported commodities while using captive women for their own social and economic benefit.

The Atlantic slave trade transformed indigenous African slavery in myriad ways. Before the Atlantic system developed, for example, an African parent in desperate circumstances might "pawn" a child to someone with sufficient resources to keep him or her alive. It was a desperate move, but sometimes necessary; no one viewed a pawned child as mere property of his or her master. Rather, the chances were good that the child would be incorporated into the new master's village society.

This common process of incorporating dependent outsiders often took the form of "fictive kinship." Over time, descendants of pawned children or war captives would come to be identified with local lineages and recognized as members of the community. The patrilineal nature of most African societies, where a child inherits the lineage status of his or her father, helped that process along. It meant that a child born from a slave mother and a man of full lineage status would become a member of the father's lineage, and thus would be accepted as a full member of the community. Such African practices stood in contrast to the situation in the Americas, where European masters seldom acknowledged responsibility for their own slave-borne offspring.

Asante kingdom
(ca. 1700–1896) A rising state in eighteenth-century West Africa in the rainforest region of what is now Ghana. Asante's wars of expansion produced prisoners who were often sold into the Atlantic slave circuit.

Dahomey
(ca. 1650–1894) African kingdom in present-day southern Benin, reaching its height of influence in the eighteenth century. Its leaders sought regional power by raiding for slaves in other kingdoms and selling them for firearms and European goods.

Armed Women with the King at their Head, plate II from "The History of Dahomey" by Archibald Dalzel, engraved by Francis Chesham (1749–1806) pub. 1793 (engraving), Norris, Robert (d.1791) (after)/Private Collection/The Stapleton Collection/The Bridgeman Art Library

Armed Dahomey Female Warriors Dahomey was a rising West African power in the eighteenth century, infamous for its militarism and systematic use of the slave trade to secure the weapons needed to expand its power. Dahomey was also known for its battalion of fierce and well-trained women soldiers, called *Mino* ("our mothers") in the Fon language, and "Amazons" by Europeans. The *Mino* were accorded high status. Led by female officers, they took on some of the social attributes of men and were not allowed to marry or bear children during their term of service.

African slave raiders profited from the complementary preference of African masters for female slaves and European plantation owners for male ones. Male slaves could be exported, while female captives were more likely to be sold within West Africa's own slave markets. In each case, the fates of their children were likely to be quite different. In Africa, the women's offspring would often be assimilated into the host community; in the Americas assimilation into European society was hardly an option.

● **CONTEXT&CONNECTIONS** Arab societies, like most African ones, are patrilineal, meaning that a child inherits the clan status of his or her father. Children of Arab fathers and slave mothers would thus usually be considered Arabs and full members of the community, a sharp contrast with colonial North American practices. For this reason it is exceptional to find segregated "black" communities in contemporary Arab lands, even though the slave trade between Africa and Arab lands began much earlier than the Atlantic one. ●

As an antislavery activist, Equiano perhaps had an interest in downplaying the negative aspects of indigenous slavery. But he addresses the issue of slavery in Africa in a forthright way, whether the account is based on his own childhood memories or on accounts he had heard from other slaves:

> *Each master of a family has a large square of ground.... Within this are his houses to accommodate his family and slaves; which, if numerous, frequently cause these tenements to present the appearance of a village.**

In such a village, where there was so little physical distance between master and slave, where conditions of housing and diet were relatively equal, and where the ability to exploit the labor of slaves carried with it a responsibility to protect them, there was little chance that the type of chattel slavery characteristic of the American plantation could ever develop. But the transformation of West African systems of slavery under the impact of the Atlantic trade is suggested by a passage from the *Interesting Narrative* where Equiano, being taken to the coast, is purchased by an African master, a wealthy widow whose *"house and premises were the finest I ever saw in Africa."* Equiano sketches the traditional practice of incorporating outsiders:

> *When mealtime came, I was led into the presence of my mistress, and ate and drank before her with her son. That filled me with astonishment; and I could scarcely avoid expressing my surprise that the young gentleman should suffer me, who was bound, to eat with him who was free.... Indeed everything here, and their treatment of me, made me forget that I was a slave. The language of these people resembled ours so nearly, that we understood each other perfectly. They had also the very same customs as we.... In this resemblance to my former happy state, I passed about two months; and now I began to think I was to be adopted into the family....**

As in times past, his new mistress could have kept the young man, and by marriage he and his descendants would likely have become integrated into that society. However, by this time traditional systems had been transformed under the influence of the Atlantic trade. His new mistress now had the option of selling him for cash; in Equiano's account, she sold him back into the slave export channel that led to the coast.

As warfare increased, the resulting climate of insecurity often enabled warrior chieftains to gather followers, with sharper political hierarchies reflecting greater inequality. African merchants and political leaders who traded in slaves thus gained power and status. Traditional institutions could be corrupted as a result, as when judges near Equiano's home region were corrupted by the slave trade, abusing their authority to banish wrongdoers in order to benefit from the slave trade. In such ways, on scales large and small, the Atlantic market transformed traditional institutions.

---

*Olaudah Equiano, *The Interesting Narrative of the Life of Olaudah Equiano, or Gustavus Vassa, the African*, ed. Vincent Carretta, 2d ed. (New York: Penguin, 2003), pp. 36, 52–53.

By the later eighteenth century, as more African states came to rely on slaves not just as commodities for export but also as soldiers and laborers, some African "societies with slaves" started to become "slave societies" where slavery became essential to the functioning of state and society. While this intensification of slavery under the influence of the Atlantic trade enhanced the power of some Africans, by far the biggest political and economic advantages went to European slave traders and plantation owners.

● **CONTEXT&CONNECTIONS** Ironically, abolitionism was one of the main arguments used by Europeans to justify their partition of Africa during the *New Imperialism* (Chapter 26) of the late nineteenth century. In their "scramble for Africa," European societies might justify their military invasions and often brutal colonial occupations by claiming the need to eliminate conditions of slavery, conditions that their own nations had originally helped to create. ●

Some historians have warned that we should not exaggerate the impact of the Atlantic slave trade on continental Africa. It is true that some African societies were still part of trans-Saharan and Red Sea commercial networks with slave markets of long standing (see Map 19.2). It is also true that many African societies had no connection at all with external slave markets. Despite the Atlantic slave trade, farming and herding remained the principal economic activities in Africa.

However, on a continent where land was plentiful but people were scarce, the loss of population through the export of slaves harmed economic growth. Europe and Asia experienced surges in population during the eighteenth century, due in large part to the introduction of productive new food crops from the Americas. While such crops were introduced in Africa as well, the total population of the African continent remained stagnant, strongly suggesting that the large-scale export of slaves had a deeply damaging effect on Africa's overall economic productivity.

Europe and the Atlantic World, 1650–1807

By the eighteenth century, the Atlantic Ocean was awash with people, goods, plants, animals, diseases, religious and political ideas, and cultural forms such as music and storytelling traditions, all circulating freely among Europe, Africa, and the Americas. The Atlantic world emerged as a transcultural zone where enterprising adventurers, even former slaves like Olaudah Equiano, sought their fortunes. Meanwhile, Britain and France—now surpassing the Spanish, Portuguese, and Dutch as the world's dominant naval powers—were locked in nearly constant conflict.

triangular trade

The network of interchange among Europe, Africa, and the colonial Americas. Consisted of raw materials and agricultural produce sent from the Americas to Europe; manufactures sent to Africa and used for the purchase of slaves; and slaves exported from Africa to the Americas.

Economic and Military Competition in the Atlantic Ocean, 1650–1763

The economic exchange among Europe, Africa, and the Americas is often called the **triangular trade**, which refers to the movement of manufactured goods from Europe to Africa, of African humanity to the Americas, and of colonial products such as sugar, tobacco, and timber back to Europe (see Map 19.2).

The image of a triangular trade is convenient, but it simplifies the global dimensions of world trade in this period. For example, Indian Ocean trade

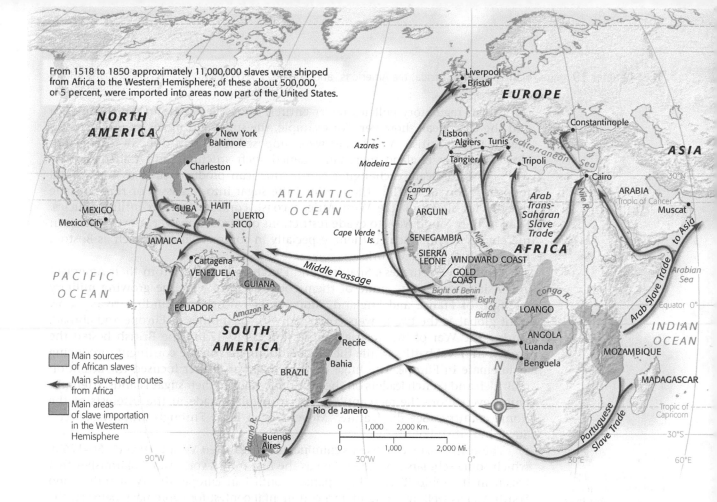

From 1518 to 1850 approximately 11,000,000 slaves were shipped from Africa to the Western Hemisphere; of these about 500,000, or 5 percent, were imported into areas now part of the United States.

Map 19.2 The Atlantic Slave Trade The Middle Passage from Africa to the Americas was the greatest forced migration in human history. The vast majority of the Africans who lived through it were put to work on Caribbean islands or coastal plantations. The Arab trade in African slaves, across the Sahara Desert and the Indian Ocean, was much older, but at no time matched the scale of the Atlantic trade.

networks connected to Atlantic networks whenever Indian cotton textiles, paid for in American silver, were exported to Africa, Europe, and the Americas. In West Africa, the use of cowrie shells from the Indian Ocean as currency (imported in enormous quantities and frequently used in African sculpture as well) also shows that trade links were not simply triangular but interoceanic. The Atlantic system was part of an emerging global economy.

Competition for commercial ascendency inevitably led to military conflict in an age when the concept of international free trade had not yet developed. Instead of believing that everyone could benefit from open markets, Europeans saw economic exchange as a zero sum game, one where enriching your own nation meant beggaring your neighbor. That is why all the major trading nations followed policies of economic **mercantilism**, regulating colonial trade by restricting colonial producers, merchants, and shippers as much as possible to the home country's own markets. Thus, for instance, New England merchants were officially prohibited from trading in the French West Indies, even if they saw good market opportunities.

mercantilism

Dominant economic theory in seventeenth- and eighteenth-century Europe that emphasized the role of international economics in interstate competition. Under mercantilism, restrictive tariffs were placed on imports to raise their prices, maximize the country's exports, and build up supplies of gold and silver bullion for military investment

British regulatory policies never entirely controlled trade in North America and the Caribbean, however. For example, the sugar and molasses produced on islands in the British West Indies were supposed to be sent directly to England. However, New England merchants defied such strictures and traded directly with the Caribbean, exchanging North American products such as timber and foodstuffs for sugar. They then refined the sugar into molasses or rum to trade directly for slaves on the West African coast, contrary to mercantilist policies. Even as they found ways to evade restrictions on trade, however, North American merchants deeply resented them, especially in commercial cities such as Boston, Philadelphia, and New York.

While the Portuguese, Spanish, and Dutch still profited from their American and Asian possessions, none of them could keep up with the growing military strength of France and England, monarchies whose longstanding rivalry now went global as the two powers competed with each other in Europe and abroad. During the War of the Austrian Succession (1740–1748), the British bested the French in naval battles, while the French dominated on the continent, producing a stalemate in Europe. The huge costs of that war further focused the attention of British and French leaders on the economic value of their sugar islands, strengthening even more the mercantilist urge to regulate trade in the interests of the home country. (See the feature "Movement of Ideas Through Primary Sources: Sugar in British Politics.")

These Anglo-French tensions culminated in the **Seven Years' War** (1756–1763), which some scholars have identified as the first truly "world war." Skirmishes that began in the Ohio River Valley sparked conflict in Europe, the West Indies, and South Asia as well, resulting in a tri-continental contest for supremacy between the British and the French that involved alliances with societies as disparate and widely scattered as the Iroquois, Prussians, and Bengalis.

A major turning point in North America was the successful British siege of Louisburg at the mouth of the St. Lawrence River, gateway to New France. Thirteen year-old Olaudah Equiano, still the property of a Royal Navy officer, was there:

> The engagement now commenced with great fury on both sides: [the French ship] immediately returned our fire and we continued engaged with each other for some time; during which I was frequently stunned with the thundering of the great guns, whose dreadful contents burned many of my companions into eternity.*

British victory in this engagement soon led to the conquest of Québec and all of New France, giving Britain a dominant position in North America. At the same time, victories in India were positioning the British for eventual mastery over South Asia (see Chapter 20).

Meanwhile, the Seven Years' War added to tensions between the British crown and American colonists. Having spent a huge sum to defend the colonies from France, the British thought Americans should now help pay for their own defense. But new taxes and restrictions on trade soon prompted the colonists to seek independence (see Chapter 22).

Seven Years' War (1756–1763) Fought simultaneously in Europe, the West Indies, North America, and South Asia, this war shifted the balance of power between Britain and France in favor of the British, making their influence paramount in India and Canada.

---

*Olaudah Equiano, *The Interesting Narrative of the Life of Olaudah Equiano, or Gustavus Vassa, the African*, ed. Vincent Carretta, 2d ed. (New York: Penguin, 2003), p. 83.

● **CONTEXT&CONNECTIONS** In the wake of the Seven Years' War, the British lost one empire and gained another. Just when the movement was stirring for independence in the American colonies, the British were displacing the *Mughals* (Chapters 16 and 20) as the dominant power in India. Historians thus refer to a "second British empire" to mark the transition from North America to South Asia as the center of late-eighteenth-century British imperial activity. By the nineteenth century, India was the "jewel in the crown" of the British empire, the most expansive the world had ever seen (see Chapter 24). ●

Life on the Eighteenth-Century Atlantic Ocean

Rimming the Atlantic, and manning the ships that transported goods and people around it, were a multitude of uprooted people. Olaudah Equiano, who spent almost half his life aboard ship, was familiar with the turbulent mass of humanity that made its living from the sea: slave traders, cod fishermen, pirates, and officers and crew fighting for king and country. Violence was common. Some were desperate enough to volunteer for life at sea; others were forced into it. Press gangs stalked the English coast looking for a chance to seize the able-bodied and force them onto British ships chronically short of sailors, a situation that Equiano and many others saw as akin to slavery.

Life aboard ship was rough. Sailors had no privacy, and discipline was tight. Captains had to be alert or they might lose control of their crews and face a mutiny. *"A ship is worse than a jail,"* stated one writer. *"There is, in a jail, better air, better company, better convenience of every kind; and a ship has the additional disadvantage of being in danger."*

Nevertheless, Equiano, *"being still of a roving disposition"* after he gained his liberty, never stayed for more than a few years on dry land. Life at sea offered opportunity for an ambitious soul from a poor background. Military prowess, acumen in trade, and seamanship all required competence, and life at sea rewarded ability, in contrast to most of British life, where ancestry and social class held sway. Even as a young slave, Equiano was able to earn a promotion to the rank of "able seaman" for his service during the Seven Years' War, making him eligible for a payment from the crown at war's end. Equiano equated that promotion with status as a freeman, so he was exceptionally bitter when his owner, who was also his commanding officer, not only pocketed his pension but also sold him to a new master. Still, life at sea gave Equiano his greatest opportunities.

● **CONTEXT&CONNECTIONS** One strength of the British navy was its relative openness to promotion based on merit rather than (as in the army) on social standing or aristocratic background. During Equiano's lifetime, for example, Captain *James Cook* (1728–1779) (Chapter 21) was becoming one of the nation's most capable naval officers. The son of a farmer, Cook rose through the ranks on the basis of his leadership abilities and navigational expertise to become one of the empire's most famous men. ●

The Atlantic Ocean also represented opportunities for fishermen, who pulled enormous hauls of cod from the **Grand Banks** off the coast of Newfoundland. Basque fisherman first discovered this area in medieval times, and salted cod had become a staple of the Mediterranean diet. By the eighteenth century, ships from many nations were exploiting this rich source of protein, which once cured was easily stored and transported.

Grand Banks

Fishing area located south and southeast of present-day Newfoundland, Canada. Noted for its immense quantities of cod, a source of protein for the residents in and around the Atlantic and of large profits for British colonial traders.

Sugar in British Politics

In the mid-eighteenth century, West Indian sugar was the most profitable resource in the British empire, with small islands like Jamaica and Barbados generating huge revenues. Plantation owners were not the only beneficiaries, as we see in this *Letter to a Member of Parliament* from 1745. The question had to do with how much the British government should tax sugar at the point of its arrival in England, that is, how high the "duty" should be. The huge profits that the sugar industry generated made a tempting target for a government trying to raise revenue to fight its increasingly expensive wars with France. The letter was published anonymously, meaning that the publisher was most likely trying to influence public opinion against a rise in the sugar tax, which the author warns would do more harm than good.

> ❯ What arguments does the author use against an increase in the sugar tax? How does the document show how closely sugar had become tied up with British economic, political, and military policies by the mid-eighteenth century?

Source: *A Letter to a Member of Parliament, Concerning the Importance of our Sugar-Colonies to Great Britain, by a Gentleman, who resided many Years in the Island of Jamaica* (London: J. Taylor, 1745). Spelling modernized.

From *A Letter to a Member of Parliament, Concerning the Importance of our Sugar-Colonies*

In the first place, I will endeavour to convince you, that whatever additional duty shall be laid on sugar, it will be at the cost of the sugar planter....

Secondly, I shall show, that such an additional duty will be an oppression and discouragement and an unequal load upon our sugar colonies at this juncture especially, and will render abortive the very scheme itself which is intended by it, of advancing the revenue. And,

Thirdly, I shall set forth the great advantages that this nation receives from the sugar colonies, and especially from the island of Jamaica, and the great advantages that it will continue to receive, if due encouragement be given to the sugar planter....

Now the case of the sugar planter is, that he is at a prodigious distance from the market ... and being already in debt, as the greatest number of the sugar planters are, and having already established his sugar works ... he must be ruined if those are not kept employed....

We have no foreign market worth notice, but Holland and Hamburg, and ... the Dutch will buy the French sugar, at the French colonies at a low price, and carry it securely to Holland in their own ships. And it is well known that the French at their colonies can and do sell their sugar much cheaper than we can in our colonies, because they have better sugar land in their islands, and nearer the seaside than we have....

[T]he sugar planter is [now] at a vast deal greater expense to make sugar.... His Negro slaves ... were sold at Jamaica at £35 per head [but now cost] £50 per head.... The sugar planter pays double the freight for his sugar home than he did before ... and double the freight out for all his utensils for making sugar, and all his furniture for his house use and family, and slaves....

[U]nless the price of sugar here at market do advance very considerably, the sugar planter can't go on, but will be ruined. If the planter, to all his other advanced charges, hath a further duty laid upon his commodity, he will be disabled from purchasing every year a fresh supply of Negroes, mules, and cattle; and as his present stock drops off, he will disabled from making the quantity of sugar he does at present ... by which means the scheme for raising more money upon that commodity, by advancing the duty, will be rendered abortive....

The principal charge which the sugar planter is at, to raise and carry on his work, is Negroes; and those are purchased in Africa by the English merchants, chiefly with the produce and manufactures of this nation, such as woolen goods.... At the same time that they are purchasing the Negroes on the coast of Africa, with those cargoes of British manufactures, they purchase also a great deal of gold, elephants' teeth, and some very valuable dying woods....

For strength to carry on his sugar work, next to the negroes, the planter must be furnished with mules, cattle, horses, etc. Of cattle the most part are raised in the colonies; some horses are raised in the colonies and some are supplied from North America.... [His equipment] ... will cost him at least 500 pounds. Add to this, the great quantity of nails, locks, hinges, bolts, and other sorts of iron ware; and lead that he must have for his buildings. And for his field work he must have great quantities of bills, hoes, axes, iron chains; also gear for his mill and his cattle ... and all this of English manufacture....

Besides this extraordinary expense ... he must have a house to live in, and furniture, and clothes, and other necessaries for himself and family, servants and slaves. To build his house he must have materials from England ... and his furniture and clothing entirely from England....

And for their food, they have a great deal, as cheese, bacon, pickles, some flour and biscuits, when cheap, and beer, ale and cider, in great quantities from England; salted beef and butter from Ireland; and salted fish, flour, biscuits and sundry other kinds of provisions for their negroes from North America.

There are in the island of Jamaica only, a hundred thousand negroes, a few more or less; every one of these ... do make use of the value of twenty shillings a year, in goods from England. In clothing they make use of a vast quantity of Manchester goods ... and many other implements, all of British manufacture. I believe ... it amounts to a hundred thousand pounds a year in British manufactures, consumed by the negroes in Jamaica only.

And now, Sir, if you'll be pleased to take a view of the whole process of the sugar manufacture, from the beginning to the time of delivering the commodity into the hands of the consumer; that is to say, from purchasing the negroes on the coast of Africa, and transporting them to the West Indies ... I am sure that you will be amazed to consider, what a prodigious number of ships, of sailors, of merchants, of trades-men, manufacturers, mechanics, and laborers, are continually employed, and reap a profit thereby....

And should the sugar colonies be so much discouraged, by the laying on of an additional duty ... you see plainly how very much our trade and navigation, and how many of our manufactures would be affected by it, and that would not be the worst of it [because] in proportion as our sugar colonies should decline, those of our neighbours, our enemies and rivals in trade and navigation would advance.

In New England, fishing became a symbol of proud independence and prosperity, symbolized by the "Sacred Cod," a wooden cod effigy still hanging in the Massachusetts State House. Men with little property but a strong work ethic could make a good living working the Grand Banks or specializing in the abundant oysters and lobsters closer to shore. New England's fishing profits, however, were connected to slavery. Merchants often bought molasses in the Caribbean with the lowest quality salted cod, used as a cheap source of protein. Thus, while cod fishing might instill an independent spirit in New England, it also provided plantation owners with a cheap way to feed captives in the West Indies and helped finance the slave trade. In the Atlantic world, slavery and freedom were two sides of the same coin.

Abolition of the British Slave Trade, 1772–1807

In 1775, now a free man, Olaudah Equiano worked as a plantation supervisor on the Central American coast. Equiano did not seem to mind, and when the job was over he even congratulated himself on a job well done: *"All my poor countrymen, the slaves, when they heard of my leaving them were very sorry, as I had always treated them with care and affection, and did everything I could to comfort the poor creatures."**

Equiano seemed to imply that slavery could be made humane. Over the next decade, however, he came to believe that slavery was inherently evil and needed to be abolished. His change in thinking was partly an outcome of deepening religious conviction. After surviving a shipwreck, Equiano joined the Methodist movement, whose founder had argued that slavery was incompatible with Christian morality. *"O, ye nominal Christians!"* Equiano wrote, *"Might not an African ask you, 'learned you this from your God, who says unto you, Do unto all men as you would men should do unto you?'"** Throughout the 1780s, more and more British Christians raised their voices in opposition to slavery. Though the slave owners and slave traders formed a powerful lobby in the British Parliament, public opinion was turning against them. (See the feature "Visual Evidence in Primary Sources: The Horrors of the Middle Passage.")

Apart from Christian conscience, other factors aided the antislavery **abolitionist** cause. In 1772, a judge had ruled that no slave, once he or she reached England, could be compelled to return to a colony where slavery was practiced. Essentially, this meant that the condition of slavery had no legal basis in British law, reflecting the pride that Britons felt in their tradition of "liberty," constitutionally guaranteed by the Bill of Rights of 1689 (see Chapter 17). But the British constitution also protected property rights. The crux of the debate was which rights should take precedence: those of a slave owner to property for which he had paid, or those of the slave to his own person?

To make the case for the superior claim of liberty over property, British abolitionists invoked public opinion. One way to make the issue more tangible for people in England was to focus on the link between their own sugar consumption, by far the highest in the world, and the evils of slavery. In his poem "Poor Africans," William Cowper wrote:

> *I pity them greatly, but I must be mum,*
> *For how could we do without sugar and rum?*
> *Especially sugar, so needful we see,*
> *What, give up our desserts, our coffee and tea?*

Abolitionist boycotts helped win the debate at the breakfast table, as more Britons came to see slavery not as something distant and abstract, but as an evil in which they personally participated by consuming slave-grown sugar.

Equiano intended his *Interesting Narrative* to be part of this accelerating abolitionist campaign. Like many authors at this time, he advertised for

abolitionist

A man or woman who advocated an end to the practice of slavery. In the late eighteenth century, a powerful abolitionist movement grew in England.

---

*Olaudah Equiano, *The Interesting Narrative of the Life of Olaudah Equiano, or Gustavus Vassa, the African*, ed. Vincent Carretta, 2d ed. (New York: Penguin, 2003), pp. 211, 61.

subscribers who would pay in advance and receive their copies once the book was written and printed. Subscriptions were a way for people to support causes they believed in. The subscribers to Equiano's book included major antislavery campaigners such as Thomas Clarkson, who wrote a university essay on the theme "Is enslaving others against their will ever justified?" and devoted himself to the abolitionist cause; Josiah Wedgwood, the highly successful ceramics entrepreneur (see Chapter 23) who designed a best-selling plate featuring the image of an African in chains saying *"Am I Not a Man and a Brother?"*; and William Wilberforce, the member of Parliament who took the abolitionist cause to the House of Commons.

After the publication of the *Interesting Narrative* in 1789, Equiano spent three years touring England, Scotland, and Ireland speaking at antislavery meetings. He was hugely successful in advancing the cause of abolitionism while doing well for himself financially. Book royalties made him the wealthiest black man in England, and when he married an English wife in 1792 her family income moderately increased his property. Proud of his new status as a married man, he announced the marriage in the new edition of his *Interesting Narrative*.

As he began an English family, Equiano remained politically active. Wilberforce had decided to press for abolition only of the slave trade, not of the condition of slavery itself. This more limited agenda had a better chance in Parliament, since many members thought it was permissible to stop slaves from being seized and transported but not for the government to strip slave owners of their property, even when that property consisted of human beings.

The British abolitionist cause, while largely religiously inspired, was also stimulated by eighteenth-century Enlightenment philosophies stressing rational thought and the quest for human liberty (see Chapter 22). The Scottish free-market economist Adam Smith, for example, argued that slavery, by preventing the negotiation of free labor contracts, distorted economies and undermined growth. And it was French thinkers who were most influential in developing the concept of *"liberty, equality, and fraternity"* as a universally applicable ideal (see Chapters 21 and 22). However, the extreme radicalism of the French Revolution, including the execution of the French king, led the British government to look on political reform with deep suspicion. Equiano even removed the names of some of his more radical subscribers from the *Interesting Narrative* to avoid guilt by association.

The abolition of the slave trade thus took much longer than its proponents had hoped. Sadly, Equiano was still waiting when he passed away prematurely at the age fifty-two (leaving behind his wife Susanna and daughter Joanna, who inherited his substantial estate).

Finally, in 1807 Parliament passed the **Act for the Abolition of the Slave Trade**, ending the trade in slaves among British subjects. Another whole generation of Africans had to wait before slavery itself was abolished in the British empire, an advance that still did not help slaves in non-British territories such as Cuba, Brazil, and the southern United States. Meanwhile, the British government, with the full backing of public opinion, pursued a global campaign to eliminate slave markets. That was a significant turnabout, considering Britain had benefited more than any other nation from four centuries of the Atlantic slave trade. Meanwhile, millions of Africans had been violently uprooted, while many of those who remained behind suffered from the Atlantic slave trade's legacy of insecurity, warfare, and population decline.

Act for the Abolition of the Slave Trade

Law passed in 1807 by the British Parliament ending the trade in slaves among British subjects. The British government then used the Royal Navy to suppress the slave trade internationally.

The Horrors of the Middle Passage

British abolitionists were well aware of the power of visual images to advance their cause, anticipating that a shocked public would pressure Parliament to end the trade in slaves. Political cartoons were one way to both express and influence public opinion.

The cartoon below refers to the case of a slave trader, Captain John Kimber, who was accused in 1792 of torturing a fifteen-year-old African girl to death when she refused to "dance" for him. ("Dancing" was a required physical activity for slaves when they were

The ABOLITION of the SLAVE TRADE.
Or the Inhumanity of Dealers in human flesh exemplified in Captn. Kimbers treatment of a young Negro Girl of 15 for her Virjin Modesty

Captain Kimber is clearly depicted as being responsible for the abuse of the African girl. He seems to be enjoying himself.

For his portrayal of the victim the artist chose to use dark ink, obscuring her features. What effect does this technique have on the viewer?

The sailor pulling the rope says: "Damn me if I like it I have a good mind to let go." The other two sailors say: "My Eyes Jack our Girls at Wapping are never flogged for their modesty," and "By G-d that's too bad if he had taken her to bed to him it would be well enough. Split me, I'm almost sick of this Black Business."

brought up to the ship's deck for exercise; slave captains routinely enforced that rule with the lash.) Kimber was acquitted, and the sailors who gave evidence against him were convicted of perjury. Abolitionists were outraged and their opponents encouraged by this legal ruling. The title of the illustration reads: "The Abolition of the Slave Trade, or the inhumanity of the dealers in human flesh exemplified in Captn Kimbers treatment of a Young Negro Girl of 15 for her virgin modesty."

The image below, the slave ship *Brooks*, was widely circulated by abolitionists to show (in the words of a modern historian) "that the slaver itself was a place of barbarity, indeed a huge, complex technologically sophisticated instrument of torture."* First

circulated by the Society for Effecting the Abolition of the Slave Trade in 1788, this engraving was widely known across Britain and the United States. Its depiction of a "close packed" slave ship made *"an instantaneous impression of horror upon all who saw it"* according to Thomas Clarkson, the prominent abolitionist who wrote the text that accompanied this image. Clarkson interviewed British sailors in slave ports like Bristol and Liverpool, who told him bloodcurdling stories of inhumanity on ships like the *Brooks*, where, another abolitionist wrote, *"human creatures [were] reduced nearly to the state of being buried alive."* The *Brooks* made ten voyages to Africa between 1781 and 1804, its captains purchasing 5,163 slaves, of whom 4,559 survived the Atlantic crossing. This image of the *Brooks* undoubtedly contributed to the abolition of the British slave trade in 1807.

---

*Marcus Rediker, *The Slave Ship: A Human History* (New York: Viking, 2007), p. 309.

How might these two images have affected viewers differently? Which might have had the greater impact on the abolitionist movement, and why?

Each adult African man aboard the *Brooks* was allocated a plank 6 feet by 16 inches with no more than 2 feet 6 inches of vertical space, too little to allow him to sit up. Not shown are the tubs of excrement that fouled the air in the slave hold.

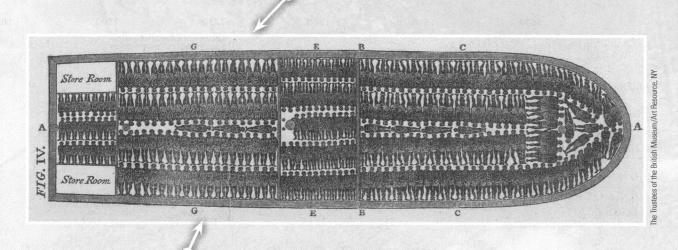

The artist who produced this engraving carefully drew every individual African on board, showing each wearing only a loincloth. Shown here are 482 slaves. On an earlier voyage, before a 1788 law that regulated the slave trade, one *Brooks* captain had crammed 609 Africans in this same space: 351 men, 127 women, 90 boys, and 41 girls.

Atlantic Slavery and the Plantation Complex in World History

The use of massed slave labor on agricultural plantations was part of world history from ancient empires through the final abolition of slavery in Brazil in 1888. Still, the type of slavery Olaudah Equiano experienced, witnessed, and fought against was exceptional in scale: the largest, most intensive, and most profitable plantation slave system ever.

Not all societies treated slaves simply as brute labor. In the Ottoman empire, slaves could rise to positions of significant power even as they suffered constraints on their freedom of movement or endeavor (see Chapter 17). In Africa, as Equiano described it, slaves were often incorporated into the communities of which they became a part, and they tended to lose their disabilities over time. Such "societies with slaves" were quite different from the "slave societies" associated with sugar.

Sugar plantations had relied on massed slave labor even before the rise of the Atlantic slave trade. From ninth-century Arab origins, the plantation complex moved westward into the Mediterranean, fed by slave-trading circuits that extended south into Africa and east toward the Black Sea. The Portuguese then transferred the sugar plantation system to islands offshore of western Africa and across the Atlantic to Brazil, from which it moved into what became the world's most intensive center of production, the West Indies (see Chapter 16).

It was ironic that Europeans were the ones who created the harsher forms of modern slavery associated with brutal plantation work in the Americas. After the fall of the Roman empire, a true "slave society," slavery had virtually disappeared from Europe. The upsurge in Christian religious conviction following the Reformation was making it more difficult to reconcile faith with slavery (see Chapter 17). And it was during the height of the Atlantic slave trade, in the eighteenth century, when Enlightenment ideas of rationality, freedom, and liberty were being developed (see Chapter 21).

Of course, the vast profits to be made by cheaply producing commodities like sugar provided individuals and nations with powerful motives for involvement in the plantation system. From the seventeenth century on, increasingly sophisticated financial mechanisms and maritime technologies had made possible the concentration of resources and the development of global markets necessary for such

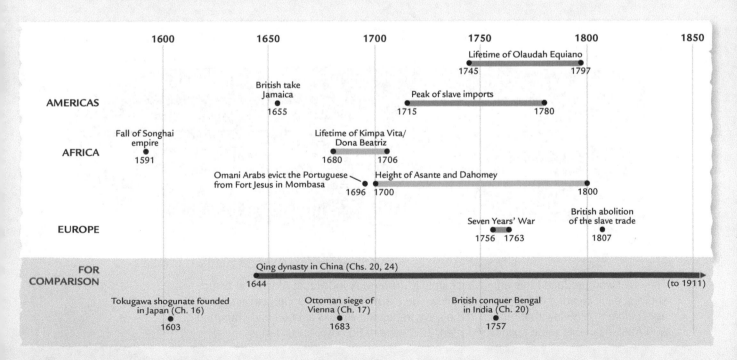

large-scale agro-industrial business operations. At the same time, competition between European states, especially France and Britain, made sustaining plantation profits a matter of great national interest (see Chapter 17).

Then, in the late eighteenth century, the beginnings of the Industrial Revolution, the independence of the United States, and a shift in British priorities toward India all lessened the importance of West Indian sugar (see Chapters 20, 22, and 23). The British, after ending the slave trade in 1807 and outlawing slavery within the British empire in 1834, became global abolitionist campaigners.

In some parts of the world, slavery has continued into the twentieth-first century, but by the 1800s the slave-based plantation complex had come to an end. Brazilian and Caribbean industries declined and new centers of sugar production, such as Hawai'i and Fiji, relied on indentured contract laborers rather than slaves.

For Africa, however, the story was not over, for those who had remained behind had suffered as well. In the short run, African life had become more dangerous and insecure, and in the long run the continent suffered from the lost vitality and productivity of millions of its sons and daughters.

Key Terms

Olaudah Equiano (560)
Great Lakes region (561)
Kimpa Vita (561)
Sahel (562)
Songhai empire (562)
Atlantic plantation system (565)

maroon communities (570)
manumission (572)
Asante kingdom (573)
Dahomey (573)
triangular trade (576)

mercantilism (577)
Seven Years' War (578)
Grand Banks (579)
abolitionist (582)
Act for the Abolition of the Slave Trade (583)

For Further Reference

Anstey, Roger. *The Atlantic Slave Trade and British Abolition, 1760–1810*. New York: Macmillan, 1975.

Blackburn, Robin. *The Making of New World Slavery: From the Baroque to the Modern, 1492–1800*. 2d ed. London: Verso, 2010.

Carretta, Vincent. *Equiano, the African: Biography of a Self-Made Man*. New York: Penguin Books, 2007.

Curtin, Philip. *The Rise and Fall of the Plantation Complex: Essays in Atlantic History*. 2d ed. New York: Cambridge University Press, 1998.

Davis, David Brion. *Inhuman Bondage: The Rise and Fall of Slavery in the New World*. New York: Oxford University Press, 2008.

Eltis, David. *Economic Growth and the Ending of the Trans-Atlantic Slave Trade*. New York: Oxford University Press, 1987.

Klein, Herbert S., and Francisco Vidal Luna. *Slavery in Brazil*. Cambridge: Cambridge University Press, 2009.

Lovejoy, Paul. *Transformations in Slavery: A History of Slavery in Africa*. 3d ed. New York: Cambridge University Press, 2011.

Mintz, Sidney. *Sweetness and Power: The Place of Sugar in Modern History*. New York: Penguin Books, 1985.

Northrup, David. *Africa's Discovery of Europe, 1450–1850*. New York: Oxford University Press, 2002.

Patterson, Orlando. *Slavery and Social Death: A Comparative Study*. Cambridge, Mass.: Harvard University Press, 1985.

Rediker, Marcus. *The Slave Ship: A Human History*. New York: Viking, 2007.

Thornton, John. *A Cultural History of the Atlantic World, 1250–1820*. Cambridge: Cambridge University Press, 2012.

MindTap **MindTap** is a fully online, highly personalized learning experience built upon Cengage Learning content. MindTap combines student learning tools—readings, multimedia, activities, and assessments—into a singular Learning Path that guides students through the course.

Empires in Early Modern Asia, 1650–1837

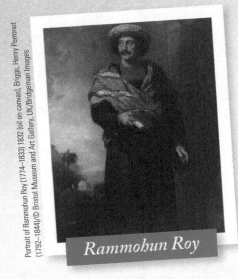

Portrait of Rammohun Roy (1774–1833) 1832 (oil on canvas), Briggs, Henry Perronet (1792–1844)/© Bristol Museum and Art Gallery, UK/Bridgeman Images

Rammohun Roy

During the lifetime of **Rammohun Roy** (1772–1833), South Asia was in transition from Mughal to British rule, and Roy's repertoire of languages reflected the cultural and religious diversity of his environment. His father, though a Hindu, was from a long line of officials serving Muslim rulers in northeastern India; thus, when still a child, Rammohun Roy (rahm-MOH-hoon ROY) added to his native Bengali by studying the court languages of Persian and Arabic. His mother's family included Hindu religious scholars, and since he was a Brahmin—a member of the highest, priestly caste—Roy also learned Sanskrit, the language of their ancient scriptures. As a teenager, he traveled across north India on a quest for knowledge and even, legend has it, debated with Buddhist lamas in Tibet. At age twenty-four he began to learn English, now essential to Bengal's politics and commerce, and found employment with the British East India Company.

Navigating such diversity, Rammohun Roy became a leading figure of the Bengal Renaissance, a rich intellectual encounter between varied spiritual and cultural traditions. As an adult, Roy embraced them all: the graceful Sufi verse of Iranian poets, the complex *Vedanta* literature at the root of Hinduism, and the message of love and forgiveness at the heart of Christianity's New Testament.

Roy was a powerful advocate for a reformed Hinduism. The faith of his ancestors, Roy believed, had degraded through the centuries. Superstition had replaced learning, and barbaric practices, such as burning widows on their husbands' funeral pyres, were thought of as religious rites. In fact, Roy's sister-in-law had been burned alive after the death of his own elder brother. Campaigning to end *suti*, the practice of widow burning, Roy wrote of his opponents:

You, however, consider women devoted to their passions and consequently incapable of acquiring divine knowledge. . . . [T]hey . . . are not allowed to marry again after the death of their

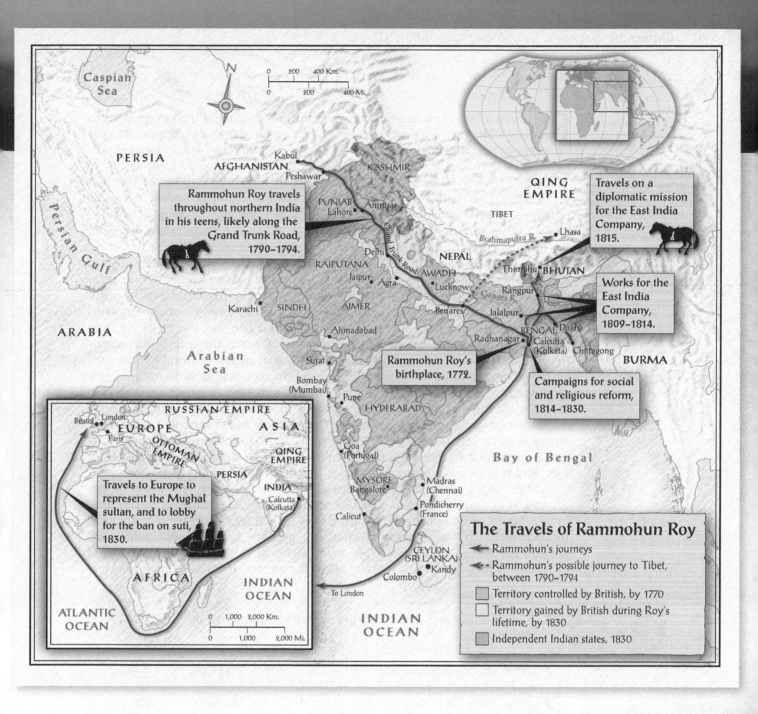

The Travels of Rammohun Roy

Rammohun Roy travels throughout northern India in his teens, likely along the Grand Trunk Road, 1790–1794.

Travels on a diplomatic mission for the East India Company, 1815.

Works for the East India Company, 1809–1814.

Rammohun Roy's birthplace, 1772.

Campaigns for social and religious reform, 1814–1830.

Travels to Europe to represent the Mughal sultan, and to lobby for the ban on suti, 1830.

The Travels of Rammohun Roy

→ Rammohun's journeys

--▶ Rammohun's possible journey to Tibet, between 1790–1794

☐ Territory controlled by British, by 1770

☐ Territory gained by British during Roy's lifetime, by 1830

☐ Independent Indian states, 1830

husbands, and consequently despair at once of all worldly pleasure; hence it is evident that death to these widows is preferable to existence. . . . [Still] to remove every chance of their trying to escape from the blazing fire, in burning them [you] first tie them down to the pile. . . . [But] the faults which you have imputed to women are not implanted in their constitution by nature; it would, therefore, be grossly criminal to sentence them to death. . . . What I lament is, that, seeing the women . . . dependent and exposed

Rammohun Roy
(1772–1833) A leader of the Bengal Renaissance in India who studied the religious texts of Islam, Christianity, and Hinduism for both religious truth and social reform. Roy argued that Hindus should return to their ancient texts, reject polytheism and superstition, and eliminate backward practices such as *suti*, or widow burning.

to every misery, you feel them no compassion, that might even exempt them from being tied down and burnt to death.*

Roy and his fellow reformers were successful in convincing the government to outlaw widow burning; however, when conservative Brahmins appealed to the British king that such a ban would violate their religious customs, Roy traveled to London in 1830 to make sure that the reformist legislation would be upheld.

Before his trip to Britain, the Mughal emperor in Delhi had bestowed upon Roy the title *Raja* ("prince") and asked him to "*bring before the authorities in England certain encroachments on his rights by the East India Company.*"† The Mughals had slipped in power and dignity since the days of Akbar (see Chapter 16): by 1830, the Mughal emperor had to beg the king of England for favors.

In a broader Asian context, the displacement of the Mughals by the British in India was part of a larger pattern of invading forces building larger and more powerful empires. In China, to give another example, Manchu invaders from the north unseated the Ming dynasty to create the Qing (ching) empire, whose emperors controlled not just China but also extensive Central Eurasian territories. As Qing generals and diplomats extended their emperor's influence, they came into increasing contact with emissaries of the expanding Russian empire. Central Eurasia then became the borderland between three powerful empires: British, Russian, and Qing.

Taken together, the expansion of the British and Russian empires showed the increasing influence of Europe in Asian affairs, though Qing China long remained unconcerned with European expansion. The Japanese were even more indifferent. Japanese rulers resisted the eighteenth-century trend toward imperial aggrandizement, consolidating power on their own islands rather than seeking further territory, and rejecting European influence as a matter of state policy.

While taking account of the Japanese exception, this chapter focuses on the expansion of empires from the late seventeenth to the early nineteenth centuries in East, South, and Central Asia. In the process, we will see how imperial leaders had to contend with factors such as changing military technologies, commercial growth, increasing social and religious interactions, expanding population, and ecological change, all of which might affect the success or failure of their policies.

FOCUS QUESTIONS	
❭	How did the Qing emperors build and maintain their empire in East and Central Asia?
❭	What factors drove Russian imperial expansion in the eighteenth century?
❭	What were the principal causes of the decline of Mughal power, and how were the British able to replace the Mughals as the dominant power in South Asia?
❭	What was distinctive about early modern Japanese history?

---

*Raja Rammohun Roy, *The English Works*, vol. 2, ed. Jogendra Chunder Ghose (Calcutta: Srikanta Roy, 1901), pp. 164, 176, 180.

†Raja Rammohun Roy, *The English Works*, vol. 1, ed. Jogendra Chunder Ghose (Calcutta: Srikanta Roy, 1901), p. 319.

The Power of the Qing Dynasty, 1644–1796

By the early seventeenth century, underlying weaknesses had made the Ming dynasty in China vulnerable to invasion and conquest (see Chapter 16). In 1644, armies from Manchuria overran Beijing, deposed the Ming dynasty, and established the Qing dynasty. From 1683 to 1796, just three long-reigning emperors ruled Qing China. It was a time of remarkable political stability, explosive population growth, economic expansion, and intellectual and artistic dynamism. The territory ruled from Beijing expanded to its greatest extent, encompassing parts of Central Asia, Tibet, and the island of Taiwan. Qing emperors ruled China until 1911.

Establishment of Qing Rule, 1636–1661

The Manchu had been nomads who lived on the steppe to the northeast of China beyond the Great Wall (see Map 20.1). By the sixteenth century, under Chinese influence, some Manchu had taken up agriculture; literacy and Confucian philosophy were influencing Manchu society as well.

Ming officials, following a time-honored strategy for maintaining peace along the borders, had earlier bestowed favors on Manchu leaders, such as the right to wear elaborate dragon-patterned robes of silk. The Manchu in turn emulated Chinese-style governance, while maintaining their own language and nomadic traditions such as fighting on horseback and a love of hunting. Then in the 1590s, when the Ming called on Manchu forces to help resist a Japanese invasion, the Manchu armies united under a ruler who declared himself leader of a new **Qing dynasty** and organized his fighters into eight "banners," named for the color of the flags that the different regiments carried in battle. Fifty years later, with Ming authority in sharp decline, some Mongol and Chinese generals switched their allegiance to the Qing, incorporating their units under separate regimental banners. Thus, the banner system allowed Manchu warriors to maintain their separate identity and command structure even while absorbing Chinese and Mongol forces into their armies.

In 1644, after one of China's own rebel armies stormed the capital and the last Ming emperor committed suicide, the Manchu established their power over Beijing and the north. However, Ming holdouts waged fierce battles against Qing forces for decades in the south. The Qing used diplomacy as well as force in dealing with this resistance: adversaries who surrendered were well treated and were incorporated into the banner system. Thus, the Manchu, earlier regarded by the Chinese as "barbarians," became masters of China itself.

To legitimize the new dynasty, Qing rulers maintained Confucianism as the official state ideology. They also retained the examination system and the Chinese system of ministries, assigning one Chinese and one Manchu official to each. The Chinese scholar-officials had the requisite knowledge and experience, but the Manchu officials, thought to be more loyal, were there to supervise the work. In their quest for legitimacy, Qing emperors stressed the continuities between their own rule and great empires of the past.

Carefully guarding their Manchu language and identity, however, the Manchu never fully assimilated into Chinese culture. Intermarriage between Manchu and Han Chinese was forbidden. (The term *Han Chinese*, which derives from an early Chinese dynasty, is used to differentiate Chinese people from other ethnic groups

Qing dynasty (1644–1911) Sometimes called the Manchu dynasty after the Manchurian origins of its rulers. The Qing (meaning "brilliant") extended their rule from Beijing as far as Mongolia and Tibet.

in China.) Qing emperors spent their summers at the great palace of Chengde (chung-deh), beyond the Great Wall, where horsemanship, hunting, and camping were reminders of nomadic life. And the Manchu continued to practice the distinctive Tibetan form of Buddhism, which aligned them more fully with their Central Eurasian subjects than with their Chinese ones.

At the same time, the Manchu made few efforts to impose their culture on Chinese subjects. One exception was a decree that all men had to cut their hair in the distinctive Manchu style, called a *queue* (kyoo), with a shaved forehead and a single long braid in back. Chinese men reluctantly complied with the Manchu order: *"Keep your head, lose your hair. Keep your hair, lose your head."*

Map 20.1 The Qing Empire, 1644–1783 Beginning from their homeland in the north, the Manchu rulers of the Qing dynasty not only conquered China but also built an empire stretching far into Central Asia, matching the contemporary expansion of the Russian empire. The Qing empire grew to more than twice the size of its Ming predecessor. Tibetans, Mongols, and other subject peoples were ruled indirectly through local authorities allied to the Qing emperors. China's contemporary rulers use this map to reject calls for autonomy by western peoples such as Tibetans and Uighurs.

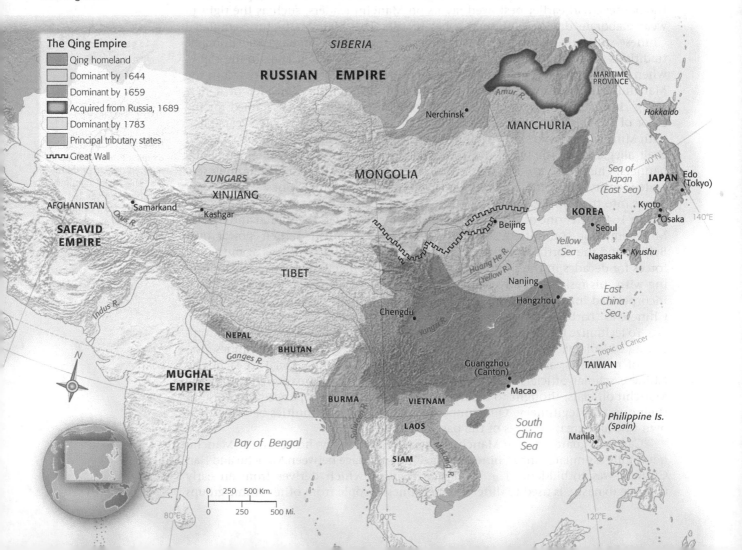

The Age of Three Emperors, 1661–1796

The success of the Qing emperors in retaining their own culture while earning the cooperation and loyalty of Han Chinese subjects found expression in the social, economic, and intellectual achievements of the late seventeenth and eighteenth centuries. When **Emperor Kangxi** (r. 1662–1722) ascended the Dragon Throne in 1662, the fate of the Qing was still in doubt. However, by 1683, he had successfully suppressed Ming resistance and annexed their last redoubt, the island of Taiwan. To military affairs, Kangxi brought knowledge of making cannons and the mathematics necessary for their effective deployment, which he learned from Jesuit tutors as a young man. Six decades of Kangxi's rule established the Qing as masters of one of the greatest empires the world had ever known. His successors Yongzheng (r. 1723–1735) and Qianlong (r. 1736–1796) consolidated that achievement. Together, these three emperors ruled for more than 130 years.

Though Kangxi retained his ancestral culture and spoke Manchu with his family and close confidantes, he studied the Chinese classics deeply and presented himself as a sage Confucian ruler. At the pinnacle of the imperial bureaucracy, he oversaw tremendous economic expansion. Confucians believed that land and agriculture are the source of wealth and that a large population is a sign of prosperity. Farmers improved agricultural productivity by planting American crops like peanuts, potatoes, and maize in previously marginal areas. China's population boomed, surging past 400 million by 1800, another important outcome of the Columbian exchange (see Chapter 15). Meanwhile, American ingredients like chili peppers transformed Chinese cuisine, and tobacco became a daily ritual for many.

Kangxi's successor, the Yongzheng (YOHNG-jung) emperor, promoted an empirical form of Confucianism based on critical examination of sources. Yongzheng then encouraged scholars to gather data in minute detail from across the empire, and compiled an 800,000-page encyclopedia, by far the largest such reference work in the world. By ordering a thorough census of landholdings and basing rural taxation on updated land registers, Yongzheng both increased state revenue through more efficient tax collection and spread the tax burden more equitably between commoners and gentry.

During the long reign of the **Qianlong** (r. 1736–1796) emperor, the power of Qing China reached its height. Coming to the throne as a young man, Qianlong (chee-YEN-loong) ruled for sixty years before abdicating: true to Confucian ideals of filial piety, he did not want his reign to exceed that of his grandfather, Kangxi. During these six decades the commercial economy became even more dynamic. Mainstays of production were luxury goods for export, especially silk and porcelain. Vast quantities of silver from Japan and Spanish America continued to flow into Qing China, financing public works as well as private investment. For some farmers, tobacco became a profitable addition to their fields. Artisans and small-scale entrepreneurs expanded the glass-making, brewing, and coal-mining industries. Thus, eighteenth-century China retained its long-established position as the largest industrial economy in the world.

The World of Women in Qing China

Cotton textile production emerged as a major commercial industry around the city of Nanjing in the lower **Yangzi River Valley**. Unlike silk, cotton cloth was affordable for all but the poorest Chinese consumers

Emperor Kangxi
(r. 1662–1722) One of the most powerful and long-ruling emperors in Chinese imperial history, who extended the Qing empire, expanded the economy, and cultivated an image as a Confucian scholar and sage.

Qianlong
(r. 1736–1796) Qing emperor who ruled during the empire's greatest territorial expansion and prosperity. Late in his reign, corruption began to infect the state bureaucracy. Rejected an English attempt to establish diplomatic relations.

Yangzi River Valley
Agriculturally productive region with the important urban center of Nanjing. The Yangzi River Delta was the site of strong industrial and commercial growth in the eighteenth century.

China: The 4th Qing Emperor Kangxi (1654–1722) at his writing desk. His temple name was Shengzu. He is considered one of China's greatest emperors./Pictures From History/Bridgeman Images

Kangxi: Emperor and Scholar The Emperor Kangxi was careful to model his image on that of China's Confucian "sage rulers" to secure the loyalty of Han Chinese scholar-officials. Kangxi was in fact a dedicated scholar with deep knowledge of the Confucian classics. At the same time, however, he emphasized his fealty to the Tibetan form of Buddhism to secure the loyalty of his Central Eurasian subjects.

and had the advantages of being comfortable, durable, and easy to clean. Traditionally, women produced textiles in China; the expansion of the cotton industry reinforced those traditions.

All Chinese women were expected to work with their hands. Wealthy women, not expected to contribute to the household income, often produced beautiful embroideries. For rural women, tending silkworms and spinning silk thread were admired accomplishments that had the additional virtue of providing income. A traditional adage summed up the division of labor: *"Men plow, women weave."** Spinning and weaving cotton within the household meshed neatly with traditions, and in commercialized regions such as the Yangzi (yang-zuh) delta, these activities drove economic growth.

Chinese women did not receive much benefit from this work. Upon marriage young women left their own families to join their husband's household, where they were subject to their husband's authority and often at the mercy of demanding mothers-in-law. Chinese widows, especially those without sons, were especially vulnerable to neglect and abuse (though their plight was perhaps not as extreme as that of the widows Rammohun Roy sought to protect in India).

Their role in textile production may in fact have made women's situation worse, since more time working at home may have increased the practice of footbinding. Originally bound feet were a distinction signifying wealth and leisure, but the fashion spread throughout the Han Chinese population. Young girls' feet were broken and compressed into 3-inch balls by binding the four smaller toes under the sole of the foot and forcing the big toe and heel together. Women with bound feet suffered constant pain, limited mobility, and frequent infections. However, the old practice of female infanticide did decline during this period, perhaps because the improved financial prospects of women in textile production softened the attitude that boys were a blessing while girls were a burden.

The Manchu had never bound their own daughters' feet; indeed, they found the practice repulsive. The cultural traditions they brought from the grasslands required that women be able to ride horses and perform other strenuous physical tasks. But footbinding was so well established among the Han Chinese that Qing officials decided not to try to abolish it.

While most Chinese women lived lives of constant toil, elite women had opportunities for education and artistic expression. Unlike the sons of elite households, who were prepared by tutors for the state examinations, girls were educated to be refined, sensitive, and cultured to bring honor to their husbands and their

---

*Susan Mann, *Precious Records: Women in China's Long Eighteenth Century* (Stanford: Stanford University Press, 1997), p. 149.

"The Weaving of Flower'd Silks," Two Women at Work, China, late 18th century (woodcut), Chinese School (18th century)/Private Collection/The Stapleton Collection/Bridgeman Images

The Weaving of Flower'd Silks, two Women at Work

Silk Weaving Silk weaving was a highly profitable enterprise in eighteenth-century China. Women played a central role in all stages of silk production, operating large and complex looms such as the one pictured here. The spinning of cotton thread and weaving of cotton cloth were also increasingly important at this time, and women dominated production in the cotton industry as well.

household. These women wrote many of the greatest poems from Qing times. Often they expressed deep emotional attachment to the other women in their lives, as in these lines from Wang Duan in tribute to the aunt who had mentored her:

> *Holding my hand, you lead me to the west garden*
> *Where, I still remember, I used to read.*
> *With deep emotion I recall your kindness in educating and cultivating me. . .**

The Qing Empire and Its Borderlands Territorial expansion, by both force and diplomacy, was one of the greatest Qing achievements. The Qing complemented the advances of the "gunpowder revolution" (see Chapter 17) by using the banner system to successfully incorporate frontier peoples into the imperial armies, extending Qing power far to the west.

---

*Wang Duan, "Xinwei chunri fanzhao Wulin fucheng Chusheng yimu ji yong ci ti Minghu yin-jian tu yuanyun," trans. Haihong Yang, "'Hoisting one's own banner': Self-inscription in lyric poetry by three women writers of late imperial China," 2010, http://ir.uiowa.edu/etd/766, p. 219.

During the century after the Manchu secured southern China and Taiwan, the Qing empire doubled in size. The Manchu then had to deal with the age-old Chinese problem of bringing stability to their unsettled western and northern frontiers. That meant asserting their control over Mongolian nomads and Turkic-speaking Muslim peoples to their west, stationing soldiers as far away as Tibet.

As in the past, the main threat came from steppe nomads, of which the most formidable were the Zunghars (ZUN-gahrs), Central Eurasian Mongols devoted to Tibetan Buddhism. The spiritual leader of both Tibetans and Zunghars was the Dalai Lama (DAH-lie LAH-mah). The Manchu used both force and subterfuge against the Zunghars, sending an army to Tibet but also supporting one of the rival contenders for the title of Dalai Lama, correctly assuming that their support would win his loyalty. Tibet began paying tribute to Beijing, which weakened the Zunghars.

Finally in 1757, Qianlong ordered that *"they must all be captured and executed."** Zunghar men were slaughtered; women and children were enslaved; and the lands were repopulated with sedentary peoples, such as the Muslim Uighurs (who still live in the western Xinjiang (shin-jyahng) province). Chinese territory was never again threatened by steppe nomads.

Elsewhere, Qing officials relied on diplomacy, much as the Ming had exacted tribute from societies outside their direct control. Annual tribute missions to Beijing symbolized the fealty even of powerful leaders, such as the emperors of Korea and Vietnam, who preserved their own political autonomy through ritual recognition of the Qing as overlords. Tribute was also sent by non-Han peoples living on the margins of Chinese society in the hills, jungles, and steppes.

Though the western regions of Tibet and Xinjiang had been brought under Qing rule, these areas were not, like Chinese provinces, administered directly by scholar-officials. Rather, local political authorities were allowed to continue under Manchu supervision as long as taxes were paid, order was maintained, and loyalty to Qing authorities was assured. The Qing appointed an official to report on Tibetan affairs, for example, but otherwise did nothing to supplant the power and influence of local Buddhist monks.

The Manchu often received Tibetan and Mongol emissaries outside the Great Wall at Chengde, the Manchu summer palace, rather than in the Forbidden City in Beijing. In fact, Qianlong had a replica of the Dalai Lama's Tibetan palace built at Chengde, an act of respect but also one implying the Dalai Lama's dependence on Manchu authority. As one historian observes, Manchu devotion to the Dalai Lama "contained always an element of menace."[†]

Unlike the Ming, however, the Qing were not interested in asserting cultural superiority over tributary societies. They viewed China as one part of a wider Manchu empire. Rather than imposing a single language on their empire, for example, Qing documents could be produced in five quite different scripts: Chinese, Manchu, Mongolian, Tibetan, or Arabic. Thus eighteenth-century Qing maps had Chinese labels for Chinese provinces and Manchu labels for non-Chinese areas, illustrating how Qianlong saw himself as a Chinese emperor when ruling lands conquered from the Ming, but as a Manchu emperor when dealing with peoples to the west. (See the feature "World History in Today's World: The Train to Tibet.")

---

*Peter C. Perdue, *China Marches West* (Cambridge, Mass.: Belknap, 2010), p. 284.
[†]Matthew Kapstein, *The Tibetans* (New York: Wiley Blackwell, 2008), p. 148.

The Train to Tibet

The $4.2 billion railway to Tibet takes passengers from Beijing to Lhasa, the Tibetan capital, skirting magnificent Himalayan peaks while climbing to an elevation above 16,000 feet (4,900 m). Passengers are given supplementary oxygen for altitude sickness, and a complex engineering system keeps the tracks level as they cross long stretches of permafrost, where the ground alternately melts and freezes. The train to Tibet is part of the Chinese government's agenda to better exploit the resources of the far interior by moving people to Tibet and other western regions from the crowded eastern and southern parts of the country.

The project has its critics. Some argue that intensive resource extraction will upset the delicate environmental balance of the Tibetan plateau. Human rights observers have focused on cultural and political issues, worrying that Han Chinese immigrants are a threat to traditional Tibetan language, culture, and religion. Tibetans themselves fear becoming second-class citizens in their own land.

The controversy exploded into violence early in 2008, when protestors took to the streets, replacing Chinese flags with Tibetan ones and, in some cases, attacking Han Chinese residents. That uprising was easily suppressed, but since 2009 over 130 self-immolations by Tibetan Buddhist monks to protest Chinese policies have deeply embarrassed the government in Beijing.

Supporters of Tibetan autonomy argue that there was never any direct imperial control of Tibetan affairs until China's People's Liberation Army invaded in 1950 and then forced the Dalai Lama, Tibet's spiritual leader, into exile in India. The Dalai Lama's advocacy of substantial Tibetan autonomy within the context of the Chinese state is thus consistent with earlier Qing imperial practice. The Chinese government, however, insists on central control.

Whatever political compromises might be made, the train to Tibet remains a symbol of the demographic changes that seem all but unstoppable as more Han Chinese move west looking for economic opportunity.

Source: Pankaj Mishra, "The Train to Tibet: What will the greatest rail journey on earth do to its destination?" *The New Yorker,* April 16, 2007.

Qing Trade and Foreign Relations Not all of the Qing empire's external relations took place within the tributary system. The Qing treated the Russians, a growing presence, on equal terms. But they were reluctant to grant diplomatic equality to other European powers, even in the nineteenth century, when the British were completing their conquest of India.

As the Russian empire expanded eastward, Kangxi worried the Russians might ally with the steppe nomads. After some skirmishes, the Russians and the Chinese agreed to the **Treaty of Nerchinsk** in 1689, according to which the Qing recognized Russian claims west of Mongolia, while the Russians agreed to disband settlements to the east. Yongzheng and Qianlong continued this policy of avoiding conflict through treaties that fixed the boundary between the two empires.

While the Russians came overland, other Europeans came by sea. European trade focused on south China, especially Guangzhou (called Canton by the Europeans). Manchu rulers associated Guangzhou with "greedy" traders rather than sober scholar-officials, and with adventurous sailors rather than dependable village-bound farmers. Accordingly, the Qing restricted European trade to this single port and required European traders to deal only with state-approved firms known as *cohongs.* Since cohong merchants had a monopoly on trade with Europeans, they found it easy to fix prices and amass huge profits.

Treaty of Nerchinsk
1689 treaty between Romanov Russia and Qing China that fixed their Central Asian border.

The structure of the China trade frustrated the British in particular. Having little to exchange for Chinese goods but silver, they saw the continued outflow of bullion toward Asia as a fiscal problem. Britain, the greatest maritime commercial power of the time, rankled at its lack of open access to the vast Chinese market.

Macartney Mission

The 1792–1793 mission in which Lord Macartney was sent by King George III of England to establish permanent diplomatic relations with the Qing empire. Because he could not accept the British king as his equal, the Qianlong emperor politely refused.

As a result, the British government sought to establish formal diplomatic relations. In 1792, King George III sent the **Macartney Mission** to negotiate an exchange of ambassadors. Qing officials allowed Lord Macartney and his party to travel from Guangzhou to Beijing but expected this representative of a "barbarian" king to recognize the superiority of the Qianlong emperor. However, Macartney refused to perform the ritual *kowtow* of full prostration before the emperor, consenting only to drop to one knee, as he would before his own king. Macartney asked that more ports be opened to foreign trade and that restrictions on trade be removed.

Qianlong's response to King George III was unequivocal: "*We have never valued ingenious articles, nor do we have the slightest need of your country's manufactures. Therefore, O King, as regards your request to send someone to remain at the capital, while it is not in harmony with the regulations of the Celestial empire we also feel very much that it is of no advantage to your country.*"* Qianlong saw China as the center of the civilized world, and he insisted that the British should appear before him only if bearing tribute in recognition of his superior position.

Qianlong's attitude was understandable. The Qing controlled the largest and wealthiest empire on earth and had no need to look beyond their borders for resources. But all was not well. As in late Ming times, inefficiency and corruption were creeping into the system. As Qianlong grew old, the power of eunuchs once again increased, their petty rivalries at court distracting from vigorous public administration. The absence of technological improvements in farming put pressure on the food supply. As more marginal lands were cleared for cultivation, deforestation led to the silting up of rivers, and floods resulted. As the situation worsened, some Chinese peasants rebelled, dreaming of restoring the Ming dynasty while viewing the non-Chinese Manchu as illegitimate, lacking the "Mandate of Heaven" (see Chapter 16).

● **CONTEXT&CONNECTIONS** Peasant rebellion was a recurring theme in Chinese imperial history. Peasants have repeatedly risen up, angered by high taxes, drought, and plague. From early times, peasants sought moral renewal as well as political change, often inspired by Buddhist visions for social reform. Though the Manchu had benefited from rural unrest in unseating the Ming, they themselves later faced religiously inspired rebels. The greatest and most destructive of all the Chinese peasant uprisings was the *Taiping Rebellion* (1850–1864; key term in Chapter 24). ●

When Qianlong abdicated in 1796, the gravity of these internal challenges was not yet clear. And while Qianlong was fascinated by a British gift of a miniature steamship with 110 tiny mounted cannon, he did not foresee how powerful the British would be in fifty years, when they returned to impose their demands by force (see Chapter 24). As the nineteenth century began, Qing officials still believed that the old ways sufficed to meet current challenges. But the threat to imperial China no longer came by land, and as the nineteenth century unfolded no Great Wall could keep out new invaders from the sea.

---

*J. L. Cranmer-Byng, ed., *An Embassy to China: Lord Macartney's Journal, 1793–1794* (Hamden, Conn.: Archon Books, 1963), p. 340.

The Russian Empire, 1725–1800

Though they themselves were a settled agrarian people, the Russians, like the Chinese, had long experience with steppe nomads. The Russian state had been founded as part of the dissolution of the Mongol empire, and Russian leaders viewed control of the steppes as necessary for the security of their heartland. Subsequent expansion to the south and east would make Russia a Great Power in Asia. After Peter the Great pushed Russia's borders further west, Russia became a major European power as well (see Chapter 17). Yet for all the splendor of the Romanov court, conditions for the majority of Russians, serfs living in rural villages, remained grim.

Russian Imperial Expansion, 1725–1800
To the west, Russia dominated the Baltic Sea region after Peter's army decisively defeated the Swedes in 1721. When the Polish kingdom collapsed after the 1770s, Russia, along with Prussia and Austria, shared in its partition. Russian power thrust to the south as well, largely at the expense of the Ottoman empire. The great prize was the Crimean peninsula, a major trade emporium on the Black Sea since ancient times. Annexed in 1783, the Crimea brought both strategic and economic benefits. Russia made its first inroads into the difficult terrain of the Caucasus Mountains at this time as well (see Map 20.2).

In the Caucasus, Russian penetration was not carried out by imperial forces but by mercenary soldiers called **Cossacks** (from the Turkish word *kazakh*, meaning "free man"). The Cossacks originated as fiercely independent horsemen, Slavic-speakers who had assimilated the ways of their nomadic Mongol and Turkish neighbors on the steppes. The Cossack code of honor was based on marksmanship, horsemanship, and group spirit.

As Russia expanded to the east across Siberia, Cossacks were at first hired by private traders who were extending the lucrative fur-trapping frontier (see Chapter 17). Though trappers and soldiers might profit from the fur trade, Russian merchants and the Russian treasury reaped the lion's share. Once the fur-bearing animals of a given area had been slaughtered to clothe the fashionable in Moscow, Paris, or Constantinople, trappers moved on to virgin terrain.

As in New France at the same time (see Chapter 18), the fur trade in Siberia exploited the expertise and labor of indigenous peoples, who the Russians called the "small people of the north." These people were vulnerable to the military technology and diseases brought from the west. If a community did not deliver its quota of furs, Cossacks might attack, carrying women and children off into slavery.

Russian soldiers and administrators subsequently followed fur traders and Cossacks into Siberia, taking formal control to make sure the tsars got their share. Thus the eastern frontier of the Russian empire extended to Alaska, which the Bering Expedition claimed for the tsar in 1741 (see Map 20.2).

The Russian empire also established influence over parts of Asia south of Siberia. In hopes of creating direct trade links with India, Peter the Great maintained armed control over the steppes on Russia's borders while pursuing a diplomatic strategy on the Central Eurasian frontier. Meanwhile, as we have seen, on the Qing frontier, skirmishes between Russian and Manchu soldiers led to the Treaty of Nerchinsk.

Cossacks

Horsemen of the steppes who helped Russian rulers protect and extend their frontier into Central Asia and Siberia.

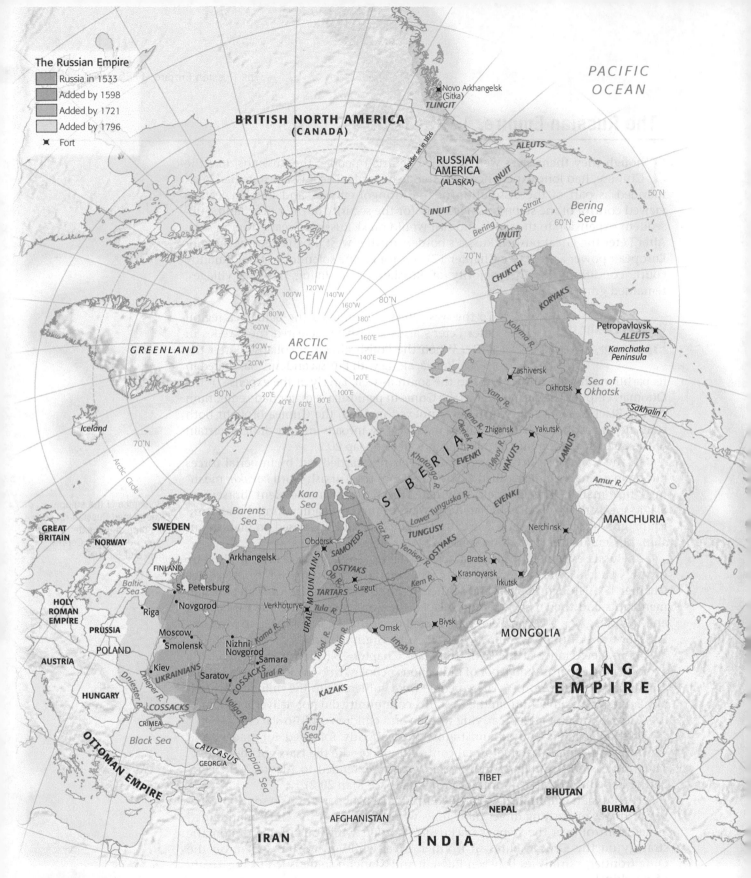

The Russian Empire

- Russia in 1533
- Added by 1598
- Added by 1721
- Added by 1796
- ✕ Fort

PACIFIC OCEAN

BRITISH NORTH AMERICA (CANADA)

Border set in 1826

Novo Arkhangelsk (Sitka)
TLINGIT

RUSSIAN AMERICA (ALASKA)

ALEUTS

INUIT

50°N

Bering Strait

Bering Sea

60°N

70°N

INUIT

INUIT

CHUKCHI

KORYAKS

Petropavlovsk
ALEUTS

Kamchatka Peninsula

GREENLAND

ARCTIC OCEAN

80°N

100°W

120°W

140°W

160°W

180°

160°E

140°E

120°E

100°E

80°E

60°E

40°E

20°E

0°

20°W

40°W

60°W

80°W

Kolyma R.

Zashiversk

Sea of Okhotsk

Okhotsk

Sakhalin I.

Iceland

70°N

Arctic Circle

Kara Sea

Barents Sea

Yana R.

Lena R.

Zhigansk

Yakutsk

SIBERIA

Khatanga R.

Olenek R.

EVENKI

Vilyuy R.

YAKUTS

LAMUTS

Amur R.

MANCHURIA

GREAT BRITAIN

SWEDEN

NORWAY

FINLAND

Arkhangelsk

Baltic Sea

St. Petersburg

Novgorod

Riga

HOLY ROMAN EMPIRE

PRUSSIA

POLAND

AUSTRIA

HUNGARY

Moscow

Smolensk

Kiev

UKRAINIANS

COSSACKS

Dniester R.

Dnieper R.

COSSACKS

CRIMEA

Black Sea

OTTOMAN EMPIRE

CAUCASUS

GEORGIA

Caspian Sea

Nizhni Novgorod

Samara

Saratov

COSSACKS

Volga R.

Kama R.

URAL MOUNTAINS

Verkhoturye

Tula R.

Obdorsk

SAMOYEDS

OSTYAKS

Ob R.

TARTARS

Surgut

Tobol R.

Ishim R.

Irtysh R.

Omsk

Biysk

KAZAKS

Aral Sea

Taz R.

Yenisey R.

Kem R.

OSTYAKS

Lower Tunguska R.

TUNGUSY

Krasnoyarsk

Bratsk

Irkutsk

EVENKI

Nerchinsk

MONGOLIA

QING EMPIRE

TIBET

BHUTAN

NEPAL

BURMA

AFGHANISTAN

IRAN

INDIA

Map 20.2 The Expansion of Russia, 1500–1800 By the end of the eighteenth century, the Russian empire extended westward into Europe, southward toward the Black Sea and Caspian Sea, and most dramatically, eastward into Central Asia, Siberia, and the Americas.

- **CONTEXT&CONNECTIONS** In the nineteenth century, Russian imperialism in Central Eurasia would become more highly militarized, a legacy of forceful intervention inherited by the Communist regime led by *Vladimir Lenin* (Chapter 28) after the Russian Revolution of 1917. The old boundary between the Qing and Romanov dynasties continued to cause tensions straight into the 1960s, when the Soviet Union and the People's Republic of China exchanged fire along their long frontier. ●

Reform and Repression, 1750–1796

During her reign, **Catherine the Great** (r. 1762–1796) consolidated control over these vast imperial frontiers. A German princess who married into the Romanov family, Catherine accumulated ever more personal power to become one of the dominating figures of eighteenth-century Eurasian politics. The Russian nobility benefited from Catherine's authoritarianism. In return for their loyalty and service in the bureaucracy and the military, Catherine gave the nobles more power over the serfs who farmed their estates. At the same time, the profitable market for grain in western Europe gave them incentive to make increasingly harsh demands on their serfs. In their elegant townhouses and country estates, the Russian aristocracy saw Western luxuries as essential to their lifestyle, and most thought little of those who toiled for them like slaves.

Catherine the Great Equestrian portraits of monarchs on white horses were common in eighteenth-century Europe, though rarely were women represented this way. Catherine, a German princess who married into the Russian royal family, removed her husband from the throne in 1762 in a bloodless coup. Tough and brilliant, she ruled under her own authority for over three decades.

- **CONTEXT&CONNECTIONS** Catherine brought cultural and intellectual influences from western Europe to the tsarist court at St. Petersburg at a time when the *Enlightenment* (Chapter 21) and its exciting new ideas were energizing reform and revolution in the West (see Chapter 22). However, while Catherine brought the latest trends in art, architecture, fashion, and even philosophy to Russia, she adamantly ruled out political reform. ●

As the serfs' situation deteriorated, unrest led to rebellion. In the 1770s, a Cossack chieftain named Yemelyan Pugachev gained a huge following after claiming that he was the legitimate tsar. Pugachev promised the abolition of serfdom and an end to taxation and military conscription. After several years of rebellion, Pugachev was captured, brought back to Moscow, and sliced to pieces in a public square. Catherine became even less tolerant of talk of reform.

Catherine's imperial policies were pragmatic, as when she restrained the Orthodox Church from converting non-Russian peoples. In the case of Siberia, the reason was financial: converts to Orthodoxy had tax protections that indigenous people lacked. In the cases of the steppes and the Central Asian frontier, Catherine saw that working with local Muslim leaders was the best way to maintain stability. In the Crimea, for example, she protected the rights of the local Tatar Muslim nobility, declaring, *"It is Our desire that without regard to his nationality or faith, each [nobleman] shall have the personal right to these lands."* Thus while conditions for Russian serfs deteriorated and force prevailed on the Siberian frontier, Catherine, like the Qing emperors, brought people of the Central Asian steppes within the Russian imperial orbit without requiring cultural assimilation. (See the feature "Movement of Ideas Through Primary Sources: Petitioning Catherine the Great.")

Catherine the Great (r. 1762–1796) German princess who married into the Romanov family and became empress of Russia. Brought western European cultural and intellectual influences to the Russian elite. Her troops crushed a major peasant uprising.

Petitioning Catherine the Great

One of Catherine the Great's innovations was to invite petitions from her subjects. Often people felt that oppression resulted from the misuse of power by local and provincial officials: if only the tsarina herself knew of these abuses, they thought, surely she would correct them. Catherine the Great encouraged this attitude and invited her subjects (other than the serfs, who had no right to address her) to submit petitions. Such a flood of petitions flowed to St. Petersburg, however, that it is unlikely that she even saw most of them, and once the French Revolution showed the dangers of stirring up public opinion (see Chapter 22), the freedom to petition the tsarina was revoked.

The first of the two petitions below was submitted by a group of Tartar nobles, that is, by the Muslim, Turkic-speaking elite of an area incorporated into the Russian empire. The Kazan Tartars had ruled the Volga River region in the fourteenth century, but in the fifteenth century this region was conquered by the Russian tsar Ivan the Terrible. Ivan slaughtered much of the Muslim population and forcibly converted many of the survivors to Orthodox Christianity. Not until the reign of Catherine did the tsars allow new mosques to be built again in Kazan.

The second petition to Catherine was submitted by a group of Jewish leaders in Belarus. The majority of the population of Belarus (meaning "white Russia") consisted of Slavic speakers closely related to Russians in language and culture. Belarus was ruled from Poland/Lithuania until the eighteenth century, after which it was incorporated into the Russian empire. The Jews of this region were known as *Ashkenazim* (see Chapter 17). Their liturgical language was Hebrew, but their everyday language was Yiddish, a dialect of German infused with Hebrew vocabulary, unintelligible to Russian speakers. To the greatest extent possible, the Ashkenazim took care of their own community affairs.

> **What attitude did the writers of these petitions express toward Catherine's imperial authority?**

> **What do these documents tell us about the relationship of religion to empire in eighteenth-century Russia?**

Source: David G. Rowley, *Exploring Russia's Past: Narratives, Sources, Images*, vol. I, To 1850 (New York: Pearson, 2006), pp. 208–209.

Petition from Tartar Nobles in Kazan Province, 1767

12. We the under-signed believe that nothing is more offensive to a person, regardless of his faith and rank, than to suffer disrespect and insults toward his religion. This makes one extremely agitated and provokes unnecessary words of abuse. But it often happens that people of various ranks say extremely contemptuous things about our religion and our Prophet . . . and this is a great affront for us. Therefore we request a law that anyone who curses our religion be held legally accountable. . . . [We further ask that] we Tartars and nobles not be forced to convert to Orthodoxy. . .

15. If any of our people are voluntarily baptized into the faith of the Greek confession [i.e., into the Orthodox Church] they should be ordered to move to settlements with Russians the very same year in which the conversion takes place. . . . We ask that, under no circumstances, are converts to be permitted to sell their houses, garden plots, and pastures to Russians or people of other ranks, but are to sell only to us Tartars; they must sell either to unconverted kinsmen or other Tartars. . . . Also, without a special personal order from Her Imperial Majesty, no churches should be built in our localities. . . .

Petition from Belarussian Jews, 1784

1. Some [Belarussian Jews] who live in towns engage in trade and, especially, in the distillation of spirits, beer and mead [honey beer], which they sell wholesale and retail. This privilege was extended to them when Belarus joined the Russian empire. Hence everyone active in

this business used all their resources to construct buildings suitable for distillation. . . . After the Belarussian region joined the Russian empire, the Jews in some towns constructed more of these in the same fashion and at great expense. The imperial monarchical decree [on Jews] emboldens them to request tearfully some monarchical mercy.

2. According to an ancient custom, when the squires built a new village, they summoned the Jews to reside there and gave them certain privileges for several years and the permanent liberty to distill spirits, brew beer and mead, and sell these drinks. On this basis the Jews built houses and distillation plants at considerable expense. . . . But a decree of the governor-general of Belarus has now forbidden the squires to farm out distillation in their villages to Jews, even if the squires want to do this. As a result [these] poor Jews [have been left] completely impoverished. . . . They therefore request an imperial decree authorizing the squire, if he wishes, to farm out distillation to Jews in rural areas.

3. . . . Jews have no one to defend them in courts and find themselves in a desperate situation—given their fear, and ignorance of Russian—in case of misfortune, even if innocent. . . . To consummate all the good already bestowed, Jews dare to petition that . . . in matters involving Jews and non-Jews . . . a representative from the Jewish community . . . be present to accompany Jews in court and attend the interrogation of Jews. But cases involving only Jews . . . should be handled solely in Jewish courts, because Jews assume obligations among themselves, make agreements and conclude all kinds of deals in the Jewish language and in accordance with Jewish rites and law (which are not known to others). Moreover, those who transgress their laws and order should be judged in Jewish courts. Similarly, preserve intact all their customs and holidays in the spirit of their faith, as is mercifully assured in the imperial manifesto. . . .

India: From Mughal Empire to British Rule, 1650–1833

Mughal India was the first of the old land-based Asian empires to be overtaken by European imperialism, a transition that was taking place during Rammohun Roy's own lifetime. None could have foreseen the coming of British domination in the seventeenth century, when the Mughal empire reached its territorial zenith under the emperor **Aurangzeb** (ow-rang-ZEB), who extended his power across India and took the title *Alamgir*, "World Seizer."

However, even during Aurangzeb's long rule (1658–1707), ambitious regional leaders had begun to resist the central power of Delhi, and after his death the empire began to fragment, leading to invasions from Iran and Afghanistan and to the emergence of autonomous regional states. As in the past history of India and other land-based empires in Eurasia, the wealth of empire attracted invaders from the mountains and steppes who were strong enough to destabilize the existing order, but not to replace it. Arriving by sea, however, the British represented something entirely new. Starting from their base in Bengal, they would fill the power vacuum left by Mughal decline.

Aurangzeb

(r. 1658–1707) Mughal emperor who used military force to extend his power but whose constant campaigns drained the treasury and whose policy of favoring Islam at the expense of India's other religions generated social and political tensions.

Aurangzeb and the Decline of Mughal Authority, 1658–1757

Aurangzeb was an energetic, capable, and determined ruler who presided over a stable and prosperous realm. The wealth he controlled was staggering. Some came from territorial conquests, but agriculture, trade, and industry were the true foundations of India's prosperity. Mughal officials encouraged the commercial farming of sugarcane, indigo, and cotton to enhance the tax base, and many peasants benefited from the focus on marketable produce. American crops like maize and tobacco were another stimulus to growth. The population did not increase as rapidly as China's in the same period: disease and periodic famine kept mortality rates high. Still, the population of India rose from about 150 million in 1600 to about 200 million in 1800. As in other land-based empires, taxes on peasant agriculture were the principal source of government revenue.

The stability of the Mughal heartland in north India was good for trade and industry. Participation in the expanding Indian Ocean economy brought in gold and silver. Silk and opium were produced for Southeast Asian markets, but the principal source of prosperity was textiles. Exports now expanded beyond established African, Persian, and Southeast Asian markets to northern Europe, where consumers found Indian cotton cloth cheaper, more comfortable, and easier to wash than domestic woolens or linens. South Asians were among the most powerful commercial agents in the world, using the silver that flowed in through Indian Ocean trade to pay cash advances to weavers, who then contracted lower-caste women to spin cotton yarn.

For Mughal rulers, commercial wealth was a mixed blessing, however. Prosperity afforded provincial leaders the cash and incentive to build up their own military forces. Aurangzeb's constant military campaigns were largely driven by the need to assert central control over restive provinces.

In the process, Aurangzeb reversed Akbar's earlier policy of religious tolerance (see Chapter 16). Whereas Akbar had courted allies among Hindus and other communities, Aurangzeb stressed the Islamic nature of his state. His imposition of a special tax on nonbelievers caused great resentment.

Historical memories of Aurangzeb were mixed. Many Indian Muslims would later look back on the power and glory of Aurangzeb's reign with nostalgia. Hindu writers like Rammohun Roy (see Chapter 20) generally had harsher memories. Writing a century after Aurangzeb's death, Roy emphasized the emperor's *"cruelty and intolerance."* Contrasting him with Akbar, whose *"memory is still adored,"* Roy judged that Aurangzeb, *"met with many reverses and misfortunes during his life time, and his name is now held in abhorrence."**

The Sikhs likewise had an ill memory of Aurangzeb. Sikhism was a new religion that emphasized equality before God, rejecting the caste system and polytheism of Hinduism while incorporating other elements of Hindu belief and ritual (see Chapter 16). Their leader Guru Tegh Bahadur (1621–1675) defended the rights not only of Sikhs but of Hindus to follow their own forms of worship. In response, Aurangzeb had him captured, brought to Delhi in an iron cage, tortured after he resisted conversion to Islam, and, finally, beheaded. Sikhism, formerly pacifistic, then became more militant. To this day, ceremonial knives are part of the daily attire of Sikh men.

---

*Raja Rammohun Roy, *The English Works*, vol. 2, ed. Jogendra Chunder Ghose (Calcutta: Srikanta Roy, 1901), p. 307.

V&A Images, London/Art Resource, NY

V&A Images, London/Art Resource, NY

Mughals at War Mughal control of South Asia was based on military supremacy, from early-sixteenth-century conquest through the reign of Aurangzeb. As this Mughal painting (in the Persian style) shows, cavalry played a central role, but the use of gunpowder weapons was also crucial to Mughal strategy.

In other regions, Aurangzeb's religious intolerance was probably less critical as a cause of rebellion than the opportunities afforded to ambitious provincial leaders by the increasing value of Indian Ocean commerce, which allowed them to amass greater wealth and arms, and thus to challenge Mughal rule. The Hindu rebellions in the western **Maratha kingdoms**, for example, were incited as much by leaders' desire for political and economic autonomy as by religious resentment.

While Aurangzeb had fairly easily subdued other regions, Maratha leaders used guerilla tactics, well suited to the region's tough terrain, to keep the Mughal armies at bay. From 1695 to 1700, Aurangzeb left Delhi to live in military encampments, spending vast sums on his campaigns. As military affairs preoccupied the emperor, corruption and incompetence crept into the government. By the time of his death in 1707, Aurangzeb was full of despair. From his deathbed, he wrote his son: *"I have not done well to the country or to the people, and of the future there is no hope."* A prolonged succession struggle ensued, tax collectors withheld government

Maratha kingdoms

Loosely bound, west-central Indian confederacy that established its autonomy from Mughal rule in the eighteenth century and challenged the invading British in the nineteenth.

funds, and the empire became even more vulnerable to regional uprisings and foreign invasions.

The initial threat came from Iran. Taking advantage of Safavid weakness (see Chapter 17), a brilliant general, **Nader Shah** (1688–1747), took the title shah for himself, establishing a new Iranian dynasty while expelling Russian and Ottoman forces. In 1739, his armies stormed into northern India. Begging for mercy, the Mughal emperor handed over the keys to his treasury, and even the fabled Peacock Throne, before Nader Shah agreed to withdraw.

This humiliating sack and plunder sounded the death knell of Mughal authority. After the Iranians withdrew, a Maratha army marched on Delhi but was defeated by Afghani invaders. If neither Iranians, nor Afghanis, nor Marathis were strong enough to rule India, it seemed likely that the Mughal empire would break into pieces, with provincial rulers ascendant. Instead it was the British who inherited Mughal imperial power.

Nader Shah

(1688–1747) Iranian ruler who invaded India from the north in 1739, defeating the Mughal army and capturing the Mughal emperor, who handed over the keys to his treasury before Nader Shah agreed to withdraw. Mughal power went into permanent decline.

Foundations of British Rule, 1739–1818

The seaborne European empires in Asia were originally geared toward commercial profit rather than territorial control. Mughal rulers paid little attention to the Dutch, British, and French East India Companies, which controlled only their own "factories," fortified outposts where they lived and kept their trade goods, and perhaps a bit of adjacent territory (see Chapter 15).

Calcutta (today's Kolkata), Rammohun Roy's city of residence, had its origins as one such "factory," founded in 1690 when the *nawab* (ruler) of Bengal granted a license to the English East India Company to settle and trade. After 1717, by Mughal command, the Company was permitted to trade duty-free, giving it a great advantage over both Indian and European competitors. Cotton cloth was a major trade item at Calcutta, as were opium (first destined for Indonesian markets and later for China), raw silk (exported to both Europe and Japan), pepper, sugar, and saltpeter, a key ingredient in gunpowder. To the south, a similar English "factory" at Madras (today's Chennai) competed for trade with the French East India Company settlement at Pondicherry (today's Puducherry).

With the decline of Mughal authority after the Iranian invasion of 1739, some European agents, like many provincial Indian rulers, seized the opportunity to expand their enterprises and retain more of their profits. Indeed, it was Company men acting on their own initiative, rather than policymakers in distant European capitals, who laid the foundations for further European expansion. One of the first and most brilliant of these "men on the spot" was the French Company's commander **Joseph Francois Dupleix** (1697–1764).

During the War of the Austrian Succession between France and Britain in the 1740s (see Chapter 18), Dupleix (doo-PLAY) took the British factory at Madras, only to be attacked in turn by a local Indian prince. Badly outnumbered, Dupleix commanded just 230 European soldiers plus some 700 *sepoys* (SEE-poyz), Indian soldiers the Europeans had employed and trained. Nevertheless, superior French firepower and organization enabled him to defeat an invading Indian force of nearly ten thousand and to establish himself as master of Madras. But for diplomatic reasons, the French ordered Dupleix to surrender those gains back to the British, who would soon follow his example with more lasting effect.

A decade later, threatened by French advances in South Asia during the Seven Years' War (1756–1763; see Chapter 19), the British fortified their trading post at Calcutta. The young nawab of Bengal, Siraj ud-Daulah (suh-RAJ uhd-duh-OO-lah),

Joseph Francois Dupleix

(1697–1764) Governor-general in charge of all French establishments in India. Dupleix used diplomacy to forge alliances with local rulers and with their help defeated a much larger British force in the 1740s.

saw these new British fortifications as a provocation. He withdrew authorization for the Company settlement and then attacked and captured Calcutta.

However, Robert Clive, a British soldier of fortune, outmaneuvered Siraj ud-Daulah. Clive had allied the East India Company with the region's Hindu commercial and banking interests, and also with Siraj's own uncle, himself an aspiring nawab. In 1757 at the **Battle of Plassey**, Bengal's leader faced only eight hundred British soldiers and some two thousand sepoys. But many of Siraj ud-Daulah's fifty thousand soldiers (secretly paid off by Clive's moneylender friends) fled the battlefield; others (allied with his ambitious uncle) betrayed him and fought with his enemy.

After the British victory, Siraj's uncle was duly installed as nawab, but that office profited him little after Company officials plundered the treasury. The chests full of silver they sent back home finally reversed the earlier outward flow of European silver into South Asia, loot that financed the construction of many a fine English country house.

Once in control of Bengal, the British could perhaps have marched on Delhi and ended the Mughal era once and for all. But Clive decided on a more subtle policy of recognizing the weakened Mughal emperor while insinuating the Company into existing Mughal institutions. The East India Company became the official revenue collector of India's rich northeastern provinces. Clive used the threat of military force to divide and conquer, extorting alliances from various nawabs, maharajahs, and sultans by offering them "protection." (See the feature "Visual Evidence Through Primary Sources: Colonel Mordaunt's Cock Fight.")

When a terrible famine in 1769 killed one-third of Bengal's population, some in Parliament blamed the East India Company, which fed its own employees and soldiers but did nothing for starving Bengalis, while insisting that they continue to pay their taxes. One member of Parliament complained: *"We have outdone the Spaniards in Peru. They were at least butchers on a religious principle. . . .We have murdered, deposed, plundered, usurped—nay, what think you of the famine in Bengal being caused by a monopoly of the servants of the East India Company?"**

The India Act in 1784 attempted to redress such abuses. **Lord Charles Cornwallis** was dispatched as governor-general and commander of British forces in India. Unlike Clive, Cornwallis was an aristocrat and a member of the British establishment. His assignment was to draw a strict line between administration and trade by implementing a policy whereby Company employees might serve as either officials or traders, but not as both. Cornwallis believed that British colonial rule could be fair and just. As his successor declared: *"No greater benefit can be bestowed on the inhabitants of India than the extension of British authority."*† That justification for colonial rule would long endure.

British influence in India spread through force, but also through diplomacy when provincial rulers looked to the British as patrons and protectors in the insecure conditions that accompanied Mughal decline. The British also absorbed Indian influences, learning Indian languages and adopting Mughal styles of dress and behavior. Because there were no English women in India, Company employees frequently consorted with local women and even took Indian wives, who provided a cultural and linguistic bridge to Indian society.

Battle of Plassey

1757 battle that gave the British East India Company control of the rich eastern Mughal province of Bengal. Sir Robert Clive used alliances with Indian rulers to defeat the larger forces of Siraj ud-Daulah, the nawab of Bengal.

Lord Charles Cornwallis

(1738–1795) British general who surrendered to American forces at Yorktown and later served as governor-general of India and Ireland.

---

*Horace Walpole, speech quoted in *Cambridge History of India*, vol. 5 (Cambridge: Cambridge University Press, 1929), p. 187.

†Quoted in Francis Watson, *A Concise History of India* (London: Thames and Hudson, 1979), p. 131.

Colonel Mordaunt's Cockfight

This 1784 painting by Johann Zoffany was commissioned by Warren Hastings, the governor-general of the British East India Company, who had it sent back to Britain as a memento. The image is based on an actual cockfight arranged between John Mordaunt and Asaf-ud-Daula, nawab of Awadh, in the latter's capital city of Lucknow. Mordaunt had been hired by the nawab to command his personal bodyguard and to arrange such amusements.

Though the British and the Indians are here portrayed as getting along well, tensions existed. Warren Hastings, later tried for wanton corruption before a court in London, was accused of having stolen the fortune of Asaf-ud-Daula's grandmother. Later, in 1857, the city of Lucknow became the epicenter of a massive revolt against British authority after the East India Company ignored local traditions of inheritance in staking its claim over all of Awadh (see Chapter 24).

This image can be analyzed as an exemplar of *orientalism*, a concept developed by the late Palestinian-American scholar Edward Said. Said argued that Westerners' self-image in this period developed in opposition to their concept of the "Orient" as an exotic, sensual, irrational space of "otherness."

The liveliness and dynamism of the Indians on the left and in the background seem to contrast with the more formally posed British figures. **What differences are there in the depiction of the Europeans and Indians in this portrait? How might this painting be interpreted as an example of Western artistic "orientalism," of the rendering of Indians as exoticized "others"?**

Tate, London/Art Resource, NY

The Europeans are more stiffly posed but are painted with greater attention to their individual characteristics than the surrounding Indians. They are also elevated *above* the cockfight, symbolically distanced from both Mordaunt, a man of lower class, and Asaf-ud-Daula, a foreigner and an "oriental." As a group they pay little attention to the main event: cockfighting is beneath them.

1. Mordaunt stands tall near the center of the action, separated from the other European figures on the right. Cockfighting was not a "gentlemanly" sport, but then Mordaunt was both illiterate and illegitimate, and, needing to make his own way in the world, he had headed for India. His distance from the other Europeans marks his status as servant of the nawab rather than as an officer of the Company.

2. The rulers of Awadh were Shi'ite Muslims who built many mosques and fostered religious learning. Asaf-ud-Daula did so as well, but he was also famous for warm hospitality, ribald humor, and sensuality. Some have seen Asaf-ud-Daula's posture in this painting as indicating sexual arousal; an intimation of homosexuality can be seen in the background just over his left shoulder. The nawab had many adopted children, but despite having a wife and access to hundreds of concubines, it was said he had no children of his own.

3. We can identify most of the European figures in the painting, including John Wombell, the chief accountant for the East India Company in Lucknow, and, seated to his left, the artist himself, Johann Zoffany. Seated in the front of the European group, holding a cock, is Lieutenant Golding of the Company's Corps of Engineers.

4. Claude Martin, shown here in dress uniform, was an infamous French adventurer. A self-made man, he had a commission with the British East India Company while serving simultaneously as Asaf-ud-Daula's Superintendent of the Arsenal. He accumulated a fortune, which he used to support a number of much younger Indian mistresses, to patronage Mughal artists, and to pursue eccentric passions: in 1785, he organized a hot-air balloon ascent over Lucknow.

In the field of law, we see one example of the complex intercultural processes that developed. A visiting Chinese sailor witnessed a Company court proceeding at Calcutta in the 1780s; in his memoirs, he provided a snapshot:

> *The head judge sits, and ten guest judges [the jury] sit on his side. The head guest judge is the elder of the guest merchants. . . . On the day they consider the suit and then decide the outcome, if one of the guest judges does not agree they must hear the case again. Even if this happens two or three times, no one views this as inconvenient.**

The Chinese visitor was struck by the elaborate procedures of a jury trial. But while the Company men used British-style jurisprudence among themselves, they did not try to replace South Asian legal traditions with their own. Instead, a situation of legal pluralism developed, in which Indian litigants could pursue their

*Xie Qinggao, *Hailu jiaoyi*, ed. An Jing (Beijing: Shangwu yingshugan, 2002), translation by Valerie Hansen.

cases in either local courts or in British ones. The British East India Company hence employed both Muslim and Hindu legal advisers to guide them in implementing a multilayered judicial system.

The expansion of British power in India was not a planned exercise in imperialism. In fact, one Company official had declared in the 1770s: "*The dominion of all India is what I never wish to see.*" But the vacuum left by declining Mughal power combined with the greed and ambition of "men on the spot" to push British frontiers forward. In the west, when Maratha armies threatened the British East India Company's factory at Bombay (today's Mumbai), the British engaged in a series of alliances and interventions in that region. Finally, in 1818 they defeated the Marathas, and from thence moved toward control of all South Asia. Without central planning or foresight, the British had gone from maritime prowess to mastery over one of the world's most populous and productive regions.

Rammohun Roy: Liberal Imperialism and the Bengali Renaissance

Rammohun Roy's early life corresponded to the period when the British East India Company was accumulating more and more South Asian territory and affecting Indian economic and social life ever more deeply. In those early years, he tells us, "*I proceeded on my travels, and passed through different countries, chiefly within, but some beyond, the bounds of Hindustan, with a feeling of great aversion to the establishment of the British power in India.*"[*]

However, after he returned in 1814 to live in Calcutta Roy developed friendships with some of its British residents and changed his mind. "*Though it is impossible for a thinking man not to feel the evils of political subjection and dependence on foreign people,*" he wrote, "*yet when we reflect on the advantages which we have derived and may hope to derive from our connection with Great Britain, we may be reconciled to the present state of things which promises permanent benefits to our posterity.*"[†]

● **CONTEXT&CONNECTIONS** Later Indian nationalists disagreed about Rammohun Roy's legacy. *Mohandas K. Gandhi* (Chapter 28) criticized him for an elitist, pro-British attitude. Rabindranath Tagore, winner of the Nobel Prize for Literature (1913), saw Roy's legacy differently: "*[Roy] knew that the ideal of human civilization does not lie in the isolation of independence, but in the brotherhood of interdependence of individuals as well as of nations. . . . [He] devoted himself to . . . rescuing from the debris of India's decadence the true products of its civilization, and to make our people build on them as the basis . . . of an international culture.*"[‡] ●

Roy thus vigorously supported the development of an English-language college for Calcutta. When some British scholars argued that the Company should endow a Sanskrit-language school, Roy rejected the idea: "*the pupils will there acquire what was known two thousand years ago with the addition of vain and empty*

---

[*]Raja Rammohun Roy, *The English Works*, vol. 1, ed. Jogendra Chunder Ghose (Calcutta: Srikanta Roy, 1901), p. 318.

[†]"A Letter on Grant's Jury Bill," *India Gazette*, January 22, 1833; cited in Amiya P. Sen, *Rammohun Roy: A Critical Biography* (New York: Penguin, 2012).

[‡]Rabindranath Tagore, "Rammohun Roy, the Path Maker and Luminous Star in Our Hour of Decadence," an address delivered by Rabindranath Tagore as President of the Preliminary Meeting of the Rammohun Roy Centenary held at the Senate House, Calcutta, on February 18, 1933. http://www.thebrahmosamaj.net/articles/rammohun_pathmaker.html.

subtleties."* The English language, which he associated with science, inquiry, and liberty, would liberate young Bengalis from the passivity that had come from centuries of Mughal rule and from the clouds of superstition then darkening Hindu civilization.

Some British officials also supported English-language schooling for Indian boys, but differed sharply with Roy on the *purpose* of that education. One such Englishman argued that the goal of schooling should be *"to create a class of persons, Indian in blood and color, but English in taste, in opinions, in morals, and in intellect."*† For Roy, progress would come not through such wholesale assimilation, but rather through the creative intertwining of multiple influences. The Bengal Renaissance looked to reform, not to displace, local languages, cultures, and religious traditions.

Critical reasoning always guided Roy's assessments of religion, whether Hindu, Jain, Muslim, or Christian. Even as a teenager, his criticism of contemporary Hindu practices caused a deep rift with his father and separation from his family. After studying the ancient philosophy of the Jains, whose doctrine of *ahimsa* required absolute nonviolence toward all living things, he rejected it as impractical. From Islam, he took a profound and insistent belief in the unity of God. He rejected, however, the concept of prophetic revelation and criticized what he saw as Muslims' intolerance, which, he thought, stemmed from their doctrinaire tendencies.

Christianity was a relatively new influence in Roy's adult years, when larger numbers of missionaries came to Bengal. Studying their texts, Roy came away with a deep appreciation of the moral quality of the teachings of Jesus Christ and applauded the Christian humanism he saw practiced by some members of Calcutta's British community. On the other hand, he rejected the idea of the Holy Trinity, insisting on the unity of God, drawing the ire of some missionaries. Other European Christians, however, shared his philosophical viewpoint. The *Brahmo Sabha* religious community that Roy founded in Calcutta in 1828 became aligned with the Unitarian Church in England, which he visited when in London. Both *Brahmo Sabha* in India and Unitarianism in Britain and the United States avoided complex rituals and theologies, stressed quiet contemplation of the unity of Godhood, and affirmed a humanistic emphasis on good works.

Thus, Roy's intellectual and spiritual path led him to emphasize the compatibility of reformed Hinduism with British Christianity. He was indeed deeply grateful for British officials' support in his campaign against *suti*, bringing a petition before the British House of Commons celebrating *"that this barbarous and inhuman practice has been happily abolished."*‡ As the first prominent Indian to visit England, he was well-received by political and cultural leaders and, after his early death, was respectfully buried in English soil.

However, history would frustrate Roy's vision of social improvement through the fusion of Indian, Islamic, and European beliefs. As the economic changes that came with British rule cut more deeply into Indian society, more Hindus began to resent official patronage of a foreign religion; some saw the abolition of suti as an intrusion of Christian beliefs on their own religion and culture. Many Muslim Indians also came to regard Christianity as a threat to their traditions.

*Raja Rammohun Roy, *The English Works*, vol. 2, ed. Jogendra Chunder Ghose (Calcutta: Srikanta Roy, 1901), p. 325.

†T. B. Macauley, "Minute on Education," 1835, http://www.columbia.edu/itc/mealac/pritchett/00generallinks/macaulay/txt_minute_education_1835.html.

‡Raja Rammohun Roy, *The English Works*, vol. 2, ed. Jogendra Chunder Ghose (Calcutta: Srikanta Roy, 1901), p. 333.

• **CONTEXT&CONNECTIONS** Not long after Roy's death, a huge uprising against British authority and Christian influence, the *Indian Revolt of 1857* (Chapter 24) would create serious obstacles along his favored path of Anglo-Indian accommodation. •

Meanwhile, as the fates of Britain and India became entwined in the early nineteenth century, Tokugawa Japan stood on the other end of the continuum of Asian-European interaction. At the same time that Rammohun Roy was sailing to England, the Japanese shogun reaffirmed the total ban on European entry into his domains.

Tokugawa Japan, 1630–1837

After Hideyoshi's failed invasion of China (see Chapter 16), early modern Japan remained largely aloof from empires and empire building. Unlike Korea and Vietnam, Japan did not pay tribute to the Chinese emperor. It was subject to no foreign power and followed its own distinctive political, economic, and cultural dynamic. The Tokugawa (toe-koo-GAH-wah) shoguns and daimyo lords ruled over a rapidly growing society with a flourishing economy and major accomplishments in fields such as poetry, theater, and architecture.

The story of early modern Japan divides roughly into three periods. From 1630 to 1710, the Tokugawa system was at its height. But from 1710 to 1790, financial and environmental problems stymied the Tokugawa. Population growth stalled, and a widening gap between rich and poor led to social tension. After 1790, increased foreign interactions tested the Tokugawa commitment to isolationism.

Stability and Prosperity in Early Tokugawa Japan, 1630–1710

While the Japanese emperor remained a shadowy figure secluded in the ritual center of Kyoto, real political power rested with the Tokugawa shoguns in the political capital at Edo (Tokyo). The shoguns, literally "commanders of force," successfully brought peace and stability to the Japanese islands, even while the provincial lords, the daimyo, retained substantial authority within their own domains (see Chapter 16). Seventeenth-century Japan reaped the fruits of peace.

The nation brought back into production valuable resources that had been neglected during the violence and insecurity of the sixteenth century. Farmers improved irrigation, replacing dry field agriculture with rice paddies, and cleared forests and terraced hillsides to bring more fields into production. Fishermen increased harvests from the surrounding seas.

The shoguns and daimyo tapped into this productive wealth through an efficient tax system based on precise surveys of land and population. Farmers, no longer subject to arbitrary taxes, boosted production. At the same time, Chinese demand for silver and copper stimulated mining. Some of the new wealth went toward the improvement of roads and irrigation works, further stimulating economic growth. An increase in coinage and a great expansion of internal trade marked the shift from local and regional self-sufficiency to a truly national economy. This economic dynamism led to the expansion of Japanese cities. Many castle towns, originally civil war strongholds, now developed into cultural and commercial centers. The most spectacular example was the capital Edo (ED-doe), which grew from a small village to a city of more than a million people by 1720.

A pressing social issue was to define a peacetime role for the samurai warriors. Samurai were expected to give absolute loyalty to their lords and to display courage and valor in battle. However, the samurai code—or *bushido* ("the way of the warrior")—instructed them to cultivate civil as well as military arts, and in times of peace to emphasize the former: *"Within his heart [the samurai] keeps to the ways of peace, but . . . keeps his weapons ready for use. The . . . common people make him their teacher and respect him."** In the more peaceful Tokugawa atmosphere, some samurai positioned themselves as intellectual and cultural leaders, establishing schools, writing Confucian treatises, and patronizing the arts. Still, they maintained absolute allegiance to their daimyo lords, for whom they were ever ready to die.

The dynamism of the times tested boundaries. Regulations requiring peasant villages to be self-sufficient were widely ignored as farm families increasingly geared their production toward urban markets. In gender relations, some activities contradicted the Tokugawa theory of strict Confucian hierarchy. Elite women made prominent literary contributions, and women of other social classes claimed some mobility and economic opportunity. While women in samurai households were most subject to tight patriarchal control, urban merchant and artisan families were less restrictive. Thus, women participated as performers as well as audience members in some of the new forms of dance and theater.

New artistic forms arose in Japan's burgeoning cities. Poets experimented with a simple new form called *haiku*, and urban audiences patronized the new *kabuki* (ka-BOO-ki) theater, more realistic and emotive than previous forms of Japanese drama. These artistic trends marked the social fluidity of urban life, a worry to Tokugawa leaders who wanted everyone to keep to his or her place. Constant edicts ordering people to dress in clothes and live in houses appropriate to their social status are a good indication that many were *not* doing so.

● **CONTEXT&CONNECTIONS** Japan was certainly not unique in its imposition of sumptuary laws regulating how people should dress based on gender and social status. In medieval Europe purple was the color of royalty; in Ming China, it was the five-clawed dragon that was restricted to imperial display. Merchants in both Europe and Japan, meanwhile, defied aristocratic restrictions by wearing silk: the rising *bourgeoisie* (Chapter 16) would not be prevented from flaunting its wealth. Regulation of women's dress was even more common. ●

Tokugawa artists expressed the social fluidity of their urban milieu in works expressing *ukiyoe*, a "floating world" of languid pleasures: *"living only for the moment, turning our full attention to the pleasures of the moon, the snow, the cherry blossoms . . . diverting ourselves in just floating, floating; caring not a whit for the pauperism staring us in the face."*† The works of *ukiyoe* artists, though often exquisite, betray a sense of complacency in the face of the mounting challenges eighteenth century Japanese society was experiencing.

....

Challenges, Reform, and Decline, 1710–1790

In 1710, Japan was rich, populous, and united. But the eighteenth century brought new challenges. One problem was ecological. During the seventeenth century the population of Japan had doubled to over 30 million people.

---

*Quoted in Ryusaku Tsunoda et al., *Sources of the Japanese Tradition* (New York: Columbia University Press, 1958), pp. 399–400.

†Quoted in Richard Lane, *Images from the Floating World* (New York: Putnam, 1978), p. 11.

Library of Congress Prints and Photographs Division[LC-DIG-jpd-02255]

The Art of the Floating World This 1745 work by Utagawa Toyoharu captures the spirit of *ukiyoe* in Tokugawa Japan. Ukiyoe artists often depicted courtesans and their patrons, and their conversations and pleasant pastimes, in a languid and sensual manner. Here reflections-within-reflections and deep three-point perspective pull the viewer into a world unconcerned with the hustle and bustle of life outside.

Farms became smaller and smaller, and without improvements in technology or sources of energy, Japan had nearly reached its limit in food production. As in China, irrigation had led to silting up of rivers and increased flooding. In addition, economic growth and urban construction had depleted Japan's timber resources. Wood became more expensive, and excessive logging led to soil erosion.

Yoshimune (r. 1716–1745), one of the greatest Tokugawa shoguns, issued edicts emphasizing frugality and curtailment of unnecessary consumption. True to the Confucian tradition, Yoshimune interpreted social problems as resulting from moral lapses. But his edicts could not change people's behavior.

Nevertheless, Yoshimune did sponsor some successful reforms. Most importantly, he reformed tax collections to eliminate local corruption, and he set strict limits on interest rates to relieve indebted farmers. He also sponsored the cultivation of sugar and ginseng to replace imports from Korea and Southeast Asia and promoted planting sweet potatoes on marginal land to increase the food supply. Support for fishing resulted in greater supplies of seafood and also of fertilizer needed to refresh the exhausted soil.

Yoshimune sought to bring merchants under greater control. Increased government involvement in commerce especially suited larger trading houses that were anxious to secure government-backed monopolies. But these policies tended to undermine entrepreneurialism, and they gradually made Japanese business more regulated and monopolistic and less dynamic and inventive.

For all his effort and energy, Yoshimune's reforms mainly amounted to "struggling to stand still."* Japan's social problems arising from the ecological and economic crises continued to escalate, as incidents of rural unrest nearly doubled in

Yoshimune

(1738–1795) Eighth Tokugawa ruler to hold the title of shogun. A conservative but capable leader under whose rule Japan saw advances in agricultural productivity.

---

*Conrad Totman, *Early Modern Japan* (Berkeley: University of California Press, 1993).

the later eighteenth century. Hundreds of thousands perished during the famine of the 1780s. It was becoming clear that the Tokugawa shoguns' conservative domestic policies were as inadequate as their continued attempts to seclude themselves from the outside world.

Tokugawa Japan and the Outside World, 1790–1837

The shoguns' conservative policies were most evident in foreign affairs. In the seventeenth century, alarmed by the early success of Christian missionaries, Tokugawa leaders had outlawed the faith (see Chapter 16), and they promulgated a series of **Seclusion Edicts** that strictly limited contact with Europeans, forbidding Japanese even to risk exposure through travel overseas. Those policies continued into the nineteenth century.

However, pragmatism did sometimes temper the policies of isolation. For one thing, Japanese seclusion applied only to Europeans. Trade with Chinese and Korean merchants grew, and overall Japanese foreign trade thereby increased. While contact with Europeans was limited, the scientific and philosophical books that reached Japan through the annual Dutch trade mission found an eager audience, especially among samurai. For centuries the Japanese called Western knowledge **Dutch learning**, and the ability to read Dutch became a sign of worldly sophistication. Nevertheless, for most Japanese aspiring to cultural sophistication it was still China, long the predominant external influence, which provided the templates for science and philosophy.

However, some Tokugawa thinkers, many of them samurai, downplayed even China's influence. They exalted Japan's indigenous Shinto religion and its emphasis on the spiritual forces of the natural and ancestral worlds. In rejecting foreign influences such as Buddhism, Confucianism and Dutch learning, advocates of Shinto reinforced the Tokugawa trend toward nativism and isolationism.

In contrast to the Qing, Russians, and British, Tokugawa Japan simply opted out of empire building. Its only territorial expansion was to lightly populated northern islands, especially Hokkaido (ho-KIE-do), where the indigenous Ainu people lived by hunting, gathering, and fishing and were no match for Japanese weapons. Even as external pressures increased in the late eighteenth century, the Tokugawa focus on self-sufficiency remained.

● **CONTEXT&CONNECTIONS** Japanese attitudes toward empire would change dramatically in the later nineteenth century, when Japan's naval defeat of China led to the acquisition of Taiwan and Korea (see Chapter 24). Japanese imperialism became even more aggressive in the first half of the twentieth century. Before and during the Second World War, the country conquered much of East and Southeast Asia (see Chapter 29). ●

In 1791, the first American ship landed in Japan, and the next year a Russian delegation sent by Catherine the Great arrived to establish trade relations. Although these events tested the shoguns' commitment to their isolationist policies, their response was unequivocal: the shogun reaffirmed the full force of the Seclusion Edict of 1639. The Japanese attacked foreign whaling vessels and fired on an 1837 American expedition, forcing it to flee.

This Japanese response was even less accommodating than that of the Qianlong Emperor in China, who at least allowed regulated trade with the British to continue even as he turned aside the Macartney Mission. Russia and the Western powers were, however, persistent. Soon Japan's leaders, like those in China, would face an ultimatum: open your doors to foreign trade, or advanced industrial weapons will blow them down (see Chapter 24).

Seclusion Edicts

Series of edicts issued by the Tokugawa shoguns that, beginning in the 1630s, outlawed Christianity and strictly limited Japanese contact with Europeans. Only a single annual Dutch trading mission was allowed, with the stipulation that no Bibles or other Christian texts were to enter the country.

Dutch learning

Traditional Japanese title for Western knowledge. Knowledge of Dutch in Tokugawa Japan was a sign of worldliness and sophistication.

World Economies and the Great Divergence

As our own times change, often our views of the past change as well. The recent economic successes of China and India have led some historians to reconsider Asia's place in the development of the modern world economy (see Chapters 31 and 32).

In the late seventeenth century, Mughal India was one of the world's most prosperous empires; Tokugawa Japan was urbanizing and commercializing; and the rulers of Qing China were cultivating the continuing expansion of the world's largest economy. By the early nineteenth century, however, the Industrial Revolution in Europe was rapidly shifting the global balance of economic power westward (see Chapter 23), ensuring the military and technological supremacy of Europe. The relationship between Britain and China shows just how suddenly and dramatically the change occurred. In 1793, the emperor Qianlong easily rebuffed British emissaries seeking stronger commercial and diplomatic ties; in 1839, ironclad British steamships destroyed China's coastal defenses and imposed their own terms of trade on humiliated Qing rulers (see Chapter 24).

In the past, many historians assumed that an exceptional bundle of European characteristics paved the way for industrial modernity. These factors included an early lead in scientific inquiry (see Chapter 21); the development of commercial capitalism and the relatively high status of merchants; competition between nations for economic and military advantage; and higher labor costs leading to increased innovation in manufacturing (see Chapters 16 and 17). In this view, Europe's early modern commercial empires translated smoothly into global economic dominance in the industrial age. Those assumptions have now been critiqued by historians who insist on a more global perspective, arguing that, prior to 1800, Europe's industrial potential was not unique.

That is the argument of historian Kenneth Pomeranz in his comparative study of what he calls the "great divergence" between the economies of Great Britain

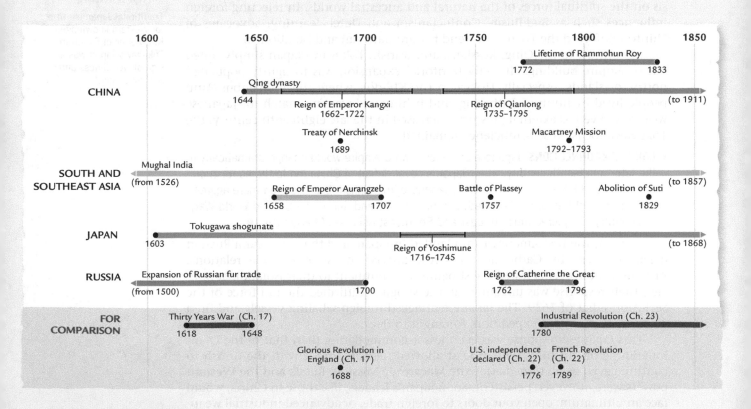

and China's Yangzi River Delta in the early nineteenth century.* According to Pomeranz, contingencies and accidents, not deep historical or cultural differences, explain Britain's early lead in industrial development. For example, Britain's coal deposits were much more easily accessible than China's. Access to the resources of the Americas was another key factor (see Chapters 18 and 19): American sugar plantations contributed greatly to the capital and organizational expertise that would later propel industry, and access to American timber and other natural resources freed the British from the ecological constraints of their own small island. In addition, Britain's maritime focus gave it a compelling interest in steam power that did not exist in Qing China, where security interests focused on Central Asia, not on the sea coast.

---

*Kenneth Pomeranz, *The Great Divergence: China, Europe, and the Making of the Modern World Economy* (Princeton: Princeton University Press, 2000).

It was also simple good fortune that monopoly trading companies like the British East India Company were in the right place at the right time to shift their priorities to providing raw materials for European industry and cultivating global markets for the products of European factories. Rammohun Roy was perhaps naïve to think that the Company's commercial activities would help elevate the Indian economy. In fact, political control would allow the Company to manipulate tariffs and markets to their own advantage, and at the expense of Indian manufacturers (see Chapter 23).

Though the debate among historians continues, a growing consensus emphasizes that vigorous economic growth in contemporary China and India marks a return to an earlier status quo when Asian economies were at the global forefront. Their relative poverty for the past two hundred years now looks to have been an aberration, and their current ascent a return to historical norms.

Key Terms

Rammohun Roy (590)
Qing dynasty (591)
Emperor Kangxi (593)
Qianlong (593)
Yangzi River Valley (593)
Treaty of Nerchinsk (597)

Macartney Mission (598)
Cossacks (599)
Catherine the Great (601)
Aurangzeb (603)
Maratha kingdoms (605)
Nader Shah (606)

Joseph Francois Dupleix (606)
Battle of Plassey (607)
Lord Charles Cornwallis (607)
Yoshimune (614)
Seclusion Edicts (615)
Dutch learning (615)

For Further Reference

Bayly, C. A. *Indian Society and the Making of the British Empire.* New York: Cambridge University Press, 1990.

Brower, Daniel R., and Edward J. Lazzarini. *Russia's Orient: Imperial Borderlands and Peoples, 1700–1917.* Bloomington: Indiana University Press, 1997.

Crossley, Pamela. *The Manchus.* Oxford, England: Blackwell Publishers, 2002.

Dalrymple, William. *White Mughals: Love and Betrayal in Eighteenth Century India.* New York: Penguin, 2004.

Dasgupta, Subrata. *Awakening: The Story of the Bengal Renaissance.* Delhi: Random House, 2011.

Kappeler, Andreas. *The Russian Empire: A Multiethnic History.* Harlow, England: Longman, 2001.

Keay, John. *The Honourable Company: A History of the English East India Company.* London: HarperCollins, 1991.

Matsunosuke, Nishiyama. *Edo Culture: Daily Life and Diversions in Urban Japan, 1600–1868.* Honolulu: University of Hawai'i Press, 1997.

Perdue, Peter C. *China Marches West: The Qing Conquest of Central Eurasia.* Cambridge, Mass.: Harvard University Press, 2005.

Richards, John. *The Mughal Empire.* New York: Cambridge University Press, 1996.

Totman, Conrad. *Early Modern Japan.* Berkeley: University of California Press, 1993

 **MindTap** is a fully online, highly personalized learning experience built upon Cengage Learning content. MindTap combines student learning tools—readings, multimedia, activities, and assessments—into a singular Learning Path that guides students through the course.

21

European Science and the Foundations of Modern Imperialism, 1600–1820

Sir Joseph Banks (1743–1820), 1771–72 (oil on canvas), Reynolds, Sir Joshua (1723–92)/Private Collection/Photo © Agnew's, London/Bridgeman Images

Joseph Banks

When the young botanist **Joseph Banks** (1743–1820) sailed aboard the *Endeavour* as part of a British expedition across the Pacific Ocean, his interest went beyond flora and fauna to include the people he encountered on the voyage. From the Amerindians of Tierra del Fuego (the southern tip of South America), to the Polynesians of the Pacific, to the Aboriginal peoples of Australia, Banks kept careful notes of his interactions with peoples of whom Europeans had little previous knowledge. His concern with these cultures went beyond mere curiosity. He was interested in understanding the relationships *between* societies. For example, when Banks learned that Tahitians understood the speech of the Maori (MAO-ree) of New Zealand, he recognized that there was a family connection between the two peoples. Banks was a pioneer of *ethnography*, the study of the linguistic and cultural relationships between peoples. However, he was mystified by the behavior of the Polynesian people he and his shipmates met when they stepped ashore on the island of Tahiti:

*T*hough at first they hardly dared approach us, after a little time they became very familiar. The first who approached us came crawling almost on his hands and knees and gave us a green bough. . . . This we received and immediately each of us gathered a green bough and carried it in our hands. They marched with us about 1/2 a mile and then made a general stop and, scraping the ground clean . . . every one of them threw his bough down upon the bare place and made signs that we should do the same. . . . Each of us dropped a

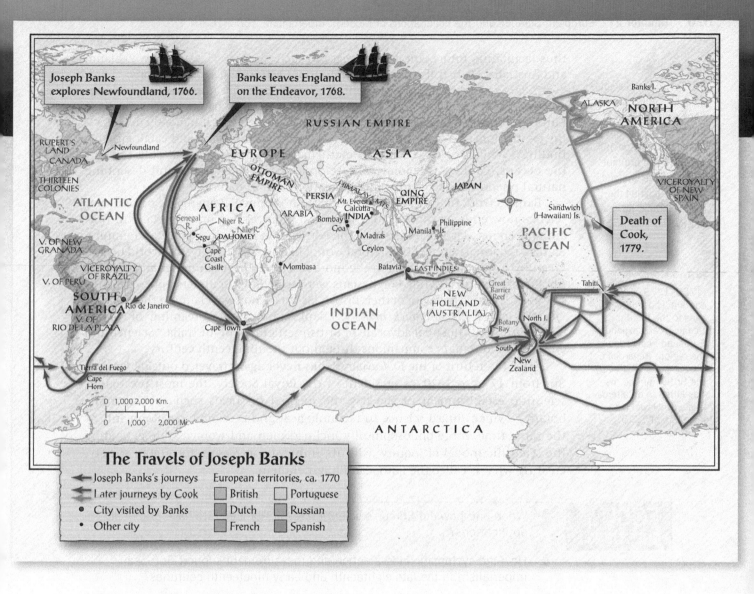

Joseph Banks explores Newfoundland, 1766.

Banks leaves England on the Endeavor, 1768.

Death of Cook, 1779.

The Travels of Joseph Banks

- ← Joseph Banks's journeys
- ← Later journeys by Cook
- • City visited by Banks
- • Other city

European territories, ca. 1770
- British
- Dutch
- French
- Portuguese
- Russian
- Spanish

bough upon those that the Indians had laid down, we all followed their example and thus peace was concluded.*

Such ceremonies became a bit less mysterious to Banks after he began to learn the Tahitian language and made friends with a high priest who helped him understand Polynesian customs. Still, even after years of contact, the cultural gulf between the Tahitians and the Englishmen remained.

Banks returned to England in 1771 after a three-year journey. The crewmen who had survived the *Endeavour*'s three years at sea were among the few at that time who had sailed around the world. Their captain, **James Cook** (1728–1779), became an instant celebrity. He had accomplished his mission of charting the Pacific Ocean,

---

*J. C. Beaglehole, ed., *The Endeavour Journal of Joseph Banks*, 2d ed., vol. 1 (Sydney: Halsted Press, 1962), p. 252. Here as elsewhere, some revisions of Banks's punctuation and usage have been made.

Joseph Banks

(1743–1820) English botanist on Captain James Cook's first voyage in the Pacific, who categorized different species of plants and brought them back to England. Also established the Royal Botanic Gardens at Kew.

James Cook

(1728–1779) British sea captain whose three voyages to the Pacific Ocean greatly expanded European knowledge of the region. Regarded as a great national hero by the British public, he was killed in an altercation with Hawai'ian islanders in 1779.

thus facilitating future European voyages to such places as Hawai'i, New Zealand, and Australia. He had also carried out important astronomical observations.

In fact, scientific inquiry was central to the *Endeavour*'s mission. The drawings and specimens of plant and animal life Banks brought back greatly expanded European knowledge of the natural world. He was interested not merely in collecting exotic flora and fauna but also in systematically classifying and cataloging his findings. While Cook was using his mathematical and navigational skills to chart the oceans, Banks was helping to develop a system for naming and describing natural phenomena to clarify familial relationships in nature.

Banks's work on the *Endeavour* produced no immediate, tangible benefit. But science now enjoyed considerable social and political support. Especially in Britain and France, leaders understood the connection between science and empire. Banks's reconnaissance of the natural world, like that of the physical world undertaken by Cook, was a prelude to the more assertive European imperialism of the nineteenth century. While Polynesians were struggling to understand what they saw as the strange behavior of their British visitors, Cook was claiming their islands *"for the use of his Brittanick majesty."* Banks came home dreaming of *"future dominions,"* an influential advocate of British settlement in Australia.* Science and empire would remain companions throughout the nineteenth century.

After the return of the *Endeavour*, Banks never again traveled outside Europe. But from 1778 to 1820, as president of the Royal Society, the most prestigious scientific establishment of the day, he focused on fields such as "economic botany," which linked science to technological and economic development. At the same time, more philosophically inclined men and women were extending the scientific model of inquiry, with its emphasis on reason, to human society, creating what is called the European Enlightenment.

FOCUS QUESTIONS

> When and how did Europe's scientific revolution begin to have practical applications?

> How did systematic classification and measurement support European imperialism in the late eighteenth and early nineteenth centuries?

> How did the societies of Oceania and Australia experience encounters with Europeans in this period?

> How did Enlightenment thought derive from the scientific revolution, and how did it differ from previous European thought systems?

From Scientific Revolution to Practical Science, 1600–1800

Joseph Banks was heir to a tradition that stretched back to the sixteenth century, when Nicolaus Copernicus first published his theory of a heliocentric solar system and Galileo Galilei upset church authorities by providing strong

*Quoted in Patrick O'Brien, *Joseph Banks: A Life* (Chicago: University of Chicago Press, 1987), pp. 105, 264.

evidence that the earth rotates around the sun (see Chapter 16). For most Europeans in the eighteenth century, the Christian faith, whether Catholic or Protestant, still held most of the answers to basic questions about relationships between God, humanity, and the natural world. By then, however, especially among the elites of northern Europe, men and women who embraced rational inquiry were becoming increasingly prominent. Aided by royal and aristocratic patronage, they began to pursue the "new science."

The development of science was important not only from a purely intellectual standpoint. Western science became "revolutionary" in global terms as its practical applications increased the political and military power of Europeans on the world stage. As president of the Royal Society and in his own research, Joseph Banks contributed to developments linking scientific inquiry to real-world applications and economic purposes on his own English estate, in Britain more generally, and across the expanding British empire.

The Development of the Scientific Method

In seventeenth-century western Europe an intellectual debate divided thinkers into two camps: the "ancients" and the "moderns." The "ancients," who carried forward the scholarly traditions of the humanists (see Chapter 15), emphasized the authority of Aristotle and other classical authors as the foundation on which knowledge in fields such as medicine, mathematics, and astronomy should be built. The "moderns" had a bolder idea.

Rejecting the infallibility of classical authority as well as Christian theology, the "moderns" argued that human reason provided the key to knowledge. It was an optimistic viewpoint that contradicted the traditional Christian conception of humanity as "fallen" from God's grace, tainted by original sin, and capable of salvation only through divine mercy. The "moderns" believed instead that humankind was endowed by God with reason and through that reason could apprehend and accurately describe God's creation. *"All our knowledge begins with the senses, proceeds then to the understanding, and ends with reason. There is nothing higher than reason,"* wrote the German philosopher Immanuel Kant (1724–1804).*

● **CONTEXT&CONNECTIONS** In imperial China, Confucian scholars also had long debated the reliability of input from the senses. Doubt characterized the late *Ming dynasty* period, when the Neo-Confucianism of Wang Yangming focused on the priority of inward contemplation (key term in Chapter 16). The eighteenth century, however, saw a reemphasis on the more empirical tradition of Confucianism during the reign of the Yongzheng emperor, when "evidential learning" led to the compilation of what was then the world's largest encyclopedia (see Chapter 20). For most Hindus and Buddhists, on the other hand, the issue was hardly debatable: the material world is illusory, and our senses are distractions from the truth, not guides toward it. ●

One seventeenth-century thinker who applied reason using a *deductive* approach—arguing from general principles to specific truths—was the Frenchman **René Descartes** (1596–1650). Descartes (DAY-cart) argued that the axioms of true philosophy had to be firmly grounded in the human capacity to reason. He associated rationality with mathematics and thought that logic could result in a

René Descartes
(1596–1650) French scientist, mathematician, and philosopher who developed the deductive method of reasoning (moving from general principles to particular facts).

---

*Immanuel Kant, *Critique of Pure Reason*, ed. and trans. Wolgang Schwarz (Berlin: Scientia Verlag Aalen, 1982), p. 217.

Robin Treadwell/Science Source

Elisabeth and Johannes Hevelius The German-Polish astronomer Johannes Hevelius was an innovator in celestial observation and data collection, using telescopes of his own design to study lunar topography. A member of London's Royal Society, Hevelius is shown here with his second wife, Elisabeth, who came to him begging for instruction when she was just a teenager. They married and collaborated from that point on. After Johannes died, Elisabeth Hevelius achieved independent recognition for her continued work.

Sir Francis Bacon
(1561–1626) English politician, essayist, and philosopher who argued for inductive reasoning—working from observation of natural phenomena to larger truths.

unified system of truth. Emphasizing systematic doubt as a key to knowledge, he questioned even his own existence. His famous solution, *"I think, therefore I am,"* demonstrated that his ability to reason was the proof of his existence. Descartes also believed he had to doubt the existence of God before proving to himself that God did, in fact, exist. For Descartes, proof of God's existence came from rational thought rather than inherited wisdom or sacred texts.

While Descartes' philosophy was based on introspection, others were laying the foundations for modern science based on experimentation and observation of the natural world. The Englishman **Sir Francis Bacon** (1561–1626) was one of the main proponents of an *inductive* approach to science: working from modest, carefully controlled observations toward larger truths. Like Descartes, Bacon believed that doubt produced knowledge. *"If a man will begin with certainties,"* he wrote, *"he shall end in doubts; but if he will be content to begin with doubts he shall end in certainties."** (See the feature "Movement of Ideas Through Primary Sources: A Japanese View of European Science.")

As Copernicus and Galileo had demonstrated (see Chapter 16), astronomy was a prime example of how empirical scientists used systematic observation and the application of mathematics to unlock the secrets of a rationally ordered cosmos. Tycho Brahe (1546–1601), a Danish nobleman, also contributed to this effort. Using observations made with only the naked eye, in 1573 Brahe challenged the Aristotelian concept of an eternally unchanging celestial sphere by demonstrating that a bright supernova had emerged beyond the earth's atmosphere.

One of Brahe's assistants, the younger German mathematician Johannes Kepler (1571–1630), then applied Brahe's data to an analysis of the orbit of the planet Mars, using a Copernican framework placing the sun at the center of the solar system. Kepler's calculations, published in 1609, showed that planetary motion could be most simply explained by plotting the planets' orbits along elliptical rather than circular paths. But both Aristotle and Christian teaching insisted that all celestial motion was circular, the perfect form of movement for a perfect heavenly domain. Kepler thus reinforced Galileo's challenge to the traditional Christian idea that the "perfect" heavens

---

*Sir Francis Bacon, *Advancement of Learning*, with a preface by Thomas Case (London: Oxford University Press, 1906), p. 35.

above are governed by different physical laws than the "sinful" earth below. This was a real breakthrough for science: the notion that identical laws of nature prevail throughout the entire universe, and that those laws can be elegantly described through mathematics.

At first, such radical new ideas caused discomfort, as when an English poet of the early seventeenth century expressed his feeling of disorientation in a Copernican universe: *"The sun is lost, and the earth, and no man's wit / Can well direct him where to look for it . . . / 'Tis all in pieces, all coherence gone."** Tensions between "faith" and "reason," whether religion or science offered the surest path to truth, would continue far into the future (see Chapter 23). A century later, however, the prestige of science was on the rise. More Europeans became comfortable with the idea that it is our God-given ability to reason and to use our senses to observe nature that gives us the means to comprehend the brilliance of creation, and to strive toward truth on the basis of science.

The achievements of the Englishman **Isaac Newton** (1642–1727) confirmed that increasingly confident and optimistic worldview. Newton followed Descartes' lead in using reasoned, deductive thinking to establish general principles that tied together his own findings and those of other scientists. He was also a brilliant observer of the natural world, following Bacon's inductive approach to experimental science. Newton described a predictable natural world in which all matter exerts gravitational attraction in inverse proportion to mass and distance: the universal law of gravitation. To achieve the mathematical rigor necessary to describe the acceleration and deceleration of bodies in motion, Newton became one of the inventors of differential calculus.

Now, by the early eighteenth century, an English poet could write: *"Nature and Nature's laws lay hid in night; God said Let Newton Be! and all was light."*[†] The association between God and Newton in this poem shows that the tension between science and faith was beginning to ease. Newton himself was a devout Christian, and while many continued to believe that God actively intervened in nature, those who adopted Newton's outlook tended to see the universe as a self-functioning outcome of God's perfect act of creation. God was like a master clock maker who, having set his elegant machine in motion, did not need to further interfere.

● **CONTEXT&CONNECTIONS** Deists like Newton embraced the ethics of the New Testament and retained their belief in God, while rejecting the idea of His active intervention in the natural world or human affairs. Others with a similar viewpoint included *Rammohun Roy* (Chapter 20) and Thomas Jefferson. Jefferson and many other deists were also Freemasons, members of lodges that used secret rites and rituals to promote reason, charity, and brotherly love (see Chapter 22). ●

Newton confidently declared that he could use mathematics to *"demonstrate the frame of the system of the world."* Joseph Banks inherited not only Newton's optimism but also his position as president of the Royal Society. Starting with Newton and continuing with Banks, this assembly of leading thinkers served as a nerve center for European science.

Isaac Newton
(1642–1727) Skilled theoretical and experimental scientist who did more than anyone to create a new, systematic architecture for science by stating the universal law of gravitation. Also one of the inventors of differential calculus, he undertook extensive experiments with optics that led to much more powerful telescopes.

---

*John Donne, "An Anatomy of the World," The Poetry Foundation, http://www.poetryfoundation.org/poem/173348

[†]Alexander Pope, "Epitaph Intended for Sir Isaac Newton," in *Pope: Selected Works*, ed. Herbert Davis (London: Oxford University Press, 1966), p. 651.

A Japanese View of European Science

In the history of modern science, a common pattern has been repeated around the world. Those who generated new ideas, such as Galileo, were often attacked for their assault on tradition, but later their innovations were absorbed into the status quo. When Europeans then took the new science to other continents, once again these ideas and approaches challenged established tradition. Here we have an example from anatomy, with a Japanese observation of the dissection of a human corpse.

For medieval Europeans, the main authority in anatomy was the ancient Greek physician Galen who, though he dissected many birds and animals, had theories about the inner workings of the human body that were based largely on speculation. Then, in 1543, a Belgian physician published a new scheme of human anatomy based on actual dissection of human cadavers. Adherents of Galen's view were upset, as were those many Christians who saw the violation of dead bodies as sacrilegious. Over the next two hundred years, however, dissection became a routine process.

In the eighteenth century, the Tokugawa shoguns had severely limited Japanese contacts with Europeans. But through the annual Dutch trade mission to Nagasaki, a few books entered the country, and some curious Japanese scholars learned Dutch so they could read them (see Chapter 20). Below, a physician named Sugita Gempaku (1733–1817) describes how, having looked at a Dutch anatomy text, he was astonished to see how accurate it was when he witnessed the dissection of a human body.

> What was the basis of earlier Japanese views of anatomy, and how were they contradicted by the Dutch textbook?

> How did Gempaku's experience indicate that there were beliefs in Japanese society restricting the routine examination of human corpses for medical research?

Source: Japan: A Documentary History, ed. David J. Lu (Armonk, N.Y.: M. E. Sharpe, 1997), pp. 264–267. Used with permission of M. E. Sharpe, Inc.

A Dutch Lesson in Anatomy

Somehow, miraculously I obtained a [Dutch] book on anatomy. [Then] I received a letter from . . . the Town Commissioner: "A post-mortem examination of the body of a condemned criminal by a resident physician will be held tomorrow. . . . You are welcome to witness it if you so desire."

The next day, when we arrived at the location . . . Ryotaku reached under his kimono to produce a Dutch book and showed it to us. "This is a Dutch book of anatomy called *Tabulae Anatomicae*. I bought this a few years ago when I went to Nagasaki, and kept it." As I examined it, it was the same book I had and was of the same edition. We held each other's hands and exclaimed: "What a coincidence!" Ryotaku continued by saying, "When I went to Nagasaki, I learned and heard," and opened this book. "These are called *long* in Dutch, they are the lungs," he taught us. "This is *hart*, or the heart." . . . However, they did not look like the heart given in the Chinese medical books, and none of us were sure until we could actually see the dissection.

Thereafter we went together to the place that was especially set aside [for] us to observe the dissection. . . . That day, the butcher pointed to this and that organ. After the heart, liver, gall bladder and stomach were identified, he pointed to other parts for which there were no names. "I don't know their names. But I have dissected quite a few bodies from my youthful days. . . . Every time I had a dissection, I pointed out to those physicians many of these parts, but not a single one of them questioned 'What was this,' or 'What was that?'" We compared the body as dissected against the charts both Ryotaku and I had, and could not find a single variance from the charts. The Chinese *Book of Medicine* says that the lungs are like the eight petals of the lotus flower, with three petals hanging in front, three in back, and two petals forming like two ears. . . . There were no such divisions, and the position and shapes of intestines and gastric organs were all different from those taught by the old theories. The official physicians . . . had witnessed dissection seven or eight times. Whenever they witnessed the dissection, they found that the old theories contradicted reality. Each time they were perplexed and could not resolve their doubts. Every time they wrote down what they thought was strange. They wrote in their books, "The more we think of it, there must be fundamental differences in the bodies of Chinese and of the eastern barbarians." I could see why they wrote this way. . . .

We decided that we should also examine the shape of the skeletons left exposed on the execution ground. We collected the bones, and examined a number of them. Again, we were struck by the fact that they all differed from the old theories while conforming to the Dutch charts. . . .

On the way home we spoke to each other and felt the same way. "How marvelous was our actual experience today. It is a shame that we were ignorant of these things until now. As physicians . . . we performed our duties in complete ignorance of the true form of the human body." . . . Then I spoke to my companion, "Somehow if we can translate anew this book called *Tabulae Anatomicae*, we can get a clear notion of the human body inside out. It will have great benefit in the treatment of our patients. Let us do our best to read it and understand it without the help of translators." . . .

The next day, we assembled at the house of Ryotaku and recalled the happenings of the previous day. When we faced the *Tabulae Anatomicae* we felt as if we were setting sail on a great ocean in a ship without oars or a rudder. With the magnitude of the work before us, we were dumbfounded by our own ignorance. . . . At that time I did not know the twenty-five letters of the Dutch alphabet. I decided to study the language with firm determination, but I had to acquaint myself with letters and words gradually.

Practical Science: Economic Botany, Agriculture, and Empire

Reliant on the natural world for medicine as well as food, people have always studied plant life. It was only with the rise of modern botany, however, that scientists began to systematically collect and organize a catalogue of the world's flora.

Carl Linnaeus (1707–1778) was the pioneering figure in this area. As a medical student, Linnaeus first studied plants for their medicinal properties, but as his enthusiasm for plant collecting grew, he enlarged his focus. He traveled across Sweden gathering plant specimens, restored the botanical gardens at his university, and eventually sent nineteen of his students on voyages around the world to gather specimens for study. Two of Linnaeus's students were aboard the *Endeavour* with Joseph Banks.

Like Newton, Linnaeus combined close scientific observation with theoretical system building. In 1735, he published his classification of living things, *Systema Naturae*. The Linnaean system orders species into hierarchical categories still in use today—genus/order/class/kingdom—in which any new plant from anywhere in the world can be classified. To Linnaeus, this orderly relationship among living things was another demonstration of the harmony of God's creation.

Linnaeus also developed the binomial ("two name") system of Latin names for organisms, with the first name indicating the genus and the second the species. Though the world's plants already had names used by the people who were familiar with them, those local names fit no consistent network of classification. Now, as Linnaeus's students brought more and more specimens back to Europe, they received new names that made them, for the first time, part of a single knowledge system.

Though Joseph Banks was perhaps a less original botanical thinker than Carl Linnaeus, he was exceptionally adept at deriving practical economic lessons from his work. Banks was a leading figure in the drive for "improvement." In agriculture, "improvement" meant using scientific methods to increase the productivity of existing land and to bring new land under cultivation. Both Banks and King George III (r. 1760–1820), sometimes called "the farmer king," eagerly supported the effort to bring to agriculture the insights gained from natural science. Since the seventeenth century, English farmers had learned to improve the soil by sowing clover and turnips in fields that had previously been left fallow. They also practiced selective breeding of livestock to boost the production of wool, meat, and milk.

Joseph Banks was among the wealthy "gentleman farmers" in England who could afford to invest in water engineering technology pioneered by the Dutch, reclaiming low-lying land by using windmills to pump water from diked marshes. Banks's estate exemplified all the other measures that were improving agricultural productivity in eighteenth-century England, including experimenting with crop rotations and crossbreeding farm animals. The outcome of this "agricultural revolution" was more arable land for planting and greater efficiency in production. The timing was significant, since increased food supplies would support urbanization during the Industrial Revolution (see Chapter 23).

● **CONTEXT&CONNECTIONS** The use of canals, dikes, and irrigation ditches to control water for agricultural production is as old as civilization itself. In Chinese history, imperial states actively sponsored and controlled large-scale water projects, building canals, irrigation channels, and dams (see Chapters 16 and 20). Grain agriculture in northwestern Europe, in contrast, was less dependent on irrigation, and here royal support for labor-intensive water control projects was far less common. Some historians argue that long-term differences in the roles of Chinese and European states can be explained through such differences in water management. ●

This agricultural revolution led to greater inequality, however. Previously, English village society, like peasant societies elsewhere, was oriented toward stability and security. Farm families all shared common access to pastures and woodlands. But in the seventeenth and eighteenth centuries, members of the English gentry, like the Banks family, accumulated larger landholdings under new laws allowing them to "enclose" common lands as private property. Collective food security in the countryside now mattered less than productivity and profitable crop sales.

Having lost access to the commons, many rural families could no longer sustain themselves. Those who could not find work serving the gentry drifted to cities or coal mines looking for employment. One person's "improvement," therefore, could be another's ticket to unemployment. Banks himself received numerous protests from displaced farmers, and his London house was once stormed by protesters of a trade law that benefited landholders like Banks while raising the price of bread for the urban poor. Hunger also resulted in rural areas when new laws barred the poor from hunting wild game, a traditional way to supplement their diets: "poaching" royal and aristocratic game became a hanging offense. Notwithstanding popular resistance to enclosure and hunting restrictions, the law was on the side of the upper class: the interests of "gentlemen" were well represented in Parliament and in the courts; those of the poor were not.

Joseph Banks was also an advocate for "improvement" on the imperial stage, playing a pivotal role in globalizing the practical application of science through his advocacy of "economic botany." To this end, he developed a pioneering experimental facility at Kew Gardens, *a great botanical exchange house for the empire.* * Scientists brought new plant specimens from around the world to Kew to be examined, catalogued, and cultivated, and the benefits of this "economic botany" could then be disseminated in Britain and its colonies.

Throughout the expanding British empire, in such places as the West Indies, South Africa, and India, British governors and commercial concerns established botanical gardens as part of the effort to achieve "improvement" on a global scale. Unlike the haphazard Columbian exchange, this was biological diffusion aided by science. For example, when the British Navy needed secure supplies of timber from tall trees for ship construction, English botanists identified South Asian mahogany as a possible supplement to British and North American oak and shipped seeds from India to botanical gardens in the British West Indies for study. Another famous example is the story of breadfruit, a nutritious plant food first encountered by Joseph Banks on the island of Tahiti. Banks saw the potential for transferring breadfruit from Polynesia to the West Indies as inexpensive food for slaves, and through his influence the Royal Navy sent the *Bounty* in 1787 to bring specimens to Kew Gardens. (The *Bounty* failed at its task when the crew mutinied against their captain; however, subsequent attempts to diffuse tropical crops like breadfruit across the British empire succeeded.)

The emphasis on science and "improvement" also served to justify the dominance of the British elite at home and abroad. Advocates of enclosure argued that those who were thrust aside would ultimately benefit from scientifically rational

---

*Quoted in Richard Drayton, *Nature's Government: Science, Imperial Britain, and the 'Improvement' of the World* (New Haven: Yale University Press, 2000), p. 108.

Botany and Art Most scientific expeditions, starting with Banks' own journey to the Pacific and Australia, employed artists to catalog in fine detail the new flora they encountered. This exquisite rendering of a Corypha Elata plant, native to northern Australia, was produced by an anonymous Indian artist employed by the British.

agriculture. The same attitude applied across the empire. Francis Bacon had earlier applied this idea to British colonization in Ireland: "*We shall reclaim them from their barbarous manners . . . populate, plant and make civil all the provinces of that kingdom.*"* If "barbarous" peoples like the Irish were not using the land efficiently, the argument went, it could be legally seized from them by those who would make it "civil."

Banks regarded Australia as "empty" land, because its aboriginal inhabitants had not "improved" it. Aboriginal Australians might not understand the necessity of fencing off vast land holdings for sheep—thus barring them from their ancestral hunting and gathering lands—but no one, the "improvers" would say, should stand in the way of progress.

The British would long justify their empire by claiming that it created the best possible life for the local inhabitants. Banks shared in that view. Economic botany, he once wrote, "*would help to banish famine in India and win the love of the Asiatics for their British conquerors.*"*

---

*Quoted in Richard Drayton, *Nature's Government: Science, Imperial Britain, and the 'Improvement' of the World* (New Haven: Yale University Press, 2000), pp. 55, 118.

Museums, Science, and Empire

The work of museums in the collection, analysis, classification, and preservation of natural and cultural phenomena can be traced back to the foundation of the British Museum in 1759. Today, museums must often contend with legacies of imperialism marking their collections, such as demands for repatriation of prized items.

From the sixteenth century, the inquisitive thrust of the new science had an acquisitive dimension as well. Gentlemen and aristocrats competed to assemble "cabinets of curiosities"—shelves full of interesting and exotic specimens—both for their own amusement and to provoke their visitors' envy and astonishment.

Then the eighteenth century brought a new seriousness of purpose, the rise of a more rigorous culture of evidence and classification. Sir Hans Sloane (1660–1753) pioneered this more focused approach. Sloane was a member of the Royal Society who traveled to Jamaica, collecting not only flora and fauna, but also cultural artifacts characteristic of its largely African population (see Chapter 19). As Sloane's acquisitions and reputation grew, others sent him samples from their own collections, forming the basis of the donation that would found the British Museum. Joseph Banks contributed ethnographic material from his Polynesian voyage.

Modern museums descended from this tradition are not, however, without their controversies. One is determining the proper ownership of artifacts. The British Museum's Elgin Marbles, for example, were taken from Athens by a British ambassador to the Ottoman empire two centuries ago and then sold to the British government. The government of Greece has long demanded their return, seeing the marbles as a cornerstone of their national culture. Similarly, some of the most exquisite examples of bronze statuary from the West African kingdom of Benin (see Chapter 16) are on display at the British Museum, having been looted during the British sack of the royal palace in 1897. Like the Greek government, the royal family of Benin has demanded the repatriation of their cultural patrimony.

Museums are an example of the longstanding entanglement of science and empire. While we all have a great deal to learn from visiting the world's great museums, we should keep in mind the question of how those objects arrived in their current settings and ask whether descendants of the original owners might still have a legitimate claim upon them.

Measuring and Mapping: Exploration and Imperialism in Africa, India, and the Americas, 1763–1820

In an age of expanding European empires, the scientific quest for classification and quantification had global implications. In the late eighteenth and early nineteenth centuries, increased sophistication in the measurement of time and the mapping of space firmly linked science and empire.

Europeans' acquisition of more detailed information on world geography was an essential step toward global control. As European expeditions gathered geographical information across the globe, proliferating scientific societies communicated that knowledge internationally. Expeditions also brought back cultural artifacts from around the world, stimulating interest in the scientific study of culture. (See the feature "World History in Today's World: Museums, Science, and Empire.")

Practical Science: The Royal Society and the Quest for Longitude

As a natural scientist, Banks was most competent in the field of living organisms and their interconnections. Within the Royal Society, over which he presided from 1778 to 1820, many saw mathematics and astronomy as the superior sciences. All scientists, however, were interested in practical applications of their theories. For a nation whose rising global power depended on its maritime prowess, the most important applications of mathematics and astronomy concerned navigation. The **problem of longitude**—how to determine a ship's position on an east-west axis—occupied some of the best minds of the time.

problem of longitude

The lack of an accurate way to determine a ship's position on an east-west axis. English cabinetmaker John Harrison's invention of an accurate shipboard chronometer solved the problem.

It was a riddle that had puzzled mariners for much of human history. The best way to describe the location of any given point is with a set of imaginary intersecting lines that we know as latitude and longitude. For centuries, mariners had been able to determine their latitude, or north-south position, using Arab technologies such as the quadrant and astrolabe (AS-truh-labe) and, later, the more accurate sextant. Longitude was another matter. East-west distance traveled could be measured only if the time at any two points could be accurately compared. Until the late eighteenth century, ships' captains had no better solution than using a log and a measured rope to roughly calculate the speed and distance traveled. By this system, captains often miscalculated their position by hundreds of miles, looking in vain for land they expected to find or crashing onto rocky shores they did not. A heavy toll resulted, in shipwrecks, destroyed cargo, and lost lives, whether from drowning or dehydration.

The regular, clocklike cosmos described by scientists from Galileo to Newton offered hope. Longitude could be accurately fixed if a captain knew exactly what time it was at his current position relative to any other fixed location on earth. Observing that the motion of the heavens could be described mathematically, European scientists set out to find a way to translate celestial time into local time on board a ship. But into the eighteenth century, they had not worked out a practical solution.

● **CONTEXT&CONNECTIONS** In the early fifteenth century, Zheng He, commander of Ming China's "precious ships," determined his latitude by using the compass and innovative "star boards" that gave extremely accurate determinations of the height of various celestial objects. But Zheng He did not have any better means of determining longitude than Christopher Columbus or other European mariners. The problem of longitude was probably less critical in this case, however, since the Chinese ships spent less time crossing open seas as they navigated the coasts of Southeast Asia, India, the Persian Gulf, and Africa (see Chapter 15). ●

To an ambitious maritime power like England, the "problem of longitude" was a matter of public policy. In 1714, the British Parliament offered a cash prize to anyone who could solve it, but for decades no proposals were worthy of serious consideration. In popular speech, "discovering the longitude" came to mean "attempting the impossible."

But the astronomers in the Royal Society were persistent. The key to the problem, Isaac Newton believed, was to determine the "lunar distance" by finding a way to accurately measure the position of the moon relative to the sun by day, and to the stars by night. Doing so would require sky charts by which the future locations of these heavenly bodies could be accurately predicted. Further complicating the problem, a separate star chart would be needed for the entirely different night sky of the Southern Hemisphere.

By the 1760s, having spent hundreds of thousands of hours working on these charts, the astronomers and mathematicians of the Royal Society believed they were close to a solution. The role of the *Endeavour*, which set out in 1769, was to observe the movement of Venus across the face of the sun, an event that occurred every eight years. By using identical observations made in a wide variety of geographic locations, of which Cook's was by far the farthest from the Royal Observatory at Greenwich, astronomers would be able to predict much more accurately the future path of Venus. The solar, lunar, and stellar charts available to Cook on this journey were already much better than any other captain had ever used in the Pacific.

Meanwhile, another, potentially simpler solution would be to use a clock that accurately showed the current time at the point of departure. A captain could use stellar readings to easily calculate the time at his present location and compare that with the time at his starting point, as kept by the timepiece. Eighteenth-century clocks, however, were not accurate enough. Relying on a shipboard clock that was gaining or losing fifteen seconds a day could send a ship hundreds of miles off course.

English carpenter and clockmaker John Harrison took on the challenge of perfecting a timepiece that would be reliable enough to maintain its accuracy at sea despite the constant motion from the waves, excessive humidity, and changes in temperature. Harrison began work on his first "chronometer," as these time- pieces came to be known, in 1727. It became his life's work: the last of his four versions was not finished until 1763, when he completed a compact chronometer that was accurate in oceanic conditions within one second per day.

Harrison's challenges were not only technical. Many astronomers in the Royal Society were highly status conscious and looked down on a mere "cabinetmaker" like Harrison, and they were unwilling to give his prototypes the kind of trials that might lead to the prize. They believed that only mathematics could provide a solution.

As it turned out, both Harrison and the astronomers were on the right track. On Cook's first voyage, he used the latest astronomical charts with great success. On his second voyage, Cook also took a chronometer and was very impressed, reporting that *"it exceeded the expectations of its most zealous advocate and . . . has been our faith- ful guide through all vicissitudes of climate."** By the early nineteenth century, Harrison's chronometer was standard equipment on British naval vessels.

Mariners needed a fixed point from which the 360 degrees of longitude could be established. That "prime meridian" was set at Greenwich, the site of the Royal Observatory. Even the French, who first used Paris as the zero point, eventually accepted the British stan- dard. Greenwich had become the "center of the world," the starting point for global lines of longitude and the reference point for the world's clocks. (Today, Universal Coordinated Time [UTC] still derives from "Greenwich Mean Time.")

Just up the Thames River from Greenwich, mean- while, Joseph Banks had developed Kew Gardens as the world's leading center of botany. In both astron- omy and botany, therefore, "practical science," the ability to apply the scientific outlook to real-world applications, propelled the rising power of Britain, and of Europe, across the globe.

Harrison's Chronom- eter John Harrison solved the "problem of longitude," greatly increasing the safety and efficiency of oceanic navigation, when he perfected his chronometer in 1763. An elegant piece of craftsmanship, Har- rison's chronometer was a sophisticated and durable timepiece that kept accurate time even on rough seas and in high humidity, exemplifying the British tradition of "practical science." (National Maritime Museum, London/The Image Works)

---

*Quoted in Dava Sorbel and William J. H. Andrews, *The Illustrated Longitude: The True Story of a Lone Genius Who Solved the Greatest Scientific Problem of His Time* (New York: Walker and Co., 1998), p. 176.

Mapping Africa, Central Asia, India, and the Americas

Under the leadership of Joseph Banks, geographic exploration became a priority for the Royal Society, part of a larger European effort to map the world. As part of that focus, Banks and the Royal Society founded and funded the **African Association**, primarily in response to French competition. Until this time, Europeans in Africa had restricted themselves to small coastal settlements connected with the Atlantic slave trade (see Chapter 19). But the French seemed positioned to expand inland from their long-established outpost at the mouth of the Senegal River, a gateway to the rich and populous lands of the predominantly Muslim Sahel.

African Association

Society founded in 1788 by Joseph Banks to sponsor geographical expeditions into Africa and chart the course of the Niger River, a feat partially achieved by Mungo Park.

The founders of the African Association guessed that the key to the West African interior was the Niger River. The Niger was indeed the region's major thoroughfare, but they knew little of its origins and path. Exploring the course of the Niger would add to geographic, botanical, and ethnographic knowledge and might also promote British imperial expansion. Recruiting a young Scottish doctor named Mungo Park, whom Banks had earlier recommended as surgeon on a ship bound for Southeast Asia, the African Association sponsored a voyage of exploration to West Africa in 1795.

Park's voyage was difficult. The West African interior had been destabilized by the Atlantic slave trade, and his mission depended on the hospitality of Africans he met en route. He made it safely to Segu on the upper reaches of the Niger, an important political and economic center ever since the empire of Songhai (see Chapter 16). There his African hosts gave him an accurate picture of how people and goods moved along the river and into the wider Islamic world through North Africa and Egypt, while confirming that the Niger flowed west to east. But illness drove Park back to the coast before he could complete his mission; the precise contours of the African interior would remain obscure to European geographers for decades (see Chapter 26).

At the same time, the British were pursuing an even more elaborate geographic project in India. The British East India Company ruled rich territories from its bases at Calcutta in the northeast and Madras in the south as it began to supplant the Mughal empire (see Chapter 20). British rule in India was established not only with guns and diplomacy, but also with maps.

● **CONTEXT&CONNECTIONS** In the eighteenth century, officials in *Qing dynasty* China (Chapter 20) were also systematically compiling maps and ethnographic information about subject peoples as their empire expanded to include not only China but also parts of Central Asia. But Qing maps dealt only with a single empire, while European maps encompassed the entire globe, as Western explorers from various nations contributed to a single, expanding network of knowledge. ●

Great Trigonometrical Survey

Survey begun by the British in the late 1790s to plot the entire Indian subcontinent on a mathematically precise grid. The survey was a prelude to the expansion of Britain's Indian empire.

Beginning in the 1790s, the British undertook the **Great Trigonometrical Survey** to map the Indian subcontinent in a mathematical grid. From an astronomically determined meridian of longitude in the south of India, surveyors made precise triangulations between two other points and the first known location. Once three locations could be precisely defined in terms of longitude and latitude, the survey could proceed with further triangular measurements. Eventually the Great Trigonometrical Survey drove straight through India to the Himalayas. The highest mountain peak in the world, called Chomolungma, "Mother of the Universe," by the Tibetans, was renamed by the British "Mount Everest" after George Everest, the British surveyor-general. Such renaming occurred all over the world.

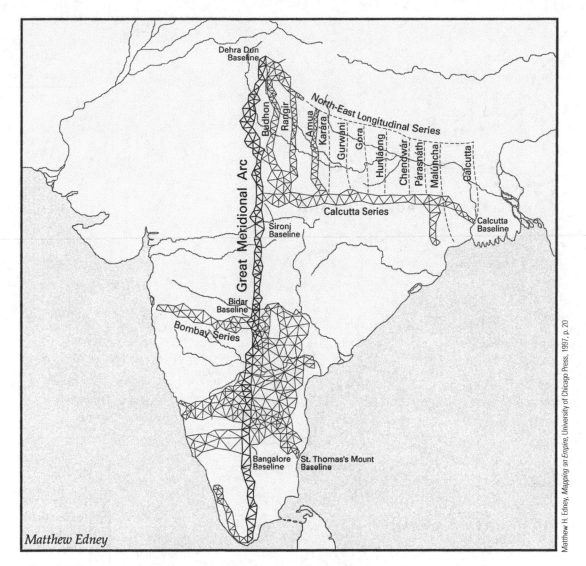

Matthew H. Edney, *Mapping an Empire*, University of Chicago Press, 1997, p. 20

The Great Trigonometrical Survey Beginning in southern India in the 1790s, British surveyors undertook a painstaking mapping project using a triangulation technique to map vast territories. By 1843, the survey had reached the Himalayas. Accurate maps were a key source of British imperial power.

The purposes of the Great Trigonometrical Survey were in keeping with Newtonian principles of rationality, harmony, and order. Previously, Europeans had seen the Mughal empire as an exotic and mystical land. The survey transformed the strange and unknowable "Hindustan" of earlier maps into a precisely ordered "India," a coherent world region. The process of mapping expressed imperial control, even over areas that had not yet been conquered. The Great Trigonometrical Survey created the skeletal structure onto which the bones, muscle, and skin of British India would be grafted.

Similar surveys were also being conducted elsewhere, including the Americas. Captain Cook's Pacific journeys helped determine the size of North America

Map 21.1 The Exploration of Western North America While Captain George Vancouver followed James Cook's Pacific expeditions and traced the Pacific coastline of North America, in the 1790s Alexander Mackenzie traced routes into the frigid interior. A decade later, Meriwether Lewis and William Clark investigated a route from St. Louis to the Oregon coast, while David Thompson traced the course of the Columbia River. U.S. Army captain Zebulon Pike led expeditions up the Mississippi River and explored the southern and western regions of the Louisiana Purchase, turning south from the Colorado Mountains into New Spain. Geographic exploration went hand in hand with expanding state frontiers across North America, as in the wider world.

(see map on page 619); then in the 1790s Captain George Vancouver and his crew charted its western coasts as far north as Alaska. At the same time, the explorer Alexander Mackenzie traveled a difficult passage from the Arctic Ocean, through what is now northern Canada, to the Pacific coast, relying on the latest technology from London (a sophisticated compass, sextant, chronometer, and telescope) as well as the knowledge of indigenous guides (see Map 21.1).

The new United States (see Chapter 22) became involved in western exploration with the **Lewis and Clark Expedition** from the Mississippi River to the Pacific coast (1804–1806), an effort, as in India, to bring what the British and Americans considered "exotic" lands into "rationality." One of President Thomas Jefferson's motivations in sponsoring the expedition was to assess the potential for an American outlet to the Pacific Ocean to facilitate trade with Asia, but the reports also made clear the huge size and vast economic potential of the American interior itself.

Like Banks and his protégés, Meriwether Lewis and William Clark carefully noted the flora and fauna on their journey, bringing the natural world of the American West into the orbit of scientific knowledge. Also like Banks, they noted the customs of indigenous peoples, speculating on their possible origins and the linguistic and cultural relationships between them. They carried surveying equipment, creating maps that settlers would later use to help them occupy the land. In the subsequent transformation of indigenous landscapes into the American West, we see another example of the intimate relationship between science and empire.

In every case, whether it was a new plant species, the height of a mountain, or the location of a harbor, Europeans added any new fact to a central bank of data, where it could be related to a centralized system of classification organized along hierarchical and mathematical lines. Control of such knowledge would radically increase the global power of Europe in the nineteenth century.

Lewis and Clark Expedition

(1804–1806) Government-sponsored team led by Meriwether Lewis and William Clark to explore a route through Native American territory to the Pacific. The expedition also documented plants and animals.

Oceania and Australia, 1770–1820

The three journeys of Captain James Cook consolidated the role of science in advancing the expansion of the British empire. Extending the reach of his first expedition, accompanied by Joseph Banks aboard the *Endeavour*, on his second and third journeys, Cook sailed near the coast of Antarctica and north to the Arctic Ocean; he also added the Hawai'ian Islands to Europe's map of the Pacific. Joseph Banks did not accompany Cook's later journeys. But from England he played a major role in the settlement of Australia, a British colony on a continent that had been virtually unknown to Europeans before Cook's voyage.

Captain Cook in Polynesia, 1769–1779

On the first voyage, Cook and Banks were aided by a Tahitian high priest named **Tupaia** (ca. 1725–1770). Tupaia (too-PUH-ee-uh) knew several Polynesian languages and, coming from a family of navigators, was able to supplement Cook's instruments and charts with a local understanding of winds and currents. He also helped Banks understand Polynesian cultural practices, such as the meaning of the peace ritual that had so mystified the Englishman when he first set foot on the island.

Tupaia

(ca. 1725–1770) A Polynesian high priest who contributed his expert navigational skills to Captain James Cook's first Pacific voyage.

In spite of Tupaia's help, miscommunications persisted. In his journals, Banks noted with frustration *"how much these people are given to thieving."* *"All are of the opinion,"* he writes, *"that if they can once get possession of anything it immediately becomes their own."** It was usually small items that went missing, but when some of their important astronomical devices disappeared, Cook was worried. Banks, with his developing knowledge of Tahitian laws and customs, was able to get the equipment back.

Theft among the British was a problem as well. Sailors kept stealing nails from the ship to trade with the islanders, for whom iron was new and valuable. However, one day when a Tahitian woman refused to sell her stone axe for an iron nail, a sailor took it anyway, and Cook decided to make an example of him. He ordered a flogging for the man and invited some Tahitian chiefs to witness the punishment. Banks describes the scene:

> *[The chiefs] stood quietly and saw him stripped and fastened to the rigging, but as soon as the first blow was given they interfered with many tears, begging the punishment might cease, a request which the Captain would not comply with.**

The Tahitians' views of property and punishment were quite different from those of the English; they were much less focused on exclusive ownership of material goods and would never use corporal punishment in a simple case of theft. Unlike Banks, who made a genuine attempt to understand the people of the island and to mediate such disputes, Cook had a strictly utilitarian attitude: he wanted to make his astronomical and navigational observations, get fresh supplies of food and water, and move on.

When Cook and his men had first arrived, they received a joyous and generous reception. Nevertheless, there were tensions. His men were exhausted from a futile trip to the Arctic in search of a "northwest passage" linking Asia and Europe, and they resented Cook's attempts to stop them from their usual practice of trading iron nails for sex. Cook was trying to protect the Hawai'ians from the venereal diseases rampant on his ship. Still, the Hawai'ians treated Cook, in particular, with great respect.

Cook departed on good terms with the islanders, but then had to return after a storm damaged his ship's mast. The mood was now much darker, and tension greeted the British as soon as they stepped ashore. Before long an argument escalated into violence, and an islander stabbed Cook to death. (See the feature "Visual Evidence in Primary Sources: The Death of Captain Cook.")

Notwithstanding the power of predictability afforded by modern science, the death of Captain Cook shows the limitations of reason in governing human interactions. No chronometers, astronomical sightings, surveys, or charts could help safely navigate the waters of cross-cultural communication.

Polynesians suffered and died in great numbers in the coming decades, killed by Afro-European diseases for which they had no immunity. Tupaia, who had aided Cook with navigation and Banks with language and culture, died of dysentery within two years of his first encounter with them. Meanwhile,

---

*Quoted in Patrick O'Brien, *Joseph Banks: A Life* (Chicago: University of Chicago Press, 1987), pp. 94, 95.

changing economies, new technologies, and imported Christianity undermined the existing order of island societies drawn into the European-dominated global system.

● **CONTEXT&CONNECTIONS** Hawai'ian history shows the increasing potency of nineteenth century imperialism. The eight main islands of Hawai'i were united in 1818 under King Kamehameha the Great, and his successors struggled to maintain their independence. After the abolition of slavery in the British empire led to a drop in Caribbean production (see Chapter 19), Hawai'ian lands were bought up by foreigners and planted with sugar cane. In the 1890s, American sugar planters spearheaded the removal of the Hawai'ian royal family from power and annexation of the islands by the United States (see Chapter 25). ●

Joseph Banks and the Settlement of Australia

The impact of Joseph Banks on the history of Australia is inscribed on one of its most famous geographic features, Botany Bay, where Banks undertook an intensive reconnaissance of eastern Australia's unique plant life. He is sometimes called "the Father of Australia" for the role he played in the foundation of the colony of New South Wales in 1788 with its capital at Sydney.

New South Wales began as a penal colony, its overwhelmingly male population consisting of prisoners, many of them Irish, who had little to lose from taking a chance on resettlement halfway around the world. The colony got off to a rocky start. Few of the convicts knew how to survive in this foreign terrain. Nor could they rely on help from the aboriginal population, which initially kept its distance and then launched a series of attacks.

The colonial economy of New South Wales strengthened with the introduction of merino sheep in 1805, descendants of the same sheep that Joseph Banks had imported from Spain to Kew Gardens. The grasslands of New South Wales proved to be ideal grazing grounds, and wool exports financed the development of colonial society. By the early nineteenth century, most settlers were free immigrants rather than convicts, the cities of Sydney and Melbourne were on paths to prosperity, and new British colonies were founded across the continent. After 1817, the name *Australia* was used to refer to this collection of colonies.

Joseph Banks regarded those developments as "improvement," another successful outcome of the application of practical science. But British settlement had a devastating impact on the original inhabitants of the continent. Aboriginal Australians had rich and complex religious and artistic traditions, as well as keen knowledge of the local environment from which, as hunter-gatherers, they derived all the necessities of life. But they had no metal tools, no hierarchical political organization, and like the Polynesians, no immunity to Afro-Eurasian diseases like smallpox. As in the Americas in previous centuries, the Aborigines experienced the European territorial advance as a plague: more than half died in the nineteenth century. The survivors fled to remote deserts and mountains, worked for Europeans on their commercial ranches, or moved to cities, a disenfranchised subclass. However, the perspectives of those displaced by "progress" (whether Australian aborigines, English peasants, or Tahitian mariners) were of little interest to Joseph Banks and others who benefited from the application of science to the extension of empire.

The Death of Captain Cook

James Cook had been sent off in royal fashion when his ships departed the Hawai'ian islands in the summer of 1779. When they returned to mend a broken mast, however, the Hawai'ians seemed disappointed and confused at their return.

Tensions ran high, especially after a high chief was flogged for stealing a pair of iron tongs. Cook's crew noticed that some men were piling stones on the beach, as if getting ready for an attack. Cook invited one of the chiefs with whom he had been

The Death of Cook, 1779, Webber, John (1750–93)/© Dixson Galleries, State Library of New South Wales/The Bridgeman Art Library

The anger of the Hawai'ians that led to this incident, Obeyesekere argues, came from Cook's unwillingness to help them in their war with Maui and his increasingly belligerent demands for food and supplies.

Obeyesekere notes that as soon as news of Cook's death reached England, his status as a Hawai'ian god became a subject of music, art, and theater. Cook's godlike status, he argues, came about not from Hawai'ian beliefs but from European myths of "conquest, imperialism, and civilization."*

---

*Gananath Obeyesekere, *The Apotheosis of Captain Cook: European Mythmaking in the Pacific* (Princeton: Princeton University Press, 1997), p. 3.

friends to come aboard his ship, but the *kahuna* (kah-HOO-nuh) was prevented by his own people from doing so. A warrior then threatened Cook with an iron dagger. Cook shot at him, and a melee broke out. On that morning, July 14, 1779, on a beach at Kealakekua Bay, Captain James Cook was stabbed to death. That fact is certain. But the cause and context of Cook's death are controversial. The engraving reproduced here, made by John Webber, the officially appointed artist of the expedition, provides some evidence but does not resolve scholarly differences in the interpretation of Cook's death.

Anthropologist Marshall Sahlins argues that Cook had first arrived during the Makahiki (ma-kah-HEE-kee) festival dedicated to the fertility god Lono. His appearance at that precise time, and his landing near the god's main temple, caused the Hawai'ians to identify him with Lono. When Cook later returned to repair a broken mast, however, the Makahiki cycle had ended. Now it was time for

Lono to be symbolically defeated, Sahlins explains, and replaced by the war god Ku. In conformity with the ritual cycle, Lono-Cook was killed.

Nonsense, says Gananath Obeyesekere, who maintains that Sahlins is guilty of typical European arrogance in saying that the Hawai'ians saw Cook as a god. In fact, Obeyesekere argues, the Hawai'ians were guided by "practical rationality," a universal common sense that would make it impossible for them to mistake a man for a god. Sahlins responds that he is the one interpreting events from within the logic of traditional Hawai'ian beliefs, while it is actually Obeyesekere who is imposing foreign beliefs on the Hawai'ians by ignoring their own cosmology and value structures. In Hawai'ian belief, he notes, there was a strong equation between status as a powerful chief and affiliation with a god like Lono.

There is no clear conclusion to this debate, as Sahlins and Obeyesekere offer differing interpretations of this image.

Area of detail

The Death of Cook, 1779, Webber, John (1750–93)/© Dixson Galleries, State Library of New South Wales/The Bridgeman Art Library

Sahlins claims that he can identify the actual killer of Cook in this image: Nuha, a powerful warrior who was "an ideal champion for the aging king in the ritualistic murder of Lono-Cook."*

Accepting the overall accuracy of this image, Sahlins even claims to be able to identify the murder weapon: "an iron spike manufactured at [a] factory in Birmingham, requisitioned by Cook 'to be distributed to them as presents toward obtaining their friendship.'"[†] ***Though John Webber was at the scene, he could not possibly have had the perspective on events that is shown in this drawing. Does the change in perspective from what he actually saw to how he represented the event diminish the reliability of the image as a historical source?***

---

*Dan Lynch, "Gananath Obeyesekere v. Marshall Sahlins: Did Hawaiians Consider Captain Cook as a God?" Unpublished paper, California State University Long Beach, 2006.

[†]Marshall Sahlins, *Islands of History* (Chicago: University of Chicago Press, 1985), p. 131.

The European Enlightenment, 1700–1800

Enlightenment

European philosophical movement of the late seventeenth and eighteenth centuries that stressed the use of reason, rather than the authority of ancient philosophers or religious leaders, in descriptions of society and the natural world.

The optimism characteristic of the new science also influenced European views on society. During the eighteenth century, **Enlightenment** thinkers argued that just as the inner workings of nature could be understood by human reason, so reason offered the means to understand and improve society. By the late eighteenth century, progress in human affairs seemed to some not only possible, but inevitable. Many thought that the lofty ideals of the Enlightenment would be realized through the efforts of those at the top of society. The new philosophical emphasis on reason did indeed impress Europe's kings, queens, and aristocracies. But there were limits to how far "enlightened" rulers would follow through on reform; few were willing to risk the traditions that gave them authority.

"Enlightened" Ideas: Politics, Economics, and Society

The contrast between two English political philosophers of different generations, Thomas Hobbes (1588–1679) and John Locke (1632–1704), shows the growing optimism of the Enlightenment. A friend of René Descartes, Hobbes applied deductive reasoning to the question of how best to sustain political order in society. In the state of nature, he pessimistically argued, anarchy prevails, and life is *"nasty, brutish, and short."* * Social and political order become possible, Hobbes argued, only when individuals relinquish their autonomy to a despotic ruler. However, Hobbes rejected the traditional "divine right of kings," the idea that God bestowed royal authority, and instead based his advocacy for absolute monarchy on reasoned arguments.

John Locke

(1632–1704) Philosopher who applied Bacon's inductive reasoning to the study of politics and argued that a stable social order is based on a contract between rulers and ruled and requires the safeguarding of "life, liberty and property."

The younger and more optimistic philosopher **John Locke** (1632–1704), a medical doctor who preferred Bacon's inductive approach, starting with experience and observation, argued in his *Essay Concerning Human Understanding* (1690) that political order derives from a contract in which individuals receive protection of basic rights, *"life, liberty and property,"* while voluntarily giving up some of their autonomy to the state. This was a contract that balanced the needs of public authority with the rights of individual subjects. What Locke described was not a democracy: in his view only propertied males were capable of participating in government. Still, everyone's basic rights would be protected.

Differences in personal experience may have helped shape the differing worldviews of these two philosophers. Hobbes had lived through the English Civil War, witnessing the anarchy and bloodshed that followed the execution of the king (see Chapter 17). Locke, on the other hand, grew up amid the peace, prosperity, and cultural achievements of the later seventeenth century, and played an important role as an adviser to King William and Queen Mary following the Glorious Revolution. The balance between the powers of king and Parliament, and the protection of individual liberties through a Bill of Rights, were real-world applications of Locke's more expansive and optimistic theories.

English constitutional thought influenced the French thinker Montesquieu (1689–1755), who traveled to England to observe its very different constitutional system. His book *The Spirit of the Laws* (1748) argues for limitations on the power of government and a rational distribution of power between social classes. Montesquieu (maw-tuh-SKYOO) believed that as societies became more advanced, their political

---

*Thomas Hobbes, *The Leviathan*, 1651.

systems would become more liberal and their people more free. John Locke had advocated separate and balanced executive and legislative powers; now Montesquieu added that judicial functions should also be protected from executive interference.

The most original economic thinker of the Enlightenment was Adam Smith. His *Wealth of Nations* (1776) emphasized the self-regulating power of markets, arguing for unfettered economic interchange within and between nations. The French term **laissez faire** (lay-say FAIR; "leave it alone") has often been applied to Smith's vision of free-market capitalism unhindered by excessive regulation.

Smith argued that economic productivity increased with a more complex division of labor. For example, an individual performing all the processes necessary to make a pin would be hard pressed to produce a single one in a day. But thousands could be produced if the work process were subdivided, each worker specializing in one part of the process.

Smith applied his concept of division of labor to international trade as well. If each nation specializes in the production of what it is best fit to produce, and trades with other nations specializing in products best fitted to their economic potential, everyone gains. For Smith, the *"invisible hand"* of the market functioned like Isaac Newton's laws of gravitational attraction, maintaining balance and harmony in economic affairs. Like Locke, he believed that protection of private property was a core function of government. Smith was also opposed to slavery because he thought that labor contracts negotiated in a free market lead to more efficient production than coerced labor obtained through force.

Like other Enlightenment thinkers, Smith was using reason to challenge received assumptions, as when his argument for competition in free markets contradicted existing economic policies based on monopoly and mercantilism (see Chapter 19). Whereas the trade restrictions of mercantilism were based on a zero-sum view of economics, in which one nation could advance only at another's expense, Smith believed that freer international trade would lead to more wealth for all. Like John Locke, Adam Smith had an optimistic view of human potential.

While philosophers across Europe aspired to the title "enlightened," it was through Paris that the intellectual currents of the Western world flowed. Indeed, we still use the French word for philosophers—**philosophes** (fill-uh-SOHF)—to describe these intellectuals today. The most important of them was **Voltaire** (1694–1778). Voltaire (vawl-TARE) was most famous as a satirist who used his reason like a searchlight to illuminate all the superstitions, prejudices, and follies of eighteenth-century European society. In his great novel *Candide* (1759), Voltaire mocked the corruption and injustice of the world around him. He believed that reason makes all phenomena and situations intelligible to the human intellect. He also thought that relativism, the ability to see yourself and your own social circumstances in a wider context, is a necessary component of enlightened thinking, since tolerance toward and understanding of others is a precondition for self-knowledge. Voltaire incurred the displeasure of religious authorities by arguing that organized religion is always and everywhere a hindrance to free and rational inquiry.

French women of means and education frequently hosted events in their *salons* (drawing rooms) at which elegantly dressed Parisians passionately debated the latest Enlightenment contributions to science, philosophy, and art. Voltaire and other notable thinkers were highly sought-after guests. But even as women organized and participated in these gatherings, few Enlightenment thinkers were

laissez faire
(French, "leave it alone") Economic philosophy attributed to Scottish Enlightenment thinker Adam Smith, who argued that businesses and nations benefit from a free market where each party seeks to maximize its comparative economic advantage.

philosophes
French intellectuals who promoted Enlightenment principles.

Voltaire
(1694–1778) The pen name of François-Marie Arouet, one of the most prominent Enlightenment writers, who used satire to critique the irrationality of French society.

A Parisian Salon Mid-eighteenth-century Paris was the center of European intellectual life. Salons were gatherings at private homes that combined entertainment with intellectual edification, including poetry readings and discussion of the latest Enlightenment philosophies. Wealthy women often hosted these lively events, competing to attract prestigious guests and distinguished authors.

Mary Wollstonecraft

(1759–1797) An English author and reformer who advocated equality of rights for women.

willing to recognize that restrictions on the role of women in society did not reflect reason, but were merely a traditional prejudice.

Some women protested their exclusion. At the same time that Sor Juana's writings were meeting resistance from church authorities in New Spain (see Chapter 18), a seventeenth-century English scientist, Margaret Cavendish, noted that restrictions on women's roles resulted from nothing more than *"the over-weening conceit men have of themselves."** Another Englishwoman, Mary Astell, challenged John Locke's idea that absolute authority, while unacceptable in the state, was appropriate within the family. Late in the eighteenth century, **Mary Wollstonecraft** went even further in her *Vindication of the Rights of Women* (1792), asking: *"How many women waste life away . . . who might have*

*Quoted in Moira Ferguson, ed., *First Feminists: British Women Writers, 1578–1799* (Bloomington: Indiana University Press, 1985), p. 86.

*practiced as physicians, regulated a farm, managed a shop, and stood erect, supported by their own industry?"** Equal access to education, full citizenship, and financial autonomy, Wollstonecraft said, would be necessary before women's full potential as individuals and as wives and mothers could be achieved.

Of all the French social classes, such daring Enlightenment ideas had the greatest impact on the bourgeoisie, or middle class. For the elite who attended salons, philosophical arguments were more a matter of fashion than of passion: members of the aristocracy had plenty of time for discussion, but little incentive to actually change social rules from which they benefited so extravagantly. On the other side of the social divide, Enlightenment ideas were of little concern to tradesmen and farmers, people who Voltaire and most other philosophes considered irrational and tradition-bound.

The French bourgeoisie, on the other hand, though economically successful, lacked the social status and political weight of aristocrats. Skepticism toward authority thus came naturally to them. Expanding literacy meant that even those who did not travel in refined circles, and who might never be invited to a salon, nevertheless had access to Enlightenment ideas.

● **CONTEXT&CONNECTIONS** In the nineteenth century, the German socialist thinker *Karl Marx* (Chapter 23) would place a strong emphasis on the historical role of the *bourgeoisie* (Chapter 16). At first they played a progressive role, he argued. Their fight against the aristocracy and its vestiges of feudal privilege were an important step toward the liberation of humankind. After the French Revolution, however (see Chapter 22), it was the bourgeoisie itself that stood in the way of further social and political progress, Marx argued, and the industrial working class created by the factory system would rise to overthrow them: bourgeois capitalism would then be replaced by a more advanced socialist system. ●

The most important publishing project of the Enlightenment was the **Encyclopedia**, or *Rational Dictionary of the Arts, Sciences and Crafts*, compiled in Paris between 1751 and 1776. More than any other work, this encyclopedia made the case for a new form of universal knowledge based on reason and critical thinking. The growth in printing and publishing facilitated the dissemination of the *Encyclopedia*, and translation into English, Spanish, and German gave it international impact.

According to the German philosopher Immanuel Kant, it was simple cowardice that stood in the way of personal and social enlightenment. It is unquestioned tradition and blind faith, *"man's inability to make use of his understanding without direction from another,"* that hinder our progress. *"Have courage to use your own reason,"* Kant concluded; *"that is the motto of enlightenment."*[†] But translating that motto into political reality meant confronting powerful vested interests, with radical, and ultimately revolutionary, implications.

Most eighteenth-century philosophes thought that if society were to become enlightened, the change would have to come from above. The mass of ill-educated and uncultured humanity, they thought, could never be expected to follow the path of reason.

Encyclopedia
(1751–1776) A collection of the works of all the great Enlightenment thinkers that promoted a new form of universal knowledge based on reason and the critical use of human intellect.

---

*Mary Wollstonecraft, *A Vindication of the Rights of Women* (Boston: Peter Edes, 1792; New York: Bartleby.com, 1999), chapter 9.

[†]Immanuel Kant, *What Is Enlightenment?* ed. and trans. Lewis White Beck (Indianapolis: Bobs-Merrill, 1959), p. 85.

Enlightenment and Reform

The idea that men of reason could reform society from above provided some eighteenth-century monarchs, so-called "**enlightened despots**," with a new rationale for absolute power. Rather than simply claiming their traditional "divine right" to rule, they could portray themselves as bringing order, harmony, and reason to their domains. Earlier, Louis XIV of France is supposed to have said, *"I am the state."* Now, the Prussian ruler Frederick the Great (r. 1740–1786) defined himself as *"first servant of the state."* Frederick implied that the kingdom was greater than the king, who needed to demonstrate his competence in action.

enlightened despots

Eighteenth-century European rulers who sought to systematically apply Enlightenment ideals to the administration of government.

Frederick was perhaps the most "enlightened" of the great monarchs of the eighteenth century. As a young man he studied music and literature and became a first-rate flute player. Under his patronage Berlin, previously known mainly for its military exploits, became a center for the arts, and the Prussian Academy of Sciences developed as a major seat of learning. Like Joseph Banks, Frederick paid close attention to practical applications of science, draining marshlands to extend Prussian agriculture and encouraging the planting of new crops, especially potatoes, to improve local diets.

Frederick absorbed French literature and the ideas of the philosophes. After meeting in 1750, he and Voltaire maintained a correspondence, trading philosophical ideas. Frederick reformed the Prussian legal system to emphasize reason and justice over tradition, advocated freedom of conscience, and allowed some freedom of the press. However, Prussia's firm military ethic still made it a tightly regimented society, its territory doubling in size as Frederick's army became one of the strongest in Europe.

Enlightenment thinking also influenced two powerful women rulers, Empress Maria Theresa of Austria and Catherine the Great of Russia. Maria Theresa (r. 1740–1780) put strict limits on landlords' power and was also the first European monarch to call for compulsory public education, moving Austria in the direction of what she called a *"God pleasing equality."* Maria Theresa's successors later carried her reforms forward, abolishing serfdom and liberalizing restrictions on the press and religion across the Habsburg lands.

● **CONTEXT&CONNECTIONS** The great Tokugawa shogun *Yoshimune* (Chapter 20), whose reign overlapped that of Empress Maria Theresa of Austria, was also an active agricultural reformer. He took a characteristically conservative course, however, in issuing repeated edicts reminding the Japanese to follow Confucian precepts and keep to their place in society. While the Japanese lords (the *daimyo*) retained tight control over their retainers, in eighteenth-century Austria (as in England) such feudal legacies as the requirement that peasants provide free labor for their lords were fading. ●

In Russia, Catherine the Great also took a lively interest in Enlightenment philosophy, and like Frederick the Great, she avidly corresponded with Voltaire. For Catherine, however, Enlightenment ideals, while enticing in theory, proved inapplicable to Russia. Under her rule, the monarchy and the Russian aristocracy became more authoritarian than ever as the conditions faced by Russia's multitude of serfs grew even more miserable. The Russian middle class, meanwhile, was too weak and dependent on the monarchy to effectively lobby for more liberal Enlightenment reforms (see Chapter 20).

In England, the balance struck between the monarchs and Parliament in 1689 forestalled any thought of despotism there, "enlightened" or otherwise (see

Chapter 17). Throughout, this period, the English constitution continued to evolve, albeit slowly and without any master plan. The Scottish and English thrones were peacefully united to form Great Britain in 1707, and over the next few decades parliamentary factions developed into organized political parties that alternated in forming governments. In 1714, a reliably Protestant German prince, crowned King George I, accepted the powers of Parliament and hence the limitations on his own authority. True, restrictions on the civil rights of British Catholics remained, and attempts to reform the House of Commons to increase the representation of merchants and professionals initially failed. Nevertheless, as the century progressed, the British parliamentary system managed social and political change without revolutionary strife.

Elsewhere in Europe, however, the eventual failure of "enlightened despots" to substantially reform their societies would lead to revolution. Ironically, as we will see in the next two chapters, the struggle to implement lofty Enlightenment ideals of reason and harmony would unleash conflicts of deep passion and dark violence.

CONTEXT AND CONNECTIONS

Science, Technology, and Revolution in World History

Initially, Europe's scientific revolution had only limited global effects. While many Asian and African producers and consumers felt the impact of Europe's involvement in the expanding early modern economy of the sixteenth and seventeenth centuries, they largely retained their own cultural and intellectual traditions. True, "Dutch learning" had entered Japan, European cartography had influenced the Qing empire (see Chapter 20), and some Iranian and Chinese artists had borrowed Western artistic techniques. However, in most of Asia and Africa (unlike

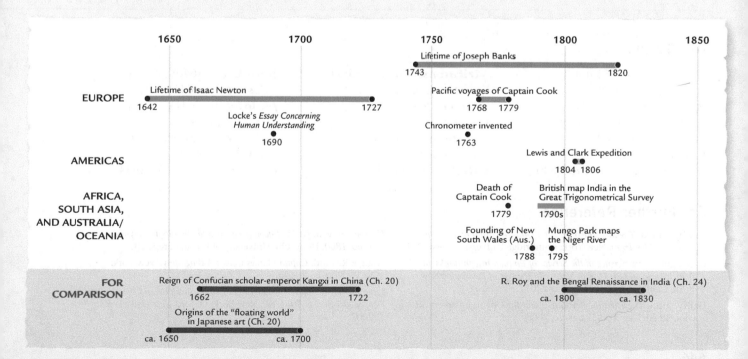

the colonial Americas), European ideas, both religious and scientific, were only marginal, if present at all.

The "practical science" advocated by Joseph Banks helped bring more and more of the world under European sway, if not always direct control, and the Industrial Revolution would magnify Europe's cultural and intellectual influence even further (see Chapter 23). Already during Banks's lifetime new technologies like the steam engine and new forms of factory organization were revolutionizing the British economy. By the late nineteenth century a flood of new technologies—railroads, steamships, telegraph lines—were boosting the productivity of industrial societies and propelling change around the world (see Chapters 24–26).

When confronted with the overwhelming material outcomes of European science and technology, people across the world would be forced to call their own beliefs and traditions into question. Should they adopt the new ideas as superior to their own, like Sugita Gempaku? Should they resist them as undermining their own way of life, as conservatives in the Russian, Ottoman, and Qing empires would advocate during the nineteenth century? Or maybe, like Japanese society, seek out a middle ground, synthesizing their own traditions with Western science and the insights of the Enlightenment (see Chapters 23 and 24)?

Many peoples across the world would have to struggle to find the freedom even to be able to make their own choices about how to adapt. In colonial Africa, for example, Western conquest was so rapid and comprehensive in the decades before 1900 that people had little time to adjust (see Chapter 26). Here, as in Polynesia and Oceania, Joseph Banks's idea that progress need take no account of indigenous interests would long prevail. Ideas of European racial superiority increasingly reinforced such attitudes.

Within Europe, science had challenged the intellectual monopoly of religious authorities, a tension that would continue into modern times with the development of evolutionary biology (see Chapter 23). Enlightenment philosophy, while it attracted the interest of kings, queens, and aristocrats, would also prove problematic for the status quo once members of the middle class began to push for reform—and revolution when necessary—in support of ideas that undercut traditional authority. The "age of reason" promised a better future, while challenging much that people had long held to be tried and true. Both the promise of progress and the unsettling consequences—such as questioning the relationship between rulers and ruled, between faith and science, between individuals and communities—would become an intrinsic part of the human condition over the next two centuries. First, Westerners had to deal with such issues themselves, as they did in revolutions in the United States, France, and Latin America, the topic of the next chapter.

Key Terms

Joseph Banks (620)
James Cook (620)
René Descartes (621)
Sir Francis Bacon (622)
Isaac Newton (623)
Carl Linnaeus (626)
problem of longitude (630)

African Association (632)
Great Trigonometrical
 Survey (632)
Lewis and Clark
 Expedition (635)
Tupaia (635)
Enlightenment (640)

John Locke (640)
laissez faire (641)
philosophes (641)
Voltaire (641)
Mary Wollstonecraft (642)
Encyclopedia (643)
enlightened despots (644)

For Further Reference

Crosby, Alfred. *The Measure of Reality: Quantification in Western Europe, 1250–1600*. New York: Cambridge University Press, 1997.

Gascoigne, John. *Science in the Service of Empire: Joseph Banks, the British State and the Uses of Science in the Age of Revolution* New York: Cambridge University Press 2011.

Henry, John. *The Scientific Revolution and the Origins of Modern Science*. 3d ed. New York: Palgrave, 2008.

Hooper, Steven. *Pacific Encounters: Art and Divinity in Polynesia, 1760–1860*. Honolulu: University of Hawai'i Press, 2006.

Hough, Richard. *Captain James Cooke: A Biography*. New York: W.W. Norton, 2013.

Israel, Jonathan. *Radical Enlightenment: Philosophy and the Making of Modernity, 1650–1750*. New York: Oxford University Press, 2002.

Jacob, Margaret. *The Scientific Revolution: A Brief History with Documents*. New York: Bedford St. Martin's, 2009.

Pagden, Anthony. *The Enlightenment: And Why It Still Matters*. New York: Random House, 2013.

Principe, Lawrence. *Scientific Revolution: A Very Short Introduction*. New York: Oxford University Press, 2011.

Salmond, Anne. *The Trial of the Cannibal Dog: The Remarkable Story* *of Captain Cook's Encounter in the South Seas*. New Haven: Yale University Press, 2003.

Slack, Paul. *The Invention of Improvement: Information and Material Progress in Seventeenth Century England*. New York: Oxford University Press, 2015.

Veth, Peter, ed. *Strangers on the Shore: Early Coastal Contact in Australia*. Canberra: National Museum of Australia Press, 2008.

MindTap

MindTap is a fully online, highly personalized learning experience built upon Cengage Learning content. MindTap combines student learning tools—readings, multimedia, activities, and assessments—into a singular Learning Path that guides students through the course.

22

Revolutions in the West, 1750–1830

Simón Bolívar

In the summer of 1805, young **Simón Bolívar** (1783–1830) traveled to Madrid, Rome, and Paris in the company of his tutor, a Venezuelan exile who had followed the allure of revolution to Europe. His teacher had required Bolívar to study the great texts of the Enlightenment (see Chapter 21), and now he was there to witness firsthand the excitement and the fear caused by the rising empire of Napoleon Bonaparte in the aftermath of the French Revolution.

One day, they climbed one of the famous hills of Rome to gain a panoramic view of the "eternal city." Bolívar was awestruck by the echoes of the city's great imperial past, which, he thought, summed up all that was truly great and all that was most tragic in history. But he saw the destiny of the Americas as greater still, and he pledged to play his part to liberate South America from the Spanish empire and thus advance the cause of liberty for all mankind:

*H*ere every manner of grandeur has had its type, all miseries their cradle....
[Rome] has examples for everything, except the cause of humanity:...heroic warriors, rapacious consuls...golden virtues, and sordid crimes; but for the emancipation of the spirit...the exaltation of man, and the final perfectibility of reason, little or nothing....The resolution of the great problem of man set free seems to have been something...that would only be made clear in the New World....I swear before you, I swear by the God of my fathers, I swear on their graves, I swear by my Country that I

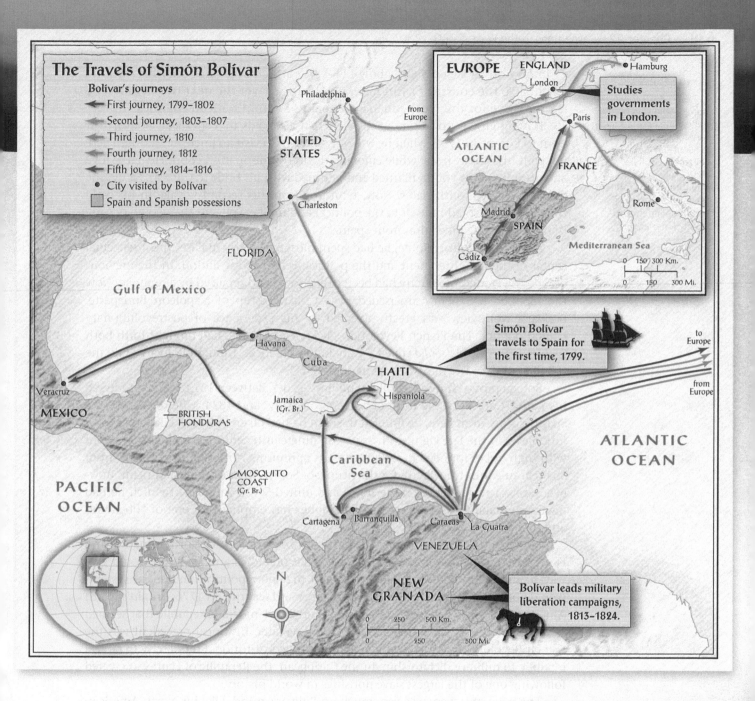

The Travels of Simón Bolívar

Bolívar's journeys

◄— First journey, 1799–1802
◄— Second journey, 1803–1807
◄— Third journey, 1810
◄— Fourth journey, 1812
◄— Fifth journey, 1814–1816
• City visited by Bolívar
☐ Spain and Spanish possessions

Philadelphia

from Europe

UNITED STATES

Charleston

FLORIDA

Gulf of Mexico

Havana

Cuba

HAITI

Hispaniola

Jamaica (Gr. Br.)

Veracruz

MEXICO

BRITISH HONDURAS

MOSQUITO COAST (Gr. Br.)

PACIFIC OCEAN

Caribbean Sea

Cartagena   Barranquilla   Caracas   La Guaira

VENEZUELA

NEW GRANADA

N

0   250   500 Km.
0   250   500 Mi.

ATLANTIC OCEAN

to Europe

from Europe

Simón Bolívar travels to Spain for the first time, 1799.

Bolívar leads military liberation campaigns, 1813–1824.

EUROPE   ENGLAND   • Hamburg

London

Studies governments in London.

Paris

ATLANTIC OCEAN

FRANCE

Rome

Madrid

SPAIN

Mediterranean Sea

Cádiz

0   150   300 Km.
0   150   300 Mi.

will not rest body or soul until I have broken the chains binding us to the will of Spanish might!*

*Excerpt from Simón Bolívar, "Oath Taken at Rome, 15 August 1805," trans. Frederick H. Fornoff, in *El Libertador: Writings of Simón Bolívar*, ed. David Bushnell (New York: Oxford University Press, 2003), pp. 113–144.

Simón Bolívar's (see-MOAN bow-LEE-var) oath changed not only his own life but also the course of Latin American history. Over the next two decades, he led the drive for the independence of Spain's South American colonies.

Having grown up in one of the richest households in Venezuela, Bolívar first went to Europe in 1799, when he was only sixteen, to visit an uncle in Madrid. There he spent his money freely while enjoying the life of the Spanish court. He fell in love and, in spite of his youth, married and returned with his bride to Caracas. Sadly, she died just eight months later. Now, returning from his second voyage in his early twenties, he devoted himself to the political and military pursuit that would occupy the rest of his life: liberation from Spain.

Apart from visiting Rome, he had spent most of this trip in Paris, the intellectual center of the Enlightenment and the political center of revolution. In the previous decade the French monarchy had been overthrown and replaced by a republic. Now the republic was being superseded by the dictatorship of Napoleon Bonaparte. Bolívar's worldview was greatly affected by his experience of postrevolutionary French politics. The French Revolution, like ancient Rome, had brought forth both *"golden virtues"* and *"sordid crimes."* Only in the Americas, thought Bolívar, could the full liberation of the human spirit be achieved.

Bolívar proved himself a brilliant military leader. Between 1813, when he entered his native Caracas at the head of a liberation army, and 1824, when he drove the Spanish army from Peru, he fulfilled the oath he had taken in Rome. Like other revolutionaries of the late eighteenth and early nineteenth centuries, Bolívar started out with high hopes founded in Enlightenment optimism. Turning independence from Spanish rule into true liberty for the people of South America proved difficult, however. Bolívar never achieved the stable and united South America of which he had dreamed, making his story, as one biographer has emphasized, one of "liberation and disappointment."*

Elsewhere in Latin America and the Caribbean, and in North America and France, other revolutionaries also believed that prejudice and tradition would give way to rationality and enlightenment, and that new political and social systems would both guarantee liberty and provide order and security. In 1776, Britain's North American colonists had broken free and founded a democratic republic that seemed to combine liberty with moderation. A more volatile historical precedent was the French Revolution, which swung violently from constitutional monarchy to radical republic to military dictatorship. In the Caribbean, the Republic of Haiti was created following one of the largest slave uprisings in world history.

The issue of slavery was very much on Bolívar's mind. Like his North American counterpart George Washington, Bolívar was a slave owner. Could the dream of liberty be compatible with the reality of slavery? Such discrepancies between dreams and harsher realities were, in fact, a central theme of the age. Reconciling the twin mandates of liberty and equality, and securing both within a stable and well-ordered state, was a tremendous challenge for revolutionaries across North and South America, the Caribbean, and France.

---

*David Bushnell, *Simón Bolívar: Liberation and Disappointment* (New York: Pearson Longman, 2004).

> What constitutional compromises did the leaders of the new United States of America make, and what were the consequences for "liberty and equality"?

> What were the major phases of the French Revolution?

> How did earlier conditions of colonialism affect the course and outcome of revolutions in Latin America and the Caribbean?

> To what extent did the revolutions in western Europe and the Americas thoroughly transform existing political and social structures?

Rebellion and Independence in America, 1763–1797

On April 19, 1775, after British soldiers marched on the town of Concord to seize and destroy arms secretly stockpiled there by the Massachusetts militia, the two sides exchanged gunfire. Surprised and confused by the colonials' irregular tactics, the British beat a retreat back to Boston, harassed along their flanks all the way.

This skirmish in a small corner of the British empire set in motion events that would have a powerful global impact. The rebels' Declaration of Independence (1776) is one of the most influential political statements in world history, and the founding of the United States was a powerful testament to the principles of Enlightenment. Nevertheless, compromises made during the nation-building process, especially about slavery, undermined the Enlightenment's highest aspirations of universal liberty and equality.

Rebellion and War, 1763–1783   A key turning point in the relations between Britain and the colonists was the British victory in the French and Indian War, the name in North America for the Seven Years' War (1756–1763) that pitted Britain against France around the world (see Chapter 19). To Britain's North American colonists, victory opened possibilities for expansion into the Ohio River Valley and other areas west of the Appalachian Mountains. But British leaders were cautious. No sooner had they defeated the French than they faced a Native American uprising. European settlements on the frontier would generate more conflict, inevitably requiring more British troops and resources. Britain's Proclamation of 1763 fixed a westward limit to colonial expansion, much to the disgust of colonists.

The British then imposed new taxes so that the colonies would help bear the cost of their own defense. Colonists bitterly resented these new taxes, such as the Stamp Act of 1765, as well as tighter restrictions on their trade with the West Indies. Resistance took the form of illegal smuggling, embargoes on British goods, and various kinds of public protests, sometimes leading to violence or destruction of property. Concluding that British policies assailed their rights as freeborn British subjects, some colonists started to call themselves "Americans," rallying to the slogan *No taxation without representation!* When they formed militias to assert their rights, the stage was set for the confrontation at Concord.

George Washington

(1732–1799) Commander of the Continental Army in the American War of Independence from Britain; also the first president of the United States of America.

Declaration of Independence

(1776) Document written by Thomas Jefferson justifying the separation of Britain's North American colonies, declaring them free and independent states.

● **CONTEXT&CONNECTIONS** Tea from South Asia played an economic role in the history of British North America and affected the political symbolism of the rebellion. At the famous "Tea Party" of May 1773, colonists threw Indian tea into Boston harbor, protesting a new British policy intended to oblige them to buy tea directly from the East India Company (see Chapter 20). The Tea Act angered local merchants who had been smuggling tea into Massachusetts, as well as consumers who anticipated that an East India Company monopoly would eventually lead to higher prices. By then, the combination of Asian tea and sugar from the West Indies (see Chapter 19) had become an expected part of their daily routine. ●

After the skirmish in Massachusetts, a Continental Congress convened, bringing together representatives from each of the thirteen colonies. **George Washington** (1732–1799) was appointed commander of its army. Washington, a Virginian, had served as an officer during British military campaigns in the Ohio River Valley. Then on July 4, 1776, Congress approved Thomas Jefferson's **Declaration of Independence**, which not only detailed the colonists' grievances but also made a stirring announcement of universal political values:

> We hold these truths to be self-evident, that all men are created equal, that they are endowed by their Creator with certain inalienable Rights, that among these are Life, Liberty and the pursuit of Happiness. —That to secure these rights, Governments are instituted among Men, deriving their just powers from the consent of the governed.

The phrase "consent of the governed" built on John Locke's theory of government as based on a contract in which individuals receive protection of their basic rights by voluntarily submitting to a legitimate government (see Chapter 21). Without that consent, Jefferson argued, rebellion was justified.

The British had some advantages in the war that began in 1776. The tens of thousands of "redcoat" soldiers in North America were well equipped and well trained. Moreover, many Loyalists in the colonies argued against rebellion. Inventor, diplomat, and continental congressman Benjamin Franklin only reluctantly exchanged his British identity for an American one, and his son William, the royally appointed governor of New Jersey, refused to do so. Many free blacks, aware that slavery had been eliminated in Britain and knowing that prominent leaders of the rebellion included slave owners like Washington and Jefferson, were Loyalist as well.

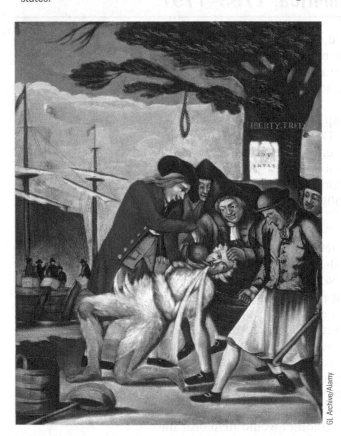

GL Archive/Alamy

Protesting Taxation Needing additional resources to control its expanded American frontier after victory in the Seven Years' War, the British Parliament imposed new taxes on the North American colonies. In this engraving, angry colonists have tarred and feathered one of the king's officials beneath a "Liberty Tree." Tarring and feathering, which often left the victim permanently disfigured, was an exceptionally violent form of vigilante justice.

● **CONTEXT&CONNECTIONS** Amerindians were divided in their response to the American war for independence. Though other Iroquois elders argued for neutrality, Joseph Brant (Thayendanegea) allied his Mohawk people with the British. After the war, Brant's descendants, exiled to Canada, remained loyal to the empire. Brant's grand-son, Smoke Johnson (Sakayengwaraton), led Mohawk forces against the United States in the War of 1812, and his great-great-granddaughter, *Pauline Johnson-Tekahionwake*, achieved fame as a Canadian poet (key term in Chapter 25). ●

The French saw support for the revolutionaries as another way to inflict damage on their perennial British nemesis; their aid proved essential for rebel success. A Franco-American treaty provided for arms supplies and French harassment of British ships in the Atlantic and Caribbean. Apart from the French alliance, the rebellious colonists had several advantages. The rural population supported the Continental Army with supplies, information on British movements, and knowledge of the local terrain. Women played a notable role. They did extra work, including blacksmithing and other "male" jobs, in the absence of their soldier-husbands, and they produced shoes, clothes, and munitions for the Continental Army. Also, since British soldiers were reluctant to search them, women made excellent spies and couriers.

Another advantage was the leadership of General Washington, who managed to maintain the morale of his troops through harsh winters, especially at Valley Forge in 1777–1778. In 1781, after Washington's army surrounded the British under Lord Cornwallis at Yorktown, French ships cut off Cornwallis's route of retreat, forcing him to surrender his army. In the Treaty of Paris (1783), the British government acknowledged the independence of the new United States of America.

● **CONTEXT&CONNECTIONS** After his surrender at Yorktown, *Lord Cornwallis* (Chapter 20) retained his high political standing and was appointed governor-general of British India. Subsequent British expansion in South Asia laid the foundation for what historians call "the second British empire" (see Chapter 20). ●

Creating a Nation, 1783–1797

An early motto of the new republic was *Novus Ordo Secolorum*: "A New Order of the Ages." The founders saw the birth of their nation as an event that would usher in a new era, *"an epoch,"* as Washington put it, *"when the rights of mankind were better understood and more clearly defined, than at any former period."* Nevertheless, in the new nation social continuities accompanied political change.

Under British rule, each of the thirteen colonies had developed a distinct political culture, and representatives of the individual states proved reluctant to sacrifice local sovereignty to create a more unified nation. The first constitution, the Articles of Confederation, allowed the federal government no tax-raising power and required it to request funds from the individual states. Under the Articles, the states were responsible for debts remaining from the war, and they levied taxes to meet those obligations. These taxes forced poorer farmers, who lived primarily through barter, to sell land to raise the necessary cash. Such farmers also stood to lose their right to vote, which was accorded only to property owners. In Massachusetts, incensed war veterans rose up in an armed rebellion, strengthening arguments for a stronger federal government with powers of taxation. Debates over the degree to which a central government should have license to tax and borrow would continue far into the future.

Mercy Otis Warren, one of the most prolific writers of her time, put it this way: "*On the one hand we are in need of a strong federal government founded on principles that will support the prosperity and union of the colonies. On the other we have struggled for liberty...[and will not relinquish] the rights of man for the dignity of government.*"* At the Constitutional Convention in 1787, central issues facing delegates were how to balance the powers of government with the rights of individuals and the power of the federal government with that of the states.

Constitution of the United States of America

(1787) Agreement that created a more unified national structure for the United States, providing for a bicameral national legislature and independent executive and judicial authority, and incorporating a Bill of Rights.

Compromise was the hallmark of the new **Constitution of the United States of America** (1787). While granting to the federal government powers of taxation, judicial oversight, international diplomacy, and national defense, specific powers, such as determining the voting franchise, were left to the states. A system of checks and balances, as earlier proposed by the French philosophe Montesquieu (see Chapter 21), ensured the separation of executive, legislative, and judicial authority. The convention struck a balance between the interests of large and small states by creating a two-house legislature, with representation in the House of Representatives based on population and that in the Senate equal at two senators for each state.

Congress amended the Constitution in 1791 with a Bill of Rights that guaranteed specific civil liberties, such as freedom of religion, of the press, of assembly, and other fundamental freedoms. However, most states restricted the vote to property-owning men. No political agency was given to women, Native Americans, slaves, or even most free blacks.

George Washington was the unanimous choice of the state electors as president. Washington, like Simón Bolívar on his European sojourn, looked to ancient Rome for inspiration. His model was the general Cincinnatus who, after leading Roman armies to victory, left the political stage to live as a simple citizen. In 1797, after two terms as president, Washington refused a third term and retired to his plantation. Washington's example of voluntarily leaving office when he felt his public service was completed powerfully reinforced constitutional limitations on executive power. (Like many subsequent world leaders, Napoleon Bonaparte did not follow Washington's example; see the feature "Visual Evidence in Primary Sources: Portraits of Power: George Washington and Napoleon Bonaparte.") Washington's Farewell Address, warning against any *"permanent alliances with any portion of the foreign world,"* would have a lasting influence on United States foreign policy.

Neither Washington nor the other leaders of the Constitutional Convention could resolve the fundamental dichotomy between liberty and slavery. Southern delegates had no intention of applying the principle that *"all men are created equal"* to the 40 percent of Southerners who were slaves. Though the abolitionist movement was gaining momentum (see Chapter 19), plantation owners prevailed. The Constitution cynically defined each slave as three-fifths of a person in calculating the size of congressional delegations, and allowed the states to define slaves as nonpersons for all other purposes.

Here was a conundrum. To bring perfect rationality and harmony to society, in line with Enlightenment ideals, one would need to start with a "blank slate" free from inherited prejudice and exploitation. The issue of slavery shows that this was not possible for the new United States. Both before and after 1776, Northern

---

*Mercy Otis Warren, Letter of September 17, 1787, to Catherine Macauley, Gilder Lehrman Collection, GLC 1800.3, pp. 1–2. http://www.digitalhistory.uh.edu/exhibits/dearmadam/letter4.html.

merchants and Southern slaveholders dominated the social and economic order. For this reason, historians continue to debate whether the war for independence should really be considered a "revolution," signified by a significant rearrangement of social and economic power. For the French Revolution, in contrast, there is no such debate.

The French Revolution, 1789–1815

The French Revolution quickly moved through three distinct stages. At first, the focus was on the relatively moderate goal of constitutional monarchy. When that proved impossible, radical republicans then led the second phase of the Revolution, seeking to fundamentally transform French society. Their rule soon degenerated into a bloody Reign of Terror.

The attempt by French revolutionaries to turn the noblest words of the Enlightenment into action was strongly opposed by the monarchy, the nobility, the church, and neighboring kingdoms, as well as by many French themselves who thought the revolutionaries were going too far. Significant numbers in the provinces resented the primacy of Paris as the revolutionary center. In the resulting disorder compromise proved impossible.

Finally, amid the turmoil emerged a military genius, Napoleon Bonaparte, who not only restored order but also extended French power across Europe. Thus, as in ancient Rome, but all in the course of one dizzying decade, monarchy was replaced by a republic, and then the republic by a new empire.

Louis XVI and the Early Revolution, 1789–1792

The complex causes of the French Revolution are still debated by historians. The heightened ambitions of the French middle class certainly must be taken into account: many members of the bourgeoisie detested the inherited privileges of the king and nobility. Though most of them were still committed to the idea of monarchy, a minority, aware of the example of the new United States, argued that the people themselves should be sovereign. These lawyers, doctors, teachers, merchants—with property and education but no titles—drew from Enlightenment ideas to promote reform and, failing that, revolution.

The vast majority of French men and women were farmers whose resentment over the feudal obligations they still owed their aristocratic overlords intensified when bad harvests in the 1780s caused hunger and hardship. Many fled to the cities, especially Paris, where overcrowding and unemployment added fuel to the revolutionary fire. Ruling over 24 million subjects from his fabulous palace at Versailles, **Louis XVI** (r. 1774–1793) was one of the wealthiest and most powerful people in the world, but he proved incapable of uniting his deeply divided people.

The most immediate cause of the revolt of 1789 was the precarious state of French finances. When Louis XVI took the throne, the French treasury was nearly empty. The loss of the Seven Years' War (1756–1763) left a pile of debt made higher by the expense of backing the American rebels. The common people were crushed by taxes, while the nobility, lavishly entertained at Versailles, paid none at all.

The economic crisis led to a political one when Louis and his ministers decided in 1789 that they had no choice but to convene an Estates-General in Paris, to which each of the three Orders of French society would send representatives.

Louis XVI

(r. 1774–1793) King of France whose inability to adequately reform the French fiscal system laid the foundation for the French Revolution. After showing reluctance to rule as a constitutional monarch, Louis was arrested and beheaded by republican revolutionaries.

Portraits of Power: George Washington and Napoleon Bonaparte

During the eighteenth and nineteenth centuries in Europe and the Americas, political leaders commissioned paintings of themselves to project images of power. Portraits such as those reproduced here could inform people not merely of the fact of power but also of the particular type of power leaders were associated with. President George Washington of the United States (in office 1789–1797) and

The stormy sky in the background might illustrate the difficult times that Washington and his comrades passed through, while the rainbow just above his upper arm might symbolize their ultimate victory.

The inkstand on the table and the books below show his importance in crafting the nation's foundational documents.

Washington wears no signs of military rank, holds a sheathed sword with its point down, and offers his open hand. The impression is one of peace.

Gérard Blot/Hervé Lewandowski

Emperor Napoleon Bonaparte of France (r. 1799–1814) were keenly aware of classical Greek and Roman models in projecting images of power, as were their portraitists Gilbert Stuart (1796) and Jean-Auguste-Dominique Ingres (1806). Washington identified himself with the democratic tradition of Athens and the republican period of Rome; Napoleon, in contrast, emphasized the imperial Roman tradition. Simón Bolívar, whose portrait at the beginning of the chapter can be compared with those here, was also keenly aware of both the republican and imperial traditions of ancient Rome.

Napoleon holds a scepter topped by a figure of Charlemagne, the early medieval king whose empire was one of his models.

Unlike Washington's open right hand, Napoleon's right fist is clenched high on his scepter, adding to the contrast between the two portraits. *In these portraits, what do such differences tell us about how the artist wished to represent each man's character, his nature as a leader, and his vision for his nation? Compare each of these portraits with that of Simón Bolívar at the beginning of the chapter, with the same question in mind.*

At his coronation in 1804, Napoleon wore two different crowns, first a laurel crown like the one shown here and then a bejeweled reproduction of Charlemagne's crown. New rulers often seek legitimacy by associating themselves with older symbols of power.

What different reactions might Napoleon's supporters and detractors have had in viewing this portrait? Napoleon did not commission this painting, and we do not know what he himself thought of it.

The First Estate consisted of the Catholic Church, the Second Estate consisted of the nobility, and the Third Estate comprised everyone else, that is, the vast majority of French men and women. It was an extreme measure: there had been no meeting of the French Estates-General since 1614.

In the provinces, elections were held for **Third Estate** delegates, many of whom were middle-class professionals. Inspired by the American Revolution, they demanded fundamental reforms, such as the creation of a representative legislative body. They collected notebooks of grievances in the French provinces to bring to Paris as a catalogue of complaints and ideas for change.

Many bishops representing the First Estate were from noble families, and the Catholic Church, by far the biggest landowner in France, was, like the aristocrats of the Second Estate, exempt from direct taxation. Since each estate had only one vote, Louis anticipated that the privileged members of the First and Second Estates would vote together, canceling out radical proposals from the Third Estate.

Delegates from the Third Estate, however, took matters into their own hands. When Louis had them locked out of the assembly hall where they planned to meet, the furious delegates met on a tennis court, declared themselves to be a **National Assembly**, and took an oath not to disband until a constitutional monarchy had been established. Reacting with fear, Louis XVI summoned eighteen thousand troops to defend his palace at Versailles, 12 miles (19.3 km) outside Paris. The French Revolution had begun.

Thus far, the contest was between the men of power—the king and his nobles—and the relatively wealthy and well-educated delegates of the Third Estate, men who *aspired* to power and influence. But the actions of the common people pushed events in a new direction. Parisians stormed the Bastille (bass-TEEL), a building that served as both a jail and an armory. They freed prisoners, armed themselves from the arsenal's stockpile, and killed the mayor.

After the Bastille uprising, Louis decided he had better compromise with the Third Estate after all. He recognized the National Assembly, which promptly declared the principle of equality before the law, eliminated the special prerogatives of the nobility, and abolished serfdom and all the remaining feudal obligations of the peasantry. In the "Declaration of the Rights of Man and the Citizen," the National Assembly declared that *"men are born and remain free and equal in rights,"* that *"the natural and inalienable rights of man"* are *"liberty, property, security, and resistance to oppression,"* that all citizens are eligible for government positions *"without other distinctions than that of virtues and talents,"* and that necessary taxation *"must be assessed equally on all citizens in proportion to their means."* Freedom of thought and religion were established, and mandatory payments to the Catholic Church were eliminated. The assembly thus articulated the ideas of the philosophes as political principles.

In one way, the National Assembly was quite traditional: this all-male body would not consider extending equality to women. They ignored the lobbying of middle-class Parisian women's groups and the arguments of author Olympe de Gouges (oh-limp duh GOOJ), who in her *Declaration of the Rights of Women*, protested: *"The exercise of the natural rights of women has only been limited by the perpetual tyranny that man opposes to them; these limits should be reformed by the laws of nature and reason."**

Third Estate

Before the French Revolution, the order of French society that included the common people (the First Estate was the clergy, the Second the aristocracy, and the Third everyone else).

National Assembly

(1789) Assembly that launched the French Revolution, formed by members of the Third Estate after the failure of the Estates-General. They agreed on the "Declaration of the Rights of Man and of the Citizen," forcing the king to sign the assembly's constitution.

*Olympe de Gouges, *Écrits politiques, 1788–1791*, trans. Tracey Rizzo (Paris: Côtes Femmes, 1993), p. 209. Reprinted in Tracy Rizzo and Laura Mason, eds., *The French Revolution: A Document Collection* (Boston: Houghton Mifflin, 1999), p. 111.

Parisian Women March to Versailles Women played a distinctive role in the French Revolution. Elite women sponsored the gatherings that spread Enlightenment and revolutionary ideals in their *salons*, while the common women engaged in direct action, as here in 1789, where they are shown marching to Versailles to force the king to return to Paris. (The Granger Collection, NYC)

Within the National Assembly, revolutionary zeal was secondary to cooperating with Louis XVI in establishing a new constitutional monarchy. But neither the king nor the assembly could control events. In the fall of 1789, the poor again took direct action. Angered by the high price of bread and distrusting the king's intentions, twenty thousand Parisians, mostly women, marched to Versailles. This "March of the Women" forced the king and his family to leave Versailles and return to his palace in Paris where the people could keep a closer eye on him.

Despite the centrality of Paris, the vast majority of French men and women were village-based peasants. Their "justice" came from courts presided over by their lord. They had to donate free labor cultivating his estates and were often forced to grind their wheat into flour at the lord's mill, where he could charge whatever he liked. While the National Assembly calmly deliberated the elimination of such feudal practices, French farmers rose up and stormed their lords' estates, sometimes content to burn the manorial rolls that listed their feudal obligations, sometimes burning magnificent country houses to the ground. Panicked aristocrats began to flee the country, seeking refuge with their relatives across Europe.

In this tense atmosphere, the National Assembly organized a Legislative Assembly to draft a new set of basic laws, following the United States's example of a written constitution and the British example of sharing power between the king and representatives of the people. But in the summer of 1791, Louis tried to escape from France, hoping to rally support from other European monarchs for his return as an absolute ruler. Instead, he was captured and held a virtual prisoner in his palace.

Meanwhile, French nobles who had fled abroad were doing their best to convince Europe's kings and aristocrats to help overthrow the revolution. The defeat of French forces by Habsburg regiments in the Netherlands in 1792 led supporters of the revolution to fear an Austrian invasion of France itself. At the same time, a poor harvest and severe grain shortage further increased tensions. In Paris, the people staged anti-monarchical demonstrations and attacked the royal palace. Hundreds of citizens and soldiers died.

The window for compromise was now closed. Some in the Legislative Assembly were happy that the experiment in constitutional monarchy had not worked. They were *republicans*, who believed that any form of monarchy undermined liberty. The next phase of the French Revolution would belong to them.

The Jacobins and the Reign of Terror, 1793–1795

Under pressure from the people of Paris, the Legislative Assembly declared a republic and instituted universal manhood suffrage. The National Assembly dissolved itself in favor of a National Convention, which immediately declared the end of the monarchy and began writing a republican constitution. They found Louis XVI guilty of treason and beheaded him in January 1793.

Under the **Jacobins**, the radical republican faction led by Maximilien Robespierre (ROBES-pee-air), the French Revolution passed through its most idealistic and most violent phase. Robespierre had been deeply influenced by the philosophy of Jean-Jacques Rousseau, who had argued that the only legitimate state was one that expressed the "general will" of the people. Rousseau envisioned a form of direct democracy practiced by enlightened citizens, but he rejected the checks on government power proposed by Montesquieu and implemented in the Constitution of the United States. Instead Rousseau had talked of constructing a "Republic of Virtue."

Perfect equality was part of the Jacobin plan to wipe the slate clean and transform society from bottom to top. The republic confiscated lands belonging to the church and to the nobility and abolished slavery in the French empire. In the name of "*liberty, equality, and fraternity*" everyone, rich and poor alike, was to be addressed as "*Citizen*." The year 1793 would be "*Year One*" of a new calendar, marking the victory of reason over the old Christian faith. Time itself would have a revolutionary new beginning.

But no fresh start was really possible; the past could not be so easily erased. Devout Catholics, especially in the provinces, deeply resented the Jacobins' moves against the Catholic Church. Meanwhile the seizure of private property by the Jacobins, fighting to save the Revolution, deeply shocked the bourgeoisie. Many who had initially supported the Third Estate and plans for constitutional monarchy now recoiled from the revolutionary excess of Robespierre and his followers. (See the feature "Movement of Ideas Through Primary Sources: Edmund Burke's Reflections on the French Revolution.")

Jacobins

The most radical republican faction in the National Convention. They organized a military force that saved the republic, but their leader Maximilien Robespierre, head of the Committee of Public Safety, ruled by decree and set in motion the Reign of Terror.

Robespierre then imposed an even harsher dictatorship after the kings of Prussia and Austria declared counterrevolutionary war on France. Not for the last time in world history, a revolutionary leader declared that to save the revolution, its most cherished principle—liberty—would have to be sacrificed. A dictatorial Committee of Public Safety replaced the fledgling democratic institutions of the republic. The committee quashed its enemies with a so-called Reign of Terror in which forty thousand people were beheaded.

The symbol of the Revolution now became the guillotine (gee-yuh-TEEN), in which the condemned had their heads removed by the quick fall of a sharp, heavy blade. That the guillotine became a symbol of revolutionary violence is ironic. The philosophes were horrified by grisly public executions, where the executioner often needed several swings of his heavy axe to fully decapitate the condemned. Dr. Joseph Guillotin had intended his invention as an enlightened means of execution, clean and swift. Now his attempt at humane reform had been transformed into an efficient instrument of terror.

Though their methods were harsh, the Jacobins were successful in securing the republic against Austrian and Prussian invaders. They fielded an enormous army of conscripts who first stemmed the tide of invasion and then went on the offensive. Mass conscription had cultural and political ramifications as well. Most of the soldiers were peasants who had never before traveled far from home, where they practiced local customs and spoke distinct regional dialects. Once trained for defense of the republic, many developed a stronger sense of national identity, transformed, in one historian's words, "from peasants into Frenchmen."

Reduced foreign threats, however, emboldened the Jacobins' domestic enemies. People in the provinces were angry at the radicalism they associated with Paris, and most members of the middle class favored a more moderate republic. Many Jacobins themselves now lost their heads, including Robespierre himself. "*Revolutions*," a French journalist commented, "*devour their children.*"

The Age of Napoleon, 1795–1815

The National Convention reasserted power and created a new constitution with a more limited electorate and a separation of powers. From 1795 to 1799, however, the country remained sharply divided. The Directory, which formed the executive branch of the new government, faced conspiracies by both the Jacobins and by monarchists. Meanwhile, French armies continued to gain victories as a young general named **Napoleon Bonaparte** (1769–1821) took northern Italy from the Austrians. In 1799 two members of the Directory plotted with Napoleon to launch a coup d'état and form a new government.

Like George Washington, Napoleon looked to ancient Rome for inspiration. But unlike the American general, Napoleon followed Rome's imperial example, transforming the republic into an empire (see Map 22.1, page 664). In a series of referendums the French people voted their approval of Napoleon's enhanced power, tired of chaos and bickering politicians, and proud of his armies' successes. Napoleon neutralized political opposition by bringing all but the most fervent monarchists into his administration. In 1801, he reached a compromise restoring papal authority, gaining the allegiance of Catholics who had felt oppressed by the

Napoleon Bonaparte

(1769–1821) Military commander who gained control of France after the French Revolution. He declared himself emperor in 1804 and attempted to expand French territory, but failed to defeat Great Britain and abdicated in 1814. He died in exile after a brief return to power in 1815.

Edmund Burke's Reflections on the French Revolution

British parliamentarian Edmund Burke (1729–1797) has been called "the father of conservatism," a reputation that came mostly from his denunciation of the excesses of the French Revolution in a letter he wrote to a French aristocrat, published as *Essays on the French Revolution*. In fact, Burke's politics were generally liberal: he upheld the rights of Parliament and limitations on those of the king; supported the American Revolution, Catholic rights in his native Ireland, and the abolition of the slave trade; and spoke strongly against the corruption of the British East India Company (see Chapter 20).

In the *Essays*—written in 1790 before the execution of Louis XVI, the bloodshed of the Reign of Terror, and the dictatorship of the Jacobins—Burke argued that the French had been mistaken in basing their case for liberty on abstract ideals such as "the rights of man." Instead, he explained how liberty was better protected with a constitution grounded on inherited cultural and political

institutions. Using abstract ideas to overrule custom and tradition pushed the revolutionaries, he said, toward corruption and dictatorship. Critics of Burke, defenders of Enlightenment thinking such as Thomas Paine (*The Rights of Man*) and Mary Wollstonecraft (*A Vindication of the Rights of Women*), rejected his arguments, though it was not long before the violence unleashed by the Jacobins and the tyranny imposed by Napoleon seemed to vindicate Burke's position.

> What were the main arguments Burke used to criticize the French Revolution, and how did he assert the superiority of British constitutional development? (You may want to review England's "Glorious Revolution" in Chapter 17 and compare it to the French Revolution.)

Source: Edmund Burke, *Works* (London: 1867).

From Essays *on the French Revolution*

The question of dethroning [a king] will always be, as it has always been, an extraordinary question of state....As it was not made for common abuses, so it is not to be agitated by common minds. The speculative line of demarcation, where obedience ought to end, and resistance must begin, is faint, obscure, and not easily definable. It is not a single act, or a single event, which determines it. Governments must be abused and deranged indeed, before it can be thought of; and the prospect of the future must be as bad as the experience of the past....The wise will determine from the gravity of the case...but, with or without right, a revolution will be the very last resource of the thinking and the good....

The [British] parliament says to the king, "Your subjects have inherited this freedom," claiming their franchises not on abstract principles "as the rights of men," but as the rights of Englishmen,

and as a patrimony derived from their forefathers. You will observe that from Magna Carta [onward] it has been the uniform policy of our constitution to claim and assert our liberties as an entailed inheritance derived to us from our forefathers, and to be transmitted to our posterity...without any reference whatever to any other more general or prior right....Thus...in what we improve, we are never wholly new; in what we retain, we are never wholly obsolete....

You [in France] chose to act as if you...had everything to begin anew. You began ill, because you began by despising everything that belonged to you....Respecting your forefathers, you would have been taught to respect yourselves. You would not have chosen to consider the French as a...nation of low-born servile wretches until the emancipating year of 1789....You would not have been content to be…a gang of Maroon slaves, suddenly broke loose from the house of bondage, and therefore to be pardoned for your abuse of the liberty to which you were not accustomed.…

Compute your gains: see what is got by those extravagant and presumptuous speculations which have taught your leaders to despise all their predecessors, and all their contemporaries, and even to despise themselves, until the moment in which they became truly despicable.…France, when she let loose the reins of regal authority, doubled the license of a ferocious dissoluteness in manners, and of an insolent irreligion in opinions and practices; and has extended through all ranks of life, as if she were communicating some privilege, or laying open some secluded benefit, all the unhappy corruptions that usually were the disease of wealth and power. This is one of the new principles of equality in France.…

Remember that your parliament of Paris told your king, that, in calling the states together, he had nothing to fear.…It is right that these men should [now] hide their heads.…They have seen the French rebel against a mild and lawful monarch, with more fury, outrage, and insult, than ever any people has been known to rise against the most illegal usurper, or the most [bloody] tyrant. Their resistance was made to concession; their revolt was from protection; their blow was aimed at a hand holding out graces, favors, and immunities.…

They have found their punishment in their success. Laws overturned; tribunals subverted; industry without vigor; commerce expiring, the revenue unpaid, yet the people impoverished; a church pillaged, and a state not relieved; civil and military

anarchy made the constitution of the kingdom; everything human and divine sacrificed to the idol of public credit, and national bankruptcy the consequence.…The principle of property, whose creatures and representatives they are, was systematically subverted.…

After I have read over the list of the persons and descriptions elected into the Third Estate, nothing which they afterwards did could appear astonishing. Among them, indeed, I saw some of known rank; some of shining talents; but of any practical experience in the state, not one man was to be found. The best were only men of theory.…Nothing can secure a steady and moderate conduct in such assemblies, but that the body of them should be respectably composed, in point of condition in life, of permanent property, of education, and of such habits as enlarge and liberalize the understanding.…

Judge, Sir, of my surprise, when I found that a very great proportion of the assembly (a majority, I believe) was composed of practitioners in the law. It was composed, not of distinguished magistrates…but…of obscure provincial advocates…the fomenters and conductors of the petty war of village vexation.…To these were joined men of other descriptions, from whom as little knowledge of, or attention to, the interests of a great state was to be expected, and as little regard to the stability of any institution; men formed to be instruments, not controls. Such in general was the composition of the Third Estate in the National Assembly; in which was scarcely to be perceived the slightest traces of what we call the natural landed interest of the country.

Map 22.1 Napoleonic Europe in 1810 Although the enlargement of France by 1810 was only temporary, Napoleon's campaigns had lasting effects on the map of Europe. By consolidating territory in German- and Italian-speaking areas, challenging the power of traditional aristocracies, and exemplifying the power of nationalism, Napoleon helped lay the foundations for the later emergence of new nation-states (see Chapter 23).

Jacobins. Then, in 1804, he crowned himself Emperor Napoleon I, though only after securing the approval of the legislature and ratifying the move through a national plebiscite.

By the orderliness and rationality of his administration, Napoleon seemed an "enlightened despot," fulfilling the hopes of the eighteenth-century philosophes. He sponsored the creation of the Bank of France to stabilize finances, enforced use of the metric system of weights and measures to rationalize trade and accounting, and initiated a new system of laws, the Napoleonic Code, recognizing the legal equality of all French citizens. To create it, eminent jurists used the deductive Cartesian approach (see Chapter 21). Starting from general principles (rather than inherited custom), they constructed a reasoned system of civil law.

● **CONTEXT&CONNECTIONS** The Napoleonic Code became highly influential across Europe and, exported with the French overseas empire, worldwide. However, the French long refused to treat conquered Africans as citizens to whom the Code applied, ruling instead through administrative fiat. Then in the 1950s and 1960s, when African nationalists successfully organized for reforms and independence, the Napoleonic Code formed the template for new legal systems in nations such as Mali, Senegal, and Côte d'Ivoire (see Chapters 26 and 30). ●

Historians have also seen in Napoleon's campaigns the origins of modern **nationalism**, the belief that individuals are bound together by ties of language, culture, and history. National identity was not entirely new, but in France in the wake of the Revolution and Napoleonic campaigns, national feeling became much stronger. Earlier, members of the nobility were tied by marriage to aristocracies in other countries and had only limited feelings of "French" identity. Peasants, meanwhile, were tied more strongly to their local communities and provincial cultures than to the French state in Paris. But when conscripts returned to their villages, full of pride as soldiers for France, they now saw themselves as citizens of a nation rather than subjects of a king. Napoleon cultivated that sense of patriotism and national pride, promising them not liberty but glory.

French nationalism grew in parallel with Napoleon's military achievements. Though the emperor abandoned his planned invasion of England after the British defeated his navy in 1805, Napoleon's forces seemed unstoppable on the continent of Europe. French armies, commanded by the greatest general of the age and by military officers chosen for their talent rather than their aristocratic connections, swept through Iberia and Italy; asserted control over the Netherlands, Poland, and the western half of Germany; and inflicted embarrassing losses on the Austrians and Prussians. Simón Bolívar, living in Paris after his visit to Rome, was disappointed by Napoleon's imperial pretensions, but like many, he admired Bonaparte's political and military skills.

● **CONTEXT&CONNECTIONS** Nation-states, what one historian has called "imagined communities," where "peoples" form "governments" within "nations," became common only in modern times. Earlier, great empires always included diverse peoples; multiethnicity was as characteristic of ancient Rome as of the later Ming, Mughal, Ottoman, Austrian, and Russian empires (see Chapters 16-17). In Holland, France, and England in the seventeenth century, however, national solidarity began emerging when people started to think of themselves as belonging to "Dutch" or "French" or "English" nations which transcended loyalty to any particular leader or dynasty. Nineteenth-century Europeans more clearly articulated the concept of "nationhood" (see Chapter 23) and through their empires exported the idea across the globe. Now "national" thinking is nearly universal, though still problematic: there have been many nations (like Nigeria) without coherent "peoples," and many peoples (like the Kurds) without their own nations (see Chapter 27). ●

nationalism

The defining ideology of the nation-state, emphasizing the rights and responsibilities of citizens toward the nation as superior to those based on regional, religious, familial, or other identities. Nationalism often asserts a common ethnic and linguistic heritage in legitimizing state power.

In reaction to French invasion, feelings of nationalism intensified across Europe. When the French had first crossed the Rhine River, many Germans greeted them as bearers of Enlightenment, of liberty and equality. After Napoleon and his troops behaved more like occupiers than liberators, however, many Germans were bitterly disappointed. Likewise, on the Italian peninsula, French invasion caused the subjects of disparate monarchies to assert a common "Italian" identity in rallying against the intruders (see Chapter 23).

In the end, it was Napoleon's ambition that caused his own downfall. In 1812 he mounted a massive attack on Russia. The Russian army could in no way prevent this assault, but they used their vast landscape to military advantage. When Napoleon reached Moscow, he found that the city had been abandoned and largely burned to the ground by its own people. Retreat through the harsh Russian winter decimated the French army. Of the 700,000 troops that had invaded Russia, fewer than 100,000 returned.

A broad coalition of anti-French forces now went on the offensive, invaded France, forced Napoleon to abdicate, and restored the Bourbon monarchy by placing Louis XVIII (r. 1814–1824) on the throne. Dramatically, Napoleon escaped his exile, returned to Paris, and re-formed his army before finally being defeated by British and Prussian forces at the Battle of Waterloo in 1815. By this roundabout route, France finally became a constitutional monarchy. Napoleon died in exile on a remote South Atlantic island.

Napoleon's impact beyond France itself was substantial. His amalgamation of small western German states into the Confederation of the Rhine set the stage for the development first of nationalism among Germans, who were bound together by language and culture but politically fragmented, and later of a centralized German nation-state. Similarly, on the Italian peninsula after Napoleon's

Battle of the Pyramids The Napoleonic Wars came to North Africa with the French invasion of 1798 and their defeat of the Mamluk army. Subsequently, the British victory over Napoleon's Mediterranean fleet forced him to abandon Egypt. Muhammad Ali, an Ottoman general, soon filled the power vacuum created by the French invasion (see Chapter 23).

NAPOLEON DEFEATING THE MAMELUKES, AT THE BATTLE OF THE PYRAMIDS, NEAR CAIRO.

Library of Congress Prints and Photographs Division| LC-DIG-pga-05741|

conquest, modern Italian nationalism and the quest for a unified Italian nation began. As far away as Egypt, Napoleon's invasion in 1798 destroyed the status quo, stimulating Egyptians' national consciousness and setting the stage for the emergence of a more powerful Egyptian state (see Chapter 23).

For Simón Bolívar, Napoleon's most relevant impact occurred in Spain where, by overthrowing the monarchy, Napoleon gave an opening to the forces of South American liberation. Within France's own overseas empire, the most dramatic developments took place on the Caribbean island of Saint-Domingue (san-doe-MANG).

The Haitian Revolution, 1791–1804

The colony of Saint-Domingue was by far France's richest overseas possession. Occupying the western half of the island of Hispaniola, Saint-Domingue accounted for as much as a third of French foreign trade. Half a million African slaves toiled on the colony's plantations under conditions so harsh that the planters had to constantly import more Africans to keep enough slaves working in the fields (see Chapter 19).

As the reverberations of 1789 reached Saint-Domingue, revolution in Haiti also moved through several stages. Initially, the central conflict was between the whites who dominated the plantation economy and the *gens de couleur* (zhahn deh koo-LUHR), free men and women of mixed race, who about equaled the whites in number. Artisans and small farmers, some gens de couleur were even prosperous enough to own a few slaves themselves. Many were literate, and having followed the events of the American and French Revolutions, they demanded liberty and equality for themselves. By 1791, civil war broke out between the planters and the gens de couleur.

While neither group wanted to end slavery, civil war between them created an opening for a vast slave uprising organized by a *Voudun* (voh-doon) priest called Boukman (because he was literate). Voudun beliefs and rituals derived from West and Central Africa, and as a religious leader Boukman had great authority among African slaves, while his position as his master's coach driver gave him the mobility to organize thousands of slaves to rise up at his signal. When they did so, in the summer of 1791, the rebels were spontaneously joined by tens of thousands of other slaves from across the island, as well as by maroons, runaway slaves who lived in the mountains (see Chapter 19).

Just as French peasants had burned the manor houses of their aristocratic overlords, now Boukman's slave army attacked the planters' estates in Saint-Domingue. Forty thousand marched on the city of Le Cap, where whites and gens de couleur had taken refuge. The slaughter lasted for weeks, until planter forces finally captured and executed the rebel leader; they fixed his head to a pole with a sign that read: *"This is the head of Boukman, chief of the rebels."*

● **CONTEXT&CONNECTIONS** Ironically, the Haitian Revolution played a role in delaying the abolition of the slave trade in the British empire. In 1791, planters in the British West Indies, and their allies in Britain, used fear of revolt to lobby effectively against *abolitionist* legislation, a delay that pushed back the end of the British slave trade until 1808, much to the disappointment of *Olaudah Equiano* (Chapter 19). ●

Portrait of Toussaint Louverture (1743–1803) on horseback, early 19th century (colour engraving), French School (19th century)/Bibliotheque Nationale, Paris, France/Archives Charmet/Bridgeman Images

Toussaint L'Ouverture This contemporary engraving shows the Haitian revolutionary leader Toussaint L'Ouverture in an equestrian pose associated with civil and military power. Toussaint brought Enlightenment ideals to the elemental struggle of Haiti's slaves for liberation. His leadership was sorely missed in Haiti after he was tricked into negotiations with France and died in a French prison.

Toussaint L'Ouverture

(1744–1803) Leader of the Haitian revolution. Under his military and political leadership, Haiti gained independence and abolished slavery, becoming the first black-ruled republic in the Americas. He died in exile in France.

In 1792, the French government sent an army to restore order. But then a new commander emerged. François-Dominique Toussaint was born a slave but had been educated by a priest and had worked in his master's house rather than in the fields. The name by which he is remembered, **Toussaint L'Ouverture** (1744–1803), reflects his military skill: *L'Ouverture* refers to the "opening" he would make in the enemy lines. But Toussaint's political, intellectual, and diplomatic strengths were equally important in turning Haiti into an independent nation freed from the savage inequalities of slavery.

Like Olaudah Equiano (see Chapter 19), Toussaint L'Ouverture (too-SAN loo-ver-CHUR) had diverse experiences that allowed him to bridge the worlds of slave and master. He could organize the slaves to fight while forging alliances with whites, gens de couleur, and the foreign forces that intervened in the conflict. By 1801, his army controlled most of the island. Toussaint supported a new constitution that granted equality to all and declared him governor-general for life.

Initially, some radical French revolutionaries supported the rebels, but Napoleon had other ideas, and in 1802 he sent an expedition to crush Toussaint's army. Toussaint was open to compromise as long as slavery would not be restored and freely agreed to meet with French officers to discuss the matter. They betrayed him: sent to France and harshly treated, Toussaint died in prison.

Meanwhile, many of the soldiers sent by Napoleon to Haiti, lacking immunity to tropical diseases, succumbed to malaria and yellow fever. In Haiti, it was mosquitos more than firepower that drove away the French, just as it was frostbite more than cannon that later ejected them from Russia.

● **CONTEXT&CONNECTIONS** Historians now recognize the role of disease in the Atlantic revolutions. Africans had often arrived in the Americas with disease immunity, which European settlers also developed from childhood exposure. Troops fresh from Europe, in contrast, were extremely vulnerable. Toussaint and other rebels could use differential immunity to their advantage, for example by luring European troops into swampy, malaria-infested areas. ●

The subsequent independence of Haiti terrified slave owners in the United States. Some plantations stepped up security measures, while the U.S. government refused to grant Haiti diplomatic recognition. Venezuela was even more directly affected. In 1795, a Venezuelan who returned from Haiti, a free *zombo* (of mixed African-Amerindian ancestry), led a rebellion of slaves and free persons of color, sending the elite of Caracas into a panic. Simón Bolívar was just twelve at that time, but later he would seek the support of the Haitian government and would argue for the abolition of slavery.

The Latin American Wars of Independence, 1800–1824

Simón Bolívar and other Latin American revolutionaries looked to the ideals of the Enlightenment and the examples of the United States, France, and Haiti in charting their own wars of independence. Also shaping the course of revolution here were relations between *criollos* (American-born Spaniards) and people of African, Amerindian, or mixed descent (see Chapter 18). Beyond widespread agreement on the need to expel the Spanish, the divergent interests of these groups made it difficult to establish common political ground.

Francisco Miranda, Simón Bolívar, and South American Independence

His Venezuelan predecessor, Francisco Miranda (1750–1816), anticipated Simón Bolívar's path. While Bolívar came of age only during the French Revolution, Miranda had earlier traveled to the United States where, in 1783, he met with George Washington and Thomas Jefferson, seeking their inspiration and support for a parallel uprising against Spain. He then toured Europe, escaping Spanish attempts to capture him, and participated in the French Revolution. In Paris, the Jacobins jailed and nearly executed him for denouncing their dictatorship. When he finally returned to South America in 1806, Miranda's goal was to inflame continental revolution against Spain and to forge a unified Gran Colombian state. (See the feature "World History in Today's World: Competing Visions of South American Cooperation.")

Miranda was a living embodiment of the Atlantic Ocean as a transmission zone for revolution. While in Paris, he had been inducted into the society of the Freemasons, a transnational group whose members' belief in Enlightenment rationality took the form of secret rites and rituals emphasizing honesty, integrity, charity, and brotherly love. Though they met in secret, masons were among the most influential intellectual and political actors of the eighteenth century. Members included Benjamin Franklin, Voltaire, George Washington, and the Austrian composer Wolfgang Amadeus Mozart. In 1803, while in Europe, Simon Bolívar was himself inducted into a masonic lodge in Cádiz, Spain.

By the time Bolívar went back to Venezuela in 1807, finding that Francisco Miranda had returned as well, conditions were ripening for Latin American independence. In 1808 Napoleon put his own brother on the Spanish throne, forcing the Spanish king to abdicate. Rejecting the Napoleonic regime as illegitimate, South American elites created *juntas* (ruling groups) to assert temporary local rule.

Loyalists thought these juntas (HUN-tahs) should be disbanded as soon as the legitimate king returned to power. But republicans like Miranda, Bolívar, and

Competing Visions of South American Cooperation

For two centuries, South American unity has been an elusive goal. Francisco Miranda's vision of Gran Colombia was only partly realized by Simón Bolívar and did not last beyond 1830. Still, any discussion of South American unity is sure to invoke the names Miranda and Bolívar.

Since 1991, the Common Market of the South, or Mercosur, has promoted interregional collaboration under the leadership of Venezuela, Brazil, and Argentina. In 2012, however, a competing organization, the Pacific Alliance, was established by Chile, Mexico, Colombia, and Peru.

Apart from the geographic split, the two organizations are also divided by political philosophy and economic policy. The Mercosur governments have mostly been controlled by populist political parties emphasizing a central role for the state. The Pacific Alliance, on the other hand, was created by more conservative political leaders who stress neoliberal, free-market policies. The Pacific Alliance member states are also much friendlier to the United States than those of Mercosur, where traditional suspicions of U.S. intervention and economic domination run deep.

For now, the Pacific Alliance seems to have greater potential. Chile, Mexico, Colombia, and Peru have already eliminated 90 percent of trade tariffs as well as visa requirements. Their plan is for a common market, as they pursue negotiations toward trade pacts with both the United States and the European Union.

The governments of Brazil, Argentina, and Venezuela reacted to the rise of the upstart Pacific Alliance as a threat to their longer term goal of fuller integration, eventually with a common currency and a South American legislature. That agenda has stalled for a number of reasons. Economic disputes between booming Brazil and debt-plagued Argentina have made cooperation over trade issues difficult, and the death of Venezuelan leader Hugo Chávez removed the most charismatic proponent of socialist defiance of the United States.

There have been calls for cooperation between the competing blocs. In 2013, the government of Uruguay proposed that Mercosur embrace a "multiplicity of memberships" to allow its members to work more closely with the Pacific Alliance, and Chilean President Michelle Bachelet organized meetings to identify points of collaboration. Still, as in the days of Miranda and Bolívar, South American unity remains a far-off dream.

their Argentinean counterpart José de San Martín (1778–1850) saw the chance to win complete independence. This division of opinion meant that to win independence, South American republicans would have to fight against powerful local loyalists as well as Spanish troops.

A principal grievance for men of Bolívar's background was that *peninsulares*, the direct representatives of royal authority in Spanish America, dominated the affairs of church and state. Ambitious criollos felt that the existing system was an impediment to their rightful place as leading members of their communities. Criollo merchants, for example, were continually frustrated by restrictions on trade imposed by the peninsulares.

But the struggle involved more than just imperial representatives and local elites. In most places, building a popular base of support for independence required appealing to Indians, Africans, mestizos, and other people of mixed descent, who together made up the majority of the population.

For example, Bolívar's home city of Caracas, facing the sea, was culturally and economically connected to the Caribbean. Slave plantations were an important part of its economy, and Bolívar spent part of his childhood on such a plantation. In addition, Caracas had a large community of *pardos*, free men and women of mixed African-Spanish-Native American ancestry. As in Haiti, unity across these deep divides of class and race was hard to achieve.

In the Venezuelan interior, Bolívar would need the cooperation of *llaneros* (yah-NEYR-ohs), tough frontier cowboys of mixed Spanish-Amerindian descent (like the *gauchos* of Argentina and the *vaqueros* of Mexico). Farther south, Bolívar's armies eventually entered the Viceroyalty of Peru, where the main social divide was between the Spanish-speaking colonists of the coastal areas and the still considerable Amerindian population of the Andes. Simón Bolívar (unlike George Washington) constantly faced the challenge of forging alliances between disparate racial and ethnic groups.

Meanwhile, local elites had taken power in Caracas. Their conservative junta saw local control as temporary, and sent the well-traveled Bolívar on diplomatic missions to London and Washington in 1810. But Bolívar betrayed them by lobbying the British to support his own plan for independence. Upon his return, Bolívar attended the first Congress of Venezuela, which on July 3, 1811, following the passionate advocacy of Francisco Miranda, became the first body in Latin America to declare independence from Spain.

However, racial, ethnic, and regional divisions inhibited any strong sense of "Venezuelan" identity upon which a new nation could be founded. The constitution restricted voting rights to a small minority of criollo property owners and did nothing to abolish slavery. In addition, the llaneros of the interior felt threatened by a constitutional provision that extended private property ownership to the previously uncharted plains. If wealthy ranchers fenced off the lands where they herded wild cattle, the cowboys might lose their livelihood and their independence.

Taking advantage of these divisions, forces loyal to Spain were soon on the offensive. A massive earthquake in the spring of 1812 compounded a sense of foreboding as support for the republic wavered. Miranda began negotiations with Spanish officials for an armistice. Bolívar regarded Miranda's actions as treasonous and had him arrested, a harsh turn against his older colleague that caused some to view Bolívar with suspicion. Amid such acrimony, the young republic collapsed.

Bolívar then set out on the military path he would pursue for the next twelve years, proclaiming a *"war to the death."* Captured Spaniards would be executed, he declared, while American-born Spanish loyalists would be given a chance to mend their ways. In the summer of 1813, Bolívar's army was strong enough to enter Caracas, but again divisions within Venezuelan society worked against him. To broaden his movement's appeal, Bolívar had forged alliances with groups that had been excluded from the first congress and constitution, including llaneros and slaves. Many criollos, however, distrusted Bolívar's army, regarding his black and cowboy soldiers as mere bandits and outlaws.

In addition to such internal dissension, the cause of independence suffered a setback in 1815 after Napoleon's defeat at Waterloo and the restoration of the Spanish monarchy. The Madrid government then reasserted its political and economic control over its American dominions. Seeking greater efficiency through administrative reform, the new Spanish king reinforced the preference for peninsulares in positions of colonial command, while dispatching fifty ships and over ten thousand soldiers to restore imperial authority.

Put on the defensive, Bolívar retreated to the island of Jamaica, where he once again sought British help. He also traveled to Haiti, pursuing support from its government with a pledge to seek *"the absolute liberty of the slaves who have groaned beneath the Spanish yoke in the past three centuries."** Most importantly from a military standpoint, he recruited battle-hardened British mercenaries to serve as his elite force.

Returning once more to Venezuela in 1817, Bolívar established himself in the interior and was recognized as the supreme commander of the various patriotic forces. He offered freedom to slaves who joined his army, and he revived his alliance with the llaneros of the plains. Bolívar's toughness in battle and his willingness to share the privations of his men—once spending a whole night immersed in a lake to avoid Spanish forces—won him their loyalty.

In 1819, even while the Spanish still held Caracas, delegates to the **Congress of Angostura** planned for the resuscitation of independent Venezuela. Bolívar argued for a strong central government with effective executive powers, fearing that a federal system with a strong legislature would lead to division and instability. Rather than stay to see these plans carried out, however, he went south and west to confront imperial forces in the Spanish stronghold of Bogotá. Seeking a broader foundation for Latin American liberty, he began his fight for *Gran Colombia*, a proposed constitutional union encompassing today's Venezuela, Colombia, Panama, Ecuador, and Peru (see Map 22.2).

Bolívar and his troops suffered greatly on their trek into the frigid Andes, but their morale remained high. The Spanish forces, on the other hand, became demoralized. Led by generals who could not match Bolívar's strategic brilliance, they quickly gave way, first in Bogotá and then in Ecuador. Meanwhile, further south, other liberators were scoring equivalent successes. José de San Martín (hoe-SAY deh san mar-TEEN) took the region of Rio de la Plata (today's Argentina), while Chile's successful republican forces were led by Bernardo O'Higgins (the Spanish-speaking son of an Irish immigrant). Together San Martín and O'Higgins had occupied the coastal regions of Peru, leaving only its Andean region in loyalist hands.

The situation in the Andes had been tense since an Amerindian uprising in 1780 led by **Tupac Amaru II** (1741–1781), a descendant of the last Inca ruler. Tupac Amaru (TOO-pack ah-MAR-oo) had been baptized and educated by Jesuit priests and for a time served the Spanish government. But the poverty, illiteracy, and oppression faced by his people caused him first to petition for reform and then, when his pleas were ignored, to raise an Andean rebellion.

Spanish authorities savagely suppressed Tupac Amaru's revolt, forcing him to witness the torture and death of his own wife and family before his own execution. The coastal criollo elite of Peru in and around Lima supported this repression of Andean rebellion, fearing a race war in which they might be victims. The Spanish tried to enforce cultural assimilation by banning indigenous cloth and the use of the indigenous Quechua (KETCH-wah) language. But the Amerindians of the mountains avoided the ban, and as much contact with Spanish officials as possible. Though these highland Amerindians were potential allies of Bolívar, they remained aloof, more concerned with the autonomy of their own communities than the independence of nations.

Congress of Angostura

(1819) Congress that declared Venezuelan independence after Simón Bolívar gave an opening address arguing for a strong central government with effective executive powers.

Tupac Amaru II

(1741–1781) José Gabriel Condorcanqui Noguera, a descendant of the last Inca ruler; called himself Tupac Amaru II while leading a large-scale rebellion in the Andes against Spanish rule. He was defeated and executed.

---

*Excerpt from Simón Bolívar, "Oath Taken at Rome, 15 August 1805," trans. Frederick H. Fornoff, in *El Libertador: Writings of Simón Bolívar*, ed. David Bushnell (New York: Oxford University Press, 2003), p. 77.

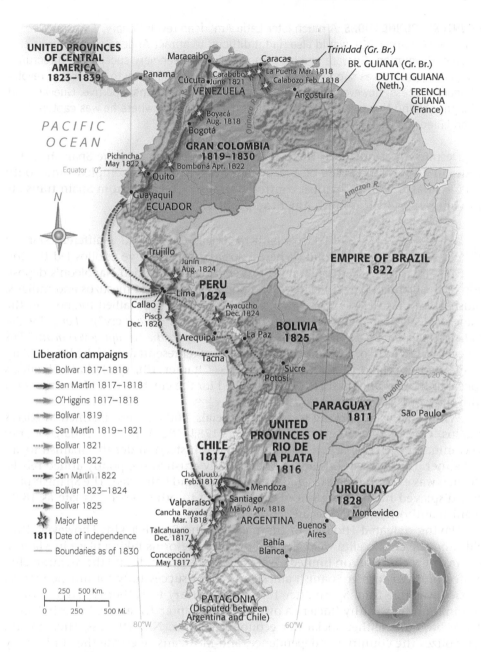

UNITED PROVINCES OF CENTRAL AMERICA 1823–1839

Maracaibo

Panama

Cúcuta • June 1821 Carabobo

Trinidad (Gr. Br.)

Caracas

La Puerta Mar. 1818
Calabozo Feb. 1818

BR. GUIANA (Gr. Br.)

DUTCH GUIANA (Neth.)

FRENCH GUIANA (France)

VENEZUELA

Angostura

PACIFIC OCEAN

Boyacá Aug. 1818

Bogotá

GRAN COLOMBIA 1819–1830

Orinoco R.

Pichincha May 1822

Equator 0°   Bomboná Apr. 1822

Quito

Amazon R.

Guayaquil

ECUADOR

N

Trujillo

Junín Aug. 1824

EMPIRE OF BRAZIL 1822

Lima

PERU 1824

Callao

Ayacucho Dec. 1824

Pisco Dec. 1820

Arequipa

La Paz

BOLIVIA 1825

Liberation campaigns

Tacna

Sucre

Potosí

Paraná R.

20°S

→ Bolívar 1817–1818

➤ San Martín 1817–1818

→ O'Higgins 1817–1818

→ Bolívar 1819

➤ San Martín 1819–1821

⋯ Bolívar 1821

→ Bolívar 1822

⋯ San Martín 1822

→ Bolívar 1823–1824

⋯ Bolívar 1825

✦ Major battle

1811 Date of independence

— Boundaries as of 1830

PARAGUAY 1811

São Paulo

CHILE 1817

UNITED PROVINCES OF RIO DE LA PLATA 1816

Chacabuco Feb. 1817

Mendoza

URUGUAY 1828

Valparaíso

Santiago

Maipó Apr. 1818

Cancha Rayada Mar. 1818

ARGENTINA

Buenos Aires

Montevideo

Talcahuano Dec. 1817

Bahía Blanca

Concepción May 1817

0   250   500 Km.

0   250   500 Mi.

PATAGONIA (Disputed between Argentina and Chile)

80°W   60°W

Map 22.2 Independence in Latin America Paraguay led the way toward Latin American independence in 1811. The United Provinces of Rio de la Plata (the core of today's Argentina) followed in 1816. The next year, José de San Martín and Bernardo O'Higgins secured Chilean independence. By 1819, Simón Bolívar had secured the independence of Venezuela and Ecuador, uniting them into the independent state of *Gran Colombia*. Combined Chilean and Colombian forces defeated the Spanish at Ayacucho in 1824, finalizing the independence of Spanish Latin America.

● **CONTEXT&CONNECTIONS** A much later Latin American revolutionary, *Ernesto "Che" Guevara* (Chapter 30), would also find it difficult to attract Andean allies. During the Cuban Revolution, Guevara and his compatriots had been very successful in recruiting poor peasants as supporters. When he went to Bolivia to try to repeat that revolutionary success, however, the local Amerindians remained unsupportive. Guevara and his men found themselves isolated in the cold mountains, where he was captured and killed. ●

Despite Amerindian disinterest, Bolívar's troops engaged the Spanish in the Andes in 1824 at the Battle of Ayacucho. Their victory was complete, and South America was free from Spanish control. But would freedom from Spain translate into liberty for diverse South American peoples?

Mexico, 1810–1821

Mexico's path to independence had a different starting point. Whereas socially conservative criollos led the initial struggle in Venezuela, in Mexico Napoleon's deposition of the Spanish king quickly led to a popular uprising of mestizos and Indians. Parish priest **Miguel de Hidalgo y Costilla** (1753–1811) rallied the poor in the name of justice for the oppressed, issuing his famous *Grito* ("cry"): *"Long live Our Lady of Guadalupe! Long live the Americas and death to the corrupt government!"* His appeal to the Virgin of Guadalupe, a dark-skinned representation of the Virgin Mary as she had appeared to a lowly peasant (see Chapter 18), symbolized Hidalgo's appeal to Indians and mestizos. Hidalgo called for the creation of a Mexican nation with the words *"¡Mexicanos, Viva México!"*

While this was shocking to Spanish officials, Hidalgo also alarmed Mexico's criollos. One of them, Agustín de Iturbide (1783–1824), refused Hidalgo's offer to command the rebel army, leading his troops instead under the Spanish loyalist banner. Iturbide's well-trained soldiers easily crushed the poorly armed rebels: Hidalgo was excommunicated and then captured and beheaded. The Spanish publicly displayed his mutilated head as a warning to other rebels. As late as 1820, Spanish authority seemed secure.

Having defeated Hidalgo in the name of the Spanish king, however, Iturbide and the criollo elite were alarmed by liberal reforms taking place in Madrid, where a new constitution limited royal power. Now Iturbide and the Mexican elite turned on their former Spanish allies and fought successfully for independence. Mexico was free from Spain after 1821, but contrary to Father Hildago's vision, domination by wealthy hacienda owners (see Chapter 18) assured that independence brought neither social nor economic reform. Nevertheless, Hidalgo still symbolizes the country's independence, and Mexicans celebrate the anniversary of the *Grito de Dolores*, September 16, as Mexico's national day.

● **CONTEXT&CONNECTIONS** The social divisions left unaddressed at the time of Mexican independence in 1821 festered until the outbreak of the Mexican Revolution in 1910, when mestizos and Indians organized by *Emiliano Zapata* (Chapter 25) rose again to challenge the large landowners and big ranchers. ●

Miguel de Hidalgo y Costilla

(1753–1811) Mexican priest who launched the first stage of the Mexican war for independence. Hidalgo appealed to Indians and mestizos and was thus viewed with suspicion by Mexican criollos. In 1811, he was captured and executed.

Brazil and the Caribbean, 1808–1835

The age of Atlantic revolutions played out much differently in Brazil, which became an empire under the former Portuguese ruling family, and in the Caribbean, where rule from Europe and, as in

Father Hidalgo In 1810, Father Hidalgo rallied the common people of Mexico, especially mestizos and Indians, under the banner of the Virgin of Guadalupe for independence from Spain. Mexican elites opposed him, however, and cooperated with Spanish authorities to crush the uprising. Hidalgo was executed.

Brazil, slave plantation economies continued. (Independent Haiti was the exception.)

Brazil had followed its own distinct path toward independence. In 1808, the Portuguese royal family fled Napoleon's invasion, seeking refuge in Brazil. In 1821, the king returned to Portugal, leaving his son Pedro behind as his representative. Pedro, however, declared himself sympathetic to the cause of independence, and in 1824 Pedro I (r. 1824–1831) became the constitutional monarch of an independent Brazil.

Brazil's independence was therefore managed by its social and economic elites and was a deeply conservative affair. Like the United States, Brazil became independent with its merchant and slave-owning elites intact. Encountering less political and economic disruption than the Spanish-speaking Americas, Brazil was poised to attract immigrants and capital investment, and to deepen penetration of its vast interior.

Nevertheless, deeper social fissures were exposed during the constitutional transition, leading to the largest *urban* slave uprising in the history of the Americas, the Malê Revolt, or Muslim Uprising, of 1835. The population of the northeastern city of Salvador de Bahia, where the uprising took place, was not only majority African, but primarily Yoruba (from what is now western Nigeria). Muslim scholars led the revolt, and even used Arabic in their correspondence to avoid detection. The response of the authorities was harsh. The Muslim clerics who led the uprising were quickly executed. Both sides were well aware of the Haitian example. As in Brazil, slavery endured late into the nineteenth century in Cuba and other Spanish possessions in the Caribbean.

- **CONTEXT&CONNECTIONS** Yoruba religious life in Brazil was a complex mix of Christianity, Islam, and belief in the power of the traditional *orisas*, the Yoruba gods (see Chapter 19). As in today's Nigeria, followers of all three traditions were found in nineteenth-century Brazil, though even more common was a blending of monotheistic and traditional beliefs and practices. The *syncretism* (Chapter 18) of the Malê rebels, for example, included the use of African amulets as protective devices, though sometimes incorporating Koranic passages. ●

Meanwhile, in the Caribbean, Jamaica was the scene of another significant slave uprising in 1831–1832, the Christmas Rebellion, under the leadership of a Baptist preacher. Inspired by the British abolitionist movement and the peaceful outlawing of the slave trade, the rebels demanded that they be paid for their labor and free to leave their plantations in search of better opportunity. As always, the plantation owners ferociously repressed the rebellion. But that was their last hurrah. Just two years later, in 1834, Parliament freed all slaves in the empire, with compensation due to former slave owners. In Jamaica and elsewhere, blacks swiftly abandoned the sugar fields. Abolition thus came to the British Caribbean without either revolution, as in Haiti, or national independence, as in the Spanish Americas.

Revolutionary Outcomes and Comparisons to 1830

The circulation of revolutionary ideas and revolutionary experiences connected the Atlantic world in the late eighteenth and early nineteenth centuries: Simón Bolívar's goals and achievements grew directly from earlier struggles in the United States, France, and Haiti to transform politics in the name of liberty and equality. By 1830, however, the outcomes of revolution in Europe and across the Americas were quite different.

In Europe, the excesses of French politics led to a strong counterreaction of conservatism in defense of tradition over change. Europe's revolutionary flame was extinguished when princes, priests, and aristocrats used the defeat of Napoleon to suppress reform (even, after all that had happened, placing yet another "Louis" on the throne of France!). Leading this attempt by European conservatives

Map 22.3 Europe in 1815 After the disruptions in the political map of Europe caused by the French Revolution and the expansion of Napoleon's empire (see Map 22.1), in 1815 European diplomats restored earlier boundaries and established a conservative status quo at the Congress of Vienna. One important change was the appearance of a larger Prussian kingdom, now including Rhineland territories in the west of Germany, a territorial expansion that would later form the foundation for German unification (see Chapter 23). Austria competed with Prussia for influence, founding a German Confederation centered in Vienna.

to turn back the clock was Prince Metternich of Austria, who orchestrated the **Congress of Vienna** (1815), which restored the balance of power among Britain, France, Austria, Prussia, and Russia (see Map 22.3). Aristocrats once again flaunted their wealth in the capitals of Europe, no longer afraid of revolutionary violence.

However, the spread of nationalism and the association of that idea with progressive reform proved a constant challenge to European rulers. When Greek nationalists won their independence from the Ottoman empire in 1829, the event did not at first appear to threaten the European status quo. But it was not long before ethnic minorities in the Austrian and Russian empires also began organizing

Congress of Vienna

(1815) Conference at which the balance of power among European states was restored after the defeat of Napoleon Bonaparte.

along national lines, while the idea of a single, powerful German nation began to spread as well. Other ideals of the French Revolution also remained alive, such as the idea that equality could only be achieved through a more equitable distribution of wealth. Before long a rising generation of revolutionaries would try once again to overturn Europe's status quo (see Chapter 23).

The United States of America, following George Washington's farewell advice, stayed largely aloof from European affairs. In the first half of the nineteenth century the new country focused on expansion, with relatively high wages and cheap land attracting swelling numbers of European immigrants. In 1803, anxious for funds to fight on other fronts, Napoleon agreed to the Louisiana Purchase. Vast new territories were thus added to the United States, and soon Lewis and Clark's expedition was pointing the way west (see Chapter 21). These lands were not, however, unoccupied. Over the course of the nineteenth century, violence and dislocation would mark U.S. westward expansion. And since the issue of slavery remained unresolved, regional tensions increased, ultimately exploding in a violent civil war (see Chapter 25). Conversations, and disagreements, about the true meaning of "liberty" would continue in the United States far into the future.

In Haiti, the transition from slave colony to free republic proved exceedingly difficult. Freed slaves fled the plantations to establish their own farms on small plots of land, and a massive decline in overall production followed. The sharp decline in plantation exports robbed the new government of its tax base. The political transition to independence proved equally problematic. The personal ambitions of early Haitian rulers, fueled by tensions between the mixed-race gens de couleur and Haitians of African/slave descent, created political divisions and a long-standing culture of corruption and dictatorship. Centuries of an economic and social system based almost solely on sugar and slavery had left Haitians ill-prepared to achieve either democracy or prosperity.

In Latin America, Simón Bolívar's attempt to create a state of *Gran Colombia* fell apart. The great liberator ended his life in disappointment, as all across the region military commanders seized power in a patchwork of often squabbling new republics. Lacking strong traditions of local governance, these new republics were easily dominated by military dictators who allied with wealthy landowners and church officials. Concentrated wealth, a legacy of the colonial era, provided a poor foundation on which to build democracy. And before long, as Bolívar foresaw, the fragmentation of *Gran Colombia* left South America vulnerable to external powers such as Great Britain and the United States.

caudillos

Latin American military men who gained power through violence during and after the early nineteenth century.

By 1830, those ruling in much of Latin America were **caudillos** (cow-DEE-yos), strong-arm rulers who looked after their own interests and those of the military above all else, usually with the support of the dominant landowners and the Catholic Church. In Venezuela, for example, one of Bolívar's top commanders, José Antonio Páez, separated the country from *Gran Colombia* while establishing an authoritarian style. In Mexico, it was one of Iturbide's commanders at the time of independence, General Antonio López de Santa Anna (1794–1875), who came to typify the venality and weakness of caudillo rule, serving as president nine different times starting in 1833, and eventually losing half of Mexico to the United States (see Chapter 25). Soon, reformers across Latin America were striving to create liberal constitutional orders to replace the caudillos.

Although Africans, Amerindians, and people of mixed descent played important roles in the Latin American wars of independence, their efforts were not to be rewarded with power or privilege, even where slavery was abolished. Benefiting most from independence were the criollos who had consolidated their political and economic dominance by assuming positions of authority vacated by departing peninsulares. As for the church, while individual priests might side with the downtrodden, the Catholic hierarchy still allied itself with the wealthy and powerful.

Nowhere were the goals of liberty, equality, and fraternity decreed by French revolutionaries fully realized. But Enlightenment concepts were now a permanent part of the political conversation around the Atlantic and, as the nineteenth century progressed, across the world.

CONTEXT AND CONNECTIONS

The Global Legacies of Revolution

To go through a "complete revolution" means to experience a bottom-to-top transformation, a thorough reordering of society. Of the cases considered in this chapter, only the brief period of extreme republicanism in France under the Jacobins and the Haitian revolution approach that definition. In the other cases—in the United States, in France under the National Assembly and Napoleon, across Latin America—in spite of significant political change, notable continuities with prerevolutionary societies remained.

Enlightenment philosophers were, of course, the ones who suggested that custom and tradition should be tossed aside if and when they stood in the way of a rationally ordered society. They were more conservative on the question of how to achieve that end, however, generally trusting that sophisticated, cosmopolitan elites

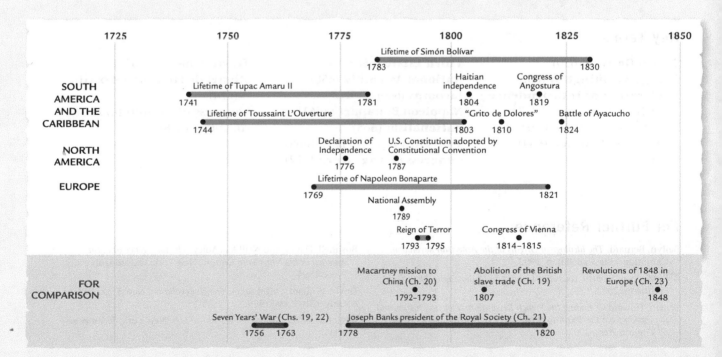

would lead the way. In Britain's North American colonies, it was indeed the more privileged and well educated who led the war of independence and the creation of the new republic. Even so, the doctrine of popular sovereignty required them to look beyond their own self-interest as planters, merchants, and professionals and take seriously the aspirations of the broader society (if not of blacks, Amerindians, or women).

In every other case, however, the old order's resistance to change required revolutionaries to mobilize excluded members of society to generate the power they needed, as when Simón Bolívar assembled his coalition of criollos, cowboys, and slaves to throw off Spanish rule. Even if, as in France and Haiti, revolutionaries did not originally plan it that way, those at the bottom usually rose up demanding to be heard (peasants burning manor houses in France, Parisians seizing the Bastille, Haitian slaves attacking sugar plantations and their owners, mestizos and Indians rallying to the banner of Father Hidalgo in Mexico).

Once the genie of mass agitation was out of the bottle, middle-class revolutionaries were generally anxious to put it back: to define liberty in a way that protected property, and to limit voting rights to those "responsible" enough to use them wisely. That was the path advocated by philosopher John Locke and reflected in the British constitution. In contrast, the more radical restructuring of society in France led to the Jacobin dictatorship and ultimately to Napoleon's empire, precedents that both historians and aspiring revolutionaries would closely investigate for centuries to come.

As we will see, the eighteenth-century revolutions left enduring global legacies. Later revolutionary leaders in Russia and China found inspiration in the events of 1789 (see Chapters 23 and 27), while anticolonial nationalists in Asia and Africa would look to the history of North and South American liberation to inspire their own quest for independence from European empires (see Chapter 30). The French and Haitian examples were especially inspiring to revolutionaries mobilizing masses of people to achieve wholesale change. For conservatives, on the other hand, the dangers of mass mobilization outweighed the benefits: they recalled Edmund Burke's warning that radical revolution leads to dictatorship.

Key Terms

Simón Bolívar (650)
George Washington (652)
Declaration of Independence (652)
Constitution of the United States of America (654)
Louis XVI (655)

Third Estate (658)
National Assembly (658)
Jacobins (660)
Napoleon Bonaparte (661)
nationalism (665)
Toussaint L'Ouverture (668)
Congress of Angostura (672)

Tupac Amaru II (672)
Miguel de Hidalgo y Costilla (674)
Congress of Vienna (677)
caudillos (678)

For Further Reference

Bailyn, Bernard. *The Ideological Origins of the American Revolution*. Cambridge, Mass.: Belknap, 1992.

Bell, Madison Smartt. *Toussaint Louverture: A Biography*. New York: Pantheon, 2007.

Brown, Howard G. *Ending the French Revolution: Violence, Justice, and Repression from the Terror to Napoleon*. Charlottesville: University of Virginia Press, 2007.

Bushnell, David, and Neill MacAuley. *The Emergence of Latin America in the Nineteenth Century*. New York: Oxford University Press, 1994.

Doyle, William. *Origins of the French Revolution*. New York: Oxford University Press, 1999.

Englund, Steven. *Napoleon: A Political Life*. New York: Scribner's, 2004.

Geggus, David P. *The Impact of the Haitian Revolution in the Atlantic World*. Columbia: University of South Carolina Press, 2002.

McNeill, J. R. *Mosquito Empires: Ecology and War in the Greater Caribbean, 1620–1914*. New York: Cambridge University Press, 2010.

Reis, João José. *Slave Rebellion in Brazil: The Muslim Uprising of 1835 in Bahia*. Baltimore: Johns Hopkins University Press, 1993.

Van Young, Eric. *The Other Rebellion: Popular Violence, Ideology, and the Mexican Struggle for Independence, 1810–1821*. Stanford: Stanford University Press, 2001.

Wood, Gordon S. *The American Revolution*. New York: Modern Library, 2002.

MindTap

MindTap is a fully online, highly personalized learning experience built upon Cengage Learning content. MindTap combines student learning tools—readings, multimedia, activities, and assessments—into a singular Learning Path that guides students through the course.

23

The Industrial Revolution and European Politics, 1765–1880

Mikhail Bakunin

In the summer of 1848, Russian émigré **Mikhail Bakunin** (1814–1876) rushed to Paris as revolution once again engulfed the French capital. The fire of revolt quickly spread to Berlin, Vienna, Budapest, Rome, Milan, and all across Europe. History was on the revolutionaries' side, Bakunin thought. Freedom was coming: kings, princes, and popes would be tossed aside.

Those were distant memories by the summer of 1851, as Bakunin sat in solitary confinement in the imposing Peter and Paul Fortress in the Russian capital. He had been taking part in a rebellion in Prague when Austrian forces captured him, sentenced him to death, and then turned him over to Russian authorities, who gave him the chance to write a "confession" to the tsar. *"There was in my character,"* he wrote, *"a radical defect: Love for the fantastic, for out-of-the-way, unheard of adventures, for undertakings which open up an infinite horizon and whose end no man can foresee."**

Though Bakunin was dispirited and in poor health, with little chance of ever seeing his family or the light of day again, his message to Tsar Nicholas still conjured up the heady days of 1848:

Now what shall I say to you, Sire, of the impression produced on me by Paris! This huge city, the center of European enlightenment, had suddenly been turned into the wild Caucasus: on every street, almost everywhere, barricades had been piled up like mountains.... NOBLE WORKERS in rejoicing, exulting crowds, with red banners and patriotic songs [were] reveling in their victory! And in the midst of this unlimited freedom, this mad rapture, all were

---

*Cited in E. H. Carr, *Mikhail Bakunin* (New York: Vintage, 1937), p. 1.

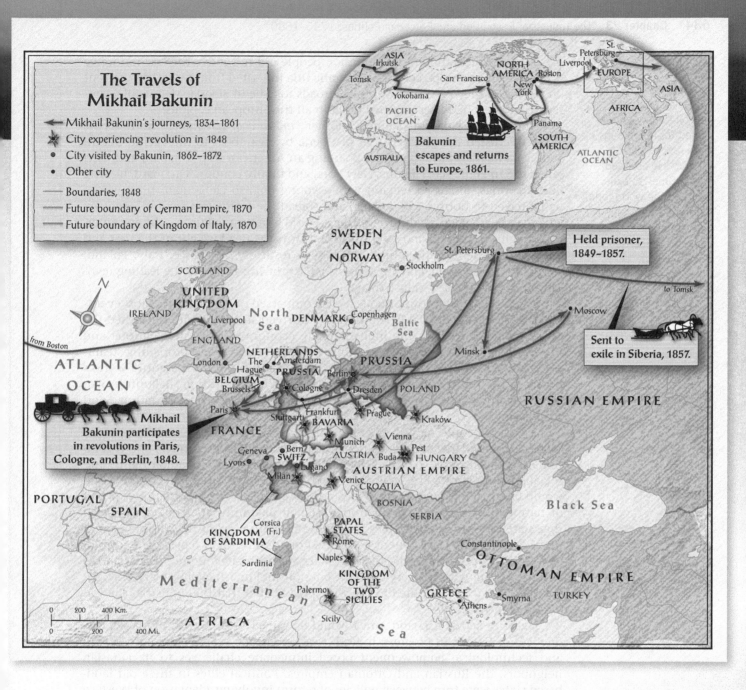

The Travels of Mikhail Bakunin

← Mikhail Bakunin's journeys, 1834–1861
✦ City experiencing revolution in 1848
● City visited by Bakunin, 1862–1872
● Other city

— Boundaries, 1848
— Future boundary of German Empire, 1870
— Future boundary of Kingdom of Italy, 1870

Bakunin escapes and returns to Europe, 1861.

Held prisoner, 1849–1857.

Sent to exile in Siberia, 1857.

Mikhail Bakunin participates in revolutions in Paris, Cologne, and Berlin, 1848.

so forgiving, sympathetic, loving of their fellow man.... [N]owhere have I found so much noble selflessness, so much truly touching integrity ... with such heroism as I found in these simple, uneducated people, who always were and always will be a thousand times better than their leaders! ... It seemed that the whole world had been turned upside down.*

*The Confession of Mikhail Bakunin, trans. Robert C. Howes (Ithaca: Cornell University Press, 1977), pp. 54–55.

Bakunin's celebration of the common people did not move the tsar to forgive him. He was stripped of the aristocratic title inherited from his father and sent on a long journey by sleigh over frozen roads to exile in Siberia. Meanwhile, conservative rulers had re-established order in all the European capitals.

Undeterred, Bakunin planned another *"unheard of adventure."* In 1861, he escaped, crossed the vast expanses of Siberia by steamboat to the Pacific Ocean, avoided a Russian naval patrol by boarding an American ship to Japan, and then sailed to San Francisco, Panama, New York, and finally London. On board, he sang Russian songs, discussed religion with a young English clergyman (from whom he managed to borrow 250 dollars), and spread the words *freedom* and *revolution* wherever he traveled. Bakunin circled the world to return to Europe, the epicenter, he thought, of humankind's quest to overthrow the dead weight of the past and build a truly democratic future. He traveled restlessly, to France, Italy, Poland, Germany, Switzerland, and Sweden, his fame growing as one of the leading revolutionaries of Europe's industrial age.

Mikhail Bakunin's tumultuous life encompassed one of history's most eventful periods: the Industrial Revolution. Coal-driven steam engines unleashed the power of fossil fuels in the industrializing economies of western Europe and the United States, driving the machinery of new factories and propelling steamships and locomotives. More efficient transportation bound the entire world's people more tightly in networks of trade and communication. Bakunin's own early travels were by cart, sleigh, and sailing ships, his later ones by railroad and steamship.

As more people moved to cities, often living in squalid conditions, rapid social change further stimulated debates among European reformers and revolutionaries, for example, between liberals, who emphasized individual rights, and socialists, who stressed the collective good. Reformers in other parts of the world would take inspiration from these ideals of 1848, and also from the emotive power of nationalism surging across Europe. Mikhail Bakunin's anarchism—his belief that states are inherently oppressive—stood in contrast with the communism of his archrival, Karl Marx, whom he accused of attempting to replace one form of government oppression with another. Marx was ultimately more influential. His writings, along with the very different ones of the English evolutionary biologist Charles Darwin, contributed to the widespread belief that the industrial age was a time of progress.

Societies across Asia and Africa would be forced to cope with myriad consequences of European progress; indeed, western Europe's rapid economic growth and technological empowerment posed immediate challenges to its Eurasian neighbors, the Russian and Ottoman empires. Political elites in these old land-based states were torn between policies of reform involving adaptation of Western models of law and governance and conservative policies that stressed continuity over change.

The Industrial Revolution tremendously empowered western European nations relative to other societies. Therefore, it is essential to understand Europe's nineteenth-century economic, political, and ideological developments, models that would be exported around the world.

> What were the most important outcomes of the Industrial Revolution?

> What were the main features of European political development during and after the revolutions of 1848?

> Why were the ideas of Karl Marx and Charles Darwin of such great significance for world history?

> What were the principal challenges to political reform in the Russian and Ottoman empires in the nineteenth century?

The Industrial Revolution: Origins and Global Consequences, 1765–1870

It would be difficult to exaggerate the consequences of the **Industrial Revolution**. The productive capacity of human societies had not received such a boost since the emergence of agriculture eleven thousand years earlier. With the unlocking of fossil fuels as the key source of energy, total global output of manufacturing rose over 400 percent between 1750 and 1900. The same period also saw a massive shift of production from east to west: India and China accounted for over half of the world's manufacturing production in 1750, but Europe and the United States accounted for nearly three-quarters by 1900 (see Table 23.1). Global population doubled in the same period.

Innovations—new forms of energy, new technologies, new ways of organizing human labor—were the foundation of the Industrial Revolution. By burning

Industrial Revolution

Changes that began in late-eighteenth-century Britain and transformed the global economy by creating new markets for raw materials and finished goods; accompanied by technological changes that revolutionized production processes, living and working conditions, and the environment.

Table 23.1 Manufacturing Production of Selected Countries, 1750–1900, as Percentage of Global Total

	1750	1800	1830	1860	1880	1900
China	33.1	33.3	29.9	19.5	12.5	6.3
India/Pakistan	24.4	19.7	17.9	8.4	2.8	1.7
Russia	4.7	5.4	5.4	7.1	7.8	8.9
France	3.9	4.1	5.4	8.0	7.8	6.8
Japan	3.9	3.4	2.7	2.7	2.5	2.4
Germany	3.2	3.4	3.8	4.9	8.4	13.1
Italy	2.4	2.7	2.2	2.7	2.5	2.6
Great Britain	1.6	4.1	9.8	19.9	22.8	18.5
United States	—	0.7	2.7	7.1	14.7	23.7
World	100	100	100	100	100	100

Adapted with permission from David Christian, *Maps of Time: An Introduction to Big History* (Berkeley: University of California Press, 2004), p. 404, Table 13.1.

coal to drive steam engines, applying those steam engines to power machinery, and organizing mechanical processes in factories to centralize and rationalize the division of labor, industrial societies achieved unprecedented economic growth. Britain took the lead, soon followed by continental Europe and the United States. By the middle of the nineteenth century, industrialized societies were poised to translate economic power into military and political predominance on the world stage.

The Industrial Revolution was a global process. Improvements in transportation and communications—the steamship, railroad, and telegraph—created a worldwide market for raw materials. At the same time, as industrial production outstripped domestic demand, industrialists sought world markets to expand production even further.

Origins of the Industrial Revolution, 1765–1850

The British empire stimulated Britain's early modern economy. Timber and furs from Canada, sugar from the Caribbean, cotton textiles from India, and tea from China were part of a global trade network dominated by British shipping. Trade profits generated investment capital for industrial production, and Britain's trade and communications infrastructure supported British merchants seeking to expand global markets and sources of raw materials.

● **CONTEXT&CONNECTIONS** Apart from Britain's lead in global commerce and the easy availability of its coal deposits, the nation's social and cultural norms may also have spurred industrial innovation. Elsewhere in Europe the titled nobility remained aloof from commerce. In Britain less rigid lines divided aristocrats, members of the gentry like *Joseph Banks* (key term in Chapter 21), and merchant families. ●

James Watt

(1736–1819) Scottish inventor who developed the world's first powerful and cost-effective steam engine; one of the most important contributors to Britain's Industrial Revolution.

In 1765, **James Watt** (1736–1819) helped launch "the age of steam and iron" when he unveiled the first workable steam engine. Building on earlier experiments with vacuum pumps, Watt's steam engine was fired by coal, a cheap and abundant source of energy in the English midlands, where coal production increased tenfold between 1750 and 1850. Now the working power of human muscles, wind and water, and horses and oxen would be supplemented, and even replaced, by the ignition of fossil fuels—first coal, then later petroleum—an energy revolution that would eventually alter the balance between human beings and the biosphere. (See the feature "World History in Today's World: The Anthropocene: A New Geological Epoch?")

Equally important were improvements in iron production. Iron smelters worldwide had long used wood charcoal to fuel their furnaces, but doing so limited production to small batches. Meanwhile, much British coal was too impure to burn at the high temperatures necessary for iron production. Then inventors devised a way of purifying coal to make a more concentrated product called coke, and by the 1760s coal could be used to make low-cost, high-quality iron in plentiful amounts.

Meanwhile, other entrepreneurs were focusing on the social organization of production. In his *Wealth of Nations*, Adam Smith had argued that division of labor was a key to increased productivity (see Chapter 21). A shoemaker could make a fine pair of shoes, for example, but not as efficiently as a group of workers who each focused on a single step in the process. Smith's insight paved the way for the factory system of production.

The Anthropocene: A New Geological Epoch?

Geologists employ much larger time frames than historians. In fact, 31 of the 32 chapters in *Voyages in World History* are entirely encompassed by a single geological epoch: the Holocene, marking the 11,700 years since the end of the last ice age.

Now some geologists think it is time to insert a new benchmark: the *Anthropocene* ("human epoch"). They argue that the planet's physical features have been so strongly affected by the human species since 1800 that this new designation better describes earth systems in the very recent past. According to this view, the Anthropocene began about two centuries ago with the intensive use of fossil fuels during the Industrial Revolution.

According to an article published by the Royal Swedish Academy of Sciences, using atmospheric carbon dioxide measurements to track fossil fuel impacts, the preindustrial level of 270–275 parts per million (ppm) had been elevated to 310 ppm by 1950. In 2014, carbon dioxide peaked at over 400 ppm. This "Great Acceleration," as the authors call it, "is reaching criticality. Whatever unfolds, the next few decades will surely be a tipping point in the evolution of the Anthropocene."[*] That tipping point could mean a catastrophic and irreversible regimen of global warming.

The International Union of Geological Sciences is currently considering a proposal that the Holocene be formally declared to have ended in the year 1800, and that the current epoch should be named the Anthropocene. That term, they state, "has emerged as a popular scientific term used by scientists, the scientifically engaged public and the media to designate the period of Earth's history during which humans have had a decisive influence on the state, dynamics and future of the Earth system."[†]

Historians have long recognized that the Industrial Revolution was also an energy revolution. Now geologists are affirming that the global effects of those changes were even more revolutionary than previously thought.

[*]Will Steffen, Paul J. Crutzen, and John R. McNeill, "The Anthropocene: Are Humans Now Overwhelming the Great Forces of Nature?" *Ambio*, vol. 36, no. 8 (December 2007): 1. http://www.ambio.kva.se.

[†]Working Group on the Anthropocene, http://quaternary.stratigraphy.org/workinggroups/anthropocene/.

In the 1760s, entrepreneur and abolitionist **Josiah Wedgwood** began to experiment with a more complex division of labor in his ceramics factory. By breaking the production process down into specialized tasks, his factory produced greater quantities of uniform dinnerware at less expense. Wedgwood advanced the factory system of production even further when, in 1782, he was the first to install a steam engine, combining Smith's division of labor and Watt's steam power. The age of mass production had begun: the days when a master potter and a few apprentices painstakingly produced pottery by hand were ending.

Wedgwood modeled his designs on those found on imported Chinese porcelain, the finest in the world and avidly collected by the British elite. Once Wedgwood brought the price down, even the less affluent could afford a few pieces of "china" for their cupboard. Middle-class consumers (then and now) played a key role in the expansion of industrial markets.

Josiah Wedgwood

(1730–1795) English ceramics manufacturer who combined the use of steam power with factory organization to greatly increase the output and lower the cost of his products. He was a prominent supporter of the abolition of slavery.

● **CONTEXT&CONNECTIONS** Josiah Wedgwood was also an advocate of the abolition of slavery and a subscriber to *Olaudah Equiano's Interesting Narrative* (Chapter 19). Wedgewood mass-produced plates showing an African in shackles declaiming "*Am I not a man and a brother?*" ●

It was in the textile industry, however, where division of labor and steam power combined to full potential. Traditionally, India had been by far the world's largest producer of cotton textiles, and Indian calico cloth flooded the British market. Unhappy with such competition, British wool producers convinced Parliament to impose high tariffs on Indian calicoes, making them less affordable.

However, the tariffs did not apply to imports of raw cotton, which surged as British entrepreneurs developed a decentralized "putting-out" system to produce cotton cloth domestically. They would provide raw materials to a rural family, and in a traditional gender division of labor, the women spun the cotton into thread that the men then wove into cloth. Since spinning took more time than weaving, men frequently had to wait for the women to catch up.

These old methods of spinning and weaving held back production, giving industrialists an incentive to mechanize the process. British inventors first mechanized spinning and then developed steam-driven power looms. By the 1830s, the manufacture of cloth had been fully mechanized and consolidated into factories.

Of course, inexpensive labor was needed to make the factories profitable, and Britain's agricultural revolution helped create such a workforce (see Chapter 21). Driven off the land by "improving farmers," many desperate English peasants moved to the mines and emerging factory towns. Their lives were no longer governed by the seasons and the constraints of muscle power; instead, harsh whistles herded them down mine shafts or through factory gates with relentless regimentation.

Artisans were displaced as well. In its efficiency, the factory system led to a deskilling of labor and a depression of wages for skilled craftsmen, many of whom actively resisted. In the early years of the nineteenth century, some organized secret societies to assault the machinery that was depriving them of their traditional livelihoods. (Those machine smashers were called "Luddites," a term that even today may be used for those who resist technological change.) In response to such incidents, Parliament made industrial sabotage a capital crime, and sent the army to protect property and restore order. No one would be allowed to stand in the way of "improvement," even if the costs and benefits of industrial progress were unequally shared.

The energy revolution of coal and steam, together with the more efficient social organization of the factory system, transformed virtually every field of manufacture. Britain's early lead in industrialization combined with its strength in international commerce to make it the dominant global power. Following Britain's lead, coal-rich Belgium also developed a substantial network of steam-fired factories, followed by France, Germany, and northern areas of the United States.

Global Dimensions of the Industrial Revolution, 1820–1880

From its inception, the Industrial Revolution was a global process. Improvements in transportation and communications dramatically increased the pace of global interactions. Industrial economics bound people around the world ever more tightly as producers and consumers. Militarily, the nineteenth century brought constantly increasing mobility of soldiers and their ever more sophisticated weaponry. Culturally and intellectually, European tastes and ideas achieved unprecedented status among global elites. By century's end, most of humankind was participating in the global commodity markets of industrial capitalism.

● **CONTEXT&CONNECTIONS** *Globalization* is the term we use to refer to the contemporary shrinking of the world—what some have called the "annihilation of time and space"—by rapid transport and communications (see Chapter 31). In fact, world historians see a precedent in the nineteenth century for the more recent wave of globalization. In the first industrial era, railroads, steamships, and telegraphs were also making the world a much smaller place, and economists point out that then, as now, relatively free markets played a pivotal role in boosting global trade. ●

Water transport, via coastal shipping, rivers, and canals, had always been more efficient than transport by land, but as the price of iron dropped, railroads became a viable alternative. By midcentury a dense network of railroads covered western Europe, increasing both urbanization and mobility (see Map 23.1). In North America, transcontinental railroads crossed the United States and Canada. If Mikhail Bakunin had arrived in San Francisco just ten years later on his round-the-world voyage, in 1871 rather than 1861, he would likely have used the transcontinental railroad to cross from the Pacific to the Atlantic, instead of going by ship. By 1880, railroad construction had also begun in Russia, British India, and Mexico.

By 1850, steamships also had improved transportation in industrial nations, especially in the United States, where large waterways like the Mississippi River conveyed people and goods over great distances. With steamships and railroads supporting access to markets, the availability of inexpensive iron plows made possible the agricultural settlement of the Great Plains and the east-to-west integration of North America (see Chapter 25).

Map 23.1 Continental Industrialization, ca. 1850 Ease of access to iron and coal spurred industrialization in parts of Europe, such as northeastern France, Belgium, and northwestern regions of the German Confederation. Railroads supplemented rivers and canals as efficient transport by 1850 and by the end of the century tightly integrated the nations in Europe.

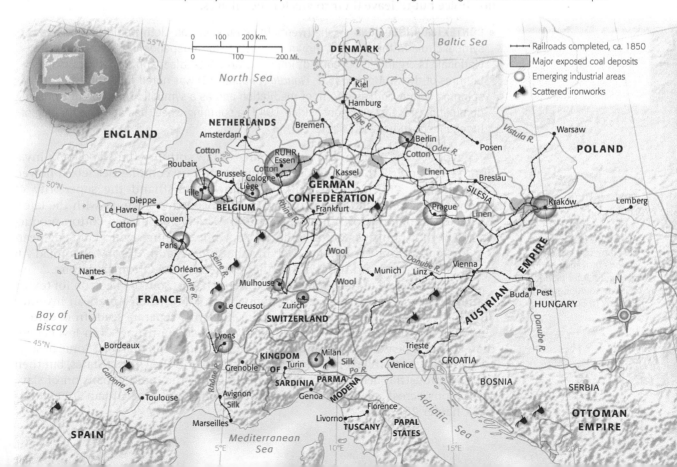

The international influence of steamships was just as revolutionary. The first steam-powered crossing of the Atlantic took place in 1838 and of the Pacific in 1853. Though sailing ships remained common, by the 1870s steamships were dramatically reducing transportation times and shipping costs and enhancing the military advantage of Western nations around the world. With the completion of the Suez Canal in 1869 (linking the Mediterranean and Red Seas) steamships cut transportation time from Europe to South Asia from months to weeks. Such advances enabled the expansion of European imperialism in Africa and Southeast Asia and the tightening of control over existing colonies, like British India (see Chapters 24 and 26).

With the newly invented telegraph, information moved even more quickly than people and goods. The first long-range telegraph message was sent in 1844. In 1869, a submarine cable was laid beneath the Atlantic Ocean. Telegraphs allowed traders to accurately compare prices instantaneously across continents. Shipping companies used the telegraph to lower their costs and increase global trade. Military officers with telegraphic information had a powerful tactical advantage.

Industrialization expanded the need for raw materials, especially cotton. After the British gained control (see Chapter 20), the export of raw Indian cotton replaced the export of finished cloth, partly because of the lower cost of factory-made textiles, and partly because of the tariffs aiding British industry. Unemployed Indian spinners, weavers, and dyers then fled to the countryside. Such were the complex and uneven outcomes of industrialization: British villagers were forced off the land and into cities, while at the very same time Indian artisans had no choice but to leave their towns for the villages.

● **CONTEXT&CONNECTIONS** In the twentieth century, cotton cloth would play a large symbolic role in the quest of Indian nationalists for independence from Britain. Nationalists organized boycotts of imported British textiles, and sometimes made bonfires of them. *Mohandas K. Gandhi* (Chapter 28) was noted for sitting and spinning cotton both as a form of meditation and as a symbolic rejection of British domination; for those reasons, since 1947, a spinning wheel has adorned the flag of independent India (see Chapter 30). ●

Egypt became another important source of raw cotton. After Napoleon's invasion (see Chapter 22), an ambitious Ottoman military commander seized power. **Muhammad Ali** (r. 1808–1848) had witnessed firsthand the superiority of European weaponry and knew that his regime needed to keep up with the latest advances. Muhammad Ali (moo-HAH-muhd AH-lee) encouraged cotton production to pay for railroads, factories, and guns, while sending science and engineering students to study in France. Defying the sultans' authority, Muhammad Ali reoriented Egypt toward the West, further weakening the Ottoman empire.

The Deep South of the United States was the largest source of cotton for textile manufacturers, with its production surging after 1793, when American inventor Eli Whitney created the cotton gin to more efficiently separate seeds from cotton. Undoubtedly, slaves picking cotton in the American South saw even less benefit than Egyptian peasants from supplying cotton to industrial markets. Some observers had thought that slavery would gradually die out in the United States, but then the new industrial demand for cheap cotton led to the rapid expansion of slave plantations across regions newly conquered from their Amerindian inhabitants (see Chapter 25).

Muhammad Ali

(r. 1808–1848) Egyptian ruler who attempted to modernize his country's economy by promoting cotton cultivation and textile manufacturing and by sending young Egyptians to study in Europe.

The web of industry drew in commodities from around the world. Palm oil from West Africa helped lubricate industrial machinery. Cattle hides from the *pampas* (PAHM-pahs) grasslands of Argentina spurred a proliferation of leather goods. Mexican plantations exported sisal for making rope. These examples all show how Africans and Latin Americans participated in the Industrial Revolution primarily as suppliers of raw materials.

As we will see in the following three chapters, the Industrial Revolution challenged ways of life in the Americas, Africa, Asia, and the Pacific. In fact, similar challenges faced the peoples of Europe. In the machine age, artisans lost customary control over their crafts, some began to view traditional political and religious institutions as anachronistic, and millions of new city dwellers traded longstanding bonds of community for urban anonymity. Pessimists saw the rapid social and cultural changes of industrial society as markers of moral decay and social disorder. But for many Europeans, Mikhail Bakunin among them, the new industrial age represented fresh possibilities for the liberation of the human spirit.

Reform and Revolution in Nineteenth-Century Europe, 1815–1880

In 1815, the great powers of Europe had banded together to quell the fires of the French Revolution and its aftermath (see Chapter 22). Their success did not last long. Monarchy and aristocratic prerogative no longer sat well with Europe's rising bourgeoisie and new industrial working class. Proponents of change embraced the ideals of the Enlightenment and the example of the French Revolution while debating the political ideals of liberalism, socialism, and anarchism.

Tensions rising from industrial change reached a crescendo in 1848, when revolutions across Europe seemed ready to sweep the old order away. Shock and disappointment befell revolutionaries like Mikhail Bakunin when conservative, authoritarian leaders re-established control. Still, Bakunin, like many others, kept alive the hopes and high ideals of 1848.

Nineteenth-Century Ideologies: Liberalism, Socialism, Romanticism, Anarchism, and Nationalism

Mikhail Bakunin embodied the new sensibilities of his time. His writings show the influence of the five different, sometimes contradictory ideologies emerging from industrializing Europe: liberalism, socialism, romanticism, anarchism, and nationalism.

Liberalism, most strongly associated with urban middle classes and most strongly developed in Britain, implied open-mindeness and the need for social and political reform, a trend resisted by many continental monarchs and their supporters, especially in the military. Liberals favored freedom of conscience, freedom of trade, the protection of property rights, and limitations on the political power of religious authorities. They emphasized constitutional government and further extension of voting rights (at least to men with sufficient property and education).

Socialism was better developed in France and Germany, where its advocates debated whether workers' rights would be better advanced through the overthrow of the state or by working within existing institutions. In the later nineteenth century, when workers gained the vote in Britain, France, and Germany, the trend was toward *evolutionary* socialism, with parliamentary parties dedicated to workers' rights and fuller social equality. Where workers had no vote, as in Russia, it was the revolutionary strand of socialism that predominated.

Romanticism was less of a political program than a cultural style, one that prioritized emotional intensity and authenticity as a backlash against Enlightenment rationalism. Romantic painters evoked forests, mountains, and moonlight, as a counterpoint to the gritty, crowded conditions of cities and factories. German composers developed highly influential musical romanticism, culminating in the long, complex, and powerful operas of Richard Wagner (1813–1883). Landscape architecture in Europe moved from parks and gardens of classical linearity to a wilder, less cultivated look.

Romanticism was strongly connected to *nationalism*, the most powerful political ideology of the industrial age. While liberals emphasized the rights of individuals, and socialists largely focused on the interests of workers, nationalists believed in the destiny of peoples. While liberalism and socialism had universal application, nationalists often restricted their vision to "their own" people, often with a romanticized appeal to their nation's destiny for greatness. For peoples (like the Germans) who did not yet have nation-states to represent them, nationalists (like Wagner) sought to develop cultural and historical pedigrees. The revolutionary potential of the national idea was most clear where nationalists sought to separate their group from multinational empires, such as the Poles from Russia, the Greeks from the Ottomans, and the Hungarians from Austria.

Mikhail Bakunin debated adherents of each of these ideologies while promoting his own brand of *anarchism*. Liberals, he thought, were on the right track in their advocacy of individual freedom. However, he sharply criticized them for favoring such rights only for the middle class, saying *"when the masses are restless, even the most enthusiastic liberals immediately reverse themselves and become the most fanatical champions of the State."** In this critique of liberalism, Bakunin agreed with the socialists, who also saw the liberal defense of property rights as a way for the middle class to protect its interests against working people.

Where Bakunin differed with the socialists was in his belief that governments are by nature repressive: the leaders of a socialist state, he predicted, would look after their own interests, not those of the masses. *"The free human society may arise at last,"* he wrote, *"no longer organized … from the top down … but rather starting from the free individual and the free association and autonomous commune, from the bottom up."**

Though Bakunin was a romantic figure himself—passionate, fearless, and unconventional—he warned that romanticized nationalism was being used by conservative leaders to gain the patriotic support of the very workers who should, he thought, oppose them. Only if workers saw through such tricks would their revolutionary actions achieve *"what they really want, the free self-organization and administration of their own affairs from the bottom upward, without any interference or violence from above."** Instead of seizing the state, Bakunin thought revolutionaries should destroy it.

---

*Mikhail Bakunin, "God and the State," "The Program of the Brotherhood, 1865," "Some Preconditions for a Social Revolution," in *Bakunin on Anarchy*, ed. Sam Dolgoff (New York: Dover, 1972), pp. 234, 134, 338.

● **CONTEXT&CONNECTIONS** Except in small utopian communities organized along communal lines, Bakunin's anarchist vision has never been effectively put into practice. But his influence remained great among twentieth-century radicals like *Emma Goldman* (Chapter 27), and the 1960s witnessed a resurgence of interest in the life and thought of Mikhail Bakunin among some student rebels. ●

Victorian Britain, 1815–1867

In 1815, Britain was dominated by those who associated change with the excesses of the French Revolution. The landed classes still dominated in Parliament and imposed stiff tariffs on imported grain, raising the price of bread. Meanwhile, unemployment was high among soldiers returning from the wars against Napoleon, while the enclosure movement and the new factory system were driving many out of villages and into urban slums.

Conditions in cities were appalling. Wages were low, and many employers preferred children, especially girls, as factory workers because they were nimble, could fit into tight spaces, and were easy to control. Industrial cities were unhealthy places, as German socialist leader Friedrich Engels observed during a visit to Manchester in 1844:

> *Right and left a multitude of covered passages lead from the main street into numerous courts, and he who turns in thither gets into a filth and disgusting grime.... Inhabitants can pass into and out of the court only by passing through foul pools of stagnant urine and excrement. At the bottom flows, or rather stagnates, the Irk, a narrow, coal-black, foul-smelling stream, full of debris and refuse, which it deposits on the shallower right bank. In dry weather, a long string of the most disgusting, blackish-green, slime pools are left standing on this bank.**

Disease spread rapidly in such neighborhoods, becoming even more deadly after increased contact with India brought cholera to England. In London, thousands died from infected water supplies.

Better-off families moved to pleasant suburbs, isolated from filth, disease, and the pollution spewed by what poet William Blake called England's *"dark, satanic mills."* The prevailing view of the upper class was that the poor were responsible for their own fate, an attitude satirized by novelist Charles Dickens in *A Christmas Carol*, when Ebenezer Scrooge says that if people are so poor that they are likely to die, *"they should do so and decrease the surplus population."*

Mining Coal Apart from employing adult male labor, Britain's mine owners also relied on adolescent boys and "pit ponies" to extract coal from ever-deeper shafts and to transport it to the surface. Mining was dangerous work, and even those who survived the frequent accidents were likely to die early from lung disease. The "pit ponies" were often stabled underground, seeing the light of day perhaps only once a year, during an annual shutdown holiday.

---

*Excerpt from *The Marx-Engels Reader*, Second Edition, edited by Robert C. Tucker. Used by permission of W. W. Norton & Company, Inc.

Before 1832, the British middle and lower classes had no right to vote and thus no direct means of influencing policy. Attempts by industrial workers to form unions were outlawed by Parliament. Factory workers might find solidarity in churches: Methodism's egalitarian ethos allowed workers to assert spiritual, if not social and political, equality. Others sought solace in gin and opium.

By the time of Queen Victoria (r. 1837–1901), however, a reform impulse animated British politics. Charitable organizations grew in size, their leaders arguing that the poor could improve their lot if only they would adopt middle-class values like thrift and sobriety. Many saw that the government also had a role to play, especially in improving health and sanitation.

In the tradition of British "practical science" (see Chapter 21), the government sponsored scientific studies to improve urban planning, water supplies, and hygiene. Early Victorian reform drew on a philosophy called *utilitarianism*, which brought the enlightenment belief in rationality to issues of social reform. For example, utilitarians successfully lobbied for reform of Britain's appalling prisons, bringing in air and light, and a new emphasis on rehabilitation. Similarly, investigations of child labor led to public outcry and legislation that regulated abhorrent labor conditions. Restrictions on the activities of Catholics were finally lifted. And by the 1850s wages had increased: even less-skilled workers were beginning to benefit from British pre-eminence in industry and trade.

The conservatism of the post-Napoleonic period was giving way to a more open political environment. Parliament responded to the frustrations of the growing but still disenfranchised urban middle class by passing the **Reform Bill of 1832**. The bill brought Parliament into closer accord with the social changes brought on by industrialization. First, seats in Parliament were redistributed to take account of the growth of cities. Second, the bill lowered the property requirements for voting so that better-off members of the middle class, such as male shopkeepers, could vote. This new Parliament better reflected urban interests, as when it slashed tariffs on imported grain, lowering bread prices for workers at the expense of profits for the rural gentry.

Reform Bill of 1832

Bill that significantly reformed the British House of Commons by lowering property qualifications for the vote. Still, only wealthier middle-class men were enfranchised.

- **CONTEXT&CONNECTIONS** One interested foreign observer of the parliamentary debate over the Reform Bill in 1832 was *Rammohun Roy* (Chapter 20), who had traveled to London in support of legislation abolishing widow burning in India. Meeting with leaders of the utilitarian movement, Roy stressed their commonality of purpose with the social reforms of the Bengal Renaissance. •

John Stuart Mill (1806–1873), who Mikhail Bakunin admiringly called an *"apostle of idealism,"*[*] was a powerful voice of British liberalism. In his book *On Liberty* (1859), Mill argued that liberty involved freedom not only from arbitrary government interference but also from *"the tendency of society to impose ... its own ideas and practices as rules of conduct on those who dissent from them."*[†] His emphasis on freedom from both political oppression and social conformity led Mill to conclusions that were radical for the time: he thought the vote should be extended not only to working men but also to women.

John Stuart Mill

(1806–1873) English philosopher and economist who argued for the paramount importance of individual liberty and supported greater rights for women.

By the 1860s, further social change again necessitated political reform. The Reform Bill of 1867 nearly doubled the number of voters, and at the end of the 1880s

---

[*]Paul McLaughlin, *Mikhail Bakunin: The Philosophical Basis of His Theory of Anarchism* (New York: Algora Publishing, 2002), p. 113.

[†]John Stuart Mill, *On Liberty* (London: Longman, Roberts and Green, 1869), p. 5.

another reform bill gave nearly all British men the vote. Through these gradual steps toward greater electoral inclusion, Britain was becoming a democracy. (Women, however, were not fully enfranchised until as late as 1928.) Meanwhile, the easing of restrictions on trade unions increased the bargaining power of the working class.

The combination of economic success and relatively peaceful political reform made many mid-Victorians supremely confident of their nation and optimistic about its future. (See the feature "Visual Evidence in Primary Sources: The Great Exhibition and the Crystal Palace.") The British constitution was evolving to suit new circumstances, just as Edmund Burke had predicted (see Chapter 22). On the European continent, in contrast, many societies were rocked by revolution and unsettled by changing national borders.

France: Revolution, Republic, and Empire

In 1815, diplomats at the Congress of Vienna restored the Bourbon dynasty to power in France (see Chapter 22). After the revolutionary and Napoleonic years, however, it was impossible to return to the past, and in 1830 a popular uprising overthrew the Bourbon monarch.

Some of those who organized street protests against the king clamored for a return to republican government. Many middle-class liberals, however, feared that a republic would favor working-class interests at the expense of private property. Their leaders advocated a constitutional monarchy and invited Louis Philippe, a nobleman more interested in business than in royal protocol, to take the throne. King Louis Philippe, the "bourgeois king," certainly maintained a more open regime than that of the Bourbons, though voting was restricted to a small minority of property-owning men. Republicans despised him.

In early 1848, police in Paris fired on a crowd of demonstrators, and 1,500 republican barricades went up around the city. Louis Philippe abdicated and fled the country. "*No sooner had I learned that they were fighting in Paris,*" Bakunin wrote in his confession to the tsar, "*than ... I set out again for France.*"* Suddenly, for the first time in fifty years, France was a republic in which the people themselves were sovereign. The change was so dramatic that men met in a newspaper office to plan the country's future, divided on how to proceed.

An influential socialist, Louis Blanc (loo-EE blawnk), argued that private ownership of industry was inefficient and unfair, leaving many unemployed and giving workers no say in how the factories were run. He called for cooperative workshops to be set up by the government and run by the workers. Employment would be guaranteed for all. Bakunin strongly disagreed with Blanc's government-centered approach, which "*advised the people to rely in all things upon the State.*"† Instead, he thought, workers should seize the factories and run them cooperatively without interference from either bourgeois owners or state functionaries.

Blanc's socialist ideas were also opposed by middle-class defenders of property rights, and under their influence the republic implemented only a weakened version of his plan. The state funded some public works projects, such as planting trees, and guaranteed those who could not find work enough money to live on. Almost all this money was spent in Paris, a fact resented by the rural majority.

---

*The Confession of Mikhail Bakunin, trans. Robert C. Howes (Ithaca: Cornell University Press, 1977), p. 56.

†Mikhail Bakunin, "Socialism," in Bakunin on Anarchy, ed. Sam Dolgoff (New York: Knopf, 1972), p. 121.

The Great Exhibition and the Crystal Palace

London's Hyde Park was the site of mid-Victorian Britain's monument to industrial, technological, and commercial progress: the Great Exhibition of the Works of Industry of All Nations. Queen Victoria herself opened the Exhibition to great public acclaim in 1851. Her husband, Prince Albert, one of the principal planners, was at her side. The Great Exhibition received over 6 million visitors, some traveling from continental Europe and the United States, and raised enough money through admission fees to endow the great Victoria and Albert Museum and the Natural History Museum, both of which still stand near Hyde Park today. The Crystal Palace, an imposing glass and iron structure built to enclose the Exhibition and protect attendees from the weather, was itself a wonder of industrial technology.

Over half the exhibit space was devoted to the tools and products of British manufacturers, and

The Crystal Palace, completed in time for the opening of the Great Exhibition in 1851, was 1,851 feet (564 m) long, with an interior height of 128 feet (39 m). It used more than a million square feet of glass, more than any other building up to that time.

Recent innovations in glass manufacturing provided the architects with the large panes necessary to give the building the "crystal" effect of clear walls and ceilings. Queen Victoria bestowed a knighthood on creator Joseph Paxton, who designed the building in just ten days, for his achievement.

Another innovation was the provision of public toilets, first just for men and later for women as well. Visitors paid a penny to use the facilities, hence the term "to spend a penny" in British English for making a lavatory trip.

SSPL/The Image Works

The huge central transept was the site of concerts, circuses, and tightrope walking; music was provided by the world's largest organ.

When the Great Exhibition ended, the Crystal Palace was taken apart and re-erected in a South London suburb. The Crystal Palace Football Club is a reminder of the role the surrounding grounds then played in sporting life, even after the building was destroyed by fire in 1936.

great attention was paid to colonial contributions to the country's wealth and power. Collecting Indian artifacts and containing them within the exhibition hall, for example, was an implicit assertion of the legitimacy of Britain's imperial claim over South Asia and another expression of the ongoing relationship between science and empire (see Chapter 21).

The Great Exhibition had an enduring global influence. Later, other nations would also erect monumental buildings and put their achievements on display, inviting all nations to participate in "world's fairs" such as those held in Paris (1878), Chicago (1893), and, more recently, Shanghai, at China's World Expo (2010).

Visitors to the Great Exhibition passed through a series of courts focused on the history of art and architecture (from ancient Egypt through the Renaissance) and natural wonders of the world. The main attractions, however, were exhibits of the latest industrial technology: *"every conceivable invention,"* as Queen Victoria noted in her diary.

Visitors gasped in amazement at the Koh-I-Noor diamond, the largest cut diamond in the world at that time; took their first ever look at photographs at the display of the recently invented daguerreotype; witnessed the powerful and fast-loading revolving pistol of Samuel Colt; and wondered at the latest ingenuities of industrial machinery and design. ***How would the wonders of technology displayed in London in 1851 compare with those that might be assembled for a similar "Great Exhibition" today?***

Some one hundred thousand objects were spread over 10 miles (16 km) of viewing space.

Prince Albert emphasized that the Great Exhibition demonstrated the orderly progress of British society. *"We have no fear here either of an uprising or an assassination,"* he bragged to his cousin, King William of Prussia, who had survived a revolutionary uprising just three years earlier, in 1848.

V&A Images, London/Art Resource, NY

The largest exhibit was a huge hydraulic press used for bridge building, with a series of metal tubes, each weighing well over 1,000 tons.

An even more popular display was a simple statue of a female Greek slave, demurely hidden in a small red tent and wearing only a simple chain. Exoticism and sexual allure, it seems, were just as interesting to the Victorians as mechanical might.

Even in Paris, the tide was turning away from republicanism in the summer of 1848. One of Bakunin's fellow Russian exiles heard a commotion outside his window, and saw a group of *"clumsy, rascally fellows, half peasants, half shopkeepers, somewhat drunk"* as they *"moved rapidly but in disorder, with shouts of 'Vive Louis-Napoleon!'"* In response, the Russian socialist shouted *"'Vive la République!'"* But *"those who were near the windows shook their fists at me,"* he remembered, *"and an officer muttered some abuse, threatening me with his sword."**

With the rise of **Louis Napoleon** (1808–1873), revolutionary dreams were crumbling. Louis Napoleon represented, in his own words, *"order, authority, religion, popular welfare at home, national dignity abroad."* He was popular with liberals fearful of socialism, peasants resentful of Parisian domination, and everyone who recalled with pleasure the glorious days of his uncle, Napoleon Bonaparte. After being elected president, Louis Napoleon organized and won a plebiscite making him Napoleon III, emperor of France.

Louis Napoleon

(1808–1873) Conservative nephew of Napoleon Bonaparte who was elected president of the Second Republic before winning a plebiscite making him Emperor Napoleon III in 1852. Was forced to abdicate in 1870 after losing the Franco-Prussian War.

● **CONTEXT&CONNECTIONS** As in the 1790s, France went swiftly from constitutional monarchy to republic to empire (see Chapter 22). Karl Marx was among those who noted the parallels between the aftermaths of the French revolutions of 1789 and 1848. *"All great world-historic facts and personages appear twice,"* Marx commented bitterly, on what he saw as a second-rate version of the original Napoleon, *"the first time as tragedy, the second time as farce."*[†] ●

Napoleon III presided over the Second empire (1852–1870), a period of stability, prosperity, government investment in infrastructure and support for industry, and expanding French power. As president, Louis Napoleon eliminated Blanc's socialist program, seeking instead to stimulate the economy by selling government bonds to finance railway construction and by backing semipublic financial institutions to provide capital for commerce and industry. Although Napoleon III was authoritarian, he respected the rule of law and basic civil liberties. Like Napoleon Bonaparte, he gained support by appealing to French nationalism and by expanding the overseas French empire (see Chapter 26).

The Habsburg Monarchy, 1848–1870

News of the 1848 uprising in Paris spread like wildfire across Europe. The dominant power in central Europe was the Austrian empire, still ruled by the Habsburg family. Protestors, university students prominent among them, took to the streets of Vienna in early 1848 demanding new rights. The befuddled emperor reportedly asked, *"Are they allowed to do that?"* Prince Metternich, the conservative architect of the Congress of Vienna, resigned his position as chancellor and fled to England.

While nationalism held nations like France together, it had the potential to tear multiethnic empires like Austria apart, when Italian, Hungarian, Czech, Croatian, and other Habsburg subjects agitated for national rights. In Budapest, a Hungarian assembly created a new constitution ratifying religious freedom, equality before the law, and an end to the privileges of the old feudal nobility.

---

*Alexander Herzen, *My Pasty and Thoughts*, trans. Constance Garnett (Berkeley: University of California Press, 1982), pp. 333–334.

[†]Karl Marx, *The Eighteenth Brumaire of Louis Napoleon*, Part VII, 1852, https://www.marxists.org/archive/marx/works/1852/18th-brumaire/ch01.htm.

Revolution also swept Milan, the chief city of Austria's northern Italian possessions, and Prague, where Bakunin was captured by Austrian forces.

As in France, peasants were shocked by the radicalism in the cities, and their support helped Habsburg authorities under the young Emperor Franz Joseph II (r. 1848–1916) re-establish control within their German-speaking territories. But by 1859 Italian rebels won independence from Austria, and in 1866 Prussian forces defeated the Habsburg army. The discontent of subject nationalities continued.

With crises looming, the emperor proclaimed a Dual Monarchy in 1867 under which he would be simultaneously emperor of Austria and king of Hungary, allowing each state its own separate institutions. Through this compromise Austria retained its Great Power status and settled the long struggle between German rulers and Hungarian subjects, though many other ethnic and national grievances in the empire remained unresolved.

● **CONTEXT&CONNECTIONS** Religious differences compounded ethnic divisions in Central Europe (see Chapter 17). The Austrians themselves were Catholic, as were the emperor's Croatian and Italian subjects; Hungary was divided between Catholics and Protestants; Serbs were Orthodox Christians, while Bosnians were Muslims, a legacy of Ottoman influence in the Balkans. Tensions between them helped spark world war in the next century (see Chapter 27). ●

The Unification of Italy, 1848–1870

In 1848, Italian liberals dreamt of a new political order based on ties of language, culture, and history. But they would have to overcome significant regional differences and the long-standing division of the Italian peninsula into numerous states. The north, much of it under Austrian rule, was subject to the same forces of industrialization and urbanization as western Europe, while the south was still largely peasant and traditional in its Catholicism. Differences in dialect made it difficult for Italians to understand one another. Such divisions had enabled conservatives to stifle liberal reforms and attempts at unification.

Like other Italian idealists of the time, **Giuseppe Garibaldi** (jew-SEP-pay gar-uh-BAWL-dee) (1807–1882) believed in the need for a *risorgimento*, a political and cultural renewal of Italy that would restore its historic greatness. After being condemned to death for leading an uprising in Genoa, Garibaldi, with romantic swagger, fled to South America and then took part in a Brazilian rebellion.

The revolution of 1848 called Garibaldi back to Italy. Rebels on the streets of Turin demanded liberal reforms; protestors in Milan forced Austrian authorities onto the defensive; and in Rome rebels declared a new Roman republic and chased the pope, ruler of vast central Italian domains, out of the city. Garibaldi headed to Rome to resist French forces dispatched by Louis Napoleon to restore papal rule. Garibaldi's defeat ended the short-lived Roman republic, another victory for the "forces of order" that had sent Bakunin to his lonely prison cell.

Another chance for Italian unification came in 1860 after a rebellion broke out in southern Italy. With the kingdom of Naples tottering, Garibaldi landed on the island of Sicily, overthrew its corrupt ruler, and crossed to the mainland. His army marched north, bringing Naples and Sicily into a new, united Italy in 1861. Garibaldi's exploits stirred Mikhail Bakunin, and when the two finally met in 1864, their warm embrace was cheered by an enthusiastic crowd. Inspired by the spontaneous mass support for Garibaldi's campaign, Bakunin felt the hopefulness of 1848 returning.

Yet once Garibaldi and the revolutionaries had paved the way, more conservative leaders commandeered the process and founded Italy as a constitutional monarchy

Giuseppe Garibaldi (1807–1882) Italian nationalist revolutionary who unified Italy in 1860 by conquering Sicily and Naples. Though he advocated an Italian Republic, the new country became a constitutional monarchy instead.

Defense of the Roman Republic In 1848, Giuseppe Garibaldi and his followers declared a Roman Republic. Here we see their successful defense of the republic against invaders from the kingdom of Naples in 1849. Later, however, French forces laid siege to Rome and restored the pope to power. Finally, in 1871 Rome became the capital of a unified Italy.

Battle of Palestrina, May 9, 1849. Second Roman Republic, Italy, 19th century/De Agostini Picture Library/A. de Gregorio/Bridgeman Images

with a limited electorate and a relatively weak legislature. Still, while this outcome dashed the hopes of more radical republicans, it did put unified Italy on the list of European great powers, especially after 1870, when the French garrison protecting the pope withdrew, bringing the city of Rome into the new Italy as its capital.

Sharp divisions remained, however. For many, the concept of being "Italian" was something entirely new. Especially in the south, church and family retained their traditional importance, and local customs predominated over the much newer national ideals. Many in the north felt more comfortable with European culture than with the Mediterranean lifestyle of their new countrymen. In contrast to France, where revolution and empire had helped give the French people a shared sense of national solidarity, Italians had a longer road ahead in forging their common identity.

Germany: Nationalism and Unification, 1848–1871

From the standpoint of world history, the most important European political development of the nineteenth century was the creation, in 1871, of a unified Germany. Almost immediately, Germany became a significant force in world affairs.

After 1815, the Congress of Vienna (see Chapter 22) had recognized a tapestry of forty-two separate polities, only loosely affiliated within a German Confederation. Prussia, with its capital in Berlin, was the most powerful member, though its ambitions to dominate the Confederation were strongly resented by Habsburg Austria. As a result of this rivalry, when Prussia sponsored the expansion of a German customs union from the 1820s onward to increase inter-German trade, it excluded Austria.

A potent legacy of the Napoleonic era was the very *idea* of German nationhood. France had demonstrated the power of national unity, and now more

Germans aspired to go beyond confederation to nationhood of their own. But would the process of nation building be controlled by liberals, strongest in the west, or by monarchical conservatives, represented by Prussia? That was the key question when the revolutionary flame of 1848 swept across the German states.

Having left Paris, Bakunin found himself in Dresden, the capital of the kingdom of Saxony, when an insurrection broke out. He helped lead the democratic forces until Prussian soldiers came to the rescue of the Saxon army. As Bakunin fled to Prague, it was clear that the Prussian government would oppose unification based on a popular uprising.

Indeed, Friedrich Wilhelm IV of Prussia (r. 1840–1857) took a hard line, using military force to crush demonstrators who stormed an arsenal and seized a royal palace in Berlin. Although the king did grant Prussia a constitution with a representative assembly elected through universal manhood suffrage, he and his ministers remained free to ignore it and rule as they liked. Friedrich Wilhelm saw the Prussian constitution as an expression of royal beneficence, not as a matter of rights.

Elsewhere, however, there was significant support for a unified Germany under a liberal constitution. A committee of prominent liberals organized an election, and in 1848 delegates at the **Frankfurt Assembly** drafted a constitution that embodied progressive principles, such as freedom of assembly and freedom of the press. Seeking a symbol of unity, they offered the crown to the Prussian king as constitutional monarch of a democratic German state. But Friedrich Wilhelm refused to accept what he called *"a crown from the gutter,"* rejecting the very principle of popular sovereignty upon which the proposed constitution was based.

Friedrich Wilhelm's refusal killed any hope of unifying Germany under a liberal constitution. But the forces of industrialization, the building of railroads, and rapid urbanization were creating conditions in which a unified Germany seemed more desirable than ever. In the 1860s, under the initiative of Prussian chancellor **Otto von Bismarck** (1815–1898), Prussia supervised the creation of a new German nation. "Germany" became a reality in 1871 when a coalition of armies led by Prussia defeated those of Napoleon III, forcing the emperor to abdicate. The victors then crowned Prussian king Kaiser Wilhelm II emperor of Germany in the grand Versailles Palace, a tremendous blow to French national pride, and a signal that militarism would be the foundation stone of the new German state.

Bismarck had told a committee of the German Confederation in 1862: *"Not through speeches and majority decisions are the great questions of the day decided—that was the mistake of 1848—but by iron and blood."** Bismarck's victories over Denmark, Austria, and most especially France sparked German national pride, inspiring many with a romantic vision of a grand German state fulfilling the people's destiny as a great world power. From Bakunin's perspective, Bismarck was *"an out-and-out aristocrat ... with a militarist and bigoted bugbear of an emperor as chief."*[†]

Inspired by Prussian victories, many Germans now envisioned a grand German state fulfilling the people's destiny as a great world power. German manufacturing boomed, and the gross national product doubled between 1870 and 1890. But the German achievement had unsettling implications for the other great powers, which now faced an invigorated competitor for markets and empire.

Frankfurt Assembly

Assembly held in 1848 to create a constitution for a united German Confederation; elected Friedrich Wilhelm IV as constitutional monarch, but Wilhelm refused the offer on the principle that people did not have the right to choose their own king.

Otto von Bismarck

(1815–1898) Unified Germany in 1871 and became its first chancellor. Previously, as chancellor of Prussia, he led his state to victories against Austria and France.

---

*Quoted in Otto Pflanze, *Bismarck and the Development of Germany*, vol. 1 (Princeton: Princeton University Press, 1990), p. 184.

[†]Mikhail Bakunin, "Critique of Economic Determinism and Historical Materialism," in *Bakunin on Anarchy*, ed. Sam Dolgoff (New York: Knopf, 1972), p. 315.

New P

rights to working people, they thought, socialism could develop through democratic rather than revolutionary means.

Bakunin, while he agreed with Marx that revolution would be necessary, saw dangerous seeds of dictatorship in his German competitor's philosophy. A government founded on Marxist principles, Bakunin warned, *"will not content itself with … governing the masses politically … it will also administer the masses economically, concentrating in the State the production and division of wealth.… It will be the reign of scientific intelligence, the most aristocratic, despotic, arrogant, and elitist of regimes."**

Though by the time of Marx's death in 1883 there had been no socialist revolutions, his ideas were spreading and his followers increasing. And, as we will see when examining communist regimes of the twentieth century (Chapters 27–30), Bakunin's prophecy proved perfectly accurate.

Karl Marx

(1818–188:
author and
who founded
branch of sc
wrote *The M*
the Commu
(1848) and
(1867).

Charles Darwin

(1809–1882) English natural historian, geologist, and proponent of the theory of evolution.

Charles Darwin, Evolution, and Social Darwinism

Prior to publishing his groundbreaking book *On the Origin of Species by Means of Natural Selection* in 1859, the British scientist **Charles Darwin** (1809–1882) had spent many years gathering evidence. Geologists had already determined that the earth was millions of years old and that its surface features had changed greatly over time. Darwin believed that long-term biologic change, or evolution, also characterized natural history. His search was for the mechanism of the evolutionary process.

In the Galápagos Islands off the coast of South America, Darwin observed that finches and turtles differed from those on the mainland and even in other areas of the islands. He theorized that the variations resulted from the adaptation of species to different environments. His principal contribution was the idea that natural selection drove this process.

Darwin explained that the origins of all life on earth resulted from the imperative of survival. Organisms with traits that gave them a better chance of survival passed those traits along to their offspring. Over time, random genetic mutations lead to the accumulation of diverse traits and, when beneficial genetic variations are passed through generations, to the increased success of some species and the appearance of new ones. Failure to adapt to changing conditions, meanwhile, could lead to extinction. Like Newton's theory of gravitation, Darwin's evolutionary theory was elegant, universally applicable, and a substantial advance in understanding.

In *The Descent of Man* (1871), Darwin made it clear that human beings had also undergone natural selection in their evolution as a species, contradicting Biblical accounts of human creation. In Europe, but even more strongly in the United States and the Islamic world, many religious leaders denounced his work.

Religious ideas themselves were not standing still. In western Europe and North America, evangelical Protestantism, with an emphasis on a more personal and emotionally intense relationship with the divine, was inspiring many to seek out converts in the slums or to become missionaries abroad. In the Islamic world, an important nineteenth-century development was the emergence of the Wahhabis, who emphasized a return to the purity of early Islam. Across religions, critics of industrial modernity complained of a shift from spiritual life to a new obsession with the production and consumption of material goods. In offering a purely materialist explanation for the origin of our species, Darwin offended those who believed that

*Mikhail Bakunin, "Critique of Economic Determinism and Historical Materialism," in *Bakunin on Anarchy*, Sam Dolgoff ed. (New York: Knopf, 1972), p. 319.

faith, not science, was the key to knowledge. (See the feature "Movement of Ideas Through Primary Sources: Religious Leaders Comment on Science and Progress.")

Yet Darwin's insights were quickly accepted by virtually all natural scientists, and his ideas resonated with broader intellectual trends. The intense competitiveness of industrial capitalism, after all, was bringing on more complex and productive economic enterprises, leading to a belief in progress bolstered by popular views of evolution as "improvement." Even Karl Marx saw Darwin's theory of evolution as reinforcing his own view that human history proceeds through stages (feudalism, capitalism, socialism) on a progressive path forward.

Some, however, applied Darwin's concept of adaptation and survival in the natural world directly to human society, with dangerous implications. *Social Darwinism* was the idea that differences in wealth and power could be explained by the superiority of some and the inferiority of others. Analogies from nature were thus used to justify social inequality. Social Darwinism was also used to explain Europe's increasing global dominance: European imperialism was an inevitable natural process—the "survival of the fittest"—in which "inferior peoples" would be displaced. Darwin himself did not draw such social and political corollaries from his work, but Social Darwinism became deeply entrenched in European thought as racists looked increasingly to science to justify their prejudices.

Challenges to Reform in the Russian and Ottoman Empires, 1825–1881

The Russian and Ottoman empires seemed to be on different trajectories in the nineteenth century. Russia, one of the great powers of Europe, had the world's largest army and a vast Eurasian empire. The Ottomans, in contrast, were contracting, having lost territories across their domain. Sensing Ottoman weakness, the Russians went on the offensive in the **Crimean War**, anxious to gain warm water Black Sea ports and access to the Mediterranean. Had Britain and France not intervened on the Ottomans' side (fearing a too powerful Russian neighbor), the tsars may well have succeeded.

Crimean War
(1853–1856) War fought in the Crimean peninsula between the Russian and Ottoman empires. France and Britain sent troops to aid the Ottomans and prevent Russian expansion.

Yet the Crimean War highlighted a crucial similarity between the Russian and Ottoman empires. Both had already been put on notice by Napoleon Bonaparte's invasions (see Chapter 22) that burgeoning power lay to their west. Half a century later, that western advantage had grown much greater not only in armaments, but also in finance, logistics, medical science, engineering, and myriad other fields. When the war finished in a deadlock, elites in both Istanbul and St. Petersburg needed to take stock of how to remain competitive in this new environment. Should they emulate the reforms of western Europe through more liberal policies, or follow the advice of conservatives to reject foreign influences and remain true to their own traditions?

Emancipation and Reaction in Russia

Mikhail Bakunin was from a generation of educated Russians inspired by the revolutionary changes to the west and anxious to transform their homeland. "*Russia figures as a synonym for brutal repression,*" he said; "*thanks to the execrable [policies] of our sovereigns, the name 'Russian' ... stands for 'slave and executioner.'*"*

---

*Mikhail Bakunin, "On the 17th Anniversary of the Polish Insurrection," in *Bakunin on Anarchy*, ed. Sam Dolgoff (New York: Knopf, 1972), p. 59.

Religious Leaders Comment on Science and Progress

While the nineteenth century saw the rise of secular ideologies such as liberalism, socialism, and nationalism, religion continued to shape the views of most people around the world. The excerpts below illustrate the implications of modern industrial ideologies for religious faith as interpreted by a Sunni Muslim scholar and a Roman Catholic pope.

The first selection comes from Sayyid Jamāl ad-dīn al-Afghani (1838–1897). He was educated in Islamic schools in Afghanistan and Iran and then spent twenty years in British-ruled India, also traveling to western Europe and the Ottoman empire. Al-Afghani saw pan-Islamic unity as necessary for effective resistance to European dominance and worked to heal divisions between the Sunni and Shi'ite Muslim communities. His efforts did not go unchallenged. Sufi mystics and Wahhabi purists, for example, had little use for his attempt to reconcile Islam with Western science.

The second passage is by Pope Pius IX (r. 1846–1878), who became a staunch conservative after republican revolutionaries forced him to temporarily flee Rome in 1848. Pius IX greatly increased papal authority when he proclaimed the doctrine of papal infallibility, which stated that the pope's statements on central issues of faith were to be regarded as coming directly from God and could not be challenged. His criticism of the loss of spiritual focus in the face of materialism has been a consistent theme of the Roman Catholic Church ever since.

❭ How do Pius IX and al-Afghani differ in their views of the relationship between religion and the ideas and ideals of industrial modernity?

❭ Are there any connections between these nineteenth-century debates and current controversies concerning science and faith in the Christian and Islamic worlds?

Sources: Excerpt cited and translated in Nikki Keddie, *Sayyid Jamāl ad-dīn "al-Afghani": A Political Biography* (Berkeley: University of California Press, 1972), pp. 161, 186. Reprinted by permission; excerpt, Pope Pius IX, *Quanta Cura (Condemning Current Errors)*, from www.ewtn.com.

Sayyid Jamāl ad-dīn al-Afghani

1. "Lecture on Teaching and Learning" (1882)

If someone looks deeply into the question, he will see that science rules the world. There was, is, and will be no other ruler in the world but science.... In reality, sovereignty has never left the abode of science. However, this true ruler, which is science, is continually changing capitals. Sometimes it has moved from East to West, and other times from West to East.... The acquisitions of men for themselves and their governments are proportional to their science. Thus, every government for its own benefit must strive to lay the foundation of the sciences and to disseminate knowledge....

The strangest thing of all is that our *ulama* [scholarly community] these days have divided science into two parts. One they call Muslim science, and one European science. Because of this they forbid others to teach some of the useful sciences. They have not understood that science is that noble thing that has no connection with any nation, and is not distinguished by anything but itself. Rather, everything that is known is known by science, and every nation that becomes renowned becomes renowned through science....

How very strange it is that the Muslims study those sciences that are ascribed to Aristotle with the greatest delight, as if Aristotle were one of the pillars of the Muslims. However, if the discussion relates to Galileo, Newton and Kepler, they consider them infidels. The father and mother of science is proof, and proof is neither Aristotle nor Galileo. The truth is where there is proof, and those who forbid science and knowledge in the belief that they are safeguarding the Islamic religion are really enemies of that religion. The Islamic religion is the closest of religions to science and knowledge, and there is no incompatibility between science and knowledge and the foundation of the Islamic faith....

2. "Answer of Jamāl ad-dīn to Renan" (1883)

All religions are intolerant, each one in its way. The Christian religion, I mean the society that follows its inspirations and its teachings … seems to advance rapidly on the road of progress and science, whereas Muslim society has not yet freed itself from the tutelage of religion…. I cannot keep from hoping that Muslim society will succeed someday in breaking its bonds and marching resolutely in the path of civilization after the manner of Western society…. No I cannot admit that this hope be denied to Islam.

Pope Pius IX

Quanta Cura (Condemning Current Errors), 1864

For well you know, my brothers, that at this time there are many men who applying to civil society the impious and absurd principle of "naturalism," dare to teach that "the best constitution of public society … requires that human society be conducted and governed without regard being had to religion any more than if it did not exist; or, at least, without any distinction between true religion and false one." From which false idea … they foster the erroneous opinion … that "liberty of conscience and worship is each man's personal right, which ought to be legally proclaimed and asserted in every rightly constituted society; and that a right resides in the citizens to an absolute liberty, which should be restrained by no authority whether ecclesiastical or civil, whereby they may be able openly and publicly to manifest and declare any of their ideas whatever, either by word of mouth, by the press, or in any other way." Whereas we know, from the very teaching of our Lord Jesus Christ, how carefully Christian faith and wisdom should avoid this most injurious babbling.

And, since where religion has been removed from civil society, and the doctrine and authority of divine revelation repudiated, the genuine notion itself of justice and human right is darkened and lost, and the place of true justice and legitimate right is supplied by material force … [then] human society, when set loose from the bonds of religion and true justice, can have, in truth, no other end than the purpose of obtaining and amassing wealth, and … follows no other law … except … ministering to its own pleasure and interests.

Amidst, therefore, such great perversity of depraved opinions … and (solicitous also) for the welfare of human society itself, [we] have thought it right again to raise up our Apostolic voice.

Yet Bakunin still held high hopes for Russia. The history of peasant uprisings in Russia, such as Pugachev's rebellion (see Chapter 20), assured him that Russians would not *"patiently resign themselves to their misery"* forever. He saw the Russian *mir*, or village, with its collective decision making and community ownership of land, as a foundation on which an anarchist future could be built. In the short term, however, revolutionary prospects in Russia were bleak, as the tsar's secret police sent Mikhail Bakunin and hundreds of other dissenters into exile

● **CONTEXT&CONNECTIONS** While Karl Marx disparaged peasants, comparing them to a *"sack of potatoes,"* Mikhail Bakunin idolized them. He believed that with their traditions of community decision making, peasants could form the foundation of a liberated Russia. In the end, it was the communist dictator Joseph Stalin who settled the issue, brutally resettling millions of rural Russians and Ukrainians on state-run farms during the *collectivization* of the 1930s (Chapter 28). ●

Russia was still overwhelmingly rural. It had a powerful aristocracy but a weak middle class and almost no modern industry. Russian society was divided between a landowning nobility and serfs so poor, illiterate, and lacking in rights that aristocrats could win or lose these "souls" (as they called their serfs) in a game of cards. The nobility profited from this system, as did the government, which depended on serf conscripts for the huge army. Yet the Crimean War had shown that modern wars could not be won without an industrial foundation. Russia's social structure, lacking both a self-confidant property-owning class to build factories and a proletariat to work in them, was inadequate to the task.

Tsar Alexander II (r. 1855–1881), who came to the throne near the end of the Crimean War, understood the need for change. In 1861 he issued his **Emancipation Edict** freeing the serfs. However, to avoid antagonizing the nobility, the edict required that serfs pay for their own emancipation, even though the amount of land they were allocated was insufficient.

At the same time, the tsar's government began taking action in support of industrialization. During the 1870s government support led to a boom in railroad construction, stimulating the coal and iron industries. High tariffs on foreign goods promoted the development of Russian factories, although growth continued to lag well behind western Europe's. While by 1880 British, French, and German workers were enjoying some benefits of increased productivity, such as better clothing and housing, Russian workers still suffered the dangerous and squalid conditions that had marked the first phase of industrialization.

Another challenge for Alexander's government was the question of nationalities. In Germany, nationalism helped overcome regional and class differences to unify the young nation. The use of nationalism by conservative elites was impossible in the Russian empire, however, where over half the people were not Russian. As in multiethnic Austria, here nationalism was a divisive force. The tsarist state harshly suppressed ethnic minorities, as during an 1863 rebellion in Poland.

By that time, Bakunin's generation was losing influence to a younger group of Russian revolutionaries with little patience for philosophical debate. The secret police were everywhere, forcing dissidents underground. Russian anarchists, agreeing with Bakunin that freedom could be achieved only through the abolition of the state, its bureaucracy, and its army, despaired of doing so through a popular uprising. Some anarchists accepted the need for violence and even terrorism to achieve their ends: a bomb killed Tsar Alexander II in 1881, causing a further

Emancipation Edict

1861 edict by Tsar Alexander II that freed the Russian serfs. However, serfs had to pay their former owners for their freedom, and the land they were allocated was often insufficient to produce the money needed to meet that cost for freedom.

Emancipated Serfs As with freed slaves in the U.S. South during the late nineteenth century, living conditions for most Russian serfs were not immediately transformed by emancipation in 1861. Most were illiterate and, like the wheat threshers shown here, had to rely on their own labor power. (Adoc-photos/Art Resource, NY)

crackdown on dissidence and establishing a link between anarchism, violence, and assassination foreign to Bakunin's thinking.

With the stifling of liberal, socialist, and even nationalist thought, Russian intellectuals and artists instead focused on the question of whether and to what degree Russia should learn from and adopt western European cultural and constitutional models. "Westernizers" answered in the affirmative, while "Slavophiles" declared that Russia should stand by her Slavic traditions, Orthodox Christianity, and tsarist state. The debate was irresolvable, but it did produce some magnificent music. Peter Ilich Tchaikovsky followed Western classical models to become Russia's best-known composer, while "Slavophiles" like Nicolai Rimsky-Korsakov emphasized Slavic and Central Eurasian themes.

Meanwhile, the assassination of Alexander II had shut the window on further reforms. Reform instigated from above can be revoked from above, and Alexander's son and successor did just that. A more conservative attitude toward nationalities is one example. While Alexander II had given considerable freedom to his Finnish subjects, his son declared that everyone in the empire should learn Russian. State support for Orthodox Christianity increased, and repression of Jews intensified. While the building of railroads and encouragement of industry continued, modest steps toward representative government, even at the local level, were shelved. The Slavophile slogan *"Orthodoxy, Autocracy, and Nationality"* guided Russian policy in the later nineteenth century.

Reform and Reaction in the Ottoman Empire

Though still large and powerful, after 1800 the Ottoman empire was under increasing pressure. The Ottomans lost control of Egypt to the independent regime of Muhammad Ali, Greece to an independence movement in 1829, and Algeria to French invaders in 1830, and they were also slipping in the Balkans, the mountainous region of southeastern Europe they had controlled since the days of Süleyman the Magnificent (see Chapter 17). Even sooner and more insistently than their Russian counterparts, Ottoman leaders recognized the need for reform.

Having modernized the military by eliminating the outmoded Janissary Corps (see Chapter 17) Ottoman rulers next laid the foundations for extensive overhaul of the empire's governmental, legal, and educational systems. The resulting **Tanzimat Reforms** (1839–1876) were an ambitious attempt at top-down modernization. In the Tanzimat (TAHNZ-ee-MAT) period, the Ottoman government established new European-style primary and secondary schools to supplement the traditional Islamic schools, introduced colleges of military science and medicine, and sponsored student study in France and Germany. The urban elite began to travel more widely and to read French, Armenian, and Turkish newspapers, and European-style buildings were erected in Istanbul to modernize the capital. The legal system was revamped so that the same civil code applied to everyone, Muslim and non-Muslim alike, with full equality before the law. Finally, to facilitate trade with the West, the Tanzimat reformers introduced a new commercial code modeled on western European rather than Islamic principles.

The Tanzimat Reforms led to better administrative efficiency and greater investment and economic growth. They also opened up a longstanding divide between more secular, European-oriented elites, especially in the Western-facing capital city of Istanbul, and more conservative, religiously oriented Turks in the rural interior. Like Slavophiles who stressed Orthodox Christianity as a foundation of Russian society, Muslim religious leaders worried that by borrowing so many ideas from the West the government was undercutting the traditional religious and cultural foundations of their society. They also resented their loss of control over the educational and legal systems that had been a principal source of their power and prestige. Meanwhile, even, some educated Turks (as well as minority Armenians and Greeks) were dissatisfied with the centralized and bureaucratic nature of the Tanzimat program and argued for a constitutional monarchy guided by the principles of liberalism.

Issues of nationality and ethnic identity were another significant challenge for Ottoman reformers. Traditionally, legal pluralism characterized a system where Christian Orthodox, Armenian Apostolic, or Jewish law would prevail in separate courts for the empire's diverse minority communities (see Chapter 17). But that system proved incompatible with modern nationalism, which stressed a tight identification of religion, ethnicity, and political loyalty. While Tanzimat

Tanzimat Reforms

(1839–1876) Restructuring of the Ottoman empire; control over civil law was taken away from religious authorities, while the military and government bureaucracies were reorganized to gain efficiency.

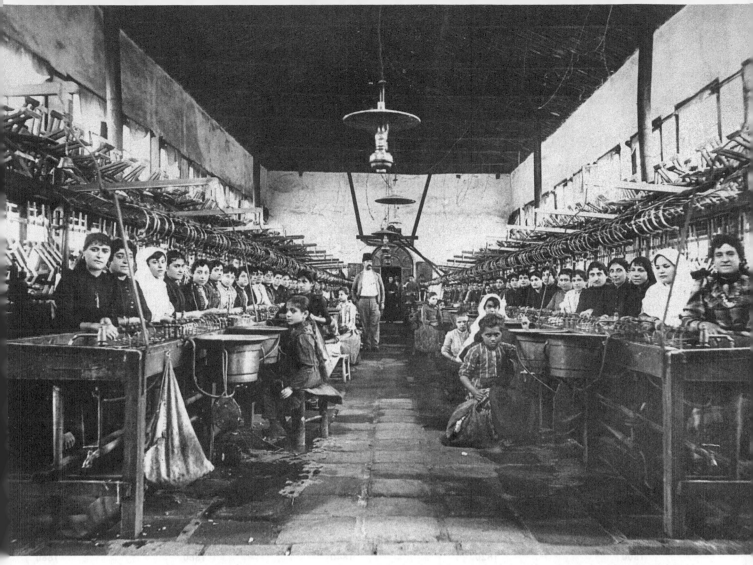

Turkish Factory In the global industrial processes of the nineteenth century, the role of many world regions was solely as suppliers of raw materials and consumers of finished products. Here we see that in the western Ottoman empire, factory production itself became a part of economic life. In this factory girls and women are weaving silk thread into cloth; the factory supervisor, however, is a man. In Japan as well (see Chapter 24), early textile production relied primarily on women's labor. As in England and India, skilled male artisans lost work when displaced by factories employing less skilled laborers, including young women and children.

(Roger-Viollet/The Image Works)

reformers hoped that a unified "Ottoman" identity could be fostered across the empire, in reality non-Turkish subjects of the Sultan were now more likely to see themselves as separate national groups and to turn to outside powers for protection, as when Orthodox Slavs looked to Russia in defiance of Ottoman authority.

Though Ottoman reforms went deeper than Russian ones, the Tanzimat program was also subject to autocratic whim. Just as Russia had relapsed after the assassination of Tsar Alexander II, so the Tanzimat Reform agenda lost momentum with the accession of Sultan Abd al-Hamid (AHB-dahl-ha-med) II (r. 1876–1918). With the backing of conservatives, he suspended proposals for constitutional reform and ruled arbitrarily. In Istanbul, as in St. Petersburg, after 1880, reactionary policies triumphed over reformist ones, with catastrophic results: just two generations later, both of these once-great imperial states would collapse (see Chapter 27).

Global Repercussions of the Industrial Revolution

Europe's prominent place in world affairs was not, of course, something that began with the Industrial Revolution. As described in Chapters 15–18, maritime expansion and access to American resources, especially silver, had enriched European societies in the early modern period. But in the late eighteenth century, much of the world's population—most notably in China—was only marginally affected (see Chapter 20).

It was the Industrial Revolution that placed western Europe firmly at the center of world power. Economically, that meant heightened competition for the raw materials necessary for factory production, many of which (cotton and rubber, for example) were available only outside Europe. As other European states, especially Germany, caught up with Britain's early lead, competition for such resources, as well as for markets for industrial products, intensified. By the late nineteenth century, heightened economic competition would drive a "New Imperialism" that led to direct European control over hundreds of societies (see Chapters 24–26).

Militarily, the Industrial Revolution changed the global balance of power dramatically. Earlier maritime and gunpowder technologies were not a European monopoly, as their effective use by the Ottoman empire demonstrated (see Chapter 17). Now, with steam-powered battleships, more powerful field artillery, and rapidly repeating rifles, the technological and financial costs of keeping up with the rising industrial powers of the West escalated decade by decade. Not even the mighty Russian military was able to keep pace.

The global tensions that resulted from European industrial supremacy had social, cultural, and political implications as well. As we have seen, in both the Russian and Ottoman empires, nineteenth-century elites debated whether to assimilate western European cultural traits as a spur to modernization or to abide by their established cultural and religious traditions. By the late nineteenth century, such debates resonated around the world. For example, while Chinese leaders vacillated on whether and how they might meet the Western challenge by borrowing Western ideas, Japanese reformers won a decisive victory with the Meiji Restoration in 1868 (see Chapter 24). By 1880 the Japanese government had learned, like the Russians and Ottomans before them, that industry was key to success, perhaps even survival, in the harshly competitive Western-dominated world order.

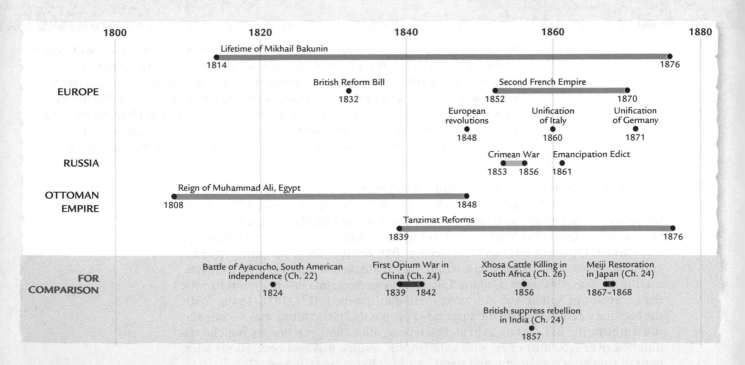

The social consequences of the Industrial Revolution, including the movement of many more people to cities, were also global. Social change led to intellectual ferment. Latin Americans, Africans, and Asians, as well as Europeans, were soon discussing the merits of the key ideas—nationalism, socialism, liberalism—that had formed the background for Mikhail Bakunin's political activism and anarchist philosophy. The revolutionaries of 1848 took aim at the traditional foundations of European social and political authority, attacking the inherited position of kings, landed aristocrats, and religious leaders. Such tensions appeared elsewhere in the world as well whenever new conditions and new ideas undermined customary authority. Faced with aggressive European expansion and a resulting social and political disequilibrium, Africans, Asians, Arabs, Amerindians, and others began to question how they might best adapt. In the industrial age, the mandate for change became insistent.

Meanwhile, within Europe, the rise of a unified Germany significantly altered the balance of power, removing Britain from its previous pinnacle of supremacy and alarming the French and the Russians as well. After 1890, Germany would become more aggressive in challenging the British empire, helping propel a scramble for colonies in Africa and Asia (see Chapter 26), and in the twentieth century the explosion of aggressive militarism present at the birth of Germany in 1871 would lead to two devastating world wars (see Chapters 27–29). Industrial progress, it seems, was a mixed blessing.

Key Terms

Mikhail Bakunin (684)
Industrial Revolution (685)
James Watt (686)
Josiah Wedgwood (687)
Muhammad Ali (690)
Reform Bill of 1832 (694)

John Stuart Mill (694)
Louis Napoleon (698)
Giuseppe Garibaldi (699)
Frankfurt Assembly (701)
Otto von Bismarck (701)
Karl Marx (702)

Charles Darwin (704)
Crimean War (705)
Emancipation Edict (708)
Tanzimat Reforms (710)

For Further Reference

Allen, Robert C. *The British Industrial Revolution in Global Perspective*. New York: Cambridge University Press, 2009.

Anderson, Benedict. *Imagined Communities: Reflections on the Origin and Spread of Nationalism*. London: Verso, 1991.

Auerbach, Jeffrey. *The Great Exhibition of 1851: A Nation on Display*. New Haven: Yale University Press, 1999.

Bakunin, Mikhail. *Bakunin on Anarchy: Selected Works by the Activist-Founder of World Anarchism*. Sam Dolgoff, ed. and trans. New York: Knopf, 1972.

Hanioglu, M. Sükrü. *A Brief History of the Late Ottoman Empire*. Princeton: Princeton University Press, 2010.

Hobsbawm, Eric. *The Age of Capital, 1848–1875*. New York: Simon and Schuster, 1975.

Mayr, Ernst. *One Long Argument: Charles Darwin and the Genesis of Modern Evolutionary Thought*. Cambridge, Mass.: Harvard University Press, 1993.

Randolph, John. *The House in the Garden: The Bakunin Family and the Romance of Russian Idealism*. Ithaca, N.Y.: Cornell University Press, 2007.

Rapport, Mike. *1848: Year of Revolution*. New York: Basic Books, 2010.

Reeves, Richard. *John Stuart Mill: Victorian Firebrand*. London: Atlantic Books, 2008.

Rosen, William. *The Most Powerful Idea in the World: A Story of Steam, Industry, and Invention*. New York: Random House, 2010.

Sperber, Jonathan. *Karl Marx: A Nineteenth Century Life*. New York: Liveright, 2013.

Stearns, Peter. *The Industrial Revolution in World History*. 4th ed. Boulder: Westview, 2012.

Tilly, Louise. *Industrialization and Gender Inequality*. Washington, D.C.: American Historical Association, 1993.

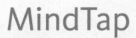 **MindTap** is a fully online, highly personalized learning experience built upon Cengage Learning content. MindTap combines student learning tools—readings, multimedia, activities, and assessments—into a singular Learning Path that guides students through the course.

24 The Challenge of Modernity in China, Japan, and India, 1800–1910

Portrait of a Japanese man named Fukuzawa Yukichi, a samurai and officer on the 1862 Takenouchi mission to Europe, employed as an interpreter of Dutch and English, 1862 (albumen print), Potteau, Jacques-Phillippe (1807–76)/Pitt Rivers Museum, Oxford, UK/Bridgeman Images

Fukuzawa Yûkichi

In 1859, the government of Japan sent its first delegation to visit the United States. On the crossing **Fukuzawa Yûkichi** (foo-koo-ZAH-wah yoo-KEE-chee) (1835–1901), a twenty-four-year-old samurai, studied *Webster's Dictionary*, but it did not prepare him very well for his experiences in San Francisco. *"There were many confusing and embarrassing moments,"* he later wrote, *"for we were quite ignorant of the customs of American life."**

At his hotel, he was amazed when his hosts walked across expensive carpets with their shoes on. Fukuzawa attended a dance wearing the outfit of a samurai, with two swords and hemp sandals:

*To our dismay we could not make out what they were doing. The ladies and gentlemen seemed to be hopping around the room together. As funny as it was, we knew it would be rude to laugh, and we controlled our expressions with difficulty as the dancing went on. . . . Things social, political, and economic proved most inexplicable. . . . I asked a gentleman where the descendants of George Washington might be. . . . His answer was so very casual that it shocked me. Of course, I know that America is a republic with a new president every four years, but I could not help feeling that the family of Washington would be revered above all other families. My reasoning was based on the reverence in Japan for the founders of the great lines of rulers—like that for Ieyasu of the Tokugawa family of Shoguns.**

*From The Autobiography of Yukichi Fukuzawa, by Eiichi Kiyooka, 1960, pp. 114–116.

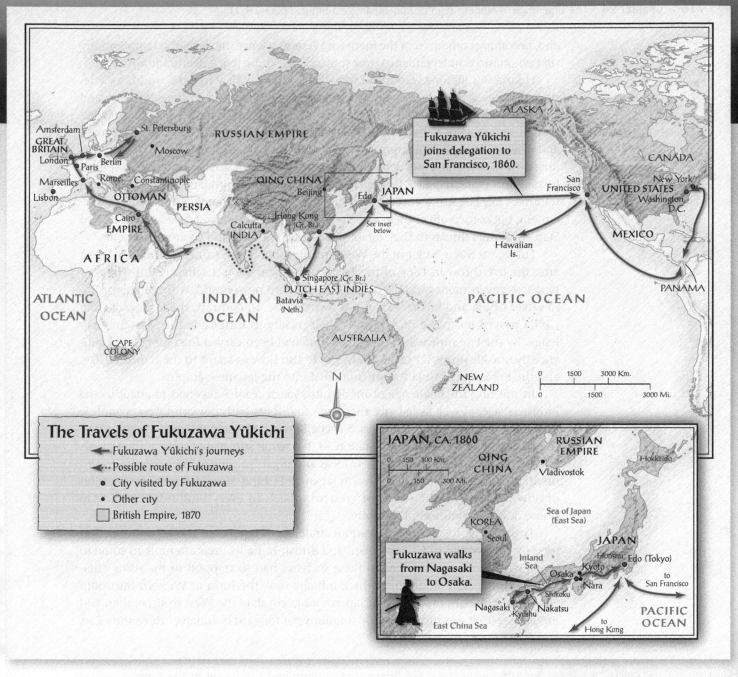

The Travels of Fukuzawa Yûkichi

←— Fukuzawa Yûkichi's journeys
◄- - Possible route of Fukuzawa
• City visited by Fukuzawa
• Other city
☐ British Empire, 1870

Fukuzawa Yûkichi joins delegation to San Francisco, 1860.

Fukuzawa walks from Nagasaki to Osaka.

JAPAN, CA. 1860

T hough he was much more knowledgeable about the Western world than most Japanese, Fukuzawa said of himself and his American hosts, *"neither of us really knew much about the other at all."**

Fukuzawa had grown up in a low-ranking samurai family that was expected to give unconditional support and service to their lord, but he was an ambitious nonconformist. As a young man he dedicated himself to "Dutch learning" (see Chapter 20)

*From *The Autobiography of Yukichi Fukuzawa*, by Eiichi Kiyooka, 1960, p. 115.

Fukuzawa Yûkichi

(1835–1901) Japanese writer, teacher, political theorist, and founder of Keio Academy (now Keio University). His ideas about learning, government, and society greatly influenced the Meiji Restoration. Considered one of the founders of modern Japan.

and, becoming convinced of the merits of Western science, he developed a philosophy that emphasized independence over subservience and science over tradition.

Fukuzawa's lifetime was one of remarkable change. All across the world, societies struggled to adapt to the new industrial age with its advances in transportation and communications technologies, the spread of new religious and secular ideologies, and the dynamics of a changing global economy. In western Europe, rulers, reformers, and rebels all struggled for control over the direction of change, while at the same time Russian and Ottoman elites debated calls for liberal reform versus conservative appeals to tradition (see Chapter 23). Societies in East Asia were similarly divided. Japanese reformers like Fukuzawa embraced change along Western lines as a means of empowerment, but conservatives there and elsewhere in East Asia saw Europe and the United States as hostile threats to their established social, political, and economic systems.

Fukuzawa was a leader of the Westernizing faction that came to dominate Japan after the overthrow in 1868 of the Tokugawa shogunate (see Chapter 20). The new Japanese government was able to resist the Western powers and, with military victories over China and Russia, expand its own empire. In contrast, the leaders of Qing China proved incapable of reforming their society to turn aside the Western challenge. By the late nineteenth century, China had been carved into spheres of influence by outside powers. Korean leaders were also slow to adapt to the industrial age, and the Korean peninsula was incorporated into the Japanese empire.

In meeting the challenge of modernity, South Asians also had to adapt to the industrial age, as well as balance their own traditions with powerful new economic forces and cultural influences. A major rebellion in 1857 signaled how deeply many Indians resented British rule. The failure of that revolt stimulated Indian intellectuals and political leaders to develop new ideas and organizations to achieve self-government. Indian nationalists, like those in Japan and China, struggled with the question of how to deal with the power of Western models in everything from clothing to house design to political philosophy.

This chapter focuses on the various strategies of resistance and accommodation used by the peoples of China, Japan, and British India in their attempts to come to terms with the industrial age. All these societies had to respond to the rising challenges of industrial modernity, which initially took the form of Western intrusion. Fukuzawa Yûkichi's proposal that Japan should emulate the West to strengthen and modernize itself was just one of the solutions put forward in nineteenth-century East and South Asia.

FOCUS QUESTIONS

> What were the main forces that undermined the power of the Qing dynasty in the nineteenth century?

> What made it possible for Japan to be transformed from a relatively isolated society to a major world power in less than half a century?

> What were the principal ways that British-ruled Indians responded to imperialism?

> How and why did Chinese, Japanese, and Indian societies respond differently to the challenges of industrial modernity?

China's World Inverted, 1800–1906

Four decades after China's emperor dismissed Britain's diplomatic advances (see Chapter 20), the British returned with firepower to forcibly open Chinese markets. Suddenly faced with Europe's industrial might, Qing officials agreed to a series of unequal treaties. Soon after, a major rebellion shook the Qing dynasty to its foundations. While some officials, humiliated by the decline in imperial prestige, entertained reform, they were outmaneuvered by conservatives who opposed adopting Western political, educational, and economic models.

The conservatives' policies were a disaster. By the end of the nineteenth century, soldiers from Britain, France, Russia, the United States, and Japan had occupied Beijing's Forbidden City, as Imperial China lost its ancient status as the "Middle Kingdom" to become a chessboard on which the great powers moved their pieces, dividing China into spheres of influence.

Fukuzawa Yûkichi, who had helped implement Western-style reform in Japan, observed in 1899: *"I am sure that it is impossible to lead [the Chinese] people to civilization so long as the old government is left to stand as it is."** Seven years later the last Manchu emperor abdicated, but by then China's long-dominant role in East Asia had been usurped by Japan.

Qing China Confronts the Industrial World, 1800–1850

In the late eighteenth century, the British East India Company faced an old problem for Western traders in China: apart from silver, they had few goods of value in Chinese markets. But in the 1770s, after they came to dominate opium-producing regions in India, the British began exchanging illicit opium for tea, silk, and other valuable commodities. The strategy was commercially brilliant, since narcotics create their own demand through the spiral of drug addiction. But it was ethically problematic and even hypocritical. Opium induces such lethargy and such a sense of hopelessness that those in its clutches neglect their own health and the care of their dependents. Even while the British sought to stamp out opium addiction at home, the East India Company was smuggling opium into China in open disregard of Chinese governmental authority. Widespread addiction undercut China's economy through lost productivity.

By 1839, Sino-British relations were in crisis. The Qing government declared that drug traders would be beheaded and sent a scholar-official named Lin Zezu (lin say-SHOE) to Guangzhou to suppress the opium trade. In a letter to Queen Victoria, Lin made his government's position clear:

[By] introducing opium by stealth [the British] have seduced our Chinese people, and caused every province in the land to overflow with that poison. They know merely how to advantage themselves; they care not about injuring others!...

---

*From *The Autobiography of Yukichi Fukuzawa*, by Eiichi Kiyooka, 1960, p. 277.

*Therefore those foreigners who now import opium into the Central Land are condemned to be beheaded and strangled.**

To the British, however, the issue was not so much opium as free trade. Commercial interests were lobbying the British government for more open access to Chinese markets, which had traditionally been highly regulated. And according to an extreme interpretation of liberal economic theory, free trade is always and everywhere best for everyone. If the Chinese did not agree, then they would have to be *forced* to open their markets.

The first **Opium War** (1839–1842) was a severe shock to the Qing government. The British used their iron-clad gunboats to blockade the Chinese coast and bombard coastal cities such as Guangzhou and Shanghai. Being so easily defeated by "Western barbarians," many Qing commanders committed suicide in disgrace. In 1842, as the British sailed up the Yangzi River and prepared to blast apart the walls of Nanjing, Qing officials realized that they would have to negotiate.

With no bargaining power, the Qing felt compelled to agree to the humiliating terms of the **Treaty of Nanjing**, the first of a series of unequal treaties that eroded Chinese sovereignty. The agreement opened five "treaty ports" to unrestricted foreign trade and gave possession of Hong Kong, upriver from the great port of Guangzhou, to the British. The treaty's provision of extraterritoriality, making Britons subject to British rather than Chinese law at the treaty ports, was a crushing blow to Chinese pride.

The Treaty of Nanjing only whetted British and other European appetites. Using supposed Qing violations of the Nanjing treaty as a pretext, in the second Opium War of 1856 the British and French burned Qianlong's magnificent summer palace to the ground, and briefly occupied the Forbidden City. In 1860, the Qing agreed to another, even more unequal treaty that opened more ports to Western trade and allowed "international settlements" in key Chinese cities such as Shanghai and Guangzhou. These settlements, where only Europeans were allowed to live, were foreign enclaves on Chinese soil. The British also mandated that the Manchu would no longer refer to them as "barbarians" in imperial documents.

Opium War

In the first Opium War (1839–1842), Britain invaded the Qing empire to force China to open to trade. In the second Opium War (1856–1860), an Anglo-French force once again invaded to enforce the unequal treaties that resulted from the first war and extract further concessions.

Treaty of Nanjing

(1842) One-sided treaty that concluded the first Opium War. Britain was allowed to trade in additional Chinese ports and took control of Hong Kong. The provision for extraterritoriality meant that Britons were subject to British rather than Chinese law.

The Taiping Rebellion, 1850–1864

The Opium Wars and the unequal treaties that followed had exposed Qing weakness, leading some Chinese to conclude that the Manchu had lost the "Mandate of Heaven" (see Chapter 16). Indeed, as early as the 1790s, some peasant rebels had questioned Qing imperial legitimacy. Such challenges would cascade in the decades to come.

Behind the political chaos of nineteenth-century China was a startling fact: the population had grown by over 100 million between 1800 and 1850. Farmers brought more marginal lands into production; agricultural yields declined; villages were repeatedly flooded. People were suffering from neglect, misrule, and hunger. Although imperial governments had long been responsible for flood control and famine relief, the Qing bureaucracy, fighting foreign invaders, instead raised taxes for its military in the midst of the people's suffering.

*Mark A. Kishlansky, ed., *Sources of World History*, vol. 2 (New York: HarperCollins College Publishers, 1995), p. 268.

● **CONTEXT&CONNECTIONS** Chinese historians long used a cyclical theory to explain the rise and fall of imperial dynasties. At the beginning, strong leaders with Confucian virtue are active in administration, assuring ethical behavior by scholar-officials. Imperial decline and the consequent loss of the Mandate of Heaven would begin when emperors became distracted from day-to-day administration: courts became corrupt; canals silted up; peasants revolted; warlords defied imperial authority; and famine and calamity stalked the land. The theory of dynastic cycles seems applicable to the late *Ming dynasty* period (key term in Chapter 16) and to the Manchu as well. Of course, apart from issues of political leadership, modern historians also take account of demographic, environmental, and economic factors in charting the rise and fall of dynasties. ●

In the mid-nineteenth century, further peasant revolts shook the empire, including a major Muslim uprising in the northwest. The situation was especially desperate in Guangdong province, where the **Taiping Rebellion** (1850–1864) began, and then spread throughout southern China, sending the empire into chaos. The leader of the Taiping (tie-PING) was Hong Xiuquan (hoong shee-OH-chew-an). Hong had traveled to Guangzhou for the imperial examinations where, having failed in several attempts, he then studied with Western missionaries and added a unique interpretation to their message.

Hong claimed to be the younger brother of Jesus Christ, come to earth to establish a *"Heavenly Kingdom of Great Peace."* Mixing Christianity with peasant yearnings for fairness and justice, Hong attracted hundreds of thousands of followers to his vision of reform. In their Heavenly Kingdom, the Taiping proclaimed, *"inequality [will not] exist, and [everyone will] be well fed and clothed."**

● **CONTEXT&CONNECTIONS** Movements such as the Taiping are referred to as *millenarian*. Some Christians believe that after the second coming of Christ a millennium (one thousand years) of earthly peace and prosperity will follow. Another such millenarian movement occurred at the very same time in South Africa. During the tragic *Xhosa Cattle Killing* (Chapter 26), a young prophetess predicted that departed ancestors would rise from the dead to purge evil from the land, borrowing the concept of the resurrection of the dead from Christian missionaries. In both China and South Africa in the mid-1850s, religious *syncretism* (Chapter 18) followed from contact with European missionaries, influencing mass millenarian movements. ●

Many in the disciplined core of the Taiping movement were, like Hong, from the Hakka ethnic group. The Hakka were only brought under imperial control during Ming times and had never fully assimilated Confucian ideas of hierarchy. Women had relatively independent roles, and their feet were never bound. Hong's "long-haired rebels" refused to wear the long, braided ponytail (or *queue*) mandated by Manchu authorities as a sign of subservience. *"Ever since the Manchus poisoned China,"* Hong said, *"the influence of demons has distressed the empire while the Chinese with bowed heads and dejected spirits willingly became subjects and servants."*†

In late 1850 some twenty thousand Taiping rebels defeated an imperial army sent to crush them; they then went on the offensive and captured the city of

Taiping Rebellion
(1850–1864) Massive rebellion against the Qing led by Hong Xiuquan, who claimed to be the younger brother of Jesus Christ come to earth to create a "Heavenly Kingdom of Great Peace." The imperial system was greatly weakened as a result of the uprising.

---

*Franz Michael and Chang Chung-li, *The Taiping Rebellion: History and Documents*, vol. 2 (Seattle: University of Washington Press, 1971), p. 314.

†Jen Yu-Wen, *The Taiping Revolutionary Moment* (New Haven: Yale University Press, 1973), pp. 93–94.

Nanjing, just upriver from Shanghai. Tens of thousands of Manchu were systematically slaughtered. Hong moved into a former Ming imperial palace and declared Nanjing his capital.

After 1853, however, the Taiping rebels gained no more great victories. Their rhetoric of equality alienated landowners and educated elites: influential members of the gentry organized militias to fight them. The Taiping were unable to recruit experienced administrators because their religious beliefs were at odds with the Confucian ideals of scholar-officials, and corruption seeped into the movement when some leaders abandoned the plain living advocated by Hong and indulged in expensive clothing, fine food, and elaborate rituals.

From their base at Nanjing, the Taiping threatened the rapidly developing European interests in Shanghai. So now, in the early 1860s, the British and French, who had done so much to undercut the Qing, rallied to the dynasty's defense. In 1864, Qing forces, supported by European soldiers and armaments, stormed and took Nanjing. A Manchu official reported: *"Not one of the 100,000 rebels in Nanjing surrendered themselves when the city was taken but in many cases gathered together and burned themselves and passed away without repentance."** A staggering 30 million people had been killed by the end of the Taiping Rebellion, and China's rulers were more beholden to European powers than ever before.

"Self-Strengthening" and the Boxer Rebellion, 1842–1901

Self-Strengthening Movement

Nineteenth-century Chinese reform movement with the motto "Confucian ethics, Western science." Advocates of Self-Strengthening sought a way to reconcile Western and Chinese systems of thought.

In the wake of the Opium War and Taiping Rebellion, some educated Chinese began arguing that only fundamental change would enable the empire to meet the rising Western challenge, as more and more representatives of industrial capitalism arrived by steamship looking for markets and cheap labor. Some joined together in the **Self-Strengthening Movement**, with the motto *"Confucian ethics, Western science."* China, these reformers said, could acquire modern technology and the scientific knowledge underlying it while retaining the ethically superior Confucian tradition. As one of their leaders stated, *"What we have to learn from the barbarians is only one thing, solid ships and effective guns."*†

Reformers supported the translation of Western scientific texts (the first since the days of Jesuit influence in the seventeenth century) and established new educational institutions that merged the study of Confucian classics with coursework in geography and science. And for the first time some young Manchu and Chinese men ventured to Europe and the United States to study Western achievements firsthand. They were sowing seeds of change along the same lines as Fukuzawa Yûkichi in Japan.

Conservatives, however, scoffed at the Self-Strengthening Movement. A prominent Neo-Confucian rejected education in science and engineering, sneering that no one *"could use mathematics to raise a nation from a state of decline or to strengthen it in times of weakness."*‡ Like Muslim scholars in the Ottoman empire, Chinese

---

*Franz Michael and Chang Chung-li, *The Taiping Rebellion: History and Documents*, vol. 3 (Seattle: University of Washington Press, 1971), p. 767.

†Teng Ssu-yü and John K. Fairbank, *China's Response to the West: A Documentary Survey, 1839–1923* (Cambridge, Mass.: Harvard University Press, 1954), pp. 53–54.

‡Quoted in Patricia Buckley Ebrey, *Cambridge Illustrated History of China* (London: Cambridge University Press, 1996), p. 245.

History/Bridgeman Images

A Qing Arsenal A major focus of the Self-Strengthening Movement was military modernization. Here Qing officials survey cannon at an arsenal built in 1865, after the suppression of the Taiping Rebellion. The reformers hoped to achieve self-sufficiency in military infrastructure with the aid of foreign advisers; however, the corruption and inefficiency of the imperial bureaucracy prevented them from achieving that goal, a great contrast to Japanese achievements in military production in the following decades.

scholar-officials derived their power and prestige from training in a historically successful body of knowledge. To accept foreign principles in education would undercut their influence, and to emphasize military over scholarly pursuits would go against Confucianism. *"One does not waste good sons by making them soldiers,"* went an old saying.

● **CONTEXT&CONNECTIONS** The relatively low status of soldiers in imperial China stood in contrast to the social norms of both Japan and western Europe. The Middle Kingdom had no equivalent to the valiant knights of European lore or the steadfast *samurai* who had long been the bedrock of Japanese society. Indeed, in the sixteenth century, *Matteo Ricci* (Chapter 16) had applauded the Ming Chinese who, in contrast to rulers on his own violent continent, emphasized culture and learning over military affairs. ●

Conservative attitudes coalesced at the top of the imperial hierarchy when, during the reign of two child emperors, real power lay in the hands of a conservative regent, the **Empress Ci Xi** (1835–1908), an intelligent and ambitious concubine who came to dominate the highest reaches of the Qing bureaucracy. Conservatives rallied around Ci Xi (kee SHEE). She discouraged talk of reform and diverted funds meant for modernization, such as programs to build railways and strengthen the military, to prestige projects like rebuilding the ruined summer

Empress Ci Xi
(1835–1908) The "Dowager Empress" who dominated Qing politics in the late nineteenth century, ruling as regent for the emperor Guangxu. She blocked the Hundred Days' Reforms and other "Self-Strengthening" measures.

palace. Indeed, instead of building a real warship, she ordered an ornamental marble boat to decorate the palace lake.

Ci Xi resented the unequal treaties with European nations, and the arrogance of their representatives infuriated her. Despite limited beginnings of industrialization and the acquisition of some modern armaments, however, the Qing military was still no match for its rivals. In 1884, during a dispute over rights to Vietnam, French gunboats obliterated the Qing southern fleet within an hour. Southeast Asia, no longer tributary to the Qing, would now belong to France (see Chapter 26).

The Japanese, pursuing a policy of rapid industrialization and militarization, were also a threat. In 1894 an uprising against Korea's imperial dynasty drew in both Japanese and Chinese military forces, resulting in the Sino-Japanese War. The Qing, having lost their southern fleet to France, now lost almost their entire northern fleet to Japan. The treaty that ended the war gave Japan possession of both Korea and the island of Taiwan.

After these military defeats, Chinese reformers finally won official support in 1898, when the young Guangxu (gwahng-SHOO) emperor issued a series of reform edicts. Guangxu was inspired by a group of young scholars who had traveled to Beijing to present a petition urging that the government found a state bank, sell bonds to support large-scale railroad building, and create a modern postal system. The most fundamental reform concerned education. Expertise in poetry and calligraphy would no longer be required. Instead, examination questions would focus on practical issues of governance and administration. Beijing College was to add a medical school, and all the Confucian academies were to add Western learning to their curricula.

Ci Xi quickly intervened to suppress Guangxu's reforms, confining him, along with his most progressive advisers, to the palace. Some advocates of Self-Strengthening were charged with conspiracy and executed; others left the country or lapsed into silence.

Meanwhile, the aggression of external powers intensified. Germans seized the port city of Qingdao (ching-DOW) and claimed mineral and railway rights on northeastern Shandong peninsula (birthplace of Confucius). The British expanded their holdings from Hong Kong, and the Russians increased their presence in Manchuria (see Map 24.1). Public anger grew, directed at the Manchu for letting the empire slip so dramatically.

Boxer Rebellion

(1898) Chinese uprising triggered by a secret society called the Society of Righteous and Harmonious Fists, a fiercely anti-Western group. Intended to drive out Westerners, it resulted instead in foreign occupation of Beijing.

Throughout the tumultuous nineteenth century, Chinese had sought security by joining secret societies. One of these, the "Society of Righteous and Harmonious Fists," also known as the Boxers because of their emphasis on martial arts, now rose to prominence. The Boxers were virulently antiforeign. In 1898 they attacked European missionaries and Chinese Christian converts, thus beginning the **Boxer Rebellion**. Empress Ci Xi decided to side with these antiforeign rebels and declared the Boxers a patriotic group: *"The foreigners have been aggressive towards us, infringed upon our territorial integrity, trampled our people under their feet.... They oppress our people and blaspheme our gods."** (See the feature "Visual Evidence in Primary Sources: The Boxer Rebellion: American and French Views.")

---

*Victor Purcell, *The Boxer Uprising: A Background Study* (New York: Cambridge University Press, 1963), p. 224.

Map 24.1 Asia in 1910 By 1910, empire was the status quo across Asia. In addition to the established British, French, and Dutch possessions, the United States (Philippines) and Japan (Korea and Taiwan) were new imperial players. The Russian empire was also a powerful presence, expanding at the expense of Iran, though its defeat by Japan in 1905 showed the limits of its influence in East Asia. Qing China was still technically a sovereign state; however, important coastal regions were under de facto European colonial control.

Territories held by
Western powers
- Great Britain
- France
- Netherlands
- United States
- Russian Empire
- Japan and its territories
- Independent Asian states
- Ottoman Empire
- Major railroads

RUSSIAN EMPIRE

SIBERIA

Sea of Okhotsk

JAPANESE EMPIRE

PACIFIC OCEAN

INDIAN OCEAN

CHINA

INDIA

OTTOMAN EMPIRE

ARABIA

AFRICA

DUTCH EAST INDIES

The Boxer Rebellion: American and French Views

The Boxer Rebellion (1898–1901) marked the death throes of the Qing dynasty. The decision of the Dowager Empress, Ci Xi, to support the "Righteous Society of Harmonious Fists" against the "Western barbarians" was calamitous. The Qing had to pay huge reparations, and though they did finally institute real political and social reforms, it was too late. In 1912, a new Republic of China marked the final end of China's long imperial history.

One of the Boxers' principal grievances was against Christian missionaries, who came to China in increasing numbers in the second half of the nineteenth century. Unlike Matteo Ricci (see Chapter 16), who had adapted his Christian message to Confucian traditions and Chinese cultural norms, the European and American missionaries who arrived in the 1800s expected converts not only to accept Christianity, but also to conform to Western family models, styles of dress and housing, medical systems, and other cultural practices.

As with the Indian rebels of 1857 (discussed later in this chapter), who were driven in part by their belief that the British planned to use Christianity to subvert local cultures and traditions, so too the Boxers singled out missionaries as particular enemies. In the summer of 1900, 239 foreign Christians were killed by the Boxers across north China; Chinese converts and sympathizers were murdered

President William McKinley (in office 1897–1901) wields a sword, while the figure of Uncle Sam attacks with a bayonet at the end of his rifle. The two figures represent the five thousand American soldiers sent as part of the China Relief Operation in 1900 to break the Boxer siege of Western delegations in Beijing.

National Archives, Washington, D.C.

"*Life, Liberty, and the Pursuit of Happiness under Treaty Rights*," inscribed on the American flag, justifies their actions in defense of the unequal treaties, which, since the Treaty of Nanjing in 1842, had made it impossible for the Qing rulers of China to regulate international trade.

The Boxer rebels are shown as savages, with frenzied expressions. They march with heads on pikes, reach to stab a prostrate woman, and have murdered the child at her feet. The baby is wrapped in a tattered American flag, an image that would arouse strong emotions.

In spite of the United States's participation in the occupation of the Forbidden City, McKinley's Open Door Policy advocated free trade with China without territorial annexation.

as well. As the Boxers marched on Beijing, foreigners took refuge in a walled compound. Although the Qing commander acted to protect them, twenty thousand foreign soldiers (from Britain, France, Russia, Japan, and the United States) also arrived to occupy the capital and rescue the besieged.

Another principal grievance of the Boxers was the partition of China into Western "spheres of influence." But in the end, their uprising only led to further foreign interference. Though the United States, with its Open Door Policy, proclaimed its opposition to the further partition of China, the division of the world's oldest and most populous empire continued unabated.

The political cartoons here, one from the United States and the other from France, are both from the period of the Boxer Rebellion but demonstrate different attitudes toward the conflict. In neither case does it seem that the Chinese will have much to say about the outcome.

China leaps up in alarm, shown here in the stereotypical late-nineteenth-century Western fashion, with exceptionally long fingernails and a long flowing queue of braided hair. *Compare the Chinese characters in the two cartoons. Both are caricatures, but what different impressions do they make on the viewer?*

Queen Victoria of Great Britain (left) seems shocked as Kaiser Wilhelm of Germany aggressively takes the first slice of the Chinese "pizza."

The United States is missing from this scene.

Tsar Nicholas of Russia eyes Wilhelm's action and seems to be ready to join in; looking over Nicholas's shoulder, France is unarmed and, while she seems interested, appears less engaged. *Compare the Western figures in the two cartoons. What arguments for or against the Western invasion of China might the two artists be making?*

The Japanese figure on the right studies the "pizza" as if he is planning a chess move. He holds no weapon, but his menacing sword lies on the table ready for action.

Imperial support for the Boxers proved disastrous. In the summer of 1900, on the grounds that foreigners in China had to be protected, twenty thousand troops from over a dozen different nations marched on Beijing and occupied the Forbidden City. Another humiliating treaty followed. The Qing were required to pay 450 million ounces of silver (twice the country's annual revenue) to the occupying forces.

Finally, the Manchu government implemented substantial reforms, abolishing the examination system and making plans for a constitutional order with some degree of popular representation. At long last, an imperial decree abolished the cruel practice of footbinding. But it was much too late. In 1912, revolutionaries overthrew the decrepit Qing dynasty (see Chapter 27).

● **CONTEXT&CONNECTIONS** The worst of times in China have often come during a period of chaos and uncertainty between the fall of one dynasty and the consolidation of power by another. That pattern would be repeated in the first half of the twentieth century. After the fall of the Qing dynasty in 1912, decades of civil war followed. A semblance of stability returned only after the Second World War, with the end of Japanese occupation and the foundation of the People's Republic of China in 1949 under Mao Zedong (see Chapters 28 and 29). ●

The Rise of Modern Japan, 1830–1905

When Fukuzawa Yûkichi wrote that China could never move forward under Qing leadership, he was in a good position to judge. He had been instrumental in Japan's own transformation from weakness and isolation to industrialization, centralized state power, and imperialism. After the Meiji (MAY-jee) Restoration of 1868, Japan adapted to the new industrial age by looking to the West not just for its technology but also for principles of education, economic organization, and state building. Yet socially, culturally, and spiritually, the Japanese retained their ancient traditions. By borrowing foreign ideas and adapting them to Japanese culture, Japanese society actually achieved the "self-strengthening" that eluded Chinese reformers.

After the arrival of a U.S. fleet in 1853, isolation from the West was no longer possible. Having observed the devastating consequences of the Opium Wars, Fukuzawa and others advocated radical reform based on rapid acquisition of Western knowledge and technology. As elsewhere, the reform was opposed by conservative defenders of the status quo. But in Meiji Japan, reformers took charge of imperial policy, laying the foundations of military and industrial modernization, and fulfilling Fukuzawa's vision that his country would be recognized as an equal in Asian affairs by the Europeans and Americans.

Late Tokugawa Society, 1830–1867

Growing up, Fukuzawa was ashamed of the gap between his family's samurai status and its low income. Samurai were not supposed to deal with mundane affairs such as shopping and handling money. But since they could not afford servants, the Fukuzawa family had no choice but to do so. Fukuzawa remembered how they would do their shopping at night, with towels over their faces to hide their shame. Particularly acute was the scornful treatment he endured: *"Children of lower samurai families like ours were obliged to use a respectful manner of* *address in speaking to the children of high samurai families, while these children invariably used an arrogant form of address to us. Then what fun was there in playing together?"** Although Fukuzawa's father was an educated man and well versed in the Chinese classics, no achievement on his part could raise his family's status.

Even so, the Fukuzawa family had higher status than most people. Below them were the farmers, then the artisans, and then the merchants (who were seen more as economic parasites than as productive members of society). Lowest of all were the outcasts who performed such unsavory tasks as working in leather and handling the bodies of executed criminals.

As a young man, Fukuzawa tested the attitude of the peasants by addressing them first in the haughty tones of the samurai and then speaking to them in the dialect of an Osaka merchant. The peasants abased themselves with humility when Fukuzawa spoke as a samurai, but they treated him with scorn when he imitated the speech of a merchant.

The young Fukuzawa longed to escape the social strictures that limited his ambitions. Education proved the key. Fukuzawa received no formal education until he was fourteen, and then it was the traditional curriculum of Confucian classics taught in Chinese. Frustrated, he obtained his family's permission to travel to the port city of Nagasaki, which was the site of the annual Dutch trade mission and the center of "Dutch learning" (see Chapter 20). Fukuzawa's study of Western medical and scientific texts convinced him of the superiority of Western over Chinese styles of education.

In 1853, shortly after Fukuzawa had begun his Western studies, American **Commodore Matthew Perry** (1794–1858) steamed into Edo harbor, his "black ships" sending shock waves through Japanese society. Perry's mission was to impress the power of American technology on the Tokugawa government and force it to establish diplomatic relations and open Japanese ports to foreign trade. Fearing that the Americans and Europeans might unleash a destructive barrage, the Tokugawa government submitted and, in 1858, signed an unequal treaty with the United States and five European powers granting access to treaty ports and rights of extraterritoriality.

Among those who accused the shogun of having humiliated the nation by signing the 1858 treaty were some daimyo lords who hoped to use the crisis to increase their independent power. Some even acquired modern weapons to fire at passing European ships. In the early 1860s, it was not clear whether the Tokugawa government still possessed enough authority to enforce its edicts.

Seeking some breathing space, in 1862 the shogun sent a delegation to Europe hoping to delay further unequal treaties. Fukuzawa, a member of this delegation, later published his observations of European life in a widely read book called *Western Ways*. (Fukuzawa became the Japanese public's main source of information on the Western world; in fact, *all* translations of Western books were known as *Fukuzawa-bon*.)

The situation was becoming dangerous by the time of his return in 1863. Apart from rebellious daimyo, the Tokugawa government was also opposed by a militant group of *rônin* (ROH-neen). Samurai without masters, these rônin were a floating population of proud men of limited means, stridently antiforeign and

Commodore Matthew Perry

(1794–1858) American naval officer and diplomat whose 1853 visit to Japan opened that country's trade to the United States and other Western countries.

*From *The Autobiography of Yukichi Fukuzawa*, by Eiichi Kiyooka, 1960, p. 18.

Commodore Perry´s Arrival in Japan This Japanese print shows the arrival of Commodore Matthew Perry´s steam-powered "black ships" near Edo (modern Tokyo) in 1853. After submitting to Perry´s demand that Japan be opened to Western trade, Japanese leaders in 1859 sent the Tokugawa mission to San Francisco, on which Fukuzawa Yûkichi served, as an attempt to discover more about the U.S. government and its motives in East Asia.

nostalgic for a glorious past when their military skills were highly prized. *"The whole spirit,"* Fukuzawa said, *"was one of war and worship of ancient warriors."** Fukuzawa, who had now learned English and was working as a government translator, was a potential target for their anger. For years he never left his home at night, fearful of being assaulted by anti-Western thugs.

The Meiji Restoration, 1867–1890

The challenge of the West required a coordinated national response, and neither the weakened Tokugawa government nor the rebellious daimyo could provide one. But another possible source of national unity was the imperial court at Kyoto. Some anti-Tokugawa rebels flocked to the banner of a new child emperor under the slogans *"Revere the Emperor!"* and *"Expel the Barbarians!"*

*From *The Autobiography of Yukichi Fukuzawa*, by Eiichi Kiyooka, 1960, p. 164.

In 1867, supporters of the emperor clashed with the shogun's forces. Fukuzawa was teaching in Edo at the Keio Academy he had founded, lecturing on economics from an American textbook while a battle raged nearby: *"Once in a while . . . my pupils would amuse themselves by bringing out a ladder and climbing up on the roof to gaze at the smoke overhanging the attack."** He remained neutral, for his own safety and that of his students, and feared that the imperial forces would prove to be just as antiforeign as those of the shogun.

The armies of the imperial party were successful. In 1868, the **Meiji Restoration** brought a new government to power at Edo, now renamed Tokyo. Fukuzawa was delighted to discover that reformers dominated the administration of the Meiji ("enlightened") child emperor. They began to utterly transform the closed, conservative society Fukuzawa had known as a child. Most were, like him, men from middle and lower samurai families that placed a strong emphasis on scholarship.

> **Meiji Restoration**
> (1868) A dramatic revolution in Japan that overthrew the Tokugawa, restored national authority to the emperor, and put the country on a path of political and economic reform. Meiji industrialization turned Japan into a major world power.

The Meiji reforms replaced the feudal domains of the daimyo with regional prefectures under the control of the central government. Tax collection was centralized to solidify the government's economic control. The Meiji government allowed commoners to carry arms for the first time, as it created a national conscript army equipped with the latest weapons and led by officers trained in modern military organization. All the old distinctions between samurai and commoners were erased: *"The samurai abandoned their swords,"* Fukuzawa noted, and *"non-samurai were allowed to have surnames and ride horses."*† Fukuzawa expressed hope for the transformative power of individualism: *"It is time to make it possible for wealth, honor, and happiness to be entirely the fruits of a man's own efforts."*‡

Fukuzawa coined two of the Meiji reform's most popular slogans: *"Civilization and Enlightenment"* and *"Rich Nation, Strong Army."* Viewing education as the key to progress, the government set up a national system of compulsory schooling and invited Fukuzawa to head the Education Ministry, but he preferred to keep his independence by founding a newspaper.

The policy of the Meiji oligarchs was to adopt Western methods to strengthen Japan so it could resist Western intrusion and engage the world as an equal. Some Japanese remained critical of this new direction, including the forty-two thousand samurai who participated in the Satsuma Rebellion of 1877. Their leader, Saigō Takamori, ritually disemboweled himself when the battle turned against his men, and he became a hero to conservatives. But the Meiji reformers countered by creating their own cult of Saigō, using the same clever strategy by which they had used a traditionalist slogan—*"Revere the Emperor"*—to mobilize support for radical reforms.

As in Europe, the rewards of increased industrial productivity were unequally distributed in Meiji Japan. Landowners benefited the most from advances in agriculture. Rice output increased 30 percent between 1870 and 1895, but peasants often paid half their crop in land rent, and now had to pay taxes to the central government as well.

---

*From *The Autobiography of Yukichi Fukuzawa*, by Eiichi Kiyooka, 1960, p. 210.

†Fukuzawa Yûkichi, *The Speeches of Fukuzawa: A Translation and Critical Study*, ed. Wayne Oxford (Tokyo: Hokuseido House, 1973), p. 93.

‡Yûkichi Fukuzawa, *An Outline of a Theory of Civilization*, rev. trans. David A. Dilworth and G. Cameron Hurst III (New York: Columbia University Press, 2008), Kindle pp. 3000–3001.

To make ends meet, many rural families sent their daughters to work in factories the government was setting up. Poorly paid and strictly supervised, young women lived in factory dormitories, their dexterity and docility exploited for the benefit of others. Fukuzawa was critical and argued that *"the position of women must be raised at once,"* stressing education for girls as the first step toward greater gender equality.*

A twenty-year-old woman named **Kishida Toshiko** (KEE-she-dah toe-she-ko) went even further, speaking eloquently for women's rights in meetings across the country. *"Equality, independence, respect, and a monogamous relationship are the hall marks of relationships between men and women in a civilized society,"* she said. *"Ah, you men of the world, you talk of reform, but not of revolution. When it comes to equality, you yearn for the old ways, and follow, unchanged, the customs of the past."*† She even leavened her criticism with a little humor: *"If it is true that men are better than women because they are stronger, why aren't our sumo wrestlers in the government?"*‡ Kishida was soon arrested, fined, and silenced. The men at the top of Meiji society chose the slogan *"Good Wife, Wise Mother"* to reinforce traditional patriarchy, defining proper women as submissive, subservient, and legally inferior.

The gender debate exemplifies another of Fukuzawa's contributions: his encouragement of open discussions, creating a space for "public opinion" in Japanese politics. Even if he disagreed with Kishida's advocacy of full and immediate equality for women, when she traveled the country making her case she was embodying Fukuzawa's principle of *enzetsu*, "public speaking." (It was a concept so new in Japanese society that Fukuzawa had to make up a word for it.) In becoming a modern nation, Japan was also becoming a mass society where rulers had to take account of popular feelings and opinions.

Fukuzawa was particularly proud of his part in stimulating public opinion to pressure the Meiji oligarchs for a formal constitution. In 1873 he had returned from another mission to Europe particularly impressed with the newly unified Germany. Responding to the call for a constitution, Meiji oligarchs now looked not to the model of liberal Britain, but to that of imperial Germany. The Japanese constitution of 1889 was therefore based on the German one, where the emperor rather than elected representatives controlled the real levers of power.

● **CONTEXT&CONNECTIONS** Like Germany under Chancellor *Otto von Bismarck* (Chapter 23), Meiji Japan achieved unification through conservative nationalism rather than through liberalism based on individual rights. The slogan *"For the sake of the country"* urged individuals to sacrifice for the larger good. And as in Germany, militarism combined with nationalism to make Japan more aggressively imperialistic. ●

Meiji Japan went even further than Germany in giving the state control of industrial development. The government itself constructed railroads, harbors, and telegraph lines, making direct investments in industry as well. The Meiji

Kishida Toshiko

(1863–1901) An early Japanese feminist who urged that as part of the Meiji reforms, women should have equal access to modern education and be allowed to take part in public affairs.

*Fukuzawa Yûkichi, *Fukuzawa Yukichi on Japanese Women: Selected Works* (Tokyo: University of Tokyo Press, 1988), p. 138.

†"The Meiji Reforms and Obstacles for Women Japan, 1878–1927," excerpts from the speeches of Kishida Toshiko, http://www.womeninworldhistory.com/WR-04.html.

‡http://womenshistory.about.com/library/qu/blqutosh.htm?pid=2765&cob=home.

ministers and the oligarchs behind them did not leave economic development to market forces, viewing economic planning as more conducive to social harmony than market competition. (When translating the word "competition" for an economics textbook, Fukuzawa used the word *kyōsō*, literally, "race-fight." A treasury official objected, however: *"I understand the idea,"* said the official, *"but that word 'fight' is not conducive to peace. I could not take the paper with that word to the chancellor."**)

Even after the government sold off its industrial assets and encouraged private capital to play a leading role in commerce and industry, a tight connection between state and private enterprise continued. After 1880, Japanese industry was dominated by **zaibatsu** (zye-BOT-soo), large industrial cartels that collaborated closely with the civil service. (Some of the nineteenth-century zaibatsu, like Mitsubishi, still exist today.) Liberal, free-trade economic notions were never as strong in Japan as in Britain and the United States.

In fact, the Japanese trend, reflecting a global one, was away from liberalism and toward militarism. In 1875, Fukuzawa Yûkichi had cited Mill's *On Liberty* (see Chapter 23) when applauding liberal reforms. As Japan's military competition with her neighbors heated up, however, Fukuzawa took a more nationalistic view, de-emphasizing individual rights and women's rights, while placing a greater emphasis on Japan's collective imperial destiny.

By the 1890s, the great powers, including Japan, were coming to see global competition as a zero-sum struggle for survival. A more cynical Fukuzawa could now write, *"There are only two ways in international relations: to destroy, or to be destroyed....A nation does not come out on top because it is in the right. It is right because it has come out on top."[‡]*

zaibatsu

Large corporations that developed the Japanese industrial economy in close cooperation with the imperial government.

Japanese Imperialism, 1890–1910

Japan was now in a position to be a player in an imperial game whose rules had been established by Europe and the United States. Late in life, believing Japanese national prestige required the acquisition of an empire, Fukuzawa embraced Social Darwinist concepts, promoting the idea that the Japanese were racially superior to other Asians and destined to lead the continent forward. His opinion mattered, not only because of his books and his newspaper, but also because graduates of his own Keio Academy were now rising to power in the Meiji bureaucracy.

Japan flexed its imperial muscle first in Korea, where its forces confronted those of China while both were responding to an uprising in 1894. Japanese victory in the consequent **Sino-Japanese War** (1894–1895) caused a wave of national pride. In addition to acquiring control over Korea and Taiwan, the Meiji government forced Qing China to grant access to treaty ports and rights of extraterritoriality similar to those enjoyed by European powers. At the same time, Japan renegotiated its own treaties with Europe, this time on a basis of equality. Chinese bitterness at the humiliation ran deep. (See the feature "World History in Today's World: Senkaku or Diaoyu Islands?")

Sino-Japanese War

(1894–1895) A war caused by a rivalry over the Korean peninsula; ended with a one-sided treaty that favored Japan, which obtained treaty rights in China as well as control of Korea and Taiwan.

---

*From *The Autobiography of Yukichi Fukuzawa*, by Eiichi Kiyooka, 1960, p. 190.

‡Quoted in Helen M. Hopper, *Fukuzawa Yûkichi: From Samurai to Capitalist* (New York: Pearson Longman, 2005), p. 120.

Senkaku or Diaoyu Islands?

The eight tiny, unpopulated islands in the East China Sea seem an unlikely touchstone for international conflict. But the disputed islands, called *Senkaku* by the Japanese and *Diaoyu* by the Chinese, have sparked repeated confrontations, wars of words that analysts worry might escalate.

The stakes are higher than they may appear. The islands straddle strategic shipping lanes, and their waters may prove rich in oil and gas. Moreover, this territorial dispute brings back divisive historical memories. Japanese conservatives, tired of focusing on transgressions from World War II, are anxious to project a stronger military profile after decades of pacifism. For their part, Chinese nationalists recall with deep resentment the violence inflicted on their ancestors by the Japanese empire, such as the infamous Rape of Nanjing (see Chapter 28). Japan, they believe, has never properly apologized.

Tensions escalated in 2012 when Japanese politicians proposed having the government buy some of the islands from their private owners. "No one will ever be permitted to buy and sell China's sacred territory," responded the Chinese foreign ministry.* Anti-Japanese demonstrations broke out across China, with attacks on Japanese car dealerships and factories. Though calm was restored, both Japanese and Chinese leaders have continued to stoke the nationalist instincts of their citizens by keeping the controversy alive.

In the spring of 2014, the Chinese government took matters one step further by asserting control of the islands' airspace, backing down when U.S. bombers defied that claim. Still, the Chinese defense minister told his American counterpart: "China has indisputable sovereignty over the Diaoyu Islands" and would "make no compromise, no concession, no treaty."[†] Meanwhile, some Japanese, watching how easily the Russian government annexed Crimea in 2014 (see Chapter 32), worried whether the United States would indeed live up to its treaty obligations and back their claim in the case of a Chinese military offensive. Rarely has so little geography contained such grave dangers.

*"Japan Protests at Chinese Ships Near Disputed Islands," *BBC News*, July 11, 2012.

[†]Quoted in Helene Cooper, "Hagel Spars with Chinese over Islands and Security," *New York Times*, April 8, 2014.

Japan pressured Korea to adopt reforms. At first the Korean king allied himself with the Japanese; then in 1896 he sought protection from the Russians. For the next eight years, Korean reformers allied with Japan while the king and other conservatives promoted Russian interests. Meanwhile, Meiji rulers saw the presence of Russian troops in the Qing province of Manchuria as a direct threat to their own "sphere of influence" in northeastern Asia.

The result was the **Russo-Japanese War** of 1904–1905. Just as the Japanese Navy had decimated the northern Qing fleet ten years earlier, now it scored another major victory, destroying or disabling most of Russia's Pacific fleet. While the United States brokered peace negotiations, the Japanese government posted advisers to all the important Korean ministries. In 1910, after a Korean nationalist assassinated the Japanese prime minister, the Meiji government formally annexed Korea.

Japan's victory in the Russo-Japanese War had global consequences. Russia was a traditional European great power, with the world's largest military. Its defeat meant that Japan must now be counted among the great powers of the world. And there was also the question of race. The defeat of a European power by an Asian one inspired nationalists across Asia and Africa with the thought that European superiority was not inevitable.

Russo-Japanese War
(1904–1905) War caused by territorial disputes in Manchuria and Korea. Japan's defeat of Russia was the first victory by an Asian military power over a European one in the industrial age. (1772–1833)

● **CONTEXT&CONNECTIONS** The war with Japan was unpopular in Russia, and defeat added to mounting tensions in the capital of St. Petersburg. After suppressing

Peace Negotiations This print by Kiyochika Kobayashi shows Japanese and Chinese negotiations at the end of the Sino-Japanese War. By the harsh terms of the Treaty of Shimonoseki (1895), the Qing empire ceded the island of Taiwan to Japan, recognized Japanese rights over Korea, and agreed to make substantial reparation payments. The Qing and Meiji diplomats in this portrait are clearly differentiated by their clothing, reflecting the divergent Meiji and Qing attitudes toward adoption of Western ways. (RMN-Grand Palais/Art Resource, NY)

a rebellion in 1905, Tsar Nicholas II finally approved limited reforms. However, as in Qing China after the Boxer Rebellion, they were too little and too late. The Romanov dynasty collapsed in the wake of the First World War to be replaced by the Bolsheviks led by *Vladimir Lenin* (Chapter 27). ●

As Japanese imperial ambitions grew in Asia and the Pacific, Germany, France, Britain, and the United States were also expanding their presence in the region. The world was becoming a smaller place, and the imperial aspirations of the great powers, now including Japan, would become a touchstone of conflict in the twentieth century.

British India, 1818–1905

By the early nineteenth century, the British were the "new Mughals," the dominant political force on the Indian subcontinent. Hundreds of millions of artisans and farmers felt the effects when the British used that political power to drain India of raw materials for Britain's own industrialization.

Unlike the rulers of Qing China and Tokugawa Japan, who initially retained their authority as they struggled to adapt to industrial modernity, Indian elites were subject to direct colonial control. Even so, as the story of Rammohun Roy demonstrated (see Chapter 20), South Asians carried on the same type of debate that could be heard in China and Japan: whether to adjust to the new circumstances by rejecting Western models, by embracing them, or by trying to balance them with indigenous traditions. The first of those choices inspired a major rebellion in 1857, but the British suppressed the revolt and consolidated their rule even further. Indian nationalists then began developing new ideas and organizations in response to the problem of British rule, and by the beginning of the twentieth century they had laid the foundations of modern Indian nationalism.

The Last Phase of Company Rule in India, 1835–1857

The authority of the British East India Company had spread across the subcontinent after the Battle of Plassey in 1757, though as late as the 1830s many Indians were still just beginning to feel the impact of British rule. At that time, Rammohun Roy (see Chapter 20) was one of only a handful of Indians who had learned English and begun to assimilate European ideas.

Over the next two decades, however, the implications of British rule for Indians, both peasants and elites, greatly intensified. The reasons were largely economic, stemming from the international impact of the industrial revolution. While Mughal rulers had promoted the South Asian commercial economy's connection with Indian Ocean markets, the British yoked the Indian economy to British commercial and industrial interests.

As we have seen, one result was Indian *deindustrialization*, notably in the textile manufacturing centers of the northeastern region of Bengal (see Chapter 23). By 1830, unemployment among India's textile workers was reaching a critical level, leaving India "to fall backward in time . . . losing most of its artisan manufacturing abilities, forcing millions of unemployed craftsmen to return to the soil."* In Bengal we find that the rural-to-urban migration of English industrialization was actually reversed.

Technological and social changes caused shifts in Anglo-Indian social and cultural interactions as well. Steamships, telegraphs, and (after 1869) the Suez Canal, shortened the distance between Europe and India. Company employees who had previously spoken Indian languages, worn Indian clothing, and established relationships with Indian women were now more likely to bring British wives with them, use English both privately and in their official capacities, and hold themselves aloof from Indian society. In segregated British towns, officials now carefully followed the rituals of Victorian social life, dressing formally for dinner no matter how high the temperature and replacing local curries with tinned meats from home. Every British outpost had a "club" where British officials and merchants gathered to socialize. Indians—no matter how accomplished—were excluded, except as servants.

Such cultural distancing contributed to a tense political situation in the 1850s. Meanwhile, increasing British intrusion on Indian customs and ways of life provoked a powerful counter-reaction, especially after an increase in the number of British missionaries stoked Indian concerns that the British were seeking to overturn their cultural traditions and convert them to a foreign religion. This fear,

---

*Stanley Wolpert, *India* (Berkeley: University of California Press, 1991), p. 51.

combined with economic strains and the loss of support for the British presence from some of India's traditional elites, created a volatile situation.

The Indian Revolt of 1857 and Its Aftermath

The **Indian Revolt of 1857** began with a mutiny among the sepoys (SEE-poyz), the two hundred thousand Indian soldiers under British command. The immediate cause of the revolt was Britain's introduction of a new, faster-loading rifle. The loading procedure required soldiers to bite off the greased ends of the guns' ammunition cartridge casings. The rumor spread among Muslim troops that the cartridges had been greased with pig fat; many Hindus believed that fat from cattle had been used. Since contact with pork was forbidden to Muslims and cattle were sacred to Hindus, both groups suspected that the British were trying to pollute them as part of a plot to convert them to Christianity. (See the feature "Movement of Ideas Through Primary Sources: Religion and Rebellion: India in 1858.")

A group of soldiers killed their British officers after some soldiers were arrested for refusing to use the new cartridges. They marched to Delhi and rallied support for the restoration of the aging Mughal emperor. The revolt quickly spread across northern and western India, where the rani (queen) of Jhansi (JAN-see), one of the Maratha kingdoms, rode into battle with her troops. Violence was terrible on both sides, the rebels sometimes killing British women and children, and the British strapping rebels to cannon and blowing them to pieces. The resulting bitterness would long poison race relations in the British Raj, further accelerating the process of segregation.

British observers believed that the cause of the rebellion was simply the backwardness of the Indian people. Earlier liberal beliefs in Indian capacity were now challenged by the Social Darwinist notion that South Asians (like Africans) were naturally and permanently inferior, both culturally and genetically.

The Indian rebels knew what they were fighting against but were less unified about what they were fighting for. In South Asia the cultural, linguistic, and religious landscape was exceptionally diverse, making it all the more necessary to develop a sense of identity embracing all the peoples under British rule. Lack of unity and coordination among regional rebellions, however, made it easy for the British to retake control.

By 1858 the revolt was over, and the British government responded by disbanding the East India Company and abolishing the last vestiges of Mughal authority. In 1876, Queen Victoria added "Empress of India" to her titles. The British now emphasized alliances with conservative Indian elites, such as the maharajahs and sultans who were allowed to keep nominal control over "princely states," while the British retained real power for themselves, centralizing the colonial administration and enhancing its fiscal responsibilities. At the top of that system stood the Indian Civil Service, elite government officials selected on the basis of a rigorous examination. In theory, anyone who passed the examination could join the Indian Civil Service. Since the exams were only administered in England, however, Indian candidates did not have a realistic chance.

Westernized Indians, following the example of the earlier Bengal Renaissance in their quest to balance indigenous and imported cultural traditions, were dismayed when the British mocked them for trying to assimilate English culture, and were disheartened when the British turned to the remnants of the old aristocracy for allies. In 1885 they organized a new political movement called the Indian National Congress.

Indian Revolt of 1857

Revolt of Indian soldiers against British officers when they were required to use greased ammunition cartridges they suspected were being used to pollute them and cause them to convert to Christianity. The revolt spread across north India.

Religion and Rebellion: India in 1858

The following passage was written in the Urdu language in 1858 by an Indian Muslim, Maulvi Syed Kutb Shah Sahib. Maulvi Syed saw the Indian Revolt as a chance to drive the British out of India. In this letter to Hindu leaders, he urged Hindu-Muslim cooperation to accomplish that goal, arguing that the British were consciously defiling both religions in an attempt to force conversions to Christianity.

One of the grievances Maulvi Syed mentions is British laws concerning widows. Islamic law encourages the remarriage of widows, following the example of Muhammad, whose wife Khadijah was a widow. Among Hindus, however, patriarchal beliefs dictated that a wife's life was essentially over once her husband died. Thus the custom of sati encouraged widows to throw themselves on the fire when their husbands were cremated to demonstrate their devotion and to allow them to be reunited in the next life. In fact, relatively few Hindu women, usually from the highest castes, actually did so. In 1829, with the approval of the Bengali reformer Rammohun Roy, the British abolished sati and issued another order that widows should be allowed to remarry (see Chapter 20).

Another controversy to which the author refers is the "doctrine of lapse," a colonial ruling that if an Indian prince died without a male heir, direct control over his territory would go to the British, ignoring local traditions of adoption and inheritance. In 1856, the city of Lucknow and the rich province of Awadh had been taken over by the British through this device.

> What reasons does Maulvi Syed give to justify the rebellion? Which of those reasons does he feel are most important?

> If you were an Indian follower of Rammohun Roy (see Chapter 20), how would you respond to Maulvi Syed's arguments?

Source: Records of the Government of the Punjab and Its Dependencies, New Series, No. VII (Lahore: Punjab Printing Company, 1870), pp. 173–175.

Maulvi Syed on British Christians

The English are people who overthrow all religions. You should understand well the object of destroying the religions of Hindustan [India]; they have for a long time been causing books to be written and circulated throughout the country by the hands of their priests, and, exercising their authority, have brought out numbers of preachers to spread their own tenets....

Consider, then, what systematic contrivances they have adopted to destroy our religions. For instance, first, when a woman became a widow they ordered her to make a second marriage. Secondly, the self-immolation of wives [sati] on the funeral pyres of their deceased husbands was an ancient religious custom; the English...enacted their own regulations prohibiting it. Thirdly, they told people it was their wish that they...should adopt their faith, promising that if they did so they would be respected by Government; and further required them to attend churches, and hear the tenets preached there.

Moreover, they decided and told the rajahs that such only as were born of their wives would inherit the government and property, and that adopted heirs would not be allowed to succeed, although, according to your [Hindu] Scriptures, ten different sorts of heirs are allowed to share in the inheritance. By this contrivance they will rob you of your governments and possessions, as they have already done with Nagpur and Lucknow.

Consider now another of their designing plans: they resolved on compelling prisoners, with the forcible exercise of their authority, to eat their bread. Numbers died of starvation, but did not eat it, others ate it, and sacrificed their faith. They now perceived that this expedient did not succeed well, and accordingly determined on having bones ground and mixed with flour and sugar, so that people might unsuspectingly eat them in this way. They had, moreover, bones and flesh broken small and mixed with rice, which they caused to be placed in the markets for sale, and tried, besides, every other possible plan to destroy our religions.

They accordingly now ordered the Brahmins and others of their army to bite cartridges, in the making of which fat had been used. The Muslim soldiers perceived that by this expedient the religion of the Brahmans and Hindus only was in danger, but nevertheless they also refused to bite them. On this the British resolved on ruining the faith of both, and [lashed to the cannons] all those soldiers who persisted in their refusal [and blew them to pieces]. Seeing this excessive tyranny, the soldiery now, in self-preservation, began killing the English, and slew them wherever they were found, and are now considering means for slaying the few still alive here and there. It is now my firm conviction that if these English continue in Hindustan they will kill everyone in the country, and will utterly overthrow our religions; but there are some of my countrymen who have joined the English, and are fighting on their side....

Under these circumstances, I would ask, what course have you decided on to protect your lives and faith? Were your views and mine the same we might destroy them entirely with a very little trouble; and if we do so, we shall protect our religions and save the country....

All you Hindus are hereby solemnly adjured, by your faith in Ganges; and all you Muslims, by your belief in God and the Koran, as these English are the common enemy of both, to unite in considering their slaughter extremely expedient, for by this alone will the lives and faith of both be saved....

The slaughter of cows is regarded by the Hindus as a great insult to their religion. To prevent this a solemn compact and agreement has been entered into by all the Muslim chiefs of Hindustan, binding themselves, that if the Hindus will come forward to slay the English, the Muslims will from that very day put a stop to the slaughter of cows, and those of them who will not do so will be considered to have abjured the Koran, and such of them as will eat beef will be regarded as though they had eaten pork....

The English are always deceitful. Once their ends are gained they will infringe their engagements, for deception has ever been habitual with them, and the treachery they have always practiced on the people of Hindustan is known to rich and poor. Do not therefore give heed to what they say. Be well assured you will never have such an opportunity again.

Popperfoto/Getty Images

Princely States After the Indian Revolt of 1857, the British placed a greater emphasis on cooperating with traditional Indian authorities, sometimes recognizing their nominal sovereignty over "princely states." Here a British "resident" is surrounded by maharajas and nawabs of the northwestern Punjab province in 1895. Such rulers maintained luxurious lifestyles while helping stabilize colonial rule. The same use of "native authorities" would characterize British Africa (see Chapter 26).

The Origins of Indian Nationalism, 1885–1906

After 1857, amid all the political and social tensions, the Indian economy grew. As in Europe, railroads played a major role (see Map 24.2). The British imported tracks and engines, benefiting British manufacturers and workers, while Indian taxpayers financed 50,000 miles (80,500 km) of rail construction. The primary economic purpose of the railways was to speed the export of Indian raw materials, such as cotton, in support of British industry, as well as the import of British manufactured goods, such as the iron goods and finished textiles that were displacing India's own manufactures. Fukuzawa Yûkichi was critical of these impacts: *"Have the European countries,"* he asked, *"really respected the rights and interests and integrity of the countries with which they have come into contact? . . . Wherever the Europeans come, the land ceases to be productive."**

*Cited in Carmen Blacker, *The Japanese Enlightenment, A Study of the Writings of Fukuzawa Yukichi* (New York: Cambridge University Press, 1969), p. 131.

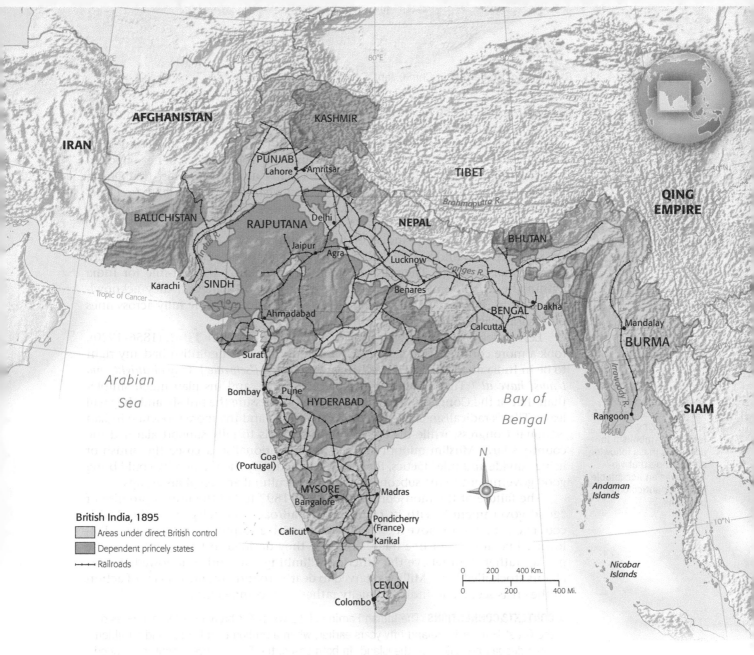

Map 24.2 Indian Railroads, 1893 After the Indian Revolt of 1857, the British stabilized their rule by allying themselves more strongly with traditional Indian rulers. Some of the "princely states" were very extensive and their rulers, such as the Nizams of Hyderabad, were quite wealthy. Even in the princely states, however, the British were clearly predominant. After 1857, the British built an extensive railroad and telegraph network to tighten their control, though improved transport and communications had the unintended consequence of helping bring Indians together from across the subcontinent, fueling the growth of Indian nationalism.

Still, developing networks of transportation and communication brought benefits to Indians. Railroads, along with telegraphs and a postal service, created a communications infrastructure that put India's diverse peoples and regions in closer contact than ever before and served as a crucial precondition for nationalist organization.

India's emerging middle class, now often educated in English following a British school curriculum, had the clearest vision of "India" as a single, unified

Indian National Congress

(1885) Formed by wealthy, Western-educated Indians to advance the cause of Indian involvement in their own governance. In the twentieth century, it would become the vehicle for India's independence under the leadership of Mohandas K. Gandhi.

Bal Gangadhar Tilak

(1856–1920) Indian nationalist who demanded immediate independence from Britain, mobilizing Hindu religious symbolism to develop a mass following and arguing that violence was an acceptable tactic for anticolonial partisans.

political space. In the beginning, however, the relatively advantaged men of the **Indian National Congress** cared most about the interests of their own social class. For example, the Congress campaigned to have the Indian Civil Service examination administered in India so that Indians would have a better opportunity to compete. They challenged their rulers to live up to the promise that Queen Victoria had made in 1858, that *"our subjects, of whatever race or creed, be freely and impartially admitted to office in our service, the duties of which they may be qualified by their education, ability, and integrity."**

At the beginning, the Indian National Congress was fighting not to change the system but to find a place within it, believing that slow reform was better than revolutionary change. They did not seek independence, but self-rule for India within the British empire. And self-rule could not be achieved, they acknowledged, until India's people learned to respect one another more fully across lines of religion, caste, and language.

Less patient Indian nationalists, notably **Bal Gangadhar Tilak** (1856–1920), took a more confrontational approach, questioning why the British had any right to be in India at all. Tilak (TIH-lak) declared: *"Swaraj ['self-rule'] is my birthright, and I must have it!"†* Tilak's appeal was more emotional, and his plan much simpler than that of the Congress: organize the masses to pressure the British, and they will leave. Tilak's radicalism challenged both the British and the more moderate Indian National Congress, while his use of Hindu symbols to rally support alarmed the country's large Muslim minority. While Indian nationalists accused the British of using "divide and rule" tactics, the British claimed only their neutrality could bring good government to the subcontinent's diverse cultural and religious groups.

The failure of the monsoon rains in 1896–1897 tested the British promise of "good government." With its command of railroads and telegraphs, the British could be expected to move food from regions with a surplus to those in need. Following liberal ideas of free trade, however, they decided to leave matters to the market rather than relieve the suffering. Climbing grain prices followed as merchants stockpiled food. Millions starved to death. To Indians, British lack of action in the crisis seemed to indicate cruelty rather than competency.

● **CONTEXT&CONNECTIONS** The Indian Famine of 1896–1897 brought back memories of the Great Hunger in Ireland fifty years earlier, when a million people died and a million more despairing exiles left the island. In both cases, the British government, convinced of the superiority of market forces over state economic intervention, refused to implement sufficiently active relief programs to save the lives of their colonial subjects. ●

The British government, meanwhile, continued to use spectacular public rituals to display its power and legitimize its rule. The most impressive was the "durbar" procession, a combination of circus, parade, and political theater held at Delhi in 1903, which featured maharajahs in ceremonial garb, hundreds of parading elephants, tens of thousands of marching soldiers, and elaborate salutes to the new King Edward VII, Emperor of India.

Grand political theater notwithstanding, conflict arose in 1905 when British bureaucrats, for no reason other than administrative expediency, decided to split

---

*Proclamation by the Queen to the Princes, Chiefs, and the People of India, November 1, 1858.

†Quoted in Stanley A. Wolpert, *Tilak and Gokhale: Revolution and Reform in the Making of Modern India* (Berkeley: University of California Press, 1991), p. 191.

in two the culturally and economically integrated northeastern province of Bengal. No Indians were consulted about the **Partition of Bengal**, which created a predominantly Muslim province in the east. Nationalists again accused the British of using communal rivalries to reinforce their power by separating Hindus from Muslims.

● **CONTEXT&CONNECTIONS** At the end of the colonial era, British India was in fact partitioned between two separate states: the Republic of India (with a Hindu majority) and Pakistan (with a Muslim majority). The partition line of 1905 is now a national border, with Bengali-speakers divided between the Indian state of West Bengal and the separate nation of Bangladesh (see Chapter 30). ●

Protesting the Partition of Bengal, the Indian National Congress organized a boycott of British goods. Bengali activists made huge bonfires of English cloth across the province. Conditions were now ripe for the development of mass nationalism, bringing together the Western-educated elite of the congress and the millions of urban and rural Indians struggling toward a better future. The new spirit was captured by Rabindranath Tagore, a Nobel Prize winning poet whose grandfather had been a close colleague of Rammohun Roy:

> *Where the mind is without fear and the head is held high . . .*
> *Where the world has not been broken up into fragments by narrow domestic walls . . .*
> *Where words come out from the depth of truth;*
> *Where the clear stream of reason has not lost its way into the dreary desert sand of dead habit . . .*
> *Into that heaven of freedom, my Father, let my country awake.**

Tagore's vision came a step closer to realization in 1906 when Mohandas K. Gandhi (1869–1948), then a little-known lawyer, returned home from leading South Africa's Indian community in protests against racial discrimination. Gandhi (GAHN-dee) would soon come to symbolize a new India, forging alliances between leaders and people to lead his country toward independence (see Chapter 28).

India: Swami Vivekananda, Jaipur, c.1895/Pictures From History/Bridgeman Images

Swami Vivekananda Since the nineteenth century, Hindu spirituality, including the practice of yoga, has had a global appeal. Swami Vivekananda (1863–1902) played an important role, developing a large following in Europe, and in the United States after he addressed an international religious gathering in Chicago at the time of the Columbian Exposition (see Chapter 25). Like members of the earlier Bengal Renaissance, Vivekananda advocated a reformed Hinduism purged of superstition and caste prejudice.

Partition of Bengal
(1905) A British partition of the wealthy northeastern Indian province of Bengal for administrative expediency; became a touchpoint of anticolonial agitation.

---

*Rabindranath Tagore, "Chitto Jetha Bhayashunyo (Where the Mind Is Without Fear)," http://allpoetry.com/Where-The-Mind-Is-Without-Fear.

Asia in the Modern World

Even prior to 1800, Asian societies were contending with the challenges of modernity. Commercial expansion and the growth of cities in the seventeenth and eighteenth centuries were signs of economic and social dynamism but strained the cultural traditions and political institutions in Mughal India, Qing China, and Tokugawa Japan (see Chapter 20). This was the world of Fukuzawa Yûkichi's childhood, one in which his family's samurai traditions were no longer in sync with the evolution of Japanese society.

Rapid population growth was an even greater modern challenge: China's population grew from about 110 million in 1600 to 330 million in 1800, India's from approximately 100 million to 225 million, and Japan's from 12 million to 30 million. During the eighteenth-century agricultural revolution in Britain, innovators like Joseph Banks brought greater productivity to rural areas (while displacing many farmers in the process; see Chapter 21). In contrast, the growth of food production in Asia was largely *extensive* rather than *intensive*, requiring peasant communities to bring marginal lands under cultivation to keep pace with population growth. In manufacturing as well, Asian growth was based on the abundance of cheap labor rather than on innovations leading to higher productivity per worker.

By the early nineteenth century, the Industrial Revolution in the West had greatly magnified the difference in economic productivity between western Europe and South and East Asia (see Chapter 23). By the mid-nineteenth century, industrialization and its new technologies gave European nations both the motive and the means to intervene more forcefully in Asian affairs.

India was already feeling the impact in the late eighteenth century (see Chapter 20). In gradually expanding British East India Company authority at the expense of the Mughal empire, the British took advantage of the centrifugal force of Indian regionalism. At first, the British largely accommodated themselves to Indian languages and cultures, but after 1800, and especially after the rebellion of 1857, they formed a tightly bound ruling clique. In responding to British rule, Indian reformers faced the challenge of resisting British political and cultural intrusions while at the same time absorbing British influences.

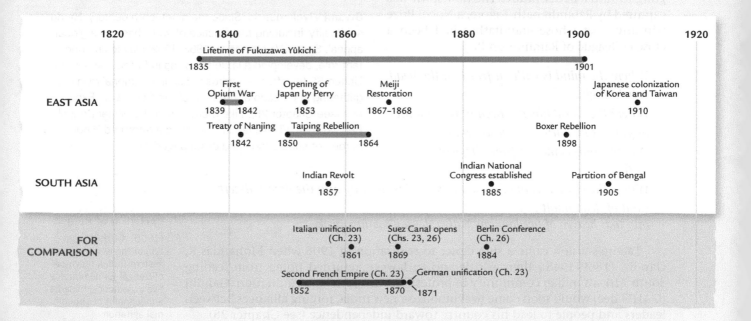

742

China's confrontation with the industrial West came much more suddenly. Only two generations separated the British diplomatic mission of 1793, arrogantly dismissed by the Qianlong emperor (see Chapter 20), and the humiliation of the first Opium War of 1839. The remainder of the nineteenth century saw China's Confucian elite, in the midst of foreign invasions and domestic rebellions, struggle to find a response. The changes advocated by partisans of Self-Strengthening might have been enough to propel the empire toward modernization, but the resistance of conservatives doomed all such initiatives. The occupation of the Forbidden City in 1900 by foreigners once disparaged as "barbarians" was the deepest possible humiliation, one from which twentieth-century Chinese leaders would strive to recover.

Japan also had its conservatives who resisted change, and before 1868 it was by no means clear that Fukuzawa's relentless advocacy of reform along Western lines would be successful. After the Meiji Restoration, however, Fukuzawa's plans were implemented. By 1910, the Japanese had defeated both the Chinese and the Russians, renegotiated unequal treaties, and built the infrastructure of a modern industrial state. Meiji authorities could boast that they, alone among Asian leaders, had transformed their nation from a victim into a player in the global competition for military prestige and economic growth.

It would take another century for China to return to its long-standing position as the largest economy in Asia, joining independent India as one of the world's fastest-growing countries (see Chapter 32). Even as its economy surpassed that of Japan in 2011, however, China still lagged far behind the United States, which, even back in 1900, had set the pace, simultaneously the world's largest industrial and agricultural producer.

Key Terms

Fukuzawa Yûkichi (716)
Opium Wars (718)
Treaty of Nanjing (718)
Taiping Rebellion (719)
Self-Strengthening Movement (720)
Empress Ci Xi (721)

Boxer Rebellion (722)
Commodore Matthew Perry (727)
Meiji Restoration (729)
Kishida Toshiko (730)
zaibatsu (731)
Sino-Japanese War (731)

Russo-Japanese War (732)
Indian Revolt of 1857 (735)
Indian National Congress (740)
Bal Gangadhar Tilak (740)
Partition of Bengal (741)

For Further Reference

Anderson, Marnie S. *A Place in Public: Women's Rights in Meiji Japan*. Cambridge, Mass.: Harvard University Asia Center, 2011.

Cohn, Bernard S. *Colonialism and Its Forms of Knowledge: The British in India*. Princeton: Princeton University Press, 1996.

Dalrymple, William. *The Last Mughal: The Fall of a Dynasty, Delhi 1857*. New York: Vintage, 2008.

Fogel, Joshua A., ed. *Late Qing China and Meiji Japan: Political and Cultural Aspects*. Norwalk, Conn.: Eastbridge Press, 2004.

Fukuzawa, Yûkichi. *The Autobiography of Yûkichi Fukuzawa*. Eiichi Kiyooka, trans. New York: Columbia University Press, 1960.

Hobsbawm, Eric. *The Age of Empire, 1875–1914*. New York: Vintage, 1989.

Jansen, Marius B. *The Making of Modern Japan*. Cambridge, Mass.: Harvard University Press, 2000.

Rawksi, Evelyn Sakakida. *The Last Emperors: A Social History of Qing Imperial Institutions*. Berkeley: University of California Press, 2001.

Spence, Jonathan. *God's Chinese Son: The Taiping Heavenly Kingdom of Hong Xiuquan*. New York: W. W. Norton, 1997.

Wiley, Peter Booth. *Yankees in the Land of the Gods: Commodore Perry and the Opening of Japan*. New York: Penguin, 1991.

Zachmann, Urs Matthias. *China and Japan in the Late Meiji Period: China Policy and the Japanese Discourse on National Identity, 1895–1904*. New York: Routledge, 2009.

 **MindTap** is a fully online, highly personalized learning experience built upon Cengage Learning content. MindTap combines student learning tools—readings, multimedia, activities, and assessments—into a singular Learning Path that guides students through the course.

State Building and Social Change in the Americas, 1830–1910

Pauline Johnson-Tekahionwake

g14 collection/Alamy

Pauline Johnson-Tekahionwake (1861–1913) watched nervously as several older male poets recited their verse. It was the winter of 1892, and the hall in Toronto was packed for an "Evening with Canadian Authors." Her ambition was to be a well-known, financially independent poet, and here was her chance to make an impression. She chose to recite "A Cry from an Indian Wife," a poem that focused on her concern with Canada's First Nations, its indigenous inhabitants:

*T*hey but forget we Indians owned
the land
From ocean unto ocean; that
they stand
Upon a soil that centuries agone
Was our sole kingdom and our right alone.
They never think how they would feel today,
If some great nation came from far away,
Wresting their country from their hapless braves,
Giving what they gave us—but war and graves . . .
Go forth, nor bend to greed of white man's hands,
By right, by birth we Indians own these lands,
Though starved, crushed, plundered, lies our nation low . . .
Perhaps the white man's God has willed it so.*

*Excerpt from *Flint and Feather: The Complete Poems of E. Pauline Johnson (Tekahionwake)*. Toronto and London: The Musson Book Co., Ltd., 1912.

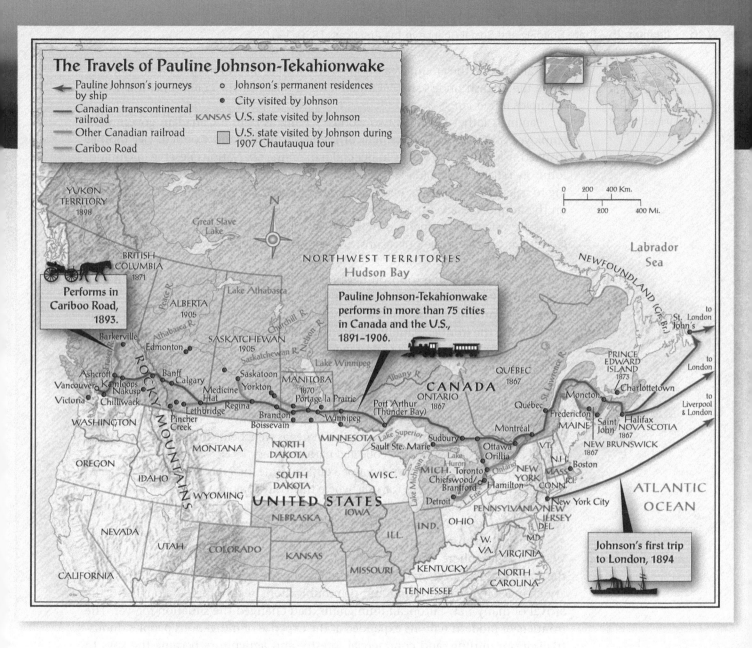

The Travels of Pauline Johnson-Tekahionwake

- ← Pauline Johnson's journeys by ship
- ━ Canadian transcontinental railroad
- ━ Other Canadian railroad
- ━ Cariboo Road
- ● Johnson's permanent residences
- ● City visited by Johnson
- KANSAS U.S. state visited by Johnson
- ☐ U.S. state visited by Johnson during 1907 Chautauqua tour

Performs in Cariboo Road, 1893.

Pauline Johnson-Tekahionwake performs in more than 75 cities in Canada and the U.S., 1891–1906.

Johnson's first trip to London, 1894

Patriotic Canadians might have heard these as dissonant words; nevertheless, they gave Johnson's powerful performance loud applause.

"A Cry from an Indian Wife" reflected Johnson's own mixed ancestry. Her father's family was Mohawk, an Iroquois (IR-uh-kwoi) band that had established a close alliance with the British during the colonial period. As a child, Pauline would listen to Mohawk legends and tales of a family history that included Joseph Brant, the Mohawk leader who had fought with the British in the American War of Independence (see Chapter 22). The British family connection went deeper when Pauline's father married an Englishwoman. Their wedding photograph shows optimism toward this

Pauline Johnson-Tekahionwake

(1861–1913) Canadian poet of mixed English and Mohawk ancestry.

cultural mixture: the groom wears both British medals and an Iroquois wampum belt, while the English bride's stiff Victorian attire is offset by the ceremonial tomahawk she holds in her lap.

Pauline's father balanced two worlds, serving as both a Canadian government employee and a respected member of the Six Nations Band Council. Her mother instilled strict Victorian values in her children on the Six Nations Reserve in Ontario. Johnson-Tekahionwake (da-geh-eeon-WA-geh) would have a lifelong challenge trying to balance her Mohawk heritage with her English ancestry. Though she grew up on the Iroquois reserve, she spoke only English, and though fascinated by Mohawk tales, she was most influenced by British literature. She was a loyal and patriotic Canadian, yet she spoke out against her country's policies toward indigenous First Nations societies.

As an adult, Pauline Johnson began to use her father's Mohawk family name, Tekahionwake ("double life"), in advertisements for a new career: traveling across Canada performing her poetry. Variety shows had become a popular form of entertainment on the frontier. Pauline Johnson-Tekahionwake became one of the nation's best-known entertainers. Her performances drew attention to her dual heritage. She took the stage in a dramatic buckskin outfit to perform poems such as "A Cry from an Indian Wife," after intermission reappearing in a Victorian evening gown to recite poems of nature and love. Having found a way to earn a living through her art—a challenge for a woman of her time—Johnson-Tekahionwake crossed Canada nineteen times, often performing in the United States as well, before retiring to Vancouver on the Pacific coast, where she collected native stories.

But the late nineteenth century was a difficult time for a mixed-race person. Racial divisions were sharpening in Canada, where the white majority thought that Amerindian peoples were doomed to disappear in the face of industrial and commercial progress, symbolized by the very railroad that Johnson used to reach her audience.

Indeed, the nineteenth century was a time of relentless change across the Western Hemisphere. In 1830, much of North and South America still lay outside the control of European-derived governments. By the end of the century revolutionary changes in transportation and communications technologies, along with the arrival of many new European immigrants, had changed the situation forever. The frontiers of modern nations expanded at the expense of indigenous peoples. Industrialization, mining, and commercial forestry and agriculture became the keys to wealth and power in the Americas.

Perhaps the most striking feature of this period was the rise of the United States as both the dominant hemispheric power and a global force. Canada was also a growing economic power, where many shared in rising prosperity. In Latin America, where industrialization lagged behind, only privileged elites enjoyed the benefits of state building.

Telegraphs, steamships and railroads, massive new cities, and enormous industrial fortunes helped consolidate the power of national states, while posing challenges to many older ways of life. Social readjustments in the nineteenth-century Americas included the abolition of slavery, the arrival of new immigrants, the struggle of workers for rights and representation, changing gender relations, and as Johnson-Tekahionwake's story indicates, difficult times for indigenous peoples.

Political Consolidation in Canada and the United States

Consolidation of state power was a major feature of nineteenth-century North America. Canada overcame deep regional divisions to become a nation, while the United States emerged from the Civil War with the federal government more powerful and ambitious than ever before. In both cases, governments extended their authority more deeply into society and more broadly across the continent. Through activities and acquisitions in the Caribbean and Pacific, by century's end the United States had become an imperial power as well.

Confederation in Canada

Canada was a product of slow evolution rather than revolutionary transformation. In 1830, British North America consisted of more than half a dozen disconnected colonies. Yet by 1892, when Pauline Johnson-Tekahionwake made her debut on a Toronto stage, Canadians possessed a strong national identity even while affiliating themselves with the British empire. Like many, Johnson-Tekahionwake was proud of being both Canadian and British: "*And we, the men of Canada, can face the world and brag/That we were born in Canada beneath the British flag.*"*

British North America contained a diversity of peoples and landscapes. Upper Canada, with its capital at Toronto on the northern shore of Lake Ontario, was the fastest-growing region, where cheap land attracted English, Irish, and Scottish immigrants. Lower Canada, the lands along the St. Lawrence River known as Québec, retained its French-speaking Catholic majority, the *Québecois* (kay-bek-KWAH). The Atlantic colonies were primarily populated by seafaring people dependent on the bounty of the Atlantic Ocean. And at the opposite end was British Columbia, its Pacific capital of Victoria more accessible to San Francisco than to Toronto.

Far from the main population centers lay trading posts that brought commercial opportunity to the frontier, but also guns, alcohol, and violence to indigenous

---

*Excerpt from *Flint and Feather: The Complete Poems of E. Pauline Johnson (Tekahionwake).* Toronto and London: The Musson Book Co., Ltd., 1912.

A Métis Man and His Wives The métis of the Canadian frontier were culturally and biologically mixed descendants of French traders and First Nations women. Protective of their independence, many métis resisted incorporation into the Canadian confederation, often in alliance with First Nations communities. These rebellions were defeated by Canadian forces in 1869 and 1885.

responsible government

Nineteenth-century constitutional arrangement in British North America that allowed colonies to achieve dominion status within the British empire and elect parliaments responsible for internal affairs. The British appointed governors as their sovereign's representative and retained control of foreign policy.

communities (see Chapter 18). Several First Nations, such as the Cree, Ojibwa (oh-JIB-wuh), and Sioux (soo), still lived freely on the Great Plains. Mingled among them were communities of French-speaking *métis* (may-TEE), frontiersmen of mixed European-Amerindian descent. Farther from the main areas of European settlement and British control were the Inuit hunters of the far north.

Having learned from the American War of Independence to accommodate settlers' political ambitions, the British government offered Britons who emigrated to British North America (or to Australia, New Zealand, or South Africa) limited participation in government, while still appointing a governor from London. By 1830, however, British North Americans were calling for **responsible government**, which would give many powers of the British-appointed governor to a prime minister, leader of the dominant party in parliamentary elections. As the climate for reform increased in Britain (see Chapter 23), an official report recommended responsible government for Canada, as well as a cut in tariffs on imports to Canada that led to a boom in cross-border trade with the United States.

Most French-speakers also favored these changes. As far back as 1763, the British Parliament had guaranteed equal rights for French-speaking Catholics. Despite the influx of British settlers, most Québecois trusted that British constitutional models would protect their linguistic, religious, and cultural traditions.

Likewise, many First Nations peoples in Canada favored continuing association with the British empire. For the Johnson family, whose ancestors had fought alongside the British for generations, the beneficence of Britain and of Queen Victoria was unquestioned. With such consensus, and with British support, the birth and evolution of Canada took place peacefully, especially once the American Civil War (1861–1865; discussed in the next section) gave Britain an added incentive to stabilize its North American territories.

Thus in 1867, the British Parliament passed the British North America Act, creating the **Confederation of Canada** with a federal capital at Ottawa. Though only four of the current Canadian provinces were included in the original confederation, its legal framework was established. Canada was now a "dominion" within the British empire. Local affairs were in the hands of the Canadian and provincial governments. However, Queen Victoria appointed a governor-general to represent the Crown, and Britain continued to control Canada's foreign relations.

Political consolidation and economic growth went hand in hand after 1867 with the building of the **Canadian Pacific Railway** (1867–1884). The railway led to the incorporation of new provinces (Manitoba, the Northwest Territories, and British Columbia), while utterly transforming Canada's Great Plains.

Before the Industrial Revolution, the plains' tough grasses supported only buffalo and, later, horses and cattle. Now, with the advent of cheap steel plows and the inexpensive transport provided by the railway, grain production boomed. Canadian wheat exports rose from 10 million bushels in 1896 to 145 million bushels in 1914. Over a million farmers and their families moved out onto the prairie, taking advantage of free land and the cheap agricultural implements churned out by the new industrial plants. They were the audience for Pauline Johnson-Tekahionwake as she took her act to the town halls and opera houses springing up in farming centers and mining camps. Marking the rise of the Canadian west, Alberta and Saskatchewan (sa-SKACH-uh-won) entered the confederation in 1905 (see the map on page 745).

● **CONTEXT&CONNECTIONS** Locked up in the North American prairie was a staggering potential of calories for human consumption, but without domesticated herds or steel tools to cut through the tough grassland soil, Amerindians could extract only a limited amount, mainly by hunting buffalo. Then, with the *Columbian exchange* (key term in Chapter 15), came cattle, along with the horses needed to manage them. By the late nineteenth century, the American buffalo had been hunted nearly to extinction and its habitat overrun, first by open cattle ranges then by farmers using steel plows to turn the soil and plant imported grains like wheat, displacing native grasses. From this transformed landscape, vast supplies of grain and meat entered global markets. ●

A stable and effective federal government promoted economic growth in Canada. Twenty-five years of Conservative Party dominance ended in 1896, followed by four consecutive elections won by the Liberals, with a strong centrist base. The Liberal Party emphasized "race fusion," acknowledging Canada as a bicultural land where English and French, Protestant and Catholic, could live in peace, forging a Canadian identity based on mutual tolerance. Canadians did not always live up to that ideal: Amerindians and Asian immigrants experienced sometimes brutal racism. Still, a unique nationalism accommodating Canada's affiliation with the British empire was taking shape.

Confederation of Canada

(1867) Confederation of former British colonies united under a single federal constitution, a dominion within the British empire.

Canadian Pacific Railway

(1881–1885) The railway's completion led to the transcontinental integration of Canada and opened Canada's Great Plains to European settlement.

Sectionalism and Civil War in the United States

Unlike Canada, the United States entered the nineteenth century with a strong constitution and a lively sense of national identity. (See the feature "Movement of Ideas Through Primary Sources: Alexis de Tocqueville's *Democracy in America*.") The Louisiana Purchase of 1803 gave the young country a sense of unbounded opportunity, opening paths westward (see Map 25.1). But westward expansion also provoked crisis. As new states entered the Union, would they be slave states or free? Could balance between the North and South be maintained? Would American nationalism prove stronger than American sectionalism?

Map 25.1 U.S. Expansion, 1783–1867 The United States expanded dramatically during the decades after independence. Vast territories were purchased from France (the Louisiana Purchase) and Russia (Alaska), acquired by treaty with Great Britain (the Pacific Northwest) and Spain (Florida), and annexed from Mexico after its defeat in the Mexican-American War (the desert Southwest and California). Contemporaries in the United States regarded this transcontinental growth as the nation's "manifest destiny."

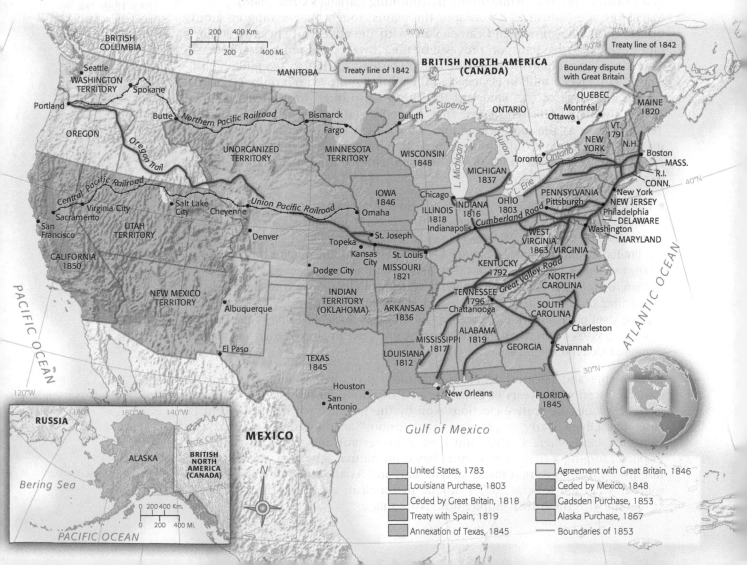

Legend:
- United States, 1783
- Louisiana Purchase, 1803
- Ceded by Great Britain, 1818
- Treaty with Spain, 1819
- Annexation of Texas, 1845
- Agreement with Great Britain, 1846
- Ceded by Mexico, 1848
- Gadsden Purchase, 1853
- Alaska Purchase, 1867
- Boundaries of 1853

An important context for those questions was the massive economic expansion of the United States in the first half of the nineteenth century, what historians have called a "market revolution." The technological advances of the Industrial Revolution led to an economy focused on factories, cities, and market-oriented farming in the North and, in the South, on the massive expansion of cotton planting resulting from industrialized textile production (see Chapter 23).

Better roads and, especially, canals and railways linked producers with markets as never before. The completion in 1825 of the 363-mile Erie Canal, for example, connected the Great Lakes with New York City, drastically lowering the costs of transporting grain to eastern cities and across the Atlantic. The Southern economy was also booming: by 1860 cotton made up more than half the value of U.S. exports. But the economies of North and South were diverging further as a result.

Populism and expanded democracy marked the presidency of **Andrew Jackson** (in office 1829–1837). Unlike previous American presidents, Jackson, a hero of the war with Britain in 1812, presented himself as representing the common man, emphasizing his humble roots rather than his experiences as a slaveholder and plantation owner. Jackson's emphasis on populist democracy was symbolized by his inauguration party: he threw the doors of the White House open to one and all, and a near riot broke out. Indeed, the United States was becoming more democratic as new states entering the Union allowed all free men to vote and the established eastern states reduced or eliminated property qualifications. Expanded voting rights brought popular passions to political campaigns, as catchy songs, stirring advertisements, and vigorous attacks on opponents' character became the norm.

As Jackson took office, sectional tensions between North and South, between the industrializing and agricultural parts of the country, were on the rise. Most Northern congressmen favored an enhanced federal role in support of the infrastructure for economic growth, while in the South, states' rights advocates were dominant.

Meanwhile, westward expansion was exacerbating these regional tensions. Already in 1820, the question of whether the new state of Missouri would allow slavery had bitterly divided the nation. The question intensified after 1848 when the U.S. victory in the Mexican-American War (discussed later in this chapter) added California and new territories in the Southwest to the Rocky Mountains and Great Plains. Would those vast spaces be settled by free white homesteaders or by plantation owners and black slaves?

The Democratic Party, which had become identified with Southern planter interests, declared that the issue should be decided by "popular sovereignty," meaning by the voters within the new states. **Abraham Lincoln** (in office 1861–1865), a leader of the new Republican Party founded by antislavery activists in 1854, disagreed. To put the issue in the hands of territorial voters, Lincoln declared, would be little more than giving them *the liberty of making slaves of other people.* More than most Northern politicians, Lincoln stressed the moral dimension of the question, viewing slavery as a *"monstrous injustice."* Other Republicans opposed slavery not because it was wrong but because they thought that slavery was incompatible with the spread of the free, independent farmers they saw as the bedrock of society.

For many white Southerners, Lincoln and the Republican Party threatened freedoms long protected by the sovereignty of the states. To them, Republicans represented a hard-edged industrialism that contrasted with Southerners' perception

Andrew Jackson
(in office 1829–1837)
The seventh president of the United States; a symbol of the expansion of voting rights and an aggressive advocate of westward expansion.

Abraham Lincoln
(in office 1861–1865)
Sixteenth president of the United States and the country's first Republican president. His election on an antislavery platform led eleven states to secede from the Union, plunging the country into the American Civil War.

Alexis de Tocqueville's *Democracy in America*

The French historian Alexis de Tocqueville first traveled to the United States in 1831 at the age of twenty-six, and at age thirty he published the original French version of *Democracy in America*. Later, as a deputy in the French National Assembly, he was a political moderate and opposed both the Socialists and Louis Napoleon (see Chapter 23). Based on extensive travels and personal observations, *Democracy in America* is still regarded as one of the most insightful analyses of the "American character" ever written.

> What does de Tocqueville see as the most essential features of American civilization, and what does he identify as its strengths and weaknesses?

> Are the Frenchman's observations still relevant to an understanding of the United States today?

Source: Alexis de Tocqueville, *Democracy in America*, http://xroads.virginia.edu/~HYPER/DETOC/toc_indx.html.

Author's Introduction

Among the novel objects that attracted my attention during my stay in the United States, nothing struck me more forcibly than the general equality of condition among the people....The more I advanced in the study of American society, the more I perceived that this equality of condition is the fundamental fact from which all others seem to be derived and the central point at which all my observations constantly terminated.

On Patriotism

As the American participates in all that is done in his country, he thinks himself obliged to defend whatever may be censured in it; for it is not only his country that is then attacked, it is himself.... Nothing is more embarrassing in the ordinary intercourse of life than this irritable patriotism of the Americans. A stranger may be well inclined to praise many of the institutions of their country, but he begs permission to blame some things in it, a permission that is inexorably refused.

Geography and Democracy

The chief circumstance which has favored the establishment and the maintenance of a democratic republic in the United States is the nature of the territory that the Americans inhabit. Their ancestors gave them the love of equality and of freedom; but God himself gave them the means of remaining equal and free, by placing them upon a boundless continent. General prosperity is favorable to the stability of all governments, but more particularly of a democratic one, which depends upon the will of the majority, and especially upon the will of that portion of the community which is most exposed to want....In the United States not only is legislation democratic, but Nature herself favors the cause of the people.

In what part of human history can be found anything similar to what is passing before our eyes in North America? The celebrated communities of antiquity were all founded in the midst of hostile nations, which they were obliged to subjugate before they could flourish in their place.

Even the moderns have found, in some parts of South America, vast regions inhabited by a people of inferior civilization, who nevertheless had already occupied and cultivated the soil. To found their new states it was necessary to extirpate or subdue a numerous population.... But North America was inhabited only by wandering tribes, who had no thought of profiting by the natural riches of the soil; that vast country was still, properly speaking, an empty continent, a desert land awaiting its inhabitants....

Three or four thousand soldiers drive before them the wandering races of the aborigines; these are followed by the pioneers, who pierce the woods, scare off the beasts of prey, explore the courses of the inland streams, and make ready the triumphal march of civilization across the desert.... Millions of men are marching at once towards the same horizon; their language, their religion, their manners differ; their object is the same. Fortune has been promised to them somewhere in the West, and to the West they go to find it....

Religion and Democracy

The Americans combine the notions of Christianity and of liberty so intimately in their minds that it is impossible to make them conceive the one without the other....

In France I had almost always seen the spirit of religion and the spirit of freedom marching in opposite directions.... [American Catholics] attributed the peaceful dominion of religion in their country mainly to the separation of church and state. I do not hesitate to affirm that during my stay in America I did not meet a single individual, of the clergy or the laity, who was not of the same opinion on this point....

Associations and Civil Society

In no country in the world has the principle of association been more successfully used or applied to a greater multitude of objects than in America.... The citizen of the United States is taught from infancy to rely upon his own exertions in order to resist the evils and the difficulties of life; he looks upon the social authority with an eye of mistrust and anxiety, and he claims its assistance only when he is unable to do without it.... If some public pleasure is concerned, an association is formed to give more splendor and regularity to the entertainment. Societies are formed to resist evils that are exclusively of a moral nature.... In the United States associations are established to promote the public safety, commerce, industry, morality, and religion. There is no end which the human will despairs of attaining through the combined power of individuals united into a society.

Tyranny of the Majority

I know of no country in which there is so little independence of mind and real freedom of discussion as in America. In any constitutional state in Europe every sort of religious and political theory may be freely preached and disseminated....

In America the majority raises formidable barriers around the liberty of opinion; within these barriers an author may write what he pleases, but woe to him if he goes beyond them.

of their gracious way of life based on virtues like valor and honor. After all, some argued, sick or elderly slaves were cared for by their masters, while industrial workers injured on the job were thrown into the street.

After Lincoln's election in 1860, these divisions could no longer be bridged. Eleven Southern states declared their independence as the Confederate States of America, plunging the country into civil war (1861–1865). Some people, thinking the war would soon be over, brought picnics to witness the first battles. They did not account for the technological changes that made modern warfare more deadly. Increasingly precise weapons and powerful explosives, combined with tactics that threw waves of uniformed soldiers upon each other, led to mass suffering. Over six hundred thousand people died, the most in any American armed conflict.

● **CONTEXT&CONNECTIONS** Battles between Union and Confederate armies in the U.S. Civil War often featured desperate charges against well-entrenched forces supported by artillery, in which thousands of young men might be killed. That mode of fighting anticipated the brutal trench warfare in World War I (see Chapter 27). Because European politicians and generals had not learned the lessons of the U.S. Civil War, they went to war in 1914 with no inkling of the scale of slaughter they were putting in motion. ●

The North had clearly superior resources in the Civil War: railroads for moving men and material, iron foundries to produce guns and munitions, and textile factories to produce uniforms. The Confederates had less tangible advantages: superior military leadership and soldiers who were fighting to defend their homes and traditions. However, the South's export-oriented agricultural economy left the Confederacy vulnerable to a Union naval blockade since it depended on British markets for tobacco and cotton and on British factories for arms and ammunition. By 1865, the productivity of Northern farms and factories overwhelmed Southern resistance.

In 1863, Lincoln had issued the Emancipation Proclamation, making the abolition of slavery, not simply the preservation of the Union, a goal of the war. By the time of Union victory in 1865, the U.S. Senate had already passed the Thirteenth Amendment, abolishing slavery. With Union victory, the question became how the Northern victors would treat their vanquished foes. The assassination of Abraham Lincoln in 1865 meant that the most able American politician would not be there to help resolve that issue.

Reconstruction

(1865–1877) Period immediately after the American Civil War during which the federal government took control of the former Confederate states and oversaw enforcement of constitutional provisions guaranteeing civil rights for freed slaves.

Federal troops occupied the South to enforce federal law as part of a process known as **Reconstruction**, which was deeply resented by most white Southerners. In spite of further constitutional amendments intended to protect the civil and voting rights of freed slaves, "Redeemers" and secret societies like the Ku Klux Klan terrorized freed men and women, while Southern politicians in the Democratic Party sought to end Reconstruction and restore race-based governance. The presidential election of 1876 was the turning point. Amid a dispute over electoral votes, the Republican candidate, Rutherford B. Hayes, secured the election when he agreed to withdraw federal troops from the former Confederacy, putting an end to Reconstruction.

Some felt Reconstruction had unconstitutionally magnified the power of the federal government. But for Southern blacks, "states' rights" was a disaster. Vigilante violence against blacks increased dramatically, and Southern state legislatures enacted segregationist policies that came to be known as Jim Crow laws.

The American Civil War had several important global implications. First, the conflict showed how tightly interconnected the global economy was in the age of industry. When the fighting disrupted cotton exports from the American South, a surge in the price of raw cotton on global markets resulted, hitting British textile manufacturers hard, while benefiting alternative cotton producers (such as those in Egypt; see Chapter 26). Other globally relevant lessons of the American Civil War were the pivotal role of industry in determining its outcome and the degree of civilian mobilization required to keep large armies in the field for such an extended period. Not until the world wars of the twentieth century, however, would the terrible cost of industrialized conflict be fully realized.

The Gilded Age

After the Union victory, the United States experienced a spurt of population growth and productivity. As in Canada, the opening of the Great Plains brought huge economic dividends. The spread of railroads and steamships lowered transport costs and made commercial agriculture possible in more regions. Increased agricultural production led to falling grain prices in the cities, where industrial employment surged. Silver and gold booms brought a flood of investment capital to the nation's banks, while overwhelming Amerindians with invading settlers in the Black Hills of Dakota and the Sierra Nevada Mountains of California.

● **CONTEXT&CONNECTIONS** Nineteenth-century gold strikes took place across the world. In California after the Mexican-American War, the Gold Rush brought hundreds of thousands from eastern U.S. states as well as Europe, China, the Pacific Islands, and Mexico. When the California mines played out, some prospectors followed news of fresh strikes north to Canada and Alaska, or crossed the ocean to Australia. The greatest gold strikes of all were in South Africa beginning in 1884 (see Chapter 26). ●

Urbanization was a key development in the United States, as the percentage of Americans living in cities rose from roughly 10 percent in 1850 to over 30 percent by 1890. Most dramatic was the growth of Chicago: the "city with broad shoulders" served as the principal hub for the processing and transport of agricultural goods from the West, growing from merely thirty thousand citizens in 1850 to over 2 million by 1900.

During the last two decades of the nineteenth century, American steel firms and railroad companies exceeded any level of economic organization the world had ever seen. Mark Twain, the great American author and humorist, called it a **Gilded Age** (gilded with gold on the outside, concealing base metal within). For beyond the fortunes of the most privileged lay deep inequalities: grinding rural poverty across the South; an urban working class crammed into filthy unsafe tenements in the industrial North; and political favors for sale to the highest bidder. By 1890, less than 1 percent of the U.S. population controlled 90 percent of the nation's wealth.

In reaction to such economic pressures and inequalities, farmers in the Plains states organized a movement against the corporate and railroad interests that controlled the storing and shipping of grain. At the same time, industrial workers began to form unions to fight for better pay and working conditions, sometimes with violent results. One notorious example occurred in Chicago. Across the country on May 1, 1886, workers peacefully demonstrated in favor of an eight-hour work day. (Thus May 1st became recognized as international workers' day nearly everywhere except, ironically, in the United States.) In Chicago, after police killed two strikers on May 3, local anarchists called a workers' rally in Haymarket Square.

Gilded Age

Period of economic prosperity in the United States in the last two decades of the nineteenth century, when the opulence displayed by the wealthy masked the poverty, political corruption, and unsafe living and occupational conditions for the working class.

The Granger Collection, NYC

Orphans of the Gilded Age Jacob Riis captured this image of street children in New York in the 1880s. Riis, a Danish-American social reformer, used such photographs to bring the middle class's attention to the distress of those left behind by surging American economic growth.

Late in the peaceful rally, police moved in and someone threw a bomb toward them; shots followed, and several policemen and workers died. Authorities arrested some German and Czech anarchists as the press stoked anti-immigrant and anti-labor fervor; historians continue to debate the guilt or innocence of the four men who were hung.

● **CONTEXT&CONNECTIONS** The most prominent anarchist in the United States was *Emma Goldman* (Chapter 27), an immigrant from Russia who was radicalized by the "Haymarket martyrs" and fought for workers' freedom from both governmental and corporate oppression. ●

In spite of the Haymarket affair, the labor movement in the United States gradually grew stronger and better organized. Still, few advocated socialism. When most Americans demanded equality, what they really meant was equality of opportunity. It was their deep belief in individual opportunity that inspired Americans' characteristic sense of optimism.

In 1893, the United States celebrated its self-confidence at the World's Columbian Exposition held in Chicago. The fair featured a dazzling model city, with the world's first Ferris Wheel as a response to the new Eiffel Tower of Paris. It was the first time that many spectators arriving from farms and small towns had ever seen electric lights, a telephone, or a "horseless carriage" with a diesel engine.

Like London's Great Exhibition before it (see Chapter 23), the Columbian Exposition was a monument to industrial and technological progress.

Even as crowds flocked to the Columbian Exposition, the U.S. economy suffered a great jolt, the Panic of 1893. The exuberance of Gilded Age capitalism had been founded on price speculation. In 1893, the bubble burst when a bank failure in Argentina led to a run on U.S. banks. A sharp decline in investment and employment followed. From the new "progressive" wing of the Republican Party came calls for greater government regulation of irresponsible corporate speculators.

● **CONTEXT&CONNECTIONS** The overall pattern of the late-nineteenth-century international economy was volatile, with periods of exuberant growth followed by deep downturns. Marxists at the time argued that this boom-and-bust cycle would inevitably bring capitalism crashing down (see Chapter 23). Contemporaries referred to the slump of the early 1890s as the "Great Depression," a title usurped by an even more devastating global economic collapse in 1929 (see Chapter 28). ●

The Panic of 1893 was a short-term economic setback, but that same year, at least one observer noted a more fundamental shift. In his essay "The Significance of the Frontier in American History," historian Frederick Jackson Turner argued that the availability of an open frontier underlay the democracy and lack of class enmity in American life, compared with the harsher social conflict in Europe. With that frontier "closed," how would Americans adjust? The United States was in fact no longer a youthful frontier society. In the three decades following the Civil War, it had become the world's leading industrial *and* agricultural producer, with increasingly complex global interests.

Indeed, toward the century's end, the United States was trading continental frontiers for global ones. In addition to its activities in the Pacific (see Chapter 24), the United States intervened in Latin America, occupying Cuba and Puerto Rico (as well as the Philippines) after the Spanish-American War (1898–1900). In Cuba, U.S. occupation derailed an indigenous independence movement and sponsored an oligarchy sympathetic to U.S. corporate interests. Then, in 1903, the United States, anxious to create a U.S.-controlled canal on the Isthmus of Panama, supported Panamanian aspirations for independence from Colombia (breaking the last link of Simón Bolívar's Gran Colombia; see Chapter 22). Having annexed Hawai'i and declared a U.S. protectorate over the Philippines, the United States would soon control the fastest route westward from Atlantic to Pacific. It was clear to the world's people that the United States was now playing the imperial game, both within its own hemisphere and beyond.

Reform and Reaction in Latin America

Like Canada and the United States, Latin American nations had to overcome regional and sectional differences to develop effective national institutions. But where Canada and the United States were fundamentally secure within their borders, many Latin American nations faced severe external challenges, both political and economic. In the middle of the nineteenth century, Mexico lost northern territory to the United States and then suffered a decade of French occupation. Domination by Europe and the United States skewed Latin American economic production toward foreign markets. Overreliance on exports of agricultural produce and natural resources and imports of industrial goods and technologies hindered the development of integrated national economies.

Economic Dependency in Latin America

The Industrial Revolution had profound economic consequences for Latin Americans. Already during the colonial period their economies had been geared toward high-value exports like gold and silver, exchanged for luxury goods consumed by Spanish officials and local elites, the *criollos*. The benefits of trade were very unequally shared. Except in areas with slave plantations, international trade was fairly limited and local self-sufficiency still common. That changed quickly after about 1820, with surging foreign investment directed toward increasing export production.

Latin Americans fell into an economic trap that historians have called a "dependency complex." Rather than developing their own industrial base or integrating their national and regional markets, they depended almost exclusively on exporting raw materials, typically agricultural produce or minerals, in order to import manufactured goods. Relying on lightly processed exports to obtain higher-value industrial goods reinforced the sharply drawn social inequalities inherited from colonialism. (See the feature "World History in Today's World: The Roller Coaster of Commodity Prices.")

While rough-and-ready military men often dominated national politics, it was the oligarchs at the top of the social pyramid, descendants of "good" Iberian families, who controlled economic life, using their international connections to profit as intermediaries between local producers and global markets. Meanwhile, the lack of local industry and the focus on international rather than domestic trade stunted the growth of a vigorous middle class.

Economic dependency undermined peasant communities. With the transition to labor-intensive plantation crops for export, they often lost control over their own land and labor, forced by taxes, debt peonage, and sometimes direct coercion to leave their villages to work for miserable wages in mines and on plantations (see Chapter 18). Economies were growing in ways that made many people poorer, a process that one historian has called "the poverty of progress."

● **CONTEXT&CONNECTIONS** In the 1960s, radical sociologists identified the "development of underdevelopment" as a key feature of the modern world economy, focusing on economic dependency as an exploitative framework of international capitalism, funneling resources from "third-world" societies in Latin America, Asia, and Africa, to enrich the already dominant "first world" (see Chapter 30). ●

Conservatives, Liberals, and the Struggle for Stability in Mexico

After Mexico won independence from Spain in 1821, the government fell into the hands of ineffective soldier-politicians, the *caudillos* (cow-DEE-yos) (see Chapter 22). General Antonio López de Santa Ana (1794–1876), who served as president of Mexico nine different times while losing half the country to the United States, was the most notorious.

The Roller Coaster of Commodity Prices

In the twenty-first-century era of globalization, South American nations have been rising stars. Brazil's economy, for example, grew by 4.2 percent annually from 2004 to 2010 (see Chapter 32).

But has Brazil and its neighbors escaped the long-standing trap of economic dependency, overreliance on the export of a limited range of agricultural products, minerals, and energy sources? That question came into renewed focus when a sharp fall in commodity prices from 2014 into 2015 demonstrated the exceptional vulnerability of South American countries to roller-coaster fluctuations in the world economy.

A staggering drop in oil prices, for example, sent Venezuela into a state of shock. From a 2011 peak of $117 a barrel, and a mid-2014 price of $108 a barrel, the price of crude oil plunged by more than half, to less than $50 a barrel in early 2015. While the country's non-oil exports have remained flat for twenty years, crude oil has accounted for over 90 percent of export revenue. Venezuela is now paying the price for failing to translate oil wealth into a more diversified portfolio.

The Brazilian economy is not as reliant on a single commodity, but its growth estimates have also been revised downward. Soybean exports, especially to China, peaked at a price of $621 a metric ton in 2012, but then bottomed out at less than $390 a ton at the end of 2014. (In fact, slowing demand from China affected economies across Latin America.) The Brazilian government found itself with declining tax revenues even while bearing the costs of the 2014 World Cup and the 2016 Summer Olympics. Meanwhile, some farmers found it was no longer worth the cost to plant soybeans on fields they have only recently cleared from the tropical forest (although the steep environmental costs of that land clearance cannot be recovered.)

Of course, global commodity prices eventually will recover. But volatility will undoubtedly remain, and Latin America's legacy of economic dependency will continue to challenge governments and businesses far into the future.

A major problem for Mexico was its northern state of Texas. Traditionally, Mexico's wealth in people, resources, settled agriculture, and culture was in its central and southern parts. Texas, in contrast, was an untamed frontier with only a few officials and missionaries mixed in with *vaqueros* (vah-KAIR-ohs; cowboys), Amerindians such as Apache and Comanche, and the occasional American adventurer. None of them paid much attention to Mexican authorities.

In the 1820s, Mexico attempted to stabilize this distant frontier by inviting English-speaking settlers into Texas. Most were Americans who planned to use slave labor to produce cotton. But since Mexico had already abolished slavery, the importation of slaves was illegal. President Santa Ana would either have to enforce that law or allow slaveholding Texans to flout his authority.

By 1836, when Santa Ana came north with his troops, thirty thousand American settlers lived in Texas. Unhappy with Mexican rule, these settlers allied with discontented Spanish-speaking Texans to fight for independence. Despite victories at the Alamo and elsewhere, Santa Ana lost Texas. In the new Republic of Texas, a referendum prepared the way for U.S. annexation in 1845. Mexico's loss of territory to the United States continued when a U.S. administration provoked war with Mexico in 1846, sending its forces all the way to Mexico City. The Treaty of Guadalupe Hidalgo (1848) gave the United States the northern half of Mexico. Mexico's "Norte" had become the American Southwest.

Mexican liberals, distraught by their country's weakness and inspired by the European revolutions of 1848 (see Chapter 23), supported *La Reforma*, a movement to get rid of caudillo rule and create a more progressive nation. One of their leaders, Benito Juárez (beh-NEE-toh WAH-rez) (1806–1872) became the country's first Amerindian president.

Juárez and the liberals succeeded against conservative resistance and enshrined the principles of *La Reforma* in the Mexican Constitution of 1857. The new constitution restricted the privileges of the Catholic clergy and the military. Most liberals saw the church as restricting individualism and progress while upholding the power of the large landowners. The constitution also contained a Bill of Rights, ending the old caste system and making everyone equal before the law.

Conservatives reacted angrily to such reforms, especially limitations on the church's power and the seizure of its land. While some priests followed the example of Father Hidalgo in supporting the rights of the majority (see Chapter 22), Mexican bishops allied with the *hacendados*, the large landowners who had opposed Hidalgo's revolution in 1810 and who now rejected the liberal constitution.

Contention between liberals and conservatives created an opening for the French emperor Napoleon III (see Chapter 23) who sent troops to Mexico in 1861. His stated intention was to force payments of Mexican debt, but his real motive was to resurrect a French empire in the Americas. The liberal government fought back. In 1862, on the fifth of May (*Cinco de Mayo*), a small army of Mexicans defeated a much larger French force at the Battle of Puebla. But Mexico lost the war after conservatives helped the French invaders take Mexico City. While pressure from Europe and the United States eventually forced the French to withdraw, the struggle between Mexico's liberals and conservatives continued.

In 1876, **Porfirio Díaz** (1830–1915) came to power. Like the old caudillos, he ruled as a dictator, and during his long tenure as president (1876–1880 and 1884–1911), he ignored the ideals of *La Reforma*, such as freedom of speech and assembly. He was, however, a firm believer in free trade and foreign investment, actively courting investors from Britain and the United States. Such economic development had political implications: the power of the state expanded, for example, as improved rail transportation gave the government greater access to the entire country.

Apart from railroads and mining, most new investment was in agriculture. As was typical of Latin American economic dependency, holders of large estates responded to the expansion of markets with extensive planting of export crops like cotton, sugar, and hemp. Commercial agriculture brought great wealth to Mexico's landowners, its urban commercial class, and foreign investors. However, these groups prospered at the expense of many formerly self-sufficient peasants.

Porfirio Díaz ruled Mexico as an elected dictator, winning rigged elections from 1884 on. By the early twentieth century, however, a younger generation of middle-class Mexicans chafed at the old dictator's political monopoly. Among their leaders was Francisco Madero, who ran for the presidency in 1910 under the slogan *"Effective Suffrage and No Reelection,"* and then launched a revolution when Díaz once again claimed victory. Finally, the aged Díaz fled to Europe.

Removing a dictator is usually easier than creating a new political order, and that proved true in Mexico from 1910 to 1928. In 1913, Madero was assassinated by a military officer, who in turn was deposed by the liberal Venustiano Carranza. Though Carranza held Mexico City and controlled the federal army, two former partners in his revolutionary coalition, **Emiliano Zapata** (1879–1919) and Pancho Villa (1878–1923), now turned against him.

Porfirio Díaz

(1830–1915) President of Mexico from 1876–1880 and 1884–1911. While he ignored Mexican civil liberties, Díaz courted foreign investment to develop infrastructure and provided much-needed stability.

Emiliano Zapata

(1879–1919) Leader of a popular uprising during the Mexican Revolution; mobilized the poor in southern and central Mexico to demand "justice, land, and liberty."

Villa and Zapata This photograph from 1915 shows Pancho Villa (*center*, sitting on the presidential throne in the National Palace) with Emiliano Zapata (*right*) at his side, his trademark hat on his knee. Forces loyal to Venustiano Carranza soon chased the two revolutionaries from Mexico City, however. Both were later assassinated. (Underwood & Underwood/Historical/Corbis)

In the north, the dashing Villa came to represent for many the romance of revolution as he and his comrades, mostly cowboys and small ranchers, fought big property owners for land and water rights. In the south, Zapata galvanized support among hardscrabble southern peasants, many of them Amerindians, with the demand for "*¡Justicia, Tierra, y Libertad!*"

Although Carranza's government instituted a new constitution in 1917, trying to balance the different interests that had emerged during the revolution, chaos continued to engulf the country into the 1920s. Carranza's agents assassinated Zapata in 1919; Carranza himself fell to an assassin in 1920, and Villa in 1923. Other leaders and causes emerged, and as many as 2 million people had been killed in the revolution by 1929, when the Party of the Mexican Revolution finally restored stability (see Chapter 27).

.... **Spanish-Speaking South America**

Simón Bolívar's vision of a great confederation had failed (see Chapter 22), leaving nine separate South American nations by the 1830s. As in Mexico, their economies fell into the trap of economic dependency, exporting relatively low-value raw materials and importing higher-cost finished products. And as in Mexico, this economic system made them highly vulnerable to the price swings of global commodity markets. While plantation owners, commercial intermediaries, political elites, and foreign investors might prosper, peasants and laborers rarely did.

The story of Venezuela was fairly typical. The president, José Antonio Páez (1790–1873), had been a self-made military leader in the liberation campaigns. Páez (PAH-ays) consolidated his power in typical caudillo fashion by forging an alliance with the old criollo aristocracy, who overlooked Páez's rough manners since he was able to control the common people for them. Nevertheless, in the 1860s, after a brief civil war, Venezuelan reformers established a more liberal regime, abolishing slavery, building railroads, and expanding school facilities. Still, economic inequalities remained entrenched, with an export-oriented agricultural sector controlled by a Venezuelan oligarchy closely tied to foreign investors.

Argentina was more economically successful. Railroads now made it easier to get Argentine cattle to market, and the development of refrigerated steamship compartments in the 1860s brought Argentine beef to European consumers. As the economy boomed, the capital, Buenos Aires, became one of the world's great cities. Cosmopolitan politicians, merchants, and lawyers enjoyed the city's elegant plazas and pleasant cafés. A growing working class, many of them recent immigrants from Italy, worked in meatpacking plants and other export-oriented industries. From their neighborhood cafés arose the sensual *tango*, Argentina's gift to musical culture.

Apart from Argentina, the most successful South American republic was Chile, another country with a largely European demographic profile. As elsewhere in Latin America, conservatives and liberals squared off, as did centralizers and believers in provincial

Buenos Aires The Argentine capital of Buenos Aires was an exceptionally prosperous city in the first decade of the twentieth century. As in Paris, New York, and Berlin, automobiles were beginning to compete with horse-drawn carriages along its spacious boulevards. But Argentina's prosperity was overly dependent on volatile international commodity markets, and revenue from its exports went disproportionately to those at the very top of society.

autonomy. But in Chile a conservative consensus emerged early on, supported by the powerful Catholic Church.

Political consensus may have been easier to achieve in Chile because of its success in competing with its neighbors, Peru and Bolivia. Starting in the 1840s, the three countries greatly benefited from *guano* (GWA-noh), or bird droppings, along the Pacific coast: guano makes an excellent fertilizer and was in high global demand. Of course, shoveling guano was not pleasant: tens of thousands of Chinese laborers, escaping from the disruption of the Taiping Rebellion (see Chapter 24), were desperate enough to cross the ocean as indentured laborers to do the job.

As guano deposits declined, Peru, Bolivia, and Chile began to develop nitrate mines in the same region as an alternative source of fertilizer. The intensifying competition led to the **War of the Pacific** in 1879. Chile's victory enhanced its reputation, and Chileans developed a stronger sense of national identity. But the war was disastrous for Bolivia, which became a landlocked country and one of the poorest societies in the Americas (see Map 25.2).

Still, even in Chile and Argentina, the most economically successful South American societies of the late nineteenth century, industrialization lagged far behind the pace set by the United States and Canada. Production of raw materials and importation of manufactured goods remained the norm, as did foreign investors' hold on much of the profit from growth.

War of the Pacific
(1879) War among Bolivia, Peru, and Chile over the natural resources of the Pacific coast. Chile emerged victorious, gaining international prestige, while Bolivia's loss made it a poor, landlocked country.

From Empire to Republic in Brazil

Brazil's large size, distinct ecology and demography, and relationship to Portugal led on to a unique path. After Brazilian liberals declared the country's independence from Portugal in 1822, the heir to the Portuguese throne, already living in Brazil, agreed to serve as the new nation's constitutional monarch. Brazil therefore achieved independence more smoothly than other South American nations (see Chapter 22).

Still, Brazil's principal political tensions were quite similar to those of its republican neighbors. Brazil's progressive middle-class liberals were at odds with the country's conservatives, mostly large estate owners and military men who stressed traditional values such as the authority of the Catholic Church. The abolition of slavery, although a major liberal priority, was not achieved until 1888, later than anywhere else in the Americas.

By then, coffee had replaced sugar as the primary export: in response to rising demand among newly affluent middle-class consumers in Europe and the United States, Brazil became the world's largest coffee exporter. The government took an active role in stimulating the production of rubber, now in great demand for industrial purposes, by granting gigantic land concessions in the Amazon. As a result, the Amazonian city of Manaus grew as fast as the mining towns of the western United States, its opulent opera house a symbol of the excesses that came with quick money.

Their growing export economy boosted the confidence of Brazilians as they abolished first slavery and then the monarchy, proclaiming a republic in 1889 with the motto *"Order and Progress"* proudly displayed on the country's new green and gold flag. But Brazil still found itself in the same dependency trap as other South American nations. The rubber boom collapsed when production spread to Central Africa and Southeast Asia, and coffee exports sharply declined during the global economic slump of the 1890s.

Map 25.2 Latin America, ca. 1895 By 1895, all of the nations of South and Central America were independent except for British, French, and Dutch Guyana and Honduras. Panama seceded from Colombia in 1903 with military backing from the United States, which was anxious to further its canal interests. Many Caribbean islands remained British, French, and Dutch colonies. However, Cuba was freed from Spanish rule in 1898, the same year the United States took control over Puerto Rico. Railroad networks seen in Mexico, Chile, Argentina, and southern Brazil were a sign of foreign investment in exports like minerals and livestock products.

● **CONTEXT&CONNECTIONS** The rubber industry of the late nineteenth century was notorious for labor exploitation and abuses. The most infamous case occurred in the Congo Free State, the Central African domain of *King Leopold II of Belgium* (Chapter 26), where the violence and avarice of European rubber companies left as many as 10 million Africans dead. In the Amazon as well, rubber barons and their agents expropriated Amerindian lands and subjected Amerindian workers to slave-like servitude. ●

The Nineteenth-Century Americas in Perspective

All across the Americas, changes resulted from integration into global markets and consolidation of state power. Amerindian sovereignty came to an end, ever larger numbers of European immigrants altered racial demographics, and changes were taking place in gender roles. Pauline Johnson-Tekahionwake was not the only woman seeking greater autonomy in late-nineteenth-century society, when an increasingly organized women's movement was articulating a platform of voting rights and social equality.

The Fates of Indigenous Societies

The nineteenth century was decisive for America's indigenous peoples. Before the Industrial Revolution, Amerindian societies in regions as diverse as the Andes, the Arctic, Amazonia, and the Great Plains retained control over their own political, social, and cultural lives. Some, like the Johnson family and other Iroquois on the Six Nations Reserve, maintained connections with settler societies while balancing old traditions and new influences. But by the end of the century Amerindian sovereignty had disappeared.

In Mexico, for example, following independence in 1821, Mayan-speaking villagers on the Yucatán (yoo-kah-TAHN) peninsula continued to live much as before, with little reference to Spanish-speaking government officials. They grew maize, beans, and other staple crops in communities deeply rooted in the pre-Columbian past. While Christian, their Catholicism mixed local and imported beliefs. Though connected to wider networks as producers and consumers, their self-sufficiency nevertheless allowed them to choose their own terms of contact with the outside world.

That autonomy was challenged in the 1840s with a boom in plantation agriculture. At first, planters of sugar and *henequen* (a fibrous plant used for rope making) could not attract Amerindian workers at the wages they offered. Just at this time, however, Mexican tax collectors were becoming more aggressive because of the expensive wars with Texas. Forced to earn cash to pay their taxes, formerly self-sufficient peasants had to seek work on plantations. Many were then entrapped by debt peonage: never able to repay their employers, they could not leave to seek better wages elsewhere.

Meanwhile, a small group of Maya militants began a guerrilla campaign in 1847 known as the **Yucatán Rebellion**, attacking both Mexican government officials and local hacienda owners. With the Mexican army occupied against the United States, the rebels soon controlled over half of the Yucatán peninsula. Once the war in the north was over, however, Mexican forces redeployed against the Maya rebels and gradually reimposed government authority. Elite Mexicans, liberal and conservative alike, viewed the Maya rebels as primitive folk standing in the way of the "progress" of nation building and market expansion.

Yucatán Rebellion (1847) Maya uprising on Mexico's Yucatán peninsula, challenging the authority of the Mexican government and local landowners. Some Maya communities defended their sovereignty into the 1890s.

Scattered fighting continued until 1895. By then Maya resistance had been broken: the need for cash to pay their taxes had driven them to low-wage peonage on plantations producing for export. Taxes tied them to the Mexican state; their labor tied them to the global economy. The autonomy for which they had fought was gone.

In the United States, the dominant society had no use for Amerindians even as subservient laborers. Driven primarily by the discovery of gold in Georgia and insistent pressure for fresh land on which to grow slave-produced cotton, the U.S. Congress passed the **Indian Removal Act** in 1830. President Jackson supported and oversaw the forced migration of southeastern Amerindians such as the Creek and Cherokee to a designated "Indian Territory" in today's Oklahoma. Ironically, in 1827 the Cherokee had emulated the U.S. model in drafting a constitution in an attempt to protect their independence. That experiment ended tragically with a forced march west that killed over four thousand on what the Cherokee call the *Nunna daul Tsuny*, the *"Trail Where They Cried"* or the *"Trail of Tears"* (see page 798).

The life and customs of the indigenous communities of the Great Plains were quite different from those of the agricultural Maya and Cherokee. Plains Amerindians lived in mobile bands and depended on buffalo hunting for both food and goods to trade. The ancient buffalo-hunting culture of the Plains took on new impetus with the arrival of horses in the sixteenth and seventeenth centuries. Formerly semi-agricultural people, like the Cheyenne and the Lakota (luh-KOH-tuh) moved onto the Plains year-round and used horses and rifles to hunt.

Then after 1846, when Great Britain ceded Oregon to the United States, large numbers of settlers sought their fortune on the "Oregon Trail." By the time of the American Civil War, a series of forts in the Dakota Territory protected settlers-in-transit from Amerindian attacks.

For a time it seemed that negotiations between the Lakota and the U.S. government might preserve stability. An 1868 treaty, for example, forbade white settlement for all time in the Black Hills, sacred to the Lakota and other Plains societies. Four years later, however, gold was discovered, and waves of white prospectors descended on mining camps in the heart of sacred Lakota land. To leaders like **Sitting Bull** (ca. 1831–1890) treaties with the U.S. government now seemed worthless, and they prepared for war.

In the summer of 1876, Lakota and Cheyenne warriors defeated Lieutenant Colonel George Custer and his forces at the Battle of Little Bighorn, killing Custer and over half of his men. Although Custer's demise was the outcome of a military blunder, the American press portrayed it as a heroic *"last stand"* against *"savages."* Amid calls for swift vengeance, some advocated not just the defeat of the Lakota confederation but also the total annihilation of Amerindians.

Then, just a few years later, European immigrants and American settlers began arriving in the Dakota Territory as permanent homesteaders, a dramatic change made possible by railroads. In 1890, the U.S. government abrogated its treaty with the Lakota to open lands for these settlers. Now confined to reservations, the Lakota, who had depended on open lands where buffalo grazed, found their way of life imperiled.

Some despairing Plains Amerindians were attracted to the teachings of a mystic named Wovoka (wuh-VOH-kuh), leader of the Ghost Dance Movement. Wovoka's followers believed that he was a messiah sent to liberate them and that by dancing the Ghost Dance they would hasten a new age in which the invaders would disappear from the earth and the native peoples would live in peace and prosperity.

Indian Removal Act

(1830) Legislation leading to the dispossession of Amerindian peoples in the southeastern United States. Thousands of Cherokee died when forcibly marched to Oklahoma along the "Trail of Tears."

Sitting Bull

(ca. 1831–1890) Lakota chieftain who led Amerindian resistance to white settlement of the Black Hills. After defeating U.S. cavalry and Lieutenant Colonel George Custer at the Battle of Little Bighorn in 1876, he was killed in 1890 during conflict surrounding the Ghost Dance Movement.

● **CONTEXT&CONNECTIONS** Scholars have compared the Ghost Dance Movement and the *Xhosa Cattle Killing* (Chapter 26) as examples of "millenarian" spiritual movements combining indigenous and Christian beliefs and promising to bring about a new age of peace and justice. Resurrection of the dead, an idea common to both the Xhosa prophetess Nongqawuse in the 1850s and Wovoka on the Great Plains in the 1880s, was borrowed from Christian preachers and adapted to the needs of indigenous societies faced with invasion and cultural marginalization. ●

The U.S. government regarded the Ghost Dance Movement as subversive and ordered the arrest of Sitting Bull in the mistaken belief that he was one of its leaders. Early in 1890, Sitting Bull died in a skirmish when tribal police tried to detain him. Two weeks later, U.S. soldiers fired into a group of Lakota captives, killing between 150 and 300 people. Nearly half of the victims of this Wounded Knee Massacre were unarmed women and children. An editorial writer at a South Dakota newspaper had this to say:

*The Whites, by law of conquest, by justice of civilization, are masters of the American continent, and the best safety of the frontier settlements will be secured by the total annihilation of the few remaining Indians. Why not annihilation? Their glory has fled, their spirit broken, their manhood effaced; better that they die than live the miserable wretches that they are.**

Such violent racism in support of a policy of genocide was not uncommon. (The author of this editorial, L. Frank Baum, would later write the beloved children's story *The Wonderful Wizard of Oz.*)

Rather than pursuing outright annihilation, however, the federal Bureau of Indian Affairs separated Amerindian children from their parents to prevent them from learning the language, culture, and rituals of their own people—a form of cultural genocide. Amerindian armed resistance was over. The frontier wars persisted only in entertainment, courtesy of Buffalo Bill Cody's tremendously popular Wild West shows, where Americans flocked to be thrilled by stylized reenactments of the frontier wars.

Traveling across Canada in the 1890s, Pauline Johnson-Tekahionwake saw firsthand the tragedy of the Plains Amerindians in the sad spectacle of *"a sort of miniature Buffalo Bill's Wild West"*[†] in which Blackfoot warriors, seeking coins from travelers, caricatured their old war maneuvers. Some might have been veterans of the **Métis Rebellions**, the uprisings of mixed-race and First Nations peoples that had inspired Johnson to write "A Cry from an Indian Wife."

The métis settlement in the Red River Valley of what is now the Canadian province of Manitoba represented an older form of European-First Nations interaction.

The Granger Collection, NYC

Chief Joseph Chief Joseph (Hinmah-too-yah-lat-kekt, "Thunder Rolling Down the Mountain") was a Nez Perce Amerindian leader and a famous man of peace. The discovery of gold led the U.S. government to renege on its treaty with the Nez Perce, shrinking their reservation to a tenth of its former size. In 1877, Chief Joseph led his people, pursued by U.S. cavalry, in a desperate attempt to reach Canada. He was captured and exiled to Oklahoma. Only in 1885 were Joseph and his remaining followers allowed to return to their homes in the Pacific Northwest.

Métis Rebellions

(1867 and 1885) Rebellions by the métis of the Red River Valley settlement in Manitoba, a group with mixed French-Amerindian ancestry that resisted incorporation into the Canadian Confederation. In 1885 their leader, Louis Riel, again led them in rebellion against Canadian authority.

---

*L. Frank Baum, *Aberdeen Saturday Pioneer*, December 20, 1890.

†Pauline Johnson-Tekahionwake, cited in Betty Keller, *Pauline: A Biography of Pauline Johnson* (Toronto: Douglas and Macintyre, 1981), p. 94.

During the heyday of the fur trade, mixed-race families were not uncommon and sometimes established their own communities (see Chapter 18).

The first of two Métis Rebellions came immediately after Canadian confederation in 1867. London had transferred authority over the vast territories of the Hudson's Bay Company to the Canadian government without consulting the people who lived there. The métis leader Louis Riel organized his community to resist incorporation into Canada, which they feared would lead to loss of their lands and the erosion of their French language. Riel declared an independent provisional government, but soon accepted British guarantees that Canada would protect the language and Catholic religion of his people. Negotiations led to the incorporation of the province of Manitoba into Canada in 1870.

At the same time, Canadian policies assumed that increasingly desperate First Nations peoples of the plains would disappear as a distinct population. The buffalo were dwindling; alcohol was becoming a scourge. Amerindian hunting traditions and lack of capital made a transition to commercial farming almost impossible. In exchange for exclusive reserves and small annuities, band after band gave up claim to the lands of their forebears as the railroad brought in settlers and commerce.

The Indian Act of 1876 asserted the authority of the Canadian state over First Nations communities. As in the United States, children were separated from their families and sent to "industrial schools," given English names, and forbidden to speak their own languages. (See the feature "Visual Evidence in Primary Sources: The Residential School System for First Nations Children.")

In the Pacific Northwest, where Pauline Johnson-Tekahionwake lived out her retirement collecting tales of the Squamish (SKWAW-mish) people, Canadian officials banned traditional rituals such as the *potlatch*, where men solidified their social position by distributing their wealth as gifts. The potlatch expressed the core cultural values of the First Nations of the Pacific West, but the idea of giving away your possessions could not have stood in greater contrast to the ethos of industrial and commercial capitalism on which Canada was then being built.

Meanwhile, the flood of arriving settlers would make the métis a minority in their own land. In 1885 Louis Riel once again organized resistance, this time forging alliances with disaffected Cree, Assiniboine, and other First Nations peoples. Métis partisans attacked a government outpost as Riel's indigenous allies burned down white homesteads. But they were no match for three thousand troops sent west by rail. Riel was arrested, convicted of high treason, and hanged. When Pauline Johnson-Tekahionwake recited "A Cry from an Indian Wife" in 1892, these events were still fresh in the minds of her audience.

If we compare the Yucatán Rebellion, the struggles of the Lakota, and the Métis Rebellions, we might first be struck by this difference: whereas the Mexican government and economic oligarchy wanted to incorporate the Maya peasantry as laborers in the commercial plantation system, the United States and Canada had no use for Amerindians even as workers. But the three cases have this in common: in the Yucatán, the Black Hills, and Manitoba, people rose up to defend their long-established cultures against foreign intrusion and commercial agriculture. All three societies had creatively merged indigenous and imported ideas: Maya beliefs and Catholicism, Lakota traditions with horse-based buffalo hunting, French and First Nations cultures in the days of the fur trade. Now all these peoples lost their ability to control their interactions with the national societies being constructed around them.

Immigration, Abolition, and Race

During Pauline Johnson-Tekahionwake's lifetime, the picture of Canada's society was complicated by the arrival of new immigrants: Chinese, Italians, Russians, and others. Early in the twentieth century, half of the population on the prairies was born outside of Canada. The same was true throughout the Americas. The United States was the most favored destination, but Argentina and Brazil also attracted many European immigrants.

In Brazil and the Caribbean, the abolition of slavery was connected to immigration patterns and policies. Slavery was abolished in Haiti in 1803, on the British West Indies in 1833, and on the remaining French islands fifteen years later. Unable to keep the former slaves as poorly paid wage earners, landowners turned to indentured workers. In the English-speaking Caribbean, indentured laborers came largely from British India, part of a broader South Asian diaspora (scattering) that also took contract workers to South Africa, Malaya, and Fiji. In Cuba, where slavery was not abolished until 1878, over a hundred thousand Chinese workers came to the island as indentured workers to supplement slave labor.

● **CONTEXT&CONNECTIONS** Demand for cane sugar was still rising in the 1830s when newly freed slaves abandoned Caribbean plantations, driving down production. Entrepreneurs responded by starting new plantations wherever conditions of heat and humidity were appropriate. Instead of slavery, the new plantations relied on indentured laborers brought across the seas from impoverished lands, for example, Filipinos to Hawaii and Indians to Fiji and South Africa. ●

Like Cuba, Brazil was bringing in new migrants even before slavery was abolished, such as contract laborers from Japan to work on coffee farms. (Today the largest group of Japanese-descended persons outside Japan is found in Brazil.) Much larger and more influential in Brazilian culture, however, was the Afro-Brazilian population with its origins in the old sugar plantation system. Brazilian art, music, dance, and religious worship all show a deep African influence.

Reflecting the racism of their age, the rulers of republican Brazil were embarrassed by the country's African heritage. Their motto was *"Order and Progress,"* and in their minds black people represented neither. To "improve" the country racially, the government recruited immigrants from Europe. Incentives lured Germans, Italians, and others to the economically dynamic southern part of the country. The northeast, the base of the old plantation system, remained more African in population and culture.

Even so, Brazil retained the traditional flexibility and ambiguity in race relations inherited from the colonial period. While the elite class was predominantly white and the poorest class predominantly black, there was a vast intermediate stratum of mixed descent. Complex racial designations classified people by speech, education, style of clothing, and other factors in addition to color. Racial classification, therefore, could be a matter of negotiation rather than simple appearance: as they say in Brazil, *"Money whitens."*

Racism was also evident in immigration to the United States. For example, the Anglo-Protestant majority portrayed Irish Catholics as drunk, violent, and lazy. Demeaning stereotypes also greeted new immigrants from southern and eastern Europe, such as Italian Catholics and Russian Jews. Prejudice against Chinese and Japanese immigrants on the west coast was even more intense, and Congress banned Chinese immigration altogether in 1882. Still, in 1913, fully 15 percent of the population (more than at any time since) had been born outside the United States.

The Residential School System for First Nations Children

After the conquest of Amerindian communities, nineteenth-century governments in both the United States and Canada implemented residential school systems designed to separate Amerindian children from their families and thus from the culture of their people. Children in these often church-run schools were given new names, converted to Christianity, forced to speak only English, and punished for speaking the language of their own people. Physical and sexual abuse were common, and rates of infectious disease, especially tuberculosis, were high. In Canada, attendance by First Nations children at residential schools was compulsory until 1948.

In this photograph, "Thomas" wears long braided hair and leans against a large fur robe. He holds what appears to be a toy gun, perhaps given to him as a prop by the photographer.

Assuming the photographer posed the boy, what impression does he seem to have wanted the photograph to have on its viewers?

One writer says that this image shows "the disorder and violence of warfare and of the cross-cultural partnerships of the fur trade...that had dominated life in Canada since the late sixteenth century."* How does the image show that?

Saskatchewan Archives Board, Regina Industrial School

*John S. Milloy, *A National Crime: The Canadian Government and the Residential School System, 1879 to 1906* (Winnipeg: University of Manitoba Press, 1999), p. 4.

Finally, in 1998 the Canadian government formed the Aboriginal Healing Foundation to support community projects in reparation for the damage done by this attempted cultural genocide of First Nations peoples. In 2008, the Canadian prime minister made a formal statement of apology, recognizing that "the consequences of the Indian residential schools policy were profoundly negative and that this policy has had a lasting and damaging impact on aboriginal culture, heritage, and language." The statement highlighted the "tragic accounts of the emotional, physical, and sexual abuse and neglect of helpless children, and their separation from powerless families and communities."

These two photographs were taken at the Regina Industrial School in the Canadian province of Saskatchewan and published in the *Annual Report* of the Canadian Department of Indian Affairs in 1904. They record the appearance of a First Nations child identified only as "Thomas Moore" (his true name was not recorded), supposedly upon his first arrival and again a few years later.

Saskatchewan Archives Board, Regina Industrial School

Apart from his hair and clothing, what is different and meaningful about Thomas's facial expression and posture in the second photograph?

The wall against which Thomas is leaning in this photograph seems much more solid and permanent than the fur robe in the earlier picture, perhaps symbolizing the superior strength of Christian Canadian society.

The goal of the Canadian government was to replace buffalo hunting with settled agriculture, a transformation perhaps symbolized by the potted plant included in this photograph. ***Taken together, what do these two photographs tell us about the ideology behind the residential school system in turn-of-the-century Canada?***

In Australia as well, aboriginal children were taken from their parents, forced into residential schools, and denied the chance of learning their own language and culture.

Some doubted whether these new arrivals, with their unfamiliar foods, languages, and customs, could ever be assimilated.

Racism continued to drive policy toward Americans of African descent, where the "one drop rule," in contrast with Brazil's more complex race-status hierarchy, classified all individuals with any appearance of African descent as black. In 1896, the Supreme Court upheld the legality of racial segregation in the South. Those African Americans who tried to escape racism by moving to northern states or beyond to Canada were disappointed by the prejudice they still faced. For example, after a thousand black farmers fled Oklahoma to the Canadian prairies to escape disenfranchisement and segregation, the Canadian government subjected them to arbitrary and humiliating medical examinations.

Meanwhile, recent immigrants from Europe, in spite of prejudices against them, fared better than U.S. African Americans. Many Irish Americans, for example, found good work as police officers and firemen, jobs that were closed to blacks. The cruel irony was that African Americans, whose ancestors had witnessed the birth of the republic, now watched as new arrivals from Europe leaped ahead of them.

Harsh racial rhetoric and even harsher racial realities pervaded the Americas. Encounters among Amerindians, Africans, Asians, and Europeans seemed decisively to favor the latter. For all the variation among the nations of North and South America, they had one thing in common: light-skinned men were in charge.

Gender and Women's Rights

In 1848, the Seneca Falls Convention, sometimes seen as the beginning of the modern women's movement, was held in upstate New York. Inspired by the abolitionist movement and the revolutions of the same year in Europe (see Chapter 23), the women met to proclaim universal freedom and gender equality, declaring:

> Now, in view of this entire disfranchisement of one-half the people of this country, their social and religious degradation…and because women do feel themselves aggrieved, oppressed, and fraudulently deprived of their most sacred rights, we insist that they have immediate admission to all the rights and privileges which belong to them as citizens of these United States.

Such proclamations would eventually transform gender relations in the United States, Canada, and the world. In the short run, however, most women, like Pauline Johnson-Tekahionwake, had to explore their own possibilities without much external support. Just as she investigated her own complex identity through life and art, her public performances also explored her identity as a woman. The costume change she made halfway through her recitals—from buckskin to evening gown, from Tekahionwake to Pauline Johnson—transformed her from a passionate and even erotic persona to a distant and ethereal one.

For many middle-class women in the United States and Canada, the bicycle became a symbol of a new mobility and a new kind of freedom. For Pauline Johnson-Tekahionwake, the canoe played this role. Some of her nature poems, such as "The Song My Paddle Sings," were based on canoe trips she took as a young woman on the Six Nations Reserve:

> …The river rolls in its rocky bed;
> My paddle is plying its way ahead…
> And up on the hills against the sky,

A fir tree rocking its lullaby,
Swings, swings,
Its emerald wings,
*Swelling the song that my paddle sings.**

In her canoe poems, Johnson-Tekahionwake is always in control, even when, as is often the case, she has a male companion. The independence asserted in her poetry was reflected in her personal life as well. She had several significant relationships but no marriage, and though money was a constant worry, she was financially independent. Perhaps Johnson-Tekahionwake's autonomy arose from her mixed heritage, deriving from both the matriarchal tradition of the Mohawk and the new possibilities for women proclaimed at Seneca Falls.

How exceptional were Pauline Johnson-Tekahionwake's attitudes and experiences? Women's progress toward equality and autonomy varied tremendously according to geographic location and class standing. Among wealthier women in major commercial cities like Toronto, Chicago, or Buenos Aires, some were politically active, seeking legal equality and the vote for women. Some organized campaigns for social improvement, working to limit abuses of child labor, to improve sanitary conditions, or to fight the evils of alcohol. Some daughters of the middle class took advantage of new educational opportunities. Female doctors, lawyers, and university professors were few, but there were many new openings for schoolteachers and nurses. The invention of the typewriter and the emergence of large corporations also created a vast new job market for female secretaries, many from the working class.

Often, young women from the working or middle classes viewed employment as temporary, lasting only until they married. According to the "cult of true womanhood" dominant at the time, woman's role was in a "separate sphere," where she would maintain a refined home as a sanctuary from the brutal and competitive "men's world" of business and industry. Even though women like Johnson-Tekahionwake might reject the "cult of true womanhood," many urban middle-class women and poorer women who aspired to be middle class embraced the idea.

Of course, American women lived diverse lives. A middle-class homemaker in Buenos Aires had greater comfort than a Swedish pioneer getting her family through the winter on the Canadian prairie. An Irish nun teaching immigrant children in Chicago would be difficult to compare with a Maya mother sending her sons off to work on a Yucatán plantation. For her part, Pauline Johnson-Tekahionwake enjoyed a life of mobility and autonomy that would have been unimaginable to her foremothers.

Bicycle Advertisement This advertisement from 1896 associates the bicycle with the newfound mobility and independence of the "new woman." In the poems of Pauline Johnson-Tekahionwake, it was often a canoe that allowed women to "be content."

---

*Excerpt from *Flint and Feather: The Complete Poems of E. Pauline Johnson (Tekahionwake)*. Toronto and London: The Musson Book Co., Ltd., 1912.

The Americas: Hemispheric and Global Connections

After growing up in a world of horses and canoes, Pauline Johnson-Tekahionwake made her career as a performer traveling by railroad and steamship, planning her trips and advertising her upcoming shows with the help of the telegraph. Mass audiences for news and entertainment were an important outcome of the increased pace of communications and transport in the late nineteenth century. Widespread access to inexpensive newspapers and common experiences of dance hall revues were part of the nation-building process, helping to create national cultures not just in the rapidly growing cities, but also across the vast frontier spaces of North America. In the early twentieth century, the invention of the radio and wider use of automobiles would magnify that trend toward mass national culture, as would cinema and, later, television.

Popular culture in North America, including the new popularity of spectator sports like baseball, ice hockey, and football, though scorned by cultural elites, marked the rising influence and spending power of the middle class and, increasingly, of industrial workers as well. At the same time, urban opportunity attracted immigrants from around the world. In 1910, almost a fourth of all Canadians and 15 percent of the U.S. population were foreign born.

The Industrial Revolution had quite different effects in Latin America. Here small elites continued to dominate culture, politics, and economics. Mexico and Central and South America all inherited colonial social systems based on the hacienda, where large landowners dominated local societies. In the nineteenth century, the commercialization of agriculture in response to new industrial markets further magnified the pattern of exceptionally concentrated landholding. Foreign investors, with little interest in tying local and regional markets together, constructed railroads to smooth the export of raw materials to Europe and North America. Likewise, foreign investment in mining and agriculture encouraged reliance on a narrow range of commodities demanded by the industrial powers.

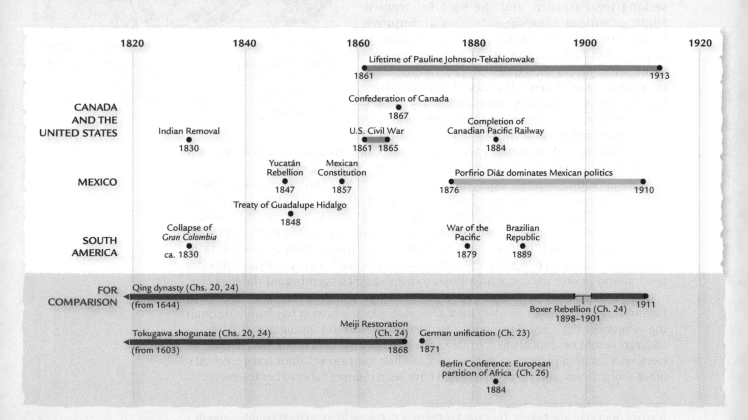

The Industrial Revolution thereby reinforced and expanded the power of Latin American elites, but the vast majority of people saw little benefit, losing land and control over their own labor as commercial plantations spread. Cities such as Buenos Aires and Mexico City grew dramatically, but they were dominated by the oligarchs who controlled export channels and access to foreign capital. Entering the twentieth century, Latin American economies had become more dependent than ever on the export of raw materials and the import of manufactured goods, often producing what they did not consume and consuming what they did not produce.

For much of the nineteenth century, the British were the dominant investors, adding the Latin American economies to their "informal empire." By the end of the century, however, the United States had overtaken Britain as the leading source of investment in Latin American economies and was asserting itself more aggressively in politics as well. In many nations, the power of local oligarchies became closely tied to American corporate interests, themselves actively supported by American political and, sometimes, military power. Such an imbalance of wealth and power in the Western Hemisphere found expression in the old complaint: "*Poor Mexico, so far from God and so close to the United States.*" Mexico's devastating territorial loss in 1848 was a preview of more aggressive U.S. imperialism to come.

At century's end, the United States projected its power not only across Latin America but across the Pacific as well, joining Europeans in a wave of empire building across the globe, the subject of the next chapter.

Key Terms

Pauline Johnson-
Tekahionwake (746)
responsible government (748)
Confederation of Canada (749)
Canadian Pacific Railway
(749)

Andrew Jackson (751)
Abraham Lincoln (751)
Reconstruction (754)
Gilded Age (755)
Porfirio Diáz (760)
Emiliano Zapata (760)

War of the Pacific (763)
Yucatán Rebellion (765)
Indian Removal Act (766)
Sitting Bull (766)
Métis Rebellions (767)

For Further Reference

Bender, Thomas. *A Nation Among Nations: America's Place in World History*. New York: Hill and Wang, 2006.

Bushnell, David, and Neill Macauley. *The Emergence of Latin America in the Nineteenth Century*. 2d ed. New York: Oxford University Press, 1994.

Conrad, Margaret. *A Concise History of Canada*. New York: Cambridge University Press, 2012.

Dickason, Olive Patricia. *Canada's First Nations*. 3d ed. New York: Oxford University Press, 2001.

Edwards, Rebecca. *New Spirits: America in the Gilded Age*. New York: Oxford University Press, 2005.

Fausto, Boris and Sergio Fausto. *A Concise History of Brazil*. 2d ed. New York: Cambridge University Press, 2014.

Fernández-Armesto, Felipe. *The Americas: A Hemispheric History*. New York: Modern Library, 2003.

Frazier, Donald S. *The United States and Mexico at War*. New York: Macmillan, 1998.

Gray, Charlotte. *Flint and Feather: The Life and Times of E. Pauline Johnson, Tekahionwake*. Toronto: HarperCollins, 2002.

Kolchin, Peter. *Unfree Labor: American Slavery and Russian Serfdom*. Cambridge, Mass.: Belknap, 1990.

McPherson, James. *Battle Cry of Freedom: The Civil War Era*. New York: Oxford University Press, 2003.

Wasserman, Mark. *Everyday Life and Politics in Nineteenth Century Mexico*. Albuquerque: University of New Mexico Press, 2000.

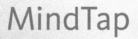 **MindTap** is a fully online, highly personalized learning experience built upon Cengage Learning content. MindTap combines student learning tools—readings, multimedia, activities, and assessments—into a singular Learning Path that guides students through the course.

Khama, c.1910 (gelatin silver print)/Private Collection/© Michael Graham-Stewart/Bridgeman Images

King Khama III

In the short space of twenty years, between 1870 and 1890, European powers drew colonial boundaries on their maps of Africa without the consent, and in most cases without even the knowledge, of those they planned to rule. In many places, Africans mounted spirited resistance, but the Europeans' technological superiority proved impossible to overcome. As the British poet Hilaire Belloc observed: *"Whatever else happens, we have got the Maxim gun, and they have not."**

During his lifetime, **King Khama III** (ca. 1837–1923) of the Bangwato (bahn-GWA-toe) people of southern Africa witnessed the great changes that came with the advance of the European empires. As a child, he was familiar with the occasional European hunter or missionary crossing the kingdom; as a king, he was forced to take drastic action to prevent the complete subjugation of his society:

A t first we saw the white people pass, and we said, "They are going to hunt for elephant-tusks and ostrich-feathers, and then they will return where they came from." … But now when we see the white men we say "Jah! Jah!" ("Oh Dear!"). And now we think of the white people like rain, for they come down as a flood. When it rains too much, it puts a stop to us all…. It is not good for the black people that there should be a multitude of white men.†

---

*Hilaire Belloc, *The Modern Traveler* (London: Edward Arnold, 1898), p. 41.

†King Khama of the Bangwato, quoted in Neil Parsons, *King Khama, Emperor Joe and the Great White Queen: Victorian Britain Through African Eyes* (Chicago: University of Chicago Press, 1998), p. 103.

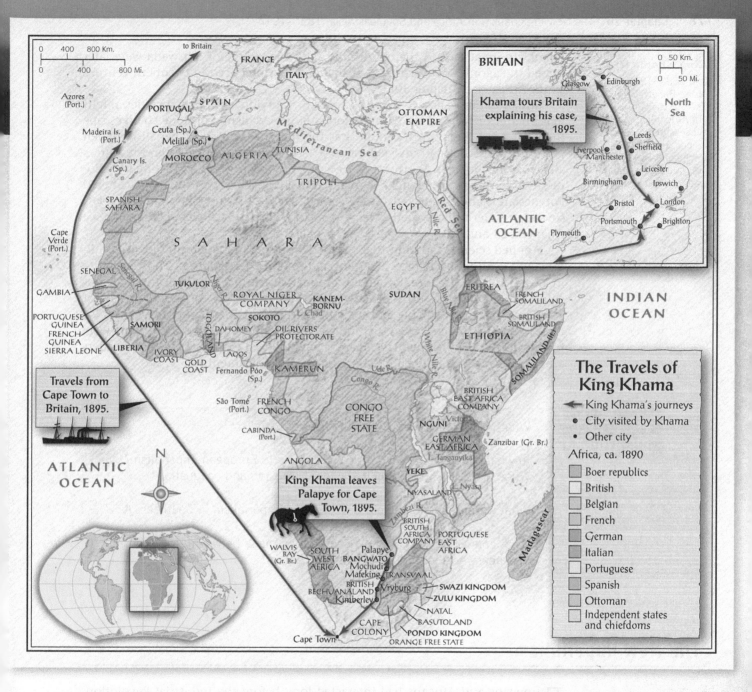

The Travels of King Khama

- ← King Khama's journeys
- • City visited by Khama
- • Other city

Africa, ca. 1890
- Boer republics
- British
- Belgian
- French
- German
- Italian
- Portuguese
- Spanish
- Ottoman
- Independent states and chiefdoms

Khama tours Britain explaining his case, 1895.

Travels from Cape Town to Britain, 1895.

King Khama leaves Palapye for Cape Town, 1895.

In 1895, King Khama (KAH-ma) and two neighboring kings began a long diplomatic mission, journeying by horse, railroad, and steamship from their homes in what is now Botswana, across South Africa, and all the way to London. They were in a difficult position. The frontier of white settlement already established in South Africa was moving northward, and the discovery of diamonds and gold had added further momentum to European expansion. The kings' goal was to have the British government declare a protectorate that would allow the Bangwato people to retain their farming and grazing lands and at least some control over their own affairs. The British public responded positively to their appeals, the colonial secretary argued in their favor, and they even had an audience with Queen Victoria.

King Khama III
(ca. 1837–1923) King
of the Bangwato, a
Tswana-speaking south-
ern African group. His
successful diplomacy
helped establish the
Bechuanaland protector-
ate, putting the Bang-
wato and other kingdoms
under British rather than
South African rule.

Thanks in great part to their effort and skill, the people of Botswana were later spared the agonies of *apartheid* ("separateness") as practiced in twentieth-century South Africa (see Chapter 30).

Still, Khama's success was only partial. Individual African societies might make better or worse deals with the forces of imperialism, but none could escape them. The late nineteenth century was the time of the New Imperialism, when powerful industrial nations vied for control of colonial territories and resources all across the globe. In Southeast Asia as well, Europeans were competing for colonies, while American, French, German, and British flags went up over scattered Polynesian islands, Meiji Japan took control over Korea and Taiwan, and the last sovereign Amerindian societies were defeated in the United States and Canada (see Chapters 24 and 25).

Applied science and industrial productivity generated the technological, military, and economic advances that powered the New Imperialism. Those societies in possession of the tools of empire—modern firearms, telegraphs, and steamships—were able to assert their power as never before. In Africa and Southeast Asia, local leaders were able to resist only by manipulating European rivalries for their own ends, though even such independent states as Siam and Ethiopia were incorporated into the unequal global system based on empire. Indigenous leaders around the world could relate to King Khama's predicament.

FOCUS QUESTIONS

> What were the main causes of the New Imperialism?

> In what different ways did Africans respond to European imperialism? When and how did they militarily resist invasion and occupation?

> What were the main outcomes of the New Imperialism in Southeast Asia?

> What connections and comparisons can be made between Africa and Southeast Asia in the late nineteenth century?

The New Imperialism

Europeans and Africans had interacted long before the Industrial Revolution. After the sixteenth century, especially in western Africa, their relationship increasingly focused on the slave trade, though direct European involvement was limited to coastal fortifications (see Chapter 19). Until the late nineteenth century, Europeans in Africa's interior included only a small group of settlers moving out from Cape Town and a few intrepid explorers.

The Industrial Revolution altered this pattern. By 1808, when the British Parliament abolished the slave trade, the economic needs of European economies were shifting: the slave-based West Indian sugar plantations were declining in importance, while factory owners sought inexpensive sources of raw materials and new export markets for their manufactures. In the mid-1800s, European explorers fanned out across the continent to assess its cultural and physical geography, identify its resources, and evaluate the transportation potential of its rivers. Pressed by evangelical Christians once involved in the abolitionist movement, the British government took an active role in stamping out the slave trade.

For most of the nineteenth century, African merchants and African political authorities facilitated the new trade connections as Europeans still largely remained at the coasts. Then, something dramatic happened. As King Khama noted, suddenly after 1870 Africans confronted *"a multitude of white men."* The era of **New Imperialism** had begun. Heightened competition among industrial states for African raw materials and markets was a major factor in European colonial expansion. Geopolitical rivalries, personal ambitions, and religious convictions were additional motives.

At the same time, the "tools of empire" available to the invaders expanded beyond more accurate rifles. Steamships and telegraphs allowed quicker coordination between European centers of command and European officials on the ground. Because African rivers drop sharply from highlands to the sea, sailing ships could not travel far inland. But steam-powered ships could readily penetrate the continent's interior, and beginning in the 1890s, railroads too conveyed troops and colonial administrators. Advances in medical technology were also vital: in the 1840s it was discovered that quinine, from the bark of a South American tree, provided protection against malaria. Routes to the interior of Africa, once known as "the white man's graveyard," were now open.

New Imperialism

An increase in European imperial activity during the late nineteenth century, caused primarily by increased competition between industrial states for raw materials and markets and by the rise of a unified Germany as a threat to the British empire.

Political and Economic Motives

Though the French and Portuguese had long-standing coastal enclaves, the British dominated European-African interactions for the first two-thirds of the nineteenth century. Long the world's most important maritime power, by this time the British had taken the lead in industrialization as well, aggressively pursuing new sources of raw materials and markets across the globe. Before 1870, however, the British were reluctant to add vast new holdings to their formal empire. In Latin America and in China, the British had asserted their economic dominance without the expense of direct colonial occupation, an approach supported by free-trade ideology. At first, it seemed that relations with Africa would follow that pattern of "informal empire."

● **CONTEXT&CONNECTIONS** In Latin American countries such as Argentina, national oligarchies maintained social, financial, and legal orders conducive to British capital investment, making colonial conquest unnecessary (see Chapter 25). In contrast, military invasion had been necessary to open China's doors to trade at the time of the *Opium Wars* (key term in Chapter 24), and Britain went on, with others, to divide China into "spheres of influence." Both Latin American and East Asian experiences thus differed from the direct colonial partition that affected Africans and Southeast Asians. ●

The global dynamic of European imperialism changed after 1871 with the unification of Germany, the fastest-growing industrial economy in the second half of the nineteenth century. Having defeated the French (see Chapter 23), the Germans wanted to assert their equality with the British by acquiring an empire of their own. For their part, the French wanted to restore their country's international standing after its humiliating defeat by the Germans. Imperial expansion in Africa and Southeast Asia accomplished that goal and gave legitimacy to the government of the French Third Republic.

With the United States and Japan also asserting themselves as military powers in Asia, by the 1880s the whole international system was becoming much more competitive; the liberal belief that every nation's economic needs could be met through free trade in open markets was starting to dim. European policymakers began to see secure and protected colonial markets as essential to further industrialization.

Imperial expansion in the age of the New Imperialism was closely tied to industrial capitalism, coinciding with the **Second Industrial Revolution** in the latter half of the nineteenth century. A rapid acceleration in industrial technology meant that electricity, steel, and petroleum superseded coal, steam, and iron. Large chemical and metal industries required secure access to natural resources like tin, oil, and rubber from around the world. Believing free markets were not adequate to their needs, nationalistic policymakers reintroduced mercantilist economic strategies from the early modern era (see Chapter 17).

Chartered companies—state-backed monopolies—were once again used to secure markets, sources of raw materials, and overseas investment opportunities. Just three decades after the British East India Company became defunct in 1858, a new charter was granted to the British South African Company. As in the eighteenth-century days of mercantilism, private corporations with their own armies and administrative personnel allowed European nations to pursue imperial expansion on the cheap.

Meanwhile, domestic politics spurred more active imperialism when politicians used patriotic appeals to cultivate popularity with newly enlarged electorates. Leaders of the French Third Republic appealed to "national honor" in extending their colonial frontiers. In Britain, the Conservative Party became the "party of empire," using appeals to pride in global dominance to win elections. German leaders believed that if the public's attention could be focused on military glory and imperial expansion, then nationalism would strengthen German unity and weaken the appeal of socialism.

Ideology and Personal Ambition

In the late nineteenth century, Europeans advanced the idea of a "civilizing mission"—that the "natives" needed European stewardship for their own "improvement"— cloaking their self-interest in humanitarian justifications. Earlier, the French and mid-Victorian Britons had approached Africa with a more liberal orientation emphasizing African potential for civilizational equality. Of course, their concept of "civilization" was ethnocentric: they sought to raise Africans and other "natives" to the "superior" European level. Still, they had placed no limit on what Africans with proper education and social circumstances might achieve. Missionaries inspired by the abolitionist movement focused on the salvation of African souls and the redemption of the continent from spiritual practices they regarded as primitive superstition, but many thought it would be Africans themselves who would ultimately uplift the continent spiritually and materially.

The career of **David Livingstone** (1813–1873), the great Scottish missionary, exemplifies this belief in Africans' intellectual and spiritual capacity. Livingstone spent the better part of his life exploring the continent and preaching Christianity to its people. His dream was to have African Christians take over positions of church leadership. In pursuit of this goal, he spent time among the Bangwato, serving as a tutor to one of the kings who accompanied Khama to London.

On the other side of the continent, Samuel Ajayi Crowther, the first African bishop of the Church of England, was fulfilling Livingstone's goal. Born in what is now western Nigeria, Crowther was sold into slavery in 1821. By then the British

Second Industrial Revolution

The more technologically sophisticated and capital intensive industrialism of the later nineteenth century. Electricity, steel, and petroleum superseded coal and iron, and large corporations now required secure access to natural resources from around the world.

David Livingstone

(1813–1873) Scottish missionary and explorer idolized in Britain for his commitment to the spiritual and moral salvation of Africans.

were committed to abolition, and the Royal Navy seized the Portuguese ship on which he was held captive, dropping the twelve-year-old off at Freetown in Sierra Leone, earlier established as a home for such "re-captives." After education in Sierra Leone and England, and having served on a mission to the Niger River, Crowther was ordained as an Anglican priest. One of his enduring contributions to African Christianity was his translation of the Christian texts into his own native Yoruba and other African languages.

In 1864, Crowther became the Anglican bishop of West Africa. But some white missionaries resented his appointment and refused to follow his directives. Unlike Livingstone, they viewed blacks as permanent children, incapable of handling high office. Such racism forced Crowther into retirement, and an English bishop replaced him. In the harsher racial environment fostered by the New Imperialism, the dream of African church leadership withered.

Some African Christians responded to clerical racism by rejecting European religious authority altogether. In founding their own churches, African Protestants often looked to the ancient Ethiopian Church for inspiration, stressing the historical fact that African Christianity could flourish under African control. (See the feature "Movement of Ideas Through Primary Sources: Pan-Africanism and African Identity.") African Catholics, in contrast, did not have the option of autonomy, bound as they were to the authority of Rome. It would be many years before African priests and bishops would rise to prominence.

Bishop Crowther's story shows that by the later nineteenth century liberal optimism in African capacities was fading. By the end of the century, Social Darwinism, the idea that humanity consists of a set of clearly demarcated racial groups arranged along a hierarchy of ability, had become Europe's conventional wisdom. Now most white people saw themselves as sitting atop an unchangeable hierarchy of races, a belief that justified colonial expansion as part of the natural order of things.

● **CONTEXT&CONNECTIONS** The shock of the *Indian Revolt of 1857* (Chapter 24) had contributed to the hardening of British racial attitudes. ●

The change in later Victorian times is shown in the contrast between David Livingstone and the young journalist and explorer Henry Morton Stanley (1841–1904), who set off to find Livingstone in Central Africa when he was feared lost. Unlike Livingstone, who lived peacefully among Africans and acknowledged their help and hospitality, Stanley organized his expedition along military lines, treating Africans so harshly that the British government insisted that he stop flying the Union Jack. Stanley later traced the great Congo River from its source deep in Central Africa to its outlet on the Atlantic and, having been rebuffed by Britain, formed an alliance with the ambitious **King Leopold II of Belgium** (r. 1865–1909) to profit from his discoveries.

Belgium was a small kingdom that had become independent only in 1830. Leopold envied Queen Victoria's vast empire and, convinced that great wealth could be gained in Africa, declared, *"I must have my share of this magnificent African cake!"* Against a background of intensified competition for markets and raw materials for industry and the surging nationalism of European politics, Leopold's initiative to use the Congo River as a gateway to a vast Central African empire was the spark that set off a mad rush for African territory.

Concerned that Leopold's imperialism might destabilize the balance of power in Europe, Germany's Otto von Bismarck brought together representatives of the European colonial powers at the **Berlin Conference** in 1884 to establish

King Leopold II of Belgium

(r. 1865–1909) Ignited a "scramble for Africa" when he claimed the large area of Central Africa he called the Congo Free State. The ruthless exploitation of Congolese rubber by Leopold's agents led to millions of deaths.

Berlin Conference

(1884) Conference organized by the German chancellor Otto von Bismarck in which representatives of the major European states divided Africa among themselves.

Pan-Africanism and African Identity

Pan-Africanism stresses the shared destiny of people of African descent around the world, especially between continental Africans and people of African descent in the Americas. Among the first great Pan-African thinkers was Edward Wilmot Blyden (1832–1912). A child of free blacks from the Virgin Islands, Blyden spent many years living in West Africa.

In his early writings, Blyden focused on the potential for African uplift that would follow from a significant repatriation of American blacks back to their continent of origin. He lived in Liberia, an independent republic founded by free American blacks in 1847, and in Sierra Leone, where the British colony sent "re-captives" they had liberated from Atlantic slave ships.

Later, after European conquest and partition, Blyden, while himself a Christian, came to emphasize Islam as a more suitable pathway toward literacy and civilizational progress for Africans, adding the study of Arabic to his educational recommendations. (In Liberia, Blyden taught Arabic as well as classical Greek and Latin.)

By regarding all people of African descent as partaking of a common destiny and by emphasizing higher education as a pathway toward racial improvement, Blyden anticipated the projects of later Pan-Africanists, including the influential African American writer and activist W. E. B. Du Bois (1868–1963). Both men stressed the need for black racial solidarity to overcome the political disabilities and psychic traumas resulting from slavery, racism, and colonization.

> Blyden was not opposed to European-style education, but worried about the side effects it might have on Africans. Why was he worried?

> How does Blyden use history to illuminate what he sees as the main differences between Christian and Muslim Africans?

Source: *Black Spokesman: Selected Published Writings of Edward Wilmot Blyden*, ed. Hollis R. Lynch (New York: Humanities Press, 1971).

Race and the African Personality

[F]or every one of us—there is a special work to be done ... a work for the Race to which we belong. It is a great Race—great in its vitality, in its powers of endurance and its prospect of perpetuity. It has passed through the fiery furnace of centuries of indigenous barbarism and foreign slavery and yet it remains unconsumed. Well, now, there is a responsibility which our personality, our membership in this Race involves. It is sad to think that there are some Africans, especially among those who have enjoyed the advantages of foreign training, who are blind enough to the radical facts of humanity as to say, "Let us do away with the sentiment of Race. Let us do away with our African personality and be lost, if possible, in another Race."

That is as wise ... as to say let us do away with gravitation, with heat and cold and sunshine and rain. Of course, the other Race in which these persons would be absorbed is the dominant Race, before which, in cringing self-surrender and ignoble self-suppression, they lie in prostrate admiration.... Your place has been assigned to you in the Universe as Africans, and there is no room for you as anything else....

Therefore, honour and love your Race. Be yourselves, as God intended you to be or he would not have made you thus.... If you are not yourself, if you surrender your personality, you have nothing left to give the world.... There is hardly anything new in a material sense, that the so-called civilized African can contribute to the world's resources, but if his individuality is preserved and developed on right or righteous lines, he will bring intellectual and spiritual contributions which Humanity will gladly welcome.

Christianity, Islam, and Africa

Having enjoyed exceptional advantages for observation and comparison in the United States, the West Indies, South America, Egypt, Syria, West and Central Africa, we are compelled, however reluctantly, to [say that] wherever the Negro is found in Christian lands, his leading trait is ... servility. He is slow and unprogressive. Individuals may be found here and there of extraordinary intelligence, enterprise and energy, but there is no Christian community of Negroes anywhere which is self-reliant and independent....

On the other hand, there are numerous Negro [Muslim] communities and states in Africa which are self-reliant, productive, independent and dominant, supporting, without the countenance or patronage of the parent country, Arabia, whence they derived them, their political, literary, and ecclesiastical institutions....

Now, what has produced this difference in the effects of the two systems upon the Negro race? [Islam] found its Negro converts at home in a state of freedom and independence.... When it was offered to them they were at liberty to choose for themselves.... [They] become Muslims from choice and conviction, and bring all the manliness of their former condition to the maintenance and support of their new creed.... [T]he Arab superstructure has been superimposed on a permanent indigenous infrastructure; so that what really took place, when the Arab met the Negro in his own home, was a healthy amalgamation, and not an absorption or an undue repression ... shaping many of its traditional customs to suit the milder and more conciliatory disposition of the Negro.

Christianity, on the other hand, came to the Negro as a slave, or at least as a subject race in a foreign land. Along with the Christian teaching, he and his children received lessons on their utter and permanent inferiority and subordination to their instructors.... The religion of Jesus was embraced by them as their only consolation in their deep disasters.... It found them down-trodden,

oppressed, scorned; it soothed their sufferings [and] subdued their hearts.... These are great advantages, but ... all tendencies to independent individuality were repressed and destroyed. Their ideas and aspirations only in conformity with the views and tastes of those who held rule over them....
[N]o amount of allegiance to the Gospel relieved the Christian Negro from the degradation of wearing the chain he received with it.... Everywhere in Christian lands he plays, at the present moment, the part of the slave, ape, or puppet....

The Mohammedan Negro has felt nothing of the withering power of caste. There is nothing in his colour or race to debar him from the highest privileges, social or political, to which any other Muslim can attain. Mohammedan history abounds with examples of distinguished Negroes. The eloquent *Azan*, or "Call to Prayer" ... was first uttered by a Negro, Bilâl by name, whom Mohammed ... appointed the first Muezzin....

Now, it must be evident that Negroes trained under the influence of a [Muslim] social and literary atmosphere must have a deeper self-respect ... than those trained under the blighting influence of caste, and under the guidance of a literature in which it has been the fashion for more than two hundred years to caricature the African, to ridicule his personal peculiarities, and to impress him with a sense of perpetual and hopeless inferiority.

The sympathy ... between the Arab missionary and the African is more complete than that between European and the Negro. With every wish, no doubt, to the contrary, the European seldom or never gets over the feeling of distance, if not of repulsion, which he experiences on first seeing the Negro.... The African convert ... acquires a very low opinion of himself, learns to depreciate and deprecate his own personal characteristics, and loses that "sense of the dignity of human nature" which observant travelers have noticed in the Mohammedan Negro.

rules for the partition of Africa. No Africans were present. The European delegates declared that the boundaries of European possessions in Africa would be recognized only where the claimant established *"effective occupation."* For Africans, this meant twenty years of constant warfare and instability as European governments launched a wave of invasions to secure the effective occupation of the territories they claimed, setting off the "scramble for Africa." Millions of Africans would die.

Africa and the New Imperialism

As late as 1878, Europe's colonial presence was almost entirely restricted to the African coast (see Map 26.1). The all-out scramble for control of African territory was therefore something new. In contrast to India, where British power had been expanding since the eighteenth century, most Africans confronted European power only *after* the development of industrial technology like machine guns, field cannon, telegraphs, and steamships. The suddenness of the onslaught caught Africans off guard. Should they fight back? Seek diplomatic options? Ally themselves with the intruders? African leaders tried all of these options, with little success.

Although European imperialists reduced Africa to a set of simple stereotypes, with "tribal Africa" representing the "heart of darkness," in reality it was a continent of immense cultural and geographic complexity. Africa's own historical dynamics, including the rise of Muslim states in West Africa, the creation of the Zulu empire in the far south, and the expanding nineteenth-century trade in ivory and slaves in East Africa, are an essential context for understanding Europe's partition of the continent.

Western and Eastern Africa After the abolition of the transatlantic slave trade, European merchants shifted their business in West Africa from the purchase of human beings to the search for commodities needed to supply expanding factories at home. While Egypt became a major source of raw cotton for British industry (see Chapter 23), the most important product coming from sub-Saharan Africa was palm oil for use as an industrial lubricant. Starting in the 1820s, African farmers planted and processed oil products for the export market, and many West African merchants became wealthy in this trade. Factory-produced cloth and iron goods were becoming cheaper at the same time, as higher demand was increasing the price Europeans would pay for palm oil. At least in some regions, Africans found the terms of trade moving in their favor.

Initially, as West African economies became more integrated into world markets, political power remained with African kingdoms and chiefdoms. In an influential essay in 1868, a British-educated African surgeon named John Africanus Horton called for African kingdoms to reform themselves by incorporating Western constitutional practices, as their contemporaries were doing in Japan (see Chapter 24). Like Bishop Crowther, Dr. Horton had established his career at a time when it was thought that the future lay with European-educated Africans. Now, as the forces of conquest gathered, Horton's idea that African traditions might be merged with Western models to secure the continent's progress quickly became obsolete.

● **CONTEXT&CONNECTIONS** European-educated African Christians like John Africanus Horton, ambitious to reconcile local cultures and institutions with the progress and

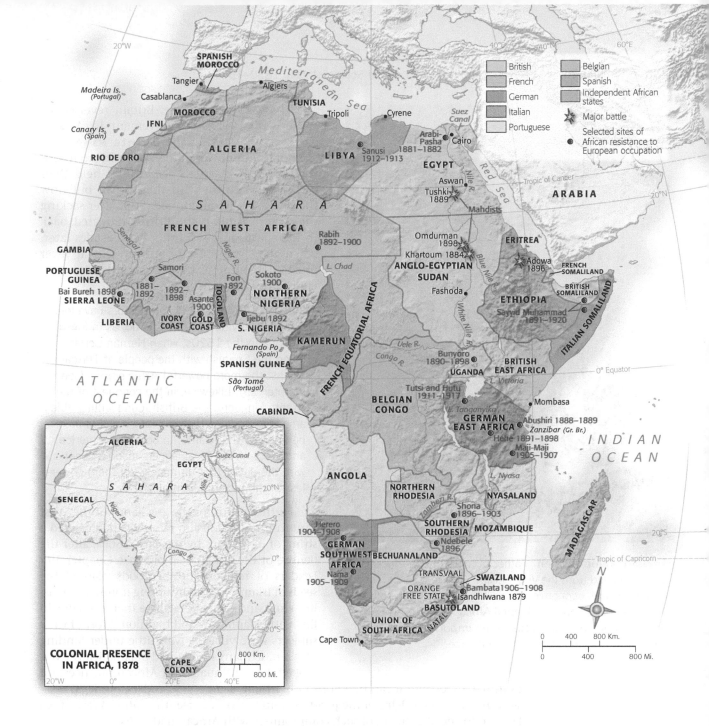

Map 26.1 Africa, 1878 and 1914 The dramatic expansion of European imperialism in Africa is seen in the comparison of maps from 1878 and 1914. Before the "scramble for Africa" the European colonial presence was largely limited to small coastal enclaves, with some movement inland only in Algeria and the Cape Colony. By 1914, Europeans dominated the entire continent, with only Liberia and Ethiopia retaining their independence. The British were the main power in eastern and southern Africa, the French in western and northern Africa, and the Belgians in Central Africa.

modernity they associated with Europe, had much in common with *Rammohun Roy* and the earlier Bengal Renaissance (Chapter 20). In India as well as Africa, these reformers' efforts were stifled by imperial officials and other whites for whom, by the end of the century, racial hierarchies had become fixed and immutable. ●

Historical/Corbis

Edward Wilmot Blyden   Father of modern Pan-Africanism, Blyden moved from the Virgin Islands to West Africa, advocating political, economic, and cultural cooperation between American blacks and continental Africans. Above all, Blyden was an educator who stressed the importance of black empowerment and black self-confidence.

In 1874, for example, Britain reversed its earlier policy of noninvolvement in Africa's interior by attacking the **Asante kingdom**, the dominant power in the West African forest. In the 1820s, Asante's armies had held their own in a skirmish with the British, but now they were badly outgunned. Still, after sacking the Asante capital, the British retreated back to the coast, only returning two decades later, when the "scramble for Africa" was at fever pitch, to complete their conquest (discussed later in this section).

● **CONTEXT&CONNECTIONS** Conquerors have long used the "divide and rule" tactic, as in Meso-america in the 1520s, when Hernán Cortés allied the Spanish with the people of Tlaxcala against the more powerful *Aztec empire* (see Chapter 15). Likewise, in the conquest of the Asante kingdom, the British found willing allies among chiefdoms that had long resisted incorporation by the Asante. In both Mesoamerica and West Africa, local leaders made a "deal with the devil" that ultimately left them powerless in the face of alien rule. ●

Further north, in the grasslands of the West African interior, Muslim reformers had created a string of new states by the early 1800s, after the demise of the Songhai empire (see Chapter 19). Leaders of religious brotherhoods planted the seeds of Islamic reform by urging nominally Muslim kings and emirs to regulate their domains in line with Islamic law and tradition. Most of their subjects were villagers with little understanding of Islam, so many leaders had pragmatically overlooked the continuation of African practices, for example, by using African traditions rather than Islamic jurisprudence in legal decision making. The origins of the jihad movements of nineteenth-century West Africa lay in reformers' criticism of such compromises with African traditions.

One of the most important West African jihad leaders was Shehu Usuman dan Fodio (1754–1817). In what is now northern Nigeria, dan Fodio called for local emirs to put their governments in line with Islamic law. When one emir tried to assassinate him, Usuman dan Fodio (OO-soo-mahn dahn FOH-dee-oh) retreated to the desert, built a large army, conquered his enemies, and consolidated the emirates into the new Sokoto (SOH-kuh-toh) caliphate. From here the jihadist impulse spread both east and west.

Throughout the nineteenth century, West African Muslim populations became stricter in their practice, and Islam gained large numbers of new adherents. Nana Asma'u, Shehu Usuman's daughter, established an enduring reputation across the Sahel for establishing Islamic schools and advocating religious education for

Asante kingdom

Dominant power in the West African forest in the eighteenth and early nineteenth centuries. The Asante capital was sacked by British forces in 1874 and again in 1896. In 1900, Yaa Asantewa's War represented a final attempt to expel the British.

women. Her writings in Arabic and Hausa, especially her poems, are still widely read.

At first, the leaders of West African jihadist states were focused on reforming their own Muslim societies and paid little attention to Europeans. However, when the French began to move further up the Senegal River in the 1870s, territorial ambitions clashed and conflict followed.

The West African Muslim who organized the most sustained resistance to the French invasion was **Samori Toure** (ca. 1830–1900). From a relatively humble merchant background, Samori Toure (sam-or-REE too-RAY) built a new state on the upper Niger by training soldiers to use imported rifles. At first his ambitions were merely political, but in 1884 he declared himself to be *"commander of the faithful,"* leader of a jihad against lax Muslims and unbelievers. Even then, Samori avoided confronting the French, focusing instead on controlling trade routes in slaves, salt, and gold. But once the French had conquered his neighbors, they turned their firepower on him.

Unable to prevail in conventional warfare, in 1891 Samori retreated to the east with his army and launched a grueling guerrilla campaign. But success at guerilla war requires support from the local population. Samori's forces had none, earning the hatred of the local people by taking whatever they needed. Cut off from access to imported ammunition and gunpowder, Samori's soldiers learned to manufacture their own from local materials but eventually succumbed. After the French captured and exiled Samori in 1893, they were masters from the Senegal to the Niger Rivers.

The French march to the east threatened British control of Egypt and the Nile Valley. British forces thus moved to achieve "effective occupation" over the savanna region still dominated by the Sokoto caliphate. After Usuman dan Fodio's death, the caliphate became decentralized into a number of separate emirates, so the British did not face the combined armies of a unified caliphate. British rifles and machine guns mowed down the emirs' cavalry charges, and British field cannon easily breached their city walls. Some emirs fought, some fled, and some surrendered, as British forces took control of what is now northern Nigeria.

In West Africa, the lack of alliances among African peoples facilitated European imperialism. Without organizational or ideological foundations for a broader unity, African leaders dealt only with the local manifestations of the scramble for Africa. Possessing a broader overview of African developments, the Europeans used their superior communications technology and geographical knowledge to great advantage.

The nineteenth century was even more violent in East Africa, where a new slave trade began even as the Atlantic trade was diminishing. Along the coast, the Swahili city-states had long focused outward, on Indian Ocean trade (see Chapter 16). In the early nineteenth century, however, interior peoples began to bring increased supplies of ivory to the coast in response to rising demand in the West for billiard balls, piano keys, combs, and other products manufactured from expensive elephant tusks. Soon well-armed caravans, often financed by Indian bankers and organized by Arab or Swahili merchants, were marching into the interior. These militarized trading ventures decimated elephant herds and, even more tragically, intensified the East African slave trade. Appeals from David Livingstone and other European observers to end the Arab-dominated trade provided a strong humanitarian argument for greater British involvement in the interior of East Africa.

Samori Toure

(ca. 1830–1900) Founder of a major state in West Africa who adopted the pose of a jihadist leader in competition with neighboring kingdoms. After being forced into confrontation by the French, he launched a long but unsuccessful guerrilla campaign against them.

By the 1880s, the British and the Germans were scrambling for East African territory, especially Lake Victoria (as the British renamed it) and the headwaters of the Nile. Already devastated by the slave trade, East Africans were unable to stop them.

Southern Africa

In southern Africa as well, the dynamics of African history intersected with European imperialism. Long before the Dutch established their settlement at Cape Town (see Chapter 16), the ancestors of King Khama and his people—Bantu-speaking farmers, herders, and ironworkers—had populated the land.

● **CONTEXT&CONNECTIONS** About four thousand years ago, the distant Bantu-speaking ancestors of peoples like Khama's Bangwato were moving outward from the region of Eastern Nigeria in a complex series of migrations. Some moved south into the Central African rain forest, and others went east to the *Great Lakes region* (Chapter 19), then southward through the eastern savannas. Bantu speakers, farming peoples with relatively dense populations, large herds of cattle, and iron tools, then displaced indigenous foraging societies as the dominant cultural force across southern Africa. ●

In the late eighteenth century, drought led small chiefdoms in southern Africa to band together to secure permanent water sources. The most successful of the new states was the Zulu empire of **Shaka** (r. 1820–1828). He formed a standing army of soldiers from different clans, emphasizing their loyalty to him and to the Zulu state rather than to their own chiefdoms, and chose his generals on the basis of merit rather than chiefly status. Young women were organized into agricultural regiments, and no one was allowed to marry without Shaka's permission.

Shaka's conquests were known as the *mfecane* (mm-fuh-KAHN-ay), "the crushing." Many chiefdoms were violently absorbed into the Zulu empire, though some neighboring chiefs submitted voluntarily. In either case, conquered peoples were merged into Zulu society and became Zulu, as what had been a small chiefdom became a mighty nation. The mfecane set in motion a chain reaction as other leaders copied Zulu military tactics and carried the frontier of warfare a thousand miles north. The Bangwato and other societies in the interior fled, abandoning much of their land.

At the same time that the mfecane was disrupting southern African societies, descendants of earlier Dutch and French colonists, called Boers, were seeking land for further expansion. The Boers moved into territories temporarily depopulated in the wake of Zulu warfare, causing frontier conflicts that alarmed British authorities.

● **CONTEXT&CONNECTIONS** In the twentieth century, the Boers would more commonly be referred to as Afrikaners. They speak the Afrikaans language, derived from the seventeenth-century Dutch used by their ancestors when they left Cape Town to strike out on the frontier (see Chapter 16). It was Afrikaner nationalists who created the racist *apartheid* state after 1948 (Chapter 30), but who later compromised with the African National Congress and *Nelson Mandela* (Chapter 31) to build a multiracial, democratic South Africa. ●

The British were a new factor in southern Africa in the early 1800s, having taken Cape Town from the Dutch during the Napoleonic Wars. Though their main concern was the security of Cape Town and the maritime route to India, they became embroiled on the frontier, where the Boers, searching for land and resenting British interference, came into conflict with African societies.

Shaka
(r. 1820–1828) Founder and ruler of the Zulu empire. Zulu military tactics revolutionized warfare in southern Africa. Through the *mfecane*, or "crushing," Shaka violently absorbed many surrounding societies into his empire.

Cecil Rhodes
(1853–1902) British entrepreneur, mining magnate, head of the British South Africa Company, and prime minister of the Cape Colony; played a major role in the expansion of British territory in southern Africa.

The Boers had never been able to subdue African resistance to their encroachment, but British firepower now overwhelmed some Xhosa (KOH-suh) chiefdoms, which lost rich grazing lands to the colonists. Neither negotiation nor military resistance could stem the European tide. Contact with colonial society also deeply divided Xhosa society. Traditionalists saw those Xhosa who converted to Christianity and grew crops for colonial markets as having abandoned their own people and traditions.

Then disaster struck. A cattle disease, inadvertently introduced by the Europeans in the 1850s, wiped out large numbers of Xhosa cattle. Facing starvation as well as invasion, some Xhosa turned to the prophecies of a young woman, Nongqawuse (nawng-ka-WOO-say) (ca. 1840–1898), who said the spirits told her that if the people slaughtered their remaining cattle, ancestral warriors would return, evil would be purged from the land, and new cattle herds would emerge from the ground. Belief in the power of ancestors, and in the power of certain women to communicate with them, was traditional to the Xhosa. But the idea that the resurrection of the dead would accompany a new era of peace was borrowed from Methodist missionaries, an example of syncretism (see Chapter 18).

Lacking other means of resistance, many Xhosa followed Nongqawuse's prophecy and killed their cattle. When the prophecy did not come true, hunger spread throughout the land. The **Xhosa Cattle Killing** of 1856–1857 ensured the success of British conquest. Over one hundred thousand African lives were lost, while the survivors were incorporated into Britain's Cape Colony.

Unlike the Xhosa, the Zulu and most other southern African societies retained their sovereignty into the 1870s. Their colonial fate was not determined until mineral discoveries—diamonds in 1868 and gold in 1884—combined with the "effective occupation" required by the Berlin Conference finally motivated the British to conquer the rest of the South African interior.

In 1879, British authorities issued an ultimatum demanding that the Zulu king Cetshwayo disband his regiments. Cetshwayo (chet-SWAY-yoh) refused to comply. Zulu warriors did defeat the British at the major Battle of Isandhlwana (ee-san-DLWAH-nah), but like the Battle of Little Bighorn (see Chapter 25), this defeat only made the invaders more determined. Zulu warriors had been trained to rush the enemy in dense regimental ranks, a successful tactic under Shaka that British cannon and machine guns rendered suicidal. Soon the British sacked the Zulu capital and sent Cetshwayo into exile.

The main figure of the New Imperialism in southern Africa was **Cecil Rhodes** (1853–1902), a mining magnate who advocated a British empire

Xhosa Cattle Killing (1856–1857) A large cattle die-off in Africa caused by a European disease. Some Xhosa accepted Nongqawuse's prophecies that if the people cleansed themselves and killed their cattle their ancestors would return and bring peace and prosperity. The result was famine and Xhosa subjection to the British.

The Granger Collection, NYC

THE RHODES COLOSSUS
STRIDING FROM CAPE TOWN TO CAIRO.

Cecil Rhodes Victorian imperialist Cecil Rhodes dreamed of British imperial control of eastern and southern Africa "from Cape to Cairo." Combining political and economic clout, Rhodes was prime minister of the Cape Colony, owner of some of the world's richest gold and diamond mines, and head of the British South Africa Company. He later endowed the Rhodes Scholarship program to bring elite Americans of British descent to Oxford University in England so that the United States might share Britain's imperial purpose.

"from Cape to Cairo." His British South Africa Company (BSAC) was a chartered company with its own army and ambitions for conquest. It was to avoid annexation by the BSAC that Khama traveled to London.

Earlier the Boers, resentful of British intrusion and proud of their independence, had created several republics in the northern interior of South Africa. British recognition of their independence would not long endure, for in 1884 the greatest gold discovery in world history took place right in the heart of Boer territory. The clash between Boer aspirations for independence and Cecil Rhodes' drive for gold inevitably led to the South African War (1899–1902).

The British had no trouble taking control of the towns and railway lines, but the Boer combatants blended into the civilian population and launched guerrilla attacks in the countryside. To separate civilians from soldiers, the British put Boer civilians into "concentration camps" (the first use of that term). Over twenty thousand, many of them women and children, died of illness. Though the South African War was between the British and the Boers, tens of thousands of Africans were also killed.

The British won the war but then compromised with their defeated foes. The **Union of South Africa** (1910) was created by joining British colonies with former Boer republics under a single constitution, creating, as in Canada, a self-governing dominion within the British empire (see Chapter 25). British and Boer leaders compromised by emphasizing what they had in common: the need for cheap African labor.

British mine owners and Boer farmers thus both embraced the Union as "an alliance of gold and maize." In 1913 the Native Land Act, passed by the new, all-white South African parliament, limited Africans to "native reserves" that included only a tiny proportion of their traditional landholdings. The goal was to strip indigenous communities of their agricultural self-sufficiency and thus drive Africans to work in mines and on white farms at the lowest possible pay, laying the economic foundations for what would later be called apartheid.

Union of South Africa

Self-governing dominion within the British empire created in 1910 from a number of British colonies and Boer republics after the South African War. This compromise protected both British mining and Boer agriculture at the expense of African interests.

● **CONTEXT&CONNECTIONS** Two distinct types of European colonialism developed in Africa. In settler colonies like South Africa, restrictions on African landholding drove Africans onto European farms and into European mines to work for very low wages. French Algeria, British Rhodesia (today's Zimbabwe), and the "white highlands" of Kenya were other settler colonies. Elsewhere, as across West Africa, Africans retained control of their own land and labor while growing commercial crops for export and paying taxes to the colonial state. It was in settler colonies that decolonization after the Second World War would be most violent (see Chapter 30). ●

Because of King Khama's negotiations with the British government, his people were not part of the Union of South Africa and were ruled instead by the British Colonial Office. The Zulu and the Xhosa, meanwhile, like other Africans incorporated into South Africa, experienced the harshest form of colonial racism. As mineworkers and low-wage laborers on settler farms, they struggled at the lowest level of the global economy.

Meanwhile, in neighboring German Southwest Africa (today's Namibia), another chilling precedent was being set for the twentieth century. In 1904, after a Herero rebellion was put down by superior European firepower, the German commander ordered that the Herero be driven into the Kalahari Desert and prevented from returning. Tens of thousands of them died in the century's first *genocide*, an attempt to destroy an entire people and their culture.

African Resistance to Conquest

Between 1880 and 1900, European powers occupied and partitioned Africa. France and Britain held the largest African empires; Portugal and Germany each had substantial territories in the east and south; Italy and Spain were relatively minor players; and King Leopold of Belgium claimed the vast Congo in the center of the continent.

In spite of European technological superiority, Africans fought back. The Nile Valley was one arena of resistance. Its strategic value increased with the construction of the **Suez Canal** between the Mediterranean and the Red Sea in 1869. Financed by French and English capital, the canal became the main shipping route between Europe and Asia.

The Egyptian *khedive* (a descendant of Muhammad Ali, see Chapter 23) thought that revenue from the canal would allow Egypt to maintain its independence. But cotton prices, and Egyptian government revenue, dropped sharply after 1865, when the end of the American Civil War brought U.S. cotton back onto the world market. Unable to pay the country's debts, the khedive was forced to sell Egypt's shares in the Suez Canal to the British and to accept European oversight of government finances. European officers were imposed on the Egyptian military, which was reorganized as an Anglo-Egyptian force.

In 1882, nationalist Egyptian military officers rebelled against the khedive and his European backers but the British quickly suppressed the uprising and then forced the khedive to accept a governor-general to oversee the Egyptian government. The British thus came to dominate Egypt, much as they dominated the "princely states" in India (see Chapter 24), taking real power into their own hands while allowing indigenous rulers their traditional titles and luxurious lifestyles.

Once in control of Egypt, the British needed to secure the Upper Nile Valley as well. Here they faced resistance from a jihadist state in Sudan, where a cleric named **Muhammad Ahmad** (1844–1885) proclaimed himself to be **the Mahdi** (MAH-dee), the "guided one" that some Muslims believe will come to announce the end of days and the final judgment of humankind. In 1881, he declared a holy war against Egypt, which also brought him into conflict with Britain. The Mahdi's forces took the strategic city of Khartoum in 1884, killing the British commander of a combined Anglo-Egyptian force. When Muhammad Ahmad died of typhus a few months later, however, his movement lost direction.

The jihadist movement regained momentum in the 1890s under the *khalifa* ("successor") to the Mahdi, as the British now sought "effective occupation" over the entire Nile Valley. The Battle of Omdurman (1898) was the bloodiest battle between European and African forces during the entire period. Though outnumbered two to one, Anglo-Egyptian forces used their Maxim guns to terrible effect. The British lost forty-seven soldiers; over ten thousand Sudanese forces were killed, some shot as they lay wounded on the field.

French conquests in the interior prompted the British to "effectively occupy" coastal territories and thus in 1896 to finally put an end to Asante independence. The Asante king reluctantly accepted a British protectorate, but his people rebelled after the new British governor demanded the "Golden Stool," the sacred symbol of the nation and its kings. (By legend, a chief priest had caused the Golden Stool to descend from the heavens; for an outsider to touch it would be a horrible desecration.)

As they prepared for war some Asante fighters, no strangers to British firepower, doubted the outcome. A queen mother, Yaa Asantewa (YAH ah-san-TAY-wuh),

Suez Canal

(1869) French-designed canal built between the Mediterranean and the Red Seas that greatly shortened shipping times between Europe and Asia; dominated by European economic interests.

Muhammad Ahmad, the Mahdi

(1844–1885) *Mahdi* is the term some Muslims use for the "guided one" expected to appear before the end of days. Muhammad Ahmad took this title in Sudan and called for a jihad against British-dominated Egypt.

stood forward and spoke: *"[If] you the men of Asante will not go forward, then we ... the women will. I shall call upon my fellow women. We will fight the white men. We will fight till the last of us falls in the battlefields."** The Yaa Asantewa War of 1900 was a military defeat for the Asante, but it caused later British governors to treat the Asante royal family with greater respect and to acknowledge Asante traditions.

The British also faced stiff resistance in the southern African kingdom of the Ndebele (nn-day-BEH-lay). Descendants of a Zulu regiment that had moved northward, the Ndebele were militarily formidable, but no match for the British South Africa Company of Cecil Rhodes. Lobengula, their king, tried to protect his people by signing a treaty granting the British mineral rights while retaining his own authority on the land. Even so, Lobengula recognized that the invaders were unlikely to keep their promises. *"Did you ever see a chameleon catch a fly?"* he asked a missionary. *"The chameleon gets behind the fly and remains motionless for some time, then he advances very slowly and gently ... [then] he darts his tongue and the fly disappears. England is the chameleon and I am that fly."*† Sure enough, the Ndebele were absorbed into the British colony of Rhodesia after losing two wars of resistance in the 1890s.

● **CONTEXT&CONNECTIONS** Lobengula's quandary was very familiar to nineteenth-century Amerindian leaders. Just as *Sitting Bull* (Chapter 25) led the Lakota into confrontation with the United States after the government broke its promise to leave the Black Hills in their hands for all time, so Lobengula rallied Ndebele warriors to defend their land and people when the British broke their treaties. ●

Coordinating resistance was even more difficult in regions where traditional political organization was less centralized. The Maji Maji (MAH-jee MAH-jee) Revolt in German East Africa was led by a religious prophet, Kinjekitile (kihn-JAY-kee-TEE-lay), who attempted to forge an alliance among numerous small chiefdoms. In the 1890s, German military conquest had met little opposition, with local leaders deciding to follow the traditional course of paying tribute in cattle to more powerful overlords while continuing to mind their own affairs. That arrangement did not suit the Germans, however, who were interested not in cattle, but in exportable commodities. By 1905, people in the region had grown angry after the Germans forced them at gun point to grow cotton. African farmers were left with little time to tend their own food crops. The payment they received was barely enough to pay colonial taxes, and cotton robbed their fields of fertility.

Maji Maji meant "powerful water," a reference to a sacred pool that attracted pilgrims from a wide area, which Kinjekitile used as a rallying point. He promised his followers that bathing in the sacred stream would make them immune to German bullets. Of course, this did not happen, and the Germans ruthlessly suppressed the uprising. But they also learned not to press their advantage too far, and they no longer enforced mandatory cotton growing. Rebellions, after all, were expensive. The Maji Maji rebellion was just one of many that showed how Africans' willingness to fight could force the Europeans to moderate their policies. While military defeat was inevitable, their resistance was not futile.

Nonetheless, the imperial powers consistently demeaned Africans, as exemplified by a new fad of displaying "natives" as a curiosity at Western expositions.

---

*Yaa Asantewa, cited in David Sweetman, *Women Leaders in African History* (London: Heinemann, 1984), pp. 34–35.
†Neil Parsons, *A New History of Southern Africa*, 2d ed. (London: Macmillan, 1993).

One wonders what King Khama and his colleagues thought when, dressed in Victorian garb, they were taken to see a "Somali village" and its "primitive" residents on display at London's Crystal Palace. The worst excess came in 1906, when a Central African named Ota Benga was displayed in a cage at the Bronx Zoo in New York. He later committed suicide. The disrespect and cruelty fostered by such racism long endured.

The New Imperialism in Southeast Asia, Austronesia, and the Pacific

As in Africa, Europeans had long competed for access to trade in Southeast Asia and had established some imperial bases, but here as well it was only in the late nineteenth century that the New Imperialism led to nearly complete Western domination. In mainland Southeast Asia, the French allied with Vietnamese emperors to extend their power over what became French Indochina. The British expanded from India into Burma and Malaya. The Dutch dominated the thousands of islands that make up insular Southeast Asia; the United States joined the imperial club when it took the Philippines from Spain (see Map 26.2). Meanwhile, the British consolidated their control over Australia and New Zealand, and Europeans, Americans, and Japanese hoisted their flags across the islands of the Pacific (see Map 26.2).

Mainland Southeast Asia

The French occupied Vietnam by displacing its imperial rulers, who had modeled themselves on the Ming dynasty (see Chapter 16). In 1802, after decades of disorder, the Nguyen (noo-WEN) family had established a new dynasty, with Catholic missionaries representing French influence at the Vietnamese court. Emperor Napoleon III (see Chapter 23) then moved the French from indirect influence to direct control when he sent an army of occupation. In 1862 the besieged Nguyen ruler ceded the commercial center of Saigon to France, opened three "treaty ports" to European trade, and gave the French free passage up the Mekong (MAY-kong) River. By 1884, the French were in control of all of Vietnam but still faced guerrilla resistance. The French army of conquest, in what French authorities called a campaign of "*pacification*," killed thousands of rebels and civilians before establishing firm control.

By then French forces had also conquered the neighboring kingdom of Cambodia and had taken Laos by agreement with the kingdom of Siam (discussed in the next section). In 1897, they combined these territories into the **Federation of Indochina**, or simply French Indochina. French colonial authorities took over vast estates on which to grow rubber and turned rice into a major export crop. The profits went almost entirely to French traders and planters, though some Chinese and Vietnamese merchants in Saigon also benefited from the increase in commerce that came with the tighter integration of Southeast Asia into global markets.

Federation of Indochina

(1897) Federation created by the French after having conquered Vietnam, Cambodia, and Laos—an administrative convenience, as the societies that made up the federation had little in common.

● **CONTEXT&CONNECTIONS** Resistance to foreign occupation is a consistent theme in Vietnamese history and has been an important part of the country's identity since the early fifteenth century, when Ming armies were driven back to China (see Chapter 16). In the twentieth century, Vietnamese armies would battle the French, Japanese, and Americans (see Chapter 30) before facing another Chinese invasion in the late 1970s. Every single time, the Vietnamese forced the withdrawal of foreign invaders. ●

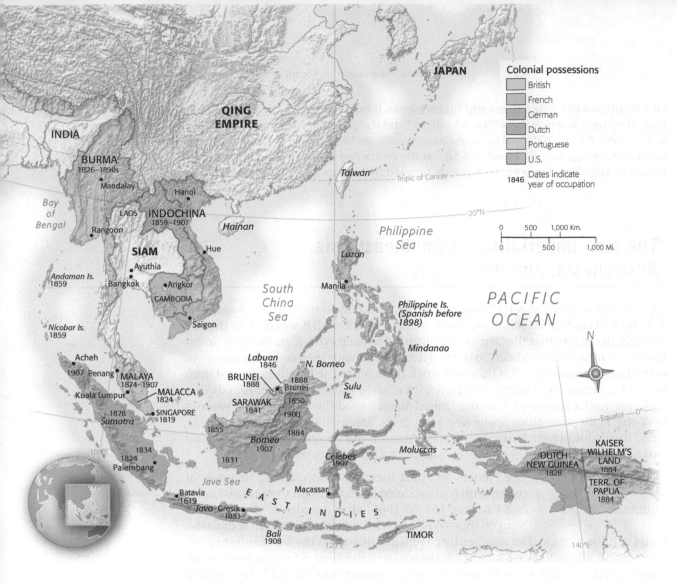

Map 26.2 The New Imperialism in Southeast Asia, 1910 European nations had controlled parts of Southeast Asia, such as the Dutch East Indies and the Spanish Philippines, since the sixteenth and seventeenth centuries. The New Imperialism of the nineteenth century strengthened the European presence in those societies while bringing the entire region, with the exception of Siam (Thailand), under Western colonial rule. In remote regions, such as the highlands of central Borneo, the process of conquest was not complete until the early twentieth century.

Burma was likewise incorporated into the British empire in stages. By the 1870s, Britain controlled the south, while in the north a reformist Burmese king attempted to modernize the country under indigenous rule. British representatives had no patience for these experiments. They refused to take off their shoes in the king's presence, a terrible affront to court protocol. Finally, in 1886 British forces invaded from India and took the capital of Mandalay. While suppressing a number of regional rebellions, they brought administrators from India and began building railroads to the rich timber resources of the Burmese jungles.

The trading city of Singapore had been Britain's most valuable possession in Southeast Asia since 1819. It attracted many Chinese immigrants and became the center of the Chinese merchant diaspora in the region, while Indians arrived as

Roger-Viollet/The Image Works

French Colonialism in Indochina Like other European colonialists, the French argued that they were developing their imperial territories for the good of their subjects through both a "civilizing" cultural mission and economic development projects such as road building. As this photograph from Southeast Asia indicates, however, it was the "natives" who did most of the work and their colonial overlords who grabbed the lion's share of profit.

clerks and office workers. Initially, the British were content to control the port and grow rich on the trade between the Indian Ocean and the South China Sea, leaving politics to the dozens of Muslim sultanates of Malaya. But after completion of the Suez Canal in 1869, British merchants became anxious to exploit the rich tin resources of the Malay Peninsula, for which the Second Industrial Revolution had dramatically increased demand.

In Malaya, as in Africa, local rivalries supported a policy of "divide and conquer." British "residents" gave local rulers "advice" on the governance of their sultanates; if a sultan refused, they would simply recognize another ambitious man as ruler and work through him. As in Egypt and the princely states of India, indigenous rulers remained in place but power was squarely in the hands of Europeans. The British prided themselves on having brought efficient administration to yet another corner of the globe. Meanwhile, they expanded plantations of commercial crops such as pepper, palm oil, and rubber.

Insular Southeast Asia, Austronesia, and the Pacific

The Dutch had been the dominant European presence in the islands of Southeast Asia since the seventeenth century (see Chapter 16). After the Dutch East India Company was disbanded in 1799, colonial authorities imposed even harsher economic conditions. In 1830, for example, Dutch authorities forced rice farmers on the island of Java to convert to sugar production. One Dutch official declared that *they must be taught to* *work, and if they were unwilling out of ignorance, they must be ordered to work."** Through such coercion the Dutch could buy sugar at low prices and then sell it for a great profit on world markets. The Europeans demanded cash taxes, and most people could obtain colonial currency only by working for Europeans or by growing cash crops for export. Peasants thus became tied to international commodity networks as they became dependent on the sale of crops like sugar and coffee.

Dutch authorities asserted more and more formal administrative control over Java and Sumatra, where individual sultans had previously been left in charge of local affairs. At the same time, the increasing presence of other European powers motivated the Dutch to seek control of hundreds of other islands. They killed or sent into exile anyone, such as rebels on the Hindu-ruled island of Bali, who resisted. The New Imperialism thus significantly deepened Dutch power over the Indonesian archipelago.

Meanwhile, the United States had claimed a direct territorial stake in the Pacific when it annexed the Hawai'ian Islands in 1898 (see Chapter 25). The further extension of American imperialism to the Philippines came as a result of the Spanish-American War of 1898–1900. That conflict, initially centered on the Caribbean island of Cuba, spread to include the Philippines, where Spain had been in power since the foundation of Manila in 1571.

Filipino resistance to Spanish authority led, in 1896, to an independence revolt. But in 1899, the Spanish handed the islands over to the United States by secret treaty. The Filipino revolutionaries continued to struggle for independence, now against a U.S. army of occupation. Over sixteen thousand Filipino combatants died.

Some in the United States protested that waging war against people fighting for independence was contrary to American principles. The writer Mark Twain joined the Anti-Imperialist League, declaring that American motives in the Philippines were no more pure than those of European imperialists and just as driven by economics. Observing the debate in American public opinion, the British poet of empire Rudyard Kipling urged America to shoulder its imperial responsibilities:

Take up the White Man's burden—
Send forth the best ye breed—
Go bind your sons to exile
To serve your captives' need;
To wait in heavy harness,
On fluttered folk and wild—
Your new-caught, sullen peoples,
Half-devil and half-child.†

Kipling worried that the British empire was in decline and that only an imperialistic United States could save the world for "Anglo-Saxon civilization." Americans needed to *"take up the White Man's burden,"* Kipling argued, for the benefit of the *"new caught, sullen peoples"* (that is, Filipinos) themselves.

---

*Cited in D. R. SarDesai, *Southeast Asia Past and Present*, 4th ed. (Boulder: Westview, 1997), p. 92.
†Verse from "The White Man's Burden" by Rudyard Kipling, from *Rudyard Kipling's Verse Definitive Edition* by Rudyard Kipling, 1920, Doubleday.

The African American writer W. E. B. Du Bois (doo BOYZ) offered a differing view of American imperialism. Noting that the New Imperialism had led to white domination across the world, he predicted in 1903 that *"the problem of the twentieth century is the problem of the color-line."** His prophecy would prove to be as accurate for the civil rights movement in the United States as it was for twentieth-century decolonization movements in Southeast Asia, Africa, and the entire colonial world.

British motivation for expansion in Australia and New Zealand predated the New Imperialism. By the 1870s, in fact, white immigrants had already reduced Australian Aborigines to a defeated and subservient people even as the continent's economy boomed, fueled by wool exports and gold discoveries. In New Zealand, however, British settlers had faced tougher resistance from the Polynesian-speaking Maori people. Though an 1840 treaty created the framework for British-Maori coexistence, guaranteeing the Maori land rights and giving them the status of British subjects, by the 1860s warfare had broken out. British victory followed, and by 1890 indigenous Maori, like their Hawai'ian cousins, had lost nearly all of their land.

The territorial acquisitions of the New Imperialism culminated in the Pacific. Japan annexed Okinawa. French Polynesia was established. Germany took New Guinea, and Samoa was divided between Germany and the United States. By century's end, there were no more unclaimed territories on which to plant the flag of empire. (See the feature "Visual Evidence in Primary Sources: National Flags.")

Case Studies in Imperialism

Case studies from Africa and Southeast Asia demonstrate the economic and political implications of the New Imperialism. The history of rubber shows how industrial and technological developments could lead to violence and death. The story of how the rulers of Siam (Thailand) and Ethiopia retained their independence shows how these exceptions prove the rule of Western dominance.

. . . .
A Case Study of the New Imperialism: Rubber

During the Second Industrial Revolution, the spread of products such as waterproof clothing and factory conveyor belts, telephones, electrical lines, and bicycles generated a booming trade in rubber. At first the only source was the Brazilian Amazon, where "rubber barons" built palatial homes while indigenous Amerindian peoples suffered from the introduction of diseases to which they had no resistance (see Chapter 25). Soon, global demand for rubber outstripped the Brazilian supply, leading to the cultivation of plantation rubber in Southeast Asia by the French in Indochina, the British in Malaya, and the Dutch in their East Indies. But it would take some years for those new Asian sources of supply to come onto the market, and Central Africa was, meanwhile, the only other source of wild rubber.

Market conditions in the 1890s thus brought a frenzied search for rubber to Central Africa, leading to the infamous abuses in the Congo Free State. This was the personal domain of King Leopold II of Belgium, who now found a way to turn his vast territories into quick cash. The Belgian king leased out

*W. E. B. Du Bois, *The Souls of Black Folk* (New York: Vintage, 1990).

National Flags

Banners and flags have a long history as markers of individual and group identity. Flags took on even more important symbolic power in the nineteenth century with the rise of European nation-states and the spread of their empires. In the West, where flags had earlier been closely associated with royal families, they now became the symbols of entire nations. The imposition of a nation's flag beyond the nation's frontier became a defining symbol of imperialism.

Here are nineteenth-century flags from societies that struggled to retain their independence: Liberia (West Africa), Ethiopia (East Africa), Siam (or Thailand, Southeast Asia), the Hawai'ian kingdom, and the Cherokee nation (United States). Creating these flags and asserting the right to fly them were important expressions of resistance to colonialism.

Courtesy Rick Wyatt. www.crwflags.com

The West African Republic of Liberia was founded in 1847 by freed American slaves. An earlier version of the flag had a cross rather than a star in the upper left. When the flag was first presented, *"many eyes were suffused with tears.... Who that looked back to America and remembered what he saw and felt there, could be otherwise than agitated?"*[*]

Courtesy Rick Wyatt. www.crwflags.com

This flag, first used in 1897, features the "Lion of Judah" as a symbol for Ethiopia. Red stands for power and faith; yellow for peace, wealth, and love; and green for land and hope. These became the colors of global African nationalism, and they can now be found on the flags of nations such as Ghana, Zimbabwe, Guyana, and Grenada. The flag has deep religious symbolism for Jamaican Rastafarians.

*Cited in Carl Patrick Burrowes, *Power and Press Freedom in Liberia, 1830–1970* (Trenton: Africa World Press, 2004), p. 60.

This flag dates from 1891. One of several different flags from Siam, it was flown above the palace only when the king was present. At the center is the royal coat of arms, with a trident and golden crown above. Later, the flag of Thailand evolved to emphasize national rather than royal identity, with horizontal stripes of red, white, and blue. **How do these flags combine indigenous and imported design elements?**

This flag was commissioned by Kamehameha the Great, the first Hawai'ian to unify the islands, in 1816, and it flew until 1893. The eight bars represent the major Hawai'ian Islands, and the British Union Jack reflects the attempts of Hawai'ian monarchs to use an alliance with Britain as protection against the United States and other imperialist powers. This is the current state flag of Hawai'i.

After the U.S. government forcibly moved the Cherokee people to Oklahoma (see Chapter 25), the nation adopted a constitution to mark their quest for sovereignty in their new home. The date on this flag (currently in use) commemorates that constitution. Each of the seven yellow stars represents one of the original Cherokee clans; the black star represents those who lost their lives on the "Trail of Tears."

Violence in King Leopold's Congo Here two victims of King Leopold's policies, Mola and Yoka, display their mutilated limbs. Mola's hands were eaten by gangrene after being tied too tightly by Leopold's agents. Yoka's right hand was cut off by soldiers who planned to receive a bounty at headquarters by using the hand as proof of a kill. Once the world learned about this extreme violence, humanitarian voices rose against Leopold. (Courtesy, Anti-Slavery International, London)

huge "concessions" to private companies, which ordered their agents to use whatever means necessary to maximize the harvest. The result was a reign of terror. Like the farmers forced to grow cotton in East Africa, the families of rubber collectors went hungry because they could not tend their own fields. Women were locked in cages to force their husbands to meet impossible quotas. When those rubber quotas were not met, the killing began. Belgian officers and agents paid Free State soldiers to bring back the hands of those they killed. These soldiers would sometimes chop off the hands of the living and bring them back to the Belgian trade stations for a cash reward. Eventually 10 million people died, mostly from hunger. In the West, middle-class consumers happily purchased bicycles and newfangled automobiles, unaware of the horror that produced the rubber for their tires.

Leopold brazenly claimed to be a great humanitarian, bringing "civilization" to the "dark continent," even as stories of the torture he sponsored began to reach Europe. Investigations by a suspicious shipping clerk in Brussels revealed the full horror of Leopold's crimes, and he helped form the Congo Reform Association to demand that they be ended. Finally, in 1908 King Leopold sold his African empire to the Belgian government, reaping a huge profit. A heritage of violence still affects the Congo today, while Brussels is filled with the many grand monuments that Leopold built with his bloodied fortune.

Enduring Monarchies: Ethiopia and Siam

Given the overwhelming strength of European domination in the age of the New Imperialism, it seems surprising that Ethiopia and Siam (present-day Thailand) managed to retain their independence. Factors such as competent leadership were important, but the continuing independence of these two states merely confirmed overwhelming European domination in Africa and Southeast Asia.

The ancient Christian kingdom of Ethiopia first met modern European firepower in 1868 when a British relief column was sent to rescue several British subjects held hostage by the Ethiopian king. The British easily crushed the African army they encountered. Though the Ethiopian leader had killed himself on the field of battle, leaving the kingdom defenseless, the British then withdrew. In the 1860s the "scramble for Africa" had not yet begun.

Menelik II (r. 1889–1913) was determined to strengthen his state against further assault. Ethiopia, like Tokugawa Japan, had long had a decentralized political structure in which rural lords, commanding their own armies, were as powerful

Menelik II

(r. 1889–1913) Emperor who used diplomacy and military reorganization to retain Ethiopian independence, defeating an Italian army of invasion at Adowa in 1896.

as the emperor himself. Menelik (MEN-uh-lik) consolidated power at the imperial court and created his own standing army, equipped with the latest repeating rifles. He also used his credentials as a Christian to enhance his diplomatic influence in Europe, where his ambassadors played the European powers against one another to Ethiopia's advantage.

Menelik was also fortunate that the European assault on Ethiopia came from Italy, the weakest of the European imperial powers. The Battle of Adowa (1896) was an Ethiopian victory, though Italy did take the strategically important region of Eritrea on the Red Sea. Britain, by then dominant in northeastern Africa, was convinced that Menelik would maintain security on the Egyptian frontier and allow European traders free access to his kingdom. Since this was a cheaper solution than occupying the country by force, the British sponsored the development of modern infrastructure, such as banks and railroads, during Menelik's reign. The benefits, as usual, went to Ethiopian elites and European investors. The Ethiopian majority continued to scratch out a meager existence.

Simultaneously, the kings of Siam also faced the danger of absorption into European empires, with the British expanding from India in the west and the French threatening from Indochina in the east. But two long-ruling kings, Mongkut (r. 1851–1868) and Chulalongkorn (r. 1868–1910), secured the ancient kingdom's sovereignty. Both used internal reform and diplomatic engagement to deal with the threats of the New Imperialism.

As a young man, Mongkut (MANG-koot) lived in a Buddhist monastery. When he emerged to become king in 1851, his monastic experience interacting with men from all social classes helped him become a popular leader. Having learned English, mathematics, and astronomy from Western missionaries, he could interact effectively with Europeans as well.

Observing China's fate after the Opium Wars (see Chapter 24), Mongkut was determined to meet the Western challenge. Conservatives at court opposed his reforms as undermining Buddhist traditions. Nevertheless, Mongkut invited Western emissaries to his capital and installed them as advisers. Though Mongkut favored the British, he balanced their influence with French and Dutch advisers. He also opened Siam to foreign trade, giving merchants from various countries a stake in his system.

● **CONTEXT&CONNECTIONS** The Siamese tradition of welcoming foreigners to the royal court and relying on them as advisors was established well before the reign of Mongkut. In the seventeenth century, for example, Iranian and French merchants competed for influence at court (see page 488). ●

Most importantly, Mongkut chose an English tutor for his son and heir, **Chulalongkorn**. Coming to power in 1868, the same year as the Meiji Restoration in Japan, Chulalongkorn (CHOO-luh-AWHN-korn) appointed able Siamese advisers who understood that their traditions and sovereignty could be preserved only through reform. Chulalongkorn altered the legal system to protect private property, abolished slavery and debt peonage, expanded access to education, and encouraged the introduction of telegraphs and railroads. Moreover, he centralized governmental power through a streamlined bureaucracy that reached from the capital into the smallest villages.

Like his father, Chulalongkorn was an able diplomat who played Europeans off one another. Lacking a strong army, he gave up claims to parts of his empire, such as Laos, to protect the core of his kingdom. Not only did this appease the French and the British, but it also gave his kingdom a more ethnically Thai character. (See the feature "World History in Today's World: Political Conflict and the Thai Monarchy.")

Chulalongkorn
(r. 1868–1910) King of Siam (Thailand) who modernized his country through legal and constitutional reforms. Through successful diplomacy he ensured Siam's continued independence while neighboring societies were absorbed into European empires.

Political Conflict and the Thai Monarchy

Thailand is one of forty-four nations that have retained a monarchical system of government (others include the United Kingdom, Saudi Arabia, Spain, Brunei, Swaziland, Morocco, the Netherlands, and Jordan). Like many of these states, Thailand is a constitutional monarchy where the king is expected to be above day-to-day politics. In fact, one of the general arguments in favor of monarchism is that the royal family helps unite the nation by transcending political factions.

Since coming to the throne in 1946, the world's longest-serving monarch, King Bhumibol Adulyadej (Rama IX) has indeed represented continuity and stability. The king's image is displayed, and revered, everywhere in Thailand (and across the world in the now ubiquitous Thai restaurants). Criticism of the king and his family is outlawed.

In the past few years, however, a wound has opened in Thai society that the king, now old and infirm, seems unable to heal: a disagreement between rural Thai voters, especially in the north of the country, and the urbanites in the south, especially in the capital of Bangkok. Rural voters have consistently supported members of the populist Thaksin family, whose policies of economic redistribution are strongly opposed by the military and by the urban middle class.

In 2014, the military intervened to remove Yingluck Shinawatra, Thailand's first female Prime Minister, from office, even after she had received a clear majority of votes. As a member of the Thaksin family, the military saw Shinawatra as unfit for leadership, engineering her impeachment and indictment on corruption charges.

Meanwhile, King Bhumibol seems unable to bridge the political chasm between poor and rich, north and south, canceling his annual birthday speech late in 2014 for reasons of ill health. The questions now are who will succeed the aged king after he passes away, and will his successor be able to reconcile the deep divisions in Thai society? By law, Thais are not even allowed to address the question of royal succession. It seems that the Thai military, rather than the Thai monarchy, holds the keys to the country's future.

Source: "Thai Politics: Yingluck in the Dock," The Economist, January 15, 2015.

Chulalongkorn was fortunate that the British and the French were anxious to avoid conflict between their Indian and Indochinese empires. Because their traders and missionaries were allowed to establish themselves in the kingdom, and because the Siamese leader was able to ensure peace and stability in his domain, the French and British agreed in 1896 to recognize the independence of the kingdom of Siam as a buffer between their empires (see Map 26.2).

As with Ethiopia, effective political leadership secured the independence of Siam through internal reform, centralization of government power, and deft diplomatic maneuvering. Nevertheless, had the British or French wished to conquer Ethiopia or Siam, they could have done so. The achievement of Menelik and Chulalongkorn in the 1890s was to position their countries to take advantage of inter-European rivalries.

In the age of the New Imperialism, African and Southeast Asian societies could retain their sovereignty only under unusual circumstances. King Khama's situation was much more common. He did his best with the diplomatic resources at his disposal, but his kingdom was too small and too poorly armed to survive as an independent state. Unlike Menelik and Chulalongkorn, most African and Southeast Asian rulers did not command sufficient resources to protect themselves from

W. and D. Downey/Hulton Royals Collection/Getty Images

King Chulalongkorn of Siam This photograph from 1890 shows King Chulalongkorn of Siam with his son, the Crown Prince Vajiravudh Rama, who was studying in Britain. Chulalongkorn used deft diplomacy to maintain the independence of Siam (Thailand) during the height of the European scramble for colonial territory. Father and son are dressed in European style, but the warm embrace of their hands was a Southeast Asian touch. British males rarely showed such affection in Victorian portraits.

the New Imperialism. Even in Ethiopia and Siam, the economic impact of Western industrial capitalism brought new and difficult challenges to rural peoples, who were now bound, like their counterparts in colonial empires, to a global economy to which they contributed much more than they received.

The New Imperialism in World History

In the second half of the nineteenth century many small-scale societies and kingdoms that had maintained their autonomy could no longer resist the imperial ambitions of aggressive European nation-states. The story of their often spirited resistance and ultimate defeat was a global one: from the Great Plains of Canada and the United States (see Chapter 25), to Vietnam and the Philippines, to the interior of East Africa. If even a mighty empire like Qing China succumbed (see Chapter 24) smaller states like King Khama's Bangwato could not hope to defend themselves.

When King Khama and his colleagues traveled to London in 1895, they were visiting the epicenter of global financial and military power. By then, however, the British could no longer be complacent. They had lost their early industrial lead to emerging economies in Germany and the United States, and the British empire, while still by far the world's largest, faced challenges from its newly ambitious competitors in the age of the New Imperialism.

Before 1850, European maritime prowess had only intermittently been translated into political domination, though British control over India set a precedent (see Chapter 20). It was the Industrial Revolution that provided the means and motivation for further imperial expansion (see Chapter 23). Initially, though, it seemed that the British would be content with "informal empire" rather than more direct forms of administrative domination: in China and Latin America that policy was generating great profit without the expense of conquest and control.

By the late nineteenth century, however, refinements in chemical and metallurgical processes—the Second Industrial Revolution—led to more sophisticated production techniques, much larger industrial corporations, and intensified competition for raw materials and markets. As Britain's new competitors developed newer and more efficient industrial infrastructure, such competition unleashed the rapid expansion of empires in the last quarter of the century. The "scramble for Africa" was the most dramatic example of the new global quest for imperial dominion.

By 1900, when foreign troops occupied the Forbidden City in Beijing (see Chapter 24) and the process of partition and conquest in Africa, Southeast Asia, and the Pacific neared completion, the organizing principle of a world unified by industrial markets was clear. Western Europe and the United States stood astride the globe, seemingly reinforcing the Social Darwinist claim of their

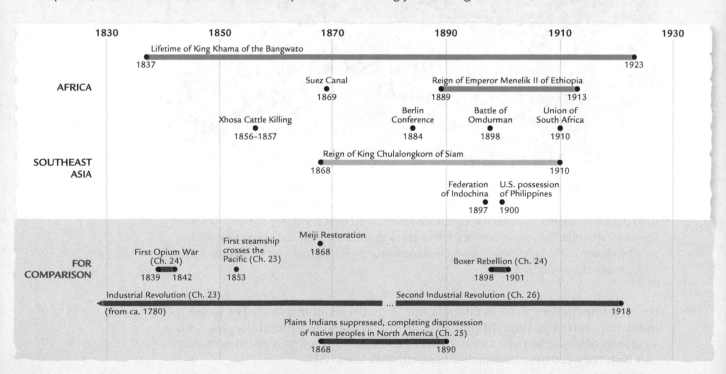

natural superiority, with only Japan offering a clear example of non-European achievement in the race to industrialized military power.

Africa, Southeast Asia, and the Pacific offered a safety valve for European and Japanese competition in the late nineteenth century, but entering the twentieth century the flags of empire crowded against each other across the world, and European conflicts would turn inward during two great world wars (see Chapters 27 and 29). The First and Second World Wars drew the world's peoples into devastating conflict arising from inter-European competition, but ultimately undercut Western domination. By mid-century, anticolonial nationalists would effectively organize themselves to campaign for national independence. Today, it seems that the West's global dominance, which had once appeared so enduring, might only have been a passing episode in world history.

Meanwhile, King Khama's mission to London had important long-term consequences. Because of his efforts, the Bangwato and the other peoples of Botswana entered the British empire as a protectorate administered by the Colonial Office and avoided incorporation into apartheid South Africa (see Chapter 31). The people of today's Botswana, a peaceful and relatively prosperous state, thereby avoided the terrible violence of twentieth-century apartheid—a small victory, perhaps, when measured against the great events of the time, but one of which Khama's descendants are justifiably proud.

Key Terms

King Khama III (778)
New Imperialism (779)
Second Industrial
 Revolution (780)
David Livingstone (780)
King Leopold II of Belgium (781)
Berlin Conference (781)

Asante kingdom (786)
Samori Toure (787)
Shaka (788)
Cecil Rhodes (788)
Xhosa Cattle Killing (789)
Union of South Africa (790)
Suez Canal (791)

Muhammad Ahmad,
 the Mahdi (791)
Federation of Indochina (793)
Menelik II (800)
Chulalongkorn (801)

For Further Reference

Baker, Chris, and Pasuk Phongaichit. *A History of Thailand*. 3d ed. New York: Cambridge University Press, 2014.

Cleall, Esme. *Missionary Discourses of Difference: Negotiating Otherness in the British Empire, 1840–1900*. New York: Palgrave Macmillan, 2012.

Headrick, Daniel. *The Tools of Empire: Technology and European Imperialism in the Nineteenth Century*. New York: Oxford University Press, 1981.

Hochschild, Adam. *King Leopold's Ghost: A Story of Greed, Terror and Heroism in Colonial Africa*. Boston: Houghton Mifflin, 1999.

Lockard, Craig. *Southeast Asia in World History*. New York: Oxford University Press, 2009.

Markus, Harold G. *The Life and Times of Menelik II: Ethiopia 1844–1913*. New York: Oxford University Press, 1975.

Martin, B. G., ed. *Muslim Brotherhoods in Nineteenth Century Africa*. New York: Cambridge University Press, 2003.

Owen, Norman G., ed. *The Emergence of Modern Southeast Asia*. Honolulu: University of Hawai'i Press, 2004.

Packenham, Thomas. *The Scramble for Africa, 1976–1912*. 2d ed. London: Longman, 1999.

Peiers, J. B. *The Dead Will Arise: Nongqawuse and the Great Xhosa Cattle Killing Movement of 1856–1857*. London: James Currey, 1989.

Reid, Richard. *A History of Modern Africa: 1800 to the Present*. 2d ed. London: Wiley-Blackwell, 2011.

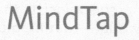 **MindTap** is a fully online, highly personalized learning experience built upon Cengage Learning content. MindTap combines student learning tools—readings, multimedia, activities, and assessments—into a singular Learning Path that guides students through the course.

27

War, Revolution, and Global Uncertainty, 1905–1928

Emma Goldman

Emma Goldman (1869–1940) was one of the most provocative figures of the early twentieth century—in her native Russia, in her adopted country of the United States, and across the world. When she was a girl, her father tried to stifle her dreams. As a young immigrant in New York, she experienced grinding poverty. As a result Goldman became a tireless and outspoken campaigner for workers' and women's rights.

A notorious radical, the press dubbed "Red Emma" the *"most dangerous woman in the country."* The U.S. government imprisoned her for her 1917 campaign against military conscription and then deported her back to Russia, which also ejected her when she became a fierce critic of Soviet totalitarianism. Later in life she had no permanent home, traveling through the United States, Canada, and Europe pleading the cause of anarchism.

Emma Goldman saw oppression in all large institutions, in governments as well as corporations, in religious institutions and political parties. She defined her anarchism as:

*T*he philosophy of a new social order based on liberty unrestricted by man-made law; the theory that all forms of government rest on violence, and are therefore wrong and harmful, as well as unnecessary... Anarchism alone stresses the importance of the individual, his possibilities and needs in a free society. Instead of telling him that he must fall down and worship before institutions, live and die for abstractions... Anarchism insists that the center of gravity in society is the individual—that he must think for himself, act freely, and live fully. The aim of Anarchism is that every individual in the world shall be relieved from the

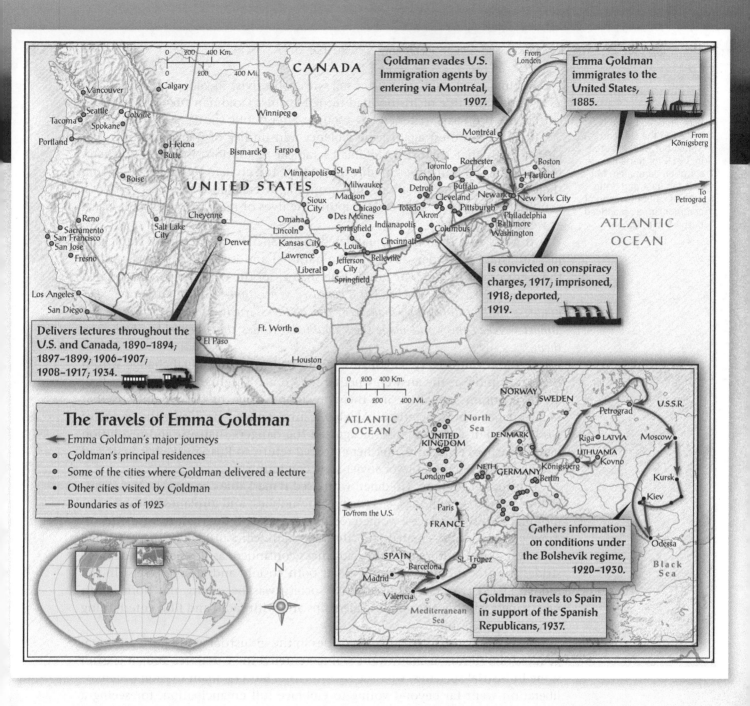

The Travels of Emma Goldman

Goldman evades U.S. Immigration agents by entering via Montréal, 1907.

Emma Goldman immigrates to the United States, 1885.

Is convicted on conspiracy charges, 1917; imprisoned, 1918; deported, 1919.

Delivers lectures throughout the U.S. and Canada, 1890–1894; 1897–1899; 1906–1907; 1908–1917; 1934.

Gathers information on conditions under the Bolshevik regime, 1920–1930.

Goldman travels to Spain in support of the Spanish Republicans, 1937.

The Travels of Emma Goldman

← Emma Goldman's major journeys
● Goldman's principal residences
● Some of the cities where Goldman delivered a lecture
● Other cities visited by Goldman
— Boundaries as of 1923

interference and oppression of others.... My faith is in the individual and in the capacity of free individuals for united endeavor.*

*Emma Goldman, "Anarchism: What It Really Stands For," p. 64, and "Was My Life Worth Living," pp. 442–443, from *Red Emma Speaks: An Emma Goldman Reader*, comp. and ed. Alix Kates Shulman, 3d ed. (Amherst, N.Y.: Humanity Books, 1998).

Emma Goldman
(1869–1940) Russian-born anarchist who moved to the United States but was deported in 1919 for her anticonscription campaign. Militant feminist and critic both of capitalism and of communism as practiced in the Soviet Union.

At a time of triumphant patriotism, with collectivist ideologies on the rise, it seemed the tide of history had turned against Goldman's beliefs. Still, she battled on, both as a writer and as a sought-after public speaker.

It was her protest against the violence and futility of the First World War (1914–1918) that solidified Goldman's radical reputation. Industrially driven total war caused immense suffering for soldiers and civilians alike. In mobilizing their empires for the war effort, the European powers made their local conflict a genuinely global one, severely disrupting the lives of many Africans and Asians as well.

At war's end, diplomats squandered the chance to create a more stable and just international order, as competing national and imperial interests planted the seeds of conflict for the future. The shadow of the First World War loomed over the 1920s: *"The war has left a confused generation,"* Goldman wrote. *"The madness and brutality they had seen, the needless cruelty and waste which had almost wrecked the world made them doubt the values that their elders had given them."**

A true revolutionary, Goldman did not believe that gradual change within the status quo was the answer, whether for women's rights, for political justice, or for economic equality. She therefore found hope in the revolutions that rocked major world societies in Mexico, China, and Russia during the period of world war. But Goldman also recognized the dangers that war and revolution had unleashed, especially after her enforced return to Russia gave her firsthand knowledge of the brutality of Soviet-style communism.

During her lifetime, Goldman witnessed remarkable changes. In the industrialized world, telephones, electricity, automobiles, and airplanes became commonplace. In some places, women fought for and won the right to vote. African American musicians created jazz, the first significant influence of the United States on global culture. Scientific advances continued, as physicists made huge strides toward understanding nature at both cosmic and atomic levels. In the industrialized world, urbanized mass society was becoming the norm, with newspapers gaining enormous readerships and with radio and film entertaining and informing millions.

Meanwhile, urbanizing mass societies in the industrial world put traditional gender roles in flux as many more women entered the workforce and, at least in some industrial societies, won the right to vote. But Goldman's vision of female liberation went far beyond voting to embrace full emancipation, foreseeing a day when *"the road toward greater freedom [will be] cleared of every trace of centuries of submission and slavery."**

---

*Emma Goldman, "Was My Life Worth Living," p. 436, "The Tragedy of Women's Liberation," p. 159, from *Red Emma Speaks: An Emma Goldman Reader*, comp. and ed. Alix Kates Shulman, 3d ed. (Amherst, N.Y.: Humanity Books, 1998).

FOCUS QUESTIONS

❯ How can the First World War be regarded as a "total war," both for the domestic populations of the main combatants and for the entire world?

❯ How did the postwar settlements fail to resolve global political tensions or stabilize the international economy?

❯ How did the outcomes of revolutions in Mexico, China, and Russia add to the uncertainty of the postwar world?

❯ How did Emma Goldman's agenda for women's rights transcend the acquisition of voting rights?

World War I as Global "Total" War

World War I (1914–1918) represented a radical change in warfare. This was "total war," requiring complete mobilization of national resources and engaging masses of civilians. Governments assumed unprecedented powers to regulate social, political, and economic life, straining traditional social and political systems. Nothing would remain the same. The British called it simply the Great War.

The war was also a truly global struggle. While colonial peoples had been caught up in earlier European conflicts, the global involvement of World War I was unprecedented. Young men from the United States shipped out to Europe, Indian soldiers marched to Baghdad, Southeast Asians worked behind the lines on the western front, West Africans fought in the trenches: all had life-changing experiences.

Causes of World War I, 1890–1914

On June 28, 1914, in the Balkan city of Sarajevo, a Serbian nationalist assassinated Archduke Franz Ferdinand, heir to the Austrian throne. The Balkan region had long been an unstable zone between the Austrian and Ottoman empires (see Map 27.1). As the Ottomans declined, Austrians were asserting themselves and provoking local nationalists who did not want to escape one empire only to be dominated by another (see Chapter 23).

Despite their cultural similarities as Slavs and their long history of coexistence, the inhabitants of the Balkans emphasized religious differences as they developed competing nationalisms. Serbians looked to their fellow Orthodox Christians in Russia for support; Croatian nationalists allied themselves with Catholic Austria; Bosnian Muslims sided with the Ottoman empire.

These local Balkan tensions led to full-scale war because of the rising militarism, aggressive nationalism, and intense imperial competition that had preoccupied the leading industrial nations in the age of the New Imperialism (see Chapter 26). In the late nineteenth century, tensions between the great powers, now including Japan and the United States, had found an outlet in colonial rivalries outside of Europe. By 1900, however, there were no more African, Asian, or Pacific lands left to conquer. The assassination of Archduke Franz Ferdinand therefore ignited the fuse under a Europe bristling with heavily militarized national competition.

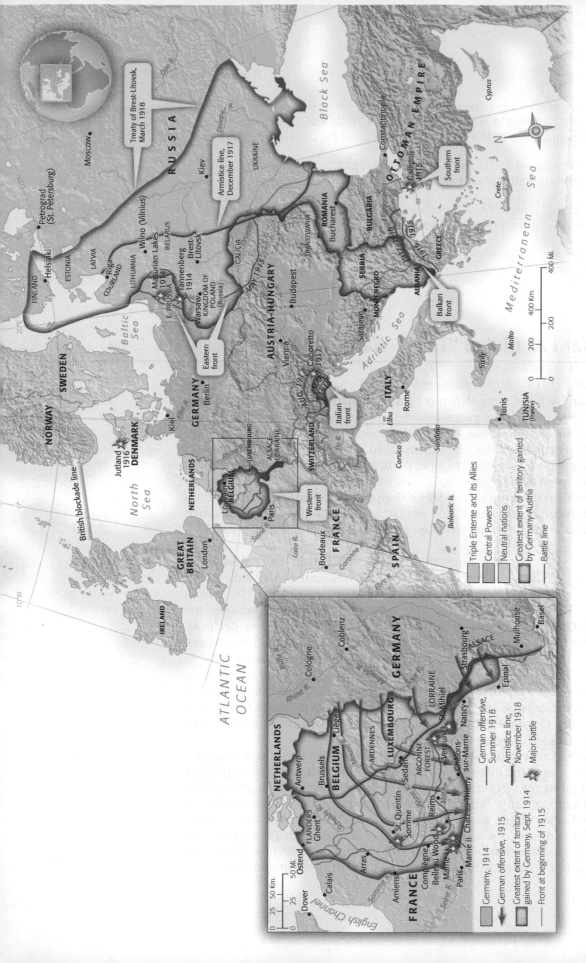

Map 27.1 World War I, 1914–1918 By the end of World War I, horrific violence along the western front in Belgium, Luxembourg, and northeastern France, and on the eastern front in the Russian empire and eastern Europe, had led to the deaths of over 8 million soldiers, with 20 million wounded. On the southern front, defeat led to the dissolution of the Ottoman empire. While these three theaters saw the fiercest fighting, the global effects of the conflict made it truly a world war.

Germany epitomized the era's militarism, especially after 1890 when **Kaiser Wilhelm II** (r. 1888–1918) dismissed Otto von Bismarck (see Chapter 23) to pursue a more aggressive foreign policy. His naval buildup caused Britain to reverse its practice of avoiding commitments on the continent. Likewise, the French and Russian governments, faced with rising German power, overcame their long-standing mutual distrust. A series of treaties produced a combination of alliances that divided Europe into two opposing blocs—the Triple Entente (ahn-TAHNT) of France, Britain, and Russia against the Triple Alliance of Germany, Austria, and Italy—leaving diplomats with no flexibility.

Thus the Balkan crisis detonated an explosive confrontation between two hostile and heavily armed camps. The Austrian government threatened Serbia with war if it did not comply with a set of humiliating demands. The Serbs appealed to Russia, while the Germans backed up the Austrians. The Ottoman empire, fearful of Russian and British designs, allied itself with Germany. After a period of indecision, Italy joined with Britain, France, and Russia.

Public opinion compounded the war atmosphere. In urbanized, industrial societies, foreign affairs were no longer the exclusive purview of diplomatic elites. Expanding electorates had daily access to inexpensive newspapers that struck a nationalistic tone. Emma Goldman criticized *"the jingo howls of the press"* that created war fever as a way to sell newspapers, and the *"blood and thunder tirades"** of cynical politicians using patriotic appeals as a cheap way to gain votes. Indeed, declarations of war met with popular excitement and patriotic demonstrations. Only in Russia, where the tsar and his ministers ignored public opinion, did the government act without a popular mandate.

According to Emma Goldman, a fundamental cause of war was the profit-driven greed of arms manufacturers. She singled out the huge German industrial conglomerate of Krupps that *"for personal gain and profit,"* she said, had sent its emissaries all across Europe *"inciting national hatreds and antagonisms."** Goldman warned that U.S. corporations were contributing to war fever for the same reason.

Whatever the complex of causes, Europeans responded to the declarations of war with remarkable naïveté, believing it would be quick and conclusive and that their side would win. Even the German Social Democratic Party, which had long urged *"workers of the world unite!"* now supported a military mobilization that would pit German workers against French and British ones. Not having fought a general war since the defeat of Napoleon in 1815 (see Chapter 22), Europeans simply could not conceive of the horrors of modern industrialized warfare.

● **CONTEXT&CONNECTIONS** Both the *Crimean War* (key term in Chapter 23), between Russia and the Ottoman empire (1853–1856), and the U.S. Civil War (1861–1865) (see Chapter 25) had anticipated the higher mortality and logistical challenges of industrial warfare. Both conflicts took place away from western Europe, however, and the great powers did not learn those lessons. ●

Total War in Europe: The Western and Eastern Fronts

Britain had pledged to defend neutral Belgium, so when the Germans attacked Belgium en route to France war became inevitable. Unlike 1870, when the Prussians quickly took Paris, in 1914 the German advance was stopped 20 miles (32.2 km) short (see Map 27.1).

Kaiser Wilhelm II
(r. 1888–1918) German emperor whose foreign policy and military buildup changed the European balance of power and laid the foundation for the Triple Alliance and the Triple Entente.

---

*Emma Goldman, "Preparedness: The Road to Universal Slaughter," *Mother Earth*, 10, no. 10 (December 1915).

From "Shell Shock" to Posttraumatic Stress Disorder

In 1915, "shell shock" was a new concept, invented by a British doctor to explain a disturbing phenomenon: British soldiers were returning from the front blind, deaf, or paralyzed without any apparent physical cause. Military leaders were alarmed because over 80 percent of "shell shock" victims were never able to return to service. Those who returned to civilian life were often looked down on as cowards, suffering social isolation as well as psychological trauma. Meanwhile, victims who remained at the front suffered from a variety of nervous disorders. One wartime poet described their "*dreams that drip with murder*" and their "*stammering, disconnected talk.*"*

Today, we know a great deal more about the psycho-emotional difficulties resulting from intensive combat. The current term *posttraumatic stress disorder* (PTSD) originated in the 1960s, during the U.S. war in Vietnam (see Chapter 30) when U.S. soldiers faced not only incessant artillery and rifle fire, but deep uncertainty and insecurity as they moved through jungle terrain. Their enemies could be hidden in the foliage above or emerge suddenly from trapdoors below.

The Veteran's Administration (VA) hospital system in the United States thus developed expertise in dealing with PTSD. Apart from veterans of the Vietnam conflict still suffering four decades later, the VA system must now also find ways to deal with large numbers of younger PTSD sufferers from more recent wars. For example, the U.S. National Institutes of Health estimates that PTSD afflicts 20 percent of all veterans of the country's invasion and occupation of Iraq (see Chapter 32).[†]

Contemporary diagnoses of PTSD reach far beyond the shocks faced by soldiers in battle to include stress disorders arising from rape, torture, child abuse, accidents, natural disasters, and other traumatic events. The research of neuroscientists may lead to medications that can ameliorate the symptoms of PTSD, but to this point patients seem to benefit most from programs that include "exposure treatment," where they can talk through their original source of trauma in an emotionally secure environment. Ultimately, of course, the only sure cure for war-related PTSD is peace.

---

*Cited in British Broadcasting Company, "Shell Shock," *Inside Out Extra*, March 3, 2004, http://www.bbc.co.uk/insideout/southwest/series1/shell-shock.shtml.

[†]National Institutes of Health, "PTSD: A Growing Epidemic," *Medline Plus*, Winter 2009, http://www.nlm.nih.gov/medlineplus/magazine/issues/winter09/articles/winter09pg10-14.html.

---

western front

During World War I, the line separating the elaborate trenches of German and Allied positions, which soon became almost immobile. Trench warfare was characteristic of the western front.

Stalemate on this **western front** resulted in a new tactic: trench warfare. On one side, French and British soldiers fortified entrenched positions with razor wire; on the other side, Germans did the same. Miserable in the muddy trenches, soldiers were called on to charge "over the top," and try to overrun enemy positions. With machine-gunfire and bombs bursting around them, sometimes choking on poisonous mustard gas, they had little chance of survival, let alone victory. Battle lines of trenches and tunnels established early in Belgium and northern France hardly shifted.

The casualties of trench warfare were horrific. In 1916, at the Battle of Verdun more than half a million French and German troops lost their lives, and the Battle of the Somme killed nearly a million British and German soldiers. Young men from the same neighborhood, school, or village often volunteered and trained together, and then might all be killed within a few minutes. Many had married as they headed off to war; for decades afterward, war widows lived lives of regret for their lost youth, 630,000 of them in France alone.

The survivors of trench warfare lost not only their companions but also their physical and mental health. "Lost generation" was the term used to refer to the young adults who came of age during the Great War, not just those who died, but also those who lost their hopes and dreams. (See the feature "World History in Today's World: From 'Shell Shock' to Posttraumatic Stress Disorder.")

Civilians also suffered. Consumer goods became extremely scarce as domestic industries shifted toward the production of war materiel. To undermine the German war effort, the British navy blockaded Germany's seaports, and in response German submarines targeted British shipping in the Atlantic Ocean. Before 1914, Germany and Britain had been major trade partners. Now their navies crippled international trade. Since European prosperity depended on an interlinked world economy, hardship was the result.

● **CONTEXT&CONNECTIONS** The sharp decrease in international trade during World War I brought to an end the stunning growth of the world economy that had begun in the mid-nineteenth century. With the Great Depression, World War II, and the Cold War still ahead (see Chapters 28, 29, and 30), it was not until the 1990s that the momentum of international trade fully recovered, bringing a new round of economic "globalization" (see Chapter 31). ●

Protracted total war transformed European government and society. Because a nation had to tap all its energies in the interests of survival, governmental power expanded. Large corporations and the state were already in close cooperation in Germany before the war, but in Britain national economic planning represented a shift away from economic liberalism. Everywhere, the First World War began a long-term trend toward greater government involvement in economies. Anarchist notions of breaking down large companies and putting workers themselves in charge of the factories now seemed antiquated.

Indeed, government bureaucracies of all kinds expanded dramatically. Unions lost the right to strike. Traditional liberties—freedom of speech, freedom of assembly—were curtailed. The British Parliament even began to regulate the hours

Library of Congress Prints and Photographs Division [LC-US262-39197]

French Women and Total War With so many men away at the front, French women often took over management of family farms. Heightened authority came with a steep price, however. Here French women in the Somme region are pulling a plow, their horses and oxen having been either killed in the crossfire or requisitioned by one of the competing armies.

of the nation's pubs. Less time spent drinking, it was thought, would improve industrial efficiency.

For European women, the war brought opportunities as well as costs. The nursing profession expanded, and with so many men absent, women became more important in factories. In France, many women ran family farms. Such circumstances undermined the idea that the woman's place was in the home, while men dominated the public sphere. But women paid a high price as well, toiling on extra shifts, raising children without any help, and despairing for their brothers, sons, and husbands at the front.

Nowhere were the consequences of total war greater than in eastern Europe. When the Russian army entered the Balkan conflict, warfare spread as far as Romania and Bulgaria. But the **eastern front** between German and Russian forces was the main battle line (see Map 27.1). Russia was still a primarily rural empire, a fatal weakness under conditions of industrialized total war. German invaders took hundreds of thousands of prisoners and treated them with extreme harshness.

Morale among Russian peasant conscripts was poor to begin with and deteriorated rapidly. Mutinies were common: soldiers and sailors, mostly descendants of serfs, felt little loyalty toward their aristocratic officers. Sometimes they killed their own commanders rather than head into futile battles; frequently they simply abandoned their weapons and walked home. American journalist Louise Bryant described them: *"great giants of men, mostly workers and peasants, in old, dirt-colored uniforms from which every emblem of Tsardom had been carefully removed."**

Famine stalked the Russian countryside as war disrupted food production. Factories closed when Russian industrialists lost access to Western capital. Despite deteriorating circumstances, Tsar Nicholas II refused to consider surrender. By 1917, the Russian people were demoralized and exhausted.

eastern front

The front in Russia during World War I. The German army moved quickly across eastern Europe into Russia; low morale plagued the poorly equipped Russian army in the face of superior German technology.

Total War: Global Dimensions

Total war required access to global resources. Battles were fought in Africa and the Middle East; Japan declared war on Germany to seize German concessions in China; Britain and France depended on their Asian and African empires for manpower and materiel. By the time the United States entered the war in 1917, the Great War truly was a world war.

The decision by the Ottoman empire to side with Germany opened a **southern front** that extended the war to the Middle East and North Africa. During the late nineteenth century, German banks, commercial houses, and manufacturers had invested heavily in the Ottoman economy, and the Ottomans saw a German alliance as protection against the French, British, and Russians.

The most important strategic Ottoman position was the Dardanelles, a narrow strait connecting the Black Sea with the Mediterranean. In 1915, British forces, including many Australian and New Zealand Army Corps (ANZAC) troops, attacked the heavily fortified Ottoman position at Gallipoli. Ottoman forces, entrenched on higher ground, put up a tenacious defense, with great mortality on both sides. After a quarter million casualties, the British withdrew.

In the wake of Gallipoli, the British could spare neither men nor materiel from their home islands to fight on the southern front, so they mobilized regiments

southern front

The front in World War I caused by the Ottoman empire's decision to ally with the German army. Britain mobilized colonial forces from India, Egypt, and Australia to engage Ottoman forces at Gallipoli; British forces also occupied Mesopotamia and Palestine.

---

*Quotes from Louise Bryant, *Six Red Months in Moscow* (New York: George H. Doren, 1919), p. 21.

from their African and Asian colonies. For example, black soldiers from the West Indian Regiment of the British Army, mostly from Jamaica, were deployed against the Ottomans in Palestine. Egyptian soldiers under British command were the main force there. The invasion resulted in British control over Jerusalem. Meanwhile, Indian soldiers engaged Ottoman forces in Mesopotamia.

Knowing that many Arab subjects of the Ottoman empire were unhappy with Turkish rule, the British also forged an alliance with Arab leaders, with the dashing T. E. Lawrence, "Lawrence of Arabia," organizing Arab attacks on Ottoman railways and fortifications. Lawrence was an amateur archaeologist whose knowledge of Arabic and of the culture of Bedouin desert nomads proved vital to British intelligence. He was also an innovator in guerilla tactics; by dynamiting railroad bridges, he tied up the better-equipped Ottoman army.

Though the French did little fighting outside Europe, they also looked to their empire for support. When the number of volunteers from their imperial possessions did not meet wartime demand, French colonial officials pressured local African leaders to supply, by force if necessary, more conscripts for the French army. The most famous regiment of colonial recruits was the **Senegalese Sharpshooters**, many of whom died or were maimed on the western front. Soldiers from North Africa—Morocco, Tunisia, and Algeria—were also conscripted in large numbers.

Most of the Arab, Indian, and African soldiers mobilized by the British and French were Muslims, creating the potential for divided loyalty, especially since some saw the Ottoman sultan as *caliph*, successor to the political powers of the Prophet Muhammad. The British commander of the Palestinian campaign was therefore careful when entering Jerusalem—holy to Islam as well as to Christianity and Judaism—to assure his Egyptian and Indian troops, as well as the city's residents, that all their religious sites would be respected.

Battles between German East Africa and British-controlled Kenya also demonstrated the scope of total war in East Africa. On one side were African soldiers led by German officers, and on the other a largely Indian army commanded by the British. The German commander's main goal was to tie down the Anglo-Indian forces to keep them from being redeployed to the Middle East. He therefore repeatedly struck and then retreated, requisitioning local food reserves and destroying what was left to deny sustenance to his opponents. Famine and disease stalked the land; total war reached even the remote interior of East Africa.

In Southeast Asia, the French recruited young Vietnamese men for the Indochinese Labor Corps. The French assigned tedious work like digging fortifications and maintaining roads to the Vietnamese conscripts, allowing the army to concentrate more troops on the front line. At the same time, Indochinese rice

Senegalese Sharpshooters

Mostly Muslim soldiers from French West Africa who were conscripted by the French empire in World War I and developed a reputation as fearsome fighters.

Postcard depicting a Senegalese soldier, 1915 (coloured photo), French School (20th century)/Private Collection/Archives Charmet/Bridgeman Art Library

Gloire à la plus grande france

Franco-African Soldier Total war meant the mobilization of African and Asian colonial subjects. This young man, fighting for "the greater glory of France," is a Senegalese Sharpshooter, most likely a West African Muslim. He stands proudly, with German helmets perched atop his head.

and rubber were directed to support the French war effort. Chinese workers were recruited to the western front as well.

The Indians, West Africans, and Vietnamese conscripted by the British and French, as well as the civilians in colonial territories who produced coffee, rubber, tin, and other goods for imperial forces, contributed much to the war effort but received little in return. Later, anticolonial nationalists would base claims to greater self-government or independence on the sacrifices made during the war.

● **CONTEXT&CONNECTIONS** The Great War was decisive in moving the Indian nationalist *Mohandas K. Gandhi* (Chapter 28) toward mass nationalism and direct action. Gandhi urged loyalty to Britain during the war, expecting political concessions on the question of Indian self-government in return. Disappointed by the British response, during World War II Gandhi changed tactics and launched a *"Quit India"* campaign (Chapter 29), this time refusing to sanction Indian support for the British empire even during the war. ●

The End of the Great War

To achieve victory, one side would have to break the stalemate on the western front. After imposing a humiliating peace on Russia in early 1918, Germany seemed poised to do so, quickly redeploying troops westward. Just then, however, the United States entered the war to bolster French and British forces.

In 1914, the United States had only a small army, and Americans were still inclined to follow George Washington's advice that the republic should not *"entangle our peace and prosperity in the toils of European ambition."* Initially, President **Woodrow Wilson** (in office 1913–1921) kept the United States out of the war, but true neutrality proved impossible. With Germany's trade blocked by the British navy, America supplied industrial and military provisions to France and Britain. Between 1914 and 1916 American exports to these two countries grew from $824 million to $3.2 billion, bringing industrial expansion to the United States without any military cost.

America's entry into the war was largely in response to Germany's use of submarine warfare, itself a reaction to the British embargo on Germany. In 1915, the Germans sank the *Lusitania*, a civilian passenger ship with many Americans on board. After President Wilson protested, the Germans promised to stop attacking ships without warning. Meanwhile, business interests in the United States urged a rapid military buildup. While citing national security reasons, they also knew, as critics like Emma Goldman pointed out, that military spending was highly profitable.

Early in 1917 the Germans, aiming to stop American arms shipments to Britain, resumed submarine attacks. Proclaiming *"The world must be made safe for democracy,"* Wilson asked Congress to declare war. U.S. public opinion, inflamed by sensationalistic news reporting, was now swinging in favor of war. Goldman responded by mocking a former president—*"the blood and thunder tirades of bully Roosevelt"*—and dismissing the idealism of Wilson as *"the sentimental twaddle of our college-bred President."**

Goldman then went further by turning her antiwar message into action. Her public campaign against conscription led to her arrest, conviction, and a two-year prison sentence, with the judge recommending that she be deported upon her

Woodrow Wilson

(in office 1913–1921) President of the United States during and after World War I. Wilson's idealistic view, enshrined in his Fourteen Points, was that Allied success in the war would lead to the spread of peace and democracy.

---

*Emma Goldman, "Preparedness: The Road to Universal Slaughter," *Mother Earth*, 10, no. 10 (December 1915).

release. Goldman found that even in a liberal democracy, total war brings a grave loss of freedom.

Conscription went forward. Though the Germans were speeding troops westward from the Russian front, the arrival of a million-strong American force turned the tide in favor of the British and the French. On November 11, 1918, the Germans agreed to an armistice ending the war. The United States was now in a position to influence the peace talks that followed, taking a place alongside the major European powers. Germany was excluded from the bargaining table, as were the Asians and Africans whose fates were also to be determined.

The Postwar Settlements

As diplomats headed for France to attend the **Paris Peace Conference** in 1919, American authorities were forcing Emma Goldman and 247 other political deportees onto a ship in New York bound for the Russian capital, St. Petersburg. Meanwhile, an unprecedented outbreak of influenza was racing around the world. Between 1918 and 1920 as many as 50 million people died, far more than had lost their lives during the war itself. Wartime violence and dislocation had paved the way for an epidemic that further deepened global distress. The world seemed changed in some fundamental way, and the future was uncertain. In this atmosphere, representatives of the Allied powers—Britain, France, Italy, and the United States—gathered in Paris.

Paris Peace Conference

(1919) Conference that resulted in the Versailles treaty, which added to post–World War I tensions. A war-guilt clause and reparations payments destabilized Germany, and efforts to create stable nations from former imperial provinces in eastern Europe were problematic.

The Paris Peace Conference

The principal leaders at the Paris Peace Conference—Woodrow Wilson of the United States, Georges Clemenceau of France, and David Lloyd George of Britain—faced an enormous task. Germany had to somehow be reincorporated into Europe. The collapse of the Austrian and Ottoman empires required entirely new political systems in central Europe and western Asia (see Map 27.2). Germany would have to relinquish its colonies in Africa and the Pacific. The world's map had to be redrawn.

Wilson's high-minded "Fourteen Points," presented before the war's end, contained specific recommendations based on a few clear principles. Wilson stressed the importance of free trade, the right of peoples to national self-determination, and the creation of a permanent international assembly to provide safeguards against future wars. The British goal, on the other hand, was to safeguard its imperial interests, while the French priority was punishment of Germany.

Meanwhile, representatives from Africa, the Arab world, Southeast Asia, and other societies with deep concerns over the outcomes tried, with little effect, to influence the negotiations. Lacking a voice at the Paris Peace Conference, many of the world's people could only wait to see what the great powers would decide for them. (See the feature "Movement of Ideas Through Primary Sources: Dissenting Voices at the Paris Peace Conference.")

In the end, the Versailles treaty fell far short of Wilson's goals. The Allies did agree to Wilson's plan for a **League of Nations**. But tensions resulted from French insistence on punishment for Germany; from the failure to create coherent states in eastern Europe; from the imperial ambitions of Britain and France; and from the lack of participation in the League of Nations by both Russia, embroiled

League of Nations

Assembly of sovereign states, advocated by Woodrow Wilson, that was intended to provide a permanent diplomatic forum in the hopes of avoiding future conflict.

Dissenting Voices at the Paris Peace Conference

In 1919, delegates from the victorious nations traveled to France for the Paris Peace Conference. Concerned about the outcome of those negotiations, representatives from defeated nations like Germany, and spokesmen for societies entangled in European empires, also came to Paris. In the end, the resulting Versailles treaty left deep bitterness and future problems for central and eastern Europe, the Middle East, and the entire colonial world.

The first document is part of a letter written in May 1919 from Count von Brockdorff-Rantzau, leader of the German delegation, to French Prime Minister Georges Clemenceau, regarding a draft of the Versailles treaty. His suggestions for amendment were ignored.

The second extract is from a resolution passed by the General Syrian Congress of Damascus trying to stop the great powers from applying Section 22 of the League of Nations treaty to their country, which would allow the French to take control of Syria (and give the British control of Palestine). The Syrian resolution had no effect, and the French drove their leader, Faisal al-Hashemi, out of Syria.

The third document was drafted for submission to the Paris Peace Conference by Nguyen Ai Quoc (Nguyen the Patriot), a young Vietnamese nationalist then living and working in Paris, who would later become globally known under the name Ho Chi Minh. Nguyen's proposal was ignored by the French, who continued their colonial occupation of Indochina without any significant changes.

Another unofficial lobbying effort came from the Pan-African Congress, bringing together delegates from the United States, the West Indies, and Africa to Paris to speak for global African interests. Contrary to their pleas, European colonialism in Africa was further entrenched at Paris when the British, French, and Belgians took control of former German colonies as "mandated territories."

> **Why were these various perspectives ignored by the great powers? If these voices had been taken seriously, how might the Versailles treaty have differed?**

Sources: German and Syrian delegations: Cited in James H. Overfield, *Sources of Global History Since 1900*, 2d ed. (New York: Wadsworth/Cengage, 2012), pp. 99–101, 102–103. Ho Chi Minh: Peter Anthony DeCaro, *Rhetoric of Revolt: Ho Chi Minh's Discourse for Revolution* (Westport, Conn.: Greenwood, 2003), Appendix A, p. 101. Pan-African Congress: *African American Political Thought: Integration vs. Separatism, from the Colonial Period to the Present*, ed. Marcus D. Pohlmann (Oxford: Taylor & Francis, 2003), pp. 195–199.

Germany: "Leader of the German Peace Delegation to Georges Clemenceau"

I have the honour to transmit to you herewith the observations of the German delegation on the draft treaty of peace....

We were aghast when we read in documents the demands made upon us....The more deeply we penetrate into the spirit of this treaty, the more convinced we become of the impossibility of carrying it out. The exactions of this treaty are more than the German people can bear.

With a view to the re-establishment of the Polish State we must renounce indisputably German territory [including] Danzig, which is German to the core....The purely German district of the Saar must be detached from our empire, and the way must be paved for its subsequent annexation to France, although we owe her debts in coal only, not in men....

Germany, thus cut in pieces and weakened, must declare herself ready in principle to bear all the war expenses of her enemies, which would exceed many times over the total amount of German State and private assets....The sum to be paid is to be fixed by our enemies unilaterally....No limit is fixed, save the capacity of the German people for payment, determined not by their standard of life, but solely by their capacity to meet the demands of their enemies by their labor. The German people would thus be condemned to perpetual slave labor....

In other spheres also Germany's sovereignty is abolished....Her chief waterways are subjected to international administration; she must construct in her territory such canals and such railways as her enemies wish....The German people are excluded from the League of Nations, to which is entrusted all work of common interest to the world. Thus a whole people must sign a decree for its own...death sentence.

From Syria: "Congress of Damascus Resolution"

We ask that the Government of this Syrian country should be a democratic civil constitutional Monarchy on broad decentralization principles, safeguarding the rights of minorities, and that the King be the Emir Faisal, who carried on a glorious struggle in the cause of our liberation....

Considering the fact that the Arabs inhabiting the Syrian area are not naturally less [capable] than other more advanced races...we protest against Article 22 of the Covenant of the League of Nations, placing us among the nations in their middle stage of development which stand in need of a mandatory power....

We do not acknowledge any right claimed by the French Government in any part whatever of our Syrian country....We oppose the pretensions of the Zionists to create a Jewish commonwealth in the southern part of Syria known as Palestine, and oppose Zionist migration to any part of our country....Our Jewish compatriots shall enjoy our common rights and assume the common responsibilities....

We also have full confidence that the Peace Conference will realize that we would not have risen against the Turks...but for their violation of our national rights, and so will grant us our desires in full...since we have shed so much blood in the cause of our liberty and independence.

From Vietnam: "Eight Points"

While waiting for the sacred right of nations to self-determination to be recognized, the people [of] Indochina, present the following demands to the governments of the Allied powers in general, and the French government in particular:

1. General amnesty for all Vietnamese political prisoners.
2. Equal rights for Vietnamese and French in Indochina, suppression of the Criminal Commissions which are instruments of terrorism aimed at Vietnamese patriots.
3. Freedom of press and of opinion.
4. Freedom of association and assembly.
5. Freedom of travel at home and abroad.
6. Freedom to study and the opening of technical and professional schools for natives of the colonies.
7. Substitute rule of law for government by decree.
8. Appointment of a Vietnamese delegation alongside that of the French government to settle questions related to Vietnamese interests.

From Africa: "Manifesto of the Second Pan-African Congress"

The absolute equality of all races, physical, political, and social, is the founding stone of World Peace and human advancement....The beginning of Wisdom in inter-racial contact is the establishment of political institutions among suppressed Peoples. The habit of democracy must be made to encircle the earth....Surely...there can be found in the civilized world enough of human altruism, learning and benevolence to develop native institutions for the native's good rather than continuing to allow the majority of mankind to be brutalized and enslaved....

The world must face two eventualities: either the complete assimilation of Africa with two or three of the great world states, with political, civil and social power and privileges absolutely equal for its black and white citizens, or the rise of a great black African State, founded in Peace and Good Will, based on popular education, natural art and industry and freedom of trade, autonomous and sovereign in its internal policy, but from the beginning a part of a great society of peoples in which it takes its place with others as co-rulers of the world.

Map 27.2 Territorial Changes in Europe After World War I The Versailles treaty altered the map of Europe dramatically through the application of Woodrow Wilson's policy of "national self-determination." New nations appeared in central and eastern Europe, carved from the former Russian, Austro-Hungarian, and Ottoman empires, though the complex ethnic composition of the region often made it impossible to draw clear lines between "peoples" and "states." The handover of the key regions of Alsace and Lorraine from Germany to France caused much bitterness among German nationalists.

in revolution, and the United States, retreating into isolationism. The First World War was not, as President Wilson had promised *"a war to end all wars,"* nor had the world been *"made safe for democracy."*

● **CONTEXT&CONNECTIONS** One of those who petitioned the peace conference to apply the principle of self-determination to his country, Vietnam, was *Ho Chi Minh* (Chapter 30). After his petition was ignored, Ho joined the French Communist Party, later traveling to Moscow. During the Second World War, he led the tenacious resistance of his Viet Minh army against Japanese invasion (see Chapter 29). Ho declared Vietnamese independence after the Japanese withdrew, but the French tried to reclaim their colonial powers. After the Viet Minh defeated the French in 1954, they faced a U.S. invasion that lasted beyond Ho's death in 1969. With victory in 1975, the communist government of newly unified Vietnam renamed Saigon as Ho Chi Minh City in his honor. ●

The Weimar Republic and Nation Building in Europe

After surrender and the kaiser's abdication, German liberals and socialists cooperated in the creation of the new **Weimar Republic**. Many years after the revolutions of 1848 (see Chapter 23), Germany finally had a liberal, democratic constitution.

Weimar Republic
(1919–1933) The government of Germany created after World War I, based on a liberal democratic constitution. The new republic was immediately faced with huge war debts, political turmoil, and rising inflation.

The Weimar Republic faced enormous challenges. At war's end the German people were hungry, cold, and dispirited, and the huge reparation payments demanded by France crippled their recovery. National pride was wounded by the Versailles treaty's requirement for the complete demilitarization of the Rhineland, the German province bordering France, and severe restrictions on German rearmament.

It was in difficult circumstances that German centrists tried to foster the liberal political culture needed to sustain a free society. They faced opposition on the left from communists, who led uprisings in Berlin and Munich in 1919, and on the far right from the organizers of the Beer Hall Putsch, an attempt to seize power by angry war veterans, members of the National Socialist Party (see Chapter 28).

By 1923, the new Weimar Republic was foundering. It was unable to meet its reparation obligations, so French soldiers occupied the Ruhr Valley, Germany's industrial heartland to seize assets in lieu of cash. As the Weimar government printed more money to make up for the shortfall in its treasury, inflation spiraled out of control. People needed a wheelbarrow full of bank notes to buy a loaf of bread.

Then signs of recovery appeared. In 1925 international agreements eased Germany's reparation payments and ended the occupation of the Ruhr Valley. The German economy finally came back to prewar levels, and Berlin regained its status as a major cultural, intellectual, and artistic center. At last, Germany was offered full membership in the League of Nations. The respite was temporary, however. In just a few years another economic crisis would again drive many Germans toward the political extremes of left and right (see Chapter 28).

In the meantime, with the exception of Czechoslovakia, the new nations created by postwar diplomacy in eastern, central, and southeastern Europe proved unstable and prone to authoritarianism. A complex cultural geography meant that ethnic, linguistic, and religious groups lived scattered among each other in many places, making it impossible to use ethnic homogeneity as a simple guide for drawing new national lines on the map.

The Paris treaty recreated Poland, for example, which had been divided among Russia, Prussia, and Austria in the eighteenth century. Since the lands that became western Poland in 1920 had long been ruled from Berlin, there was a substantial German-speaking population living there, as well as a large Jewish community. Polish nationalists felt that Germans who lived in the new Poland had to either accept second-class status or move to the now reduced Germany where they "belonged." The repression of Polish Jews was even more extreme. In this tense atmosphere it proved impossible for Poland to develop a liberal, democratic political culture. In 1926, tired of the endless squabbling of politicians, conservative army officers seized power and imposed restrictions on free speech and political organization.

● **CONTEXT&CONNECTIONS** Like most Jews in the old Russian empire, including what became Poland, Emma Goldman spoke Yiddish growing up, the language of the eastern European *Ashkenazim* (Chapter 17). Also commonly spoken in New York when she arrived, Yiddish was a thriving language of poetry, philosophy, comedy, and theater. It disappeared from Poland in the 1940s, however, when nearly the entire Yiddish-speaking population, millions of people, were murdered by the Nazis as part of the *Holocaust* (Chapter 29). ●

The slide toward dictatorship in eastern, central, and southern Europe arose from a contradiction that Wilson had not accounted for: nationalism is based on the rights of *groups*, while liberalism focuses on the rights of *individuals*. Nationalists, with an "us versus them" mentality, were prone to restrict the rights of minority groups rather than follow the liberal philosophy of protecting individual rights regardless of ethnic background. The problem was particularly acute for peoples with no state to protect them, such as Europe's Jews and Roma (Gypsies).

The Mandate System in Africa and the Middle East

The fate of former German colonies and Ottoman provinces was another issue to be determined at Paris. In the end, French and British colonial interests took priority, and rights of national self-determination for African and Arab peoples received only token attention. The Allies devised the **Mandate System**, whereby the great powers ruled over territories under League of Nations auspices until their peoples might be "prepared" for self-government. Race was the unspoken determinant of who was deemed capable of self-rule.

Mandate System

System by which former Ottoman provinces and German colonies were redistributed; based on the idea that some societies were not ready for national self-determination, it expanded the empires of Britain, France, Belgium, and Japan while angering African, Arab, and Chinese nationalists.

In Africa, the Mandate System allowed the French, British, Belgian, and South African governments to take over former German colonies. Britain added German East Africa (today's Tanzania) to its empire. The French expanded their West African holdings, and the Belgians enlarged their Central African empire. While the Mandate System required reports to the League of Nations showing that they were furthering "native rights," the Europeans ruled the mandated territories like colonies, doing little or nothing to prepare them for eventual self-determination.

● **CONTEXT&CONNECTIONS** With the addition of former German East Africa to its empire as Tanganyika, Britain finally achieved *Cecil Rhodes's* dream of controlling a continuous stretch "from Cape to Cairo" (Chapter 26). ●

Still, the ideal of national self-determination inspired a new generation of African nationalists. In South Africa, for example, leaders of the African National Congress called for greater rights, including an extension of the right to vote to Western-educated African property owners and an end to residential segregation. In West Africa, returning war veterans brought a heightened consciousness of the continent's place in the wider world. More African students left for study in Europe and the United States and came back questioning the legitimacy of colonial rule. Thus, the seeds of African nationalism began to sprout in the wake of World War I.

In the Middle East, the collapse of Ottoman authority created a power vacuum. While the French and British wanted control of such rich and strategic areas as Turkey, Mesopotamia, Syria, and Palestine, they had to contend with well-organized forces of Turkish, Arab, and Jewish nationalism.

As the Ottoman empire collapsed, some of its subject peoples sought to liberate themselves. Hoping for an independent state, some Armenians supported Russia during the war. Ottoman officials responded by relocating millions of Armenians in a forced march west. As many as 1.5 million Armenians perished in what historians call the Armenian Genocide, an attempt by the Turkish military to destroy them as a people. The surviving Armenians did gain a state of their own in the postwar settlements, though other peoples in the region, such as the Kurdish-speaking population of the former Ottoman empire, did not. The Kurdish people were scattered across the new postwar states of Turkey, Iraq, Syria, and Iran (see Chapter 32).

The Middle East's postwar situation was complicated by three contradictory promises the British made during the war. In 1915, to gain Arab support against the Ottoman empire, the British had promised the prominent Hashemite family to *"recognize and support the independence of the Arabs"* after the war. Contradicting that agreement, the British signed a secret treaty with the French arranging to divide Ottoman provinces between them. Finally, the **Balfour Declaration** of 1917 committed the British government to support the creation of a "national home" for the Jewish people in Palestine. The British government was seeking additional support for the war effort from Zionists, Jewish nationalists who hoped to establish their own state on the site of the ancient Hebrew kingdoms.

Zionism had originated in the late nineteenth century among European Jews who were alarmed at persistent anti-Semitism. Zionists argued that a nation-state was necessary to represent Jewish interests in the world and give Jews a place of

Balfour Declaration

(1917) Declaration that committed the British government to help create "a national home for the Jewish people" in Palestine. Britain made this declaration to gain support from Zionists during World War I.

Hulton Archive/Getty Images

The Syrian Delegation to the Paris Peace Conference Emir Faisal al-Hashemi led a delegation to Paris to secure the independence of a Syrian Arab kingdom. He was supported by the Englishman T.E. Lawrence ("Lawrence of Arabia") shown standing behind him, second from the right. The French drove Faisal from Syria; as a consolation prize the British made him King of Iraq.

refuge in times of crisis, and had advocated for Jewish emigration to Ottoman Palestine. Still, by 1922 well over 80 percent of the people actually living in Palestine were Muslim or Christian Arabs.

After the war, the British and the French implemented their secret treaty, dividing the Middle East region between them. The French received a League of Nations mandate over Syria and Lebanon, and the British stitched together three Ottoman provinces centered on the cities of Mosul, Baghdad, and Basra into a new entity they called Iraq.

The French were not able to impose their authority on Syria without a fight. Faisal al-Hashemi had been declared king of an independent Arab state by the Syrian National Congress and had traveled to Paris as head of an Arab delegation in 1919. When the French tried to impose their authority, Faisal and his supporters resisted. Defeated by the French, Faisal then fled to Baghdad, where the British agreed to install him as king of Iraq. Lacking a local base of support in Iraq, Faisal, a Sunni Muslim, proved compliant with British authorities, who were looking for a way to balance Arab demands with their own strategic and economic interests.

Instability in Iraq could have been anticipated. An artificial creation, it was divided between a Shi'ite Arab majority in the south, a Sunni minority in the center, and a Kurdish-dominated region in the north. The choice of Faisal as king showed British favoritism toward the Sunni Arabs. Gertrude Bell, the British diplomat most responsible for the creation of modern Iraq, wrote in 1920: *"I don't for a moment doubt that the final authority must be in the hands of the Sunnis, in spite of their numerical inferiority.... Otherwise you will have a theocratic state, which is the very devil."** Shi'ite Iraqis resented Sunni political ascendancy (which would last until the American invasion of 2003; see Chapter 32).

The most complicated situation arose in Palestine. Wartime anti-Semitism had increased the appeal of Zionism among American and European Jews, and even many who had no plans to emigrate to Palestine contributed money to purchase land for those who did decide to move. Arab leaders were alarmed, fearing they would become a minority in the land where their families had lived for perhaps a thousand years.

It was impossible for the British to please both sides. When the British allowed Jewish immigration in large numbers in the early 1920s, massive Arab demonstrations erupted. When the British curtailed Jewish immigration in response, Zionist leaders were furious. The British were determined to keep Palestine because of its strategic location, but the political price was exceptionally high.

British and French leaders viewed these imperial enlargements as spoils of war and anticipated that they would retain their traditional global dominance. But the world had changed. The British had liquidated many foreign investments to fight the war and slipped from being the world's largest creditor to facing significant debts, especially to the United States. Western European economic supremacy was on the wane, while the forces of anticolonial nationalism were gathering throughout Africa and Asia.

● **CONTEXT&CONNECTIONS** Through the Mandate System, the British and the French were thus adding to their imperial commitments in Africa and Asia just when the tides of history were moving *against* European colonialism. It would have amazed the

---

*Gertrude Bell, "Letter to Her Father," October 3, 1920; cited in Scott Horton, "Bell on the Shi'a in Iraq," *Harpers Magazine*, March 19, 2008.

diplomats of 1919, secure in their dominant global roles, to learn that they might live to see the British and French empires all but disappear, supplanted by independent African and Asian nations (see Chapter 30). ●

Twentieth-Century Revolutions: Mexico, China, and Russia

Revolutions would spread across the world in the twentieth century, first in Mexico, China, and Russia, and later in societies across Asia, Africa, and Latin America. To the surprise of followers of Karl Marx, who had prophesied proletarian revolutions in advanced industrial societies (see Chapter 23), the revolutionary surge came from the fringes of the international system, in largely agricultural countries with peasant majorities. And while nineteenth-century European revolutionaries had struggled to balance nationalism with liberalism, now it was the mixture of nationalism and socialism that would prove more potent.

Consequences of the Mexican Revolution, 1919–1927

In 1910, Mexico had been first out of the twentieth century's gates of revolution (see Chapter 25). For Emma Goldman, Mexico provided a visceral feeling of excitement when she saw that *"the real and true proletarians, the robbed and enslaved peons, are fighting for land and liberty."** Her observation rang true for the forces gathered by Emiliano Zapata and Pancho Villa, but many other factions and interests were vying for power and influence as well.

The Mexican Constitution of 1917 resulted from the tug and pull between moderate and more radical delegates. A basic legal framework protecting property rights was offset by "social clauses" that enshrined the rights of workers, restricted the powers of the Catholic Church, and identified the mineral sector, including petroleum, as property of the nation as a whole, allowing later nationalization. The declaration that *"private property is a privilege created by the Nation"* opened up the possibility of land redistribution, a key goal of Zapata and his peasant constituency.

After his election as president in 1920, Álvaro Obregón tried to stabilize the country with cautious implementation of the "social clauses." His educational reforms, however, antagonized the Catholic Church and many of its supporters. Obregón was assassinated in 1928 by a member of the *Cristeros* movement, which opposed limits on the power and property of the Catholic Church.

Stability only came to Mexico in 1929, almost twenty years after the revolution began. The formation of the Party of the Mexican Revolution brought the debates between moderates and the more radical supporters of the "social clauses" into a single political party. Party leaders then used patronage, corruption, and backroom deals to try to reconcile the nation's contending needs and interests. Some leaders had less interest in government policy than in enhancing their own wealth, status, and power. Furthermore, by institutionalizing the revolution the party took away its energy and popular base.

---

*Emma Goldman, "Socialism Caught in the Political Trap," p. 107, from *Red Emma Speaks: An Emma Goldman Reader*, comp. and ed. Alix Kates Shulman, 3d ed. (Amherst, N.Y.: Humanity Books, 1998).

● **CONTEXT&CONNECTIONS** The Party of the Mexican Revolution, later renamed the Party of the Institutional Revolution (PRI), was the sole political party in power in Mexico for seven decades. Although progressive President Lázaro Cárdenas nationalized the oil sector and redistributed land to peasant communes in the 1930s (see Chapter 28), PRI leaders more often looked after their own wealth and power rather than the national interest. Finally, in 2000, Mexicans elected the leader of an alternative party to the presidency, breaking the PRI monopoly (see Chapter 31). ●

The Chinese Revolution

After the humiliations following the Boxer Rebellion (see Chapter 24), China entered the twentieth century in desperate need of a new government to unify its people and defend against foreign encroachment. In 1912, the last Qing emperor, a boy at the time, abdicated. Nationalists led by Sun Zhongshan, better known as **Sun Yat-sen** (1866–1925), declared a new Republic of China. Sun, head of the Guomindang (gwo-min-DAHNG), or Nationalist, Party, envisioned a modernized China, with a stable liberal legal system and a just distribution of resources, taking its rightful place among the world's great powers.

Sun Yat-sen

(1866–1925) The founding father of the Republic of China after the revolution of 1911; established the Guomindang, or Nationalist Party.

Sovfoto/Universal Images Group/Getty Images

May Fourth Movement May 4, 1919, was an important day in the development of Chinese nationalism. Hundreds of thousands of protesters gathered in Tiananmen Square in Beijing, angered by the Versailles treaty, which had given Chinese territory to Japan. Demonstrations across the country lasted for months, with students playing a large role. In this photograph, residents of Shanghai wave signs that say "*Down with the traitors who buy Japanese goods!*"

Japanese military superiority made such international standing difficult to achieve, however. Already ruling over Taiwan and controlling resource-rich Manchuria in the north, Japan received the German concession on the Shandong peninsula in acknowledgment of its wartime alliance with France and Britain. On May 4, 1919, Chinese university students demonstrated in Tiananmen Square in Beijing, appealing to the government to restore Chinese dignity in the face of Japanese aggression. Their **May Fourth Movement** led to strikes, mass meetings, and a boycott of Japanese goods. Chinese nationalism was on the rise, but the republican government was powerless to respond to the students' appeals.

● **CONTEXT&CONNECTIONS** Student activists who gathered in Tiananmen Square in 1989 commemorated the seventieth anniversary of the May Fourth Movement by organizing for democracy and liberty. In response, Communist authorities sent tanks and soldiers to clear the square, killing hundreds in the *Tiananmen Massacre* (Chapter 31). ●

The domestic military situation was another challenge for Sun and the Guomindang. From 1916, regional warlords mustered private armies as the country descended into a decade of disorder. Sun retreated to Guangzhou, where the Guomindang was being rebuilt by his brother-in-law and successor Jiang Jieshi, known in the West as Chiang Kai-shek (1887–1975). By 1927, the Guomindang had defeated the warlords and re-established central authority. Under Chiang's authoritarian command, however, Sun's idealistic emphasis on reform was supplanted by a growing culture of militarism and corruption.

Meanwhile, in 1921, in the wake of the May Fourth Movement, the Chinese Communist Party was formed in Shanghai. Seeking support from the new communist government in Russia, Chiang Kai-shek made a tactical alliance with the Communists. But in 1927, when he felt more secure in power, Chiang turned against them. Guomindang soldiers and street thugs killed thousands of Communists in the coastal cities, and those remaining fled to the countryside.

Mao Zedong (1893–1976), who now came to leadership of the Chinese Communist Party, argued that there was an advantage in this forced retreat, since it would be the peasants who would lead the way to socialism. Rejecting the traditional Marxist emphasis on industrial workers, Mao wrote: *"In a very short time…several hundred million peasants will rise like a tornado…and rush forward along the road to liberation."* By allying with this elemental peasant force, Mao thought, the Communists could drive Chiang from power and bring about true revolution.

● **CONTEXT&CONNECTIONS** The Nationalists and the Communists would continue to contest power for two decades. Jiang Jieshi (Chiang Kai-shek) and his Guomindang fought on the Allied side during World War II, but were driven from the Chinese mainland in 1949 by Mao Zedong's Red Army (see Chapter 30). ●

Russia's October Revolution

Even more than the Mexican and Chinese Revolutions, the Russian Revolution had a profound impact on world history. Indeed, the Bolsheviks and their leader Vladimir Lenin saw themselves as fighting not just to control one country but to change the destiny of all humanity.

May Fourth Movement

(1919) A student-led protest in Beijing's Tiananmen Square against the failure of the Versailles treaty to end Japanese occupation of Chinese territory. Such anti-Japanese protests spread across China, and focused on a boycott of Japanese goods.

Russia's first revolutionary crisis had occurred in 1905, after defeat in the Russo-Japanese War (see Chapter 24). Peaceful protesters converging on the Winter Palace in St. Petersburg to petition the tsar for reform were ridden down and murdered by mounted guards, shattering old bonds of trust.

In the ensuing crisis, Tsar Nicholas II (r. 1894–1917) conceded a series of reforms, including, for the first time, a representative assembly, called the Duma. But while property-owning men could now vote and have some voice in government, real power still lay with the tsar and his ministers and with an aristocracy that retained dominance over the military.

Nicholas had also approved a crash program of industrialization. The first phase of industrial growth only added to social instability, however. The money for industrialization came largely from higher taxes on already miserable peasants, and the new industrial workers labored under much worse conditions and at much lower pay than their Western counterparts.

While some reformers argued that the powers of the Duma should be expanded, others argued that nothing would change until the old order was entirely swept away. One of these revolutionary groups was the Social Democratic Party, communist followers of the Marxist tradition.

After 1903, the Social Democrats had split into two factions. One group, the Mensheviks, adhered to the traditional Marxist belief that a modern industrial economy would have to be built before Russia's workers would be strong enough to seize state power. The Mensheviks therefore favored an alliance with the Russian middle class that would lead to a liberal, multiparty constitutional republic.

Vladimir Lenin (1870–1924), the leader of the opposing Bolshevik faction, disagreed. Lenin's radicalism started in childhood, when his elder brother was hanged for plotting to assassinate the tsar. Lenin himself was exiled first to Siberia and then to western Europe. There he developed his theory of a *"revolutionary vanguard."* A small, dedicated group of professional revolutionists, he argued, could seize power in the name of the working class and rule in its interests. Dictatorship rather than democracy was implicit in Lenin's concept of revolutionary leadership.

World War I offered Lenin the opportunity to implement his ideas. Faced with mutiny in the army and near anarchy across the country, Tsar Nicholas abdicated in February 1917. By the summer of 1917 the Provisional Government that had replaced him was also losing legitimacy when it decided to continue to fight Germany.

By then the Russian people were simply sick and tired of war. American journalist Louise Bryant, who befriended Emma Goldman in St. Petersburg, described the passionate appeal of one war veteran at a public meeting: *"Comrades! I come from the place where men are digging their graves and calling them trenches! I tell you the army can't fight much longer!"* *"Over and over like the beat of the surf came the cry of all starving Russia,"* Bryant wrote, *"'Peace, land and bread!'"** The Provisional Government was unable to deliver on any of these demands.

Vladimir Lenin

(1870–1924) Born Vladimir Ilyich Ulyanov, Lenin led the Bolsheviks to power during the Russian Revolution of 1917. Leader of the Communist Party until his death in 1924.

---

*Quotes from Louise Bryant, *Six Red Months in Moscow* (New York: George H. Doren, 1919), pp. 48–49.

After the tsarist bureaucracy collapsed, a new form of social and political organization emerged: the *soviets* (Russian for "committees") of factory and railroad workers, of residents in urban neighborhoods, and even of soldiers and sailors in the military. The soviets represented a radical form of democracy where all participants had the right to speak and be represented, with decisions made through public discussion and consensus. It was exactly the model of democracy long advocated by Russian anarchists, from Mikhail Bakunin (see Chapter 23) to Emma Goldman.

As Russian society slid from dictatorship to near anarchy, Lenin returned from exile. His clear vision and organizational abilities put the Bolsheviks in a position to make a play for power. Given an interview with Lenin upon her arrival, Goldman found him to be *"a shrewd politician who...would stop at nothing to achieve his ends."** Her friend Louise Bryant agreed: *"He possesses all the qualities of a 'chief,' including the absolute moral indifference which is so necessary to such a part."†*

Though a sophisticated intellectual, in the summer of 1917 Lenin reduced the Bolshevik program to two simple slogans: *"Peace, Land, and Bread!"* and *"All Power to the Soviets!"* The fiery speeches and tireless organizing of another prominent Bolshevik, Leon Trotsky (1879–1940), did much to advance the communist cause that summer.

In the fall, Lenin and the Bolsheviks planned and executed a coup d'état that later communists would celebrate as the October Revolution. Hardly a shot was fired in the Provisional Government's defense. Lenin disbanded the Constituent Assembly recently elected to write a new constitution. *"A big sailor marched into the elaborate red and gold assembly chamber,"* Bryant reported, *"and announced in a loud voice: 'Go along home!'"†* Russia's brief experiment with multiparty representative democracy had ended.

Arriving in St. Petersburg in 1919, when Lenin and the Bolsheviks were fighting for the survival of their revolution, Emma Goldman at first supported their cause. *"The libertarian principle was strong in the initial days of the revolution,"* she later recalled, *"the need for free expression all-absorbing."**

Goldman was especially excited to converse with the leader of the new Women's Bureau, Alexandra Kollontai. How incredible it would have seemed during tsarist times that any woman, let alone a strong proponent of women's rights, could become a government minister! Kollontai's fierce radicalism—*"Cast off your chains! Do not be slaves to religion, to marriage, to children. Break these old ties...the world is your country!"‡*—was music to Emma Goldman's ears.

It did not take long for Goldman to become disillusioned, however, after she realized that the Bolsheviks really had no place for *"the libertarian principle."* She became one of the new Soviet Union's fiercest critics, earning the enmity of many socialists by claiming that *"it is not only Bolshevism that has failed, but Marxism itself."**

---

*Emma Goldman, "Afterword to *My Disillusionment with Russia*," pp. 387, 392, 398, from *Red Emma Speaks: An Emma Goldman Reader*, comp. and ed. Alix Kates Shulman, 3d ed. (Amherst, N.Y.: Humanity Books, 1998).

†Quote from Louise Bryant, *Six Red Months in Moscow* (New York: George H. Doren, 1919), pp. 138–139, 78.

‡Quoted in Louise Bryant, *Mirrors of Moscow* (Westport, Conn.: Hyperion, 1923), p. 112.

....
**Civil War and the
New Economic Policy,
1917–1924**

For the Communist Party, as the Bolsheviks were now called, defending the revolution was the first order of the day. To fulfill their promise to bring peace, they signed a treaty in 1918 ceding rich Ukrainian and Belarusian lands to Germany. The Communists saw this unequal treaty as a temporary setback, certain that the German communists would soon overthrow their government and establish a true and equitable peace.

The Communists also contended with powerful counter-revolutionary forces, as aristocratic generals turned their attention from the Germans to undoing the revolution. The Russian Civil War of 1919–1921 pitted the Communist Red Army, commanded by Leon Trotsky, against the "White Armies" organized by former tsarist generals with the help of the United States and Great Britain. To eliminate a rallying point for counter-revolution, the Bolsheviks coldly murdered the tsar and his family, as Lenin organized a secret police service even more terrifying than the old tsarist one.

● **CONTEXT&CONNECTIONS** The Russian experience, where members of the displaced ruling class fomented counter-revolution in alliance with foreign powers, repeated the experience of the French Revolution and anticipated the Cuban one. Like the earlier *Jacobins* (Chapter 22) and the later Cuban revolutionaries led by *Fidel Castro* (Chapter 30), the Bolsheviks justified clamping down on freedom of speech in the name of saving the revolution from its enemies. It seems that those who would take away such rights in an emergency rarely return them. ●

By 1921, when the civil war ended, Lenin was securely in control and ruling with an iron hand. The anarchic democracy of freely elected soviets was replaced by strict party discipline in all facets of life. Emma Goldman now found that the soviets, which had earlier inspired her, were being *"castrated and transformed into obedient committees."** Even within the Communist Party Central Committee, dominated by Lenin, only limited debate was permitted. Once the Communists were secure in their control of the state, all political parties and social organizations, in Goldman's words, *"were either subordinated to the needs of the new State or destroyed altogether."**

● **CONTEXT&CONNECTIONS** Goldman noted the historical continuity of Russian authoritarianism: "*Lenin takes the seat of the Romanovs, the Imperial Cabinet is rechristened the Soviet of People's Commissars.*"* More recently, commentators have recognized similar tendencies in *Vladimir Putin* (Chapter 32) as he consolidated personal power over Russia in the twenty-first century. ●

Lenin and the Bolsheviks were able to assert their claim to power not only in Russia, but across most of the former Russian empire. Though they lost lands in the west (such as Poland, Finland, and Lithuania), they retained the rich lands of the Ukraine, the vastness of Siberia, Central Asia with its potential for agricultural development, and the strategic Caucasus Mountains in the south. These regions

---

*Emma Goldman, "Afterword to *My Disillusionment with Russia*," pp. 399, 412, 413, from *Red Emma Speaks: An Emma Goldman Reader,,* comp. and ed. Alix Kates Shulman, 3d ed. (Amherst, N.Y.: Humanity Books, 1998).

were brought together in 1922 in the Union of Soviet Socialist Republics (U.S.S.R.). Allegedly a federal republic, in reality the Soviet Union was a top-down dictatorship dominated by Moscow.

After the civil war ended, Lenin instituted the **New Economic Policy** (1921–1924). Peasants were allowed to keep the land they had recently won. Restrictions on private business were lifted for all but the largest enterprises. In Goldman's analysis, the Bolsheviks could stay in power only if they moderated their demands, especially on the peasantry. The New Economic Policy, she said, *"was introduced just in time to ward off the disaster which was slowly but surely overtaking the whole Communist edifice."** The country experienced a brief respite of relative peace and the beginnings of economic recovery. But it was also during this time that, in an ominous preview of the future, the first of the Soviet labor camps was established, with the motto *"With an Iron Hand, Mankind Will Be Driven to Happiness!"*

Stalin and "Socialism in One Country"

The dynamic of Soviet policy changed when Joseph Stalin established dictatorial power. After Lenin died in 1924, Stalin exploited divisions within the Central Committee to position himself as a safe and neutral choice for leadership. By 1926, he had consolidated his power and established sole authority, driving Leon Trotsky, his main competitor, into exile. (See the feature "Visual Evidence in Primary Sources: History, Photography, and Power.)

More than personal ambition was at stake. Stalin's vision of how to move the Soviet Union forward was encapsulated by the slogan **"Socialism in One Country."** Some Communists, like Trotsky, thought socialism in Russia required the help of revolutions in advanced industrial nations and advocated a policy of fomenting proletarian uprisings in the West. Others thought that the mixed approach of the New Economic Policy, with scope for private enterprise, was necessary to nurture capital investment for further industrial development. Stalin rejected both ideas. Instead, Soviet socialism would be built through top-down government control of every aspect of life.

In 1928, Stalin launched the first of his Five-Year Plans. The entire economy was nationalized in a crash policy of industrialization. Noting that Russia was far behind more advanced economies, Stalin said, *"We must make good this lag in ten years…or we will be crushed."* After the Soviet Union cut ties with foreign economies, there was only one way Stalin could raise the capital needed for industrialization: by squeezing it out of the Soviet people. Low wages and harsh working conditions characterized new factories built to produce steel, electricity, chemicals, tractors, and other vital foundations of industrial growth. Especially productive workers received medals rather than higher wages, while poor performance could result in exile to a Siberian labor camp.

Still, by the 1930s, the Soviet Union had the world's fastest-growing industrial economy, while the capitalist nations were dragged down by the Great Depression

New Economic Policy

During the New Economic Policy (1921–1924), Vladimir Lenin's government restored some private enterprise by allowing the operation of small shops and village markets, a policy later reversed by Joseph Stalin.

"Socialism in One Country"

Joseph Stalin's slogan declaring that Soviet socialism could be achieved without passing through a capitalist phase or revolutions in industrial societies. This policy led to an economy based on central planning for industrial growth and collectivization of agriculture.

---

*Emma Goldman, "Afterword to *My Disillusionment in Russia*," p. 386, from *Red Emma Speaks: An Emma Goldman Reader*, comp. and ed. Alix Kates Shulman, 3d ed. (Amherst, N.Y.: Humanity Books, 1998).

History, Photography, and Power

As Joseph Stalin consolidated his power over the Soviet Union beginning in the late 1920s, he ordered that the history of the Russian Revolution be altered to magnify his own role. Stalin's propagandists portrayed him as having been exceptionally close to Vladimir Lenin, his close confidant and handpicked successor. In fact, while Lenin appreciated Stalin's discipline and loyalty, he regarded the younger man as of limited intelligence. In the 1930s, when Stalin began purging many of Lenin's closest allies from the

Though Lenin is shown here as a passionate orator, in fact he was not a good public speaker. To stir the masses with oratory the Bolsheviks relied on Leon Trotsky, who, as described by Louise Bryant, "*swayed the assembly as a strong wind stirs the long grass.*"

http://www.newseum.org/berlinwall/commissar_vanishes/9_10.htm

During the revolution, Lev Kamenev served as editor of the communist daily newspaper *Pravda* ("Truth"). He traveled to London to explain communist policies to the British government but was deported after one week.

Although the Bolsheviks fought against Russia's deeply rooted anti-Semitism, it returned under Stalin's rule. Trotsky, born Lev Bronstein, was the most prominent of the Jewish Bolsheviks.

Communist Party and executing many of the "Old Bolsheviks" who knew Lenin personally (see Chapter 28), the historical record was "adjusted" to remove many prominent revolutionists from the story.

Stalin's propagandists altered the photographic as well as the historical record of the revolution. This picture of Lenin speaking in Moscow in 1920 (left) is an iconographic image that was reproduced around the world. From the later 1920s, when the retouched version (below) was first produced, until the 1990s, Soviet citizens saw only the altered image in which two prominent Communists, Leon Trotsky and Lev Kamenev, had been erased and replaced with a set of wooden steps.

Stalin resented the leading role that Trotsky played as commander of the Red Army during the Russian Civil War of 1919–1921, and Trotsky was airbrushed out of all photographs from that period. In 1936 Kamenev was accused of plotting against Stalin and executed. Trotsky, exiled from Russia, died in Mexico in 1940 when one of Stalin's agents plunged an ice pick into his skull. *With today's widespread knowledge about digital editing, is it more or less likely that viewers would be fooled by such brazen alterations as seen in these photographs?*

http://www.newseum.org/berlinwall/commissar_vanishes/9_10.htm

(see Chapter 28). Some Western leftists were willing to look past Stalin's excesses to applaud Soviet achievements. But Emma Goldman pulled no punches: *"The Russian Revolution,"* she wrote, *"has demonstrated beyond all doubt that the State idea, State Socialism, and all its manifestations . . . is entirely bankrupt. . . . To call such a dictatorship, this personal autocracy more powerful than any Czar's, by the name of Communism seems to me the acme of imbecility."**

Among the Soviet Union's multitude of failures, in her view, was its backsliding on gender issues. True, women now had more educational opportunities and access to previously all-male professions like medicine. Still, even the most accomplished Soviet women had to bear the burdens of persistent patriarchy, such as sole responsibility for domestic drudgery. Though disillusioned by the Soviet model, Goldman remained committed to the idea that only a bottom-to-top revolution could bring gender equality and the true liberation of women's spirit.

Emma Goldman on Women's Rights

It may come as a surprise that Emma Goldman, a radical social critic and a staunch feminist, was not involved in the movement for women's suffrage. She admired the *"heroism and sturdiness of the English suffragettes,"** who in the years before the Great War had taken direct action to advance their cause, including public demonstrations, sit-ins, and even smashing windows, but securing the vote was never Goldman's priority.

For one thing, Goldman focused on the lives of working-class women and saw the suffrage movement as *"altogether a parlor affair, absolutely detached from the economic needs of the people."** Her hard life as a young immigrant in New York framed her outlook. The first step, she thought, was to organize women to fight for better wages and working conditions.

Even if women were now able to leave the home and seek employment—and indeed urbanizing societies relied on masses of young female labor for office and retail work—Goldman did not see progress: *"As to the great mass of working girls and women, how much independence is gained if the narrowness and lack of freedom of the home is exchanged for the narrowness and lack of freedom of the factory, sweat-shop, department store or office?"**

Many saw Goldman's views of marriage as scandalous, as when she mentioned marriage and prostitution in the same breath: *"Nowhere is woman treated according to the merit of her work, but rather as a sex,"* she wrote. *"It is therefore almost inevitable that she should pay for her right to exist, to keep a position in whatever line, with sex favors. Thus it is merely a question of degree whether she sells herself to one*

*Emma Goldman, "Afterword to My Disillusionment with Russia," pp. 393, 409, "Woman Suffrage," pp. 198, 199, "The Tragedy of Women's Liberation," p. 160, from *Red Emma Speaks: An Emma Goldman Reader*, comp. and ed. Alix Kates Shulman, 3d ed. (Amherst, N.Y.: Humanity Books, 1998).

Gaston Faris/Getty Images

Josephine Baker The most famous and wealthiest black woman in the world, Josephine Baker made her way from the slums of St. Louis to stardom in Harlem, and then in France, where she made Paris her permanent home. In the 1920s, the erotic cabaret star challenged conventional limits on women's public roles and thus joined Emma Goldman in redefining women's possibilities for the twentieth century (though from the standpoint of personal style, no two women could possibly have been more different).

*man, in or out of marriage, or to many men."** Goldman asserted that only a truly independent woman could choose marriage under conditions of equality, a very rare circumstance. Her many critics saw "Red Emma" as an unabashed promoter of "free love," a crusader against everything right and proper.

Goldman's views on contemporary motherhood were equally shocking: *"Is there anything more terrible [than] the woman, physically and mentally unfit to be a mother, yet condemned to breed: the woman, economically taxed to the very last spark of*

---

*Emma Goldman, "The Traffic in Women," p. 177, from *Red Emma Speaks: An Emma Goldman Reader*, comp. and ed. Alix Kates Shulman, 3d ed. (Amherst, N.Y.: Humanity Books, 1998).

*energy, yet forced to breed; the woman, worn and used up from the process of procreation, yet coerced to breed, more, ever more."** Goldman certainly *did* value women's role as mothers, but *not* under those kinds of circumstances.

For Goldman, therefore, girls' sex education and women's access to birth control were top priorities. Not only were these taboo subjects in "polite" society, but advocacy of birth control through the mail was a federal offense, one for which Goldman was arrested on several occasions. On the need for sex education, she was forthright: *"So long as a girl is not to know how to take care of herself, not to know the function of the most important part of her life, we need not be surprised if she becomes an easy prey to... a relationship which degrades her to the position of an object for mere sexual gratification."**

In the fight for women's access to birth control, Goldman became a friend and mentor to Margaret Sanger, a pioneering activist for women's reproductive rights and a founder of Planned Parenthood. Having worked as a nurse and a midwife on the lower East Side of Manhattan, Goldman had seen the harsh toll that serial pregnancies took on women living in poverty. At her public speeches, she courted arrest by advocating access to birth control and distributing thousands of copies of Sanger's newsletter, *The Woman Rebel.* As with marriage so with procreation, Goldman argued: only a liberated woman could properly choose the status of wife or mother. *Choice* was the sign of true independence.

Emma Goldman's definition of women's liberation was thus expansive and existential rather than narrowly political: *"True emancipation begins neither at the polls nor in the courts. It begins in woman's soul....It is necessary that woman...realize that her freedom will reach as far as her power to achieve her freedom reaches."†* As an anarchist, Goldman did not seek freedom through state institutions, in "polls" or "courts," but through women's self-actualization. Her recipe for women's emancipation was just the same as her prescription for society as a whole: *"All I want is freedom,"* she wrote, *"perfect, unrestricted liberty for myself and others."‡*

In Goldman's later years, however, individual freedoms were being constricted from both by fascists on the political right and communists on the political left (see Chapter 28). It would not be until the student movements of the 1960s that Goldman's libertarian agenda would resurface to inspire a new generation.

● **CONTEXT&CONNECTIONS** In the 1970s, Emma Goldman's insistence that women's personal lives be consistent with their political positions was especially appealing to "second-wave" feminists (see Chapter 30). A popular tee shirt of the time featured Goldman's image and a statement attributed to her: *"If I can't dance, I don't want to be part of your revolution."* ●

---

*Emma Goldman, "Victims of Morality," p. 173, "The Traffic in Women," p. 181, from *Red Emma Speaks: An Emma Goldman Reader,* comp. and ed. Alix Kates Shulman, 3d ed. (Amherst, N.Y.: Humanity Books, 1998).

†Cited in Alix Kates Shulman, "Emma Goldman's Feminism: A Reappraisal," p. 18, from *Red Emma Speaks: An Emma Goldman Reader,* comp. and ed. Alix Kates Shulman, 3d ed. (Amherst, N.Y.: Humanity Books, 1998).

‡Cited in Richard Drinnon, *Rebel in Paradise* (Chicago: University of Chicago, 1961), p. 102.

Entering the "Age of Extremes"

Over the past century, we have become accustomed to the drastic changes set in motion by the First World War. It is hard for us to imagine a world where Europe's political and economic domination was so thorough; where women were politically voiceless; where despite industrialization, the power of human and animal muscles was still the main energy source for farming; where centuries-old empires endured; and where a naïve belief in limitless progress was widely shared. War and revolution shattered such complacency.

The industrialized nature of total war came as a shock. Going into the war, cavalry regiments were essential to war planning. But the entire cavalry system was rendered anachronistic by the savage firepower of shells and machine guns. Hundreds of thousands of horses were killed, and the whole culture of "civilized" warfare between mounted "gentlemen" disappeared. Strafing aircraft and poison gas pointed to a more violent future when the lines between soldiers and civilians would blur even further. Just a generation later, during the Second World War, the targeting of civilian populations for aerial bombardment became common (see Chapter 29).

In cultural terms, total war accelerated the existing trend toward "mass societies" in which common people played a much larger role. Posters and newspapers were the principal media used to galvanize public

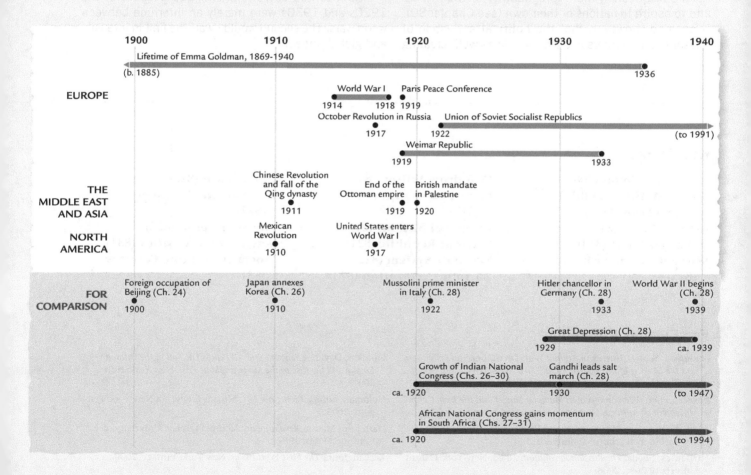

support for war, but already radio was supplementing telegraphy and new film industries had been born. By 1920, commercial radio broadcasts and the growth of cinema had created a broad platform for such dynamic cultural developments as the new African American art form of jazz music, which spread across the globe to enrich the lives of millions. Radio and film, however, also provided elites with new means to sway public opinion and could be used as mechanisms of propaganda and control, a trend that would serve authoritarian regimes in Italy and Germany in the 1920s and 1930s (see Chapter 28).

To Emma Goldman and other idealists, the revolutionary rise of the masses marked an advance toward human liberation, showing that ruling elites could no longer take the obedience of common men and women for granted. The same was true in Europe's overseas empires, where the war had caused many Africans and Asians to question the impregnability of their rulers and to aspire to nations of their own (see Chapter 30). It seemed, however, that the political activation of peasants and workers had a dark side as well, creating disordered conditions in which dictatorship could flourish, as in the absolute control established by the Communist Party in the Soviet Union under Vladimir Lenin and Joseph Stalin.

From today's perspective, communism seems to have been a historical dead end. The Soviet Union no longer exists, and the People's Republic of China, while retaining communist political control, has thrown in its lot with market economics (see Chapters 31 and 32). In the immediate postwar era, however, there were many who logically questioned whether it was liberal capitalism that might be destined for historical obsolescence. Both fascists and communists felt empowered by the uncertainty of the war's aftermath, an antiliberal trend that would be greatly magnified by the Great Depression. By the 1930s, Emma Goldman's anarchist faith in absolute individual autonomy seemed almost quaint.

As it turned out, the crisis-filled decades of the 1920s and 1930s were merely an interlude between world wars. The second would dwarf the first in intensity and global impact.

Key Terms

Emma Goldman (808)
Kaiser Wilhelm II (811)
western front (812)
eastern front (814)
southern front (814)
Senegalese Sharpshooters (815)

Woodrow Wilson (816)
Paris Peace Conference (817)
League of Nations (817)
Weimar Republic (821)
Mandate System (822)
Balfour Declaration (823)

Sun Yat-sen (826)
May Fourth Movement (827)
Vladimir Lenin (828)
New Economic Policy (831)
"Socialism in One Country" (831)

For Further Reference

Anderson, Scott. *Lawrence in Arabia: War, Deceit, Imperial Folly and the Making of the Modern Middle East.* New York: Anchor, 2013.

Chesler, Ellen. *Woman of Valor: Margaret Sanger and the Birth Control Movement in America.* New York: Simon and Schuster, 2007.

Clark, Christopher. *The Sleepwalkers: How Europe Went to War in 1914.* New York: Harper Collins, 2013.

Fitzpatrick, Sheila. *The Russian Revolution.* 3d ed. New York: Oxford University Press, 2008.

Fromkin, David. *A Peace to End All Peace: The Fall of the Ottoman Empire and the Rise of the Modern Middle East.* New York: Holt, 2001.

Goldman, Emma. *Living my Life.* Miriam Brody, ed. New York: Penguin, 2006.

Hart, John Mason. *Revolutionary Mexico.* Berkeley: University of California Press, 1997.

Keegan, John. *The First World War.* New York: Vintage, 2000.

Macmillan, Margaret. *Paris 1919: Six Months That Changed the World*. New York: Random House, 2003.

Neiberg, Michael S. *Fighting the Great War: A Global History*. New York: Cambridge University Press, 2005.

Reynolds, David. *The Long Shadow: The Legacies of the Great War in the Twentieth Century*. New York: W.W. Norton, 2014.

Schiffrin, Harold. *Sun Yat-Sen and the Origins of the Chinese Revolution*. Berkeley: University of California Press, 2010.

Service, Robert. *Spies and Commissars: The Early Years of the Russian Revolution*. New York: Public Affairs, 2013.

Strachan, Hew. *The First World War in Africa*. New York: Oxford University Press, 2004.

MindTap

MindTap is a fully online, highly personalized learning experience built upon Cengage Learning content. MindTap combines student learning tools—readings, multimedia, activities, and assessments—into a singular Learning Path that guides students through the course.

Halide Edib

From *Memoirs of Halide Adivar Edib* (N.J.: Gorgias Press). Reprinted by permission of Gorgias Press.

Halide Edib (1884–1964) grew up in cosmopolitan Istanbul, the daughter of a progressive Ottoman official who made sure she learned Arabic and studied the Quran but who also had her tutored by an English governess and sent her to a Greek-run school. In 1901, fluent in Turkish, English, Greek, and Arabic, Edib was the first Muslim girl to graduate from the American College for Girls in Istanbul. As a child of privilege, she had the luxury of exploring many different ideas and forming her identity in a safe and secure environment. Following a young woman's traditional path, after graduation, Edib married and had two children: *"My life was confined within the walls of my apartment. I led the life of an old-fashioned Turkish woman."**

Before long, Edib was moving beyond traditional gender roles, publishing her first novel in 1908 and helping to found the Society for the Elevation of Women. In 1910, she left her husband after he married a second wife, in conformity with Islamic law but against her wishes. She prevailed on her husband to obtain a divorce: she had no legal grounds to demand one herself.

Then, as with so many from her generation, the First World War changed her destiny. The Ottoman government sent Halide Edib (hall-ee-DEH eh-DEEP) southeast to Damascus and Beirut to organize schools and orphanages for girls. Soon, however, the Ottoman armies were in retreat, and she returned to the capital. In May 1918, the situation for Turkey was grim. Greek forces had seized the coastal city of Smyrna (toady's Izmir); the British had landed in Istanbul itself.

British airplanes circled menacingly overhead when Halide Edib stood to address a massive crowd before Istanbul's magnificent Blue Mosque:

*Halide Edib, *Inside India* (London: Allen and Unwin, 1937), p. 207.

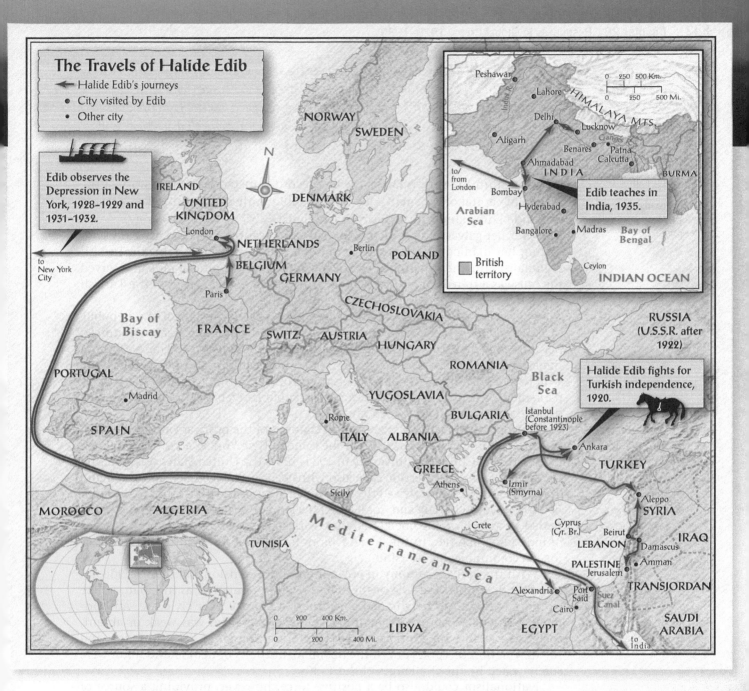

The Travels of Halide Edib

← Halide Edib's journeys
● City visited by Edib
● Other city

Edib observes the Depression in New York, 1928–1929 and 1931–1932.

Edib teaches in India, 1935.

Halide Edib fights for Turkish independence, 1920.

British territory

0   250 500 Km.
0   250 500 Mi.

Peshawar
Lahore
HIMALAYA MTS.
Delhi
Lucknow
Aligarh
Benares
Patna
Calcutta
Ahmadabad
INDIA
BURMA
to/from London
Bombay
Arabian Sea
Hyderabad
Bangalore
Madras
Bay of Bengal
Ceylon
INDIAN OCEAN

NORWAY
SWEDEN
IRELAND
UNITED KINGDOM
London
DENMARK
NETHERLANDS
Berlin
POLAND
BELGIUM
GERMANY
Paris
CZECHOSLOVAKIA
to New York City
Bay of Biscay
FRANCE
SWITZ.
AUSTRIA
HUNGARY
ROMANIA
RUSSIA (U.S.S.R. after 1922)
PORTUGAL
Madrid
YUGOSLAVIA
Black Sea
SPAIN
Rome
ITALY
BULGARIA
Istanbul (Constantinople before 1923)
Ankara
TURKEY
ALBANIA
GREECE
Izmir (Smyrna)
Aleppo
Athens
SYRIA
MOROCCO
ALGERIA
Sicily
Crete
Cyprus (Gr. Br.)
Beirut
IRAQ
Damascus
LEBANON
TUNISIA
Mediterranean Sea
PALESTINE
Amman
Jerusalem
TRANSJORDAN
Alexandria
Port Said
Suez Canal
LIBYA
Cairo
EGYPT
SAUDI ARABIA
to India

N

0   200 400 Km.
0   200 400 Mi.

Brothers, sisters, countrymen, Muslims! When the night is darkest and seems eternal, the light of dawn is nearest.... From the tops of the minarets nigh against the heaven, seven hundred years of glory are watching.... I invoke the souls of our great [Ottoman] ancestors who had so often passed in procession through this very square.... I declare in the name of the new Turkish nation presented here, that the disarmed Turkish nation of

841

Halide Edib

(1884–1964) Turkish nationalist best known for her many popular works of fiction featuring female protagonists. She was part of the army that formed the Turkish nation and later served as a member of the Turkish parliament and as a professor of English literature.

today still possesses your invincible hearts; we trust in Allah and in our rights. [The] allied powers of Europe ... have found ... an opportunity to break to pieces the last empire ruled by the crescent.... But the day will come when a greater court of justice will try those who have deprived the nations of their natural rights.*

It was a stunning performance, the first recorded instance in the history of the ancient capital of a woman addressing a public gathering. To this day, a statue of Halide Edib stands in the heart of Istanbul.

After her galvanizing speech, Edib fled east, wearing a veil and carefully concealing her manicured fingernails as she rode on horseback to join the Turkish nationalist army headquartered at Ankara. She was given official rank and served the cause as a translator and press officer to Mustafa Kemal, leader of the Turkish forces fighting for the integrity of their homeland.

They were successful in securing international recognition of the Republic of Turkey, but then she fell out of favor with the dictatorial Kemal, who forced her into exile in 1926. For the next thirteen years she traveled to France, Britain, India, and the United States, writing books and lecturing at universities. Only with Kemal's death in 1939 did she return to Turkey, winning a seat in the Turkish parliament, teaching English literature at Istanbul University, and becoming one of her country's most renowned novelists.

During Edib's years of exile, the uncertainties of the postwar world were turning into genuine global crises. When she came to New York as a visiting professor of literature at Columbia University in 1931–1932, the United States was suffering through the Great Depression. She also witnessed its global effects in Britain and France, from which she viewed the emergence of fascism with the rise to power of Benito Mussolini in Italy and Adolf Hitler in Germany. These fascist regimes represented an assault on the liberal tradition, with state power growing at the expense of individual liberties. In the Soviet Union, Joseph Stalin was further consolidating his communist dictatorship.

With the global economy in crisis and political tensions on the rise, ideologies that magnified the role of the state grew in popularity, as in Japan, where extreme nationalism heightened authoritarian control over civic life. Authoritarian tendencies gained momentum wherever liberalism was weak or absent, such as in Russia, the European colonial empires, much of Latin America, and the new nation of Turkey. Even the liberal institutions of democratic states were sorely tested by the challenges of the 1930s.

Nationalism could also be a positive force, however, providing a source of hope for many colonized Africans and Asians. The great Indian nationalist leader Mohandas K. Gandhi personified these hopes, while giving the entire world a model of peaceful political change. Like Halide Edib, Gandhi saw the fight for national independence as inseparable from the fight for justice, including equality for women, who had few rights under colonialism. Gandhi's peaceful philosophy, a source of inspiration to many, stood in sharp contrast to the renewed militarism that would soon lead to another world war.

---

*Halide Edib, *The Turkish Ordeal* (New York: Century, 1928), p. 24, n. 8. Edib did not keep a record of the speech, so this was her later reconstruction.

> How did governments in different parts of the world respond to the crisis of the Great Depression?

> Why did liberal democracy decline in influence as fascism, communism, and other authoritarian regimes rose in power and popularity?

> How successful were anticolonial nationalists in Asia and Africa during this period?

> What major events led to the outbreak of the Second World War?

The Great Depression, 1929–1939

In October 1929, prices on the New York Stock Exchange plunged; within two months, stocks lost half their value. Bank failures across Europe and the Americas brought the **Great Depression** and the global spread of economic hardship. Unemployment surged; agricultural prices plummeted. Ten years later, global markets still had not recovered.

The Great Depression in the Industrialized World

The Great Depression revealed the degree to which finance and trade integrated nearly all the world's people into a single economic system. Historians continue to debate the causes of the Great Depression, but two factors clearly stand out: the speculative excesses of the American stock market, and the international debt structure that emerged after the First World War.

By the later 1920s the global economy had recovered from postwar malaise. In the United States, financial markets reflected the frenetic pace of life during the "jazz age," with its glamorous movie stars, mass-produced automobiles, and sensational gangsters. More and more, speculators bought stock on borrowed money, trusting that markets would endlessly increase in value. When the bubble burst, ruining investors and the bankers who had lent them money, capital investment dried up, and the stock market collapse turned into a general economic crisis.

A sharp division between rich and poor magnified the problem. By 1928, only 1 percent of the U.S. population controlled 24 percent of its wealth. Since ordinary workers could no longer afford the products being churned out by American manufacturers, many plants closed. By 1932, one-fourth of workers in the United States were unemployed.

The U.S. stock market collapse soon revealed the vulnerability of the international financial system. During World War I the United States had replaced Great Britain as the world's leading creditor, and European governments were deeply in debt to American banks. The banking crisis was particularly acute in Germany, where the Weimar government was forced to borrow heavily to make huge reparations payments to France (see Chapter 27). Financiers in the United States lent Germans money, which they then paid to France, which then sent the money back to the United States as French payments on American loans. After the stock market crash, American investors called in their loans to German banks, and the

Great Depression
Economic depression beginning in 1929 with the crash of stock prices in New York followed by a series of bank failures in Europe; marked by sustained deflation, unemployment in industrial nations, and depressed crop prices.

system collapsed. By 1933, German factories produced only half the goods they had manufactured in 1929, and half the workforce was idle.

● **CONTEXT&CONNECTIONS** The Great Depression demonstrated the need for international institutions to stabilize the global financial system, and the lesson was learned. In 1944, even before the end of World War II, the *Bretton Woods Conference* created the International Monetary Fund and the World Bank to support national economies during economic downturns (key term in Chapter 29). ●

Politicians exacerbated the crisis. In 1930, the United States imposed high tariffs to protect American manufacturing from foreign imports. Great Britain enacted a series of tariff "preferences" within its empire. Though intended to save jobs, protectionist measures caused steep declines in international trade and further loss of employment. By the early 1930s, wages and prices spiraled downward in a vicious deflationary cycle.

In these circumstances, few believed that free markets could solve the problem. The British economist John Maynard Keynes argued that the massive unemployment of the time was not just a temporary corrective, as *laissez-faire* economics would have it, but a deep structural problem stemming from a lack of demand. Governments, he proposed, should take up the slack by spending freely and expanding the money supply. Even if large-scale borrowing and risks of inflation were necessary in the short run, Keynes argued, the resulting economic revival would increase the tax revenues needed to pay off deficits.

As during World War I, and in line with the recommendations of John Maynard Keynes, governments in France, Britain, and the United States now took a much more active role in domestic economies. In the United States, President **Franklin Delano Roosevelt** (in office 1933–1945) implemented his New Deal programs. Social Security created a "safety net" for many of the nation's elderly, and the Works Progress Administration put the unemployed to work on public infrastructure. Price subsidies helped stabilize farm prices while legislation strengthened workers' rights to unionize and strike. Government protection of depositors' accounts restored faith in the banking system. However, though the New Deal was quite popular, it did not get at the root of the economic problem. In 1939, unemployment in the United States still stood at 16 percent.

The same pattern of government intervention unfolded in France and Britain, while in Sweden, Norway, and Denmark, Social Democrats pledged to construct a "welfare state" that would protect their citizens through comprehensive education, health care, housing subsidies, and unemployment insurance. But while such measures reduced suffering, no merely national solution could solve the problem of depressed global markets caused by a shortage of credit.

Franklin Delano Roosevelt

(in office 1933–1945) President of the United States during the Great Depression and World War II. Created the New Deal, intended to stimulate the economy through government spending, financial sector reform, and a safety net for those most in need.

The Great Depression in Global Perspective

Depressed agricultural prices hit farmers hard everywhere, including hundreds of millions of peasant farmers in Africa, Asia, and Latin America. In very remote areas peasants might have the option of withdrawing from market production and focusing on their own family and village subsistence. But by the 1930s the vast majority had become so enmeshed in global markets that withdrawal was not an option. In Africa, for example, small-scale family farms grew cash crops like cocoa, cotton, and coffee to buy imported goods

Ullstein bild · Martin Munkacsi

Destroying Brazilian Coffee By 1932 the world market price for coffee had plunged so dramatically that Brazil, the world's leading producer, destroyed tens of thousands of tons. Burning coffee and shoveling it into the sea did little to restore vigor to the international coffee market, however. Only a revival of consumer spending could achieve that.

like cloth, kerosene lamps, and bicycles and to pay the taxes demanded by European colonial governments. Parents with extra money often invested in school fees for their children, another incentive to grow commercial crops.

When coffee and cocoa prices fell by over half in early 1930, many Africans were suddenly unable to meet their tax obligations or pay their debts. Since Western manufactures had increasingly displaced indigenous industries, they had come to depend on imported goods like iron hoes and cotton clothing, which they could no longer afford. Years of hardship followed during which school attendance declined as young people were sometimes forced to leave their villages in search of work.

Conditions were equally bleak where export commodities were produced on plantations. Brazil, the world's largest coffee producer, also experienced the steep fall in coffee prices when cash-strapped North American and European consumers cut back on consumption. Exporters destroyed huge stockpiles, hoping that decreasing the supply would increase global prices. Agricultural workers left the plantations to scratch a living out of the soil or to join the destitute in the burgeoning *favelas*, or urban slums. The situation was similar in Southeast Asia, after a global decline in automobile and bicycle production caused rubber prices to crash.

In the villages of India, the drop in crop prices further squeezed farmers who already, in the words of Halide Edib, were *"at the mercy of rain, moneylender, and tax-gatherer."** By 1932, peasant incomes had fallen by half. To avoid losing their land, many families sold the gold jewelry they were saving for their daughters' dowries. In the 1930s, billions of rupees worth of such "distress gold" were sold, and many couples delayed or canceled marriage. At the same time, many South Asian Muslims had to cancel plans to perform the hajj, the pilgrimage to Mecca and Medina that could take a lifetime of planning (see Chapter 17).

Egyptian farmers were struck equally hard. As textile factories in Europe and the United States cut production or closed, cotton prices plunged. Whereas over 16,000 people a year traveled from Egypt to Arabia for the *hajj* before 1929, only about 1,700 made the pilgrimage in 1933.

In Latin America, economic nationalism was a common response to the crisis. In Mexico, for example, President Lázaro Cárdenas nationalized the country's petroleum industry, arguing that the profits should help the Mexican people rather than enrich foreign companies. To aid rural Mexicans, he redistributed large amounts of land to peasant communities, finally fulfilling the promise of the Mexican Revolution (see Chapter 27). Like other Latin American presidents, Cárdenas went even further than leaders in the United States and western Europe in asserting state economic power in response to the Great Depression.

These were also troubled times in Halide Edib's native Turkey. Mustafa Kemal was determined to build up Turkey's own industrial base by making the country less dependent on foreign imports. He pursued import-substitution policies by erecting high tariffs to shield local manufacturers from global competition. Import substitution did create some new industrial jobs. However, such policies decreased international trade, further hampering global recovery.

Fascism, Communism, and Authoritarianism

E ven in the most liberal societies, where private enterprise and individual liberty were well established, the challenges of the early twentieth century brought greater government economic intervention. In Italy, Germany, and the Soviet Union, where liberalism had much shallower roots, those challenges created a climate in which explicitly antiliberal, authoritarian political ideologies—**fascism** and communism—flourished.

fascism

Authoritarian political doctrine based on extreme nationalism, elevation of the state at the expense of the individual, and replacement of independent social organizations in civil society with state organizations.

Fascists, most notably Benito Mussolini in Italy and Adolf Hitler in Germany, were contemptuous of representative government and of weak, vain, and vacillating politicians. They should be replaced by strong leaders who represented not self-interested factions but the people as a whole. Only then, they promised, could national greatness be achieved. Unity of purpose and the role of the state in organizing the collective will were more important in fascist thinking than individual rights. Fascists were extreme nationalists, and while racism was strongly present across the world—from the segregated cities and schools of the United States to the racially based empires of Britain and France—the German Nazis imposed racial policies of unprecedented severity. Jews were the principal target.

Communists likewise had no use for liberal democracy, following Karl Marx's description of representative democracy as a sham. *"The executive of the modern*

---

*Halide Edib, *Inside India* (London: Allen and Unwin, 1937), p. 170.

state," asserts the *Communist Manifesto*, "*is nothing but a committee for managing the common affairs of the whole bourgeoisie.*"* Unlike the fascists, however, the communists underplayed national unity while emphasizing class solidarity. In spite of evidence to the contrary, especially from World War I, many Marxists still believed that workers would unite internationally to overthrow their oppressors and create global socialism

In reality, the Soviet Union was the only existing communist society in the 1930s. As Stalin collectivized agriculture, oversaw rapid industrialization, and purged the state of his perceived enemies, the Soviet people lived in perpetual fear and deprivation. But some Western observers, their own societies wracked by economic depression, imagined that the Soviet model pointed the way toward peace, prosperity, and social justice.

Although fascists and communists hated each other passionately, they shared a common loathing for liberal democracy. Following the Great Depression, with the democratic nations struggling to restore their vitality without much success, many came to believe that either fascism or communism was the cure.

Mussolini and the Rise of Fascism

For **Benito Mussolini** (1883–1945), the state bound the people together: "*Everything for the state, nothing against the state, no one outside the state.*" After World War I, Mussolini organized quasi-military groups made up largely of former soldiers, called Blackshirts, who assaulted socialists and communists in the streets. Their belligerence intimidated middle-class politicians, whose weakness, Mussolini thought, could allow Bolshevism to spread to Italy. Mussolini's supporters called him *Il Duce* (ill DOO-chey), "the leader."

It was true that disunity made the country vulnerable. After all, the Italian nation was only six decades old: for many, local dialects and cultural traditions were still more relevant than national ones. Social tensions accompanied industrialization in the north, while the south was still mired in the poverty that had driven many to emigrate to the United States and Argentina. Neither the existing constitutional monarchy nor the Catholic Church, although it dominated the lives of most Italians, seemed able to reconcile regional and class divisions. Extreme nationalism was Mussolini's answer.

Mussolini stepped in with supreme confidence and determination, offering order, discipline, and unity. His passionate speeches contrasted sharply with the bland style of most politicians. Landowners and industrialists, favoring Mussolini's call to suppress anarchism and communism, financed the fascists as the Blackshirts harassed union leaders, broke strikes, and kept potentially rebellious farm laborers and tenants in line.

In 1922, Mussolini organized disaffected war veterans in a march on Rome. Though the elected government declared a state of siege to rebuff Mussolini's play for power, the king and the military refused to enforce it. With the support of these conservative elites, Mussolini then bullied his way into the prime minister's position. As the violence of fascist thugs escalated, however, many Italians who had been attracted by Mussolini's youth and vigor began to turn against him. He responded

Benito Mussolini

(1883–1945) Prime minister of Italy and the world's first fascist leader. Also known as Il Duce, he founded the Italian Fascist Party and formed an alliance with Hitler's Germany.

---

*Excerpt from *The Marx-Engels Reader*, ed. Robert C. Tucker, 2d ed.

by arresting opponents, assassinating socialists, and outlawing competing political parties. After 1926 Mussolini ruled as dictator.

Mussolini's definition of fascism was explicitly antiliberal: *"Liberalism denied the State in the name of the individual; Fascism reasserts the rights of the State as expressing the real essence of the individual."** One of the foundations of liberal democracy is free association, allowing people to voluntarily come together to pursue similar interests or to achieve a common objective. Mussolini instead installed a system of "corporations," in which the state itself organized all citizens involved in a common undertaking. "Corporatism" replaced independent unions with state-sanctioned ones and took over the nation's youth organizations. Even so, the fascists never actually achieved their intended degree of social control, as most Italians continued to rely on church, community, and family.

For the dull compromises of parliamentary democracy Mussolini substituted a theatrical politics that involved singing, flag waving, marching, and stirring oratory. He often invoked Rome's imperial past and promised to make it once again the center of a mighty empire. In 1935, in defiance of the League of Nations, he invaded Ethiopia to avenge Italy's humiliating defeat by King Menelik's army in 1896 (see Chapter 26). Fervent patriotism in the cause of empire proved another effective way to bind together the young Italian nation.

Some Italians were active in support of Mussolini's regime, willing to trade liberty for security and a renewed sense of national pride. Others, especially communists, paid for opposition with their lives. Most Italians probably did not care too much one way or the other and simply went on with their daily lives. As the Italian Marxist Antonio Gramsci wrote, before spending years in a fascist prison: *"Indifference is actually the mainspring of history…. What comes to pass does so not so much because a few people want it to happen, as because the mass of citizens abdicate their responsibility and let things be."†*

Hitler and National Socialism in Germany

Germany was both humiliated and financially devastated after World War I. Though the Weimar Republic had brought liberal democracy to Germany in the 1920s, the onset of the Great Depression left Germans once again desperate for solutions. With the center falling out of German politics, communists on the far left and fascists on the extreme right gained in popularity.

The German liberals and socialists who had overseen the creation of the Weimar Republic were heirs to the Enlightenment tradition that saw the use of reason as a means of achieving a just and stable social order. For many Germans, however, the war had called that belief into question. During what some historians have called an "age of anxiety" artists probed darker emotions, as with the nightmarish images painted by German expressionists.

The scientific works of the psychiatrist Sigmund Freud (1856–1939) and the astrophysicist Albert Einstein (1879–1955) were also deeply unsettling, overturning many complacent prewar assumptions. Sigmund Freud, in his quest to develop more effective interventions for neurosis, developed a view of human psychology in which unrecognized urges lay beyond the control of the conscious mind and in

---

*From *Fascism Doctrine and Institutions*, 1935, pp. 7–42. http://www.worldfuturefund.org/wffmaster/Reading/Germany/mussolini.htm.

†Antonio Gramsci, from *Avanti!*, in *Selections from Political Writings 1910–1920* (London: Lawrence and Wishart, 1977), p. 17.

which sexual complexes emanating from unremembered childhood experiences could dominate human behavior.

Meanwhile, in physics, scientists were challenging the "common sense" of the Newtonian framework (see Chapter 21) at both the atomic and cosmic levels. In his special theory of relativity, Einstein overthrew Newton's conception of time and space as an absolute grid, removing time as an independent variable by positing a four-dimensional space-time in which observation itself depends on the speed and location of the observer. Thus science itself, along with artistic modernism and psychotherapy, reinforced the climate of uncertainty in which the Weimar Republic had been born.

Into this anxious environment stepped **Adolf Hitler** (1889–1945) and his National Socialist Party, promising to restore greatness, confidence, and order. Modernism they decried as "degenerate art," while "Jewish science" was the term used to tar Freud, Einstein, and other brilliant minds as part of a conspiracy to demoralize the German people so that Jewish interests could prevail. In fact, restoring the vitality and historical mission of the Germans was Hitler's rallying cry.

Adolf Hitler
(1889–1945) Leader of the National Socialist Party who became chancellor of Germany and dismantled the Weimar constitution. His ultranationalist policies led to persecution of communists and Jews, and his aggressive foreign policies started World War II.

● **CONTEXT&CONNECTIONS** After 1933, when Nazi anti-Semitism became official policy, many German-Jewish artists, scientists, and thinkers were stripped of their academic and cultural positions and forced into exile. Of the many exiled scientists who contributed to later U.S. technological predominance, Albert Einstein was the most important as a public figure. Though Einstein's theoretical work laid the foundation for the atomic bomb (see Chapter 29), after World War II Einstein was a consistent advocate for peace and Cold War dialogue. ●

Hitler had a very different idea than did socialists or liberals of what was meant by "the people." For socialists it referred simply to the masses of workers. For liberals, who stressed individual autonomy, "the people" meant the sum total of those individuals. For Hitler, however, *das Volk* (das FOHLK), "the people," was a single organism bound by history, tradition, and race. Just as no cell is independent from the others in a living organism, so all Germans were connected by their racial destiny. Hitler defined Germans as an "Aryan" race superior to all others and identified race-mixing as a threat to that superiority. "*All the great civilizations of the past died out,*" Hitler proclaimed with stunning ignorance of history, "*because contamination of the blood caused them to become decadent.*"*

According to Nazism, Germans who did not live up to the ideal of racial pride and racial purity were like tumors that needed to be excised. Nazi targets included communists, with their internationalist doctrine; homosexuals, with their supposed rejection of traditional family values; and the physically and mentally handicapped. Proponents of the racist pseudo-science of eugenics (also popular in the United States in the 1930s) argued that selective breeding could lead to superior human beings. If the smartest "Aryan" men and women married and had children, they could produce a "master race." On the other hand, according to this racist logic, the "inferior" should be stopped from breeding: eugenic medical practices led to the sterilization of many girls from poor and ethnic minority families to stop their "genetic defects" from being passed on to another generation.

Looking for a scapegoat on whom to blame the country's problems, Hitler tapped into the centuries-old tradition of anti-Semitism. Although German Jews

*Cited in *Sources of Global History since 1900*, ed. James H. Overfield, 2d ed. (Boston: Wadsworth, 2013), p. 132.

Mary Evans Picture Library/The Image Works

National Socialist Propaganda The Nazi Party often used images of healthy blond children to emphasize German vitality and racial superiority and organized young people into party-based boys' and girls' clubs. This poster for the "League of German Girls" solicits donations to a fund to "Build Youth Hostels and Homes." In spite of the girl's smile and flowers, all of the money collected actually went into weapons production.

were thoroughly assimilated into national life, he identified them as the main threat: *"The personification of the devil as the symbol of all evil assumes the living shape of the Jew."* For the Nazis, the supposed racial characteristics of Jews contrasted with, and thereby illuminated, the virtues of the German *Volk*. Only by isolating the Jews, and ultimately eliminating them, could the goal of racial purity be achieved.

In the late 1920s, such ideas were on the far fringe. At that time, most National Socialists were poorly educated former soldiers and young men caught up in Hitler's emotional, patriotic appeals. But after the Great Depression, voters increasingly abandoned the parties of the center-right and the center-left for the communists and the fascists. Between 1928 and 1932, the National Socialist share of the vote jumped from 2.6 to 37.3 percent of the national total, and Hitler's deputies controlled more than a third of the seats in the Reichstag. Now some more affluent Germans voted for the National Socialists as a bulwark against communism.

Indeed, the German Communist Party had also gained strong support in the elections of 1932, alarming business leaders. Despite their distaste for Hitler, who most educated Germans saw as wild and unrefined, conservatives thought they would be able to control him from behind the scenes. Needing Hitler's support to form a governing coalition, which Hitler would join only if he was made chancellor, a reluctant President Paul von Hindenburg announced a new government with Hitler at its head in 1933.

A month after he took office, a fire broke out in the Reichstag (the German parliament). The arson was likely the work of a single individual, but Hitler accused the Communist Party of treason and had its members arrested. The remaining representatives then passed a law that suspended constitutional protections of civil liberties for four years and allowed Hitler to rule as a dictator. Dissenting from that vote, socialist deputies were then also arrested and sent to Dachau, the first of what would become a pan-European network of concentration camps.

Hitler dismantled Weimar's democratic institutions and became the *Führer* (leader) of an industrial state of huge potential power. Changes to German society were sudden and extreme. The Nazis abolished all other political parties and replaced Germany's federal structure with a centralized dictatorship emanating from Berlin. Like the fascists in Italy, they took over or replaced independent organizations in civil society such as labor unions. Hitler Youth replaced the Boy Scouts and church-sponsored youth groups as part of a plan, reinforced by a new school curriculum, to teach fascism to the next generation. Artists, architects, writers, and filmmakers who did not conform to the National Socialist vision were censored, harassed, and often driven into exile. (See the feature "Visual Evidence in Primary Sources: Angst and Order in German Cinema.") Hitler promised a Third Reich ("Third Empire") that would last a thousand years.

The Nazis also restricted the authority of German religious leaders. Protestant churches came under tight state control, and the Nazis seized Catholic Church properties and imprisoned priests brave enough to oppose them. Still, many Catholics joined the National Socialist Party, and Christian leaders of all denominations would later be criticized for not having done enough to resist Hitler.

Having already imprisoned the communists, the Führer (FYUR-ruhr) turned to the "Jewish problem." In 1935, the Nazis imposed the Nuremberg Laws, which deprived Jews of all civil rights and forbade intermarriage between Jews and other Germans. Some Jews emigrated, but many German Jews were so deeply assimilated into the country's cultural and social life that they could not imagine leaving. Then, on November 9, 1938, the Nazis launched coordinated attacks against Jews throughout Germany and Austria. After this *"Kristallnacht"* ("Crystal Night")—named for the smashing of windows in Jewish homes, synagogues, and stores—more Jews fled. The Nazis forced those who remained into segregated ghettos. After 1938, it was no longer possible to suppose that Hitler's anti-Semitic tirades were merely political rhetoric.

● **CONTEXT&CONNECTIONS** November 9 is a date of great resonance in German history, bringing to mind both great evil and great joy. On that date in 1938, *Kristallnacht* was a prelude to the *Holocaust* (Chapter 29), which included the murder of six million Jews. By coincidence, November 9 was also the date in 1989 when communist East Germany finally opened the Berlin Wall, presaging the end of the Cold War (see Chapter 31). ●

Part of Hitler's appeal was negative: at a time of fear and insecurity, the Führer pointed to "enemies" such as communists and Jews who could be blamed for the country's problems. Economic recovery also helps explain Hitler's popularity. While democracies vainly struggled to create jobs, German unemployment dropped from over 6 million people to under two hundred thousand between 1932 and 1938. It seemed that government economic intervention was key. German ministries fixed prices and allocated resources in close coordination with the country's largest corporations. Massive public works projects, such as the world's first superhighways and a large military buildup, put Germans back to work.

Hitler promised that traditional values of courage, order, and discipline would once again empower the German people. Women's highest calling was to stay in the home and nurture purebred Aryan children. The Nazis' massive rallies, with their precision marching, flag waving, and spellbinding speeches by the Führer himself, gave people a sense of being part of something much larger than themselves. Radio broadcasts and expertly made propaganda films spread the excitement throughout the land.

Of course, not everyone was taken in. But outspoken opposition to Hitler meant imprisonment or death. Most Germans were content to go about their daily lives, appreciative of the relative order and prosperity.

Stalin: Collectivization and the Great Purges

For all the ambition of Mussolini and Hitler, neither could match the total control of society achieved by Joseph Stalin (1879–1953). While Stalin's totalitarian

Angst and Order in German Cinema

Expressionism was one response to the horrific experience of war. Strongly emotive, expressionism captured the angst of a postwar generation torn from the securities of a world seemingly changed forever. Many expressionists challenged the viewer with strong colors, primitive outlines, violent emotion, rapid movement, and heightened sexual energy. It was art for an age of anxiety. In film, the most famous expressionist work is *The Cabinet of Dr. Caligari*, a 1920 horror film that plumbs the darkness of the human psyche; an advertising poster for the film is reproduced here.

Neoclassicism was a quite different response to postwar uncertainty, with the goal of restoring a sense of order by returning to the calm harmony associated with Greek art. The second image here exemplifies the neoclassical style. *Olympia*, directed by the great German film artist Leni Riefenstahl, was a tribute to the Berlin Olympics of 1936. While her technical brilliance is widely

The sets for this silent film featured jagged, canvas-painted backgrounds, with few right angles or settled spaces. The expressionistic look of the film, including sharp contrasts between light and dark, reinforced its theme of disorder and violence in the human psyche.

The film's emphasis on dark, uncontrollable urges reflected the increasing influence of Sigmund Freud, the great Austrian psychologist who emphasized the power of the unconscious mind.

Movie Poster Image Art/Getty Images

The story features the evil Dr. Caligari, who controls a sleepwalking man, Cesare. Caligari displays Cesare at carnivals, claiming he can predict the future. At night, Cesare performs murder on Caligari's behalf. Or does he?

The film leaves the viewer to doubt: who is the doctor and who is the patient? Who is sane and who is deranged? What is reality and what is fantasy? Such unsettling, unanswered questions were new to film when *Dr. Caligari* was premiered in Berlin in 1920, but in later decades they would become common in the genre of psychologically driven horror films.

acknowledged, Riefenstahl's work has also been judged by its propaganda value for the Nazi regime. Neoclassicism was the style preferred by Adolf Hitler.

The National Socialists denounced expressionism as a perverse form of modernism created by Jews and subversives to undermine the confidence and willpower of the German people. In 1937, Joseph Goebbels (Hitler's minister of propaganda) organized an exhibition of so-called "degenerate art" in Munich to rally the public against artistic modernism. Many "degenerate" painters, architects, designers, and filmmakers were driven into exile.

Germany's loss was America's gain. Hollywood benefited enormously from the influx of émigré film talent in the 1930s. Erich Pommer (the producer of *Dr. Caligari*) and Billy Wilder (one of the most productive and popular Hollywood directors) were Jewish refugees from fascism who significantly influenced film in the United States. Along with Jews from Poland, Russia, Lithuania, and elsewhere, they made enduring contributions to American culture.

The look of *Olympia* could not possibly be more different than that of *Dr. Caligari*. Here all is rational and orderly; right angles, classical harmony, and idealized depictions of the human body dominate. *From what you know of fascism, why were the Nazis so opposed to expressionist works like Dr. Caligari and so strongly supportive of neoclassical works like Olympia? (Try to watch clips of Dr. Caligari and the opening scene of Olympia online before you answer.)*

After silently and reverently panning across the ruins of the Parthenon, Riefenstahl's camera shows a Greek statue of a discus thrower slowly fading into the statuesque figure of a modern athlete, who gracefully completes the throw. The continuity between classical and modern is immediately asserted.

As a photographer and cinematographer, director Leni Riefenstahl (1902–2003) was one of the most influential visual artists of the twentieth century. Yet the fact that her art was placed at the service of Adolf Hitler has long clouded her reputation as a pioneering female artist.

The propaganda value of *Olympia* for Nazi racism was somewhat undermined by Riefenstahl's necessary inclusion of the victories of African American athlete Jesse Owens in the 1936 Summer Olympics; his world record-setting long jump is beautifully rendered.

control predated the global depression and was independent of it, the Soviet Union also saw an escalation of state power in the 1930s.

In 1928, Stalin had launched the U.S.S.R. on a path of rapid industrialization based on centralized Five-Year Plans. Now he turned his attention to the countryside as he sought to apply "Socialism in One Country" to rural areas as well. Lenin's New Economic Policy had allowed farmers to keep their own small plots (see Chapter 27). But Stalin completely rejected private ownership. Instead, he ordered **collectivization** of the rural sector—tearing the peasants out of their villages and marching them at gunpoint onto collective farms.

Most Russian farming communities resisted collectivization. Stalin attributed resistance solely to *kulaks* (koo-LAHKS), more prosperous peasants who, he said, were out to exploit their fellow villagers. Stalin sent the Red Army into the countryside, supposedly to help the "masses" defeat these kulaks. In reality, the Soviet state was waging war on its own people. A resulting famine killed 2 million in 1932–1933, striking the Ukrainian people especially hard.

collectivization

Stalin's replacement of peasant villages with large, state-run collective farms, following the idea of "Socialism in One Country." Millions died in famines and as a result of state terror campaigns.

● **CONTEXT&CONNECTIONS** Stalin remembered how the Ukrainians had sought independence after World War I and took revenge during the brutal imposition of collectivization. When Ukraine finally did become an independent nation in 1991 (see Chapter 31), its leaders defined the *Holodomor* famine of 1931–1932 as genocide, an attempt to kill Ukrainians so they could be replaced by Russian immigrants. This interpretation deeply offended Russian-speaking Ukrainians, including supporters of Russia's aggressive intrusion into the Ukraine in 2014 (see Chapter 32). ●

Meanwhile, the industrial sector continued its rapid expansion. The Communist Party bureaucracy treated the non-Russian parts of the Soviet Union, especially those of Central Asia, in colonial fashion, as sources of raw materials for industrial growth in the Russian heartland. In contrast with other industrial societies, the Soviet Union allowed no unemployment. But Soviet workers' wages were kept low to generate investment for further industrial expansion, while Stalin's vast system of slave-labor camps, the gulags, also boosted industrial productivity.

In the later 1930s, Stalin, always paranoid about plots against him, stepped up his repression of the Old Bolsheviks, communists whose memories of Lenin and the revolution could be dangerous to his dictatorship (see pages 832–833). During the **Great Purges**, Stalin ordered his secret police to arrest many former colleagues of Lenin, forcing them to confess to supposed crimes before they were taken out and shot. In 1937 alone, Stalin had half of the army's officer corps imprisoned or executed. It was an irrational move with another German war on the horizon, but even as he killed and imprisoned his generals, Stalin ordered a massive military buildup.

Great Purges

The execution by Stalin in the late 1930s of many "Old Bolsheviks" he regarded as competitors for power. Public trials and forced confessions marked the Great Purges.

Soviet citizens lived in a nearly constant state of terror. "Fear by night, and a feverish effort by day to pretend enthusiasm for a system of lies," writes one historian, "was the permanent condition."* A single wrong word or glance could lead to a knock on the door and exile to Stalin's gulags, embodying Stalin's dictum: *"The easiest way to gain control of the population is to carry out acts of terror."*

---

*Robert Conquest, *The Great Terror: A Reassessment* (New York: Oxford University Press, 1997), p. 252.

Authoritarian Regimes in Asia and Latin America

Beyond Europe and the Soviet Union, in many other parts of the world where liberal traditions were absent or only weakly developed, uncertainty and economic crisis strengthened authoritarianism. In both Japan and Turkey, state intervention in economic and political life increased through the inter-war years. In Brazil, a quasi-fascist regime strove to reconcile the social tensions revealed by the Great Depression.

Ultranationalism in Japan

Although the Versailles treaty had rewarded Japan with territorial concessions at China's expense (see Chapter 27), nationalists remained dissatisfied:

We are like a great crowd of people packed into a small and narrow room, and there are only three doors through which we might escape, namely, emigration, advance into world markets, and expansion of territory. The first door has been barred to us by the anti-Japanese immigration policies of other countries. The second is being pushed shut by tariff barriers.... It is quite natural that Japan should rush upon the last remaining door ... of territorial expansion.*

The Great Depression strengthened the arguments of nationalists and militarists for a more aggressive foreign and imperial policy.

In the 1920s, the country had shown signs of heading in a more democratic direction. Japan was a constitutional monarchy, with an emperor whose role was ceremonial. Though still quite limited, voting rights were extended to more Japanese men, and the cabinet was no longer chosen by imperial advisers but by the party that gained the most votes in elections.

Other factors, however, limited liberal democracy. One was the power of civil service bureaucrats, who controlled policy together with the *zaibatsu*, Japan's large industrial conglomerates (see Chapter 24). Another was the rising influence of the military and militaristic sentiment emphasizing national glory over individual liberty. In 1926, when the new emperor Hirohito came to the throne, ultranationalists saw an opportunity to expand their influence. A new requirement stipulated that the minister of defense be an active military officer with power nearly equal to that of the prime minister. After the market collapse of 1930 led to tough times for the farm families whose sons made up most of the empire's soldiers, support for an enhanced military role in government became even greater.

Ultranationalists envisioned a new Asian economic system that would combine Japanese management and capital with the resources and cheap labor of East and Southeast Asia. The turning point came with the **invasion of Manchuria**, a province of China where the Versailles settlement had allowed the Japanese to keep soldiers in the capital. In 1931, Japanese military officers blew up some railroad tracks and then blamed Chinese nationalists as a rationale for leaving their barracks and occupying Manchuria. Since they had no orders authorizing this

invasion of Manchuria

(1931) Invasion that occurred when Japanese military officers defied the civilian government and League of Nations by occupying this northeastern Chinese province, leading to the further militarization of the Japanese government.

---

*Hashimoto Kingoro, "Address to Young Men," in *Sources of Japanese Tradition*, ed. William Theodore de Bary, vol. 2 (New York: Columbia University Press, 1958), p. 289.

action, the officers were brought to Tokyo for trial, where they used the courtroom to whip up public support for the army's ambitions. As imperial fever grew, elected politicians further lost control over the military.

As in Italy and Germany, militarization brought Japanese corporations lucrative government contracts. And as in the fascist countries, Japan's economic policies seemed successful. Military spending, even if it required massive government borrowing, boosted the economy, as did the occupation of Manchuria. After 1932, expanding working-class employment further solidified the ultranationalists' political support.

The Rise of Modern Turkey

The new nation of Turkey emerged from the violent collapse of the Ottoman empire. Without the skillful military and political leadership of **Mustafa Kemal** (1881–1938), a former Ottoman officer, Turkey may well have been partitioned by the victorious Allies. For his role, Kemal earned the name Atatürk, "Father Turk."

Mustafa Kemal

(1881–1938) Also known as Atatürk, an Ottoman officer who led the nationalist army that established the Republic of Turkey in 1923. A reformer who established the secular traditions of the modern Turkish state, he served as its leader until his death.

With the success of Kemal's armies, by 1923 the great powers agreed to recognize a sovereign Turkish republic that retained the core territories and population of the old empire. Since the new republic was based on specifically Turkish nationalism, the new political framework proved awkward for the former empire's ethnic minorities, such as Armenians, Greeks, and the Kurds who predominated in the southeast.

Greek-Turkish relations were fraught with tension, leading to a massive population exchange that removed hundreds of thousands of Greeks westward across the Aegean to their "proper" country (one they might never have visited before) while a parallel movement of Turks went eastward to what was now their "own" nation. The scale of these dislocations showed once again the difficulty in applying the principle of "national self-determination" to organize national space along ethnic lines (see Chapter 27).

Turkish nationalism had been at the forefront since 1918, when Halide Edib had made her stirring speech. She later recalled how her heart had been *"beating in response to all Turkish hearts, I was part of this sublime national madness.... Nothing else mattered for me in life at all."** She went on to serve Mustafa Kemal as a loyal confidante during his military campaigns, admiring his steadfast leadership.

Once independence was secured, however, Halide Edib and Mustafa Kemal had a falling out. Whereas Edib favored the further expansion of liberal democracy, Atatürk intended to be the unchallenged leader of an absolutist state. When she criticized him, he scolded her: *"I want everyone to do as I wish.... I do not want any criticism or advice. I will have only my own way. All shall do as I command."* Edib responded, *"I will obey you and do as you wish as long as I believe you are serving the cause."* But Kemal ignored her and said, *"You shall obey me and do as I wish."*† Shortly thereafter he banned her political party and she went into exile.

Having forged a new country through war, Mustafa Kemal's goal was to put Turkey on an equal economic and military footing with the European powers, and he ordered rapid modernization to achieve that end. In the nineteenth century, the Ottoman empire had vacillated about adopting Western models (see Chapter 23). Kemal had no second thoughts in imposing a secular constitution with strict separation between mosque and state. His ideas would ideas would guide Turkey for decades to come.

---

*Halide Edib, http://gvcommunity.tripod.com/ladies/haide.htm.
†Halide Edib, *The Turkish Ordeal* (New York: Century, 1926), p. 128.

Kemalists and Islamists in the Turkish Republic

A visitor to Turkey will notice ubiquitous statues and portraits of Mustafa Kemal. Supporters of Atatürk's legacy of secular nationalism built a cult around his memory during the many years when they monopolized Turkish politics. The nation's children still learn of his exploits and memorize famous aphorisms such as: *"How happy is the one who says 'I am a Turk!'"*

But late in the twentieth century Kemalists found themselves challenged by Turks who resented having religiosity banned from public life, envisioning a greater role for religion in government. Long suppressed by the secularist military, by 2002 the expansion of Turkish democracy finally gave them a shot at governance. The Islamist Justice and Development Party (JDP) scored a definitive victory in the 2002 elections.

The JDP has dominated Turkish politics ever since, alarming Kemalists who fear that creeping Islamization will infringe on their secular lifestyles and freedoms. The use of public funds to support religious schools, for example, is strongly opposed by those who favor Atatürk's strict secularism in education. The head scarf has become symbolic of the divide between Kemalists and Islamists. Previously, women were not allowed to wear head scarves in public places, such as government offices and classrooms. In the past decade, however, they have become increasingly common.

Kemalists (and Turkish feminists) see JDP policies as rolling back Atatürk's expansion of women's rights. In 2014, President Recep Tayyip Erdoğan (see Chapter 32) publicly proclaimed that motherhood was every woman's calling, saying that women are "too delicate" for "manly" tasks. Such patriarchal pronouncements play well with the party's conservative base but arouse the ire of secularists.

Still, many daughters of the rising Turkish middle class, whose families are firm supporters of President Erdoğan, now cover their heads before going to school. Seeing them walk past a statue of Mustafa Kemal, one can easily imagine a scowl of disapproval forming on their founding father's face. Although these young women now have the freedom to express their religious convictions by wearing a head scarf, other Turks who value freedom from religion worry that religion might be imposed on them by government.

Kemal's drive to separate religion from politics included laws to improve the status of women. His policies gave girls and young women increased access to education, a move Edib strongly supported. Not surprisingly, after the emotional pain she suffered when her first husband took a second wife, she also favored the Turkish law abolishing polygamy. Edib applauded when, in 1930, Turkey became the first predominantly Muslim country in which women had the right to vote.

On the other hand, Edib critiqued the authoritarian means by which these reforms were attained. When Kemal banned women from wearing veils in all government buildings, schools, and public spaces, for example, Edib argued that while the veil should never be imposed on women, neither should it be banned by governments. *"Wherever religion is interfered with by governments, it becomes a barrier, and an unremovable one, to peace and understanding."** Education and freedom to choose were the keys to reform, she thought. Too impatient for gradual reform, Kemal simply imposed his own will on the nation. (See the feature "World History in Today's World: Kemalists and Islamists in the Turkish Republic.")

After Mustafa Kemal died in 1938, the authoritarian pattern he set in place would continue long into the nation's future, with the military playing a powerful role. But at least now Halide Edib felt secure in returning to her homeland.

---

*Halide Edib, *Inside India* (London: Allen and Unwin, 1937), p. 231.

Turkey's New Alphabet The Turkish leader Mustafa Kemal instituted a top-down program to modernize and westernize the new nation of Turkey. In 1928, he declared that Turkish would no longer be written in Arabic script but in Latin characters for all purposes, public and private. Here Kemal himself demonstrates the new alphabet.

Photo12/The Image Works

Getúlio Vargas and Brazil's "New State"

Like other parts of the world with little experience of liberal governance, many Latin American nations experienced an augmentation of their authoritarian traditions during the economic crisis of the 1930s. Brazil came closest to emulating European models of fascism.

Getúlio Vargas (in office, 1930–1945, 1951–1954) came to power in 1930 and used the state as an engine of economic growth. Like Lázaro Cárdenas in Mexico, he nationalized natural resources and promoted manufacturing through import substitution. Then, in 1937, he made a bold political move by suspending the Brazilian constitution and declaring the beginning of his *Estado Novo*, or "new state."

Vargas suppressed independent civil groups by following the corporatist model of Benito Mussolini, organizing society into "corporations" that could be directly controlled by the state. The aim of the *Estado Novo*, he said, was to stimulate the moribund Brazilian economy—*"to crisscross the nation with railroads, highways, and airlines; to increase production; to provide for the laborer"*—by putting an end to regional competition and petty political bickering. His stated goal was *"to organize public opinion so that there is, body and soul, one Brazilian thought."** That "one Brazilian thought" would, of course, be his own.

Anticolonial Nationalism in Asia, Africa, and the Caribbean

Getúlio Vargas

The President of Brazil (1930–1945, 1951–1954) who implemented neo-fascist policies in his *Novo Stado* ("New State"), magnifying the role of government in many aspects of national life, including the economy.

Colonial governments are, by their nature, autocratic, so in the 1920s authoritarianism was already the status quo across most of South and Southeast Asia, Africa, and the Caribbean. Then the economic crisis of the Great Depression led European powers to exploit their colonies even more. Harsh policies, such as forced labor, combined with the global economic decline to spread distress throughout the colonial world. As a result, movements of anticolonial nationalism gathered strength.

Gandhi and the Indian National Congress

Halide Edib traveled to India in 1935: *"India seemed to me like Allah's workshop: gods, men and nature abounded in their most beautiful and most hideous; ideas and all the arts in their ancient and most modern styles lay about pell-mell.... This India must certainly have its share in shaping the future. Not*

---

*Getúlio Vargas, "Excerpts from Speeches and Interviews, 1937–1940," in *Sources of Global History Since 1900*, ed. James H. Overfield, 2d ed. (Boston: Wadsworth, 2013), p. 160.

*because of its immemorial age, but because of the new life throbbing in it!"** Speaking before an audience at the National Muslim University, her thoughts were on some-one in the audience. Looking out at the *"fragile figure"* before her, she wrote, *"I was thinking about the quality of Mahatma Gandhi's greatness."** **Mohandas K. Gandhi** (1869–1948) had turned the Indian National Congress into the voice of India.

Before 1914, the Indian National Congress had been a reformist organization, seeking greater participation of Indians in their own governance but accepting the basic outlines of British rule (see Chapter 24). Given the contribution Indians had made to the British war effort, they expected to be rewarded with substan-tial political reform. But the British offered only modest proposals for a gradual increase in Indian participation.

Then in 1919, the **Amritsar Massacre** shocked the nation. An unarmed crowd gathered in a garden area for a religious ceremony, unaware that the British had banned public meetings. In a horrible display of the violence on which colo-nial authority was based, a British officer ordered his Indian troops to fire directly into the crowd, leaving 400 dead and 1,200 wounded. Cooperation turned to confrontation, and in 1920 the Indian National Congress launched its first mass public protest to gain *Hind Swaraj*, Indian self-rule.

By then Gandhi, a Western-educated lawyer, had discarded European dress for the spare clothing of an ascetic Hindu holy man. His philosophy was in fact influ-enced by both traditions. Western ideals of equality informed his insistence that the so-called Untouchables, those considered outside and beneath the Hindu caste hierar-chy, be given full rights and recognition as human beings. But his two main principles were from the South Asian tradition. *Ahimsa* (uh-HIM-sah), or absolute nonviolence, was at the center of Gandhi's moral philosophy. *Satyagraha* (SUHT-yuh-gruh-huh), or "soul force," was the application of that philosophy to politics. Gandhi believed that it is self-defeating to use violence to counter violence, no matter how just the cause. The moral force of his arguments earned him the title *Mahatma*, "Great Soul."

But in 1920, after the British threw Gandhi and other Congress leaders in jail, violence did accompany the first mass campaigns of civil disobedience. Deciding that the Indian people were not ready to achieve self-rule through satyagraha, Gandhi retreated to his *ashram* (AHSH-ruhm), a communal rural home, emulating the simple rural life he idealized. Meanwhile, a new generation of Congress leaders was emerging, most importantly British-educated Jawaharlal Nehru, elected as the organization's president in 1928. (See the feature "Movement of Ideas Through Primary Sources: Gandhi and Nehru on Progress and Civilization.")

● **CONTEXT&CONNECTIONS** Gandhi would spend hours sitting at a wheel spinning cotton. The gentle clicking of the wheel stimulated meditation, and also symbolized rejection of the British textiles that represented imperial economic exploitation (see Chapter 23). ●

In 1930, Gandhi re-emerged to lead another campaign of mass civil disobedi-ence. His Salt March defied a British law against Indians making their own salt. The British responded with a combination of repression and concessions. After initially jailing Congress leaders, they then compromised with the Government of India Act of 1935, which called for elections of semi-representative regional assemblies. Congress complained that this was inadequate but decided to partici-pate in the elections anyway, scoring huge victories across the country.

Mohandas K. Gandhi

(1869–1948) Indian political leader who orga-nized mass support for the Indian National Con-gress against British rule. His political phi-losophy of nonviolent resistance had worldwide influence.

Amritsar Massacre

(1919) A turning point in Anglo-Indian rela-tions, when a British officer ordered his troops to fire directly into a peaceful crowd in the city of Amritsar. Follow-ing this event, in 1920 the Indian National Con-gress, led by Mohandas K. Gandhi, began its first mass campaign for Indian self-rule.

---

*Halide Edib, *Inside India* (London: Allen and Unwin, 1937), pp. 29, 81.

Gandhi and Nehru on Progress and Civilization

The two most influential Indian leaders of the twentieth century were Mohandas K. Gandhi and Jawaharlal Nehru, representing different generations in the Indian National Congress. Gandhi, born in 1869, was the inspirational force behind Indian resistance to British colonialism in the 1920s and 1930s. Nehru, twenty years younger, participated in that resistance and later led the independent Indian republic as its first prime minister, from 1947 to 1964 (see Chapter 30).

Both men were influenced by the time they spent in Great Britain. Gandhi sailed to Britain in 1888 to pursue a law degree, and while in London he was strongly influenced by cultural trends and by philosophers who called into question the relentless materialism of late Victorian society. Among them were vegetarians and Theosophists, who emphasized intuition and mysticism over rationalism and formal theology. He was also influenced by the American writer Henry David Thoreau and the Russian novelist Leo Tolstoy, both of whom celebrated the simplicity of rural life.

Nehru's British experience was quite different. His father, a famous lawyer and a man of great wealth, sent him to study at two of the world's most famous educational institutions, Harrow School and then Cambridge University. Interacting with England's elite, the young Nehru was strongly influenced by the reformist socialism fashionable with the younger generation at the start of the twentieth century. Such socialists accepted the need for the economic development that came with capitalist industrialism but argued for a more equitable distribution of its proceeds.

Gandhi and Nehru, therefore, though close friends as well as political allies, had very different visions of India's future. While many Indians have been strongly influenced by Gandhi's philosophy, Nehru's attitude has been much more evident in Indian government policy since the country achieved independence in 1947.

> **How do Gandhi and Nehru define and evaluate the concept of "civilization"? Might it be possible to find a compromise between their two perspectives?**

Sources: M. K. Gandhi, *Hind Swaraj* (Ahmedabad, India: Navajivan, 1938 [1908]), pp. 31–33; Jawaharlal Nehru, *An Autobiography* (New Delhi: Allied, 1942), pp. 510–511.

Mohandas K. Gandhi, *Hind Swaraj* (1909)

Let us first consider what state of things is described by the word "civilization." Its true test lies in the fact that people living in it make bodily welfare the object of life. We will take some examples. The people of Europe today live in better-built houses than they did a hundred years ago. This is considered an emblem of civilization, and this is also a matter to promote bodily happiness. Formerly, they wore skins, and used spears as their weapons. Now, they wear long trousers, and, for embellishing their bodies, they wear a variety of clothing, and, instead of spears, they carry with them revolvers containing five or more chambers. If people of a certain country, who have hitherto not been in the habit of wearing much clothing, boots, etc., adopt European clothing, they are supposed to have become civilized out of savagery. Formerly, in Europe, people ploughed their lands mainly by manual labor. Now, one man can plough a vast tract by means of steam engines and can thus amass great wealth. This is called a sign of civilization. Formerly, only a few men wrote valuable books. Now, anybody writes and prints anything he likes and poisons people's minds. Formerly, men traveled in wagons. Now, they fly through the air in trains at the rate of four hundred and more miles per day. This is considered the height of civilization.... Formerly, when people wanted to fight with one another, they measured between them their bodily strength; now it is possible to take away thousands of lives by one man working behind a gun from a hill. This is civilization. Formerly, men worked in the open air only as much as they liked. Now thousands of workmen meet together and for the sake of maintenance work in factories or mines. Their condition is worse than that of beasts. They are obliged to work, at the risk of their lives, at most dangerous occupations, for the sake of millionaires. Formerly, men were made slaves under physical compulsion. Now they are enslaved by temptation of money and of the luxuries that money can buy.... Formerly, people had two or three meals consisting of home-made bread and vegetables; now, they require something to eat every two hours so that they have hardly leisure for anything else.... This civilization takes note neither of morality nor of religion.... Civilization seeks to increase bodily comforts, and it fails miserably even in doing so.

This civilization is irreligion, and it has taken such a hold on the people in Europe that those who are in it appear to be half mad. They lack real physical strength or courage. They keep up their energy by intoxication. They can hardly be happy in solitude. Women, who should be the queens of households, wander in the streets or they slave away in factories. For the sake of a pittance, half a million women in England alone are laboring under trying circumstances in factories or similar institutions. This awful act is one of the causes of the daily growing suffragette movement.

[The English] are a shrewd nation and I therefore believe that they will cast off this evil. They are enterprising and industrious, and their mode of thought is not inherently immoral. Neither are they bad at heart. I therefore respect them. Civilization is not an incurable disease, but it should never be forgotten that the English are at present afflicted by it.

Jawaharlal Nehru, "Gandhi" (1936)

I imagine that [Gandhi] is not so vague about the objective as he sometimes appears to be.... *"India's salvation consists,"* he wrote in 1909, *"in unlearning what she has learned during the last fifty years. The railways, telegraphs, hospitals, lawyers, doctors, and suchlike all have to go...."*

All this seems to me utterly wrong and harmful doctrine, and impossible of achievement. Behind it lies Gandhi's love and praise of poverty and suffering and the ascetic life.... Personally I dislike the praise of poverty and suffering.... Nor do I appreciate in the least the idealization of the "simple peasant life." I have almost a horror of it, and instead of submitting to it myself I want to drag out even the peasantry from it.... What is there in "The Man with the Hoe" to idealize over? Crushed and exploited for innumerable generations, he is only little removed from the animals who keep him company....

The desire to get away from the mind of man to primitive conditions where mind does not count, seems to me quite incomprehensible. The very thing that is the glory and triumph of man is decried and discouraged, and a physical environment which will oppress the mind and prevent its growth is considered desirable. Present-day civilization is full of evils, but it is also full of good; and it has the capacity in it to rid itself of those evils. To destroy it root and branch is to remove that capacity from it and revert to a dull, senseless, and miserable existence. But even if that were desirable it is an impossible undertaking. We cannot stop the river of change or cut ourselves adrift from it, and psychologically we who have eaten of the apple of Eden cannot forget that taste and go back to primitiveness.

Gandhi's Salt March In 1930, Mohandas K. Gandhi galvanized his supporters and received sympathetic international press coverage when he and his followers marched 240 miles (386 km) from his ashram to the sea to make salt from ocean water. It was a perfect example of nonviolent civil disobedience, since the manufacture of salt was a legal monopoly of the British Indian government.(Dinodia Photos/Alamy)

Though Gandhi used Hindu symbols to rally mass support, he and Nehru agreed that the Indian National Congress should embrace members of all faiths. That did not mollify leaders of the new **Muslim League**, who feared that under self-rule they would be oppressed by the Hindu majority. Gandhi did his best to reassure the Muslim community, and Nehru envisioned a secular state in which religion would play no part.

Based on her visit to India, Halide Edib was confident that nationalist unity could transcend religious differences. Nevertheless, distrust between the two communities increased, and Muslim League leaders began to call for the creation of a separate Muslim state, Pakistan (see Chapter 30). The British insisted that their presence as a neutral arbiter between India's diverse peoples would be necessary far into the future.

Muslim League
Political party founded in British India to represent the interests of the Muslim minority. The party eventually advocated a separate nation for Indian Muslims: Pakistan.

Colonialism and Resistance in Africa, the Caribbean, and Southeast Asia

Nationalist movements were also developing in Africa, the Caribbean, and Southeast Asia during this period. As in India, Western-educated leaders were beginning to create political structures that could mobilize large numbers of people to challenge European authority. Nevertheless, European powers continued to rule with great confidence.

A persistent feature of empire is the need for rulers to find indigenous allies to help them control and administer their territories. While the top positions were always reserved for the ruling Europeans, members of the colonized society were educated as clerks, nurses, and primary school teachers. However, in the process of being educated, they might also learn about the French Revolution and the traditional liberties of British subjects, leading them to aspire to greater freedom for themselves and their people.

The gap between aspirations and realities was stark. The French model of assimilation, for example, held out the promise that Asians and Africans could "become" French in language and culture, and even achieve French citizenship. However, most who pursued this path—speaking perfect French and immersing themselves in French culture—found that the colonialists still saw them through a racist lens as *indigenes* (ihn-deh-JEN), "natives" who were automatically inferior. The same deeply frustrating dynamic held sway in the Dutch East Indies, where people of mixed race, educated in Dutch schools, could never be the social equals of the colonizers.

The British were the most consistent in employing what they called "indirect rule," relying to the greatest extent possible on "native authorities" to carry out day-to-day administrative tasks such as collecting taxes and keeping the peace. As a result, the British had almost no concept of assimilation.

● **CONTEXT&CONNECTIONS** The British in India, after considering assimilationist models as proposed by *Rammohun Roy* (Chapter 20), reverted to their more exclusionary attitude after the *Indian Revolt of 1857*, emphasizing a sharp and permanent cultural divide between rulers and ruled (Chapter 24). Hence the British preference for "native authorities" as subordinate intermediaries, rather than Western-educated Africans, was part of a broader pattern within the British empire. ●

The European policy of relying on indigenous figureheads spurred additional resentments. In Southeast Asia, for example, the Vietnamese emperors of the Nguyen dynasty continued in office. Malaysian sultans were also given privileged positions. In Africa, "chiefs" were recognized as "native authorities," part of the supposed respect the British had for local customs. In reality, the colonialists were looking for local leaders to work at the bottom rungs of their administrations.

By the 1930s, many impatient nationalists saw the collusion of traditional elites with colonial powers as a hindrance to self-rule, as when the British divided Africans into discrete "tribes" and played their leaders against one another to secure continued control. Nigerian nationalist **Nnamdi Azikiwe** (NAHM-dee ah-zee-KEE-way) (1904–1996) deplored that policy, arguing that only when all Nigerians identified themselves with the nation as a whole, whatever their ethnic and religious backgrounds, would they be able to struggle effectively for self-rule. Having stowed away on a ship to the United States in 1925 and then graduated from the University of Pennsylvania, Azikiwe returned to West Africa in 1937 and founded the Nigerian Youth Movement while editing the *West African Pilot*, a newspaper that inspired Africans to challenge British colonial policies. Azikiwe also created a sports association focused on the increasing popularity of soccer in Nigeria to galvanize broader support for his nationalist cause.

At the same time, sporadic popular uprisings arose in response to colonial tax, trade, and land policies. In the **Igbo Women's War** of 1929, for example, women in southeastern Nigeria rebelled against colonial intrusions into their household and village affairs. Using traditional Igbo (ee-BWOH) means of protesting male abuse of authority, the women dressed up in special costumes, gathered in large numbers,

Nnamdi Azikiwe
(1904–1996) Pioneering Nigerian nationalist who, after gaining higher education in the United States, edited a newspaper and formed cultural and political organizations to unite West Africans against British colonialism.

Igbo Women's War
(1929) Rebellion led by women in colonial Nigeria who used traditional cultural practices to protest British taxation policies.

and sang songs of derision to shame the African chiefs who carried out British orders. The British modified their tax system slightly in response, but the women lacked a broader organization to connect their local efforts with a wider anticolonial struggle. A connection between broadly educated nationalists (like Azikiwe) and village-level protest would not threaten colonial rule in Africa until after 1945 (see Chapter 30).

Tensions were strongest where Europeans came not just as rulers but also as settlers, as in South Africa and Kenya. Here Africans had lost not only their sovereignty but also much of their best land. The British colony of Kenya in East Africa saw the rise of a mass protest movement in the 1920s; anticolonial feelings were strongest among Kikuyu-speaking Kenyans who lost their land to white settlers. As in the Igbo Women's War, however, local protest was not enough to gain substantial reform. Meanwhile, a young leader named Jomo Kenyatta (1895–1978) was earning a doctorate in anthropology from the London School of Economics. Only after the Second World War would Kenyatta return to lead a broad nationalist movement that connected Western-educated leaders with the mass of Kenyans, a pattern found across sub-Saharan Africa.

● **CONTEXT&CONNECTIONS** Before returning home, Jomo Kenyatta would attend the Fifth Pan-African Congress in Manchester, England, in 1946. There he met the African American activist W. E. B. Du Bois, co-organizer of the First Pan-African Congress held in Paris in 1919, as well as other Western-educated African leaders who would soon return to the continent to lead successful anticolonial revolts, among them *Kwame Nkrumah*, who would become the first prime minister of an independent Ghana in 1957 (Chapter 30). ●

In the British West Indies, modern mass nationalism developed more rapidly. Already by the 1920s Marcus Garvey (1887–1940) had amassed a huge following in Jamaica for his United Negro Improvement Association (UNIA). Following the Pan-African tradition (see Chapter 26), Garvey's "back-to-Africa" philosophy called on everyone of African descent to band together to pursue a common destiny, specifically to promote cultural and trade connections between peoples of African descent in the Americas and on the continent itself. The UNIA message resonated not only in the Caribbean, but in the United States and South Africa as well. Though a controversial figure who was convicted in the United States on trumped-up charges of mail fraud, Garvey made lasting contributions to Pan-Africanism through his unwavering insistence on the dignity of African people and their potential for economic self-sufficiency.

Meanwhile, the Great Depression was making the already difficult conditions of colonialism even worse. Across the British West Indies, for example, falling crop prices and depressed wages from 1934–1939 led to repeated outbreaks of labor unrest among agricultural workers. Colonialists were desperate for cheap supplies from the colonies to prop up their own weakened economies. The French compelled farmers in equatorial Africa to keep planting, weeding, and harvesting cotton despite a sharp drop in market prices. The British imposed a "grow more crops" campaign in East Africa, requiring peasants to dedicate land and labor to export commodities, like coffee, that were now basically worthless. But farmers could not eat cotton or coffee, and hunger resulted from these coerced diversions from subsistence crops.

In Southeast Asia, unemployment rose in Malaya, Vietnam, and the Dutch East Indies after 1929, when the drop in automobile manufacturing depressed the world market for rubber. Even where small-scale farmers stopped growing export crops and focused on food production, colonial governments still compelled cash payment of taxes. The French penalized Vietnamese peasants who did not pay taxes with forced labor on government projects and French-owned plantations.

As in Africa, however, the peoples of French Indochina still lacked the organizational means for effective resistance.

In 1930, for example, the Vietnamese Nationalist Party was harshly suppressed after raising a failed rebellion. Earlier the group had favored moderate reform, but faced with French intransigence it opted for violent resistance. Before his execution, the group's leader stated: *"If France does not want to have increasing trouble with revolutionary movements, she should immediately modify the cruel and inhuman policy now practiced in Indochina."** In the 1950s, a revolutionary movement led by Ho Chi Minh would indeed drive the French out of Vietnam (see Chapter 30).

Africa and Southeast Asia have been called the "quiescent colonies" during this period. But in larger historical perspective, the 1930s were merely a pause in the resistance to colonial occupation that began in the late nineteenth century. Nationalist leaders during this time were laying the foundations for the large-scale movements of mass nationalism that would emerge following the new worldwide military conflict that was about to erupt.

The Road to War

World War II did not sneak up on anyone. In the 1930s numerous events in Europe, Asia, and Africa heralded a coming conflict, starting with Japanese aggression in China.

China was vulnerable because of fighting between the Guomindang government of Chiang Kai-shek and Communist revolutionaries led by Mao Zedong (see Chapter 27). Attacked in 1927 by their former Guomindang allies, the Communists had retreated to the interior. During the "Long March" of 1934–1936, the Communists walked some 7,500 miles (12,000 km) to consolidate a base in the northeast.

Meanwhile, having already defied the League of Nations with its occupation of Manchuria, the Japanese empire launched a savage attack on coastal China in 1937. Chiang and Mao then agreed to cease their hostilities and fight the common Japanese enemy, but they never combined forces or coordinated their efforts (see Map 28.1).

Convinced of their racial superiority, the Japanese invaders treated the Chinese with callous brutality. During the **Rape of Nanjing**, Japanese soldiers killed hundreds of thousands of civilians, using tactics such as gang rape and mutilation of children to spread terror among the population. Total war, with its disregard of the distinction between soldiers and civilians, was being taken to a new level.

Rape of Nanjing
Japanese occupation of the city in 1937 during which they slaughtered hundreds of thousands of Chinese civilians and used other terror tactics.

Even earlier, in 1935, international institutions had shown their inability to counter military aggression during Mussolini's invasion of Ethiopia. Here total war meant Italian pilots dropping poison gas on Ethiopian villagers. The Ethiopian emperor Hailie Selassie (1892–1975) went to Geneva to beg the League of Nations for help:

I ask the fifty-two nations, who have given the Ethiopian people a promise to help them in their resistance to the aggressor, what are they willing to do for Ethiopia? And the great Powers who have promised the guarantee of collective security to small States on whom weighs the threat that they may one day suffer the fate of Ethiopia, I ask what measures do you intend to take? ... What reply shall I have to take back to my people?

*Nguyen Thai Hoc, "Letter to the French Chamber of Deputies, 1930," in *Sources of Global History Since 1900*, ed. James H. Overfield, 2d ed. (Boston: Wadsworth, 2013), pp. 202–203.

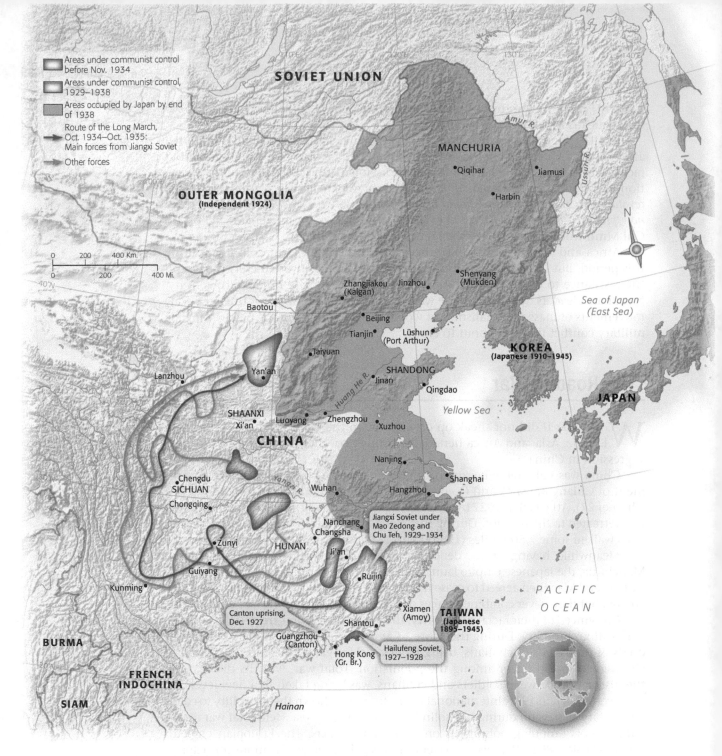

Map 28.1 The Japanese Invasion of China Six years after the invasion of Manchuria, Japanese forces began the conquest of coastal China in 1937, quickly taking Beijing, Shanghai, and other major cities. Chinese resistance, though extensive, was limited by divisions between the Guomindang government and the Communists. Expelled from coastal cities by the Guomindang after 1927, the Communists relocated first to the southern interior and then, after their dramatic "Long March," established a new base in the northeastern Shaanxi province.

The Rape of Nanjing One of the most brutal episodes during the Japanese invasion of China was the Rape of Nanjing. Here Japanese soldiers are seen using live captives for bayonet practice, with fellow soldiers and future victims looking on. Though the Chinese have long remembered such atrocities, some Japanese schoolchildren still learn nothing about them.

The emperor warned that if the international community did not take effective action, no small nation would ever be safe. The League of Nations placed economic sanctions on Mussolini but would go no further. With Italy having access to colonial resources, such as Libyan oil, and receiving aid from the German government, the sanctions had little effect.

Meanwhile, German and Italian fascists saw their movement gaining ground in Spain, where the elected government was implementing socialist policies to deal with the Great Depression. In reaction, Spanish conservatives took up arms under General Francisco Franco (1892–1975) to seize power by force. During the **Spanish Civil War** (1936–1939) Mussolini and Hitler aided Franco, while France, Britain, and the United States remained neutral. Mired in their own domestic concerns, they missed this chance to support democracy against fascism.

The Western democracies were equally tepid in response to Hitler's heightened aggression. In 1936, German military forces moved into the Rhineland region bordering France, in clear violation of the Versailles treaty. The lack of any sustained response emboldened Hitler.

Hitler had long declared that the Germans needed *lebensraum* (LEY-buhns-rowm), "living space," in which to pursue their racial destiny, and that the ethnic Germans scattered in countries to the east needed to be reunited with

Spanish Civil War
(1936–1939) Conflict between conservative nationalist forces, led by General Francisco Franco and backed by Germany, and Republican forces, backed by the Soviet Union. The Spanish Civil War was seen by many as a prelude to renewed world war.

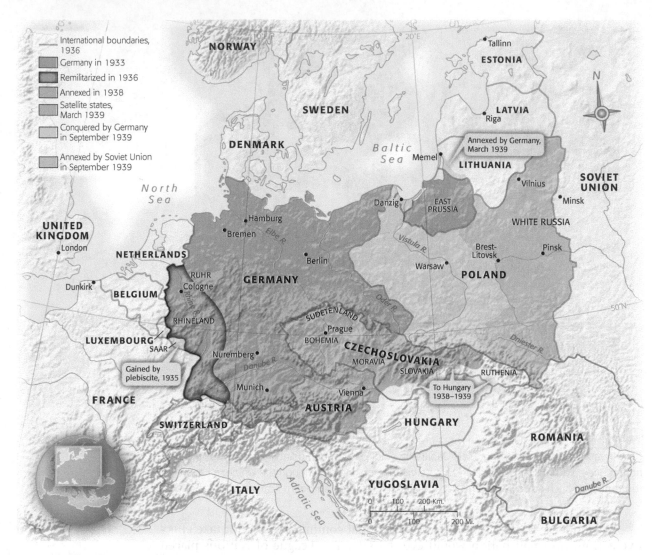

Map 28.2 The Growth of Nazi Germany, 1933–1939 The major turning point in the expansion of Nazi Germany was the annexation of the Sudetenland from Czechoslovakia in 1938. Joseph Stalin interpreted British diplomatic efforts to avoid renewed world war with alarm, and he agreed to a secret treaty to divide Poland between Hitler's Germany and his own Soviet Union. The German invasion of Poland from the west in 1939 therefore triggered the annexation of eastern Poland by the Soviet Union.

the homeland. Taking the Social Darwinist idea of a racial "struggle for existence" to the extreme, he imagined vast eastern spaces cleared of Jews, with racially inferior Slavic peoples remaining to provide slave labor under German command. While Stalin took this threat seriously, most Western leaders thought that Hitler could be contained. In fact, some Westerners sympathized with Hitler's anti-Semitism and anticommunism.

Hitler thus asserted his right to annex the Sudetenland, a province of Czechoslovakia where, he claimed, the German minority was facing discrimination (see Map 28.2). One member of the British Parliament, Winston Churchill, recommended an Anglo-French initiative to head off Hitler's expansionism. But Churchill, who would be Britain's great wartime leader (see Chapter 29), was unable to convince the British public to take a firm stand and thus risk war.

Instead, British Prime Minister Neville Chamberlain flew to Munich in 1937 to negotiate. Chamberlain's policy of *"active appeasement"* was based on the premise that Hitler would be content with minor concessions and that diplomacy could prevent a major European war. The British public, still scarred by the trauma of the Great War, largely supported Chamberlain's quest for *"peace in our time."* Germany occupied the Sudetenland unchecked, and the next year Hitler annexed Austria as well. Ever since, the term *appeasement* has meant the failure to stop an aggressor in time.

Such lack of Western resolve, shown in Ethiopia, Spain, and Czechoslovakia alike, alarmed Joseph Stalin. Stalin feared that without Western support his own army would be unable to withstand a German invasion (a problem partly of his own creation given the many officers killed during the Great Purges). Much as they hated and mistrusted each other, in the summer of 1939 Hitler and Stalin signed a nonaggression pact, secretly dividing Poland between them. Hitler was merely delaying his planned attack on Russia, while Stalin was playing for time to ready his country for war.

When Hitler invaded Poland on September 1, 1939, Britain and France immediately declared war on Germany but took no active military steps to confront the German army. Meanwhile, in the United States public opinion was largely opposed to another intervention in European politics. Soon, however, peoples across Europe, Africa, Asia, and the Americas would be embroiled in a total war the likes of which humanity had never seen.

CONTEXT AND CONNECTIONS

Suspended Between Two World Wars

After the trauma of 1914–1918, the world's people barely had a chance to catch their breath before confronting another total war, even more global and more violent. By the summer of 1940, German, Italian, and Japanese aggression and the death of democracy in Spain had sounded a warning bell that tolled across the world. Like France and Britain before, the United States was slow to take heed, avoiding involvement in the Spanish Civil War and remaining neutral even as the Germans overran France and began an aerial bombardment of Britain. By then the catastrophe of another world war was inevitable.

It is understandable that the interwar generation valued peace so highly. For those who had experienced the ravages of the Great War two decades earlier, the thought of another total war was terrible indeed. Yet even before the Great Depression, global tensions ran high, aggravated by the long list of national grievances that remained after the Paris Peace Conference (see Chapter 27).

As the 1930s progressed, international institutions such as the League of Nations proved ineffective in dealing with national aggression. The emergence of Halide Edib's own Turkey through military mobilization showed that national rights were best secured not with talk, but with action.

With the Great Depression, liberal democracy and free-market capitalism lost much of their allure. Responses from the far right and the far left—fascism, communism, and ultranationalism—offered alternatives that, whatever their cruelties, reinvigorated the Italian, German, and Soviet economies and emboldened Japan. Across the world, in nations as diverse as Brazil and Turkey, authoritarian leaders magnified the role of the state in social and economic affairs, suppressing the more democratic programs of dissidents like Halide Edib.

It seemed that the French and British had come out of the Paris Peace Conference with their status strengthened. They not only retained their global empires, but with

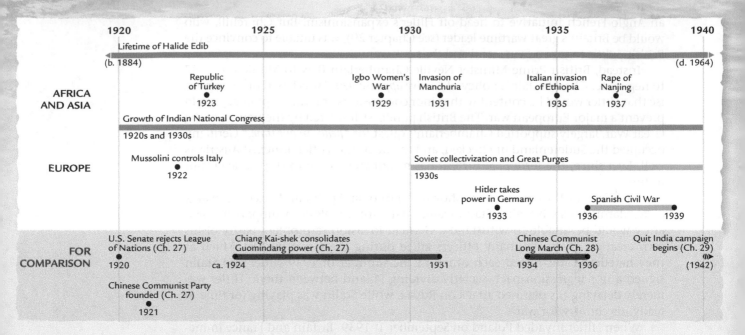

	1920	1925	1930	1935	1940
	Lifetime of Halide Edib				
	(b. 1884)				(d. 1964)
AFRICA AND ASIA		Republic of Turkey ● 1923	Igbo Women's War ● 1929	Invasion of Manchuria ● 1931	Italian invasion of Ethiopia ● 1935	Rape of Nanjing ● 1937
	Growth of Indian National Congress 1920s and 1930s				
EUROPE	Mussolini controls Italy ● 1922		Soviet collectivization and Great Purges 1930s		
			Hitler takes power in Germany ● 1933	Spanish Civil War ● 1936 ● 1939	
FOR COMPARISON	U.S. Senate rejects League of Nations (Ch. 27) ● 1920	Chiang Kai-shek consolidates Guomindang power (Ch. 27) ca. 1924 ● 1931		Chinese Communist Long March (Ch. 28) ● 1934 ● 1936	Quit India campaign begins (Ch. 29) (1942)
	Chinese Communist Party founded (Ch. 27) ● 1921				

the addition of former German colonies and Ottoman provinces, expanded them. Under the exigencies of total war, however, they had expended vast sums. The British, the dominant source of global capital investment before the war, were now in debt to American financial institutions (see Chapter 27). How could they sustain a world-embracing empire when their relative global financial standing had slipped? Only after the Second World War did the British and French discover that the costs of empire exceeded the benefits, when decolonization led to a cascade of new Asian and African nations (see Chapter 30).

Meanwhile, the United States and the new Soviet Union stood on the sidelines. The Americans, having put a toe in the cold waters of international engagement during World War I, pulled back, demilitarized, and with

the U.S. Senate's failure to ratify the League of Nations treaty, minded their own business. The Soviet Union, industrializing under Stalin's brutal dictatorship, was cut off from global economic and cultural developments. But as the French traveler Alexis de Tocqueville had predicted as early as the 1830s (see Chapter 25), the huge populations and vast resources of Russia and the United States were bound to put these two nations at the forefront of global affairs. When, in the aftermath of the Second World War, the global order based on European colonialism shattered, the United States and the Soviet Union would come to dominate the Cold War world (see Chapters 29–31). Fascism would be defeated by 1945, but the communist challenge to capitalism and liberal democracy would endure.

Key Terms

Halide Edib (842)
Great Depression (843)
Franklin Delano Roosevelt (844)
fascism (846)
Benito Mussolini (847)
Adolf Hitler (849)
collectivization (854)

Great Purges (854)
invasion of Manchuria (855)
Mustafa Kemal (856)
Getúlio Vargas (858)
Mohandas K. Gandhi (859)
Amritsar Massacre (859)
Muslim League (862)

Nnamdi Azikiwe (863)
Igbo Women's War (863)
Rape of Nanjing (865)
Spanish Civil War (867)

For Further Reference

Chang, Iris. *The Rape of Nanjing: The Forgotten Holocaust of World War II*. New York: Basic Books, 2012.

Chadha, Yodesh. *Gandhi: A Life*. New York: Wiley, 2008.

Crozier, Andrew. *The Causes of the Second World War*. Malden, Mass.: Wiley-Blackwell, 1997.

Edib, Halide. *House with Wisteria: Memoirs of Halide Edib*. Charlottesville, Va.: Leopolis Press, 2003.

Fitzpatrick, Sheila. *Stalin's Peasants: Resistance and Survival in the Russian Village After Collectivization*. New York: Oxford University Press, 1996.

Gellner, Ernest. *Nations and Nationalism*. Malden, Mass.: Wiley-Blackwell, 2006.

Griffin, Roger. *Modernism and Fascism: The Sense of Beginning Under Mussolini and Hitler*. New York: Palgrave Macmillan, 2010.

Hobsbawm, Eric. *The Age of Extremes: A History of the World, 1914–1991*. New York: Vintage, 1996.

Mango, Andrew. *Atatürk: The Biography of the Founder of Modern Turkey*. New York: Overlook, 2002.

Paxton, Robert. *The Anatomy of Fascism*. New York: Vintage, 2005.

Payne, Stanley. *Civil War in Europe, 1905–1949*. New York: Cambridge University Press, 2011.

Rothermund, Dietmar. *The Global Impact of the Great Depression, 1929–1939*. New York: Routledge, 1996.

Snyder, Timothy. *Bloodlands: Europe Between Hitler and Stalin*. New York: Basic Books, 2010.

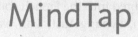

MindTap is a fully online, highly personalized learning experience built upon Cengage Learning content. MindTap combines student learning tools—readings, multimedia, activities, and assessments—into a singular Learning Path that guides students through the course.

29 The Second World War and the Origins of the Cold War, 1939–1949

Nancy Wake

By the spring of 1944, Nazi Germany had occupied France for nearly four years. In preparation for a British and American invasion at the Normandy coast, underground resistance fighters were being parachuted into the French countryside. **Nancy Wake** (1912–2011), a young Australian, was the only woman in her group. War can produce unlikely heroes, and Nancy Wake was one. While she had traveled to Paris in the 1930s looking for adventure, fun, and romance, now she was risking her life in the fight against Nazi Germany:

As the Liberator bomber circled over the dropping zone in France I could see lights flashing and huge bonfires burning. I hoped the field was manned by the Resistance and not by German ambushers. Huddled in the belly of the bomber, airsick and vomiting, I was hardly Hollywood's idea of a glamorous spy. I probably looked grotesque. Over civilian clothes, silk-stockinged and high-heeled, I wore overalls, [and] carried revolvers in the pockets.... Even more incongruous was the matronly handbag, full of cash and secret instructions for D-Day.... But I'd spent years in France working as an escape courier ... and I was desperate to return to France and continue working against Hitler. Neither airsickness nor looking like a clumsily wrapped parcel was going to deter me.*

---

*Excerpt from Nancy Wake, *The Autobiography of the Woman the Gestapo Called the White Mouse*, © 1985 Pan Publishing.

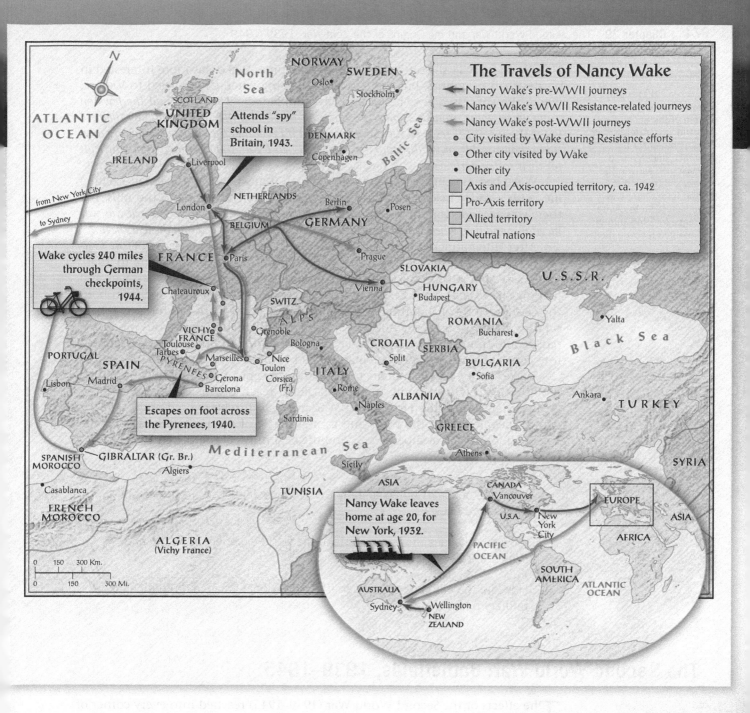

The Travels of Nancy Wake

- ← Nancy Wake's pre-WWII journeys
- → Nancy Wake's WWII Resistance-related journeys
- → Nancy Wake's post-WWII journeys
- • City visited by Wake during Resistance efforts
- • Other city visited by Wake
- • Other city
- ☐ Axis and Axis-occupied territory, ca. 1942
- ☐ Pro-Axis territory
- ☐ Allied territory
- ☐ Neutral nations

Attends "spy" school in Britain, 1943.

Wake cycles 240 miles through German checkpoints, 1944.

Escapes on foot across the Pyrenees, 1940.

Nancy Wake leaves home at age 20, for New York, 1932.

The German secret police, the Gestapo, called her "the White Mouse" and put her at the top of their "most wanted" list. But Wake evaded capture and went on to become the most highly decorated female veteran of the war.

Born in a family that was originally from New Zealand, Wake had both English and Polynesian ancestry. Even as a child she *"dreamt of seeing the world,"* and at the age of twenty she sailed from Australia to Canada and traveled by train to

Nancy Wake
(1912–2011) Highly
decorated Australian vet-
eran of the Second
World War. After serving
as a courier for the
French underground
resistance early in the
war, she traveled to Eng-
land for training and
parachuted into central
France in 1944 during
the Allied reoccupation.

New York; in 1934 she settled in Paris. At that time, Wake was more interested in parties than in politics, but she had an awakening when she traveled to Vienna, where she witnessed Jews being publicly humiliated: *"The Nazis had the Jews on a big wheel going around … maybe a dozen of them, and they were whipping them."** Later she wrote, *"I resolved then and there that if I ever had the chance I would do any-thing, however big or small, stupid or dangerous, to try and make things more difficult for their rotten party."*†

Wake became engaged to a wealthy French industrialist and lived an exciting life, with a wide circle of Parisian friends and frequent vacations to the Alps. But there was an undercurrent of tension. *"In common with many others I feared war was inevitable and then where would we all be? When would laughter end and the tears begin?"*†

After Hitler attacked Poland in 1939, there was an ominous pause before Ger-many opened a western front against France. After that invasion came in 1940, Wake served as a courier for the underground resistance, passing messages and helping the *maquis* (mah-KEE)—antifascist resistance fighters—escape from both the Gestapo and collaborating French authorities. Soon there was too much heat on the "White Mouse"; she hiked to Spain over difficult and dangerous mountain passes, and from there went to England. After training in Britain, she parachuted into central France, rejoined the maquis, and witnessed the liberation of Paris.

Wake's story puts a human face on the concept of total war. The military mobilization, civilian involvement, and global reach of this conflict were even greater than during the First World War and had unprecedented effects on the world's peoples. With the war's end came the rise of the United States and the Soviet Union as global superpowers and the beginning of their Cold War rivalry.

FOCUS QUESTIONS

❯ What factors contributed to early German and Japanese successes and later Allied ones?

❯ How did civilians in various parts of the world experience the Second World War as a total war?

❯ How did the outcome of the war affect the global balance of political and military power?

The Second World War: Battlefields, 1939–1945

The effects of the Second World War (1939–1945) reached into every corner of the globe. Japan's expansion into China made Asia and the Pacific a full-scale theater of war (see Chapter 28). As during the First World War, Africans fought for the Allies (see Chapter 27). Arab societies were disrupted by desert war in North Africa, Polynesian ones by warfare in the Pacific. But control of Europe remained

---

*This is found online in multiple sources, including http://www.abc.net.au/schoolstv/australians/wake.htm.

†Excerpt from Nancy Wake, *The Autobiography of the Woman the Gestapo Called the White Mouse*, pp. 7, 42. 1985 Pan Publishing.

central, with Britain and the Soviet Union allied against Germany (see Map 29.1). As during World War I, the United States made a delayed but decisive commitment to the war, this time fighting in both Asia and Europe.

After the German invasion of Poland in 1939, the Second World War proceeded in two phases. From 1940 to 1942, initiative and success lay with the **Axis powers**: Germany, Italy, and Japan. While the Germans and Italians advanced across continental Europe and the Mediterranean, Japanese armies were on the offensive in East and Southeast Asia. But after Germany invaded the Soviet Union in June 1941 and Japan attacked the United States in December of that same year, the momentum shifted as the Soviet Union and the United States mobilized their considerable resources. By 1944, aided by resistance movements in France, Vietnam, the Philippines, and elsewhere, the Allies were on the offensive.

Axis powers
Alliance of Germany, Italy, and Japan during the Second World War.

German *Blitzkrieg* and the Rising Sun of Japan, 1939–1942

When the German army invaded Poland, it unleashed a new form of warfare: the *blitzkrieg* (BLITS-kreeg) or "lightning war," which combined the rapid mobility of tanks and mechanized infantry with massive air power. As western Poland was quickly overrun, Stalin made use of his secret agreement with Hitler to occupy the eastern part of the country. In the German zone, true to Hitler's racial policies, the process of segregating Polish Jews began immediately, while ethnic Poles were forced into labor camps to serve German war industries. On the Soviet side, Stalin ordered the execution of the Polish officer corps, most notoriously carried out at the Massacre at Katyn Forest in 1940, where tens of thousands of Poles were killed.

While Hitler and Stalin crushed Poland, France and Britain declared war on Germany but took no military steps. Instead, during the so-called Phony War of 1939–1940, they shored up their own defenses. Nancy Wake and her fiancé moved south from Paris to Marseilles (mahr-SEY), trying to distance themselves from the anticipated German invasion.

In the spring of 1940, the Germans invaded Denmark and Norway and soon controlled Belgium and the Netherlands. They then bypassed France's Maginot Line, a series of defensive bulwarks rendered obsolete by blitzkrieg tactics. Moving swiftly through Belgium, the Germans soon occupied Paris. As British forces hastily retreated from France, the *Luftwaffe* (German Air Force) began to pummel Britain in preparation for a seaborne invasion.

● **CONTEXT&CONNECTIONS** The German drive toward Paris in 1940 was the third in seventy years. During the Franco-Prussian War of 1870–1871, Prussian-led armies occupied Paris and proclaimed the birth of a new German empire in the Hall of Mirrors at Versailles (see Chapter 23). In 1914, in contrast, the German army bogged down just 20 miles (32.2 km) outside of Paris, leading to the trench warfare of the *western front* (key term in Chapter 27). Thus a very elderly Parisian of the 1940s would have experienced three separate German assaults on her city. ●

Though unable to destroy Britain's air defenses, the Germans continually bombarded London to terrorize its citizens and sap their morale. During this "blitz," when Londoners crowded into underground train stations to escape the bombing, Britain held together under the firm leadership of Prime Minister **Winston Churchill** (1874–1965), who exhorted Britons to "*brace ourselves to our duties, and*

Winston Churchill
(1874–1965) British prime minister during the Second World War who rallied his people to stand firm during the war's dark early days. A staunch anticommunist, he coined the term *iron curtain* after the war to describe Stalin's domination of eastern Europe.

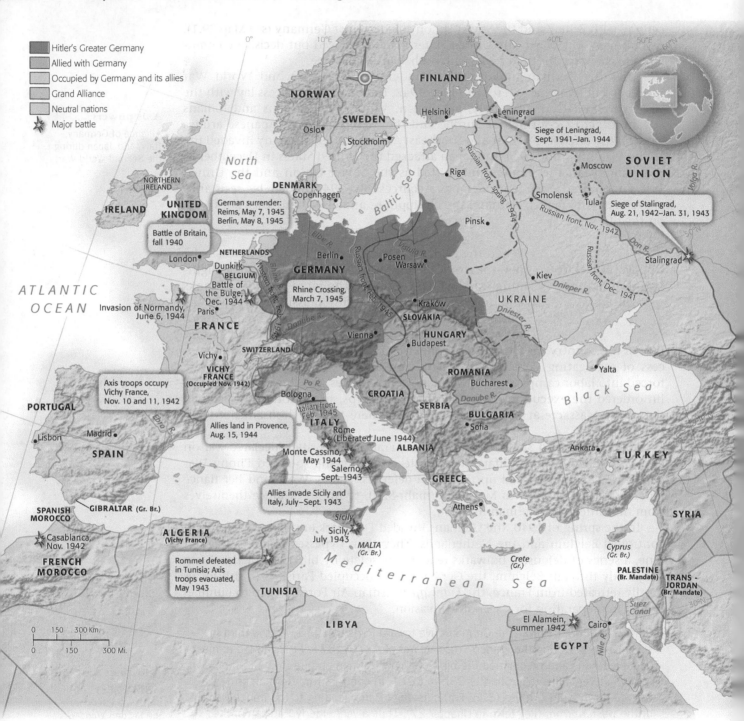

Map 29.1 World War II in Europe and North Africa Through the summer of 1941 the Axis powers, led by fascist Germany and Italy, held the momentum in the European theater of war, with Paris occupied, Britain isolated, the Soviet Union invaded, and eastern Europe and the Balkans under German domination. An important Allied triumph came with British victory at El Alamein in Egypt in 1942, but the real turning point was Soviet success in turning back the Germans at Stalingrad. After the United States entered the war, Allied invasions of Italy (1943) and of occupied France at Normandy (1944) complemented Soviet advances.

so bear ourselves that, if the British Empire and its Commonwealth last for a thousand years, men will still say, 'This was their finest hour.'" Londoners took heart that the massive Cathedral of St. Paul's in the heart of their city, though surrounded by burning rubble, stood unscathed.

German officials often found local collaborators. In both the Netherlands and Norway, for example, local fascists facilitated German conquest. As a result, collaborators with Nazism everywhere came to be called *quislings*, after the Norwegian fascist Vidkun Quisling. Meanwhile, in the Balkans, the Germans received assistance from the extreme Croatian nationalists of the Ustaše, Catholic fascists who used their German alliance to gain the upper hand over their Orthodox Serbian rivals in Yugoslavia.

The French Vichy regime was a notorious case of collaboration. After the German invaders took direct control over Paris and the north they tolerated the formation of a French-run puppet regime in the south. Some Vichy officials were motivated simply by greed or ambition, but others shared both the anticommunism and the anti-Semitism of the Nazis, later cooperating in the deportation and murder of French Jews. Vichy officials in the French colonial service extended fascist influence over parts of Africa and Asia.

At the same time, underground opposition to the Axis was found everywhere. Men and women in France, Norway, Ethiopia, Italy, Yugoslavia, Vietnam, the Philippines, and elsewhere organized covert resistance cells to defeat fascist invaders and their local allies. Polish leaders gathered in London and formed a government-in-exile. The French partisans for whom Nancy Wake worked as a courier were loyal to a maverick general, **Charles de Gaulle** (SHARL du GAWHL) (1890–1970), who formed a Free French government-in-exile in London and began to recruit an army of liberation.

War came to North Africa and southeast Europe when unsuccessful Italian invasions led to German intervention. Early in 1941, after the Italians failed to take Egypt in an offensive launched from Libya, German forces arrived to back them up, bringing tank warfare across the North African desert. Similarly, Mussolini's designs on the Balkans were undercut by his failure to conquer Greece. Again, the German high command had to divert troops to reinforce the Italian position, bringing most of Hungary, Yugoslavia, Romania, and Greece under Axis control.

Though the American president, Franklin Delano Roosevelt, privately agreed with Churchill about how much was at stake in the war, American public opinion balked at committing troops to Europe. Instead, Roosevelt declared that the United States would become the "arsenal of democracy" by negotiating a "lend lease"

Galerie Bilderwelt/Getty Images

Fascist Collaborators German invasions were facilitated by fascist collaborators. *"Dutchmen! For your honour and conscience! The Waffen SS summons you to fight Bolshevism!"* The Waffen-SS was the elite armed wing of the Nazi Party, a multi-national military force separate from the regular German army. After the war, the victorious Allies treated the *Schutzstaffel* as a criminal organization.

Charles de Gaulle
(1890–1970) French general and statesman who led the Free French Army in resistance to German occupation. Later elected president of France.

arrangement to supply American arms to Britain without need for immediate payment. In the summer of 1941, Churchill and Roosevelt met aboard a ship off the coast of Newfoundland and jointly issued the **Atlantic Charter**, reaffirming the Wilsonian principle of national self-determination: *"[We] respect the right of all peoples to choose the form of government under which they will live; and … wish to see sovereign rights and self government restored to those who have been forcibly deprived of them."* But America's moral and material support did no more than help the British to hold on.

Matters looked just as bleak in East Asia. Japan had allied with Germany, and in 1940 the Vichy government of France, complying with Japanese demands, handed over much of mainland Southeast Asia. Through naval assaults Japan also controlled southern Burma, threatening British India.

Meanwhile, as tensions grew, the United States beefed up its Pacific command in the Philippines, put a freeze on Japanese assets in the United States, and most important, cut off exports of steel and the U.S. oil on which Japan depended. The empire's military and industrial planners needed to find another source of supply and focused on acquiring the oil reserves of the Dutch East Indies, which would require taking the Philippines from the United States.

Gauging that conflict was now inevitable, the Japan high command decided to launch a preemptive surprise attack on the U.S. naval outpost of **Pearl Harbor** in Hawai'i on December 7, 1941—*"a date,"* President Roosevelt said, *"which will live in infamy."* The U.S. Pacific fleet was crippled. A few days after Pearl Harbor, the German and Italian governments also declared war on the United States. Finally, American reluctance to join the fray was overcome. Once attacked, the American people rallied to an intensive mobilization to meet Axis forces on both sides of Eurasia.

While U.S. mobilization was taking place, Japanese momentum continued, as they occupied British Hong Kong, took the Philippines, and attacked the Dutch East Indies. With victory at the supposedly impregnable British base at Singapore the Japanese captured what had been the Allies' best naval facility in East Asia, taking 80,000 (mostly Indian) British prisoners.

● **CONTEXT&CONNECTIONS** The Philippines had been ruled from Madrid for over three centuries (see Chapter 17) before being transferred to the United States as a result of the Spanish-American War of 1898–1900 (see Chapter 26). Thus between the 1890s and the 1940s Filipino partisans had fought for independence from Spain, then from the United States, and finally from Japan, before securing independence in 1946. ●

To justify expansionism in the 1930s, Japanese propagandists had touted a Greater East Asian Co-Prosperity Sphere that would supposedly free Asian peoples from Western imperialism under Japanese leadership. But the brutality the Japanese had shown in China during the Rape of Nanjing (see Chapter 28) was soon repeated elsewhere. In the spring of 1942, for example, thousands of Filipinos and hundreds of American prisoners of war died on a forced march across the Bataan (buh-TAHN) peninsula in the Japanese-occupied Philippines. Despite rhetoric about shared prosperity, it was the quest for empire that lay at the heart of Japan's war plans.

The Allies on the Offensive, 1942–1945

No one was shocked when, in June 1941, Hitler reneged on his secret pact with Stalin and invaded the Soviet Union. After the Japanese attack on Pearl

Harbor six months later, the Axis powers had brought both the United States and the Soviet Union into the war on the side of Britain. In 1943, these **Allied powers** began their effort to roll back previous Axis advances, and Nancy Wake, having escaped Vichy France by hiking across the Pyrenees, was in England, training for the Allied counteroffensive.

Hitler's eastward thrust had been successful at first, and the Germans were soon assaulting the crucial city of Leningrad (as the historic capital of St. Petersburg was then called). The three-year **Siege of Leningrad** was gruesome. Residents were reduced to hunting rats for food, and many starved. Escape was possible only during winter, in convoys of trucks across a frozen lake north of the city. While some escaped, others drowned in the icy waters as German aircraft strafed and bombed them. Of a population of 3 million, one-third perished.

Then, as the German tanks became mired in the mud that came with spring rains, and as their supply lines stretched thin, the German advance slowed. Soviet resistance stiffened, unmatched in its toughness and resiliency. Stalin's propagandists emphasized heroic stands against earlier invaders and rallied the Soviet peoples behind the "Great Patriotic Homeland War."

Allied powers

Alliance of Britain, the United States, and the Soviet Union during the Second World War.

Siege of Leningrad

(1941–1944) German siege of this Soviet city that left the city without food or fuel, resulting in over a million deaths.

Sovfoto/Getty Images

Siege of Leningrad As long as the German siege lasted, death was an everyday occurrence for the people of Leningrad (today's St. Petersburg) as a constant artillery barrage kept residents scrambling for cover. (In defiance, the great "Leningrad Symphony" by Russian composer Dmitri Shostakovich was performed in the beleaguered city in the summer of 1942. The weakened musicians received extra rations to enable them to practice, and loudspeakers broadcast the performance to the citizens of Leningrad, and to the German troops beyond.)

● **CONTEXT&CONNECTIONS** Like *Napoleon Bonaparte* (Chapter 22), Hitler had opened a second front in Russia while Britain remained unconquered and, like Napoleon, he paid a heavy price. As with the French army of 1812, the Germans found their supply lines stretched dangerously thin, and Soviet generals, like tsarist ones, were able to use the vastness of their country and its harsh climate to their advantage. Napoleon lost more than half a million troops before abandoning his campaign; during World War II, Germans suffered over 80 percent of all their casualties in the east. ●

With the United States and the Soviet Union fully mobilized, momentum shifted toward the Allies. Though this alliance between liberal democratic and communist states was an unlikely one, made possible only by their common fascist enemies, one reason for the Allied advantage in the war after 1943 was the superior coordination of the British, American, and Soviet forces. On the Axis side, in contrast, poor coordination meant that Hitler's forces had to rush in when Mussolini's faltered. The same Allied advantage held in the Pacific, where Britain and the United States collaborated closely while Japan fought alone.

The first decisive military reversal for the Axis came in North Africa, where the British finally gained the upper hand. Victory at the Battle of El Alamein in Egypt (1942) not only protected Britain's control of the Suez Canal but also secured a base for a counterattack against Italy across the Mediterranean. By 1943, British and American forces were driving northward up the Italian peninsula, aided by both Italian partisans and Free French forces, including Arab soldiers recruited from the now-liberated French colonies of Morocco and Algeria.

Faced with the Allied invasion from North Africa, Mussolini's army collapsed. Though Germany propped him up in a northern Italian enclave until 1945, he was eventually captured by the Italian resistance. To express their contempt, Mussolini's executioners hung his body by the heels from a public balcony.

In the Pacific, the Allies also gained momentum in 1942. In early summer, American aircraft sunk four of Japan's six largest aircraft carriers at the Battle of Midway. Then the United States took the offensive at Guadalcanal, the beginning of an "island-hopping" campaign to drive back the Japanese. The fighting was tough, but the huge U.S. economy was now fully geared toward military production, and new ships and airplanes rolled off assembly lines at a staggering rate, ensuring American naval dominance in the Pacific. By 1943, Allied forces were driving the Japanese back toward their home islands, as local resistance in China, Vietnam, the Philippines, and the Dutch East Indies complemented British, Australian, Canadian, and American efforts.

● **CONTEXT&CONNECTIONS** Prior to 1943, the Japanese navy had a remarkable record of success going back to the *Sino-Japanese* and *Russo-Japanese Wars* of 1894–1895 and 1904–1905 (Chapter 24). After World War II and the acceptance of a pacifist constitution imposed by the United States, Japan ceased building or deploying ships with offensive military capacity, though recent tensions with China have caused a reconsideration of that policy (see page 732). ●

Battle of Stalingrad

(1942–1943) One of the major turning points of World War II, when the Soviet army halted the German advance and annihilated the German Sixth Army. After victory at Stalingrad, the Soviets went on the offensive, driving the Germans out of Soviet territory.

Perhaps the most important turning point of the war was the **Battle of Stalingrad**. Unable to take Moscow, in late 1942 the Germans swung south toward the Soviet Union's strategic oil fields. House-by-house fighting in Stalingrad gave the Red Army time to organize a counteroffensive, and in 1943 they surrounded and annihilated the German Sixth Army. Galvanized by their victory, the Soviets launched a series of punishing attacks, and in the spring of 1944 Stalin's forces drove Hitler's army out of Soviet territory. Meanwhile, British and American bombing was starting to take a terrible toll: in the summer of 1943, the port city of Hamburg in Germany was obliterated in a firestorm that killed tens of thousands of civilians.

In late 1943 when Churchill and Roosevelt met with Stalin in Teheran (Iran), the Allies had taken North Africa, invaded Italy, and were preparing a counter-invasion of France on the coast of Normandy. Meanwhile, Soviet forces had driven the German army all the way back to the Polish border.

In anticipation of the Normandy invasion, Nancy Wake and her group parachuted into central France behind German lines. It was difficult and dangerous work. Once when her group lost their radio, and therefore contact with London, Wake bicycled more than a hundred miles over mountainous terrain to re-establish their communications: *"Every kilometer I pedaled was sheer agony. I knew if I ever got off the bike, I could never get on it again.... I couldn't stand up, I couldn't sit down, I couldn't walk and I couldn't sleep for days."**

After assisting in the Allied invasion of Normandy on D-Day, June 6, 1944, Wake reached Paris just as Allied forces drove the German army from the city she had once called home: *"Paris was liberated on 25 August, 1944, and the whole country rejoiced.... The aggressors were now the hunted.... The collaborators seemed to have vanished into thin air and the crowds in the street went wild with joy."** But there was still hard fighting to do. In the winter of 1944 a final German offensive in Belgium led to significant American casualties in the Battle of the Bulge before Allied forces regained the initiative. And Nancy Wake's happiness was tempered by personal loss: the Nazis had executed her husband and killed many of her friends.

The European war ended in a final fury. As the Red Army moved into eastern Germany, Soviet troops took their vengeance by raping, looting, and executing German civilians. When British and American aircraft firebombed Dresden, civilians who fled to underground shelters suffocated as the firestorm above them sucked the oxygen from the air. Over one hundred thousand died. With Soviet troops storming Berlin, Hitler killed himself in a bunker beneath the city. The nightmare of German fascism was over. On May 8, 1945—V-E Day—Germany surrendered.

In the Pacific, once the United States retook the Philippines late in 1944, the path toward invasion lay open (see Map 29.2). American submarines blockaded Japan, starving its military of supplies, while U.S. aircraft dropped incendiary bombs on Tokyo and other cities, reducing them to ashes. Still, most Americans thought that it would require a massive landing of troops, with tremendous casualties, to force a Japanese surrender.

Harry S. Truman (in office 1945–1953) had become president in April after the death of Roosevelt, and he made the decision to seek a quick end to the war with Japan by using a terrible new weapon. Atomic blasts at **Hiroshima and Nagasaki** killed hundreds of thousands. Some died instantly, others more gradually from radiation poisoning. (See the feature "Visual Evidence in Primary Sources: Hiroshima and Nagasaki.")

Hiroshima and Nagasaki

(1945) Two Japanese cities devastated by atomic bombs dropped by the United States in an attempt to end the Second World War. Hundreds of thousands were killed, many by slow radiation poisoning.

---

*Excerpt from Nancy Wake, *The Autobiography of the Woman the Gestapo Called the White Mouse*, pp. 225–226, 255. 1985 Pan Publishing.

Hiroshima and Nagasaki

In August 1939, President Franklin Delano Roosevelt received a letter from famed theoretical physicist Albert Einstein, a German Jew who had fled National Socialism to take up a position at Princeton's Institute for Advanced Study (see Chapter 28). Einstein informed Roosevelt that *"the element uranium may be turned into a new and important source of energy in the immediate future.... Extremely powerful bombs of a new type might thus be constructed."** Einstein warned that the German government had already begun research into the feasibility of such weapons.

Nagasaki was a major port city, in earlier times the center of Japanese trade with Europeans. After the Tokugawa seclusion edicts (see Chapter 20), Nagasaki was the site of the annual Dutch trade mission and the center of "Dutch learning." **Nagasaki Before the Atomic Bomb**.

Bad weather caused the United States to change its original plan and order the "Fat Man" bomb to be dropped on the secondary target of Nagasaki. **Nagasaki after the Atomic Bomb**.

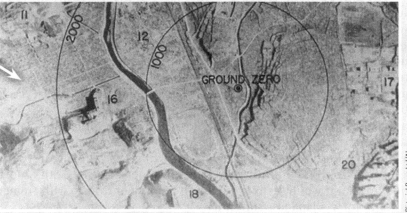

In the heart of Nagasaki stood the largest Roman Catholic Cathedral in all of Asia, Urakami Cathedral. Its ruins are still found in the memorial park marking Ground Zero. Conservative estimates put the death toll for Nagasaki at 77,000, about 30 percent of the population.

Pictorial Press Ltd/Alamy

Some of Harry S. Truman's advisors had urged the president to drop the atomic bombs on uninhabited islands as a warning that might force Japanese surrender. With only a few operational weapons, and no guarantee that they would explode as planned, Truman went ahead with the attacks on populated areas. ***The American decision to use atomic bombs on Japan in 1945 is a point of historical controversy. What are the main arguments for and against Truman's decision?***

---

*Franklin D. Roosevelt Presidential Library and Museum, http://www.fdrlibrary.marist.edu/archives/pdfs/docsworld-war.pdf.

The result was the top-secret Manhattan Project, headquartered at Los Alamos, New Mexico. Its mandate was to create an explosive device based on nuclear fission, with the greatest possible speed and without the benefit of field tests. The Manhattan Project was so secret that while serving as vice president Harry S. Truman was unaware of it, being informed only following Roosevelt's death.

In May 1945, a month after Roosevelt's death, Germany surrendered, but war in the Pacific continued, and both the United States and the Soviet Union began to redeploy forces toward Japan. Many believed that the Japanese would fight to the death in defense of their home islands and their emperor, and that perhaps a million more U.S. soldiers might die in an invasion. There was also concern in the United States that Stalin could use a protracted conflict in northeast Asia to his own benefit. Such were the circumstances under which Truman had to decide whether to deploy the new weapons.

By the end of 1945, about 140,000 people had died in Hiroshima, either from the immediate impact of the bomb or from radiation poisoning. Of those, more than one in ten were Koreans who had been forced into the service of the Japanese empire.

Fifty years later, a controversy erupted in 1995 when the Smithsonian Institution organized an exhibition on the *Enola Gay*, which dropped the bomb "Little Boy" on Hiroshima. Protestors, including veterans groups, derided the Smithsonian exhibit for asking overly critical questions about U.S. actions and for focusing too narrowly on Japanese civilian suffering.

Hibakusha ("explosion-affected people") is the Japanese term for atomic bomb survivors. Although they have played an important historical role by keeping memories alive, *hibakusha* have also faced discrimination, with some of their neighbors falsely believing that contagious genetic defects resulted from the bombings.

Victims of Hiroshima/Alinari/The Bridgeman Art Library

A survivor of Hiroshima remembered: *"We met some people from Hell. They were naked and their skin, burned and bloody, was like red rust and their bodies were bloated up like balloons.... From the burned shreds of their sailor uniforms I knew they were schoolgirls, but they had no hair left and ... they no longer appeared human."**

---

*Iwao Nakamura, "Recollections," in *Sources of Global History since 1900*, ed. James H. Overfield, 2d ed. (Boston: Wadsworth, 2013), p. 238.

Meanwhile, the Soviet Union occupied Manchuria and northern Korea, raising Japanese fears of a Soviet invasion. Immediate submission to the United States now seemed the only option to Japanese leaders. As his subjects tuned in their radios on August 14, it was Emperor Hirohito's own voice, which they had never heard before, announcing the empire's unconditional surrender. "*The enemy has begun to employ a new and most cruel bomb, the power of which to do damage is, indeed, incalculable, taking the toll of many innocent lives,*" Hirohito said. "*Should we continue to fight, not only would it result in an ultimate collapse and obliteration of the Japanese nation, but also it would lead to the total extinction of human civilization.*" Official surrender took place on September 2, 1945—V-J Day. Finally, the Second World War was over.

Map 29.2 World War II in Asia and the Pacific   The Japanese empire, like the Axis powers in Europe, dominated the early stages of the war. By 1943, however, with the United States fully mobilized to fight the Pacific war, momentum shifted to the Allies. The war ended in the summer of 1945 when President Harry Truman ordered atomic weapons dropped on Hiroshima and Nagasaki.

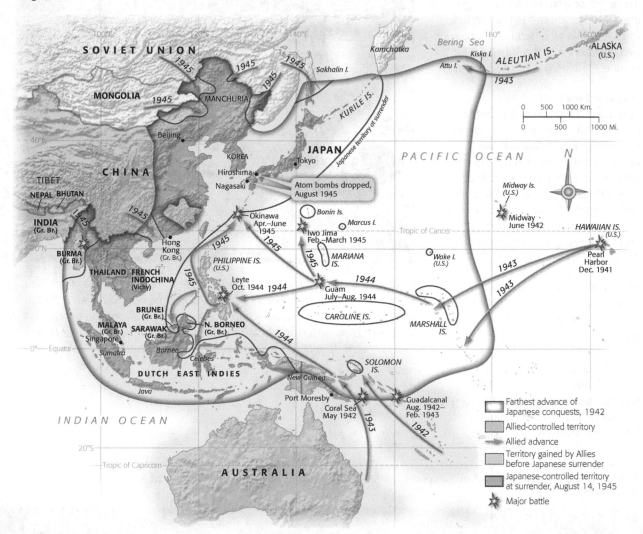

Total War and Civilian Life

Even more than during the First World War, the Second disrupted the life plans of tens of millions of ordinary people. In that sense, Nancy Wake's experience was not atypical.

In addition to witnessing the horrors of war, civilian populations were affected in myriad other ways. Consumer goods disappeared as production converted to military needs. Total war again meant intensification of government power: even the few remaining democratic societies curtailed freedom of speech and freedom of assembly. Newspapers, radio, and film were censored and often incorporated state-sponsored misinformation and propaganda.

Once again, the disruptions of total war reached civilians across the planet. Residents of remote island atolls in the Pacific found themselves trapped between U.S. and Japanese armies. Colonized Africans and Asians served as soldiers or had their labor forcibly harnessed for wartime production, their destinies hinging on the successes and failures of Allied and Axis armies. Many suffered tragic losses. Worldwide, over 50 million people were killed, including at least 25 million Soviet citizens, nearly half the total.

During the genocide known as the **Holocaust**, the Nazis murdered 6 million Jews in labor and death camps. The victims were usually starved and tortured before being killed. Of the entire European Jewish population, over 60 percent perished, including over 90 percent of Poland's Jews. The slaughter extended to millions more people as well—homosexuals, Roma (Gypsies), disabled persons, Jehovah's Witnesses, and others deemed enemies of Aryan racial supremacy.

Civilians and Total War in the United States and Europe

In the United States, families were disrupted as sons and husbands went to war and factories were converted from consumer to military production. But almost none of the fighting occurred on American soil, and the war actually benefited American society in a number of ways. Massive state spending on munitions put the country back to work, effectively ending the Great Depression.

For Americans who had long been at the bottom of the job ladder, especially women and African Americans, mobilization brought new opportunities. "Rosie the Riveter" became the symbol of women laboring on industrial production lines to produce the boots, bullets, and bombers needed by the military. Segregated African American military units, such as the famous "Tuskegee Airmen," distinguished themselves in combat, while other American blacks gained access to good industrial

Holocaust

The genocide in which the Nazis murdered 6 million Jews, known in Hebrew as the *Shoah* ("catastrophe"). The Nazis also killed hundreds of thousands of Roma (gypsies), homosexuals, Jehovah's Witnesses and others they saw as deviant.

Keystone Features/Getty Images

British War Production Total war required the complete mobilization of civilian populations behind a nation's military. As in the United States and the Soviet Union, traditional gender roles in Britain were transformed as female factory workers replaced departed servicemen. Here a British worker finalizes assembly of the nose cone of an Avro Lancaster bomber in 1943.

From Cryptography to Computer Science

Given the high stakes of total war, it is not surprising that both the Allied and Axis powers made heavy investments in applied scientific research attempting to get an upper hand. Today, we experience the legacy of those efforts whenever we use lightweight plastics, fly in a jet airplane guided by radar, or use electricity from a nuclear power plant. Modern computer science was also propelled forward by World War II.

For the British, a major challenge was Enigma, Germany's "unbreakable" coding machine. Secure in the secrecy of messages sent between the high command and ships, submarines, and aircraft, the Germans had a strong tactical advantage. To try to break Enigma the British established a secure decryption center in the suburban villa of Bletchley Park and recruited personnel highly skilled in advanced mathematics and computational theory.

Bletchley Park was a team effort, but its ultimate success stemmed from the contributions of Dr. Alan Turing, the Cambridge mathematician many see as the father of modern computer science. Some of the mathematicians at Bletchley Park eschewed mechanical solutions (like the astronomers who had

rejected Harrison's chronometer as a solution to the "problem of longitude"; see Chapter 21), but Turing realized that human computing speeds were simply too slow to crack Enigma. Unaided, even the best minds could decode no more than a tiny number of German messages.

Turing's solution was a cylinder-driven computational device, and his "Turing Machine" is a direct ancestor of modern computers. Of course, since then, progress in miniaturization has been staggering, starting with the transistor technology that was also developed during World War II. It is safe to say that the computing device in your pocket is many times more powerful than Turing's room-filling, energy-devouring machine.

The decoding of the Enigma machine saved an incalculable number of Allied lives and shortened the war, perhaps by as much as two years. Unfortunately, that happy ending did not extend to Turing's own life. He was hounded for his homosexuality, convicted of "gross indecency," and subjected to chemical castration. Alan Turing committed suicide in 1954. Finally, in 2014 Queen Elizabeth II granted Dr. Alan Turing a royal pardon. His work endures.

employment for the first time. The nation's diversity, seen by Hitler as a source of weakness, proved a strength, as when U.S. military intelligence recruited Navajo "code talkers" to use their indigenous language to encrypt messages in the Pacific theater. The Japanese never cracked the Navajo code. (See the feature "World History in Today's World: From Cryptography to Computer Science.") More broadly, the camaraderie and discipline of both military and civilian life, dedicated to a successful fight against a great evil, gave an entire generation of Americans a shared sense of purpose.

The people of the Soviet Union also experienced the "Great Patriotic Homeland War" as a powerful collective endeavor; however, their suffering and sacrifice was much greater. Even before the German invasion, workers dismantled factories and moved them to interior regions. Millions of people were likewise uprooted and put to work on farms in safer interior areas. Soviet women bore a special burden, caring for children and the elderly while taking on dangerous jobs in mines and factories. Many Soviet women also served with distinction in the armed forces. By the end of the war, tens of millions of people had been killed or uprooted, the country's agricultural and industrial infrastructure destroyed. Wartime suffering left the Soviet people with a deep determination never again to allow an invasion from the West.

Throughout western Europe civilians also witnessed the horrors of war at their very doorsteps. In every nation, families were evacuated from cities under bombardment to safer rural areas, where farming families took them in. In countries under occupation by the Nazis, the slightest sign of anti-German feeling, or any display of sympathy for the Jews, could result in imprisonment, torture, and death. After sustained bombardment, by war's end much of urban Europe lay in ruins. At least for the British, there was something positive to take away from the terrible suffering: many would later recall the feeling of mutual purpose and national solidarity of the war years with nostalgia.

Total war came to the German people only in the last stages of the conflict, but then it did so with a vengeance. Early in the war, the civilian population of Germany had experienced a lower level of mobilization. For example, since National Socialist ideology idealized German women as wives and mothers—breeders of the Aryan master race—they were not asked to contribute much to the war effort. Instead, the Nazis would enslave subject peoples to meet their labor needs. At war's end, however, German civilians paid a heavy price for their support of the Nazis. As bombs pummeled German cities, and German soldiers and civilians fell back toward Berlin, Adolf Hitler called up children and old men to reinforce his disintegrating army. In a sense, he involved the whole country in his own suicide.

The civilian experience of total war had long-term effects on Western political culture. In Europe, bitterness remained between those who resisted and those who collaborated with the Axis powers. Meanwhile, the Soviets sought to establish a zone of buffer states to insulate them from future invasion. And the people of the United States were, for the first time, fully willing to engage themselves as a great power in world affairs.

Civilians and Total War in Asia and the Colonial World

At war, the Japanese state commanded all aspects of civilian life, regulating industry and commerce, while severely restricting speech and assembly. Even so, like the Germans, most Japanese did not experience the violence of war firsthand until 1944–1945. Then Allied air assaults, and ultimately nuclear annihilation, exacted a terrible price for their nation's imperialist adventures.

Elsewhere in the Asian theater of war, European colonies were caught in the crossfire between the Allied powers and Japan. Early in the war, Japanese forces seized the colonial territories of the British, French, Dutch, and Americans. European powers were intent on liberating "their" Asian possessions, such as French Indochina and the Dutch East Indies, only to restore colonial rule. Local nationalists in places like Vietnam and Indonesia, however, saw the fight against the Japanese as the first stage of their struggle to overthrow foreign rule forever. Once the war against the Axis was over, multiple conflicts would arise between the European powers and local nationalists fighting for self-determination (see Chapter 30).

As in Europe, civilians in Asia suffered a war fought on their own soil. The Japanese regarded exploitation of Southeast Asia's natural resources as essential to their imperial mission. They treated local populations like slaves, for example by forcing Filipino men into back-breaking labor building roads and bridges. Many of them, like the Allied prisoners of war forced into similar gang labor, died from mistreatment and disease.

Sexual slavery also accompanied Japanese conquests. Rape and war, constant companions, were now put on a bureaucratic footing as officials responsible for the recreational needs of imperial troops set up brothels where teenagers and young women from the Philippines, Korea, Burma, and elsewhere were forced into service. Apart from their immediate trauma, these "comfort women" faced decades of emotional stress and social isolation. Elderly survivors are still pressing a recalcitrant Japanese government to finally admit to the historical truth.

Hunger and hardship was also the lot of Chinese civilians. Those under Japanese occupation especially suffered, but even those living in zones controlled by Chiang Kai-shek's Guomindang Army faced shortages of food and medicine. Malnutrition was common.

● **CONTEXT&CONNECTIONS** The lack of coordination between Chiang's Guomindang and Mao's rival Red Army hampered Chinese resistance to Japanese occupation (see Chapter 28), and the uneasy truce between them dissolved as soon as the Japanese withdrew. Mao Zedong's Red Army quickly went on the offensive, driving Chiang Kai-shek and the Guomindang to Taiwan. In 1949, Mao declared the foundation of the People's Republic of China (see Chapter 30). ●

Communists dominated resistance in neighboring Vietnam, where partisans led by Ho Chi Minh harassed Japanese occupation forces in cooperation with the British and Americans. In Southeast Asia the principal Allied concern was the Burma Road, by which they supplied Chiang Kai-shek's Guomindang Army. Bitterly contested jungle warfare in Burma, engaging African and Australian troops supported by Allied bombing, caught many peasant villagers in its crossfire. Late in the war, forced replacement of food crops with industrial ones, Japanese hoarding of food, and American bombing of rail and road lines contributed to the starvation of 2 million Vietnamese.

In India, the British were astonished and appalled when Mohandas K. Gandhi refused to back the British empire in the war and launched a **"Quit India"** campaign. During World War I, Gandhi and the Indian National Congress had supported the British, hoping to be rewarded with concrete steps toward Indian self-government. But Congress leaders were frustrated when the British-controlled Government of India declared war on Germany and Japan without even consulting them. While the British viewed the Congress Party as incredibly naïve for not recognizing the priority of turning back Axis assaults on freedom everywhere, Gandhi made it a matter of principle that only Indians could decide the country's course, no matter what the circumstances.

Even as British authorities once again threw Gandhi and other nationalist leaders into jail, the Indian army remained the bulwark of British defense in Asia, while Indian civilians continued to contribute labor and economic resources to the Allied war effort. As in China and Vietnam, however, wartime economic policies led to great hardship. In 1943, over 2 million people died in a famine in the northeastern province of Bengal.

British war strategies also provoked a nationalist backlash in Arab lands. Many Egyptians were outraged when the British mobilized their forces without seeking permission from the nominally independent government. As a result, Britain had to quell demonstrations in Cairo, even as it prepared for desert war with Italy. Arab nationalists had also been upset when the British allowed increased Jewish immigration to Palestine. The Grand Mufti of Jerusalem, leader of Palestinian Muslims, took a strongly anti-Zionist stand and, on the principle of "the enemy of my enemy is my friend," he urged collaboration with the Nazis. Likewise in Iraq, the government sided with Germany, leading the British to invade and occupy Baghdad in the spring of 1941.

Britain's African subjects, perhaps surprisingly, showed greater loyalty to the empire. The British mustered patriotic recruits for the **King's African Rifles** from colonies such as Nigeria and Kenya; many of these soldiers went on to serve in the tough jungle warfare in Burma. Here was another example of total war on an international scale, with African soldiers fighting in Burmese jungles to protect British India from Japanese invasion. Many of these Africans had never before traveled more than a few days' distance from home. Those who returned brought an expanded view of the world and of Africa's place in it. For many Africans, and people of African descent elsewhere, the Allied liberation of Ethiopia and restoration of Hailie Selassie as emperor in 1941 became symbolic of African dignity.

Africans from the French empire also helped defeat fascism. While most colonial officials supported the Vichy collaborators, the governor of French Equatorial

"Quit India"

Campaign by Mohandas K. Gandhi and the Indian National Congress during World War II to demand independence. They refused to support the British war effort and instead launched a campaign of civil disobedience demanding that the British "quit India" immediately.

King's African Rifles

African regiment recruited by Britain during the Second World War; saw action in Burma, fighting against the Japanese to save India for Britain.

Africa, Félix Éboué (1884–1944), stood with Charles de Gaulle. Éboué, from French Guiana in South America and a descendant of slaves, had attained French citizenship through educational achievement. Under his leadership, the colonial city of Brazzaville became a staging ground for Free French recruitment of African soldiers. Franco-African forces then played a decisive role in driving the Germans from southern France before linking up with U.S. and British forces to clear the way for the liberation of Paris.

● **CONTEXT&CONNECTIONS** Some of the African and Arab soldiers who served in the Free French armies in World War II, helping to liberate the country from German occupation, were the sons of men who had fought under the French flag in 1914–1918, as in the famous regiment of *Senegalese Sharpshooters* (Chapter 27). Memories of African contributions to French freedom are still common in Francophone West Africa. ●

Many Africans supported the Allies in the name of ideals enshrined in the Atlantic Charter: freedom and national self-determination. In South Africa, members of the African National Congress (ANC), including a young Nelson Mandela, invoked the Charter signed by Roosevelt and Churchill in their call to end racial segregation and discrimination. However, it would take another fifty years of struggle and bloodshed for democratic freedoms to become a reality for black South Africans (see Chapter 31).

The Holocaust In the midst of war, few grasped the magnitude of Hitler's assault on Europe's Jews. Only when the death camps were liberated by Allied forces in 1945 did the scale of the horror known as the Holocaust become clear. Six million Jews had been systematically murdered in the *Shoah* (Hebrew for "catastrophe").

In Hitler's manic racial scheme, most "inferior races" at least had a place as labor to support his Reich. For example, the Nazis regarded the Slavic peoples of eastern Europe as an inferior "race" destined to work under their "Aryan" superiors. (In fact, if the Germans had treated the Ukrainian and other Slavic peoples well, they might have found allies among those who had suffered under Stalin; instead Hitler's racial mania provoked stiff resistance.)

There were two "races" that Hitler claimed could play no useful role. One was the Roma, or Gypsies, a people whose ancestors had come originally from India. Across central Europe, their peripatetic lifestyle, traveling from season to season in search of work, and their clannish social behavior and resistance to cultural assimilation had long made the Roma subject to prejudice and discrimination. Now the Nazis turned informal prejudice into state oppression and murder.

Of course, Hitler's unquenchable obsession was with the Jews. As the Nuremburg Laws and the *Kristallnacht* had shown (see Chapter 28), thorough assimilation into German culture and society had given the country's Jews no protection from the Nazis. No mercy could then be expected for the Jews of Poland and the Soviet Union, exposed to the Nazi horror after the invasions of 1939 and 1941.

Early in 1942, Nazi officials met to devise a "final solution" to the "Jewish problem." According to the minutes of the Wannsee Conference, a bureaucracy would be set up to *"cleanse the German living space of Jews in a legal manner."* Jews *"capable of work"* would be sent to camps in Poland, *"whereby a large part will undoubtedly disappear through natural diminution."* Those who were not worked to death *"will have to be appropriately dealt with,"* meaning systematically murdered in "death camps." (See the feature "Movement of Ideas Through Primary Sources: Primo Levi's Memories of Auschwitz.")

Primo Levi's Memories of Auschwitz

Primo Levi (1919–1987) was an Italian Jew who joined the underground resistance to fascism in his home country. Like millions of other European Jews, he was sent to a Nazi concentration camp, but he survived and became one of the world's most renowned writers. The extract below is taken from an interview that appeared on Italian television in 1983. The interview took place as Levi was returning for the first time to Auschwitz on a Polish train. Primo Levi took his own life in 1987.

> **Apart from death itself, what were the effects of the physical and psychological torture endured by Levi and his fellow death camp inmates?**

> **Over two decades after this interview, how might we evaluate Levi's answer to the question of whether something like the horrors of Auschwitz might happen again?**

Source: Interview with Daniel Toaff, *Sorgenti di Vita (Springs of Life)*, a program on the *Unione Comunita Israelitiche Italiane, Radiotelevisione Italiana [RAI]*. From the transcript of a 1983 Italian radio broadcast, http://www.inch.com/~ari/levi1.html. The English translation is by Mirto Stone, modified for clarity. Reprinted by permission of the translator.

Return to Auschwitz

INTERVIEWER: Did you know where you were going [on the train to Auschwitz]?

PRIMO LEVI: We didn't know anything. We had seen on the cars at the station the writing "Auschwitz" but in those times, I don't think even the most informed people knew where Auschwitz was....

INTERVIEWER: What was your first [experience of] Auschwitz?

LEVI: It was night time, after a disastrous journey during which some of the people in the car had died, and arriving in a place where we didn't understand the language, the purpose.... It was really an alienating experience. It seemed we had abandoned the ability to reason, we didn't reason.

INTERVIEWER: And how was the journey, those five days?

LEVI: There were forty-five of us in a very small car. We could barely sit, but there wasn't enough room to lie down. And there was a young mother breast-feeding a baby. They had told us to bring food. Foolishly we hadn't brought water. No one had told us, and we suffered from a terrifying thirst even though it was winter. This was our first, tormenting pain, for five days. The temperature was below zero and our breath would freeze on the bolts and we would compete, scraping off the frost, full of mist as it was, to have a few drops with which to wet our lips. And the baby cried from morning to night because his mother had no milk left.

INTERVIEWER: What happened to the children and their mothers when [you arrived at Auschwitz]?

LEVI: Ah well, they were killed right away: out of the 650 of us on the train, 400–500 died the same evening we arrived or the next. They were immediately sorted out into the gas chambers, in these grim night scenes, with people screaming and yelling. They were yelling like I never heard before. They were yelling orders we didn't understand.... There was an officer ... who would ask each one of us, "Can you walk or not?" I consulted with the man next to me, a friend, from Padua. He was older than me and also in poor health. I told him I'll say I can work, and he answered, "You do as you please. For me, everything is the same." He had already abandoned any hope. In fact he said he couldn't work and didn't come into the camp. I never saw him again....

INTERVIEWER: And the food, how was it there?

LEVI: They gave us a minimal ration equivalent to about 1600–1700 calories a day, but ... there were thefts and we would always get less.... Now, as you know, a man who doesn't weigh much can live on 1600 calories without working, but just laying down. But we had to work, and in the cold, and at hard labor. Thus this ration of 1600 calories was a slow death by starvation. Later I read some research done by the Germans which said that a man could last, living off his own reserves and that diet, from two to three months.

INTERVIEWER: But in the concentration camps one would adapt to anything?

LEVI: Eh, the question is a curious one. The ones who adapted to everything are those who survived, but the majority did not adapt to everything, and died. They died because they were unable to adapt even to things which seem trivial to us. For example, they would throw a pair of mismatched shoes at you.... One was too tight, the other too big ... and those who were sensitive to infections would die. Die of shoes—of infected wounds which never healed. The feet would swell, rub up against the shoes and one had to go to the hospital. But at the hospital swollen feet were not considered a disease. They were too common so those who had swollen feet would be sent to the gas chambers....

INTERVIEWER: For the Italians, there was the language problem....

LEVI: Understanding one another is very important. Between the man who makes himself understood and that one who doesn't there is an abysmal difference: the first saves himself.... The majority of Italians deported with me died in the first few days for being unable to understand. They didn't understand the orders, but there was no tolerance for those who didn't understand. An order was given once, yelled, and that was it. Afterwards there were beatings....

INTERVIEWER: We are about to return to our hotel in Kracow. In your opinion, what did the holocaust represent for the Jewish people?

LEVI: It represented a turning point.... [It] was perhaps the first time in which anti-Semitism had been planned by the state, not only condoned or allowed as in the Russia of the Czars. And there was no escape: all of Europe had become a huge trap. It entailed a turning point, not only for European Jews, but also for American Jews, for the Jews of the entire world.

INTERVIEWER: In your opinion, another Auschwitz, another massacre like the one which took place forty years ago, could it happen again?

LEVI: Not in Europe, for reasons of immunity. Some kind of immunization must exist. It is [possible] that in fifty or a hundred years Nazism may be reborn in Germany; or Fascism in Italy.... But the world is much bigger than Europe. I also think that there are countries in which there would be the desire, but not the means. The idea is not dead. Nothing ever dies. Everything arises renewed.

INTERVIEWER: Is it possible to abolish man's humanity?

LEVI: Unfortunately, yes. Unfortunately, yes. And that is really the characteristic of the Nazi camps.... It is to abolish man's personality, inside and outside: not only of the prisoner, but also of the jailer. He too lost his personality in the concentration camp.... Thus it happened to all, a profound modification in their personality.... The memory of family had fallen into second place in face of urgent needs, of hunger, of the necessity to protect oneself against cold, beatings, fatigue ... all of this brought about some reactions which we could call animal-like. We were like work animals.

INTERVIEWER: Do you think that people today want to forget Auschwitz as soon as possible?

LEVI: Signs do exist that this is taking place: forgetting or even denying. This is meaningful. Those who deny Auschwitz would be ready to remake it.

Huw Jones/Getty Images

Auschwitz The Auschwitz Concentration Camp was a network of facilities in southern Poland built by the Nazis and included both slave labor camps and death camps. Over one million people were murdered here between 1941 and 1945, either worked to death, killed by torture and abuse, or exterminated with poison gas. The vast majority were Jews. New arrivals were mocked by the line above the gate: *Arbeit macht Frei*, "*Work makes you free.*"

The Nazi extermination of the Jews was methodical and cold-blooded. When a death camp administrator observed that people died faster if they were already short of breath when they entered the "shower rooms" that were actually gas chambers, he applied "the industrialist's logic," and forced Jewish captives to run to the showers in a panic, saving gas as well as time. Thus, thousands could be killed in a day. Scientific rationality and industrial progress were perverted to the most horrible of ends.

Not all Jews went meekly. The most militant resistance was the **Warsaw Ghetto Uprising**. Shortly after occupying Warsaw, the Nazis forced the city's Jews into a fenced-off ghetto where they found no work and very little food. In 1943, as the Nazis began to transport residents to the Treblinka death camp, the sixty thousand in the Warsaw ghetto rose up in armed revolt. Ten thousand paid with their lives, and the Nazis killed nearly all the rest at Treblinka.

Those Jews who somehow managed to escape were not assured of refuge. For decades the United States had imposed racial immigration quotas, limiting Jewish access even as refugees. In fact, in 1939, over nine hundred Jewish refugees seeking sanctuary from fascism were turned away at American ports and returned to Europe. (Many of them later died in the Holocaust.)

The government of the United Kingdom also restricted Jewish immigration, both to Britain and to its mandated territory of Palestine (see Chapter 27). In these desperate circumstances, the Zionist call for a secure Jewish sanctuary drew support from Jews and those sympathetic to their plight, though the British government, fearing an Arab uprising, continued to limit the number of refugees it would accept. Some Zionists, desperate to find a safe refuge for Europe's Jews, developed a guerrilla underground to aid illegal Jewish immigration to Palestine.

Warsaw Ghetto Uprising

(1943) Unsuccessful revolt of Polish Jews confined to the Warsaw ghetto, who rose up to resist being sent to the Treblinka death camp.

After 1939, however, it was almost impossible for Jews under Nazi rule to escape. Those who did so were helped by people such as Raoul Wallenberg, a Swedish diplomat who helped save thousands of Hungarian Jews from the death camps, and others like him who hid Jewish families or adopted Jewish children, putting their own lives and livelihoods at risk. But neither resistance nor the heroism of people who tried to aid their Jewish neighbors was enough to prevent Hitler from carrying out his plans.

In 1933, there had been 9.5 million Jews in Europe; by 1950, there were only 3.3 million left. In Poland and the western regions of the Soviet Union (Lithuania, Belorussia, and Ukraine), the Holocaust silenced the vibrant culture of the Ashkenazim (see Chapter 17). In what had been the largest concentration of Jews in the world, virtually none were left.

Along with 6 million Jews, the Nazis also slaughtered hundreds of thousands from other targeted groups. Viewing homosexuals as traitors to the master race, they imprisoned over one hundred thousand of them, and many died in concentration camps. Jehovah's Witnesses, who respect the primacy of their God by refusing to salute flags and other symbols of state authority, were also targeted. Nearly 80 percent of Europe's Roma were killed. The mentally and physically challenged of all ethnic groups were frequently sterilized and subjected to cruel medical experiments.

The Nazi death machine continued even after it became clear that the Allies would win the war. The mass graves in the camps sickened the Allied soldiers who liberated the emaciated survivors. Many Holocaust survivors found that their entire families had been killed. Sometimes, however, after scattering to different parts of the world after the war, survivors were lucky enough to find relatives who were still alive.

How could the Holocaust have happened? How could Hitler have attracted so many followers? The system certainly could not have worked without at least passive acquiescence from the German people. Moreover, anti-Semitism was strong all across Europe, and Nazi collaborators from France, Italy, Hungary, Poland, and elsewhere helped send Jews to the camps. Debates continue today about whether others could have done more to prevent the slaughter. For example, could religious leaders have played a greater role in fighting back against fascism? For her part Nancy Wake, appalled by the treatment of Jews in Austria before the war, did everything in her power to fight Nazi ideas. Too many people simply looked the other way.

Origins of the Cold War, 1945–1949

At the end of the European war, Soviet and American troops met each other joyfully at the Elbe River in Germany. Roosevelt envisioned that Allied cooperation would continue after the war in the new United Nations. Instead, the unlikely wartime partnership of liberal democracy and communism quickly dissolved, and the world divided into two hostile camps (see Map 30.2, page 909).

The New United Nations and Postwar Challenges, 1945–1947

At the Yalta Conference on the Black Sea, held in early 1945, the most important priority for ailing Roosevelt was to secure Joseph Stalin's cooperation in the founding of the **United Nations (UN)**. The UN included a General Assembly of sovereign nations and a Security Council of the major war allies:

United Nations (UN)

Organization established near the end of the Second World War to guarantee international peace and security through permanent diplomacy. A Security Council of five members, each with veto power, was created to enhance UN authority.

Britain, France, China, the Soviet Union, and the United States. Since each member of the council had veto power, its decisions could only be reached through consensus. It was hoped that the Security Council's special powers would make the UN more effective than the League of Nations.

The spirit of Allied cooperation that helped build the United Nations did not last. Roosevelt was realistic enough to know that he could not compel Stalin to give up the Red Army's control over eastern Europe, and Churchill was cynical about Stalin's assent to elections in Poland. The British and Americans had promised the Polish government-in-exile elections after the war. Stalin, however, knew that any Polish government chosen through free elections would be hostile to the Soviet Union and insisted that Poland must have a "friendly government." As soon as the war was over, it became clear that Stalin intended to assure that outcome by keeping his Red Army in occupation of Poland and installing a communist government to do his bidding.

By the summer of 1945, when Allied leaders met at Potsdam, the Soviet Red Army had occupied all of eastern Europe, and Roosevelt had died and been replaced by Truman. The Allies agreed on the plans for punishment of Germany, including a reduction in its size. But to American insistence that the peoples of Europe had the right to free elections, Stalin responded pragmatically, *"Everyone imposes his own system as far as his army can reach."* Europe was dividing into two opposing camps.

In 1946 Winston Churchill, now out of office, gave a speech in the United States in which he coined the term *iron curtain* to describe the imposition of communism in the Soviet sphere of influence:

> *From Stettin in the Baltic to Trieste in the Adriatic an iron curtain has descended across the Continent. Behind that line lie all the capitals of the ancient states of Central and Eastern Europe … and the populations around them … are subject, in one form or another, not only to Soviet influence but to a very high and in some cases increasing measure of control from Moscow.*

Ironically, in many of these countries local communists were actually a strong political force after the war, having played important roles in the antifascist resistance. But Stalin was not interested in working with them. He wanted control from the top down through men of unquestioned loyalty to Moscow, backed up by the continued presence of the Soviet army.

Nancy Wake witnessed one of the most tragic examples of Soviet domination when she traveled to Prague in 1947. Before the war, Czechoslovakia had been a prosperous society with a strong middle class and an emerging democratic tradition. But when Wake arrived to work at the British consulate, she found uneasiness: *"Although the Russians were not visible, the majority of Czechs I met used to walk around looking over their shoulders in case someone was listening to their conversation."* *

Czechs saw themselves as a bridge between East and West. Local communists fared well in a free election held in 1946 and were part of a coalition government. But Stalin wanted firmer control. In 1948, Czech communists loyal to Moscow seized power and ended their country's brief postwar experiment with democracy. *"Yes, the Germans had gone,"* Wake commented, *"but who would liberate the country from the liberators?"* *

---

*Excerpt from Nancy Wake, *The Autobiography of the Woman the Gestapo Called the White Mouse*, pp. 280, 285. 1985 Pan Publishing.

Sovfoto/Getty Images

Berlin, 1945 In April 1945, the Soviet army advanced on the German capital, supported by American and British aerial bombardment. While Adolf Hitler committed suicide in his subterranean bunker, Soviet soldiers hoisted the communist flag over the ruined city. The Red Army remained in occupation of most of eastern Europe after the war.

● **CONTEXT&CONNECTIONS** Czechoslovakia had been born through negotiations at the *Paris Peace Conference* that merged territories formerly within the German, Austrian, and Russian empires (Chapter 27). After German occupation during World War II and Soviet overrule from 1948 to 1989, Czechoslovakia finally emerged as a democratic country (see Chapter 31). Then the Czech and Slovak peoples decided to go their separate ways. In 1993, the country peacefully split into the Czech Republic and Slovakia, both of which have since become members of the European Union. ●

The United States, the Soviet Union, and the Origins of a Bipolar World

The United States and the Soviet Union were now bitter enemies, two potent "superpowers" dividing the globe in a bipolar struggle between Washington and Moscow. But full-scale war between them never developed. This was a "cold" war, often fought by proxies (smaller nations on either side) but never by the main adversaries (see Chapter 30). The deployment of nuclear weapons, first by the United States in 1945 and then by the Soviet Union in 1949, raised the stakes of total war beyond what any leader was willing to wager.

While Soviet ideology proclaimed the desirability and inevitability of socialist revolution on a global scale, Stalin was most concerned about protecting the Russian core of the Soviet Union. With large, exposed land frontiers, Soviet Russia needed buffer states along its vulnerable European and Asian frontiers. Having been invaded twice in two generations, the Soviets would not leave themselves open to another attack.

● **CONTEXT&CONNECTIONS** The Russian empire had a long history of "defensive expansion" to protect its extensive land frontiers. Both *Peter the Great* (Chapter 17) and *Catherine the Great* (Chapter 20) built territorial buffers around core Russian territories. Joseph Stalin followed the same strategy in eastern Europe, as would *Vladimir Putin* (Chapter 32) in his aggressive policies toward Georgia and Ukraine, and his efforts to build a Moscow-centered alliance for economic and strategic cooperation as an alternative to the European Union. ●

The U.S. outlook was quite different. After the war, Americans retained their characteristic optimism and idealism and stood ready to project their ideals—personal liberty, democracy, technological progress, and market-driven economic efficiency—onto the world stage. Some thought it was the beginning of an "American century," a belief reinforced by economic dominance in a world where the country's major industrial competitors had all suffered huge losses. But as Americans engaged the postwar world, they found impediments to this global vision: not everyone seemed to share American ideals. Moreover, cynical observers saw such idealism as a smokescreen for the self-interested expansion of American capitalism and American imperialism.

American policy was strongly influenced by the "Long Telegram" sent to Washington in 1946 by a U.S. diplomat in Moscow who advocated a policy of "containment." *"At the bottom of [the] Kremlin's neurotic view of world affairs,"* he wrote, *"is [the] traditional and instinctive Russian sense of insecurity."** If the Western powers held firm and maintained their unity, the author argued, Soviet expansionism could be contained.

Truman Doctrine

(1947) Declaration by President Harry S. Truman that the United States would aid all peoples threatened by communism. In reality, his doctrine of "containment" meant that the United States did not try to dislodge the Soviets from their sphere of influence.

The **Truman Doctrine** of 1947 embodied the concept of containment. The context was a civil war in Greece. Communist partisans who had fought German occupiers continued their fight for socialism at the war's end. The royalist Greek government and army were unable to put down this rebellion, and in 1947 Truman promised American aid to suppress the "terrorist activities" of the Greek communists, also promising aid to Greece's neighbor and traditional enemy Turkey and to any nation struggling for freedom: *"I believe that it must be the policy of the United States to support free peoples who are resisting attempted subjugation by armed minorities or by outside pressures."* Despite the implications of Truman's strong language, in fact Stalin conceded that Greece would be under Western control. For its part the United States took no direct action in response to the Soviet takeover of Czechoslovakia, implicitly acknowledging that Stalin would control *"wherever his army could reach."*

The Cold War stalemate was most apparent in Germany, where the Soviets occupied the eastern part of the country and the British, Americans, and French occupied the west. The capital city of Berlin, which lay within the zone of Soviet occupation, was itself divided into four sectors. With the breakdown of wartime collaboration, the Soviet Union and the Western powers never concluded an agreement on Germany's future. Instead, border tensions escalated in 1948 when the Soviets cut off access to Berlin by land and the United States responded by sending supplies to West Berlin by air. The Berlin Airlift was successful, but the crisis led, in 1949, to the creation of two separate states, the Federal Republic of Germany (or West Germany) and the German Democratic Republic (or East Germany). Each side blamed the other for preventing the reunification of Germany, but in reality neither France nor the Soviet Union was unhappy with the outcome, given that German aggression had twice in a generation posed a grave threat to their peace and security. As long as the Cold War lasted, the division of Germany was its symbolic battle line.

*George Kennan, the "Long Telegram," Moscow, 1946.

Meanwhile, the United States took an active role in rebuilding war-ravaged western Europe, most famously through the **Marshall Plan**. Although some Americans wanted the United States to withdraw from European affairs, Truman saw that the reconstruction of western European economies was essential. First, a revival of global trade, in which Europe would play a central role, was necessary for postwar American economic progress. Second, the communist parties of Italy and France were still quite strong, and continued economic difficulties might increase their popularity. In early 1948, the United States announced that $12 billion would be made available for European reconstruction.

In 1944, even before the war was over, the American-sponsored **Bretton Woods Conference** had formed a plan to prevent a repeat of the economic catastrophe that followed World War I. It created the World Bank to loan money to nations in need of a jumpstart, and the International Monetary Fund to provide emergency loans to nations in danger of insolvency. The Marshall Plan and the Bretton Woods institutions were designed to enhance the stability of a free-market international economic order. Critics pointed out that the U.S. government was creating international institutions that favored American-style capitalism.

The Soviet Union and its eastern European satellites were invited to join the Marshall Plan, but Stalin refused, aware that the socialist economic system could not bear integration with the market-based system of the West. Thus, after 1948 the Cold War division of Europe would be economic as well as political and military. While the U.S. sphere of influence consisted of market-based, industrialized economies, in the Soviet sphere, centralized planning shielded socialist economies from international market forces. To the weakest, least industrialized areas—Asian and African colonies, weak and dependent Latin American countries—the United States would promise development assistance, while the Soviet Union would advocate prosperity through socialist revolution.

Having undergone enormous industrial expansion during the war, the United States was in a much better position to aid its allies. The Soviet Union was itself in need of reconstruction. So while the United States offered the Marshall Plan, the Soviets exploited their eastern European satellites economically. Entire factories were dismantled and moved from eastern Germany to the Soviet Union. While the United States could use a combination of military strength, diplomacy, and economic aid to gain allies during the Cold War, the Soviet Union more often relied on direct military control.

Both sides also expanded their intelligence operations. The Soviet spy agency, known by the initials KGB, worked through local proxies, such as the East German *Stasi*, to maintain tight control over its satellites while trying to infiltrate Western political, military, and intelligence communities. The United States formed the Central Intelligence Agency (CIA) out of its wartime intelligence service, the first time a U.S. government agency was dedicated to collecting foreign intelligence. The CIA's first secret operation was to pay Italian journalists to write negative stories about communist parliamentary candidates.

● **CONTEXT&CONNECTIONS** The *Central Intelligence Agency (CIA)* (Chapter 30) would greatly expand the scope of its covert operations during the 1950s, acting to counter perceived Soviet influence in the postcolonial, developing world. Thus the CIA was involved in the overthrow of elected leaders in Guatemala (1953), Iran (1954), and the Democratic Republic of the Congo (1961). ●

As we will see in the next two chapters, the Cold War divided the globe. Outside Europe, communist regimes took power in the People's Republic of China, the

Marshall Plan

U.S. effort to rebuild war-ravaged Europe, named after the American secretary of state, George C. Marshall.

Bretton Woods Conference

(1944) Conference that led to creation of the World Bank and the International Monetary Fund, designed to secure international capitalism by preventing global economic catastrophes.

Democratic People's Republic of Korea, the Democratic Republic of Vietnam, and the Republic of Cuba. As the British and French empires declined in Asia and Africa, emerging new nations were often caught in the tension between the communist East and capitalist West. Some nations, such as India, were able to steer a middle course. But others, like Vietnam, Angola, Afghanistan, and Nicaragua, would be torn apart by Cold War rivalries. Two generations of humanity lived in the shadow of the Cold War, with the terrible knowledge that it could one day lead to a nuclear doomsday.

CONTEXT AND CONNECTIONS

Total War in World History

"The Second World War was the single most globalizing experience in human history." Hyperbole, perhaps, but it is difficult to think of any other series of events that have affected more people more deeply. The scale of death was unprecedented: more than 50 million all told. The number of lives sent onto entirely new trajectories in the first half of the 1940s is impossible to count. For Nancy Wake and many others who fought and survived, it was the defining period of their lives.

As the war years recede—Nancy Wake died in 2011, just weeks shy of her one-hundredth birthday—we are beginning to see the two world wars of the twentieth century as a single war during which hostilities were merely suspended. Total war was the unifying theme. Both the earlier and later conflicts mobilized civilian populations as never before and hinged on the ability to sustain industrial production. In both, imperial rulers brought colonized peoples into the war. And in both, an alliance including

Britain, France, the United States, and Russia battled a German-led coalition, including the Ottoman empire in the first war and Japan in the second.

The contrasts were in enlargement of scale, such as the development of a full-fledged theater of battle in East Asia during the second war. Technological developments were another contrast, with the rapidly moving fronts of the second war a marked difference from the static battle lines of the first, and aerial bombardment now a key to success rather than a marginal tactic. Partly for that reason, civilians were much more likely to be in the direct line of fire in World War II. From China, Spain, and Ethiopia, through the London blitz, the firebombing of Dresden, and the nuclear nightmare of Hiroshima and Nagasaki, the intensity and terror of civilian bombardment increased year by year.

The Holocaust was a benchmark of evil, though it was not altogether unique. Hitler's "final solution" followed

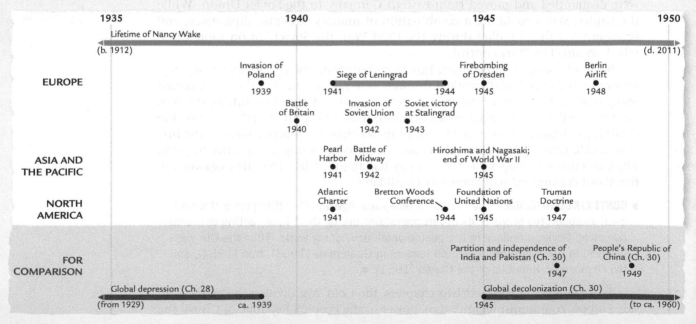

earlier twentieth-century genocides targeting the peoples of Southwest Africa and Armenians in the Ottoman empire (see Chapters 26 and 27), and it would not be the last attempt to annihilate a group of people, as later tragedies in Serbia and Rwanda would show (see Chapter 31). But the Nazis' ruthlessly methodical machinery of slaughter was unprecedented, a nightmare execution of the racist logic of Social Darwinism and the purported "struggle for existence" that had for generations infected the world (see Chapters 23 and 26). The Holocaust did not, of course, cure the world of racism. But Hitler's madness was a wake-up call for humanity: at a terrible cost, racism had lost much of its respectability.

Through both world wars, the international system had, in fact, been ordered around racial principles, with western Europeans in control of global empires that systematically denied rights of self-determination to colonized peoples in Africa and Asia. After 1945, that would quickly change. India, long the "jewel in the crown" of the British empire, became independent in 1947. In 1960, seventeen new African countries left the British and French empires to join the United Nations as sovereign states (see Chapter 30).

But for many of the world's people the road to freedom was complicated by the Cold War. The United States and the Soviet Union were unwilling to confront each other directly, since the prospect of nuclear annihilation was very real. Instead, the two sides sponsored proxy conflicts in Africa, Latin America, and Asia, undermining for decades the quest of the world's poorest and most disenfranchised for a better future. Still, however harsh the Cold War climate, the world's worst fears were never realized. Somehow, our species avoided nuclear self-destruction.

Key Terms

Nancy Wake (874)
Axis powers (875)
Winston Churchill (875)
Charles de Gaulle (877)
Atlantic Charter (878)
Pearl Harbor (878)

Allied powers (879)
Siege of Leningrad (879)
Battle of Stalingrad (880)
Hiroshima and Nagasaki (881)
Holocaust (885)
"Quit India" (888)

King's African Rifles (888)
Warsaw Ghetto Uprising (892)
United Nations (UN) (893)
Truman Doctrine (896)
Marshall Plan (897)
Bretton Woods Conference (897)

For Further Reference

Burleigh, Michael. *Third Reich: A New History*. New York: Hill and Wang, 2001.

Chang, Iris. *The Rape of Nanking*. New York: Basic Books, 2012.

Dower, John. *War Without Mercy: Race and Power in the Pacific War*. New York: Pantheon, 1987.

Dwork, Deborah, and Robert Jan Van Pelt. *Holocaust: A History*. New York: W. W. Norton, 2003.

Hopf, Ted. *Reconstructing the Cold War: The Early Years, 1945–1958*. New York: Oxford University Press, 2012.

Higgonet, Margaret, ed. *Behind the Lines: Gender and the Two World Wars*. New Haven: Yale University Press, 1989.

Iriye, Akira. *Power and Culture: The Japanese-American War, 1941–1945*. 2d ed. Cambridge, Mass.: Harvard University Press, 2004.

Keegan, John. *The Second World War*. New York: Penguin, 2005.

Larson, Erik. *In the Garden of Beasts*. New York: Crown, 2012.

Mercatante, Stephen. *Why Germany Nearly Won: A New History of the Second World War in Europe*. Westport, Conn.: Praeger, 2012.

Morgan, Philip. *The Fall of Mussolini: Italy, the Italians, and the Second World War*. New York: Oxford University Press, 2007.

Osborne, Richard. *World War II in Colonial Africa: The Death Knell of Colonialism*. Indianapolis: Riebel-Roque, 2011.

Thurston, Robert W., and Bernd Bonwetsch, eds. *The People's War: Responses to World War II in the Soviet Union*. Champaign: University of Illinois Press, 2000.

Wake, Nancy. *The White Mouse*. Melbourne: Macmillan, 1986.

Yahil, Leni. *The Holocaust: The Fate of European Jewry*. New York: Schocken, 1987.

MindTap

MindTap is a fully online, highly personalized learning experience built upon Cengage Learning content. MindTap combines student learning tools—readings, multimedia, activities, and assessments—into a singular Learning Path that guides students through the course.

30

The Cold War and Decolonization, 1949–1975

❯ The Cold War and Revolution, 1949–1962 (p. 903)

❯ Spheres of Influence: Old Empires and New Superpowers (p. 907)

❯ A Time of Upheaval, 1966–1974 (p. 921)

Stefano Rellandini/Reuters/Corbis

Ernesto ("Che") Guevara, 1960

In 1952, Alberto Granado and **Ernesto Guevara** (1928–1967), two Argentine students with promising futures in medicine, decided to take an ambitious road trip across South America on an aging motorcycle. At first, their motive was fun and adventure, *"not setting down roots in any land or staying long enough to see the substratum of things; the outer surface would suffice."* Soon, however, their encounters with Indians, peasants, and miners changed the nature of Guevara's quest:

We made friends with a [Chilean] couple.... In his simple, expressive language he recounted his three months in prison... his fruitless pilgrimage in search of work and his compañeros, mysteriously disappeared and said to be somewhere at the bottom of the sea. The couple, numb with cold, huddling against each other in the desert night, was a living representation of the proletariat in any part of the world. They had not one single miserable blanket to cover themselves with, so we gave them one of ours and Alberto and I wrapped the other around us as best we could.... The communism gnawing at [their] entrails was no more than a natural longing for something better, a protest against persistent hunger transformed into a love for this strange doctrine, whose essence they could never grasp but whose translation, "bread for the poor," was something which they understood and, more importantly, filled them with hope.*

---

*Ernesto Guevara, *The Motorcycle Diaries: Notes on a Latin American Journey*, ed. and trans. Alexandra Keeble (Melbourne: Ocean Press, 2003), pp. 75–78.

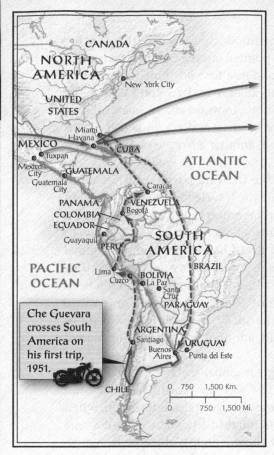

Che Guevara crosses South America on his first trip, 1951.

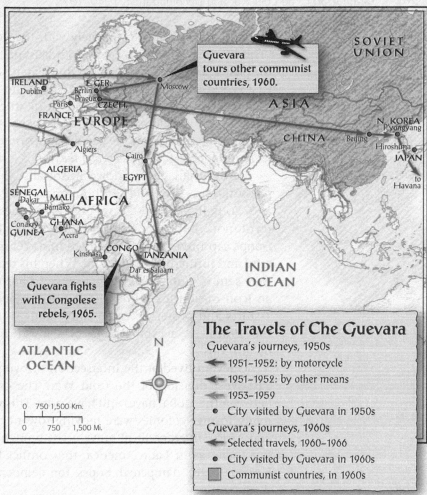

Guevara tours other communist countries, 1960.

Guevara fights with Congolese rebels, 1965.

The Travels of Che Guevara

Guevara's journeys, 1950s
- ← 1951–1952: by motorcycle
- ← 1951–1952: by other means
- ← 1953–1959
- • City visited by Guevara in 1950s

Guevara's journeys, 1960s
- ← Selected travels, 1960–1966
- • City visited by Guevara in 1960s
- ▨ Communist countries, in 1960s

B y the time Ernesto returned to Buenos Aires, he was a different man and on the path to becoming "Che," the most charismatic of twentieth-century revolutionaries.

It took one more trip to change Guevara's path from that of an Argentine doctor to that of a professional revolutionary. After completing his degree, he set out on another road trip, this time with heightened political consciousness. While in Guatemala in 1954, he witnessed the overthrow of its democratically elected socialist government by a right-wing rebel army organized and financed by the United States. Fearing arrest, Guevara fled to Mexico, where he met a group of Cuban exiles determined to overthrow their own dictator. Che joined them as a soldier and military commander, using guerrilla tactics such as quick raids and surprise ambushes to defeat the Cuban army. After the success of the Cuban Revolution in 1959, Che's fame spread around the world.

Ernesto Guevara

(1928–1967) Argentinean socialist and revolutionary, called "Che," who played a crucial role in the Cuban Revolution. After serving as a Cuban government minister, he left to organize guerrilla campaigns in the Congo and Bolivia. He was executed in 1967 by the Bolivian army.

Guevara identified completely with the downtrodden, especially those in the "Third World." In 1952, a French journalist had pointed out the tripartite division of the postwar world. The capitalist United States and its allies constituted the wealthy First World, and the socialist Soviet Union and its allies were the Second World. The Third World, lacking in industry and with little voice in world affairs, made up two-thirds of the world's population. Guevara chose to speak and act on behalf of this disempowered majority, the people Frantz Fanon, another advocate of Third World revolution, called *"the wretched of the earth."*

Rather than settling down in socialist Cuba, Guevara pursued his dream of revolution in Africa and South America. In 1965, he traveled to the Congo and in 1967 to Bolivia, in both cases organizing guerrilla armies in the name of socialist revolution. But there were to be no more glorious victories: in 1967, Bolivian troops captured Che and executed him. Yet in death he became even more powerful and influential than in life. When his remains were discovered in 1998, they were sent to Cuba, where Che received a hero's burial. By then he had long been an icon of youth culture. The familiar image of "Che," reproduced on endless T-shirts and posters, became emblematic of the social and political idealism of the 1960s. As a symbol, Che was loved and admired, or hated and feared, by millions.

Guevara lived at the intersection of two great global struggles. One was the East-West division of the Cold War. The other was the North-South division between the global haves and have-nots. This was the age of decolonization, when many former colonies were moving toward national independence. Across Asia and Africa, mass political movements brought the possibility of positive change. But there, as in Latin America, the conflict between the Soviet Union and the United States dampened hopes for democracy and reinforced trends toward dictatorship.

This chapter explores the turbulent quarter century between 1949 and 1974, when dozens of new nations were born from the dissolution of European empires; when communist revolutionaries took power in mainland China; when the United States and the Soviet Union, the new "superpowers" of the Cold War era, faced off across a deep nuclear chasm; when antidemocratic political forces in strategic parts of the world found sponsorship from the American and Soviet governments; and when young people dreamed of transforming the world. For many, Che Guevara symbolized their dreams and their disappointments.

FOCUS QUESTIONS

> What were the implications of successful revolutions in China and Cuba for the Cold War rivalry of the United States and the Soviet Union?

> How were democratization and decolonization movements in the mid-twentieth century affected by the Cold War?

> What was the role of youth in the global upheavals of 1965–1974?

The Cold War and Revolution, 1949–1962

By the 1950s, the United States and Soviet Union were amassing nuclear weapons many times more powerful than those dropped on Hiroshima and Nagasaki. Since any direct conflict between them threatened mutual annihilation, both sides were cautious not to push the other too far. Official U.S. policy remained one of "containment," of preventing an expansion of the Soviet sphere of influence but not intervening within it. Insults, propaganda, and espionage characterized U.S.-Soviet relations.

While the Cold War in Europe was a standoff, communist revolutions elsewhere increased the potential sphere of Soviet influence. In 1959, ten years after Mao Zedong had declared the foundation of the People's Republic of China, Fidel Castro and Che Guevara led a rebel army into Havana and founded a socialist government in Cuba, an island just 90 miles (145 km) from Florida. From the perspective of anticommunists in the United States and elsewhere, the "Soviet menace" was increasing.

The People's Republic of China, 1949–1962   Almost immediately after Japan's defeat, the competition between Chiang Kai-shek's Guomindang and Mao Zedong's Chinese Communist Party for control of China resumed (see Chapter 28). By the time war ended in 1949, the Communists controlled the People's Republic of China on the mainland, and Chiang Kai-shek and his Nationalist followers fled to the island of Taiwan, where they established the Republic of China (see Map 30.1).

The Communists succeeded even though the Nationalists started with a larger army, a stockpile of weapons supplied by the Allies during World War II, and control of China's largest cities. Mao's tough, disciplined army had cultivated support among the Chinese peasantry while fighting Japanese invaders. Mao used this popular base to advantage, telling his soldiers to *swim like fishes in the sea* of rural China, camouflaging their activities amid the routines of village life. Since the People's Liberation Army treated Chinese peasants with greater respect than Chiang's Guomindang, they rode mass support to success.

Once in power, the Communists revolutionized China from the bottom up. They organized peasants into agricultural cooperatives, expanded educational opportunities, indoctrinated young people in youth organizations guided by the party, and enrolled workers in state-sponsored trade unions. Within the unions, the army, and other mass organizations, mandatory "thought reform" sessions focused on the study of "Mao Zedong Thought." Those accused of deviation from socialist thought were shamed and forced to publicly confess their "errors."

The Korean War (1950–1953) put the new People's Republic of China into direct conflict with the United States. After North Korea attacked South Korea, the United States rushed to defend its ally. The mainland Chinese government, fearing that the United States intended to attack them as well, threw its massive forces into battle to reinforce the north. In the end, the south fended off invasion, but stalemate ensued along the demilitarized zone that separated the communist regime in North Korea, which allowed no freedom at all, from the stern authoritarian regime in South Korea, which allowed very little.

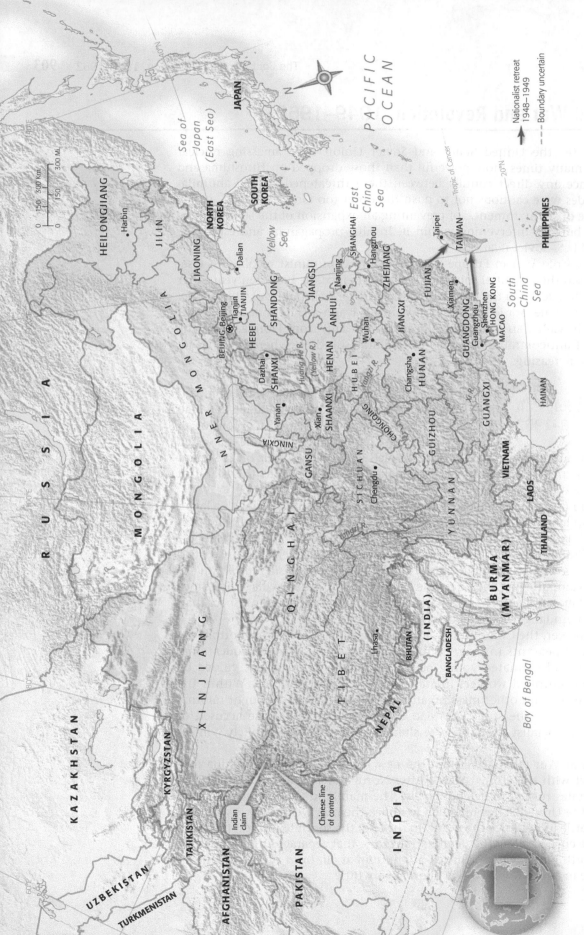

Map 30.1 China and Taiwan After World War II, the Communist forces of Mao Zedong took the offensive against the Guomindang, or Nationalist army, of Chiang Kai-shek. They drove the Nationalists off the mainland to the island of Taiwan, and Mao created the People's Republic of China on October 1, 1949. The Communists and Nationalists agreed that there was only "one China," and their continuing animosity became another zone of conflict in the global Cold War. Far to the west, tensions have arisen from border disputes between China and India.

● **CONTEXT&CONNECTIONS** South Korean and North Korean societies diverged sharply over time. South Korea, a very poor country in 1960, became a "First World" consumer society after decades of export-led economic development (see Chapter 31). After liberal reforms and free elections in 1987, South Korea became a democratic society as well. North Korea, in contrast, became more isolated after the end of the Cold War, the paranoid Kim family dynasty refusing even modest market reforms while rigidly rejecting political liberalization (see Chapter 32). ●

Initially, the People's Republic of China followed Soviet-style economic policies of state-run heavy industry and collective farming. In 1953, the Chinese adopted a Five-Year Plan and sent engineers and state planners to Russia for training. But the results were disappointing. Not only was the growth of production slower than Mao expected, but the dull, bureaucratic socialism of the U.S.S.R. did little to inspire him. Mao felt that the fire was going out of the revolution.

In 1956, Mao launched a public call for new ideas, using the phrase *"Let a hundred flowers bloom."* China's intellectuals responded by openly criticizing the Communist Party, and even Mao himself. Either the criticism was more than Mao had expected, or perhaps he had intended all along to trick opponents into the open, but during the savage repression of 1957, intellectuals were arrested, imprisoned, and exiled. Independent thinking was now a "rightist" deviation.

Having purged such "rightists," Mao still saw the Communist Party as divided into two factions, which he labeled "red" and "expert." The "experts" managing collectivization and industrial development were becoming an elite cut off from the masses. It was the "red" leadership, emphasizing socialist willpower rather than technical ability, that would rapidly bring about socialist prosperity by unleashing the true revolutionary potential of China's peasants and workers. The people, in Mao's thinking, could move mountains.

In 1958, Mao launched the **Great Leap Forward** decreeing that the agricultural collectives should be harnessed for industrial development. Rather than relying on large steel factories, revolutionaries would set up small furnaces all across the country. The "masses" were directed to pour all their energy and enthusiasm into communal production. Meanwhile, property rights were restricted, and peasants lost access to the small plots they had relied on to feed their families.

The Great Leap Forward was disastrous. The steel produced in small communal furnaces was virtually useless, and food production suffered as farm workers wasted their energies on Mao's inefficient scheme. As many as 30 million people died in the resulting famine. By 1961, the failure of the Great Leap Forward led the more pragmatic "experts" in the Communist Party to reduce Mao's authority behind the scenes (still publicly acknowledging his leadership) while reinstating rationality to economic planning.

Still, Mao's belief in the power of revolutionary enthusiasm would inspire a younger generation of revolutionaries. Che Guevara was among those attracted to the Chinese model as an alternative to both capitalism and the stodgy Soviet model of technocratic socialism.

Great Leap Forward (1958) Mao Zedong's attempt to harness the revolutionary zeal of the Chinese masses for rapid industrialization. The result was a massive economic collapse and millions of deaths from famine.

The Cuban Revolution and the Cuban Missile Crisis

In the 1950s, Cuba was an island of contrasts. Its capital, Havana, was famous for its beaches and nightclubs, where musicians fused African and Latin traditions. But Cuba's vibrant culture obscured a darker underside. The American Mafia controlled Havana's casinos, prostitution flourished, and the Cuban dictator Fulgencio Batista, supported by American business interests, allowed no democratic freedoms. Most Cubans, the poorest of them descendants of slaves, had no access to good employment, health care, or education.

● **CONTEXT&CONNECTIONS** Cuba did not abolish slavery until 1878 (see Chapter 25) and Afro-Cubans, while making enduring cultural contributions, were still at the bottom of Cuban society. For many of them, socialism brought access for the first time to education and health care. ●

Fidel Castro

(b. 1926) Cuban prime minister from 1959 to 1976 and president from 1976 to 2008. Led the successful Cuban Revolution in 1959, after which his nationalization policies led to deteriorating relations with the United States and increasing dependence on Soviet support.

Central Intelligence Agency (CIA)

U.S. federal agency created in 1947 whose responsibilities include coordinating intelligence activities abroad as well as conducting covert operations—for example, against the Soviet Union and its allies during the Cold War.

Cuban Missile Crisis

Tense 1962 confrontation between the United States and the Soviet Union over placement of nuclear missiles in Cuba. A compromise led to withdrawal of Soviet missiles from Cuba and of American missiles from Turkey.

Fidel Castro (b. 1926), like Ernesto Guevara, was an idealistic young man who renounced middle-class privilege in the name of revolution. Imprisoned in 1953 for leading an attack on an army barracks, he went into exile in Mexico City after his release in 1955. There he formed a deep friendship with Che Guevara, newly arrived from Guatemala, where the overthrow of the democratically elected government had been coordinated by the U.S. **Central Intelligence Agency (CIA)**. Che joined Castro's small rebel band for military training.

In 1956, Castro and Guevara left Mexico by boat for Cuba, finding sanctuary in the island's Sierra Maestra Mountains. Gradually they stockpiled ammunition by attacking police stations and military barracks while attracting recruits from the local population, whose assistance enabled them to outmaneuver their government pursuers. During two years of hard fighting, Che's medical background proved useful in tending wounded colleagues, but his most important role was as commander and tactician. Conditions were ruthless, and Guevara had no second thoughts about executing suspected government agents without trial or legal defense. Guevara himself often pulled the trigger. By 1958, the rebels were poised to attack Havana, and on New Year's Day 1959 Batista fled when Castro's forces marched triumphantly into the capital.

The new Cuban leader toured Washington and New York, seeking both public and official support. But relations with the United States deteriorated after Cuba's Agrarian Reform Law nationalized land owned by American corporations. Both corporate lobbyists and Cold War hawks soon portrayed Castro as a Soviet threat on America's doorstep, as the pro-Batista forces that had fled to the United States lobbied for an American-backed invasion. Faced with counter-revolution, Castro's government focused on "defense of the revolution" rather than protection of civil liberties. While neither Castro nor Guevara had ever joined the Cuban Communist Party, preferring a more populist approach over rigid Marxist orthodoxy, conflict with the United States gave them little option but to seek Soviet protection. As tensions increased, the Eisenhower administration in the United States drew up plans for invasion.

In the spring of 1961, a U.S.-sponsored group of Cuban exiles stormed ashore at the island's Bay of Pigs. The new American president, John F. Kennedy (in office 1961–1963), having had strong doubts about their prospects, had given only lukewarm support. Their invasion was a debacle and validated Castro's distrust of U.S. intentions. Meanwhile, the United States had placed an economic embargo on Cuba, making diplomacy and compromise all but impossible.

In the fall of 1962, tensions climaxed during the **Cuban Missile Crisis**. Convinced that the United States would never let his socialist experiment proceed in peace, Castro developed ever-closer ties with the Soviet Union. Nikita Khrushchev (KHROOS-chev), Soviet premier and First Secretary of the Communist Party (in office 1953–1964), took advantage of the situation to secretly ship nuclear missiles to Cuba. Khrushchev departed dangerously from the Soviets' usual policy of focusing on the security of their own borders and avoiding provocations within the American sphere of influence. When American surveillance aircraft detected the missiles, Kennedy presented an ultimatum: withdraw the missiles or court annihilation. On the brink of nuclear conflict, both sides blinked: Khrushchev agreed to remove Soviet missiles from Cuba, Kennedy quietly agreed to remove U.S. missiles from Turkey, and the world's people breathed a sigh of relief.

To help Cuba withstand the American trade embargo, the Soviets agreed to buy the island's entire sugar output at above-market prices and to subsidize the socialist transformation of the island with cheap fuel and agricultural machinery. By the mid-1960s, Cubans were better fed and better housed than they had been before the revolution; they also had free access to basic health care and were more likely to be able to read and write.

But underlying economic problems remained. As was common in Latin America since colonial times, Cuba had been subject to economic dependency (see Chapter 25), exporting agricultural produce (mostly sugar and tobacco) while importing higher-valued industrial goods. With the Soviet Union as an economic patron, Cuba's reliance on agricultural exports was as strong as ever. Economic development was further hampered by Cuba's Soviet-style command economy, characterized by bureaucratic inefficiency and low worker morale.

When Cuban workers agitated for higher wages, Che Guevara, as minister for industry, told them to be content with knowing that their hard work supported the glorious cause of socialism. Himself willing to work long hours for no personal gain, Guevara thought that others should do the same. But without material rewards for workers or incentives to inspire creativity and entrepreneurship, the Cuban economy settled into lethargy. Fidel Castro's verbose four-hour speeches exhorting Cubans to rally around the revolution did nothing to help workers facing shortages of basic goods.

In Cuba, as earlier in France and Russia, leaders faced with counter-revolution set aside early promises of democratic liberties and equated dissent with treason. Castro's government viewed all opposition to its policies as emanating from the United States and the hostile community of Cuban émigrés in Florida. Authorities on the island executed hundreds and sent thousands to prison labor camps based on the Soviet model. Guevara regarded such repression as the justifiable cost of war against capitalism and American imperialism.

Still, Guevara was bored by the endless meetings and plodding pace of government. A romantic revolutionary idealist, he left for Africa in 1965 to pursue his dreams on a global stage.

Spheres of Influence: Old Empires and New Superpowers

The Cuban Missile Crisis illustrated the dangers of one superpower intervening in the other's sphere of influence. Usually such interventions took place within a superpower's own strategic domain, as when the United States sponsored the overthrow of the Guatemalan government in 1954 or Soviet tanks crushed a prodemocracy uprising in Hungary in 1956.

But much of the world lay outside either sphere. In Asia and Africa, decolonization movements were supplanting European empires. Where former imperial powers like Britain and France managed to negotiate relatively smooth transitions, especially in Africa, they often maintained strong neocolonial influence even after independence. Elsewhere, however, in the power vacuum created by the decline of European empires, new African and Asian nations left the European orbit only to become ensnared in Cold War tensions. Some, like the Congo and Vietnam, were pulled apart in the process.

Recognizing that danger, in 1955 a group of African and Asian leaders met to discuss ways to defend their sovereignty. Their goal in founding the Non-Aligned Movement was both to avoid neocolonial influence from Europe and, by refusing to undertake formal alliances with either the Soviet Union or the United States, to sidestep superpower intervention in their affairs. It was not a simple goal to achieve, as U.S. entry into the former French zone of warfare in Vietnam would show.

Superpower Interventions, 1953–1956

During the Cold War, the United States allied with the European democracies and Turkey in the North Atlantic Treaty Organization (NATO), and the Soviet Union countered with the Warsaw Pact allying eastern European nations under its sway. Both superpowers presented themselves as champions of freedom. The Soviets, identifying colonialism and imperialism as the main barriers to liberation, supported nationalists and socialists in the Third World who were fighting to throw off European or American domination. But Moscow would not tolerate similar liberation movements within its own sphere, where the Soviets brutally crushed movements toward self-determination and freedom of speech, association, or religion (see Map 30.2).

In eastern Europe, secret police networks kept people from openly expressing anticommunist or anti-Soviet views. In East Germany, for example, the *Stasi* planted informers at all levels of society and encouraged neighbors to spy on neighbors. Hopes for reform came after the death of Stalin in 1953 and Nikita Khrushchev's denunciation of Stalinism's excesses at a Communist Party congress. Still, though Khrushchev preached limited reform, he would not tolerate popular movements for change.

In 1953, when demonstrators in East Berlin demanded better wages and working conditions, the communist authorities cracked down, plainly showing that communist rule was based more on Soviet coercion than popular legitimacy. Over the next eight years, thousands of East Berliners fled to the West. Finally, in 1961, East Germany constructed the Berlin Wall to stem the flow of skilled laborers, doctors, and engineers to West Germany, where livings standards were much higher. The Wall symbolized Cold War confrontation for the next 28 years.

The predominantly Catholic people of Poland detested the pro-Moscow government imposed on them by Stalin, especially the official atheism of the communist state. In 1956, a religious gathering attended by a million Poles turned into an antigovernment demonstration. Here the Soviet government compromised, allowing reforms such as an end to the collectivization of agriculture and some religious freedom. But it was clear that attempts to further weaken Poland's ties to the Soviet Union would not be tolerated.

The **Hungarian Uprising** tragically confirmed Soviet intolerance for real change. In 1956 Hungarian students, factory workers, and middle-class professionals rose up to protest the Soviet-imposed communist dictatorship. The Hungarian government collapsed, and though leaders of the new provisional government feared a Soviet invasion, they expected support from the Western democracies.

Hungarian Uprising (1956) Popular revolt against the Soviet-controlled government of Hungary, leading to a Soviet invasion and reimposition of communist authority.

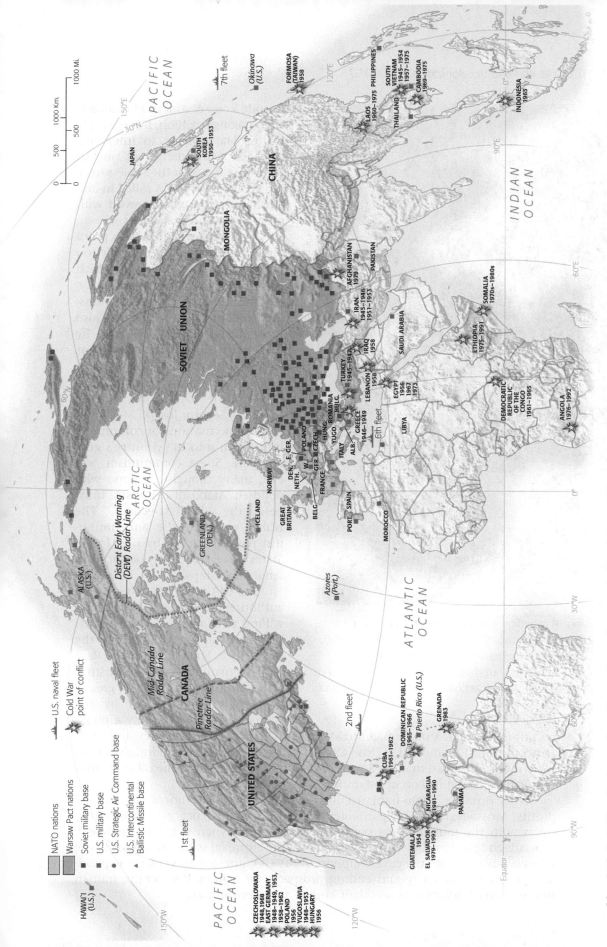

Map 30.2 Cold War Confrontations Two military alliances, the North Atlantic Treaty Organization (NATO) led by the United States, and the Warsaw Pact dominated by the Soviet Union, were the principal antagonists in the Cold War. Fearful of mutual nuclear annihilation, however, they never engaged in direct combat. Instead, the Cold War turned hot in proxy struggles around the world.

Legend:

NATO nations
Warsaw Pact nations
■ Soviet military base
■ U.S. military base
● U.S. Strategic Air Command base
▲ U.S. Intercontinental Ballistic Missile base

⚓ U.S. naval fleet
✪ Cold War point of conflict

CZECHOSLOVAKIA 1948, 1968
EAST GERMANY 1948–1949, 1953, 1958–1962
POLAND 1956
YUGOSLAVIA 1948–1953
HUNGARY 1956

HAWAI'I (U.S.)

Distant Early Warning (DEW) Radar Line
Mid-Canada Radar Line
Pinetree Radar Line

ALASKA (U.S.)
CANADA
UNITED STATES

1st fleet
2nd fleet
6th fleet
7th fleet

GREENLAND (DEN.)
ICELAND
NORWAY
GREAT BRITAIN
DEN.
NETH.
BELG.
FRANCE
SPAIN
PORT.
W. GER.
E. GER.
POLAND
CZECH.
HUNG.
ITALY
ALB.
YUGO.
ROMANIA
BULG.
GREECE 1946–1949

Azores (Port.)

MOROCCO
LIBYA
EGYPT 1956 1967 1973
SAUDI ARABIA
TURKEY 1945–1947
IRAQ 1958
LEBANON 1958
IRAN 1945–1946 1951–1953
AFGHANISTAN 1979
PAKISTAN

DEMOCRATIC REPUBLIC OF THE CONGO 1961–1965
ETHIOPIA 1975–1991
SOMALIA 1970s–1980s
ANGOLA 1976–1992

SOVIET UNION
MONGOLIA
CHINA
JAPAN
SOUTH KOREA 1950–1953
Okinawa (U.S.)
FORMOSA (TAIWAN) 1958
PHILIPPINES
LAOS 1960–1975
THAILAND
SOUTH VIETNAM 1945–1954 1957–1975
CAMBODIA 1969–1975
INDONESIA 1965

GUATEMALA 1954
EL SALVADOR 1979–1992
NICARAGUA 1981–1990
PANAMA
CUBA 1961–1962
DOMINICAN REPUBLIC 1965–1966
Puerto Rico (U.S.)
GRENADA 1983

PACIFIC OCEAN
ARCTIC OCEAN
ATLANTIC OCEAN
INDIAN OCEAN

Equator
30°N
60°N
60°E
90°E
120°E
150°E
30°W
60°W
90°W
120°W
150°W

0 500 1000 Mi.
0 500 1000 Km.

Laszlo Almasi/Reuters/Landov

The Hungarian Uprising A rebellion against their communist regime brought thousands of Hungarians onto the streets of Budapest in 1956, provoking a Soviet invasion. The Hungarians showed great courage in confronting Soviet tanks and troops, but they were bitterly disappointed when the United States and NATO provided no military support for their freedom struggle.

Despite Voice of America broadcasts encouraging rebellion, however, the United States failed to intervene, considering the danger of nuclear confrontation with the Soviets to be too great. Soviet tanks rolled in and crushed the Hungarian revolt with mass arrests and executions.

Americans were quick to point out the obvious contradiction between Soviet rhetoric, which equated socialism with democracy, and the Soviet practice of suppressing freedom. But U.S. practices also contradicted American ideals. By the early 1950s, Cold War tensions were leading many Americans to develop an almost paranoid fear of the Soviet Union, an attitude stoked by Senator Joseph McCarthy with his accusations of communist infiltration into the country's government. Since communism was evil, many thought, anyone who opposed Marxism-Leninism must be on the side of "freedom." The reality was that the anticommunist regimes backed by the United States were frequently authoritarian dictatorships.

The CIA often covertly assisted authoritarian leaders who were willing to support American interests. Iran was one example. In the early 1950s, Shah Muhammad Reza Pahlavi (pahl-AH-vee), a constitutional monarch, aspired to greater power. He was checked by the Iranian parliament, led by a popular prime minister, Muhammad Mossadegh (MOH-sah-DEHK). Pahlavi, an ardent anticommunist, cultivated a close alliance with the Eisenhower administration, which was concerned that the Soviet Union still had designs on the oil-rich lands of northern Iran it had occupied during World War II.

With Britain's Anglo-Iranian Oil Company reaping the lion's share of oil profits, Mossadegh and his parliamentary allies tried to renegotiate Iran's contracts with the multinational petroleum companies. When negotiations failed, Mossadegh threatened in 1953 to nationalize the entire oil sector. In response the Iranian military, with the covert support of the CIA, arrested Mossadegh, expanding the shah's authority and ending prospects for a more democratic Iranian future. Many Iranians now saw their king as an American puppet.

The next year, the United States similarly undermined democracy in Guatemala. Long ruled by authoritarian dictators, Guatemala had a typically dependent export economy, dominated by the United Fruit Company, which owned vast banana plantations, the only railroad, the only port, and the country's telephone system. A small Guatemalan elite benefited, but the country was a study in inequality: 72 percent of the land was owned by 2 percent of the population.

During World War II, reformist army officers had seized control and organized elections. In 1946, the new democratic government planned for land and labor reform. After another free election in 1950, the new president, **Jacobo Arbenz** (1913–1971), reaffirmed those reformist policies, arguing that democracy could not be built on the foundation of such stark social and economic inequality. The Eisenhower administration, believing the Arbenz government had been penetrated by Soviet agents, invoked the "domino theory," claiming that the "loss" of Guatemala would lead to communist victories elsewhere in the Americas. United Fruit used high-level government connections to lobby for action, and the CIA organized and financed a rebel movement, which overthrew Arbenz in 1954. Guatemala's brief experiment with democracy was over, as the country reverted to a dictatorship in the caudillo style (see Chapter 22). That was when Ernesto Guevara, an eyewitness to the U.S.-sponsored overthrow, had dedicated himself to revolution.

Jacobo Arbenz

(1913–1971) President of Guatemala from 1951 to 1954. A moderate socialist, Arbenz enacted comprehensive land reforms that angered Guatemalan elites and U.S. corporations. He was deposed by rebel forces backed by the United States.

Decolonization and Neocolonialism in Africa, 1945–1964

During World War II, Africans had become more aware of the wider world and increasingly dissatisfied with their colonial status. The French, British, and Belgians underestimated African sentiments; entering the 1950s, colonial officials still thought they were in Africa to stay.

Europeans' refusal to recognize the power of African nationalism was strongest in the settler colonies, especially South Africa, where after 1948 the Afrikaner-dominated National Party instituted **apartheid**, or "separateness." Already deeply entrenched, racial segregation now became more systematic and more centrally dictated than ever before. Over the next four decades, apartheid institutions would control where black South Africans could live and work, what they could (and could not) study, who they could love and marry, and even whether they should even be counted as "South Africans."

Elsewhere, however, by 1960 nationalist movements had freed most of the continent from colonial rule and created many new African nations (see Map 30.3). The Swahili word *uhuru* (oo-HOO-roo), "freedom," was heard around the world, and **Kwame Nkrumah** (1909–1972), the first president of independent Ghana after 1957, became an international symbol of African aspirations and Pan-Africanism.

The economic structures of colonialism remained, however, making true independence difficult. Economic development required capital and expertise, and both had to be imported. This situation created ideal conditions for neocolonialism: the continuation of European dominance even after independence had been attained.

apartheid

"Separateness" in the Afrikaner language, starting in 1948 this was the official policy of the white government of South Africa, enforcing strict racial segregation in all spheres of life, including work, education, and place of residence. Strongly opposed by the African National Congress, apartheid ended when democratic, non-racial elections were held in 1994.

Kwame Nkrumah

(1909–1972) One of the most prominent postwar African nationalists, he emphasized Pan-African unity while leading Ghana to independence in 1957.

● **CONTEXT&CONNECTIONS** As a Pan-Africanist, Kwame Nkrumah believed that only continental unity, a "United States of Africa," could empower Africans to resist the neocolonial control of Europe and the United States. Similarly, in a different era, the South American liberator *Simón Bolívar* (key term in Chapter 22) had sponsored the creation of Gran Colombia to assure true independence. Neither leader was successful in promoting broader territorial unity as protection against outside intrusion. ●

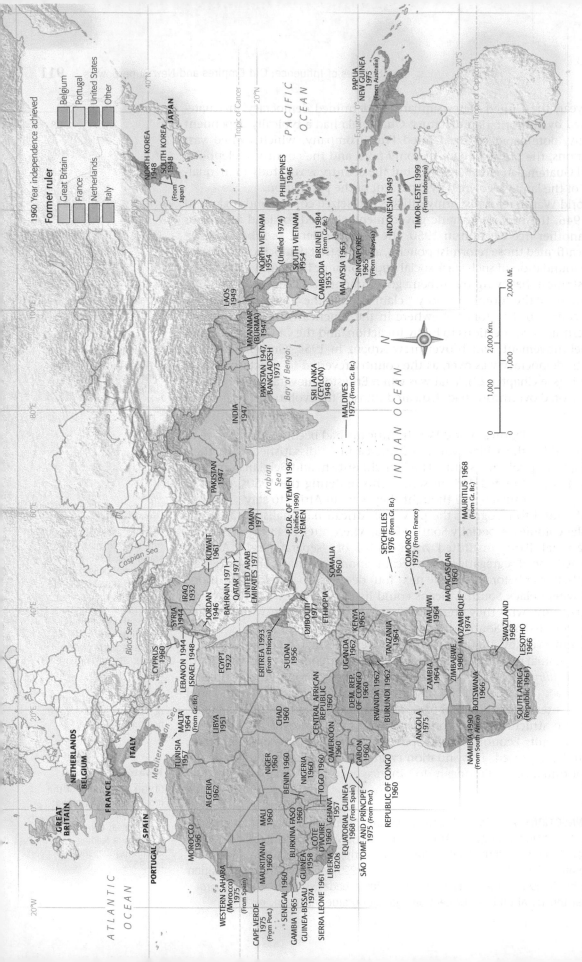

Map 30.3 Decolonization In the three decades following Indian independence in 1947, the European colonial empires in Asia and Africa unraveled, adding many new "Third World" representatives to the United Nations. Their aspirations toward dignity and development were frequently thwarted, however, by Cold War politics, continued Western economic domination, poor leadership, and ethnic and religious rivalries. In the twenty-first century, stronger economic growth has come to some of these nations of the Global South.

Former ruler

	1960 Year independence achieved
Great Britain	Belgium
France	Portugal
Netherlands	United States
Italy	Other

ATLANTIC OCEAN

GREAT BRITAIN
NETHERLANDS
BELGIUM
FRANCE
ITALY
PORTUGAL
SPAIN

Mediterranean Sea
Black Sea
Caspian Sea

MOROCCO 1956
WESTERN SAHARA 1975 (Morocco) (From Spain)
ALGERIA 1962
TUNISIA 1957
MALTA 1964 (From Gr. Br.)
LIBYA 1951
CYPRUS 1960
SYRIA 1944
LEBANON 1944
ISRAEL 1948
JORDAN 1946
IRAQ 1932
EGYPT 1922
KUWAIT 1961
BAHRAIN 1971
QATAR 1971
UNITED ARAB EMIRATES 1971
OMAN 1971
P.D.R. OF YEMEN 1967 (Unified 1990) YEMEN

CAPE VERDE 1975 (From Port.)
MAURITANIA 1960
SENEGAL 1960
GAMBIA 1965
GUINEA-BISSAU 1974
GUINEA 1958
SIERRA LEONE 1961
LIBERIA 1820s
CÔTE D'IVOIRE 1960
GHANA 1957
BURKINA FASO 1960
MALI 1960
NIGER 1960
BENIN 1960
TOGO 1960
NIGERIA 1960
CHAD 1960
SUDAN 1956
ERITREA 1993 (From Ethiopia)
DJIBOUTI 1977
ETHIOPIA
SOMALIA 1960

CAMEROON 1960
EQUATORIAL GUINEA 1968 (From Spain)
SÃO TOMÉ AND PRÍNCIPE 1975 (From Port.)
GABON 1960
CENTRAL AFRICAN REPUBLIC 1960
REPUBLIC OF CONGO 1960
DEM. REP. OF CONGO 1960
UGANDA 1962
KENYA 1963
RWANDA 1962
BURUNDI 1962
TANZANIA 1964

ANGOLA 1975
ZAMBIA 1964
MALAWI 1964
MOZAMBIQUE 1974
ZIMBABWE 1980
NAMIBIA 1990 (From South Africa)
BOTSWANA 1966
SOUTH AFRICA (Republic 1961)
SWAZILAND 1968
LESOTHO 1966
MADAGASCAR 1960

SEYCHELLES 1976 (From Gr. Br.)
COMOROS 1975 (From France)
MAURITIUS 1968 (From Gr. Br.)

Arabian Sea
PAKISTAN 1947
INDIA 1947
Bay of Bengal
SRI LANKA (CEYLON) 1948
MALDIVES 1975 (From Gr. Br.)

INDIAN OCEAN

PAKISTAN 1947, BANGLADESH 1973
MYANMAR (BURMA) 1947
LAOS 1949
NORTH VIETNAM 1954 (Unified 1974)
SOUTH VIETNAM 1954
CAMBODIA 1953
MALAYSIA 1963
BRUNEI 1984 (From Gr. Br.)
SINGAPORE 1965 (From Malaysia)
INDONESIA 1949
TIMOR-LESTE 1999 (From Indonesia)

NORTH KOREA 1948
SOUTH KOREA 1948 (From Japan)
JAPAN
PHILIPPINES 1946

PAPUA NEW GUINEA 1975 (From Australia)

PACIFIC OCEAN

Tropic of Cancer
Equator
Tropic of Capricorn

N

| 0 | 1,000 | 2,000 Km. |
| 0 | 1,000 | 2,000 Mi. |

Even before independence, the French had laid the foundations for neocolonial control of their former African colonies. Colonial policies of "assimilation" held out the promise of French citizenship for educated Africans, creating an African elite that identified strongly with French culture. Appealing to their sentiments, in 1958 President Charles de Gaulle announced a referendum to be held across French Africa. A "yes" vote meant that the former French colonies would receive control over their own internal affairs but would remain part of a larger French "community". The French government would retain control over economic policy, foreign affairs, and the military. A "no" vote meant complete and immediate independence, severing all ties to France.

All but one of the colonies voted to become members of the French community. The exception was Guinea, where a radical trade union leader, Sekou Toure (SEY-koo TOO-rey), campaigned for complete independence. The French government responded to Guinea's "no" vote by withdrawing their administrators overnight, stopping economic aid, and even ripping telephones from the walls as they vacated their offices. The French message was clear, and other African leaders learned the lesson and cooperated with France. With their currencies pegged to the value of the French franc, new nations such as the Ivory Coast, Senegal, and Mali had little control over their own economic policies.

Elsewhere, Africans had to take up arms to liberate themselves, especially where Europeans had come not just as rulers but also as settlers. For instance, over a million Europeans lived in Algeria. After the Second World War, Algerian nationalists, some of whom had fought for de Gaulle's Free French Army, demanded rights equal to those of the white settlers and a voice in their own governance. Harshly repressed, these nationalists formed the National Liberation Front (FLN—the French acronym) and, in 1954, began their armed struggle.

It was a brutal war, with the FLN sometimes launching terrorist attacks on French civilians and the French military systematically torturing Algerian resistance fighters. Over time, French public opinion soured on the violence, and in 1962 an agreement recognizing Algerian independence was finally negotiated. (See the feature "Movement of Ideas Through Primary Sources: *The Wretched of the Earth*.")

Kenya, in East Africa, also had a large settler population. There, the main nationalist leader, **Jomo Kenyatta** (JOH-moh ken-YAH-tuh) had met with other African nationalist leaders, including Kwame Nkrumah, at the Fifth Pan-African Congress before returning home from studies in England in 1946 (see Chapter 28), and he hoped to develop a mass organization to force the British into negotiations. But an impatient group of Kenyan rebels took a more militant stand, forming a secret society, stealing arms from police stations, assassinating a collaborationist chief, and naming themselves the Land and Freedom Army. The British called them the Mau Mau and depicted them as "savages" who had returned to a "primitive" state of irrationality. Hopelessly outgunned by colonial forces, the rebels used their knowledge of the forest and the support of the local population to carry on their fight.

Superior British firepower was overwhelming, though, and the government moved the rural population into fortified villages to cut them off from the rebels. By the late 1950s the rebellion was contained. Embarrassed by revelations of military abuse of African civilians, however, the British government now favored compromise with more moderate African nationalists. In 1963, Jomo Kenyatta became the prime minister of an independent Kenya.

Jomo Kenyatta
(1891-1978) The British-educated leader of Kenya's nationalist movement after World War II, Kenyatta spent years in prison before becoming the first democratically elected leader of an independent Kenya in 1963.

The Wretched of the Earth

Frantz Fanon (1925–1961) was an advocate of Third World revolution, guerrilla warfare, and socialism. Born on the Caribbean island of Martinique in the French West Indies, Fanon volunteered for service in the Free French Army and was wounded during the liberation of France in 1944. After training in Paris as a psychiatrist, he was stationed in North Africa. During the Algerian war Fanon's medical practice included psychiatric treatment of both French practitioners and Arab and Berber victims of torture. From this experience he concluded that colonialism was intrinsically violent and could only be removed by violence. He joined the Algerian National Liberation Front and became a prominent spokesman for their cause. Fanon was dying of leukemia in 1961 while writing *The Wretched of the Earth*, his bitter indictment of colonialism.

❭ What is similar and what is different between Fanon's ideas and those of Mohandas K. Gandhi (see Chapter 28)?

❭ What is Fanon's critique of European society, and how does he find hope in Third World revolution?

Sources: From Frantz Fanon, *The Wretched of the Earth* (New York: Grove, 1963), pp. 36, 39–41, 43, 45, 59, 61, 312, 315–316. Reprinted by permission; David Macy, *Frantz Fanon* (New York: Picador, 2000), p. 483.

Decolonization is the meeting of two forces, opposed to each other by their very nature.... Their first encounter was marked by violence and their existence together—that is to say the exploitation of the native by the settler—was carried on by dint of a great array of bayonets and cannons....

The naked truth of decolonization evokes for us the searing bullets and bloodstained knives which emanate from it. For if the last shall be first, this will only come to pass after a murderous and decisive struggle between the two protagonists....

The settlers' town is a strongly built town, all made of stone and steel. It is a brightly lit town; the streets are all covered with asphalt, and the garbage cans swallow all the leavings, unseen, unknown, and hardly thought about.... The settlers' town is a town of white people, of foreigners....

The native town is a hungry town, starved for bread, of meat, of shoes, of coal, of light. The native town is a crouching village, a town on its knees, a town wallowing in the mire.... The look that the native turns on the settlers' town is a look of lust, a look of envy; it expresses his dreams of possession—all manner of possession: to sit at the settler's table, to sleep in the settler's bed, with his wife if possible. The colonized man is an envious man....

The violence which has ruled over the ordering of the colonial world, which has ceaselessly drummed the rhythm for the destruction of native social forms and broken up without reserve the systems of reference of the economy...that same violence will be claimed and taken over by the native at the moment when, deciding to embody history in his own person, he surges into the forbidden quarters....

As if to show the totalitarian character of colonial exploitation the settler paints the native as the quintessence of evil. Native society is not simply described as a society lacking in values.... The native is declared insensible to ethics; he represents not only the absence of values, but the negation of values...and in this sense he is the absolute evil....

The violence with which the supremacy of white values is affirmed and the aggressiveness which has permeated the victory of these values over the ways of life and thought of the native mean that, in revenge, the native laughs in mockery when Western values are mentioned in front of him.... In the period of decolonization, the colonized masses mock at these very values, insult them, and vomit them up....

[When the urban militants] get into the habit of talking to the peasants they discover that the rural masses have never ceased to pose the problem of their liberation in terms of violence, of taking back the land from the foreigners, in terms of a national struggle. Everything is simple.... They discover a generous people prepared to make sacrifices, willing to give of itself, impatient and with a stony pride. One can understand that the encounter between militants who are being hunted by the police and these impatient masses, who are instinctually rebellious, can produce an explosive mixture of unexpected power....

Come, then, comrades, the European game has finally ended; we must find something different. We today can do everything so long as we do not imitate Europe, so long as we are not obsessed with desire to catch up with Europe.... European achievements, European techniques, and European style ought to no longer tempt us and to throw us off our balance.

When I search for Man in the technique and style of Europe, I see only a succession of negations of man, and an avalanche of murders....It is a question of the Third World starting a new history of Man, a history which will have regard to the sometimes prodigious theses Europe has put forward, but which will also not forget Europe's crimes....For Europe, for ourselves, for humanity, comrades, we must turn over a new leaf, we must work out new concepts, and try to set afoot a new man.

● **CONTEXT&CONNECTIONS** Kenyan nationalism had been stimulated immediately after the First World War when European settlers had taken over much of the best Kenyan land. In the interwar period, however, Africans found it difficult to connect such local grievances to broader organizational frameworks (see Chapter 28). Jomo Kenyatta's return in 1946, and the merging of popular demands with educated leadership, were thus part of a broader maturation in African nationalism after World War II. ●

In southern Africa, apartheid made compromise between white settlers and African nationalists impossible. Because South African leaders were adamantly anticommunist, governments in London and Washington usually overlooked their repressive policies. In response, the African National Congress, led by Nelson Mandela (see Chapter 31), organized a "defiance campaign" based on Gandhian tactics of non-violent resistance, and when that failed turned to a sabotage campaign. When Mandela was arrested and sentenced to life in prison in 1964, hopes for transforming South Africa were at an all-time low.

Still, absent the settler factor, once the British and French realized that the "winds of change" were blowing in the direction of African independence (as noted by the British prime minister in 1960), they managed the process of negotiating a handover of power peacefully, avoiding superpower intervention. Tragically, Belgium did not. The new Democratic Republic of the Congo descended into anarchy and became the site of a proxy war between the United States and the Soviet Union.

After King Leopold's brutal reign (see Chapter 26), the Belgian government had created a tightly centralized colonial administration. They did little to prepare Africans for independence: after eighty years of Belgian rule, only sixteen Africans in the entire Congo had university degrees. Still, with the Congo caught up in the nationalist excitement spreading across the continent, in 1960 the Belgians made hasty plans for independence, believing that a weak Congolese government would be susceptible to neocolonial control.

Patrice Lumumba A fiery nationalist, Lumumba faced insurmountable hurdles as prime minister of the Democratic Republic of the Congo, including political intrigues by the Belgian government and mining interests. The United States CIA cooperated in Lumumba's capture and brutal execution.

Patrice Lumumba

(1925–1961) The first prime minister of the Democratic Republic of the Congo in 1960. He was deposed and assassinated by political rivals in 1961.

The Congolese National Movement won the election, and a government was formed by Prime Minister **Patrice Lumumba** (loo-MOOM-buh) (1925–1961). At the independence ceremony in 1960 the Belgian king made a patronizing speech praising his country's "civilizing mission" in Africa. Lumumba responded with a catalogue of Belgian crimes against Africans. *"Our wounds,"* he said, *"are still too fresh and painful for us to be able to erase them from our memories."* The speech made Lumumba a hero to African nationalists, but he was now regarded as a dangerous radical in Brussels and Washington.

Lumumba faced immediate challenges. African soldiers mutinied against their Belgian officers, and the mineral-rich province of Katanga seceded. When the United Nations sent in peacekeeping forces, Lumumba suspected their real purpose was to defend Western mining interests. After turning to the Soviet Union for military aid, Lumumba was branded a "communist," and—with the complicity of the CIA—he was arrested, beaten, and murdered by rivals. Rebel armies arose in several provinces. Finally Joseph Mobutu (mo-BOO-too), an army officer long on the CIA payroll, seized dictatorial power.

Che Guevara was among those who regarded Lumumba as a fallen hero and Mobutu as an American puppet. In 1965, Che joined up with Congolese rebels in the eastern part of the country. But he was to be disappointed at the rebels' lack of discipline and ideological commitment, later writing, *"I felt entirely alone in a way that I had never experienced before, neither in Cuba nor anywhere else, throughout my long pilgrimage across the world."** When Che returned to Cuba in 1966, the Congo was firmly under Joseph Mobutu's authoritarian control. The United States was the main power broker in Central Africa, allied with Mobutu to secure the mineral riches of the Congo, some of which were vital to defense and aerospace industries.

The Bandung Generation, 1955–1965

In 1955, the leaders of former colonial states met in Bandung (bahn-DOONG), Indonesia, for the first Asia-Africa conference, strategizing to avoid both neocolonialism and superpower intervention. The careers of the Indonesian, Indian, and Egyptian representatives at the Bandung Conference illustrate how difficult it was to remain nonaligned with either the United States or the Soviet Union.

---

*Quoted in David Sandison, *Che Guevara* (New York: St. Martin's Griffin, 1997), pp. 105, 108.

In 1945, Indonesian nationalist **Ahmed Sukarno** (1901–1970) and his party declared Indonesia free of both the Dutch and the Japanese, but it was not until 1950 and the defeat of Dutch reoccupation forces an independent nation was created from hundreds of islands scattered across thousands of miles. Sukarno sponsored the development of an Indonesian language with a simplified grammar as a way to unify Indonesia's great diversity of peoples. (Indonesia is the world's fourth largest nation and its largest Muslim-majority country.)

Sukarno was widely popular at first, but he had had no experience running a country and became erratic after declaring himself "president for life" in 1963. As his popularity waned, he faced a potent communist insurgency. Suspecting that Sukarno was either sympathetic to the communists or too weak to stave them off, the Indonesian military launched a murderous crackdown in 1964.

In 1967, General Suharto, a military commander backed by the United States, ousted Sukarno, suspended the constitution, and took power. The United States was glad, as in Mobutu's Congo, to have another dependable ally in the struggle against communism, especially in a nation whose strategic importance increased with the escalation of war in neighboring Vietnam. And as with Mobutu, the United States turned a blind eye to Suharto's corruption and authoritarianism.

India's prime minister, **Jawaharlal Nehru** (juh-wah-HER-lahl NAY-roo) (1889–1964), was more successful in securing his country's nonalignment. Like other leaders of newly independent nations, Nehru faced tremendous problems. As the Muslim League had urged (see Chapter 28), in 1947 the British had partitioned their Indian colony into two separate independent states: India and Pakistan. However, a substantial Hindu minority resided in Pakistan, and an even larger Muslim minority remained in the new state of India. In a climate of fear and uncertainty, millions of people tried desperately to cross to the country where they "belonged." In the intercommunal violence that followed, as many as 10 million people were dislocated, perhaps seventy-five thousand women were raped or abducted, and more than 1 million people lost their lives.

Despite its violent birth and the enduring challenges of poverty and illiteracy, India emerged as the world's largest democracy. And while military tensions emerged on India's borders with Pakistan and China, Nehru kept his country nonaligned by purchasing military hardware from both the United States and the Soviet Union.

Next door in Pakistan, however, corruption and misrule led to a military seizure of power. A longstanding alliance began in 1958 when Pakistan's government entered into a defense agreement with the United States, which was concerned about India's military ties with the Soviet Union and anxious to have a reliably anticommunist ally in this strategic region. Despite India's nonalignment, therefore, the Cold War deeply affected South Asian politics.

Another prominent figure at Bandung was **Gamal Abdel Nasser** (1918–1970). Nasser, who came to power in a military coup in 1952, argued that Arabs should unite to fight both European neocolonialism and American imperialism. He embraced secular Arab nationalism, rejecting religion as a basis for politics, banning the Muslim Brotherhood, and elevating the military as a political force.

In 1954, Nasser successfully negotiated the withdrawal of British troops from the Suez Canal Zone (see Chapter 26). He also began plans for building the giant Aswan Dam on the Nile River to provide electricity for industrialization. He approached Britain and the United States for aid but, sticking to his nonaligned principles, refused to join an anti-Soviet alliance as a precondition. In 1956, after they refused further assistance, Nasser proclaimed the nationalization of the Suez Canal to finance the dam, outraging the British government.

Ahmed Sukarno
(1901–1970) Leader in the struggle for Indonesian independence from the Netherlands, achieved in 1949. Indonesian military leaders, backed by the United States, thought Sukarno incapable of battling communism and removed him from power.

Jawaharlal Nehru
(1889–1964) Statesman who helped negotiate the end of British colonial rule in India and served as independent India's first prime minister from 1947 to 1964. Nehru was an influential advocate of the Non-Aligned Movement, refusing to choose sides in the Cold War.

Gamal Abdel Nasser
(1918–1970) Prime minister of Egypt from 1954 to 1956 and president from 1956 to 1970. The nationalization of the Suez Canal in 1956 made Nasser a Pan-Arab hero, though the loss of the Six-Day War to Israel in 1967 badly damaged that reputation.

Bettmann/Corbis

The Nonaligned Movement After the Bandung Conference of 1955, leaders of the Nonaligned Movement continued annual summit meetings. In Belgrade in 1960 we see Jawaharlal Nehru (India), Kwame Nkrumah (Ghana), Gamal Abdel Nasser (Egypt), Ahmed Sukarno (Indonesia), and Marshall Tito (Yugoslavia). While the others were most concerned with maintaining distance from former colonial powers and the United States, Tito's goal was to avoid Soviet domination of his socialist regime.

The Suez Crisis of 1956 deepened when the British, French, and Israelis, after clandestine negotiations, sent troops to the Canal Zone. However, the intervention lacked American support, and the British and Israelis withdrew when confronted with Egyptian opposition and international criticism. A triumphant Nasser became a hero across the Arab world for standing his ground, and the Aswan Dam was later completed with Soviet aid.

Nasser's reputation in the Arab world was grounded in his support of the Palestinian cause and belligerence toward Israel. After the British relinquished their control in 1947 a United Nations plan would have partitioned Palestine into separate Arab and Jewish states. In 1948, when neighboring Arab states refused to accept that UN plan, Zionist leaders declared the independence of Israel. Egypt, Lebanon, Syria, Jordan, and Iraq immediately attacked. Nasser himself fought in the Pan-Arab army.

● **CONTEXT&CONNECTIONS** The British had taken over the Ottoman province of Palestine following World War I under the *Mandate System* (see Chapter 27). In the interwar years the British struggled to keep the peace, especially after the rise of *Adolph Hitler* in Germany increased the pressure to allow greater Jewish immigration from Europe (Chapter 28). In 1947, still recovering from war, the British handed over responsibility for Palestine to the new *United Nations* (Chapter 29). ●

As Arab refugees fled the fighting, some driven from their homes by Israeli soldiers, the Israelis routed the Arab armies, and the Israeli government expanded its borders beyond what the UN planners had envisioned. Shocked and humiliated, many Arabs thereafter looked to Nasser as their best hope to destroy Israel and return Palestinian refugees to their native land.

Nasser's reputation, however, was severely damaged after he made a series of threatening moves that prompted a preemptive Israeli attack. In the Six-Day War of 1967, Israeli forces occupied Egypt's Sinai Desert, Syria's Golan Heights, and the West Bank of the Jordan River. Israeli occupation of predominantly Arab East Jerusalem was particularly galling. U.S. support had helped make Israeli victory possible, a cause of resentment across the Muslim world. The Soviet Union gave rhetorical support to the Palestinians, but little material and military aid.

All those who participated at the Bandung meeting were aware that Cold War entanglements would compromise their ability to move their nations forward. They had different levels of success in achieving the nonalignment to which they had dedicated themselves at Bandung. Sukarno was the least successful, supplanted by a military dictatorship allied with the United States. Nehru was by far the most successful, maintaining India's status as a genuinely nonaligned democracy, though his friendship with the Soviets led the United States to arm neighboring Pakistan. In Egypt, Nasser chose to ally more closely with the Soviet Union after the Suez Crisis, but only because the Soviets were enemies of the United States, Israel's main ally. The Cold War created a difficult balancing act for Third World leaders who subscribed to the principles of nonalignment.

Vietnam: The Cold War in Southeast Asia, 1956–1974

As in Indonesia, Vietnamese nationalists had to fight colonial reoccupation forces to win their independence. After helping drive the Japanese from his country during World War II, **Ho Chi Minh** had declared an independent Democratic Republic of Vietnam in 1945, explicitly referring to the American Declaration of Independence in asserting the right of the Vietnamese people to be free from foreign rule. Ignoring Ho's declaration, France sent forces to re-establish colonial control, only to be defeated by the Viet Minh at Dien Bien Phu (dyen byen FOO) in 1954. French military officers told their government that they could not wage two counterinsurgencies—in Algeria and Vietnam—simultaneously. Since Algeria was home to a million French citizens, it was the greater priority, and the French finally withdrew from Indochina.

Ho Chi Minh
(1890–1969) Vietnamese revolutionary and Marxist who led military campaigns against Japanese invaders, French colonialists, and American and South Vietnamese forces.

At the multination Geneva Conference, Vietnam was temporarily partitioned into northern and southern regions, pending national elections. Fearing that Ho Chi Minh's Communists would win those elections, the United States supported the formation of a separate South Vietnamese regime. Conflict between the two Vietnams intensified as the United States supplied the south with weapons and military training, while North Vietnam sponsored a southern-based rebel army, the National Front for the Liberation of South Vietnam (or the Vietcong).

In 1964, President Lyndon Johnson (in office 1963–1969) began full-scale war against the communist regime in Hanoi, and by the next year two hundred thousand American combatants were in Southeast Asia. The policy of the United States hinged on success in creating a legitimate nationalist government in South Vietnam, a goal that was never achieved. Leaders in the southern capital of Saigon never came close to replicating the leadership that Ho Chi Minh had achieved in the north through years of fighting the Japanese and French.

Despite massive bombing attacks on North Vietnam, the Vietcong grew in strength. American soldiers were often unable to distinguish guerrilla soldiers from civilians. At home, Americans were incredulous when their troops brutally

Vietnamese Protest
On June 11, 1963, Thich Quang Duc, a Vietnamese Buddhist monk, burned himself to death on a Saigon street. His self-immolation was a protest of the policies of the U.S.-backed South Vietnamese government, which many Buddhists thought favored the Catholic minority.

AP images/MALCOLM BROWNE

slaughtered the villagers of My Lai (mee lie) in 1969 and spread poisonous clouds of defoliating chemicals across the Vietnamese countryside. Images of burning children fleeing napalm bomb blasts sickened global audiences. In this first "televised war," images of death and destruction were transmitted around the world.

In 1968, the Vietcong took the fight straight to the South Vietnamese capital of Saigon during the Tet Offensive. In 1969, as antiwar protests spread across American college campuses and anti-American feelings rose in much of Europe, Asia, Africa, and Latin America, the new administration of President Richard Nixon (in office 1969–1974) promised "peace with honor" through even more intensive bombing of North Vietnam and the replacement of American ground forces with South Vietnamese ones. Demoralized and corrupt, the South Vietnamese government and military were not up to the task. On April 30, 1975, after the United States withdrew its ground troops, Communist forces entered Saigon, renamed it Ho Chi Minh City, and reunified the country under their dictatorship.

● **CONTEXT&CONNECTIONS** Entering the Vietnam War, Americans were inclined to think that any fight against communism was necessarily a fight for freedom. But while the Viet Minh were dedicated Marxist-Leninist revolutionaries, their movement had its roots in Vietnam's long history of resistance to foreign intrusion: China in ancient times, Japan and France more recently, and now the United States (see Chapters 16, 26, and 29). Nationalism was thus key to Viet Minh success. ●

Meanwhile, the war in Southeast Asia had global reverberations as it galvanized opposition to U.S. military actions, especially among college students on the political left. For some antiwar protestors, the war was simply wrong and should be ended right away. As a member of the Vietnam Veterans Against the War put it in 1971: *"How do you ask a man to be the last man to die for a mistake?**"

A more radical view of Vietnam critiqued the conflict not as a "mistake" but as the logical outcome of U.S. imperialism in defense of international capital, with the heroic Viet Minh unmasking the American threat to peace and progress.

*John Kerry, Statement to the Senate Committee on Foreign Relations, April 23, 1971. http://www2. iath.virginia.edu/sixties/HTML_docs/Resources/Primary/Manifestos/VVAW_Kerry_Senate.html.

Che Guevara, as he traveled the Third World promoting the cause of revolution on the Cuban model, made this point insistently: *"Create Two, Three, or Many Vietnams!"* Guevara declared. *"And let us develop a true proletarian internationalism."** Guevara's call resonated with some young activists who rejected both the exploitative model of U.S. capitalism and the dreary state-dominated socialism of the U.S.S.R. They looked instead to the more scintillating revolutionary models of the Third World, and by 1968 dorm rooms around the world featured posters of Che Guevara and Mao Zedong. Glorification of Third World revolution became just one of the many strands of political and cultural upheaval that came to define "the Sixties."

A Time of Upheaval, 1966–1974

People who grew up during "the Sixties" remember it as a time of political, social, and cultural turmoil. The Civil Rights Movement in the United States, under the leadership of figures like Dr. Martin Luther King, Jr., paralleled other liberation movements taking place around the world. Young people took center stage, proclaiming that the world could, and should, be made a place of peace, love, and justice. In 1963, the poet-musician Bob Dylan captured the spirit of the time:

Come mothers and fathers throughout the land
And don't criticize what you can't understand
Your sons and your daughters are beyond your command
Your old road is rapidly aging
Please get out of the new one if you can't lend your hand
For the times they are a-changing.[†]

This global trend toward greater youth involvement in politics and society arose among students who had come of age after the Second World War, their dissatisfaction with the status quo peaking in 1968, a "year of revolution" that saw battles between protestors and authorities in cities as diverse as Paris, Chicago, Mexico City, and Prague.

Meanwhile, across Latin America a vast gulf separated opposing camps. On the political right, traditional economic oligarchies, foreign interests, military officers, and Catholic bishops confronted an increasingly radicalized left of students, academics, parish priests, labor leaders, and professional revolutionaries inspired by Che Guevara. The peasant-based revolutionary approach of Mao Zedong also drew the interest of Latin American revolutionaries, even as Mao's own Great Proletarian Cultural Revolution (1966–1970) spread chaos and hardship across the world's largest nation.

In most of the world, existing authorities had re-established control by the 1970s, though the Sixties spirit of idealism endured in the environmental movement, feminism, and educational reform. At the same time, diplomats stabilized the international order with a new emphasis on arms reductions and a multilateral spirit of "understanding," or *détente*.

---

*Ernesto Guevara, "Create Two, Three, or Many Vietnams," cited in *Sources of Global History since 1900*, ed. James H. Overfield, 2d ed. (Boston: Wadsworth, 2013), pp. 342–345.

[†]Bob Dylan, "The Times They Are A-Changing." Copyright © 1963, 1964 by Warner Bros. Inc.; renewed 1991, 1992 by Special Rider Music. Reprinted courtesy of Special Rider Music.

The Sixties: The Rising Expectations of Surging Youth

"The Sixties" refers more to an attitude than a strict chronology, with massive social, political, and cultural changes appearing in some places as early as the 1950s (among "beat" poets in New York, for example) but not until the early 1970s (or never at all) elsewhere. But the common denominator was generational: it was the children growing up in the wake of the Second World War who prompted the upheavals of the time. The "baby boom" phenomenon was a global one: by the mid-1960s children born at the end of the war were turning twenty and making their mark on the world.

Their agitation stemmed from their desire for so much more than their parents, who had come of age during the Great Depression and the Second World War, were willing to accept. College students were at the forefront of this trend. As college enrollments surged around the world, parents were astonished by the rebellion of their children, thinking that they should be grateful for all the work and sacrifice that had made their advanced study possible. The generation gap widened when the kids responded *never trust anyone over thirty.*

In the industrialized world, rising expectations accompanied the grand leaps of productivity that came with postwar recovery, the period from 1945 to 1975 that the French call *Les Trente Glorieuses* ("The Glorious Thirty"). And while economies were growing, social inequalities were declining, meaning that even working-class people were able to afford an extended range of consumer goods, educate their children, own property, and save for retirement. For those who had experienced the privations of the first half of the twentieth century, it was a golden time. Teenagers who previously would have been working at age sixteen to help support their families could now delay adulthood and devote time to "finding themselves," often going far beyond the cultural legacies of their forebears.

An emphasis on cultural authenticity led many young people to reject corporate commercialism and embrace "roots" music from around the world, to return to a more natural diet and vegetarianism, to join the burgeoning new environmental movement, and to reject the "rat race" of consumerism for a simpler, sometimes communal living style. The "hippie" movement of the late 1960s was awash with these and many other exploratory trends, including smoking marijuana and using psychedelic drugs to open consciousness, to *"tune in, turn on, and drop out."*

Intense interest in international influences was part of that quest, whether it meant identifying with political revolutionaries like Che Guevara or with spiritual practices of foreign cultures. Eastern religions achieved renewed popularity. (See the feature "Visual Evidence in Primary Sources: *Sgt. Pepper's Lonely Hearts Club Band.*")

The youth movement was also, fundamentally, a sexual revolution, especially after 1960, when the "pill" went on the market. Though contraceptives were opposed by religious authorities and banned in some places, their availability in a cheap, convenient form under women's control facilitated sexual experimentation.

● **CONTEXT&CONNECTIONS** In the 1950s the now elderly Margaret Sanger, a "first wave" feminist and a proponent of birth control, raised funds for research into oral contraception. Meanwhile feminists revived the ideals of her friend *Emma Goldman* (Chapter 27), supporting Goldman's position that women must have freedom of choice in partners, in employment, and in child rearing. In fact, Goldman's ideas appealed strongly to the counterculture at large, with her insistence that individuals be free from both government intrusion *and* corporate exploitation. ●

At the same time, new thinking about gender roles transformed women's rights. Even though women had achieved legal equality in much of the world, their opportunities remained sharply limited; the common expectation was that young women need not advance in their careers because they would quickly marry and devote themselves to motherhood. In the 1960s, however, "second wave" feminists demanded full equality of social and economic rights.

1968: A Year of Revolution

In the industrial world, countercultural exploration was intertwined with postwar affluence. Poorer children, of course, might not have much opportunity for self-exploration before realities like military service, the need for employment, or parenthood intervened. The same was true for less affluent parts of the world—the Soviet-dominated Second World and the teeming and diverse Third World. But even here the Sixties brought rising expectations. The global nature of youthful rebellion in the Sixties is perhaps best demonstrated by the simultaneous outbreak in 1968 of large-scale student protests in nations as diverse as the United States, France, Czechoslovakia, and Mexico.

In the "summer of love" in 1967, psychedelic art and music and slogans such as *make love, not war* emanated from U.S. college campuses. But harsher realities soon tempered the hopes of feminists, civil rights advocates, and student leaders. Drug use ruined lives, peace marches turned violent, and demonstrations resulted in mass arrests. In 1968 two voices for peace and moderation—civil rights leader Martin Luther King, Jr. and Democratic presidential candidate Robert F. Kennedy—were assassinated. Violence spread through American cities.

During the 1968 Democratic National Convention, American television viewers watched in horror as Chicago police bludgeoned youthful protesters; a few months later, Republican Richard Nixon won the presidency. To those Americans appalled by the ferment of the Sixties, Nixon was an experienced, thoughtful anticommunist who would restore order. To those who dreamt of a new age of peace and justice, Nixon represented everything that was wrong with "the establishment." The nation became even more bitterly divided after Ohio Army National Guardsmen shot four student protesters to death at Kent State University in the spring of 1970.

In Europe, Paris was a major center of student unrest. As in the United States, the number of university students had risen sharply in the post-1945 period. After three college students were arrested for occupying a dean's office, students all over France rose to their defense. In May 1968, student marchers, assaulted by riot police, built barricades of overturned cars and garbage cans.

Whereas in the United States most working Americans, including most union members, tended to side with the forces of "law and order," in France the major trade unions joined the protests. Two million French workers went on strike, some taking over factories and proclaiming that their bosses were unnecessary. Art students expressed this anarchistic spirit on posters they plastered around Paris, with slogans such as *"Be realistic, ask for the impossible!"* and *"It is forbidden to forbid!"*

In response, French president Charles de Gaulle appeared on television to proclaim: *"The whole French people...are being prevented from living a normal existence by...Reds and Anarchists...preventing students from studying, workers from working."* But he also offered concessions: an increase in the minimum wage and new elections. De Gaulle's re-election in late 1968, like the election of U.S. conservative Richard Nixon, made it clear that most voters wanted a return to "normal existence." After workers were appeased with new contracts, and French students left campus for the summer, the forces of "law and order" reasserted themselves.

In eastern Europe, students also played a prominent role in the **Prague Spring** of 1968. By the mid-1960s, discontent with the stifling conditions of

Prague Spring

(1968) An attempt by political reformers in Czechoslovakia to reform the communist government and create "socialism with a human face." The Soviet Union invaded Czechoslovakia, ending this attempt at reform and reimposing communist orthodoxy.

Sgt. Pepper's Lonely Hearts Club Band

Listen and compare two songs by the British group the Beatles, "I Want to Hold Your Hand" (1963) and "A Day in the Life" (1967), to get an idea of the depth and rapidity of cultural change in the mid-1960s. In a mere four years, John Lennon, Paul McCartney, George Harrison, and Ringo Starr went from pop stars adored by screaming adolescent girls to artists whose words, music, and rapidly evolving public images made them globally influential figures.

Tribute is paid to the Rolling Stones, the Beatles' main rival on the rock music scene, and Bob Dylan, a strong influence on their musical development. ***Given your knowledge of 1960s popular culture, what ideas and emotions would this image have evoked at the time of its first release?***

Bob Dylan

Rolling Stones tribute

Michael Ochs Archives/Getty Images

John Lennon's suggestion that Jesus, Gandhi, and Hitler all be included was vetoed. Lennon had been criticized the previous year for declaring that the Beatles were "*more popular than Jesus,*" and the inclusion of Hitler would have been even more offensive. An image of Gandhi was included at the photo shoot but was later removed at the request of the record company.

Millions anxiously anticipated the release of their new album, *Sgt. Pepper's Lonely Hearts Club Band*, on June 1, 1967. Their albums had become more complex in musical structure and more ambitious in lyrical content, influenced by the highly conceptual songwriting of Bob Dylan, an opening of the imagination commonly attributed to marijuana and psychedelic drugs, and the brilliance of their producer/engineer George Martin, with his strong background in classical music. While recording *Sgt. Pepper*, the group traveled to India for training in transcendental meditation, a journey eagerly covered by the global media and one that provided further artistic stimulation.

The album lived up to expectations. No one had ever heard anything like it before. But the album was more than just a collection of songs. Eager fans sought symbolic meanings not only in the sometimes obscure lyrics but also in the visual images that adorned the large gatefold cover of the album. The Beatles were clearly playing with ideas of celebrity and shifting identity, for example, by creating the persona of "Billy Shears" as front man of the mythical Sgt. Pepper's Band, and by posing for the album cover next to wax models of themselves circa 1964. The resulting image was studied for meaning by millions of young people around the world.

The inclusion of figurines of the Beatles (*a*) from Madame Tussauds wax museum highlights the transformation of the group's visual self-representation between 1964 and 1967.

Scattered among the historical figures and film stars are three Indian spiritual leaders (*b*), included at the suggestion of George Harrison. The influence of both Indian instrumentation and Hindu philosophy on Harrison can be heard on the album track "Within You Without You."

Famous historical figures include Karl Marx (*c*), T. E. Lawrence ("Lawrence of Arabia") (*d*), and writers Edgar Allan Poe (*e*), Lewis Carroll (*f*), and Oscar Wilde (*g*). Actors include Marlon Brando (*h*), Marilyn Monroe (*i*), and Stan Laurel (*j*).

Soviet-imposed communism was growing. Early in 1968 workers' strikes and students' protests forced the resignation of the hardline communist leadership.

The new head of the Czechoslovak Communist Party, Alexander Dubcek (DOOB-chek), promised *"socialism with a human face,"* including freedom of speech and association as well as more liberal, market-oriented economic policies. The Czech public rallied to Dubcek's cause, and students and teachers took advantage of the new atmosphere to discussed how economic justice and democratic freedoms could be achieved within a socialist framework.

Fearing that the movement toward liberalization would spread, the Soviet leadership ordered a half-million Soviet and Warsaw Pact troops into Czechoslovakia. They replaced Dubcek with a more compliant Czech communist leader. Reformers in Czechoslovakia, as well as in Poland, Hungary, and the Soviet Union itself, were put on notice: no changes to the status quo would be allowed.

● **CONTEXT&CONNECTIONS** Twenty years after the Prague Spring, *Mikhail Gorbachev* (Chapter 31) would pursue similar reforms in the Soviet Union; his efforts were unsuccessful and the U.S.S.R. slid into oblivion. At that same time, former activists from the Prague Spring were leading anti-Soviet protests, including Vaclav Havel, the first democratically-elected president of Czechoslovakia. ●

Mexico was another country where a large school-age population showed discontent. But while Mexican society was changing rapidly, Mexican politics were not. The Party of Institutional Revolution (PRI) was the elitist, bureaucratic, and corrupt descendant of the old National Revolutionary Party (see Chapter 27). Since the PRI did not allow free elections, Mexican advocates of political change had no choice but to go to the streets.

The tensions of 1968 began when riot police used force to break up a fight between two student groups. Over a hundred thousand students, with support from many of their teachers and parents, went on strike, marching through the city shouting *"¡Mexico, Libertad!"* ("Mexico, Liberty!"). The timing of the protests was particularly awkward. The Summer Olympic Games were to be held in Mexico City in October. Desperate to project a positive image to the worldwide television audience, the government decided to crack down.

Tlatelolco Massacre
(1968) Massacre that occurred when ten thousand university students, faculty, and other supporters gathered in Tlatelolco Plaza in Mexico City to protest the closing of the Mexican National University; government forces opened fire and killed three hundred people.

The result was the **Tlatelolco Massacre**, in which shooting broke out as thousands of people protested the closing of the National University. The government said the protesters fired first, a contention contradicted by many eyewitnesses watching from apartments lining the square. Hundreds were killed, but the Olympic Games went on as planned, and most of the world heard nothing about the bloodshed at Tlatelolco (tlah-tel-OHL-koh).

Although student protesters in the United States, France, Czechoslovakia, and Mexico were unable to radically change the status quo, in the longer view of history the impact of this generation seems unmistakable. The spirit of the 1960s informed social movements in the decades to come, bringing idealism and activism to music and the arts, educational reform, environmental sustainability, and gender equality. The cause of civil rights had been greatly advanced, with traditionally marginalized groups organizing to secure their rights, as when gays and lesbians came out to demand decriminalization as well as social and political equality. Of course, conservative counter-reactions to such trends continued, as in Latin America, where military governments targeted student activists for arrest, torture, and murder.

Death and Dictatorship in Latin America, 1967–1975

After his failed sojourn to Central Africa, Che Guevara was still looking for a place where a dedicated band of rebels could provide the spark for revolution. In 1967, he headed for Bolivia, convinced that its corrupt government would fall swiftly once the oppressed indigenous population rose against it. But long-exploited Andeans were wary of Spanish-speaking outsiders who claimed to be fighting on their behalf. Short on rations, Che's rebel band wandered in the frigid mountains. In September 1967, Guevara was captured by Bolivian soldiers and executed as a CIA agent stood by.

Guevara's death occurred as dictatorships arose throughout Latin America, with authoritarian governments justifying repression in the name of anticommunism. One example is the overthrow of Chile's democratic government after an alliance of left-wing parties led by the Marxist **Salvador Allende** (uh-YEN-day) (1908–1973) won a bitterly contested election in 1970. Chilean businessmen and landowners strongly opposed Allende's effort to build a socialist economy, and his nationalization of the copper mines alarmed American economic interests. In the fall of 1973, with the backing of the United States, the military staged a coup. Allende committed suicide as a force commanded by General Augusto Pinochet (ah-GOOS-toh pin-oh-CHET) stormed the Presidential Palace in Santiago.

Pinochet hired American advisors to institute free-market economic policies and welcomed foreign investment, while at the same time dismantling the institutions of Chilean democracy. Thousands of students and union leaders, like the couple Che had once met on the open road, were tortured and killed. (See the feature "World History in Today's World: Michelle Bachelet and Dilma Rousseff: From Protest to Leadership in South America.")

By the mid-1970s military governments prevailed across South America. In Argentina, thousands of students vanished as the soldiers took control. For years, desperate mothers would hold silent vigils in central Buenos Aires, holding pictures of their children, the *desaparecidos* (DEH-say-pah-re-SEE-dohs) ("disappeared ones"). Many of their sons and daughters had been killed, some drugged and pushed out of airplanes over the open sea. Successive administrations in Washington supported murderous regimes like those of Chile and Argentina, ever fearful that communism might gain advantage in "America's own backyard."

Salvador Allende

(1908–1973) Socialist leader, elected president of Chile in 1970. His government was overthrown in a U.S.-backed military coup in 1973, during which Allende took his own life.

The Great Proletarian Cultural Revolution, 1965–1974

After 1965, China's version of the "youth revolution" took a bizarre and dangerous direction when Mao began organizing young people into **Red Guard** units, who were taught that Mao himself was the source of all wisdom. His thoughts were collected in a "little red book" that became the bible of the Red Guard movement, waved enthusiastically in the air by millions of students when paying homage to the "Great Helmsman."

Mao used the Red Guards to attack his enemies within the Communist Party, the "rightists" and "experts" who had resisted him during the Great Leap Forward. An atmosphere of anarchy soon prevailed, as Red Guards attacked party offices, publicly humiliated their teachers, destroyed cultural artifacts that linked China to its past, and harassed anyone they thought needed "re-education." Educated Chinese were sent to farms and factories to humble themselves and absorb the authentic revolutionary spirit of the masses. Many died.

By 1968, this Cultural Revolution had reduced the country to chaos, its economy at a standstill. Pragmatic Communist leaders finally convinced Mao to allow

Red Guard

Young people who rallied to the cause of Maoism during the Great Proletarian Cultural Revolution. As their enthusiasm got out of control, the Red Guards spread anarchy across the People's Republic of China.

Michelle Bachelet and Dilma Rousseff: From Protest to Leadership in South America

Since the 1980s, Chile and Brazil have both fully emerged from the darkness of military authoritarianism as vibrant democracies. In Chile, Michelle Bachelet (in office 2006–2010 and 2014–2018) and, in Brazil, Dilma Rousseff (in office 2011–2018) took unusual paths to leadership, as both had earlier been imprisoned for political reasons.

Michelle Bachelet had a privileged upbringing, since her father was a brigadier general in the Chilean Air Force. When Alberto Bachelet opposed his colleague Augusto Pinochet's coup in 1973, however, he was arrested and tortured, and he died soon after. His wife and his daughter, Michelle, were also detained and abused, but were lucky when a sympathetic commander arranged for their exile. The communist German Democratic Republic accepted them and gave Michelle Bachelet a medical education. By the 1980s she had returned home, working in health care while connecting with the nascent prodemocracy movement.

Brazilian President Dilma Rousseff was politically active even as a teenager, opposing the military government that had taken power in 1964. In the late 1960s, she was a part of a revolutionary movement that allied itself with Cuba and took up arms against the dictatorship before being captured, imprisoned, and tortured. After her release and the return of Brazilian democracy, she was mentored by the hugely popular President Luiz Inácio Lula da Silva (in office 2003–2011). During that period, she served as his chief of staff and as chair of Petrobas, Brazil's state oil company (a role for which she was later implicated in a huge corruption scandal) before succeeding Lula as the Workers' Party candidate for president.

Though Bachelet and Rousseff both started from the far left of the political spectrum, and while both suffered from conservative military authoritarianism, they have followed pragmatic, neoliberal policies recognizing the central role of private capital in economic growth (see Chapter 31), even while tailoring their policies toward alleviation of poverty and reduction of economic inequality. Even today, that is a difficult balancing act. Thirty years ago, one could hardly have imagined socialists in Chile and Brazil sitting down with bankers to work out solutions to the country's problems, with the generals sitting on the sidelines obeying the rule of law!

---

the People's Liberation Army to restore governmental authority. Now, Red Guards themselves faced "downward transfer" to remote villages and labor camps. But while authorities curbed the worst excesses of the Cultural Revolution, a bitter power struggle took place behind the scenes. A radical faction called the "Gang of Four," led by Mao's wife, Jiang Qing (jyahng CHING), schemed to restore the Cultural Revolution. On the other side were pragmatists like Deng Xiaoping (DUNG shee-yao-PING), an "expert" who was struggling to regain his influence. With an aging Mao no longer in complete command, Deng and the "expert" faction reasserted themselves.

The pragmatists scored a victory in 1972 when the American president Richard Nixon came to Beijing. Relations between the two countries had long been severed. But the Chinese were worried about their long border with the Soviet Union, where armed confrontations had recently taken place. Although a die-hard anticommunist, Nixon judged that better relations with communist China would increase his own bargaining power with the U.S.S.R. and might help the United States extricate itself from Vietnam.

While the shadow of the Cultural Revolution still hung over China at the time of Mao's death in 1976, the eventual victory of Deng Xiaoping's pragmatic faction over the Gang of Four sent the People's Republic of China in an entirely new, market-oriented direction (see Chapter 31). But the people of China had paid a terrible price for Mao's political adventures: the Great Leap Forward and the Great Proletarian Cultural Revolution had killed tens of millions.

Détente and Challenges to Bipolarity

The strained relations between the United States and the Soviet Union play out in images from the early 1960s—Soviet premier Nikita Khrushchev banging his shoe on a table at the United Nations while angrily denouncing American imperialism, and President John F. Kennedy pledging to put American astronauts on the moon before the end of the decade. In 1957, the Soviets had launched *Sputnik* (SPUHT-nick), the first artificial satellite to orbit the earth. In response, America developed the Apollo space program, accomplishing the first manned mission to the moon in 1969. Indeed, the Cold War propelled continuous technological innovation, as each side poured huge resources into applied scientific research.

By the mid-1960s, a state of reluctant coexistence between the superpowers was becoming the norm. Both nations faced increasing challenges, domestic and foreign. While the United States was dealing with social discord related to the Civil Rights Movement and the Vietnam War, the Soviet Union wrestled with poor living standards. The Soviet people had guaranteed employment, universal education, and health care, but they faced persistent shortages of consumer goods, and those available were often shoddy. Moscow was looking for some breathing space in which to develop its domestic economy.

In theory, the division between East and West, between capitalism and communism, was absolute. In reality, both the United States and the U.S.S.R. were having increasing difficulty controlling their respective blocs. It was the strained relations between Moscow and Beijing after 1960 that gave Richard Nixon an opening with the People's Republic of China. Meanwhile, in 1957 the Treaty of Rome laid the foundation for what would become the European Economic Community, as western European leaders began to emerge from under the economic and political umbrella of the United States.

Although the Cold War divisions appeared likely to remain for the foreseeable future, the two superpowers began to soften their rhetoric and seek ways to live together in a spirit of *détente* (DAY-tahnt). The greatest achievement was the U.S.-U.S.S.R. Strategic Arms Limitation Treaty (SALT) of 1972, which froze the number of ballistic missiles in the possession of each nation. The specter of nuclear war never disappeared, but in the mid-1970s it began to recede.

Everett Collection Historical/Alamy

Cultural Revolution Poster Propaganda posters featuring Mao's image and references to the "little red book" were ubiquitous during the Cultural Revolution. This one depicts a soldier sacrificing himself to save a comrade while crossing a river. The slogan reads: "*Establish a new standard of merit for the people: just as the heroic 4th platoon comrade Li Wenzhong worked to defeat selfishness and promote the common good, we should convert Chairman Mao's most recent directive into action!*"

détente

The easing of hostility between nations, specifically the movement in the 1970s to negotiate arms limitations treaties to reduce tensions between the Eastern and Western blocs during the Cold War.

Idealism Amid Cold War Constraints

Painful as it was, the Second World War had opened new vistas for humanity by upending the status quo across much of the world. Hope for liberation from confining traditions became a global theme. Idealism took many forms in the post-war world, even as the Cold War and the threat of nuclear annihilation cast heavy shadows over the quest for a better future.

In the Soviet sphere, after Stalin's death in 1953 repeated uprisings in the U.S.S.R.'s captive states, even in the face of harsh reprisals, showed an intense longing for more prosperous and open societies. Those idealistic visions of a better future were consistently crushed, however, as during the Hungarian Uprising of 1956 and the Prague Spring of 1968. In the world's largest communist state, the People's Republic of China, Mao Zedong's Great Leap Forward and the Great Proletarian Cultural Revolution could themselves be viewed as versions of idealism, distorted in their enthusiasm and risking anarchy in the name of revolution. In this case, the pragmatism of Deng Xiaoping (see Chapter 31) seemed a safer alternative.

In the United States, the idealism of the "Sixties" had splintered into numerous social movements by the next decade, with traditionally marginalized groups organizing for greater equality. Advocates of Black Power, second wave feminists, Chicano and Native American rights activists, and leaders of the nascent gay rights movement all demanded recognition. Though the environmental movement offered the prospect of unity around a compelling common interest, the political left remained fractured even as conservative critics of "diversity" initiatives regained momentum with the election of President Ronald Reagan in 1980 (see Chapter 31).

A similar fracturing of social movements was evident in Western Europe, though here idealism had a more mainstream outlet: the building of a "new Europe" in the context of the European Economic Community (EEC). The path from the EEC to the European Union (see Chapter 31) was thought of in terms of economic prosperity, but also in terms of peace. With the exception of Margaret Thatcher's United Kingdom, by the 1980s the states of Europe were strongly supportive of diplomatic *détente*

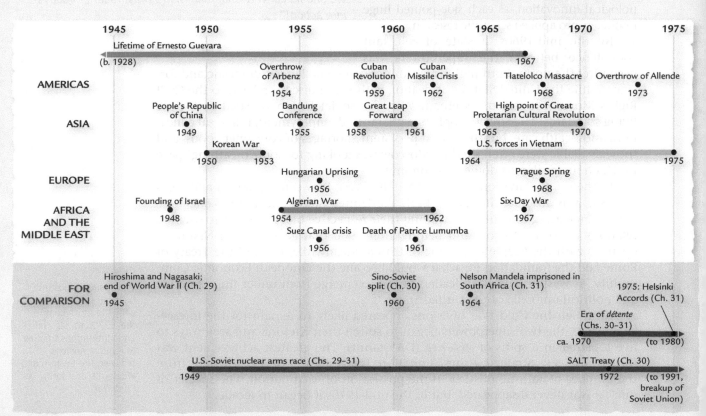

and arms reductions treaties, what the Germans called an *Ostpolitik* ("eastern politics") intended to defuse Cold War tensions. Thus in Western Europe the peace agenda of the Sixties endured.

In the Third World, dreams of revolutionary transformation persisted throughout the 1970s and 1980s, for example, in Latin America, where armed uprising might seem the only way to displace vicious military regimes, or in South Africa, where the racist apartheid regime was well-entrenched and heavily armed. It was here that young idealists might find in Che Guevara a lodestar for the new world they hoped to create. Then the Soviet Union fell, and with the onset of globalization the whole ideological context in which Guevara lived his life was gone.

In 1997, after lying for two decades in an unmarked Bolivian grave, Ernesto Guevara's body was returned to Havana, receiving a hero's welcome and full state honors. After the fall of communism in the Soviet Union, and its transformation in China into a form of market socialism, was Guevara's legacy still relevant? The inequalities and injustices that drove him to a life of revolutionary combat still exist wherever the life chances of the world's poor and their children are stunted by the greed of the powerful. But Che's solution no longer attracts many followers or sympathizers. The idea that the salvation of the "wretched of the earth" will come through mass uprisings sparked by single-minded revolutionaries now seems naïve, after a century in which all such attempts—under Lenin, Mao, Castro, and others—led to cruel and stifling dictatorships.

To young people raised after 1990, the post-war world, with its scrum of ideological conflicts feeding into the churning turmoil of the Sixties, might seem like a very distant past. Still, they might ponder their own connections to that seemingly distant world by remembering the words of American novelist William Faulkner: "*The past is never dead. It isn't even past.*"

Key Terms

Ernesto Guevara (902)
Great Leap Forward (905)
Fidel Castro (906)
Central Intelligence Agency (CIA) (906)
Cuban Missile Crisis (906)
Hungarian Uprising (908)

Jacobo Arbenz (911)
apartheid (911)
Kwame Nkrumah (911)
Jomo Kenyatta (913)
Patrice Lumumba (916)
Ahmed Sukarno (917)
Jawaharlal Nehru (917)

Gamal Abdel Nasser (917)
Ho Chi Minh (919)
Prague Spring (923)
Tlatelolco Massacre (926)
Salvador Allende (927)
Red Guards (927)
détente (929)

For Further Reference

Guevara, Ernesto. *The Motorcycle Diaries: Notes on a Latin American Journey*. Alexandra Keeble, ed. and trans. Melbourne: Ocean Press, 2003.

Hunt, Michael. *The World Transformed: 1945 to the Present*. New York: Bedford/St. Martin's, 2004.

Jeffrey, Robin, ed. *Asia: The Winning of Independence*. London: Macmillan, 1981.

Judge, Edward H., and John W. Langdon. *The Cold War: A Global History with Documents*. 2d ed. New York: Prentice Hall, 2012.

Kurlansky, Mark. *1968: The Year That Rocked the World*. New York: Random House, 2005.

Lee, Christopher J., ed. *Making a World After Empire: The Bandung Moment and Its Political Afterlives*. Athens: Ohio University Press, 2008.

Prashad, Vijay. *The Darker Nations: A People's History of the Third World*. New York: New Press, 2007.

Spence, Jonathan. *Mao Zedong*. New York: Viking Penguin, 1999.

Stark, Steven. *Meet the Beatles: A Cultural History of the Band That Shook Youth, Gender, and the World*. New York: William Morrow, 2006.

Westad, Odd Arne. *The Global Cold War: Third World Interventions and the Making of Our Times*. New York: Cambridge University Press, 2007.

Wiener, Tim. *Legacy of Ashes: The History of the CIA*. New York: Anchor, 2008.

Zubok, Vladislav. *A Failed Empire: The Soviet Union in the Cold War from Stalin to Gorbachev*. Charlotte: University of North Carolina Press, 2008.

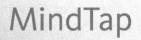 MindTap

MindTap is a fully online, highly personalized learning experience built upon Cengage Learning content. MindTap combines student learning tools—readings, multimedia, activities, and assessments—into a singular Learning Path that guides students through the course.

31

Toward a New World Order, 1975–2000

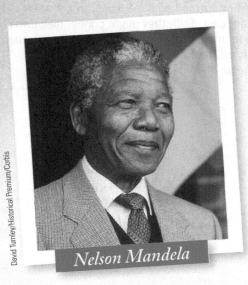

David Turnley/Historical Premium/Corbis

Nelson Mandela

Throughout the 1950s, **Nelson Mandela** (1918–2013) had campaigned for racial justice and democracy as a member of the African National Congress (ANC). Forced underground in 1961 when the South African government banned the ANC, Mandela then traveled across Africa seeking support for the creation of a guerrilla army. After returning to South Africa, he was captured and, in 1964, tried for treason and sentenced to life in prison.

Finally, in early 1990, after decades of repression and violence, South Africa's white leaders responded to international calls for Mandela's release. A few hours after he walked through the prison gates, he spoke before a large crowd in Cape Town and before a global television audience:

Today, the majority of South Africans, black and white, recognize that apartheid has no future. . . . Negotiations on the dismantling of apartheid will have to address the overwhelming demand of our people for a democratic, nonracial, and unitary South Africa. There must be an end to white monopoly on political power and a fundamental restructuring of our political and economic systems to ensure that the inequalities of apartheid are addressed and our society thoroughly democratized. . . . I wish to quote my own words during my trial in 1964. They are as true today as they were then: "I have fought against white domination and I have fought against black domination. I have cherished the ideal of a democratic and free society in which all persons live together in harmony and with equal opportunities.

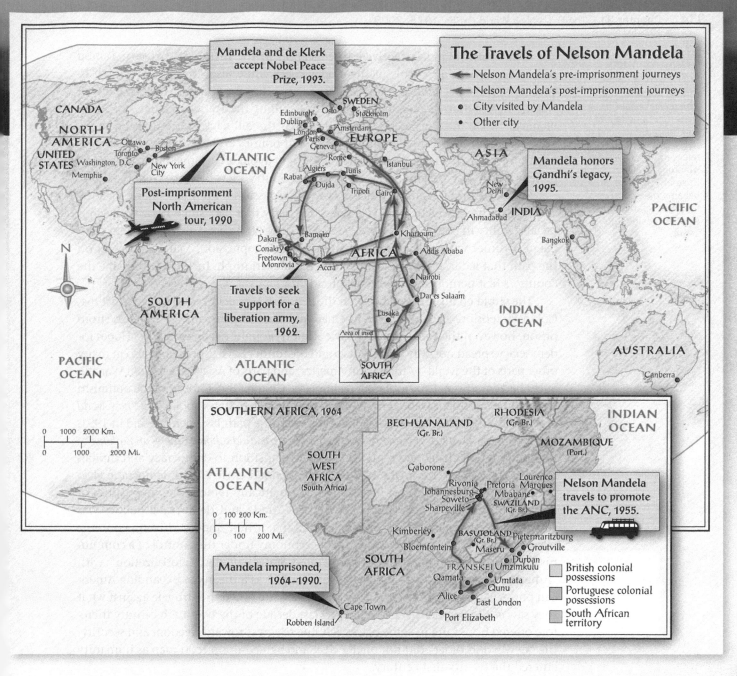

The Travels of Nelson Mandela

← Nelson Mandela's pre-imprisonment journeys
← Nelson Mandela's post-imprisonment journeys
● City visited by Mandela
● Other city

Mandela and de Klerk accept Nobel Peace Prize, 1993.

Post-imprisonment North American tour, 1990

Mandela honors Gandhi's legacy, 1995.

Travels to seek support for a liberation army, 1962.

SOUTHERN AFRICA, 1964

Nelson Mandela travels to promote the ANC, 1955.

Mandela imprisoned, 1964–1990.

British colonial possessions
Portuguese colonial possessions
South African territory

It is an ideal which I hope to live for and to achieve. But if needs be, it is an ideal for which I am prepared to die."

None of Mandela's many journeys before and after his imprisonment were as significant as his short walk through those prison gates.

---

*Nelson Mandela, *Nelson Mandela in His Own Words*, ed. Kader Asmal, David Chidester, and Wilmot James (New York: Little, Brown, 2003), pp. 46–47.

Nelson Mandela
(1918–2013) South African leader of the African National Congress and opponent of apartheid. Sentenced to life in prison in 1964; released in 1990. After winning the Nobel Peace Prize in 1993, he became the country's first democratically elected president in 1994.

As a youth, Mandela received an education in the history of his own Tembu people and in the protocols of the chief's court while also attending an English-language primary school. There a teacher assigned him the "proper" English name of Nelson; before that, he was called Rolihlahla ("pulling the branch of a tree," or "troublemaker"). He lived up to his African name at the all-black Methodist college he attended when he became embroiled in student politics and was expelled after leading a protest. In 1941, he fled to Johannesburg to avoid an arranged marriage, completed his B.A. degree, and became one of the country's few black lawyers.

Mandela combined his practice of law with a passion for politics, taking a leadership role in the African National Congress, the party that had, since 1912, worked for racial equality in South Africa (see Chapters 27 and 29). When their nonviolent campaign was met with police brutality and escalating repression, Mandela was set on the path that led to his imprisonment and his later triumph. In 1994, he became the country's first democratically elected president.

The world changed dramatically in the period of Mandela's confinement. In 1964, Cold War tensions had dominated international affairs. By the time of his release from prison, however, the collapse of the Soviet Union brought new possibilities. Hopes for democracy spread not only across Russia and the former Soviet sphere but also in many other parts of the world—Africa, Latin America, and parts of Asia—where Cold War alliances had empowered authoritarian regimes (see Chapter 30). Capturing the optimism of the time, President George H. W. Bush of the United States spoke of a *"new world order."* With the stalemate of the Cold War broken the path lay open, he said in 1991, to *"a world in which freedom and respect for human rights find a home among all nations."*

Still, myriad challenges remained. Russia's transition to democracy and capitalism was difficult, peace in the Middle East remained elusive, and democratic elections in South Africa did not instantly or automatically remove the inequalities of apartheid. The liberal association between free trade and democratic politics was contradicted by the People's Republic of China, where market-driven economic reforms created the world's fastest-growing economy under the control of a communist government. Some critics of the United States equated "globalization" with "Americanization" and saw the "new world order" as a means of expanding American power. Among them were Islamist activists who joined the struggle against what they saw as the decadent West. While the last decade of the twentieth century therefore offered hope, and in some places genuine progress toward freedom and security, the "new world order" did not offer a clear and agreed-upon road map as humanity entered the twenty-first century.

FOCUS QUESTIONS

❯ What were the major causes of the collapse of the Soviet Union?

❯ How successful were free markets and political reforms in bringing stability and democracy to different world regions?

❯ At the end of the twentieth century, in what ways were major conflicts in the Middle East still unresolved?

❯ What were the major effects of economic globalization?

The Late Cold War and the Collapse of the Soviet Union, 1975–1991

Abandoning Vietnam in 1975, the United States was divided and weary of war. Sensing an American lack of resolve, Soviet leaders expanded their military and their support for rebel movements. In 1981, however, a reassertive United States confronted the Soviet regime with the need to increase its military spending or fall behind in a renewed arms race. Meanwhile, in eastern Europe simmering discontent was threatening outright rebellion. After 1985 a new Soviet leader, Mikhail Gorbachev, initiated reforms, but it was too little, too late. In 1989, the Berlin Wall fell, and in 1991 the Soviet Union dissolved.

After Soviet communism's collapse, Germany reunified, while Poland, the Czech Republic, and other formerly communist states became stable democracies. But in Russia and some other nations that emerged from the U.S.S.R.'s breakup, establishing democratic institutions proved difficult. Where authoritarian traditions persisted, sharp inequalities attended the introduction of capitalist markets.

The United States in the Post-Vietnam Era, 1975–1990

Misadventure in Vietnam, and the resignation in 1974 of President Nixon as a result of the Watergate scandal, left U.S. society in disarray. At the same time, a steep rise in oil prices engineered by the Organization of Petroleum Exporting Countries (OPEC) shocked Americans, as did the combination of slow growth and inflation that was to afflict the U.S. economy throughout the 1970s.

When Iranian revolutionaries seized American hostages in late 1979 and a rescue attempt the following spring failed to free them, Americans felt powerless and angry. In the 1980 presidential campaign, Republican **Ronald Reagan** (in office 1981–1989) promised to restore American power and confidence. His sweeping victory brought a brash, nationalistic, and sternly anticommunist tone to American foreign policy and sharp increases in military spending. The "Reagan Revolution" was a backlash among conservatives against what they considered the liberal excesses of the 1960s and 1970s. This modern American conservative movement hoped to turn back the stronger role the government had taken for five decades in areas such as civil rights, social welfare, regulation of financial institutions, and environmental protection.

Reagan found a strong British ally in Conservative Prime Minister Margaret Thatcher, who was equally committed to rolling back the scope of government at home and to confronting the Soviet Union more forcefully abroad. However, many in Europe, as well as in the United States, were alarmed by Reagan's refusal to use the diplomatic language of détente. Europeans rallied for peace, and their leaders rejected Reagan's description of the Soviet Union as an "evil empire," preferring instead to continue the language of "peaceful coexistence." Still, when Reagan traveled to Germany in 1987 he stood before the Berlin Wall and demanded, *"Mr. Gorbachev, tear down this wall!"* Few guessed just how soon the wall would indeed come down.

Ronald Reagan
(1911–2004) Fortieth president of the United States. A staunchly anti-communist Republican, he used harsh rhetoric toward the Soviet Union and increased American military spending but compromised when negotiating arms limitations agreements.

From Leonid Brezhnev to Mikhail Gorbachev

The period from 1964 to 1982, when Leonid Brezhnev led the Soviet Union, was a time of relative stability for many Soviet citizens. While their standard of living was low, employment, education, and health care were guaranteed. Soviet citizens might never own a car, but they could take an annual vacation. While they had no freedom of speech, religion, or assembly, they did have secure old-age pensions. Perhaps for those who had lived through the ravages of Stalinism and the Second World War, basic security was enough. But for the younger Soviet generation, aware of the higher standard of living in the West, dissatisfaction with the dull status quo was growing.

Some Russian and eastern European dissidents were emboldened to assert their views after détente with the United States led to the **Helsinki Accords**, signed in 1975. This agreement committed western Europe and the United States to recognize the borders of the communist bloc countries in return for a Soviet pledge to respect basic human rights. Among those brave enough to speak out was Russian physicist Andrei Sakharov (1921–1989), the man most responsible for the development of the Soviet hydrogen bomb.

Sakharov argued that Soviet society could advance only through greater freedom of information: *"We are infinitely outstripped in computer technology,"* Sakharov and dissident colleagues wrote as early as 1970 to the Soviet leadership, *"crucial because the introduction of electronic computers into the economy is a phenomenon of decisive importance."** While Soviet computer scientists and mathematicians were world class, the centralized system they worked in denied them the avenues to creativity open to their American counterparts. There could be no Soviet equivalent to the Apple Corporation, which starting in 1977 pioneered the individual use of computers, democratizing access to this increasingly powerful technology. The idea that computing would be accessible to individuals apart from state control was inconceivable in Brezhnev's Soviet Union. *"We simply live in another age,"** Sakharov concluded.

Though he was awarded the Nobel Prize in 1975, Brezhnev prevented Sakharov from traveling to receive his award and cut him off from communications with the outside world. Soviet promises to respect human rights meant nothing in practice.

A large gap separated the Soviet Union's global ambitions from the resources generated by its inefficient economy. Huge food imports were financed by energy exports, but better and more abundant consumer options never materialized as promised. Brezhnev worsened the economic problem by making major new military commitments in the wake of the American withdrawal from Vietnam. When the Reagan administration subsequently stepped up American military spending in the 1980s, an already overstretched Soviet Union could not keep pace.

War in Afghanistan took an especially heavy toll on Brezhnev's regime. After Afghan communists seized power in Kabul in 1978 with the help of Soviet Special Forces, a Soviet occupation faced tough resistance from Islamic guerrilla fighters known as *mujahaddin* (moo-jah-ha-DEEN). The mujahaddin, aided by the United States and Pakistan, used their familiarity with the land and the populace to counter superior Soviet technology. As death tolls increased, the Soviet people grew weary of the war in Afghanistan, just as Americans had with Vietnam.

Helsinki Accords

A 1975 agreement made during the Cold War that gave recognition to the borders of communist bloc countries in eastern Europe in return for a Soviet promise, never fulfilled, to respect basic human rights.

---

*Andrei Sakharov, Roy Medvedev, and Valentine Turchin, "Letter to Comrades Brezhnev, Kosygin, and Podgorny," in *Sources of Global History since 1900*, ed. James H. Overfield, 2d ed. (Boston: Wadsworth, 2013), p. 300.

● **CONTEXT&CONNECTIONS** Afghanistan was already known as the "graveyard of empire," after local fighters repeatedly repelled British invaders in the nineteenth century. After expelling Soviet forces, many mujahaddin would turn on their former American patrons, as discussed later in this chapter. ●

When Brezhnev died in 1982, he left a difficult situation to the aging party functionaries who replaced him. Then in 1985 came a startling change when **Mikhail Gorbachev** (b. 1931) consolidated power. Believing that real reform would be necessary to save the Soviet system, and sensing the impatience of Russia's younger generation, Gorbachev denounced what he called *"the era of stagnation"* under Brezhnev. He withdrew from Afghanistan, reached out to President Reagan in pursuit of further arms limitations, and introduced policies of *perestroika* ("restructuring") and *glasnost* ("openness"). Perestroika brought an end to massive economic centralization. While the state would still dominate, industry would now use market incentives rather than bureaucratic command to manage production. Glasnost allowed formerly taboo subjects to be discussed.

Gorbachev's new policy was tested in 1986, when officials tried to cover up the Chernobyl disaster, the worst nuclear accident in history to that time, enraging both the Soviet people and their European neighbors. Gorbachev promised that the old pattern of Soviet lies would be replaced by honesty and openness.

Glasnost was effective. For the first time since the earliest days of the revolution, Russians were free to speak their minds and publish their opinions. However, the economic progress promised by perestroika failed to materialize. The Russian people still faced their dreary daily routine of standing in long lines for basics like milk, bread, and eggs. The only difference from the Brezhnev era was that they were now free to complain about it. By the end of the 1980s, Gorbachev's popularity was plummeting.

Glasnost also contributed to the unraveling of the Soviet Union. When members of disaffected ethnic groups gained a public voice for their grievances with Russian rule, the forces of repressed nationalism exploded in various republics, such as Georgia in the Caucasus Mountains and the Baltic states of Latvia, Lithuania, and Estonia. The Soviet Union began to break apart as Gorbachev agreed to a treaty giving the republics of the U.S.S.R. their de facto independence as part of a commonwealth led from Moscow (see Map 31.1).

This political fragmentation was too much for hard-line conservatives in the Communist Party who, in the summer of 1991, attempted a coup d'état. But huge crowds rallied to protect the newly elected government of the Russian Republic, which then outlawed the Communist Party of the Soviet Union. Gorbachev had failed to find a middle ground between reform and revolution. His combination of Marxism-Leninism with market reforms and political transparency was a halfway measure, doomed to failure.

Revolution in Eastern Europe

As the Hungarian uprising in 1956 and the Prague Spring in 1968 had shown, force had been necessary to keep eastern Europe in Moscow's orbit (see Chapter 30). By the mid-1980s, however, the Soviet Union was no longer willing to intervene to retain control. In Poland, for example, Catholicism was a touchstone of Polish nationalism and a historical connection with the West. The surprise announcement in 1978 that the Polish cardinal Karol Wojtyla would become Pope John Paul II powerfully affirmed that national feeling.

Mikhail Gorbachev (b. 1931) Leader of the Soviet Union from 1985 to 1991 who introduced "openness" to Soviet politics and "restructuring" to the Soviet economy. Unable to control calls for even greater changes, Gorbachev presided over the collapse of the Soviet Union.

Map 31.1 The Dissolution of the Soviet Union In the 1990s, the collapse of the Soviet Union led to the creation of new states across eastern Europe, the Caucasus Mountains, and Central Asia, regions that in the nineteenth century had been part of the Russian empire. The Baltic states of Estonia, Latvia, and Lithuania emerged as thriving democracies. Conflict was endemic in the Caucasus, however, where Russia battled separatists in Chechnya and Armenia and Azerbaijan fought for control of territory. The new nations of formerly Soviet Central Asia were dominated by strong-armed dictators.

Solidarity

Polish trade union created in 1980 that organized opposition to Communist rule. In 1989, Solidarity leader Lech Walesa was elected president of Poland as the Communists lost their hold on power.

In 1980, discontent with the communist regime reached a turning point with the formation of **Solidarity**, the first independent trade union in the Soviet bloc. In a direct challenge to the authority of the Communist Party, nearly a third of Poland's population joined Solidarity. Faced with increasing unrest, the government agreed to an election in 1989. The result was a massive victory for Solidarity and the election of its leader Lech Walesa to the position of president. The "iron curtain" was starting to crumble.

In Czechoslovakia, the young rebels of the Prague Spring of 1968 were now adults and began pushing for a new constitution. They had an additional grievance: the terrible pollution and environmental degradation caused by communism's industrial policies. Unaccountable to public opinion, the communists had not matched western European progress in protecting their nation's air, water, and forests. The police cracked down on democratic protesters, but they were unable to control events: this time no Soviet forces arrived to save them.

Communism's fall went so smoothly in Czechoslovakia that it has been called the "Velvet Revolution."

The new presidents of Poland and Czechoslovakia could not have come from more different backgrounds: Lech Walesa was a shipyard worker and labor organizer, while the Czechoslovak leader, Václav Havel, was a dramatist and intellectual. When they met as leaders of truly independent and democratic states, their complementarity was obvious, showing that for all their differences, industrial workers and artists had both been straitjacketed by communism. Now, no longer would Polish and Czech workers have to settle for the phony trade unions imposed on them by Communist Party officials, and no longer would eastern European artists have to conform to the dictates of cultural commissars.

Communism fell more suddenly and violently in Romania, where Nicolae Ceausescu (chow-SHES-koo) had ruled with an iron fist, building sumptuous palaces while his people went hungry. Isolated in his palace, Ceausescu did not realize the depth of public anger. Then, at a large public rally, Ceausescu stepped forward to receive the accolades of the crowd; instead, he was loudly jeered. Television showed Ceausescu's confusion as he heard, for the first time, his people's true opinion. His own security officials turned on him, and he and his wife were summarily executed by firing squad—the end of a brutal and vain dictator who died despised by the people he had long abused.

● **CONTEXT&CONNECTIONS** The humiliating end of Nicolae Ceausescu, with the video of his execution shown on Romanian television, was reminiscent of the ignoble treatment of the Italian fascist *Benito Mussolini*, his corpse hung by his heels from a balcony (key term in Chapter 29). Other dictators whose brutality caught up with them include Saddam Hussein of Iraq and Muammar Qaddafi of Libya (see Chapter 32). ●

The most evocative image of the fall of communism in eastern Europe was the destruction of the Berlin Wall, symbol of the Cold War since 1961. In the summer of 1989 pressure was increasing on East German authorities to allow freer transit to the West after Hungary opened its border with Austria. As huge crowds gathered at the Wall, a single gate was unexpectedly opened and a flood of East Berliners streamed across. Soon after, euphoric Berliners demolished the Wall in a festival of constructive mayhem.

If, in retrospect, the fall of communism in Europe seems to have been inevitable, it certainly did not seem so to people at the time. In East Germany, Bulgaria, Romania, and across eastern Europe, soldiers under the command of communist officials faced the awful prospect of being ordered to fire on crowds of protesters. When they did not do so, the people's sense of relief was palpable, and their feeling of joy in victory all the more intense.

Post-Soviet Struggles for Democracy and Prosperity

The failure of the communist coup in 1991 and the fall of Mikhail Gorbachev put Russian President **Boris Yeltsin** (1931–2007) in charge of defining a new path for the country. (See the feature "Visual Evidence in Primary Sources: Tanks and Protests in Moscow and Beijing.") Advised by American economists that free markets would bring prosperity, Yeltsin instituted bold economic reforms. The immediate results, however, were disappointing. A few "new oligarchs" of the post-Soviet economic elite grew

Boris Yeltsin
(1931–2007) First president of the Russian Federation, from 1991 to 1999. He rallied the people of Moscow to defend their elected government during the attempted communist coup of 1991, but his presidency was marred by financial scandals and war in Chechnya.

Tanks and Protests in Moscow and Beijing

Among the many striking images associated with the late Cold War period are these very different representations of the role that tanks played in political protests in Beijing in 1989 and Moscow in 1991. The Chinese image shows the repression of democracy, the Russian one its triumph.

As China opened up to the world in the 1980s, it was undertaking a much more successful economic restructuring than Mikhail Gorbachev's perestroika, but its leaders had done virtually nothing to emulate his program of glasnost, or "openness." By 1989, some Chinese, especially students in the capital city of Beijing, thought it was time for a change. They were inspired by a visit from Gorbachev but also by ideals of democracy they associated with the United States.

From April to August 1989, large crowds assembled in Beijing's Tiananmen Square to protest corruption and to advocate democracy. Under the giant banner of Chairman Mao that dominates the square, students erected a facsimile of the Statue of Liberty. Some Communist officials were sympathetic to the protests and urged dialogue. Chairman Deng Xiaoping rejected their advice and sent in the People's Army to dislodge the protesters. Estimates on the number of those killed range from the hundreds to the thousands.

AP Images/Jeff Widener

Taken with a long-range lens from a Beijing hotel room, this photograph of a lone individual trying to stop a line of surging tanks (which eventually went around him) summed up both the heroism and futility of the Tiananmen protests. He has never been identified. In 1989, *Time* magazine declared the "Unknown Rebel" to be one of the one hundred most influential people of the twentieth century.

By this time, it was becoming clear that fundamental changes were likely to occur in the Soviet Union. Gorbachev was in danger of losing central control as nationalists began discussing separation from the U.S.S.R. After first resisting that trend, he then agreed to a compromise that would enhance the power of the individual republics, reversing the old domination from Moscow. In the summer of 1991, a group of Communist Party officials and army officers, understanding that the Soviet Union stood on the brink of dissolution, launched the August Coup to restore central authority.

How does the manner in which the photographer has framed each of the shots affect the viewer's reactions?

Boris Yeltsin, elected president of the Russian Republic, stands on top of a tank, rallying the people of Moscow in defense of their new democratic institutions. The commander of the tank brigade had declared his loyalty to the Russian Republic and had refused to join Soviet forces against it. Contrary to the wishes of the coup plotters, this image was shown on state television and became a rallying point for further defense of democracy.

In the background is the Russian "white house," the parliament of the Russian Republic. The authority of this elected body was part of the shift away from centralized Soviet control toward newly empowered governmental institutions within the republic. After declaring a state of emergency, the coup leaders had the building shelled.

AP Images

The coup plotters were unable to muster enough military strength to overcome this resistance, which would have required a level of violence and death that was intolerable to most military commanders. Gorbachev regained his authority and declared the orders of the coup leaders null and void. It was not much of a victory, however, as the Soviet state quickly unraveled around him.

very wealthy very suddenly when state assets were auctioned off. But they often behaved more like gangsters than corporate executives, using government ties to enrich themselves and suppress competition.

Many Russians suffered when the old sureties of the Soviet system—free education and health care, guaranteed employment, old-age pensions—disappeared: the market system did not instantly make up for their loss. Even as imported consumer products became widely available, few had the means to purchase them. By the end of the 1990s, life expectancy and fertility rates were in decline, and too many Russians were hungry and cold.

Yeltsin's problems were compounded by unrest in the southern Caucasus region, where Muslim guerrillas organized a separatist movement in Chechnya (CHECH-nee-yah). Though Yeltsin used massive military force against them, he was unable to suppress the uprising. In 1999 an ailing Yeltsin handed power to a former intelligence officer, Vladimir Putin.

Putin was elected to his office in 2000 by Russian voters anxious to embrace an authority figure who promised order. Putin reined in capitalism by restoring state authority over the economy and the media, using control of oil revenues and television as bases of power. He crushed the Chechnya rebellion, stood up to the United States in global forums, and restored order to the Russian Republic. Stability was achieved, but at the expense of democracy and civil rights.

● **CONTEXT&CONNECTIONS** The stakes of *Vladimir Putin's* (Chapter 32) gambit to restore Russian dignity and power in global forums increased significantly in 2014. His invasion and annexation of the Crimean peninsula and support for rebels in eastern Ukraine brought Western economic sanctions, and the plummeting price of oil revealed underlying weaknesses in a Russian economy overly dependent on energy exports. ●

The former Central Asian republics of the U.S.S.R. faced equally difficult transitions. Located on the borderlands between China, Russia, and the Muslim world, these newly independent nations had plentiful natural resources, especially oil and gas. The potential for democracy, however, was limited because, unlike in eastern Europe, regime change came from the top down rather than through popular mobilization. Kazakhstan and Uzbekistan were typical, with independence overseen by former communist officials who paid lip service to democracy while keeping a tight rein on power and resources.

In general, the transition to liberal governance and market economics was smoother in eastern Europe. Estonia, the Czech Republic, and Poland all experienced political and economic progress in the 1990s, with a blossoming of the free associations that characterize civil society.

The reunification of Germany was more difficult. East Germans were much poorer than West Germans and usually lacked competitive job skills. The first decade after the fall of the Berlin Wall brought freedom and opportunity to eastern Germany, but also unemployment and insecurity. Still, reunification magnified Germany's diplomatic and economic centrality to Europe and its place as a global leader in science, technology, and manufacturing.

The fall of the Soviet Union was clearly a momentous turning point in modern history. It marked not only the failure of the world's longest experiment with communism but also the breakup of the formerly great Russian empire.

The Late Cold War in Latin America and Africa: Crisis and Opportunity

During the late stages of the Cold War (1975–1990), political crises afflicted many parts of Africa and Latin America. Then the collapse of the Soviet Union brought opportunities to heal political divisions and bring greater democracy. In Central America, violence between leftist insurgents and military regimes aligned with Washington gave way in the 1990s to elections and new hope for democracy and stability. Likewise in southern Africa, elections superceded warfare. But civil war and genocide in Central Africa demonstrated the destructive legacies of colonialism and superpower intervention.

From Dictatorship to Democracy in Central America

In the 1980s, a principle battleground between leftist rebels and military forces backed by the United States was Central America. Through its controversial School of the Americas, the U.S. military had trained the officer corps of many Latin American nations, a number of whom either directly intervened in politics (as in Chile and Argentina, see Chapter 30) or supported corrupt dictatorships. Latin American leftists ascribed the cruelty and corruption of such regimes to American imperialism.

Nicaragua, for example, had long been ruled by the Somoza family, dictators aligned with American economic interests. Resistance to the Somoza dictatorship was organized by the rebel Sandinista National Liberation Front. Following a major earthquake in 1972, the Somoza family stole millions of dollars of relief aid, pushing many Nicaraguans toward sympathy with the rebels. In 1979, the Sandinistas ousted the Somoza regime and formed a new government.

After Ronald Reagan took office in 1981, his administration threw its support behind anti-Sandinista insurgents known as *Contras*, illegally evading congressional oversight to get funds for the Contras by selling arms to the Iranian regime. To protect the revolution, the Sandinistas then clamped down on civil liberties, following Fidel Castro's earlier example and relying on Cuban support.

Then Soviet decline brought new possibilities for a negotiated settlement. Since Cuba's economy was undercut as Gorbachev phased out Soviet subsidies, Cuba could no longer aid the Sandinistas, and U.S. leaders no longer saw the Contras as necessary allies. Free elections were held in Nicaragua in 1989. The defeated Sandinistas respected the election results by peacefully handing over power, a major step forward for Nicaraguan democracy.

Violence also marred Guatemalan society in the 1980s. Paramilitary death squads connected with Guatemala's right-wing leaders targeted villagers, mostly indigenous Maya people, suspected of collusion with rebel armies. The killers themselves were often boys who had been kidnapped by the army and forced into service. As many as a million refugees fled from the mountains to the cities or across the border into Mexico.

- **CONTEXT&CONNECTIONS** After 1954, when *Che Guevara* (Chapter 30) had witnessed the U.S.-backed overthrow of the reformist Arbenz regime, Guatemala's leftists took up arms. In the 1980s, with violence wracking the countryside, the situation of the nation's poor was worse than ever. ●

Jean Louis Atlan/Sygma/Corbis

Sandinistas Nicaragua's Sandinistas were victorious in 1979 but U.S.-backed Contra rebels challenged their control. The Sandinistas modeled themselves on Cuban revolutionary heroes; the soldier on the right wears a red-starred beret like that of Che Guevara (see Chapter 30).

After the Cold War, the United States pressured the Guatemalan government and military to work toward a solution. A peace deal was finally brokered in 1996, when the rebels agreed to lay down their arms in exchange for land. For the first time since 1952 Guatemalans went to the polls to vote in free elections, and a government panel was soon set up to investigate paramilitary atrocities.

The relationship of the Roman Catholic Church with the politics of repression and democratization in Latin American was especially complex. During the 1970s many parish priests, influenced by 1960s radicalism, subscribed to "liberation theology" with its "preferential option for the poor." Members of the higher Church hierarchy, on the other hand, tended to maintain traditional ties to ruling oligarchs and their military allies. That division within the Catholic Church deepened after the accession of the strongly anticommunist Pope John Paul II, who quickly reined in the liberation theologians.

An especially dark chapter was the murder in 1980 of three nuns and a lay missionary from the United States by El Salvador's National Guard and the assassination that same year of the relatively moderate Archbishop Óscar Romero, who had spoken out publicly against government abuses.

But by the 1990s, the trend in El Salvador, as in Latin America as a whole, was toward democracy. In Argentina, change had come in 1982 after defeat in the Falklands War against Great Britain showed the incompetence of Argentine generals and brought about irresistible calls for change. Elections swept the military from power in Brazil as well. Even in Chile, where the Pinochet regime was deeply entrenched (see Chapter 30), pressures mounted for a free election, and in 1988 Chilean voters turned down his continued dictatorship.

Thus the democratization of Latin American nations paralleled the liberation of eastern Europe. But where countries like Poland had escaped from Soviet domination, those like Chile had freed themselves from dictatorships allied with the United States.

In Mexico, however, the problem was neither military governments nor Cold War alignments, but rather the political monopoly of the Party of Institutional Revolution (PRI), which constrained Mexican freedoms while binding the country to incompetence and corruption (see Chapter 30). Finally, in 1989, a conservative opposition party made inroads in the state of Baja California, ushering in more open electoral competition at the national level. In 2000, the election of an opposition candidate as president finally ended the PRI monopoly on Mexico's national politics.

South African Liberation

During Nelson Mandela's many years in prison, South African apartheid became more and more extreme. The government oversaw a "Bantu education" system that prepared blacks only for menial jobs. Strictly enforced residential segregation made it illegal for blacks to be in "white" areas unless they could prove they were there for employment. Meanwhile, white South Africans enjoyed a First World standard of living.

To complete racial separation, the South African government developed the system of **Bantustans**, based on the idea that Tswana, Zulu, Xhosa, and other African peoples did not belong to a common South Africa but to "tribal" enclaves where they should seek their rights. According to apartheid, these impoverished and scattered territories would form the basis for independent "nations," one for each of South Africa's "tribes." In reality, the Bantustans were simply a device to exclude blacks from South African citizenship and deprive them of any hope for rights in a unified South Africa.

Bantustans
Term used by apartheid planners for "tribal regions" in which Africans, denied citizenship in a common South Africa, were expected to live when not working for whites. They were not internationally recognized and were later reabsorbed into democratic South Africa.

● **CONTEXT&CONNECTIONS** The boundaries of the Bantustans of the 1970s derived from the Native Land Act of 1913, originally designed to turn Africans into low-cost workers (see Chapter 26). From that time, inadequate land and overcrowding had forced blacks to seek work for low wages at white-controlled mines, cities, and farms. ●

With Nelson Mandela and other African National Congress (ANC) leaders languishing in jail or in exile, in the 1970s a new generation of leaders emerged. The Black Consciousness Movement was led by Steve Biko, who argued that black South Africans faced not only the external challenge of apartheid but also an inner challenge to surmount the psychological damage it caused. The first step toward liberation, Biko said, was for blacks to eliminate their own sense of inferiority.

● **CONTEXT&CONNECTIONS** In emphasizing the need for colonized blacks to liberate themselves from an internalized sense of inferiority, Steve Biko echoed the message of Frantz Fanon in *The Wretched of the Earth* (see Chapter 30). ●

In 1976, black South African youths who heeded Biko's call were at the forefront of the **Soweto Uprising**, protesting the dismal quality of their education. When marchers refused an order to disband, police fired into the crowd, killing dozens of children. As protests spread across the country, authorities responded with their usual brutality. But Black Consciousness stayed alive in the Soweto generation even after 1977, when Steve Biko's jailers beat him to death.

Soweto Uprising
(1976) Youth demonstrations in South Africa that were met with police violence. The Soweto Uprising brought a new generation of activists, inspired by Steve Biko's Black Consciousness Movement, to the forefront of resistance to apartheid.

Soweto Uprising In 1976, schoolchildren in South Africa protested the compulsory teaching of the Dutch-based Afrikaans language in their schools. When police fired into the crowd, made up mostly of teenagers, hundreds were killed and thousands injured. The Soweto generation played a central role in bringing down apartheid over the next fifteen years. (Bettman/Corbis)

By 1983, black trade unions, church groups, and student organizations had formed a nationwide United Democratic Front. Schoolchildren boycotted apartheid schools. Resistance on the streets became violent. Sometimes African militants cruelly executed those accused of collaboration with apartheid by putting tires around their necks and setting them ablaze. In 1986, the government declared a state of emergency and sent the army into the black townships to restore order.

Meanwhile, critics outside South Africa argued that economic sanctions could help force meaningful change. In 1986, the U.S. Congress passed a comprehensive bill limiting trade with and investment in South Africa, overriding the veto of President Reagan, who saw the white government as a staunch ally and viewed Mandela and the ANC as communist sympathizers.

Feeling the pressure from domestic resistance and from sanctions, the South African government offered to release Mandela if he renounced the ANC.

His daughter Zindzi read his response at a packed soccer stadium: *"I will remain a member of the African National Congress until the day I die.... Your freedom and mine cannot be separated. I will return."** Finally, as the decline of the Soviet Union undercut the government's claim that Mandela and the ANC represented a front for Soviet-backed communism, and as sanctions undermined an already weak economy, South African President F. W. de Klerk granted Mandela an unconditional release in 1990. Despite ongoing violence, elections were held in 1994. Mandela was easily elected president, and the ANC became the dominant political force in the new South Africa.

True to the words he had spoken at his trial in 1964, Mandela emphasized inclusiveness in his government. South Africa, christened the "rainbow nation," had a new flag, a new sense of self-identity, a multiracial Olympic team, and one of the world's most democratic constitutions. A Truth and Reconciliation Commission was instituted to uncover the abuses of apartheid, while offering amnesty to those who publicly acknowledged their crimes.

Immense challenges faced Mandela as he took up his presidency. The deeply rooted inequalities of apartheid would not disappear overnight, and HIV/AIDS was beginning to take a heavy toll. At first President Mandela paid little attention to HIV/AIDS, a mistake he later acknowledged and corrected, revealing that his own son had died of the disease and urging South Africans toward a frank discussion of sexuality and sexual health. In this crisis, as in the many others he faced, Mandela's deep ethical integrity marked him as a leader of rare ability. Without Nelson Mandela, it is doubtful whether South Africa could have navigated the end of apartheid as safely and successfully as it did.

South Africa's successful first democratic, nonracial election on April 24, 1994, was one of the greatest and least expected outcomes of the post–Cold War period. But just a few weeks earlier, two thousand miles to the north in Rwanda, a genocidal slaughter had begun.

The Rwandan Genocide and Congolese Conflict The Rwandan genocide of 1994 is often presented as having "tribal" or "ethnic" roots, but Rwandans, Hutu as well as Tutsi, speak the same language, participate in the same culture, and mostly share a common Roman Catholic faith. As colonial rulers, however, the Belgians had sharply differentiated the two groups, favoring the Tutsi as local allies and giving Tutsi children preferred access to European education. Consequent resentments surfaced upon independence in 1960, when the previously disenfranchised Hutu took power and expelled many Tutsi. By the 1980s, these Tutsi exiles had organized a rebel army in neighboring Uganda.

In 1994, Hutu death squads went on a rampage when the plane carrying the Rwandan president was shot from the sky, and within a few months nearly a million people had been slaughtered, many cut with machetes. Extremist Hutu radio announcers urged young men to grab weapons and exterminate the Tutsi "cockroaches" and any moderate Hutu who tried to protect them. Since there were high rates of intermarriage, and since Hutu and Tutsi lived together in the same villages, the murderers might even kill their own neighbors and family members.

---

*Nelson Mandela, *Nelson Mandela in His Own Words*, ed. Kader Asmal, David Chidester, and Wilmot James (New York: Little, Brown, 2003), pp. 59–62.

Smartphones and "Conflict Minerals"

Internet-enabled smartphones have become ubiquitous, with the total number of users likely to surpass 2 billion in 2016. It is impossible to predict the long-term cultural and economic impacts of this global telecommunications revolution.

Engineers are constantly trying to find smaller and more efficient components for these devices, and the mineral tantalum, derived from coltan, is essential to their plans. Tantalum is irreplaceable as a material for building highly efficient, miniaturized capacitors for mobile electronics. And the quest for coltan leads directly to the Democratic Republic of the Congo, where 80 percent of the world's supply is found in the north and east of the country. Unfortunately, this is the same region deeply affected by the aftershocks of the Rwandan genocide, including foreign incursions and the depredations of murderous warlords. The smartphones on which we increasingly rely connect us, whether we know it or not, to the central African trade in "conflict minerals."

Ironically, given its high-technology applications, coltan is mined in the most primitive conditions, in places with poor roads and telecommunications, where men and boys literally scrape mud out of stream beds to locate it. The real profits come not in mining coltan, however, but in its transport and sale. This is where the warlords and smugglers get involved, and the human rights tragedy begins. Warlords are apt to recruit small boys as soldiers and to force girls into dependent domestic and sexual relationships. In addition to these human costs, the illicit and unregulated coltan trade, and the high-powered arms introduced along with it, is further threatening the endangered lowland gorilla population of the eastern Congo.

Meanwhile, profits from the coltan in our handheld devices, which might have helped Congo build its infrastructure for development, have instead gone to warlords, foreign invaders, and arms merchants. In a globalized world, the distance from the smartphones in our pockets to the war zones of eastern Congo is not great at all.

Source: "Where Apple Gets the Tantalum for Your iPhone," Lynnley Browning, *Newsweek*, February 4, 2015.

Another million Rwandans fled to neighboring countries, as United Nations peacekeepers stood by, unwilling to intervene. The conflict then spread west to further destabilize the already tottering Democratic Republic of the Congo.

The huge Congo nation, with its staggering mineral wealth, had been the great Cold War prize of the United States (see Chapter 30). Mobutu Sese Seko was the compliant dictator looking after American strategic and economic interests while stealing aid and resources so brazenly that analysts referred to his regime as a *kleptocracy*.

But with the fall of the Soviet Union and the release of Nelson Mandela, the U.S. affiliation with Mobutu Sese Seko became an embarrassment, and in 1990 Congress cut off direct aid and supported democratization efforts. Those efforts failed for two reasons. First, the political opponents of Mobutu were themselves bitterly divided; as in the early days of the Congo, most politicians represented regions and ethnic groups rather than ideas or policies. Second, the region was destabilized by the shock of genocide in Rwanda.

As a Tutsi army re-entered Rwanda to establish a new government, Hutu extremists who had perpetrated the horrible violence fled to refugee camps in neighboring Congo. When Mobutu Sese Seko sickened and died, his authoritarian rule was replaced not by freedom but by near anarchy, the country divided between multiple militias. Neighboring African countries compounded problems by sending in armies to back the various factions and vie for Congo's mineral wealth. (See the feature "World History in Today's World: Smartphones and 'Conflict Minerals.'")

Although the "new world order" of democracy and civil rights did not arrive in the Democratic Republic of the Congo, after 1995 Rwanda did make strides toward restoring peace and civility. And while a few African dictators of the old school refused to step off the stage and yield power to a new generation, signs of hope appeared in more and more places. In fact, enough progress was made toward rule of law, multiparty democracy, and economic reinvigoration on the continent that the phrase "African Renaissance" came to be used to indicate a renewed Afro-optimism as the twenty-first century approached. Democratic South Africa was just one of the now brighter lights to which those optimists might point.

Enduring Challenges in the Middle East

Throughout the twentieth century, the Middle East had been a politically unsettled region, where ethnic and religious rivalries created divisions magnified by the involvement of external powers. By the 1970s, the strategic importance of the Middle East as a source of petroleum had raised the stakes of conflict even higher.

Tension between Israel and its Arab neighbors intensified after 1973, when a brief war led Arab representatives of the **Organization of Petroleum Exporting Countries (OPEC)** to declare a boycott on oil exports to the United States in retribution for its military aid to the Jewish state. Greatly increased energy prices and the global economic slowdown that followed showed that the Arab-Israeli conflict could not be quarantined.

Meanwhile, after the Iranian Revolution of 1979, for the first time in the post-colonial era a state would be ruled under a constitution derived explicitly from Islamic law. In the 1980s, both Sunnis and Shi'ites were increasingly open to the appeals of **Islamists** who promised to restore dignity, ethical behavior, and prosperity by returning to core religious values. Islamism threatened regimes founded on the principles of secular Arab nationalism, such as Egypt, Syria, Iraq, and Jordan, while inspiring revolutionaries in Afghanistan. Meanwhile, the Israeli-Palestinian conflict endured. In spite of occasional signs of compromise, no resolution was forthcoming, although it seemed impossible that any meaningful "new world order" could ever be constructed without one.

Iran and Iraq   In the 1950s, American intervention had magnified the power of the shah of Iran while suppressing radical secular nationalism (see Chapter 30). For the next twenty years, Shah Pahlavi used oil money to modernize the country while his secret police repressed political dissidents, including conservative religious leaders who accused him of promoting decadent Western values and serving as a tool of U.S. power. On the other hand, these *mullahs* were no more sympathetic to the atheistic Soviet Union. Iranians shared their northern border with the U.S.S.R., which had occupied the north of the country in World War II and which they still regarded as a threat.

With riots and demonstrations spreading, the shah fled to the United States early in 1979. Returning from exile in Paris at the same time was **Ayatollah Khomeini** (1902–1989), whose authority was recognized by the ninety-thousand-member *ulama* (oo-leh-MAH), or community of Shi'ite religious scholars. Khomeini envisioned a tight connection between religious and governmental authority.

The path toward a just society, Islamists argued, was not through absorption of Western influences and modernity but through a return to the guiding precepts of their religion. Their argument was an explicit rejection of the secular

Organization of Petroleum Exporting Countries (OPEC)

An international organization of oil-producing nations created to set production quotas in an attempt to influence prices. OPEC's policies led to a steep rise in oil prices in the early 1970s.

Islamists

Muslims who believe that laws and constitutions should be guided by Islamic principles and that religious authorities should be directly involved in governance.

Ayatollah Khomeini

(1902–1989) Shi'ite cleric who led the Islamic Revolution in Iran in 1979 and became Supreme Leader of the Islamic Republic of Iran.

ideologies that had dominated nineteenth- and twentieth-century global political discourse. Though the radicals who seized the American embassy and hostages in Teheran were motivated more by nationalism than by religion, they responded to Khomeini's assessment of the United States as *the great Satan.*"

After Iraq invaded Iran, a surge of nationalism further consolidated support for Khomeini's government. During eight years of brutal fighting (1980–1988), over a million people were killed. Iranian civilians and soldiers suffered terribly when the Iraqi army used chemical weapons in violation of international law. That the U.S. administration of President Ronald Reagan aided the Iraqi military only furthered tensions between Washington and Teheran.

● **CONTEXT&CONNECTIONS** The battle lines of the Iran-Iraq War of the 1980s overlapped with both earlier and later ones. The armies of the Iranian *Safavid dynasty* and the Ottoman empire struggled over the same ground in the sixteenth century (Chapter 17) as did ISIS invaders and Iraqi forces beginning in 2014 (see Chapter 32). In every case, these armies struggled for control of the religious frontier between Sunni and Shi'ite majorities along the cultural frontier between Arab and Iranian populations. ●

Iranian Revolution Iranian nationalists, suspicious of both the United States and the Soviet Union, flocked to the banner of Ayatollah Khomeini to establish an Islamic Republic in 1979. Khomeini returned from exile in France as their spiritual and political leader, denouncing the United States as the "great Satan" for its longstanding support of the deposed shah. (AFP/Getty Images)

After reaching a stalemate with Iran, Iraqi President Saddam Hussein turned his expansionist ambitions toward Kuwait, a small, oil-rich state on the Persian Gulf. Hussein considered Kuwait part of Iraq's rightful patrimony, taken away from Baghdad's control during Britain's redrawing of former Ottoman boundaries in 1919 (see Chapter 27). Miscalculating that the United States, which had supported him in his war with Iran, would not oppose him now, Hussein invaded Kuwait in the summer of 1990 (see Map 31.2).

President George H. W. Bush reacted to Hussein's move by forging an international coalition against him. In the past, Hussein might have tried to counterbalance the United States by seeking an alliance with the Soviet Union, but that option no longer existed. Early in 1991, the **Persian Gulf War** began with the devastating U.S. bombing of Baghdad, after which the coalition swiftly liberated Kuwait. Hussein's army melted away, but while the path to Baghdad was open, the Bush administration calculated that removing Hussein would upset the delicate Middle Eastern balance of power. As Americans withdrew, Hussein brutally crushed a rebellion in the largely Shi'ite south.

Persian Gulf War
(1991) War that occurred when an international coalition led by the United States expelled Iraqi forces from Kuwait. Coalition forces then evacuated Iraq, and Saddam Hussein remained in power.

Afghanistan and Al-Qaeda

In 1993, the administration of new U.S. President William Jefferson (Bill) Clinton became increasingly concerned about Afghanistan. In the aftermath of the Soviet withdrawal, Afghanistan came under the control of the Taliban, Sunni Islamists advocating a severe form of fundamentalism. Women especially suffered; education for girls was eliminated completely. Mujahaddin from around the world had joined the fight against the Soviets in the 1980s, inspired by the call to holy war. After the Soviet withdrawal, some returned home to places like Egypt and Saudi Arabia determined to bring Islamic revolution to their own societies. Others found refuge in Afghanistan under the Taliban.

The most notorious was **Osama bin Laden** (1957–2011), son of a wealthy builder in Saudi Arabia. Though formerly allied with the United States against the Soviets, bin Laden despised the way America and the West propped up Israel and what he saw as illegitimate and corrupt Middle Eastern regimes, and he decried the presence of American soldiers on Saudi Arabian soil. Bin Laden and his followers in al-Qaeda (el-ka-AYE-dah) carried out truck bomb attacks on American embassies in Kenya and Tanzania in 1998. In retaliation, the Clinton administration bombed southeastern Afghanistan in an unsuccessful attempt to kill bin Laden and destroy al-Qaeda's base of operations.

Osama bin Laden
(1957–2011) Saudi Arabian leader of the Islamist group al-Qaeda, whose goal is to replace existing governments of Muslim countries with a purified caliphate; killed by U.S. commandos in 2011.

The Israeli-Palestinian Conflict

The unresolved Israeli-Palestinian conflict fueled Arab and Muslim resentments. A vicious cycle of violence rocked Israel and the occupied Palestinian territories in the 1970s and 1980s. Israel retained the territories it had occupied during the Six-Day War of 1967 (see Chapter 30), arguing that continued control of the West Bank and Gaza ensured Israeli security. But some Zionists believed that these lands, as part of the ancient Hebrew kingdom, should be permanently annexed. Thus the conservative Likud (lih-KOOD) Party, which ruled Israel for much of the period after 1977, sponsored the construction of Jewish settlements on the West Bank, violating international laws prohibiting lands taken in war from being resettled with citizens of the conquering nation. Return of the territory to its Arab inhabitants was becoming more and more difficult as Israeli settlements multiplied (see Map 31.2).

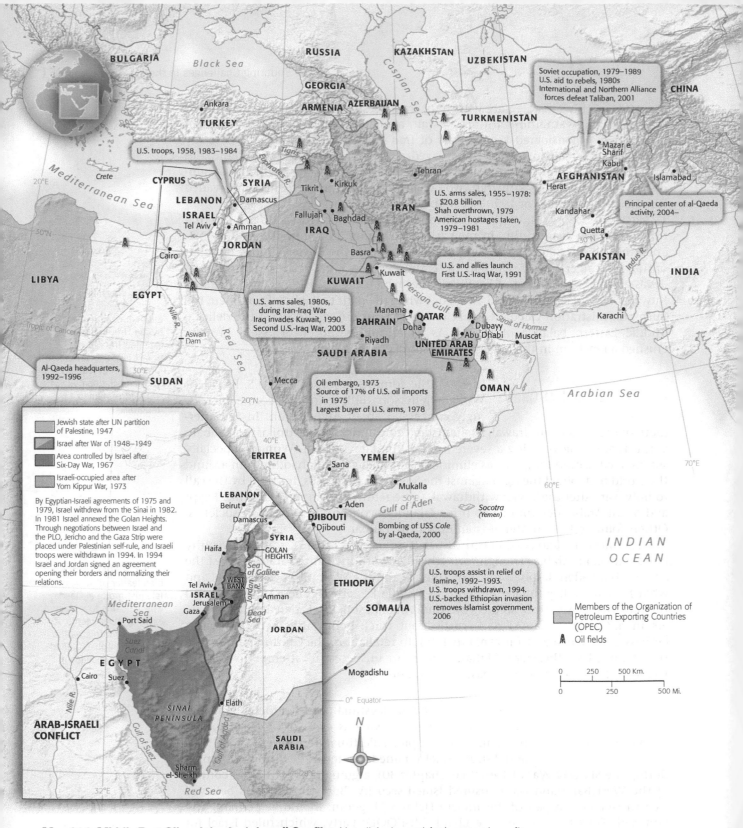

Map 31.2 Middle East Oil and the Arab-Israeli Conflict Not all Arabs and Arab states benefit from Middle Eastern oil reserves, which are highly concentrated in Saudi Arabia and the Persian Gulf. Farther west, Israel, born into a state of war when attacked by its Arab neighbors in 1948, ruled over significant Palestinian populations after taking the West Bank from Jordan and the Gaza Strip from Egypt during the Six-Day War in 1967. Whatever their other disagreements, Arabs have been unified in their denunciation of the Israeli occupation of the West Bank.

The Palestine Liberation Organization (PLO), under the leadership of Yasir Arafat (yah-SEER AHR-ah-FAT) (1929–2004), felt justified in using any means to resist the Israeli occupation, including terrorist attacks on civilians. In 1982, Israel invaded Lebanon to root out PLO bases, driving the group's leadership into North African exile. The savagery of the attacks on their refugee camps, combined with the retreat of the secular PLO, now led many Palestinians to switch their support to Islamist organizations: the Iranian-supported Hezbollah ("Party of God") in Lebanon, and in Palestine, Hamas (the "Islamic Resistance Movement"), a Sunni group related to Egypt's Muslim Brotherhood.

Violence flared again in Palestine in 1987 with the beginning of the first *intifada*, "ceaseless struggle," against the Israeli occupation of Gaza and the West Bank. The Israelis responded with security regulations restricting Palestinian mobility. Even as the intifada and the harsh Israeli response increased tensions on the ground, however, diplomatic initiatives were starting to bear some fruit.

In 1991, under European and American sponsorship, Israeli and Palestinian diplomats met to discuss possibilities for compromise, and in 1993 the Oslo

Hope for Middle East Peace This 1993 handshake between Israeli Prime Minister Yitzhak Rabin and Yasir Arafat, chairman of the Palestine Liberation Organization, gave the world hope for a Middle East peace. However, negotiations for an Israeli-PLO peace accord, mediated by U.S. President Bill Clinton, proved unsuccessful. (Reuters/Corbis)

Accords laid out a mutually agreed-upon "road map" for peace based on the idea of two separate and secure nations living side by side. President Clinton then invited Yasir Arafat and Israeli Prime Minister Yitzhak Rabin (YIT-shak rah-BEEN) to Washington for direct talks. As in South Africa at the very same time, it seemed that the post–Cold War climate meant the possibility of a new beginning.

The outcome dashed those hopes, however, when Arafat refused to accept an Israeli land-for-peace offer more generous than any previously discussed. The status of Jerusalem was one sticking point, with Israelis and Palestinians both laying claim to the city as their capital. In addition, the Israelis would not accept the Palestinian demand for a "right of return" for Arabs to the homes within Israel they had abandoned in the war of 1948. The "road map" had led nowhere.

Globalization and Its Discontents

The fall of the Soviet Union put economic globalization front and center on the world's agenda. Expanding global trade led to unprecedented growth and international economic integration. Some Asian economies surged, with the so-called "Asian Tigers," leading the way. Overcoming the disruptions of the Cultural Revolution (see Chapter 30), the People's Republic of China became the world's fastest-growing economy by adopting market principles.

When the European Economic Community transformed into the European Union (EU) in the 1990s, western Europe instantly became the world's largest single market. Expanding into the former Soviet sphere, the EU integrated parts of eastern Europe more fully into the world economy.

Amid the growth in trade and the incorporation of millions into global networks of consumption, it was also becoming clear that economic globalization brought increasing inequality. Both within nations and between them, the benefits of economic growth were not shared equally, as the gap between the global haves and have-nots increased. *Neoliberalism*, a belief in unfettered markets and unhindered international trade, proved popular with policymakers, but controversial to those who emphasized the more damaging effects of globalization.

Japan and the "Asian Tigers"

While Japan led the way in Asian economic growth in the 1950s, over the next three decades a number of other Asian economies would take off. Counted among these "Asian Tigers" were South Korea, Taiwan, and Singapore.

Japan rose quickly from the battering it took in 1945. Under occupation by the United States, Japanese leaders renounced militarism and accepted the democratic constitution Americans drafted for them. The energy and drive that had earlier gone into empire building was now focused on domestic rebirth. Fukuzawa Yûkichi (see Chapter 24) would have been proud as Japanese products came to surpass those of Europe and the United States in both quality and price.

Several factors facilitated Japanese economic success. American military protection relieved the country of the financial burden of military spending, and close collaboration between the government bureaucracy and large corporations brought planning and coordination to the national economy. Old corporations, like Mitsui, and new ones, like Sony, developed organizational structures that emphasized long-term loyalty between employers and Japanese employees, famous for their work ethic. However, company loyalty entailed endless work hours, and many Japanese women lived confining lives, raising children while rarely seeing their husbands.

● **CONTEXT&CONNECTIONS** In Japan, close coordination between large conglomerates and government civil servants began during the *Meiji Restoration*, when the government cultivated close relations with the large economic combines known as *zaibatsu* (Chapter 24). ●

In the 1970s, Japan enjoyed a rapid increase in automobile exports, especially to the United States. Japanese models first targeted consumers of inexpensive yet well-built cars. Meanwhile, manufacturers in the United States built large vehicles of indifferent quality. After oil prices surged following the OPEC oil boycott in 1973, demand for the more fuel-efficient Japanese cars skyrocketed.

At the same time, the rising price of oil revealed vulnerabilities in the Japanese economy. In addition to being dependent on food and energy imports, Japan was subject to competition from other Asian nations that began to follow the same industrial export strategy with lower labor costs. Japan responded by shifting from heavy industry toward knowledge-intensive sectors such as computers and telecommunications. Backed by large government subsidies for research and development, Japanese corporations in the 1980s increasingly focused on such high-profit activities while relocating many of their factories to other countries.

Then, even as American executives studied the Japanese model for business success, the bubble burst. In 1989, the Tokyo Stock Exchange collapsed. Real estate speculation, political corruption, and a banking crisis caused by bad loans were to blame. Demographics also played a role: Japan's low birth rate and stagnant population limited the expansion of domestic markets. To reignite the economy, the government began to emphasize leisure and consumption over savings, hoping that the country could spend its way out of crisis. While the Japanese economy stabilized, Asian growth moved elsewhere.

The South Korean government emulated the Japanese model, including close coordination between the state administration and the emerging Korean *chaebols*, economic conglomerates such as Samsung and Hyundai. It was also fiercely anticommunist, led by authoritarian personalities with close ties to the military, and paramilitary police often met student and worker protests with fatal force. The South Korean formula of authoritarian rule plus economic growth lasted until 1988, when public revulsion over the violent treatment of student protestors finally led to free elections and political liberalization.

● **CONTEXT&CONNECTIONS** In South Korea, the Summer Olympics of 1988 proved a spur to democratization, with the government anxious to showcase progressive reforms after its earlier harsh suppression of protests. That was the opposite of what had happened in Mexico twenty years earlier, when government suppression of protests leading up to the 1968 summer games culminated in the *Tlatelolco Massacre* (Chapter 30). ●

In Taiwan as well, anticommunism had led to a stern authoritarian political order dominated by Nationalist Party exiles from the mainland (see Chapter 30). As in South Korea, political liberty to match economic gains came to Taiwan only when global circumstances changed in the late 1980s, with the decline of the Soviet Union and the growth of trade with a now market-oriented Chinese mainland. In Taiwan's newly democratic political culture of the 1990s it was even possible to openly debate the previously forbidden topic of whether to declare Taiwanese independence rather than aspire to eventual reunification with the mainland. The liberal equation of rule of law, democratic processes, and free markets was being achieved.

The city-state of Singapore was the quintessence of an "Asian Tiger," its single-minded emphasis on economic growth bringing results that made it the envy of its neighbors. The success of tightly regimented Singapore led some analysts to speak of "Confucian capitalism," based on group consensus and hierarchy rather than individualism and class conflict, as an alternative to the individualistic Western model. But no generalizations about Asian capitalism could be made without taking into account the transformation of the People's Republic of China.

Deng Xiaoping's China and Its Imitators

At the start of the nineteenth century China produced about one-third of the world's industrial output (see page 685). But in 1949, after a century and a half of European economic dominance, that percentage had shrunk to less than 3 percent. The country's astonishing economic growth in the last two decades of the twentieth century restored China's historical role as a global center of manufacturing. More people were lifted out of poverty than at any previous stage in human history.

That turnabout resulted from the policies of **Deng Xiaoping** (1904–1997). After Mao's death (see Chapter 30), Deng put China on a new economic path by adopting market incentives. The first step was to grant peasants their own farm plots for private cultivation. Food production surged. Deng became a hero to millions of Chinese farming families, who could now afford small luxuries for the first time. When asked how he, a lifelong communist, justified adopting capitalist principles, Deng replied: *"It does not matter whether the cat is black or white, as long as she catches mice." "To get rich,"* he added, *"is glorious."*

Deng Xiaoping

(1904–1997) Chinese Communist Party leader who brought dramatic economic reforms after the death of Mao Zedong.

● **CONTEXT&CONNECTIONS** During the *Great Leap Forward* (Chapter 30), Deng Xiaoping was among the "experts" Mao Zedong derided for putting pragmatism above ideology. In the 1960s Deng was "sent down" to work in a tractor factory during the Great Proletarian Cultural Revolution, before re-emerging in the 1970s to defeat the radical "Gang of Four." ●

The second stage in Deng's reforms was development of the industrial sector. In the southern region of Guangzhou, near the British-controlled territory of Hong Kong, foreign investors were invited to build manufacturing plants in an embrace of international capitalism unthinkable under Mao. Many multinational corporations moved their manufacturing operations to Guangzhou to take advantage of China's cheap labor.

Chinese banks funded local investors with connections to the Communist Party. The Red Army itself became a major economic power, controlling one of the world's largest shipping lines. As manufacturing spread from Guangzhou throughout eastern and central China, a vast flow of finished goods crossed the Pacific destined for American markets. China's cities experienced a huge construction boom, attracting millions of rural migrants. The coastal city of Shanghai became a glittering cosmopolitan center, as traffic jams and billboards replaced bicycles and moralistic party posters.

Although Deng Xiaoping resigned from his post in 1987, he remained a dominant power behind the scenes until his death in 1997. During that period, both the costs and benefits of his policies became more and more apparent. A great success was the return of Hong Kong in 1997 from British to Chinese control. Communist leaders promised that under their "one country, two systems" policy the people of Hong Kong would retain their accustomed civil liberties such as rights of free speech and assembly.

The biggest test of Deng's career came in 1989. Student activists, yearning for political change to match the economic transformation of their country, organized a large antigovernment rally, erecting a replica of the Statue of Liberty in the heart of Beijing to symbolize their goals of greater freedom and an end to corruption. This student-led prodemocracy movement ended with the **Tiananmen Massacre**, in which hundreds, perhaps thousands, of student activists were killed and many more arrested.

Some Chinese officials had advocated a moderate approach and reconciliation with the students, but hardliners wanted to crush the student demonstrations. Ultimately the decision was up to Deng, who remembered the chaos caused by student rebels during the Cultural Revolution and backed the hardliners. Aware of how Mikhail Gorbachev's policy of glasnost was undermining the Soviet Union, China's communist hardliners were unwilling to put their own political monopoly at risk.

Entering the 1990s, China's economic transformation was generating other challenges as well. Environmental problems multiplied. The gap between rich and poor increased, as did imbalances between wealthier coastal regions and China's interior. As corruption spread, protests increased among the same rural population that Mao had made the center of his revolution. Still, the economic policies of Deng Xiaoping had raised China to the status of a great power. Many Chinese felt that their country had returned to its proper historical place after two centuries of humiliation by Western powers and Japan.

Hong Kong, 1997 The return of Hong Kong to China ended more than 150 years of British rule. As in India and dozens of other former colonies in prior decades, the Union Jack was lowered and "God Save the Queen" played for the final time; the flag of the People's Republic of China was then raised to mark the transfer of sovereignty

China's competitive advantage was its political stability combined with low-cost labor. By the 1990s other Asian countries were also able to build up export-oriented manufacturing centers. American consumers hardly even noticed that much of their clothing and other commodities were now produced in places like Thailand, Malaysia, Indonesia, and Vietnam. For much of the twentieth century, nationalist leaders in these countries had dreamed of catching up with the West through industrialization. Now, like China, they were moving toward that goal.

The industrial path to prosperity was now complicated, however, by the changing nature of the global economy. Manufacturing was being overtaken by marketing, financial services, and other "knowledge industries" as the highest

Tiananmen Massacre

Massacre in a public square in Beijing where, in 1989, students and workers demanded freedom and democracy. On order from the Communist Party, the Chinese military cleared Tiananmen Square with tanks and gunfire.

value-producing activities. In fact, for many Asian workers, industrialization brought little benefit. Young women with few skills other than manual dexterity made up much of the industrial workforce, and child labor was all too common. As global consumers demanded ever-cheaper products, wages remained low in China, Southeast Asia, and other industrial economies. Even in richer countries, industrial workers began to see their wages decline, or their jobs disappear, in the face of competition from low-cost Asian labor.

The European Union   Beginning in the 1980s, western European leaders, especially in France and Germany, sought to deepen cooperation throughout the European Economic Community. A European Parliament, with little real authority but great symbolic importance, was elected. Negotiations began to open borders, create a single internal market free of tariffs, and move toward a common European currency. As the Soviet Union began to dissolve, talk turned to the possibility of incorporating new members from the former Eastern bloc.

In 1992, the Treaty on European Union was signed at the Dutch city of Maastricht. It set a date of January 1, 1999, for the introduction of the euro (the EU's proposed currency), limited the amount of public debt that a nation could hold to be admitted to the union, and created a European Central Bank to coordinate monetary policy.

Some complained that a European "superstate" run by faceless bureaucrats in Brussels would undermine national sovereignty, and Great Britain, Denmark, and Sweden all rejected the euro, refusing to surrender control of their own currencies. But the signatories approved the open market provisions of the Maastricht Treaty, and with an internal market larger than that of the United States and members who represented complementary economic and human resources, the European Union was launched as a major success (see Map 31.3).

By century's end, the European Union accounted for over 18 percent of global exports. Growth rates were especially high in poorer, more agricultural countries. Spain, Greece, and Portugal, all of which had suffered from authoritarian governments, became modern democracies with significantly more educated populations. Ireland was dubbed the "Celtic Tiger" for its transformation from an agrarian society to one based on strong educational foundations and prowess in high technology (See the feature "Movement of Ideas Through Primary Sources: The End of History?").

● **CONTEXT&CONNECTIONS** Global recession in 2008 would reveal that much of the impressive growth in Ireland and the Mediterranean had been based on property speculation and irresponsible government spending. Tensions then developed between northern European governments, especially Germany, and the Mediterranean countries of the European Union, Greece in particular, over monetary policy and the need for austerity (see Chapter 32). ●

Even while pursuing market integration, some Europeans rejected what they saw as the excesses of unfettered American-style capitalism and consumerism. In Italy, partisans of the "slow food" movement focused on fresh local ingredients, careful preparation, and leisurely dining with family and friends, a direct contrast with American "fast food" culture. In France, the government reflected popular feeling when, concerned that the "new world order" really meant cultural Americanization, it subsidized French film productions to fend off domination by Hollywood. In Germany, public support for state-run pension and health care systems

Map 31.3 The European Union The European Union (EU) developed from the more limited European Economic Community, dominated by France and the Federal Republic of Germany. The United Kingdom, Ireland, Denmark, Spain, Portugal, and Greece were added in the 1970s and 1980s. The collapse of the Soviet Union led to a dramatic EU expansion into eastern Germany, central and southeastern Europe, and the Nordic and Baltic countries. Turkey's application for membership proved controversial, while Russia has resisted the inclusion of Georgia and Ukraine.

remained nearly universal, even as some economists in the United States touted the supposed advantages of "free market" alternatives.

Neoliberalism, Inequality, and Economic Globalization

Even as economists celebrated the virtues of expanding free trade, citing persistent growth, critics continued to rail against the new global economic regime of **neoliberalism**, the emphasis on free markets not only for their stimulation of trade, but also for their supposed efficiency in dealing with social issues, like education and health care,

neoliberalism

The renewed emphasis on free-market policies that accompanied globalization at the end of the Cold War.

959

The End of History?

No longer able to use the familiar compass points of East-West conflict, scholars and political analysts at the end of the Cold War struggled to find ways to describe the "new world order" and to anticipate its future direction. One of the most discussed contributions to this literature in the early 1990s was Francis Fukuyama's essay "The End of History."

Fukuyama, a Japanese American, was employed by the U.S. state department when he wrote this article. At that time, in 1989, he was associated with neo-conservatism, a movement that stressed the right and responsibility of the United States to unilaterally assert its power across the globe in the defense of American interests, including the promotion of American values of political freedom and economic enterprise. After the neoconservatives achieved great political influence under the administration of George W. Bush, however, Fukuyama broke with them over the issue of the Iraq War (see Chapter 32).

> **More than two decades after it was written, how accurate does Francis Fukuyama's prediction seem? To what extent has the triumph of liberal democracy and free-market economics marked an "end of history"?**

Source: Francis Fukuyama, "The End of History," *The National Interest*, Summer, 1989. Copyright © 1989, Francis Fukuyama. Reprinted by permission of the author.

In watching the flow of events over the past decade or so, it is hard to avoid the feeling that something very fundamental has happened in world history. The past year has seen a flood of articles commemorating the end of the Cold War, and the fact that "peace" seems to be breaking out in many regions of the world.... [T]he century that began full of self-confidence in the ultimate triumph of Western liberal democracy seems at its close to be returning full circle to where it started ... to an unabashed victory of economic and political liberalism....

What we may be witnessing is not just the end of the Cold War ... but the end of history as such: that is, the end point of mankind's ideological evolution and the universalization of Western liberal democracy as the final form of human government.... [T]he victory of liberalism has occurred primarily in the realm of ideas or consciousness and is as yet incomplete in the real or material world. But there are powerful reasons for believing that it is the ideal that will govern the material world in the long run....

The state that emerges at the end of history is liberal insofar as it recognizes and protects through a system of law man's universal right to freedom; and democratic insofar as it exists only with the consent of the governed.... [H]istory ended ... in the ideals of the French or American Revolutions: while particular regimes in the real world might not implement these ideals fully, their theoretical truth is absolute and could not be improved upon....

In the past century, there have been two major challenges to liberalism, those of fascism and of communism. The former saw the political weakness, materialism, anomie, and lack of community of the West as fundamental contradictions in liberal societies that could only be resolved by a strong state that forged a new "people" on the basis of national exclusiveness. Fascism was destroyed as a living ideology by World War II. This was a defeat, of course, on a very material level, but it amounted to a defeat of the idea as well....

The ideological challenge mounted by the other great alternative to liberalism, communism, was far more serious. Marx ... asserted that liberal society contained a fundamental contradiction that could not be resolved within its context, that between capital and labor, and this contradiction has constituted the chief accusation against liberalism ever since. But surely, the class issue has actually been successfully resolved in the West.... [T]he egalitarianism of modern America represents the essential achievement of the classless society envisioned by Marx. This is not to say that there are not rich people and poor people in the United States, or that the gap between them has not grown in recent years. But the root causes of economic inequality do not have to do with the underlying legal and social structure of our society, which remains fundamentally egalitarian and moderately redistributionist....

[T]he power of the liberal idea would seem much less impressive if it had not infected the largest and oldest culture in Asia, China.... China could not now be described in any way as a liberal democracy.... But anyone familiar with the outlook and behavior of the new technocratic elite now governing China knows that Marxism and ideological principle have become virtually irrelevant as guides to policy.... The student demonstrations in Beijing that broke out ... recently ... were only the beginning of what will inevitably be mounting pressure for change in the political system as well.... The central issue is the fact that the People's Republic of China can no longer act as a beacon for illiberal forces around the world.... Maoism, rather than being the pattern for Asia's future, became an anachronism....

Important as these changes in China have been, however, it is developments in the Soviet Union ... that have put the final nail in the coffin of the Marxist-Leninist alternative to liberal democracy.... What has happened in the four years since Gorbachev's coming to power is a revolutionary assault on the most fundamental institutions and principles of Stalinism, and their replacement by other principles which do not amount to liberalism per se but whose only connecting thread is liberalism....

[A]re there any other ideological competitors left? ... The rise of religious fundamentalism in recent years within the Christian, Jewish, and Muslim traditions has been widely noted.... In the contemporary world only Islam has offered a theocratic state as a political alternative to both liberalism and communism. But the doctrine has little appeal for non-Muslims, and it is hard to believe that the movement will take on any universal significance....

This does not by any means imply the end of international conflict per se.... There would still be a high and perhaps rising level of ethnic and nationalist violence.... This implies that terrorism and wars of national liberation will continue to be an important item on the international agenda. But large-scale conflict must involve large states still caught in the grip of history, and they are what appear to be passing from the scene.

The end of history will be a very sad time. The struggle for recognition, the willingness to risk one's life for a purely abstract goal, the worldwide ideological struggle that called forth daring, courage, imagination, and idealism, will be replaced by economic calculation, the endless solving of technical problems, environmental concerns, and the satisfaction of sophisticated consumer demands. In the post-historical period there will be neither art nor philosophy, just the perpetual caretaking of the museum of human history.... Perhaps this very prospect of centuries of boredom at the end of history will serve to get history started once again.

previously dominated by governments. For neoliberal economists, government intrusions into markets, no matter how well intended, decrease efficiency, increase corruption, and lead to unintended consequences such as diminished availability of services in high demand. For their part, critics of neoliberalism emphasize that without the regulatory oversight of democratically elected governments, neoliberal policies lead to sharpening inequalities in income and access to services, while undercutting labor, environmental, and consumer protections.

● **CONTEXT&CONNECTIONS** What are called "conservative" economic policies in the United States (limiting the size of government, balancing budgets, freeing markets from constraints) are, in most of the world, described as "liberal" or "neoliberal," in accordance with the original nineteenth-century meaning (see Chapter 23). Pressures on governments to allow companies to more easily dismiss workers, for example, might thus be described as moves to "liberalize" labor markets (see Chapter 32). ●

Neoliberalism appeared in the 1980s in the guise of "structural adjustment programs" imposed on indebted nations seeking its fiscal help by the International Monetary Fund (IMF), established as part of the *Bretton Woods* accords in 1944 (Chapter 29). After the OPEC oil boycott caused surging petroleum prices in the mid-1970s, "petrodollars" flooded the world's financial institutions, making it easy for poorer nations to borrow money for development projects. Much of that money was poorly invested, or even stolen by corrupt officials. When a global recession struck in 1980 and lenders called in those loans, many Third World nations were unable to pay.

The IMF, as the international "lender of last resort," was willing to offer emergency loans to keep those nations solvent, but only if debtors met "structural adjustment" criteria requiring sharp cuts in government spending. IMF economists argued that state interference in markets was constraining economic activity and that only by slashing state expenditures could developing countries reach sustainable levels of growth.

● **CONTEXT&CONNECTIONS** The IMF was established as part of the *Bretton Woods* accords in 1944 (Chapter 29) specifically to keep debtor nations solvent and thus to avoid the type of international credit crisis that had deepened the *Great Depression* (Chapter 28). ●

Structural adjustment programs caused suffering. In Mexico, structural adjustment meant cutting government subsidies on the price of maize meal, causing a sharp rise in the price of tortillas, and thus more hungry children. In the East African nation of Tanzania, education was put at risk after the country accepted an IMF loan in 1987 and was then forced to lay off thousands of teachers to help balance its books. Nevertheless, advocates of structural adjustment argued that, in the long term, the "magic of the market" would align production and consumption and lead to greater prosperity, the only way to create abundance for the people of countries like Mexico and Tanzania.

In the 1990s, the economics of neoliberalism dominated discussions of the many free trade pacts then being negotiated, such as the North American Free Trade Association (NAFTA) of 1994, uniting Canada, the United States, and Mexico in a market even larger than that of the European Union. NAFTA was controversial. In the United States, critics warned that the removal of tariffs on Mexican imports would mean the loss of high-paying industrial jobs as manufacturers seeking to pay lower wages moved south of the border. In Mexico, farmers worried that they would be ruined by open competition with U.S. farmers, who were heavily subsidized by their government. Even as previously high-wage industrial jobs moved south, rural Mexicans would flee north because of falling crop prices.

In the southern state of Chiapas, rebels calling themselves Zapatistas (after the Mexican revolutionary Emiliano Zapata; see Chapter 25) declared "war on the Mexican state" in 1994, with NAFTA as one of their principal grievances. The Zapatistas were part of a global movement of people who sought to reassert their collective welfare against the free-market onslaught and to protect their culture and identity against the wave of globalization. But the Zapatistas faded from the headlines, while the conservative National Action Party (PAN) advocated even greater economic liberalization, broke the monopoly of the ruling party in the Mexican presidential elections of 2000.

In South Africa after 1994, a deep irony marked the policies of the Mandela administration. That government's neoliberal emphasis on free markets, though aligned with global trends, represented a sharp break with the ANC's long advocacy of state ownership of major industries as a means of achieving social justice and racial equality. Nelson Mandela himself, always a pragmatist, understood that market-led growth was the only way to enlarge the South African economic pie and provide more opportunity for those who had historically been excluded. Part of Mandela's great political achievement, and his lasting legacy, was his ability to convince his people that while political democracy could come quickly, patience was required to move the country toward social and economic equality.

Whether economists cheered the neoliberal expansion of free trade or critiqued it as a cruel system that built equity for a few on the backs of the many, one question was no longer at issue. Socialism, in its classic twentieth-century formulations, was gone. For better or worse, capitalism was now the only game being played in the global economy. (See the feature "Movement of Ideas Through Primary Sources: The End of History?")

Beyond the "Age of Extremes"?

Eric Hobsbawm, a prominent British historian, referred to twentieth-century world history as the "Age of Extremes." Like Nelson Mandela, Hobsbawm was born while the First World War still raged, and like Mandela he could reflect back from the year 2000 on a lifetime during which rapid and unpredictable change seemed the only constant.

When Mandela and Hobsbawm were young, radio was still a new invention, telephones were a luxury, commercial aviation was in its infancy, and the British empire was the framework for the world around them, a world in which European domination was taken for granted. At the end of the century, both men had lived long enough to witness the development of instantaneous global telecommunications, a thoroughly integrated global economy, and a population that had grown from less than 2 billion to over 6 billion persons.

In the interim, momentous events had rocked the world: the Great Depression; the rise of communism and fascism; the Second World War and the Holocaust; the development of nuclear weapons and the Cold War; the collapse of the European and Soviet empires; the transformation of China and other Asian economies; and the re-creation of a brutally racist South Africa into a beacon of post–Cold War democracy and racial reconciliation. An "Age of Extremes" indeed!

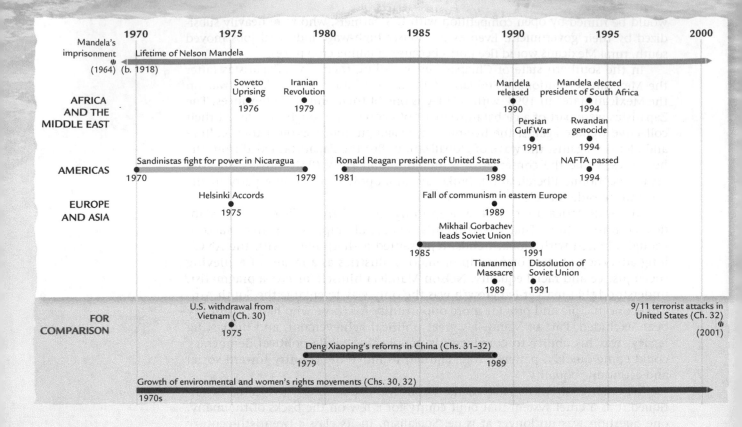

	1970	1975	1980	1985	1990	1995	2000

Mandela's imprisonment
φ
(1964) (b. 1918)
Lifetime of Nelson Mandela

AFRICA AND THE MIDDLE EAST

Soweto Uprising 1976
Iranian Revolution 1979

Mandela released 1990
Mandela elected president of South Africa 1994

Persian Gulf War 1991
Rwandan genocide 1994

AMERICAS

Sandinistas fight for power in Nicaragua
1970 – 1979

Ronald Reagan president of United States
1981 – 1989

NAFTA passed 1994

EUROPE AND ASIA

Helsinki Accords 1975

Fall of communism in eastern Europe 1989

Mikhail Gorbachev leads Soviet Union
1985 – 1991

Tiananmen Massacre 1989
Dissolution of Soviet Union 1991

FOR COMPARISON

U.S. withdrawal from Vietnam (Ch. 30) 1975

9/11 terrorist attacks in United States (Ch. 32)
φ
(2001)

Deng Xiaoping's reforms in China (Chs. 31–32)
1979 – 1989

Growth of environmental and women's rights movements (Chs. 30, 32)
1970s

The entire history of the rise and fall of the Soviet Union took place during these single lifetimes. True, communism persisted. But China and Vietnam had transformed their economies using market principles, hardly an advertisement for the superiority of Karl Marx's economic philosophy (see Chapter 23). In North Korea and Cuba, it became doubtful that communism could long survive the economic failure of their leaders. Everywhere else communism had retreated: just a handful of nations were all that was left of the great hopes and the great fears raised by communism in the twentieth century—a paltry legacy. The retreat was seen even in South Africa, where the Communist Party, close allies of Nelson Mandela and the African National Congress in the struggle against apartheid, now advocated private enterprise rather than state control as the key to economic growth and improvements in the lives of the African majority.

However, even as the world celebrated the dawn of a new millennium and U.S. President Bill Clinton talked of "*building a bridge to the twenty-first century,*" new challenges appeared. Genocide in Rwanda and other human rights abuses driven by ethnicity and religion had shown that the extreme hatreds of the old century had not been entirely left behind. More broadly, commentators observed the rise of religious extremism as a menace to secular and Enlightenment traditions. Such fears were magnified after the attacks by Islamic militants on the World Trade Center in New York and the Pentagon in Washington on September 11, 2001, and by the highly controversial U.S. invasion of Iraq a few years later. These events are too recent for proper historical analysis, but in the final chapter of this book we will attempt a survey of twenty-first-century realities in a world that has become smaller and smaller thanks to the political, economic, technological, and cultural dynamics of accelerating globalization.

Key Terms

Nelson Mandela (934)
Ronald Reagan (935)
Helsinki Accords (936)
Mikhail Gorbachev (937)
Solidarity (938)
Boris Yeltsin (939)

Bantustans (945)
Soweto Uprising (945)
Organization of Petroleum
    Exporting Countries (949)
Islamists (949)
Ayatollah Khomeini (949)

Persian Gulf War (951)
Osama bin Laden (951)
Deng Xiaoping (956)
Tiananmen Massacre (957)
neoliberalism (959)

For Further Reference

Barber, Benjamin. *Jihad vs. McWorld: How Globalism and Tribalism Are Reshaping the World*. New York: Times Books, 1995.

Garthoff, Raymond. *The Great Transition: American-Soviet Relations at the End of the Cold War*. Washington, D.C.: Brookings, 1994.

Gerlach, Christian. *Extremely Violent Societies: Mass Violence in the Twentieth Century World*. New York: Cambridge University Press, 2010.

Iriye, Akira, Petra Goedde, and William I. Hitchcock, eds. *The Human Rights Revolution: An International History*. New York: Oxford University Press, 2012.

Judt, Tony. *Thinking the Twentieth Century*. New York: Penguin, 2012.

Kagan, Robert. *Of Paradise and Power: America and Europe in the New World Order*. New York: Knopf, 2003.

Kenney, Padraic. *1989: Democratic Revolutions at the Cold War's End: A Brief History with Documents*. New York: Bedford/St. Martin's, 2009.

Mamdani, Mahmood. *Good Muslim, Bad Muslim: America, the Cold War, and the Roots of Terror*. New York: Crown, 2005.

Mandela, Nelson. *Long Walk to Freedom: The Autobiography of Nelson Mandela*. Boston: Little, Brown, 1996.

Marti, Michael. *China and the Legacy of Deng Xiaoping: From Communist Revolution to Capitalist Evolution*. Washington, D.C.: Potomac, 2002.

Sebestyn, Sebastian. *Revolution 1989: The Fall of the Soviet Empire*. New York: Vintage, 2010.

Smith, Charles D. *Palestine and the Arab-Israeli Conflict*. 7th ed. New York: Bedford/St. Martin's, 2009.

Smith, Peter H. *Democracy in Latin America: Political Change in Comparative Context*. 2d ed. New York: Oxford University Press, 2011.

MindTap

MindTap is a fully online, highly personalized learning experience built upon Cengage Learning content. MindTap combines student learning tools—readings, multimedia, activities, and assessments—into a singular Learning Path that guides students through the course.

32

Voyage into the Twenty-First Century

Ai Weiwei

The experiences of Chinese artist **Ai Weiwei** (b. 1957) exemplify some of the best and some of the worst of contemporary China. On the one hand, Ai is a global face of the "new China," a highly respected creative talent whose works are internationally admired and whose innovative contributions to the design of the Beijing National Stadium for the 2008 Summer Olympics helped the People's Republic make a strong impression on the world. More recently, however, Ai Weiwei (eye way way) has been subjected to constant police surveillance: authorities shut down his influential blog, demolished his Shanghai studio, and in 2011 detained him for almost three months. Ai is a firm believer in freedom of speech and the rule of law, and his willingness to spread those beliefs through social media has led the government to tightly restrict his freedom of expression.

As of this writing, Ai is still barred from foreign travel, but he continues to work internationally. His site-specific exhibit @Large, exploring the theme of incarceration, was mounted in 2015 at the former Alcatraz Prison in San Francisco. "*The misconception of totalitarianism is that freedom can be imprisoned,*" he says on the exhibition website. "*This is not the case. When you constrain freedom, freedom will take flight and land on a windowsill.*" Meanwhile, his reaction to house arrest is characteristically creative: "*every morning I am putting a bouquet of flowers in the basket of a bicycle outside the front door,*" Ai tweets, "*until I win back the right to travel.*"*

His father, Ai Qing (eye CHING), was one of China's leading poets, having traveled to Paris as a young man in the 1920s. He joined the Communist Party, was imprisoned by the Guomindang, and achieved fame in the 1950s before Mao declared an "anti-rightist" campaign and sent Ai Qing with his family into exile near the Gobi Desert. For twenty years his poetry was forbidden while he cleaned toilets at a "re-education" camp. His son, Ai Weiwei, grew up in bleak circumstances.

---

*For-Site Foundation, "@Large: Ai Weiwei on Alcatraz," http://www.for-site.org/project/ai-weiwei-alcatraz/.

Peter Macdiarmid/Getty Images

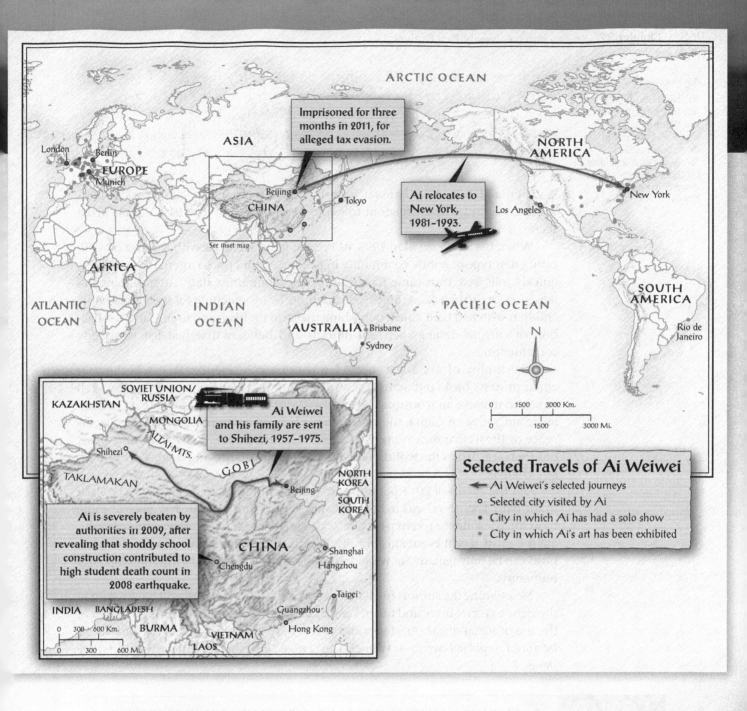

Imprisoned for three months in 2011, for alleged tax evasion.

Ai relocates to New York, 1981–1993.

Ai Weiwei and his family are sent to Shihezi, 1957–1975.

Ai is severely beaten by authorities in 2009, after revealing that shoddy school construction contributed to high student death count in 2008 earthquake.

Selected Travels of Ai Weiwei

← Ai Weiwei's selected journeys
○ Selected city visited by Ai
● City in which Ai has had a solo show
• City in which Ai's art has been exhibited

Even the thaw that came with Mao's death, and the return of his father to official favor, did not create the space Ai needed for his art. In 1981, at age twenty-four, he fled toward freedom:

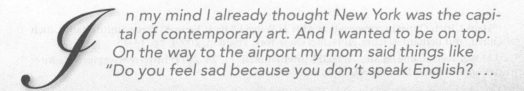

n my mind I already thought New York was the capital of contemporary art. And I wanted to be on top. On the way to the airport my mom said things like "Do you feel sad because you don't speak English? ...

Ai Weiwei

(b. 1957) A Chinese artist, blogger, and critic of the Communist government. His arrest and detention in 2011 focused global attention on the slow pace of democratization in China.

You have no money" (I had thirty dollars in my hand).... I was so naïve, but I had so much confidence. I left because the activists from our same group were put in jail. The accusation was that they were spies from the West, which was total nonsense.... [W]e all got mad and even scared—you know, "this nation has no hope."

Menial labor and financial hardship were part of Ai's New York experience, but so was freedom to explore, energized by the East Village artist scene.

When his father fell ill in 1993, Ai Weiwei returned home with the idea of replicating that type of artistic community in Beijing. A rapid rise to international success quickly followed, then came repression by the communist state. After schools collapsed in an earthquake, Ai angered the authorities by searching for the names of the children who had been killed, publishing them on his blog, and urging an investigation of corrupt dealings between officials and builders that had led to shoddy construction.

The timing of Ai's arrest in 2011 was not a coincidence. That was the year when protests broke out across the world. From the Arab Spring, to Occupy Wall Street, to massive anticorruption demonstrations in India, millions rose up to challenge authority. In China, the government clamped down harshly, fearing a recurrence of the Tiananmen protests of 1989 (see Chapter 31). Elsewhere, hopes rose, but then crashed as the world's elite regained their balance and fended off systematic change.

Did the events of 2011 point toward a different future, or were they just a flash in the pan? There is no way to be sure. Our survey of world history has given us some tools for assessing the recent past, but lacking adequate perspective, we cannot evaluate the most recent events historically. In this final chapter, therefore, our conclusions can be only tentative as we address some of the core issues facing contemporary humanity.

Meanwhile, the authors hope that as you read this, Ai Weiwei will have regained the right to travel freely and further enrich us all with his creative vision. A master at the use of social media, Ai's blogs and tweets have kept his story alive: *"Without the Internet, I would not even be Ai Weiwei today. I would just be an artist somewhere doing my shows."*

FOCUS QUESTION

> How does the study of world history enhance our understanding of key issues of the twenty-first century, such as international economics, global security, health and the environment, gender relations, democratization, and cultural globalization?

---

*"Hans Ulrich Obrist in conversation with Ai Weiwei," in Ai Weiwei, Karen Smith, Hans Ulrich Obrist, and Berhard Fibicher, *Ai Weiwei* (New York: Phaidon, 2009), pp. 14–15.

†"Ai Wei Wei: Shame on Me," SPIEGEL International, 11, 24, 2011; http://www.spiegel.de/international/world/0,1518,799302,00.html.

Emerging Economic Players

Much of the discussion about the global economy in the early twenty-first century focused on rapid economic growth rates in emerging economies in Asia, Latin America, and Africa, a phenomenon that one analyst called "the rise of the rest."* Economists paid special attention to the exceptionally strong performance of Brazil, Russia, India, and China—the so-called **BRIC** nations—though Turkey, South Africa, and other countries were part of the conversation as well. To some, an equalization of centers of world economic activity seemed to be under way.

After 2014, the picture became somewhat more clouded as the United States regained momentum, Chinese growth slowed, and plunging commodity prices damaged export-dependent economies in Russia, Brazil, and elsewhere. Yet European and Japanese economies stagnated, and with China now the world's second largest economy and Brazil in sixth place, it still seemed that the longer-term trend was toward a more multicentered global economy.

China's economic rise and the story of contemporary economic globalization go hand in hand. When Ai Weiwei was a child in the 1960s, China's contributions to the global economy were meager. In 1981, when Ai left for the United States, the country had only just begun to benefit from Deng Xiaoping's market-oriented policies (see Chapter 31). Then a startling change took place. From the early 1990s until 2010, China's economy grew at an average annual rate of nearly 10 percent a year. (By contrast, Japan's annual growth rates since 1992 have never exceeded 3 percent and have often dipped into the negative range.)

Since the Communist Party takes credit for this economic juggernaut, it must also take responsibility for the less attractive side effects. Lax environmental standards and a reliance on high-sulfur coal have made the air toxic in Beijing and other urban manufacturing centers. Millions experienced social dislocation as the government forced them from ancestral villages into hastily constructed apartment towers in mushrooming cities. Endemic corruption leads to a cynical attitude, while government attempts to restrict access to information collide with China's agenda of participating in the global knowledge economy.

India is also rising to prominence as an emerging economy, though its vibrant multiparty democracy differs sharply from China's one-party totalitarianism. And while Chinese government and business leaders focused on industrial development for export, Indians have put a greater emphasis on high technology and their huge domestic market.

Economic liberalization in the early 1990s meant the lowering of business taxes and the lifting of government restrictions, leading to an onrush of Indian entrepreneurial activity. As in China, annual economic growth rates surged toward 10 percent. Earlier, under socialist policies, Indians might wait for years to have a telephone installed or to become eligible to purchase a car. Now members of the greatly expanded middle class buy the latest-model cars and electronics on credit, take foreign holidays, and get mortgages on newly constructed homes. Such is the "new India," with globally prominent high-technology and telecommunications sectors, the world's largest film industry, and large and influential expatriate communities around the globe.

BRIC

"Brazil, Russia, India, and China," a shorthand reference to the fast-growing emergent economies of the twenty-first century. BRIC was formalized into an international organization, with the addition of South Africa in 2010, making it BRICS.

---

*Fareed Zakaria, *The Post-American World, Release 2.0* (New York: Norton, 2011), p. 1.

Sajjad Hussain/AFP/Getty Images

Two Indias Mumbai is the largest city in India, with over 18 million inhabitants. The gleaming skyscrapers seen in the background provide both commercial space for the city's booming economy and residences for its fast-growing middle class. That new prosperity stands in stark contrast to the city's slums. Dharavi, shown in the foreground, might be the most crowded place on earth.

Yet amid the undeniable economic transformation, reliance on free markets has left many Indians behind. Corruption is endemic, with billions stolen through fraudulent contracts and many rural Indians losing their land through real estate swindles. Glistening new suburbs are protected by high walls and tight security from the noise and filth of overcrowded slums, while hundreds of millions of rural Indians live without access to clean water or basic sanitation, let alone computers.

Indeed, data from India, China, Brazil, the United States, and elsewhere show a strong correlation between global economic growth and rising inequality. Critics contend that in their haste to liberalize their economies, governments have abandoned the health and educational needs of their citizens. As one economist has argued, "The ancient question of how market forces need to be tempered for the greater good of the economy and the society is now a global one"* (see Map 32.1).

In Russia, economic inequality escalated with the collapse of the Soviet Union. The rapid privatization of state assets in the 1990s benefited economic insiders, instant billionaires who formed a new economic oligarchy, while ordinary workers suffered (see Chapter 31). These post-Soviet oligarchs' lavish displays of wealth angered many, and in the early 2000s President **Vladimir Putin** played on that popular disgust to reassert state control over important sectors like energy, media, and telecommunications.

Vladimir Putin

The Russian leader who served from 2000 as either president or prime minister. Putin re-established state control over the largest sectors of the Russian economy and stimulated nationalism by reasserting the country's great power status.

---

*Robert Kuttner, "The Role of Governments in the Global Economy," in *Global Capitalism*, ed. Will Hutton and Anthony Giddens (New York: New Press, 2000), p. 163.

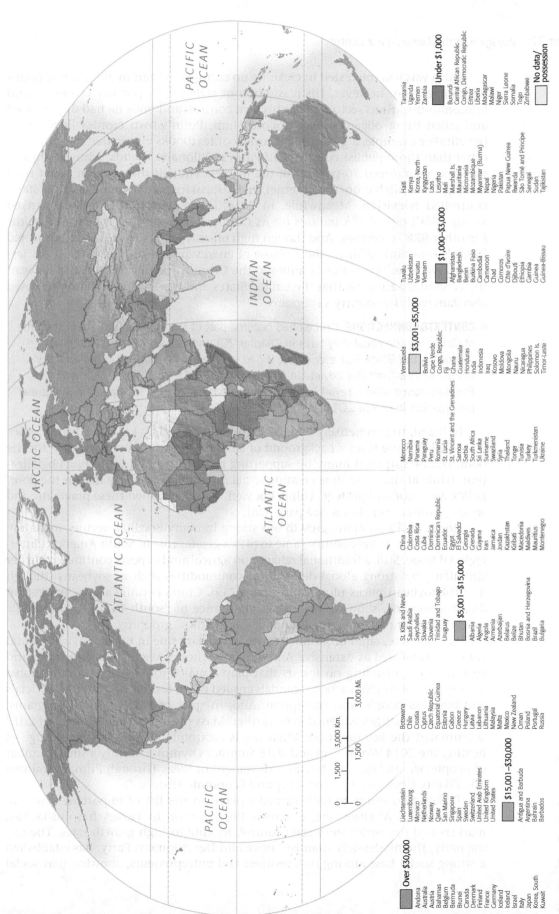

Over $30,000		$15,001–$30,000	$5,001–$15,000		
Andorra	Liechtenstein	Antigua and Barbuda		China	St. Kitts and Nevis
Australia	Luxembourg	Argentina		Colombia	Saudi Arabia
Austria	Monaco	Bahrain		Costa Rica	Seychelles
Bahamas	Netherlands	Barbados		Cuba	Slovakia
Belgium	Norway	Botswana		Dominica	Slovenia
Bermuda	Qatar	Chile		Dominican Republic	Trinidad and Tobago
Brunei	San Marino	Croatia		Ecuador	Uruguay
Canada	Singapore	Cyprus		Egypt	
Denmark	Spain	Czech Republic		El Salvador	
Finland	Sweden	Equatorial Guinea		Georgia	
France	Switzerland	Estonia		Grenada	
Germany	United Arab Emirates	Gabon		Guyana	
Iceland	United Kingdom	Greece		Iran	
Ireland	United States	Hungary		Jamaica	
Israel		Latvia		Jordan	
Italy		Lebanon		Kazakhstan	
Japan		Lithuania		Kiribati	
Korea, South		Malaysia		Macedonia	
Kuwait		Malta		Maldives	
		Mexico		Mauritius	
		New Zealand		Montenegro	
		Oman			
		Poland			
		Portugal			
		Russia			

$3,001–$5,000	$1,000–$3,000		Under $1,000		No data/ possession
Venezuela	Afghanistan	Morocco	Burundi	Tanzania	
	Bangladesh	Namibia	Central African Republic	Uganda	
Bolivia	Benin	Panama	Congo, Democratic Republic	Yemen	
Cape Verde	Burkina Faso	Paraguay	Eritrea	Zambia	
Congo, Republic	Cambodia	Peru	Haiti		
Fiji	Cameroon	Romania	Kenya		
Ghana	Chad	St. Lucia	Korea, North		
Guatemala	Comoros	St. Vincent and the Grenadines	Kyrgyzstan		
Honduras	Côte d'Ivoire	Samoa	Laos		
India	Djibouti	Serbia	Lesotho		
Indonesia	Ethiopia	South Africa	Liberia		
Iraq	Gambia	Sri Lanka	Madagascar		
Kosovo	Guinea	Suriname	Malawi		
Moldova	Guinea-Bissau	Swaziland	Mali		
Mongolia		Syria	Marshall Is.		
Nauru		Thailand	Mauritania		
Nicaragua		Tonga	Micronesia		
Philippines		Tunisia	Myanmar (Burma)		
Solomon Is.		Turkey	Nepal		
Timor-Leste		Turkmenistan	Niger		
		Ukraine	Nigeria		
			Pakistan		
			Papua New Guinea		
			Rwanda		
			São Tomé and Príncipe		
			Senegal		
			Sierra Leone		
			Somalia		
			Sudan		
			Tajikistan		
			Togo		
			Tuvalu		
			Uzbekistan		
			Vanuatu		
			Vietnam		
			Zimbabwe		

Map 32.1 Per Capita Income Despite recent surges in the economies of countries such as India, China, Russia, and Brazil, the global economy is still dominated by the United States, western Europe, Canada, Australia, and Japan. Per capita income gives only a rough estimate of people's quality of life, however. The United Nations Development Program (UNDP) uses a Human Development Report that takes account of a variety of factors in addition to income—such as education, health care, environmental standards, and gender equality—in its rankings. According to the UNDP, the island nation of Iceland ranks first in human development, Canada fourth, Japan eighth, France tenth, and the United States twelfth.* (Caption data from http://hdr.undp.org/en/statistics. Map data from *The World Almanac and Book of Facts, 2008*, ed. C. Alan Joyce (World Almanac Books, 2008).)

Putin was less interested in cleaning up corruption than in eliminating political competition, however. His reassertion of state power put key economic and telecommunications sectors under his own control, and once he had dispossessed and jailed those oligarchs who opposed him, Putin's own cronies lined up to benefit. For example, a government review of textbooks eliminated most options other than those published by one of Putin's billionaire friends, whose company was thus guaranteed 70 percent of the market. Though information about such dealings is available on the Internet, most Russians get their news from state-controlled television. Meanwhile, in 2014 Transparency International ranked Russia 136th out of 175 nations on its Corruption Perception Index, well below the other BRIC countries. And though high oil and gas prices had once burnished Russia's economic gilding, the collapse of energy prices in 2014 revealed its less impressive core. When Russia annexed the Crimean peninsula in the same year, the economic sanctions that the United States and the European Union imposed also damaged the country's economy.

● **CONTEXT&CONNECTIONS** Crimea had become part of the Russian empire at the time of *Catherine the Great* (key term in Chapter 20) and has served as a vital naval station on the Black Sea ever since. It had reverted to Ukraine after that country's independence from the Soviet Union (see Chapter 31), only to be occupied by Russian troops after a revolt in the Ukrainian capital of Kiev unseated an unpopular pro-Russian leader in 2014. ●

In Brazil, the immensely popular President Luiz Inácio Lula da Silva (in office 2003–2010) came from a background of labor organization and advocacy for the poor, but he surprised many by supporting growth through economic liberalization, while at the same time creating social programs as a safety net for the poor. Lula's successor and protégé, Dilma Rousseff, has maintained these pragmatic and socially conscious policies (see page 928).

Under Lula's program, growth was strong in many Brazilian sectors, including manufacturing, as the country came to play a greater role in South America's interregional trade. Still, a traditional reliance on agricultural exports continued, further stimulated by strong global demand for commodities such as soybeans (though in 2014 soybean prices plunged; see page 759). China became a huge market for Brazilian exports, showing the rising importance of "south to south" economic transactions among emerging economies in the BRIC grouping.

As elsewhere, rapid economic growth had a dark side in Brazil. Environmental concerns mounted as extensive Amazonian territories were cleared for farm and pasture land, intruding on forests that play a major role in cleaning the global atmosphere of surplus carbon. Scandals ensued when fast money tempted officials and business people into corruption. And, in spite of Lula's s social programs, Brazilian inequalities widened even further. Mass protests in the summer of 2013 accentuated the key question: What use is economic growth, or the prestige of hosting the 2014 World Cup and 2016 Summer Olympics, if only a small number of people benefit? (See the feature "Movement of Ideas Through Primary Sources: The Piketty Controversy: Inequality and Economic History.")

Turkey also seems to have earned a place on the list of important new economic players. As elsewhere, economic liberalization in Turkey has unshackled markets and industries from state control, leading to high growth rates. The ruling party, the moderately Islamist Justice and Development Party, has established a strong social base among businessmen and entrepreneurs, showing that social conservatism grounded in religious beliefs can be compatible with strong economic performance in a predominantly Muslim society. However, social and political tensions have also escalated, as shown by police assaults on youthful protestors in the summer of 2013 and the jailing of journalists who uncovered evidence of high-level government corruption.

● **CONTEXT&CONNECTIONS** Recent crackdowns in Turkey demonstrate once again that free market policies do not always lead to political openness, as had been predicted by nineteenth century liberal ideology (see Chapter 23). The Mexico of *Porfirio Diáz* (Chapter 25) and Chile under Augusto Pinchot (see Chapter 30) are Latin American examples where political repression accompanied free markets. ●

The emergence of former "Third World" nations as new economic players also extends to Africa. Though the continent had been seen as a venue for charity rather than investment, some African countries are now experiencing rapid growth. In 2010 South Africa, with its strong mining and industrial sectors, was formally invited to join what, as a result, became the BRICS group, while oil-rich Nigeria became the continent's largest economy.

Situations in Africa vary widely, of course, and in some regions, economic growth is precluded by the absence of rule of law (including war zones). More generally, poor infrastructure for public health, transport, and education is an impediment to growth. Still, away from the limelight, some African nations have improved dramatically in all these areas. Young, dynamic, and urbanizing populations brought a strengthened middle class to the fore. Improved telecommunications allowed many to skip landline telephones and go straight to cellular services, stimulating African economies through more efficient financial transactions via mobile banking apps.

In Ethiopia, for example, the economy grew at an annual rate of over 10 percent from 2005 to 2013, with construction cranes transforming Addis Ababa. Officials describe their country as an "African lion" equivalent to the "Asian tigers" of the 1980s (see Chapter 31). Indeed, the Ethiopian government, like those of South Korea and Taiwan earlier, has played a central role, channeling investments from China, India, Turkey, and Europe to the private sector through state banks. Remittances from Ethiopian migrants living in the United States, Europe, and the Persian Gulf have also provided an economic lift. Of course, as in other emerging economies, costs and benefits are not equally shared. The government has organized the dispossession of the poor when they "stand in the way" of development projects and has jailed the journalists who investigate and make known such human rights abuses.

● **CONTEXT&CONNECTIONS** For Ethiopian nationalists, the recent record of economic success reinforces a sense of exceptionalism tracing back to their long line of Christian kings (see Chapter 16) and the defense of Ethiopian sovereignty during the "scramble for Africa" with the defeat of Italian invaders by the armies of Emperor *Menelik II* (Chapter 26). ●

Perhaps the most startling economic transition in Africa has been the trend away from traditional Western sources of aid and investment and the debut of China as a leading player. In the first decade of the new century, over 1 million Chinese relocated to Africa to engage in a broad range of economic activities. Questions have been raised, however, about Chinese business methods and possible ulterior motives. Chinese tend to monopolize the higher-skilled positions

The Piketty Controversy: Inequality and Economic History

Few economic history books make the bestseller list, but Thomas Piketty's *Capital in the Twenty-First Century* was one of the most commented upon publications of 2014. The French economist used centuries of economic data to investigate the issue of inequality in market-driven societies.

Piketty's conclusion is that the structures of capitalism trend toward increasing inequality over time. In his analysis, the *decrease* in inequality found in developed industrial economies between roughly 1914 and 1970 was largely the result of noneconomic exigencies (wars and economic depressions) that liquidated much of the capital stock of the world's wealthiest families, as well as political factors that led to social and taxation policies favoring the middle and working classes.

But over the broader arc of history, Piketty argues, rates of return on capital have routinely exceeded rates of return on labor, meaning that everything else being equal, inherited wealth will outpace income from employment. Rates of return on capital (such as stocks, bonds, or real estate investments) might be a modest 5 percent and still far exceed national growth rates. (The last time the growth rate of the United States surpassed 5 percent was in 1984; for France, 1973.)

Piketty's work made a strong impression on liberal and progressive economists and policymakers, but was also challenged by more conservative, market-oriented analysts. One such rejoinder, from the staunchly conservative U.S. news magazine, *American Spectator*, is excerpted below. Full engagement with this debate would, of course, require a full reading of Piketty's argument and analysis of his extensive data, available at his webpage at the Paris School of Economics (http://piketty.pse.ens.fr/fr/capitalisback).

> According to to Piketty, why is increasing inequality the most likely outcome of unregulated market economics?

> What are the principle points of disagreement between Piketty and his conservative critic? Which argument do you find more convincing?

Sources: Thomas Piketty, *Capital in the Twenty-First Century*, trans. Arthur Goldhammer (Cambridge, Mass.: Belknap, 2014), pp. 571–578; James Piereson, "Thomas Piketty's 'Le Capital': Providing Intellectual Cover for Punishing the Rich," *American Spectator*, June 2014.

Thomas Piketty: *Capital in the Twenty-First Century*

The overall conclusion of this study is that a market economy based on private property, if left to itself, contains powerful forces of convergence [reduction of inequalities] associated in particular with the diffusion of knowledge and skills; but also powerful forces of divergence [sharpening of inequalities] which are potentially threatening to democratic societies and to the values of social justice on which they are based.

The principal destabilizing force has to do with the fact that the private return on capital, *r*, can be significantly higher for long periods of time than the rate of growth of income and output, *g*. The inequality *r > g* implies that wealth accumulated in the past grows more rapidly than output and wages. This inequality expresses a fundamental logical contradiction. The entrepreneur inevitably tends

to become a rentier [making money by renting out property or investing funds at interest] more and more dominant over those who own nothing but their labor. Once constituted, capital reproduces itself faster than output increases. The past devours the future. The consequences for the long-term dynamics of the wealth distribution are potentially terrifying, especially when one adds ... that the divergence in the wealth distribution is occurring on a global scale.

The problem is enormous, and there is no simple solution. Growth can of course be encouraged by investing in education, knowledge, and nonpolluting technologies. But none of these will raise the growth rate to 4 or 5 percent a year. History shows that only countries that are catching up with more advanced economies—such as Europe during the three decades after World War II or China and other emerging economies today—can grow at such rates. For countries at the world technological frontier—and thus ultimately for the planet as a whole—there is ample reason to believe that the growth rate will not exceed 1-1.5 percent in the long run, no matter what economic policies are adopted.

With an average return on capital of 4-5 percent, it is therefore likely that $r > g$ will again become the norm in the twenty-first century, as it had been throughout history until the eve of World War I.

In the twentieth century, it took two world wars to wipe away the past and significantly reduce the return on capital, thereby creating the illusion that the fundamental structural contradiction of capitalism ($r > g$) had been overcome.

To be sure, one could tax capital income heavily enough to reduce the private return on capital to less than the growth rate. But if one did that indiscriminately and heavy-handedly, one would risk killing the motor of accumulation and thus further reducing the growth rate....

A Conservative Critique

Piketty's estimates of wealth and income shares over the generations are probably as reliable and accurate as he or anyone else can make them, but even so they are estimates based upon imperfect and inexact data. His estimates of wealth, for example, do not take into account assets held by pension funds and retirement accounts, which in the United States today add up to close to $20 trillion, or around one-third of the total value of U.S. stocks and bonds.... These funds are typically not owned by members of the "top one percent" but by middle-class workers. If we could throw that $20 trillion into the pool of total wealth, Piketty's graph might look quite different.

Piketty's great fear, and one that is largely overstated, is that the concentrated ownership of wealth will create a new form of "patrimonial" capitalism in which a small number of families control the wealth of the society and pass it along to their heirs. This idea conflicts with the known tendency of wealthy families to disburse their assets over generations and to be replaced at the top by new entrepreneurs and owners of recently created capital.

It also conflicts with the dramatic rise in salaries for "super-managers" since the 1980s, which Piketty discusses. These are, as he writes, "top executives of large firms who have managed to obtain extremely high and historically unprecedented compensation packages for their labor." The "rich" today are increasingly salaried executives and managers rather than owners of stocks, bonds, and real estate, as was the case a century ago. Piketty doubts that the new "super-managers" earn these extravagant salaries on the basis of merit or contributions to business profits. He points instead to cozy and self-serving relationships they establish with their boards of directors. All that aside, the rise of "super-managers" should actually help alleviate intergenerational inequality, since people can pass on to heirs their wealth but not their high-paying jobs....

[Piketty] claims that the differential returns on capital versus labor are the driving forces of the system, but that is a partial and misleading view. The driving force of the capitalist system is relentless innovation that improves productivity and raises living standards.... Over a span of two and a half centuries, since roughly 1750, the traditional regime transformed itself through an accumulating process of technological innovation and widening circles of trade. Workers and consumers have benefited generation on generation from less burdensome forms of work and access to ever more inexpensive products that make life easier. Widely shared progress—not exploitation—is the story of the past two centuries.

in their enterprises, often employing Africans for the lowest-paying jobs without training them for higher positions. Even more troubling is China's support of certain African leaders with poor human rights and corruption records in its drive to secure the African raw materials, especially metals and fossil fuels, necessary for further industrial growth. One proposed solution is to stimulate inter-African trade through regional trading blocs, which would then strengthen overall African bargaining power in the world economy.

Such regional trade compacts became common during the 1990s, though experience has shown it is never easy to balance national interests with regional goals. The United States, Canada, and Mexico, for example, have all had complaints about the North Atlantic Free Trade Association (NAFTA) (see Chapter 31), while political disputes have hampered the effectiveness of a proposed South American common market (see page 670). The European Union (EU), by far the largest regional bloc, has struggled to balance the interests of more developed countries such as Germany and France with the needs of weaker members such as Portugal and Greece.

More ambitious than regional agreements was the drive by the **World Trade Organization** (WTO) to foster international free trade. WTO members, which have included China since 2001, accept international monitoring to assure that they maintain a level playing field by avoiding state subsidies and tariffs. The virtue of WTO policies, from a neoliberal standpoint, is the elimination of the reduction in international economic efficiency that occurs when political distortions are introduced into markets. For critics of neoliberalism, however, the regional trade blocs and the WTO regime have handicapped governments in restraining negative consequences of capitalism such as sharpening inequality and environmental degradation. For these critics, deregulation favors multinational corporations over people.

While defenders and opponents debated the merits of neoliberal globalization, the Nobel-prize winner **Muhammad Yunus** (b. 1940) of Bangladesh was thinking of practical solutions for those left behind. His Grameen ("Village") Bank pioneered microfinance, lending small amounts of money. Poor borrowers proved to be trustworthy clients even when they had no collateral to secure the loans, and small investments often led to big returns when they pooled their resources, energy, and ideas to start new enterprises. In Africa and elsewhere, it has been shown that women are particularly apt to make good use of such small infusions of capital, stimulating local economies while also addressing gender inequality. Still, such "bottom-up" approaches are dwarfed by the power and resources of the world's largest financial institutions.

World Trade Organization

Organization founded in 1995 to establish rules for international trade, with an emphasis on lowering tariffs and other barriers to the free movement of goods.

Muhammad Yunus

(b. 1940) Bangladeshi pioneer of microfinance whose Grameen ("Village") Bank gives small loans to the poor, usually women, to start small enterprises. His bank became a global model for microfinance, and in 2006, he was awarded the Nobel Peace Prize.

Global Finance: Collapse and Consequences

In the autumn of 2008, panic spread across world markets at the prospect of the insolvency of the interconnected global banking and brokerage systems. The use of complex financial instruments called "derivatives" had allowed banks to bundle and sell inflated mortgages to third parties while masking the high risks involved, infecting the financial system and creating a domino effect when the housing bubble burst. The New York Stock Exchange lost 22 percent of its value in a single week and, along with other international stock exchanges, continued to plunge thereafter. Memories of the Great Depression, when a stock market crash led to a decade of economic misery, seemed ominously relevant.

● **CONTEXT&CONNECTIONS** As painful as the 2008 financial crisis was, it was by no means as catastrophic as the *Great Depression* (Chapter 28), when the U.S. stock market crash led to a cascading series of global bank failures. For one thing, in 2008, governments had much more powerful tools of monetary intervention than in 1929. Moreover, 2008 witnessed no rush to raise national tariffs, which in the 1930s had deepened the depression by hindering international trade. ●

Most economists and government leaders determined that in the short term state intervention would be necessary to prevent more banks and brokerages from going bankrupt. Thus the outgoing administration of U.S. President George W. Bush proposed and Congress passed a program to make $700 billion available to stabilize the financial services industry. In Britain as well, where the City of London parallels New York as a global financial services center, the government organized an emergency rescue operation. Many were appalled that the very people whose risky business decisions had brought the world to the brink of ruin were being "bailed out," but the measures did forestall further financial contagion.

Still, economic recession struck. The United States and Europe faced high unemployment, and global markets were shrinking. A fundamental question of economic theory then took center stage. Was the best medium-term solution for governments to borrow money and cut taxes, running deficits in order to stimulate a broader economic recovery? Or were government deficits at the very root of the slump, meaning that fiscal austerity, cutting spending while raising taxes, was necessary to restore prosperity?

Responses varied. The United States under President Barack Obama took a Keynesian "stimulus" approach (see Chapter 28). In the United Kingdom, a conservative-led government determined that government indebtedness was the root problem and risked deflation by slashing spending while raising taxes. The French implemented a modest stimulus plan, but the Irish government took the path of austerity, implementing harsh spending cuts.

Divided responses by European Union members revealed a lack of the institutional means to coordinate national fiscal policies. The 2011 financial meltdown of Greece forced the issue. In Greece, relatively low economic productivity was paired with generous social welfare benefits. Amid the global economic crisis, with its credit rating in decline, the Greek government could no longer borrow enough money to sustain that structural imbalance. The Greek parliament passed sharp spending cuts as a condition for an emergency fiscal support package, a move opposed by the Greek voters who in 2015 voted in an anti-austerity government charged to negotiate a better deal.

● **CONTEXT&CONNECTIONS** Tensions between fiscally conservative Germans and Greeks tired of endless austerity were central to European fiscal debate. While many economists argued that *deflation* (falling prices and wages) was the nemesis of post-2008 recovery, Germans still tend to focus on *inflation* (rising prices and wages) as a perennial economic danger seeing excessive borrowing as a fiscal, and even as a moral, failure. That reflexive attitude, dating back to the great inflation of the early Weimar Republic (see Chapter 28), affected German public opinion and thus German negotiations with Greece. ●

The euro currency itself was now at risk. It seemed that only stronger fiscal coordination by the European Central Bank would allow euro-zone countries to find fiscal policies balancing their divergent national interests. Yet voters in most countries were reluctant to give up the reins of national finance to Pan-European bureaucracies.

Meanwhile, youth unemployment, especially in southern Europe, began to seem like a structural, perhaps permanent cost of deflation. In Italy, an extreme example, the youth unemployment rate in 2015 was over 41 percent. As ambitious young people left such moribund economies for opportunity elsewhere, the International Labor Office called for attention to what it called a "generation at risk."

To some it seemed that the prolonged slump of mature economies following from 2008 signaled a structural readjustment in the world economy. With U.S., Japanese, and European economies teetering on the edge of recession from 2009 to 2012, and with continued growth in much of Asia, Africa, and Latin America, it seemed that two centuries of Western economic predominance might be coming to an end. By late 2013, China had amassed foreign currency reserves of $366 *billion* dollars, much of it in U.S. Treasury bonds.

Still, by 2015 it appeared that the relative decline of more established economies might have been overstated. Although Europe and Japan continued to struggle, the American dollar remained the world's favored reserve currency, a hedge against instability elsewhere. Growing U.S. energy production (much of it resulting from environmentally controversial hydraulic fracturing technology) added to the U.S. recovery. Meanwhile China's housing boom, which had underwritten the country's recent growth, began to cool. Even though it was unlikely that the "rise of the rest" would be reversed, and while many analysts still looked to emerging markets for future growth, it seemed that zigzags would complicate the future path of the international economy.

● **CONTEXT&CONNECTIONS** Though China's rate of industrial growth has been unprecedented, the resulting contribution to global manufacturing can be viewed as a return to the historic norm. After all, *Qing dynasty* China (Chapter 20) had accounted for a full 33.1 percent of all the world's manufacturing production in 1750 (see Table 23.1, page 685). That figure had fallen to just 6.3 percent in 1900. Now the People's Republic of China accounts for an estimated 22 percent of the world's industrial output. ●

Global Security

September 11, 2001

Date of the al-Qaeda terrorist attacks on the United States in which two hijacked jetliners destroyed the twin towers of the World Trade Center in New York City. Another hijacked plane crashed into the Pentagon, and a fourth fell in a Pennsylvania field.

The optimism for a safer world that followed from the end of the Cold War did not last long. While wars between nations had indeed become less frequent, societies across the world now found themselves threatened and destabilized by non-state organizations, especially terrorist groups motivated by extreme religious ideologies, such as al-Qaeda (see Chapter 31).

Hopeful expectations for the new millennium were shattered on **September 11, 2001**, when operatives of al-Qaeda hijacked four jetliners in the United States and turned them into weapons of destruction. Thousands of New Yorkers were killed in the destruction of the Twin Towers (though the terrorists' plans to destroy the Pentagon and Congress were averted). International sympathy for the people of the United States was nearly universal.

In response, President George W. Bush declared a "war on terror," first sending U.S. forces in October 2001 to invade Afghanistan, where the Islamist Taliban government had given sanctuary and support to Osama bin Laden, and then into

Saddam Hussein's Iraq in 2003. The invasion of Afghanistan had broad international support. An international coalition, working with local anti-Taliban fighters, quickly removed the Taliban from power. The subsequent U.S. invasion of Iraq, however, generated considerable controversy. Many Americans, and even more members of the international community, knew that Iraq had no connection to al-Qaeda or 9/11.

Bush ordered the invasion in 2003, lacking United Nations sanction and with Great Britain as his only major ally. Saddam Hussein was deposed, and later tried and executed. Evidence of Hussein's violent misrule was abundant, but his supposed stockpiles of "weapons of mass destruction," used by the United States to justify its invasion, were never found.

Two years of internecine strife followed, with U.S. soldiers contending with both Shi'ite militias (supported by neighboring Iran) and Sunni terrorists backed by al-Qaeda. In the north of the country, battle-hardened Kurdish forces staked out terrain that would remain virtually autonomous even after elections created a new government in Baghdad (see Map 32.2).

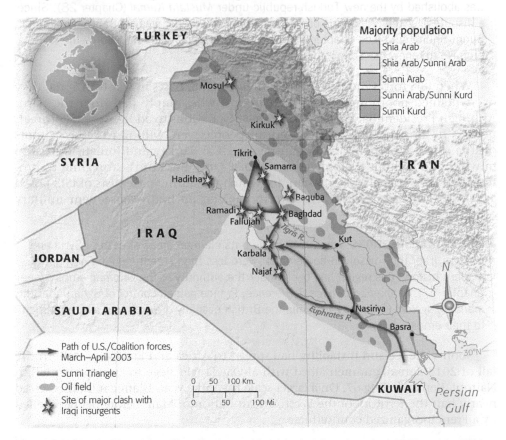

Map 32.2 Iraq in Transition Two Bush presidential administrations invaded Iraq—in 1991 to protect its oil-producing ally Kuwait from invasion, and in 2003 to oust Saddam Hussein and bring democracy to the Arab world. The first mission was successful, the second much less so. After Hussein's fall, some of the Sunnis displaced from power took up arms against the U.S. coalition, against independent Shia Arab militias, and against the now Shi'ite-dominated Iraqi government itself. Even after 2007 elections inaugurated a compromise government—with a Shi'ite prime minister, Kurdish president, and Sunni leader of parliament—it was impossible to reconcile the country's regional, religious, and ethnic divisions.

With Iraq's political future unresolved, in 2011, the United States (following the lead of its ally, Great Britain) began to withdraw its troops. Americans were now ready to end this difficult conflict after eight years and thousands of casualties, especially with the sense of closure that came with Osama bin Laden's death in a smoothly executed Navy Seals operation.

Even so, the U.S. invasion had stirred up a hornet's nest, and the world learned just how fragile Iraq still was. By 2015, the power vacuum left behind by the American invasion of Iraq was being filled by an even more extreme group, the Islamic State of Iraq and Syria (ISIS), taking advantage of regional instability to grab territory as the nucleus of a restored Sunni caliphate. With its bloodstained record of cruelty, that idea made for a chilling prospect.

● **CONTEXT&CONNECTIONS** The term *caliph* in Arabic means "successor" and is used in reference to leaders who inherited the earthly power of the prophet Muhammad. The last of the great Arab caliphates ended in 1258 when the Mongols sacked Baghdad, though Ottoman sultans also claimed the title until 1924, when the office was abolished by the new Turkish republic under *Mustafa Kemal* (Chapter 28). Since a dispute over the proper line of succession to the Prophet was central to the original Sunni-Shi'ite split (see Chapter 17), Shi'ites are especially threatened by the ISIS promise to renew the Sunni caliphate. ●

When ISIS forces moved east from their original bases in war-torn Syria, they overwhelmed poorly motivated Iraqi troops, who simply fled from the fight. Although President Barack Obama was clearly anxious to address the ISIS threat, neither he nor the war-weary American people were willing to return "boots on the ground." Neighboring countries, such as Turkey and Jordan, were also unwilling to commit themselves to combat. Only the Kurds, struggling to protect their own homeland, and Iran, for which the Sunni extremists of ISIS posed an existential threat, were proactive in backing up Iraq's subsequent military offensive.

● **CONTEXT&CONNECTIONS** When ISIS insurgents claimed areas of eastern Syria and western Iraq, they dissolved borders that were less than a century old. For most of modern history, this region had been under the authority of the Ottoman empire (see Chapter 17). At the *Paris Peace Conference*, France gained control of Syria under the *mandate system* (Chapter 27), while the British casually drew up Iraq as an addition to their empire. ●

Soon violence and instability had spread to Africa and Europe as well. In the fall of 2013 Somali gunmen allied with al-Qaeda laid siege to an upscale mall in Nairobi, Kenya, killing 67. On a larger scale the same year, Islamic militants seized nearly half the territory of the West African nation of Mali, before being repelled by a French-organized counterforce.

● **CONTEXT&CONNECTIONS** The Islamist forces in Mali, like those of al-Qaeda and ISIS, are Salafists who stress a return to the purity of Islam at its founding. That is why, when they took over territories of the former *Songhai empire* (Chapter 19), they demolished ancient shrines and destroyed documents from age-old libraries, claiming that African adaptations of Islam were idolatrous. In West Africa, as elsewhere, the terrorism of Salafist fanatics is most often directed at other Muslims, especially *Sufis* and Shi'ites (Chapter 17). ●

The Islamic State in Syria and Iraq (ISIS) The northern Syrian city of Kobani, a gateway to neighboring Turkey, was attacked by ISIS militants in late 2014. The city was successfully defended by Kurdish militias backed by U.S. airstrikes, though 200,000 refugees fled the area, part of the exodus of 4 million who fled Syria's civil war.

Gokhan Sahin/Getty Images

In Paris in 2015, two gunmen shouting *"Allahu Akbar!"* ("God is great!") stormed into the offices of a French satire magazine and opened fire, killing eleven and wounding eleven more: the magazine had published cartoons using caricatures of the Prophet Muhammad to mock Islamic terrorists. Later an accomplice took hostages in a Jewish grocery store and murdered four more people. While the French people then came together across lines of religion and ethnicity to condemn the attacks and the assault on their freedom of speech, feelings of anxiety persisted.

And what if militant groups were able to lay their hands on weapons of mass destruction? What if nuclear devices entered the global arms trade and found their way into the hands of extremist organizations or irresponsible governments? That was a real fear after Pakistan's top nuclear scientist shared his expertise with Iran and North Korea.

The United States, the European Union, and leaders of Sunni-dominant Muslim countries like Saudi Arabia imposed economic sanctions on Iran in an attempt to halt its progress toward enrichment of weapons-grade uranium. While Teheran claimed merely to be advancing a civilian energy program, the global consensus was that strict international supervision must guarantee that the Iranian program did not cross the line to military applications. With the election in 2013 of a reformist Iranian government, anxious first and foremost to address economic issues, international negotiations finally began to move in a positive direction, though a right-wing Israeli government contested U.S. efforts to mediate a diplomatic solution.

North Korea was equally worrisome. In 2006, the communist government had snubbed international opinion by openly testing a bomb and beginning to develop a nuclear arsenal. A wild card came with the death of long-time dictator Kim Jong-Il and the accession to power of his little known son Kim Jong-Un. While the younger Kim struggled to consolidate power, brutally executing his own uncle and provoking conflict with South Korea, nuclear negotiations were called off. With North Korea otherwise impenetrable, it seemed that only the People's Republic of China might have the influence to subdue the more dangerous tendencies of the Kim dynasty.

Meanwhile, a long simmering nuclear fault line separated India and Pakistan. With a history of animosity and saber-rattling, both countries (along with Israel) had developed nuclear weapons in defiance of the international Treaty on the Non-Proliferation of Nuclear Weapons. Indeed, international regulation of nuclear materials and technology is at least as important today as it was when atomic Armageddon threatened humanity at the height of the Cold War.

● **CONTEXT&CONNECTIONS** Starting in 1947, the Bulletin of the Atomic Scientists has shown a "doomsday clock" on its masthead estimating the danger of nuclear war. The original setting was seven minutes to midnight, dropping to seventeen minutes in 1991, when the United States and the tottering Soviet Union signed an arms control pact (see Chapter 31). Ominously, between 2012 and 2015, the doomsday clock was set back from five minutes to three minutes, the atomic scientists' most imminent warning of nuclear conflict since the Cold War. ●

Health and the Environment

In 2014, the virulent Ebola virus spread across the West African nations of Guinea, Liberia, and Sierra Leone. The handful of the cases that developed outside of West Africa were easily contained, but global panic still followed. In the United States, a state governor ordered a nurse who had returned from Sierra Leone to be held in quarantine, even though there was no medical rationale for doing so. Morocco reneged on its offer to host the 2015 African Cup of Nations soccer tournament, citing public health dangers that defied medical logic. The grave suffering Ebola caused was almost entirely limited to the countries first affected, and as successful measures were taken, both the disease and the panic receded.

Though people around the world overreacted to Ebola, their instinct to recognize the global nature of such health threats was not misplaced. International mobility does indeed increase the risk of pandemics, as shown earlier by the global spread of H1N1, or swine flu, itself a close relative of the flu strain that killed millions across the world in 1918–1919 (see Chapter 27 and the feature "World History in Today's World: World Historians and Disease History").

Virulent new strains of traditional killers like malaria, which until recently were confined to small geographic areas, now hop from continent to continent courtesy of mosquito hosts that find their way aboard jet airplanes. Other new strains of influenza, such as the avian flu virus from East Asia, threaten recurrent global epidemics. Meanwhile, overreliance on antibiotics in both humans and

USAID/Alamy

Fighting Ebola The rapid spread of Ebola in Guinea, Liberia, and Sierra Leone overwhelmed their health care systems and threatened the lives of thousands of African health care workers. Finally an intensive international effort was made to provide up-to-date facilities, such as the World Health Organization clinic shown here in Monrovia, Liberia.

domestic animals has spawned resistant strains of bacteria. Such developments overtax health-care systems around the world.

HIV/AIDS is, of course, another case in point. When it was first diagnosed in the 1980s, the disease was associated with two particular groups, homosexual men and intravenous drug users. Today, Africa has the largest number of AIDS victims, and more women are infected than men. For those who can afford it, medical advances have decreased suffering and extended life spans, but most of the world's HIV victims die without the benefit of effective medical intervention.

While HIV infection rates have stabilized in wealthier nations, many global health experts fear for India and China. In India, where hundreds of millions lack access to the most basic health care, the number of people living with HIV/AIDS has soared past 2.5 million. In China, even a low infection rate of 0.1 percent means that over a million people are infected. If HIV were to spread in Asia as it did in South Africa (where the infection rate grew to 25 percent of the population by 2005), those societies would be overwhelmed. Unlike most epidemic diseases, which are deadliest for the very young and very old, AIDS carries people away in the prime of their productive and reproductive lives, adding huge social and developmental costs.

Some health threats are compounded by global climate change. Scientists point to the huge cyclones that hit Burma in 2008 and the Philippines in 2013, and unprecedented drought and flooding in many parts of the world as examples. Climatologists worry that melting polar ice caps will soon disrupt the world's highly populated coastal areas, especially Bangladesh, where 55 million people

World Historians and Disease History

How has disease transmission affected world history? Since viruses and bacteria do not recognize political, cultural, or civilizational boundaries, we can only answer that question by increasing our scale of analysis to take in wider vistas of the human past. Over the past three decades, world historians have been paying greater attention to such transregional phenomena.

Studies of the fourteenth-century Black Death, for example, had too often focused solely on Europe. Today world historians pay closer attention to the epidemic's Central Eurasian origins by examining how the Mongol political ascension led to increased intercontinental exchange, possibly facilitating long-distance disease transmission. Historians are also providing a more balanced pan-Eurasian assessment of the plague's impact by looking at its effects on Chinese and Arab societies.

Analysis of European competition for control of the "new world" (see Chapters 15 and 18) provides another example. Here world historians have recognized the importance of different levels of immunity among Amerindians, Europeans, and Africans to deadly diseases, with susceptibility to malaria, smallpox, and yellow fever helping to determine the characteristics of populations and even political outcomes. A "national" view of the competing European powers and their fiscal, military, and leadership capabilities, while important, cannot achieve the more balanced assessments offered by historians who consider environmental and disease factors within larger spatial frames such as "the Atlantic world."

The story of the Spanish influenza outbreak of 1918–1919 is another historical incident where transnational approaches are required. While local histories bring us close to victims and their lives, a fuller picture requires a global view, since the disease showed no respect for national or imperial boundaries while spreading to every continent.

Disease transmission is one example of how the work of world historians has contemporary relevance. By demonstrating the transnational character of epidemic disease, world historians remind us that international health challenges require more than simply national solutions.

would be displaced by even a modest rise in sea levels. Global warming, notes one commentator, is taking the form of *"global weirding,"* where extreme weather conditions—too much or not enough rain and extremes of heat and cold—have become annual events.*

Global climate change is also affecting the spread of infectious diseases. The director general of the World Health Organization, Dr. Margaret Chan, argues: *"Many of the most important global killers are highly sensitive to climatic conditions. Malaria, diarrhea and malnutrition kill millions of people every year, most of them children. Without effective action to mitigate and adapt to climate change, the burden of these conditions will be greater, and they will be more difficult and more costly to control."*†

Some nations have taken climate challenge seriously and have made significant investments in renewable sources of energy to replace carbon-emitting fossil fuels. Germany, for example, has committed itself to a comprehensive plan for most of its energy to come from renewable sources by 2020. Both conservatives and socialists supported this initiative, and the large investments in wind and solar energy that came with it.

---

*Thomas L. Friedman, "Global Weirding Is Here," *New York Times*, February 17, 2010.

†Dr. Margaret Chan, "Health in a Changing Environment," http://www.who.int/mediacentre/news/statements/2007/s11/en/index.html.

It has proven very difficult, however, to reach a binding international agreement to limit carbon emissions. A promising start came as far back as 1992, when the United Nations instituted the talks leading in 1997 to the **Kyoto Protocol**. By 2005, for the first time, many nations agreed to mandatory limits on emissions of "greenhouse gases." The treaty lapsed in 2012, however, and has not been renewed, with India, China, and the United States stating that they will not accept legally binding reductions on carbon emissions.

A global rift pits environmentalists in the developed world against advocates for economic growth in emerging economies. China and India have depended on the burning of high-sulfur coal to fuel economic growth, and environmentalists have logically called for them to reduce emissions. The Chinese and Indian governments have argued, however, that developed countries, having *already* benefited from profligate use of fossil fuels, can *afford* cutbacks, while their own people still need accelerated growth, even at environmental expense, to lift them out of poverty.

Of course, China and India have their own reasons for cleaning up. A so-called "airpocalypse" in Beijing during the summer of 2013 made breathing painful and dangerous; it has long been true that most Chinese cancer deaths are attributable to pollution. (And the effects are not just local. A toxic cloud of coal smoke drifts from China over neighboring countries and sometimes across the Pacific Ocean. Coal shipped from the United States to China thus returns as air pollution.) The official response has been to downplay the problem but also to invest heavily in renewable energies, especially wind and solar. As bad as the air might be in China's cities, recent studies show that it is even worse in India. There, 660 million people live in areas where small airborne particles (2.5 micrometers or less) routinely cause severe lung damage. The result is a dire public health situation, especially for children.

While several countries have put a greater investment in renewable energies, the goal of **sustainable development**, of increasing economic output and productivity without severe damage to the environment, is still far away. The most immediate alternative to fossil fuels is nuclear power. However, many remain wary of its health and environmental consequences. In the spring of 2011, an earthquake in Japan reignited the global debate when the resulting tsunami led to the release of radiation from the Fukushima electricity plant, the worst nuclear incident since Chernobyl (see Chapter 31). Germany subsequently decided to shut down its nuclear energy program, gambling that enough clean energy would be available as a replacement.

Deforestation magnifies the effect of the world's rising output of greenhouse gases. Tropical forests play a large role in cleansing the atmosphere of carbon dioxide and replenishing it with oxygen. With high demand for tropical hardwoods from Central Africa and Indonesia, however, lumber companies fell vast areas of forest, sometimes bribing politicians to evade environmental regulations. In Brazil, as we have seen, farmers clear the forests for agriculture, with huge tracts of sugar cane and soybeans displacing biologically diverse ecosystems.

This section has touched on only a few of the health and environmental challenges of our times. Work is needed on every front as rising population, urbanization, and global migration make the search for solutions all the more urgent. With many geologists now agreeing that we are two centuries into the Anthropocene epoch, when human activity has dominant effects on our biosphere (see page 687), we can no longer shirk responsibility for environmental solutions.

Kyoto Protocol

(1997) International agreement adopted in Kyoto, Japan, under the United Nations Framework Agreement on Climate Change in an effort to reduce greenhouse gas emissions linked to global warming.

sustainable development

Means of increasing economic output and productivity without severe damage to the environment; for example, in the search for alternatives to fossil fuels.

Population Movement and Demography

People are on the move, both within countries and between them, usually seeking opportunity at the focal points of wealth and economic growth. That means cities. China, for example, has a staggering forty-five cities with over 2 million residents each. For the planet as a whole, 2008 was the first year when the majority of humankind lived in urban areas.*

Globally, prospects of higher wages drive millions each year to leave their homes, though they often send back much of their pay back home to support their families and intend to return. Of course, for millions of others, terrible conditions at home are the tragic inducement for movement across international borders: poverty and war drive some Africans to risk their lives crossing the Mediterranean on overcrowded boats, and desperate, low-wage migrant workers are subjected to systematic abuse in some wealthier regions, such as the Persian Gulf.

Immigration policies are controversial all around the world. In 2015, South African gangs attacked immigrants from other African countries, claiming that the outsiders were taking their jobs. In Italy, the government cracked down on illegal Roma (Gypsy) immigrants from southeastern Europe, claiming that they were responsible for an increase in crime. In the United States, immigration from Latin America has shifted the cultural and linguistic balance, generating an anti-immigrant backlash.

Religious differences can magnify concerns about immigration (see Map 32.3). Many western Europeans, for example, have been alarmed by large-scale Muslim immigration stimulated by political unrest in the Arab world. In Germany, a furious debate raged after a prominent politician wrote, "*If the birth rate of the [Muslim] migrants continues to remain higher than the indigenous population, within a few generations the migrants will take over the state and society and create a nation of dunces.*"[†] Such harsh rhetoric was on the rise in many European countries. Questions of whether and how to accept immigrants, and how best to create cultural and linguistic bridges to host societies, are thus matters of global concern.

Total world population recently surpassed 7 billion persons, a worrisome figure if we consider the resources it takes to give each of these individuals the chance at a decent life. But demographers (experts in population science) focus as much on the distribution of populations as their total size. When we consider the ratio of young to old in different societies, we find a striking imbalance. While the populations of wealthier countries grow older, Latin America, Africa, and Asia have enormous adolescent populations. Tapping into the creativity and intelligence of these hundreds of millions of young people would benefit all of us.

Back in the 1980s, worried about too many hungry mouths to feed, leaders of the People's Republic of China adopted a radical **One Child Policy** that punished parents who had a second child. Fertility declined and population growth plummeted. Now the Chinese government is relaxing the One Child Policy, worrying that there will soon be too few people of working age to support a growing number of the elderly.

One Child Policy

In China, most parents are restricted by this policy to a single child to curb population growth. The policy has led to a significant gender imbalance.

---

*United Nations, *World Urbanization Prospects* (New York: Author, 2006).

[†]Cited in "In a Rich Irony, German Jews Defend Muslims," *The Jewish Daily Forward*, January 28, 2011; http://www.forward.com/articles/134701/.

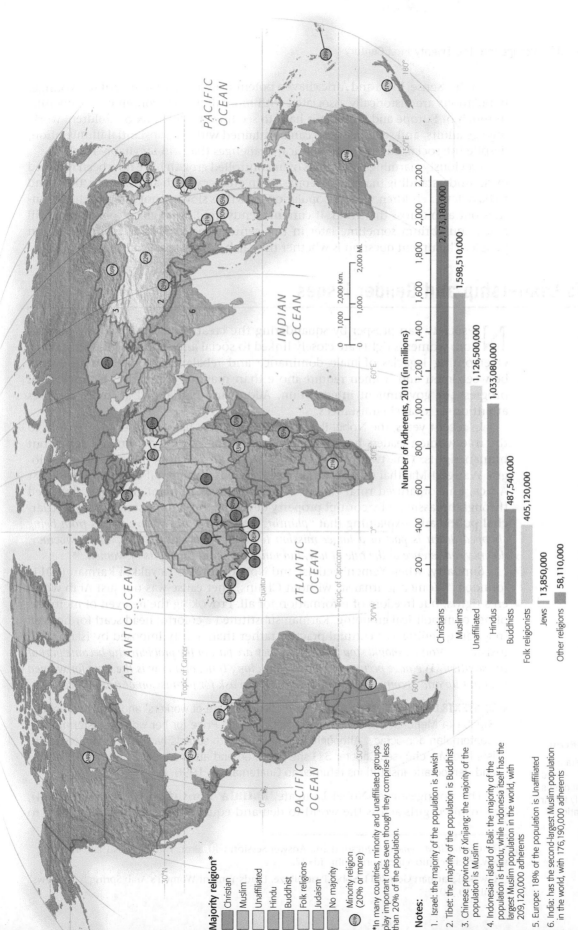

Majority religion*

- Christian
- Muslim
- Unaffiliated
- Hindu
- Buddhist
- Folk religions
- Judaism
- No majority

41% Minority religion (20% or more)

*In many countries, minority and unaffiliated groups play important roles even though they comprise less than 20% of the population.

Notes:

1. Israel: the majority of the population is Jewish
2. Tibet: the majority of the population is Buddhist
3. Chinese province of Xinjiang: the majority of the population is Muslim
4. Indonesian island of Bali: the majority of the population is Hindu, while Indonesia itself has the largest Muslim population in the world, with 209,120,000 adherents
5. Europe: 18% of the population is Unaffiliated
6. India: has the second-largest Muslim population in the world, with 176,190,000 adherents

Number of Adherents, 2010 (in millions)

Religion	Adherents
Christians	2,173,180,000
Muslims	1,598,510,000
Unaffiliated	1,126,500,000
Hindu	1,033,080,000
Buddhists	487,540,000
Folk religionists	405,120,000
Jews	13,850,000
Other religions	58,110,000

Map 32.3 World Religions Christianity, Islam, Hinduism, and Buddhism are the four major world religions, with "atheists/nonreligious" forming a majority in Communist-ruled China. The religious map of Africa is especially complex. While Muslims predominate in the north and west, and Christians in the east and south, there is a great deal of mixing along the boundaries between them, and local religions are still strong in many areas. In much of Europe and Russia, where Christian majorities are indicated, secularism is also strong and rates of church attendance quite low. While Islam predominates in North Africa and the Middle East, the nation with the largest Muslim population in the world is Indonesia, in Southeast Asia.

In that sense, India and Africa have a potential demographic advantage: younger populations are historically associated with more dynamic economies. Meanwhile, in much of Europe and Japan, it is hard to see how a stable mix of children, working-age adults, and senior citizens can be attained without substantial immigration, despite the social, cultural, and political challenges that will inevitably result.

Previously alarming predictions of uncontrolled growth have now been replaced by an understanding that when people attain greater wealth and security, they tend to have fewer children. Today, population growth is slowing not just in richer countries but also across the world. If current trends hold, total global population will reach equilibrium sometime later in this century, perhaps at a level of 9 billion people. The urgent question is whether the earth can sustain that number.

Women's Leadership and Gender Issues

No society can prosper by squandering the creative talent of half its population: women's rights are closely linked to social and economic advancement. Overcoming legacies of male dominance and rebalancing power more evenly between men and women require more than material prosperity, technological progress, or government intervention. Addressing patriarchal attitudes requires attention to local circumstances.

In recent years, the Nobel Peace Prize committee has paid special attention to the role women leaders have played in improving not only women's rights, but human rights. One twenty-first century Nobel Prize winner, the Kenyan biologist Wangari Maathai (2004), was alarmed by environmental degradation in East Africa, and organized rural women into collectives to plant trees. She persisted through harassment by corrupt property developers and imprisonment by patriarchal politicians, explaining that *"planting trees or fighting to save forests from being chopped down is part of a larger mission to create a society that respects democracy, decency, adherence to the rule of law, human rights, and the rights of women."**

Similarly, when Yemeni activist and Nobel Laureate Tawakkol Karman (2011) founded "Women Journalists without Chains," her cause was not just Arab women's rights, but freedom of information for all. Provoking the ire even of members of her own political grouping, Karman substituted a colorful head scarf for her veil (regarding veiling as a cultural practice rather than a duty imposed by Islam) and insisted: *"Women should stop feeling that they are part of the problem and become part of the solution. We have been marginalized for a long time, and now is the time for women to stand up and become active without needing to ask for permission or acceptance."*†

● **CONTEXT&CONNECTIONS** In 1992, an earlier advocate of workers' and women's rights, Rigoberta Menchú, was awarded the Nobel Peace Prize for her work in restoring Guatemalan democracy. Although government death squads had targeted union activists like Menchú (see Chapter 31) she persisted and attained global influence. Peace and democratic institutions returned to Guatemala in 1996. ●

Malala Yousafzai

(b. 1997) Pakistani Nobel Prize winner and advocate for children's rights, especially for girls' access to education.

The youngest-ever Nobel Laureate, **Malala Yousafzai** of Pakistan (2014), has inspired girls across the world to demand equal education and the power to

The Greenbelt Movement, "Question and Answer Session with Prof. Wangari Maathai," http://www.greenbeltmovement.org/a.php?id=27.

†"Tawakul Karman Gets 2011 Nobel Peace Prize, Leads Yemeni Women's Arab Spring," Asianews. it, July 10, 2011.

pursue their dreams. In 2009, eleven-year-old Yousafzai began blogging about life under the Islamist Taliban, who threatened to close girls' schools while imposing their severe form of Islamic law. Her blog gave her international prominence but incited revenge from the Taliban: one of their fighters stopped her school bus and shot her in the head.

Yousafzai went to Britain for surgery, and then launched her ongoing campaign for children's rights. After traveling to Oslo, Norway, to receive her award, Malala ended her speech to great applause by saying: *"Let this be the last time that a girl or a boy spends their childhood in a factory. Let this be the last time that a girl is forced into early child marriage. Let this be the last time that a child loses life in war. Let this be the last time that we see a child out of school. Let this end with us."**

Meanwhile in Pakistan's neighbor, India, globalization and technological change have presented new possibilities for women, at least for those fortunate enough to have an education and employment in rapidly growing sectors like information technology. Still, patriarchal attitudes remain, as shown by the persistence of the ancient **dowry system**. A girl's dowry has traditionally been the largest expense faced by Indian parents, sometimes leading the poor to lifelong indebtedness. Now the greater availability of consumer goods has had an inflationary effect, with families demanding ever-greater payments in return for marriage to their sons. Newspapers abound with reports of young brides murdered by their in-laws after their dowry payments have been made.

Because of the dowry system, the birth of a girl can seem like a tragedy, ruining the family's financial prospects. Across India, medical clinics advertise sonogram services to determine the gender of a fetus, leading to selective abortions. In the state of Punjab today, there are fewer than eight hundred girls for every thousand boys. Women's rights activists estimate that 50 million females are "missing" from the population because of selective abortion and female infanticide.

Overall disrespect for women in India has also led to an epidemic of rape, with government officials and police officers usually protecting male perpetrators while blaming the victims. Finally, in 2014, there were signs that Indian women, and Indian men of conscience, had seen enough. Huge crowds protested sickening incidents of gang rape, putting pressure on national and community leaders to finally address the issue.

In China gender discrimination remains rampant, despite strong legal and constitutional guarantees of equality and a much broader range of opportunities for educated women in the booming middle class. Lower pay for identical work is as common in China as elsewhere. Moreover, the gender ratio in China is almost as unbalanced as in India. Chinese parents, under the pressure of the One Child Policy and feeling the need for a male heir, have also practiced selective abortion.

Christopher Furlong/Getty Images

Malala Yousafzai Just twelve years old when she was attacked by militants for her stand in favor of girls' education in Pakistan, Nobel-prize winner Malala Yousafzai attained international prominence as a campaigner for children's rights while still a teenager.

dowry system
Traditional Indian marriage system in which a bride brings substantial gifts to the household of her new husband. Though illegal, it has expanded as the country's wealth has grown, leading to chronic indebtedness and the frequent murder of young brides.

---

*Malala Yousafzai, http://www.nobelprize.org/nobel_prizes/peace/laureates/2014/yousafzai-lecture_en.html.

Demographers estimate that there are as many as 70 million more males than females in the country.

Unequal access to education, unequal pay for identical work, sex trafficking, and high female death rates in childbirth are still all too common. But if women's leadership is key to overcoming such deep-seated gender inequalities, there is hope in the examples of Wangari Maathai, Tawakkol Karman, and Malala Yousafzai.

In her Nobel acceptance speech, Yousafzai also paid tribute to the 1991 winner, the Burmese democracy advocate Aung San Suu Kyi (awng san soo CHEE). For decades, Suu Kyi has been a model of persistence and patience in the difficult struggle for freedom in Burma (or Myanmar, as it was renamed by the secretive military officers who have ruled the country since 1962). After overturning election results that would have made Suu Kyi president of the country in 1990, the Burmese regime subjected her to years of house arrest. Suu Kyi was finally released in 2011 and elected to parliament in 2012, when the military allowed relatively fair elections. Still, the Burmese military holds the keys to power, allowing only gradual reform from the top down, and preventing Suu Kyi from becoming a candidate in 2015 presidential elections. In Burma and across the world, the struggles for democracy and for women's rights are inextricably linked.

A Year of Protest, Then Counter-Reactions

In 2011, hopes for expanded democracy ran high. The spark came from an unlikely place: a young Tunisian street vendor, tired of constant harassment by the police and by the corruption of municipal officials, burned himself to death in a public market. His act sparked a worldwide year of protest.

As protests spread across North Africa and the Middle East, many international observers found inspiration in the street demonstrations that became known as the Arab Spring. The massive prodemocracy encampment at Tahrir Square in Cairo was the epicenter of the movement. As in past revolutions, young people played a central role, their ability to organize and sustain massive demonstrations now greatly increased through the power of the Internet and social networking. Then came disappointment, as the military and political elites of Egypt restored control, a counter-reaction that was repeated across the Arab world and around the world.

● **CONTEXT&CONNECTIONS** As in Europe in the summer of 1848, the Arab world in 2011 saw street protests leapfrog from one capital to another, bringing high hopes for rapid and radical change. But just as in the Europe in the 1850s, those hopes were usually dashed when conservative leaders retook the initiative. Indeed, some Arab protesters would be able to relate to the travails of the Russian anarchist *Mikhail Bakunin* (Chapter 23) when, after organizing for democracy, they faced imprisonment or exile. ●

In Egypt, democratic elections in 2012 voted in the long-banned Islamist Muslim Brotherhood. However, when the Brotherhood seemed incapable of forming policies acceptable to the revolution's diverse constituencies, or even of organizing basic government services, the military stepped in, deposing the elected president and suspending the constitution. Many Egyptians applauded as the forces of "law and order" reasserted control and restored the long-standing proscription of the Muslim Brotherhood.

The greatest disappointment in the wake of the Arab Spring was unquestionably in Syria. Here the regime of Bashir Al-Assad, who became president in 2000

The Arab Spring Cairo has long been the political and intellectual center of the Arab world, and Tahrir Square in the center of Cairo was the focal point of the Arab Spring. Protesters, including many students, used social media to organize massive demonstrations that toppled the regime of Hosni Mubarak and cleared the way for free elections. The result, however, was a further military intervention in Egyptian politics after the Muslim Brotherhood, victors in those elections, proved deeply unpopular. In 2014, an Egyptian judge cleared Mubarak of all charges, including culpability in the death of hundreds at Tahrir Square. (Peter Macdiarmid/Getty Images)

with promises of reform, refused to countenance any meaningful change. A broad array of rebel groups then took up arms. While the international community disagreed over how to respond, civil war made refugees of over 4 million Syrians. It was into this power vacuum that the ruthless ISIS fighters stepped, as what had once seemed a promising chance at democratization in Syria degraded into a living hell.

While protests in the Arab world were intended to provoke fundamental constitutional change, popular movements elsewhere were less extreme, directed toward influencing existing governmental policies. In India, for example, an anticorruption activist named Anna Hazare mobilized millions using Gandhian tactics of nonviolent protest to call the country's political and business elite to account for squandering the nation's resources. Despite an anticorruption bill that finally passed in 2013 and the election of Hazare and his party to the majority in the Delhi state legislature in 2015, corruption remained deeply entrenched.

In the European Union, especially in Spain and Greece, the cause of protest was fiscal austerity. High unemployment and steep cuts to education brought students and recent graduates out into the streets, though cuts in wages, pensions, and government employment brought older workers out as well. Social benefits and free education, taken for granted for several generations, were now being withdrawn. The fault for the troubled economies, protesters argued, lay not with the ordinary people who were being hurt, but with the political and corporate elites who had mismanaged both national and international finances.

In the United States the issue was similar: in the wake of war and financial collapse, who should be held accountable for high unemployment, foreclosed homes, and the cuts in funding that led to increased college tuition? Two radically different movements emerged in response. Members of Tea Party organizations claimed that government itself was to blame and argued for a radically smaller federal government and sharp cuts in spending. "Occupy Wall Street" demonstrators, in contrast, focused on corporate greed and malfeasance as the root of the problem. While the Tea Party was absorbed into the Republican Party, and pushed it rightward, Occupy Wall Street remained outside the mainstream and had virtually no effect on public policy.

China remained relatively quiet. True, unrest was intense among some ethnic minorities, most dramatically in western China, where dozens of Tibetan monks set themselves on fire to protest government restrictions (see page 597), while tensions escalated between Han Chinese immigrants and the largely Muslim Uighur people of Xinjiang. But those protests did not affect the core areas of the Chinese population and economy. During the Arab Spring, Chinese leaders, ever fearful of a repeat of the Tiananmen demonstrations of 1989 (see Chapter 31), clamped down even further on freedom of communication.

Such was the global context for the arrest and detention of Ai Weiwei. The official media limited its coverage of events in Tahrir Square; authorities prevented the translation of foreign news reports and even blocked the word *Egypt* from search engines. It was Ai Weiwei's facility in the use of new media that made him dangerous enough to be detained after he launched an investigation into children's deaths following the Sichuan earthquake of 2008. (See the feature "Visual Evidence in Primary Sources: The Art of Ai Weiwei.")

Thus the 2011 "year of protest" passed with no major challenge to the political monopoly of the Chinese Communist Party. But hundreds of small eruptions had become common, often in out-of-the-way places with little media coverage. Will the Communist Party be able to put out all of those small fires one by one, while keeping the lid on larger-scale urban protest? Perhaps, as long as the economy continues to grow. But the lessons of history, and even the logic of Marxist philosophy, indicate that the emerging Chinese middle class will not remain content with economic benefits alone.

Once-in-a-decade changes at the top of the Communist hierarchy in 2012 led to even more draconian limits on expression. College textbooks, for example, came under scrutiny: "*Strengthen management of the use of original Western teaching materials,*" said the education minister. "*By no means allow teaching materials that disseminate Western values in our classrooms.*"* (Of course, there is *no* chance that Communist authorities will allow a book featuring Ai Weiwei into Chinese classrooms!)

But it is likely that China's booming middle class, long obsessed with the material benefits of economic growth, will sooner or later increase demands for

*Chris Buckley, "China Warns Against 'Western Values' in Imported Textbooks," *New York Times*, January 30, 2015.

basic freedoms, government transparency, and the rule of law. In 2014, protestors in Hong Kong briefly rekindled memories of the 2011 "year of protest" when they took to the streets to demand free elections. So far, it seems that the "one country, two systems" formula (see Chapter 31) has meant that Communist rulers in Beijing would increasingly impose their legal and political frameworks on relatively liberal Hong Kong. In 2014, they easily outmaneuvered the protestors. Who knows what the future will bring?

Global Art and Culture

Globalization has had mixed results. Myriad opportunities are offset by political confusion, economic anxiety, and increasing inequality. In the cultural domain, however, globalization seems more like an unmixed blessing.

Even in China, the barren propaganda of the Mao Zedong era has been replaced by a vibrant, globally connected art scene. Studios and galleries abound, especially in Beijing and Shanghai. Art schools are booming, and tens of thousands of Chinese art students study abroad.

Visual artists now push the envelope of social commentary, with ironic images of Mao Zedong and sly critiques of the Communist bureaucracy abounding. But everyone knows there are lines that must not be crossed: once artists follow Ai Weiwei's example and enter the public arena as advocates of change, the hammer falls.

Media and film are also areas where we find innovative national trajectories amid increasing transnational fertilization. The two most influential players are still Hollywood and Bollywood (the Indian industry that began in Bombay, today's Mumbai). In Africa, the rapidly expanding "Nollywood" industry of Nigeria is also becoming a regional player, with its audience globalizing as Africans move around the world (in both 2014 and 2015 Afro-British actors were nominated for Academy Awards).

● **CONTEXT&CONNECTIONS** An example of expanding transnational media is the Turkish phenomenon *Muhteşem Yüzyıl* (*The Magnificent Century*), a dramatization of life at the Ottoman court of Sultan *Süleyman* (Chapter 17). The show is one of the most popular *telenovelas* across Latin America, where it is shown in Spanish and Portuguese translation. *The Magnificent Century* is also a big hit dubbed into Arabic, inspiring Arab tourists to visit Istanbul's Topkapi Palace, where the show's intrigues actually took place.

For many people, spectator sports are a part of daily life, and here again we find the impact of globalization. Football (or soccer as it is called in the United States) is a prime example. Its modern rules developed in nineteenth-century Britain, and then traveled across the empire and beyond to become part of the texture of life around the world, feeding the hopes and dreams of young boys (and now girls, too). All across Europe, Latin America, and Africa, and increasingly Asia and North America as well, football is king. As one writer notes on the cultural globalization evident on the football pitch: "*Basque teams, under the stewardship of Welsh coaches, stocked up on Dutch and Turkish players; Moldavian squads imported Nigerians. Everywhere you looked, it suddenly seemed, national borders and national identities had been swept into the dustbin of soccer history.*"* Even if some fans bring

*Franklin Foer, *How Soccer Explains the World: An Unlikely Theory of Globalization* (New York: HarperCollins, 2004), pp. 2–3.

The Art of Ai Weiwei

Ai Weiwei practices conceptual art, with a predominant idea underlying artistic execution and materials and aesthetics embodying that driving concept. It is always relevant to ask of Ai's work: What does it mean?

Photography is one medium Ai has explored since his New York years (1981–1993). Here we see one of his most famous (and infamous) works, *Dropping a Han Dynasty Urn* (1995). Another series of photographs make up *Study of Perspective* (1995–2003), where each picture is framed at eye level with Ai's middle finger held up toward famous sites, such as Rome's Colosseum, the White House, Tiananmen Square, the Sydney Opera House, and the *Mona Lisa*. Search for *Study*

of Perspective online and consider what concept underlies the images.

Ai is also famous for large-scale public works, such as *Remembering* (2009) (shown opposite), a tribute to the children killed in the Sichuan earthquake. Another is 2011's *Sunflower Seeds* (seen with the artist in this chapter's opening), which featured millions of hand-crafted ceramic sunflower seeds strewn on the floor of London's Tate Gallery, provoking the viewer to question the relationship between nature and artifice, and between individuals and masses. The gallery's website (http://www.tate. org.uk/whats-on/tate-modern/exhibition/unilever-series-ai-weiwei/video) includes a video in which Ai Weiwei explains his rationale behind the piece:

Ai's goal is to make the viewer think. With this image, what thoughts and feelings might he be intending to provoke?

The vase Ai is dropping was genuine, two thousand years old, and quite valuable.

Ai's works question the destruction of cultural heritage in China's rush to modernize.

AP Images/Smithsonian's Hirshhorn Museum

Ai's works often confuse our assumptions about what we see as "real" and what we take to be "artificial." He often juxtaposes old materials and new forms, ideas of progress with emblems of tradition, and themes of perishing and persisting. For *Colored Vases* (2007–2010), Ai painted over valuable imperial vases with brightly colored industrial paints. In Miami, a disgruntled viewer, protesting at the globalization of art, smashed those painted vases.

to adapt an ancient porcelain technique to modern expression and to help maintain the traditional ceramics industry by employing sixteen hundred people in the production of the sunflower seeds.

Ai's work is especially appreciated in Germany, where many exhibits of his work have been launched. In *Remembering*, thousands of backpacks were fixed to the walls of Munich's *Haus der Kunst* (House of Art), one for each child killed in the Sichuan earthquake.

The backpacks are colored and arranged to spell out "*She lived happily for seven years in this world*" in Chinese characters.

Viewing the documentary film *Ai Weiwei: Never Sorry* is an excellent way to learn more about the artist. Even better would be viewing an exhibit of Ai's artwork.

Censors shut down the blog where Ai posted the kids' names, and the police severely beat him when he went to Sichuan to file a complaint. **Why were the Chinese authorities so angered by Ai's collection and dissemination of these children's names?**

Joerg Koch/AFP/Getty Images

Remembrance (2010) is a related piece, achieving a similar effect in a smaller space: one after another the children's names appear in Chinese script on a computer screen, with a voice reading each name aloud. The experience lasts for 3 hours 41 minutes before looping back to the beginning.

Ai purchased twisted steel rebar from the destroyed schools and had workers hammer it straight. His sculpture "Straight" used that reclaimed material in an undulating 38-ton steel carpet with a seam running up its center: "*The tragic reality of today is reflected in the true plight of our spiritual existence,*" he said. "*We are spineless and cannot stand straight.*"

their racism and xenophobia (fear of foreigners) into soccer stadiums, the world is still richer for the global crosscurrents displayed on the field.

When South Africa hosted the World Cup in 2010, it was a triumphant celebration for the African continent, as hundreds of millions learned more about contemporary African arts, rhythms, and cultures while watching the games. Likewise, Brazil's World Cup in 2014, although not without controversy, gave the country a chance to showcase the vibrant cultural mix in cuisine, music, clothing, and communication arising from the country's melding of African, Amerindian, and European influences.

Indeed, from soccer to basketball, from film to fashion, from home design to graphic novels, from hip hop to classical music—across the artistic landscape, the creative potential of cultural borrowing and mixing seems limitless. True, technology now allows us to experience the power of global culture from home. But as the story of Ai Weiwei and this book's entire series of travelers reminds us, *voyages* are still the best way to satisfy our curiosity and stimulate our creativity.

CONTEXT AND CONNECTIONS

Our Future Voyage

World historians need to be adept at moving across various temporal and spatial scales, from a single moment in time to the sweep of millennia, from individual lives, like that of Ai Weiwei and other travelers featured in *Voyages in World History*, to the development and interaction of global civilizations. In this chapter, we have narrowed the temporal dimension to the beginning of the twenty-first century, while attempting to keep the entire world in view. Now, in conclusion, we may widen our lens briefly to contextualize contemporary events in broader temporal perspective.

In these terms, the key issues are undoubtedly the interrelated ones of population, environment, and energy use. Though only 6.5 percent of the human beings who have ever lived were alive in 2011, they were having an unprecedented impact on the earth and its resources: land, water, and atmosphere. Our preindustrial ancestors relied principally on the power of their own muscles and those of domesticated animals, occasionally harnessing water, wind, and, in small quantities, coal. Since the Industrial Revolution, such constraints have been left behind. In just the past two decades, global energy use has skyrocketed by 39 percent, with growth rates highest in China (146 percent), India (91 percent), and Latin America (66 percent). While European energy consumption grew by just 7 percent during that period, the United States maintained its position as the largest per capita consumer of energy, each American using four times more than the global average. Are such rates of energy consumption sustainable? Will future conflicts be sparked by competition for dwindling energy and water resources?

An optimistic view of humankind's ability to support 7 billion and more people at reasonable levels of prosperity might come from reflection upon the mistake of Thomas Malthus, an early-nineteenth-century pioneer of population studies. Malthus believed that Britain was headed for an inevitable crisis as population growth came to outstrip the food supply. "*The power of population,*" he wrote, "*is indefinitely greater than the power in the earth to produce subsistence for man.*"* Yet Britain escaped the Malthusian trap by harnessing new technologies and energy sources. It remains to be seen, of course, whether an equivalent burst of technological progress can replicate that success on a global scale, where the stakes are much higher than in Malthus's time.

At any rate, the human story is about more than just production, consumption, and reproduction. Culture

*Thomas Malthus, *An Essay on the Principle of Population*, Oxford World's Classics (New York: Oxford University Press, 2008), p. 61.

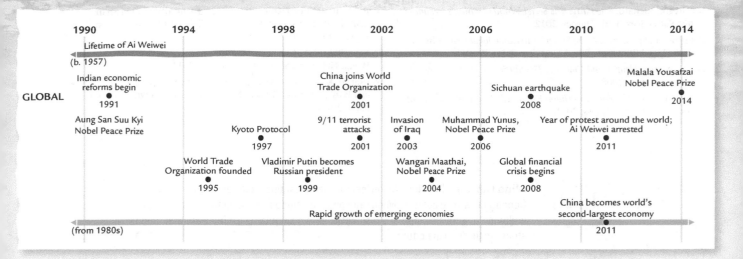

1990	1994	1998	2002	2006	2010	2014

Lifetime of Ai Weiwei
(b. 1957)

GLOBAL

Indian economic reforms begin
● 1991

Aung San Suu Kyi Nobel Peace Prize

World Trade Organization founded
● 1995

Kyoto Protocol
● 1997

Vladimir Putin becomes Russian president
● 1999

China joins World Trade Organization
● 2001

9/11 terrorist attacks
● 2001

Invasion of Iraq
● 2003

Wangari Maathai, Nobel Peace Prize
● 2004

Muhammad Yunus, Nobel Peace Prize
● 2006

Sichuan earthquake
● 2008

Global financial crisis begins
● 2008

Year of protest around the world; Ai Weiwei arrested
● 2011

Malala Yousafzai Nobel Peace Prize
● 2014

China becomes world's second-largest economy
● 2011

Rapid growth of emerging economies
(from 1980s)

matters, and at least since the Enlightenment, a vision of political, intellectual, and artistic liberation has inspired dreams of a better future. Yet progress is usually charted using only mundane economic indicators, as if increased consumption alone is the key to human fulfilment. In addition to material satisfaction, other measures were used in the United Nation's 2013 *World Happiness Report*, which found that the people of Denmark, Norway, and Switzerland were the most satisfied with their lives. Canadians ranked sixth. The United States came in at seventeenth, just below Mexico and just above Ireland.

As the human voyage continues, the African continent, where the human story began some 160,000 years ago, points the way forward. For all the challenges they have dealt with in their modern history, recent polls show that Africans are the most optimistic people on the planet. Perhaps Africans' persistent belief in and commitment to a better future for themselves and their children is a lesson for the world.

Key Terms

Ai Weiwei (968)
BRIC (969)
Vladimir Putin (970)
World Trade Organization (976)

Muhammad Yunus (976)
September 11, 2001 (978)
Kyoto Protocol (985)
sustainable development (985)
One Child Policy (986)

Malala Yousafzai (988)
dowry system (989)

For Further Reference

Ai, Weiwei. *Evidence*. Catalog of a 2014 exhibition at the Martin-Gropius Bau, Berlin. Edited by Gereon Sievernich. Munich: Prestel, 2014.

Appiah, Kwame Anthony. *Cosmopolitanism: Ethics Is a World of Strangers*. New York: W. W. Norton, 2007.

Bourguignon, François. *The Globalization of Inequality*. Thomas Scott-Railton, trans. Princeton, N.J.: Princeton University Press, 2015.

Farlow, Andrew. *Crash and Beyond: Causes and Consequences of the Global Financial Crisis*. New York: Oxford University Press, 2012.

Friedman, Thomas. *Hot, Flat and Crowded: Why We Need a Green Revolution*. Rev. ed. New York: Picador, 2009.

Klein, Naomi. *This Changes Everything: Capitalism vs. the Climate*. New York: Simon & Schuster, 2014.

Lynch, Mark. *The Arab Uprisings Explained: New Contentious Politics in the Middle East*. New York: Columbia University Press, 2014.

McGregor, Richard. *The Party: The Secret World of China's Communist Rulers*. New York: Harper, 2012.

Peterson, V. Spike, and Anne Sisson Runyan. *Global Gender Issues in the New Millennium*. 3d ed. Boulder, Colo.: Westview, 2009.

Sen, Amartya. *Identity and Violence: The Illusion of Destiny*. New York: Penguin, 2008.

Staab, Andreas. *The European Union Explained*. 2d ed. Bloomington: Indiana University Press, 2011.

Toft, Monica Duffy, Daniel Philpott, and Timothy Samuel Shah. *God's Century: Resurgent Religion and Global Politics*. New York: W. W. Norton, 2011.

Wright, Robin. *Rock the Casbah: Rage and Rebellion Across the Islamic World*. New York: Simon and Schuster, 2011.

Yousafzai, Malala. *I Am Malala: The Girl Who Stood Up for Education and Was Shot by the Taliban*. New York: Little, Brown and Company, 2013.

MindTap

MindTap is a fully online, highly personalized learning experience built upon Cengage Learning content. MindTap combines student learning tools—readings, multimedia, activities, and assessments—into a singular Learning Path that guides students through the course.

Index

Fur trade: Amerindians and, 544–546, 554; French Canadian, 545–546, 551, 554, 768; Russian, 520

Galápagos Islands, 704
Galen, 624
Galileo Galilei, 630; heliocentric theory and, 490, 620–621
Gama, Cristovão da, 473–474
Gama, Vasco da, 450, 471
Gandhi, Mohandas K. "Mahatma," 741; civil disobedience and, 859, 888; effect of World Wars I and II on viewpoint of, 816; *Hind Swaraj* and, 860–861
Garibaldi, Giuseppe, 699–700
Garvey, Marcus, 864
Gaulle, Charles de, 877, 889, 923
Gay rights, 930
Gempaku, Sugita, 624, 646
Gendered division of labor: Huron, 546; in China, 594
Gender relations. *See also* Men; Women: and race, in Spanish Americas, 540; women's rights and, 772–773
General History of the Things of New Spain (Sahagun), 434–435, 438, 448, 459, 467
Genesis (Bible), 490
Geneva Conference, 919
Genoa, colonies of, 436, 449
Genocide. *See also* Holocaust: Amerindians and, 767; Armenian, 823; in Herero rebellion, 790; in Rwanda, 964
Gens de couleur, in Haiti, 667–668, 678
Gentry. *See also* Land and landowners: British, 627, 694; Chinese, 720
Geography. *See also* Mapmaking, Ptolemy and, 449, 454
George I (England), 645
George III (England): China trade and, 598; as farmer king, 623, 626
Georgia (Caucasus): nationalism in, 937; Russian invasion of, 979 and map
Georgia (United States), 572, 766
German Confederation of the Rhine, 666
German Democratic Republic. *See* East Germany
German East Africa, 815; revolt in, 792
German(ic) languages, 487, 538
Germany. *See also* Nazi Germany: industrialization in, 688, 701; nationalism in, 677 and map; romanticism in, 691; socialism in, 691; unification of, 701, 713; Chinese territories of, 722; imperialism in, 779; African colonies of, 785 (map), 788, 790, 792, 815; New Guinea and, 794; in World War I, 815–816; at Paris Peace Conference, 818; World War I reparations and, 821, 843; after World War I, 820–821; Weimar Republic, 821, 843; Cold War division of, 896; reunification of, 942; European Union and, 958; global recession of 2008 and, 958; fiscal debate and, 977; energy initiatives of, 984–985
Ghana, independence of, 913
Ghost Dance Movement, 766
Gilded Age, in North America, 755–757

Glasnost (openness) in Soviet Union, 937, 940
Global climate change, 983; Arctic and, 983
Global Crisis: War, Climate Change and Catastrophe in the Seventeenth Century (Parker), 528
Global economy (global trade network): American civil war and, 754; American silver in, 495, 537; British empire, 686; telegraph and, 689–690; Great Depression and, 846; Bretton Wood Conference and, 897; financial crisis (2008–2012), 977
Globalization: Industrial Revolution and, 688–690; Americanization and, 934; art and, 993; Deng Xiaoping's China and, 956–957; European Union and, 954, 958, 959 (map); gender issues, 988; health and environmental issues, 985; liberalism, 960–961; inequality and, 954, 969; neoliberalism and, 959, 962; disease transmission and, 984; sports and, 993
Global warming, 529, 985
Glorious Revolution of 1688, 519
Gods and goddesses: sun-gods, 439–440, 442; Aztec Mexico, 438, 440; Inca, 443; Mesoamerican, 539; African slave, 571; Hawaiian, 639; master clock maker, 623
Gold: West African, 477; as medium of exchange, 439; East African, 471; from Americas, 455, 461, 755; African, 471, 562, 564, 777, 788–789; Brazilian, 543; on Amerindian lands, 542, 766; "distress jewelry," in India, 846
Gold Coast. *See* Ghana
Goldman, Emma, 806–808, 811, 816, 822, 825, 828–830, 834, 922; travels of, 807 (map); on women's rights, 834–836
Gorbachev, Mihkail, 939; in Beijing, 940; coup attempt against, 940; Cuba and, 943; reforms of, 926, 935, 937, 940, 957, 961
Gouges, Olympe de, 658
Government. *See also* Administration: Aztec Mexico, 438; Mughal India, 481; colonial Americas, 464; British, 694, 717; Locke's theory of, 652; Ottoman reforms, 708; Qing China, 717; Japanese industry and, 731; responsible, in Canada, 748; United States, 750, 766
Government of India Act, 859
Grameen Bank (Bangladesh), 976
Gramsci, Antonio, 848
Granada, Muslims driven from, 453
Granado, Alberto, 900
Gran Colombia, 670, 672, 673 (map), 678, 911; collapse of, 678
Grand Banks fisheries, 579
Grand Canal (China), 482
Grasslands. *See also* Great Plains, in Americas, 465
Great Britain. *See* Britain (England)
Great Depression (1930s), 846, 870; global effects of, 846; in industrialized world, 843–845; in Nazi Germany, 850; effect on colonial exploitation, 858

Greater East Asian Co-Prosperity Sphere, 878
Great Exhibition (London), 696–697
Great Lakes region: East Africa, 561, 563 (map); North America, 750
Great Leap Forward (China), 903
Great Plains (North America): agriculture in, 689, 749; Indians of, 546, 747, 766, 768
Great Proletarian Cultural Revolution, 930
Great Purges, of Stalin, 854
Great Schism (1054), 487
Great Speaker (Aztecs), 440, 459
Great Trigonometrical Survey, 633 (illus.)
Greco-Roman culture, images of power in, 656
Greece: independence of, 677 and map, 710; nationalism in, 677 and map; relations with Turkey, 856; civil war in, 896; European Union and, 958, 959 (map), 977; global recession of 2008 and, 958; financial crisis in (2011–2012), 977; fiscal debate and, 977; protests in, 992
Greek language, 448
Greenhouse gases, 985
Greenwich Observatory, 631
Grito de Dolores, 674
Guadalcanal, Battle of, 880, 884
Guadalupe Hidalgo, Treaty of, 759
Guangxu (China), 721
Guangzhou (Canton): international settlement in, 718; trade in, 597; foreign investment in, 956
Guatemala: CIA involvement in, 897; United States' intervention in, 901; democracy in, U.S. underming of, 911; death squads in, 943
Guevara, Ernesto "Che," 674, 900–901, 905; in Bolivia, 902, 927, 931; in Congo, 916; in Cuba, 906–907; Guatemala and, 911; legacy of, 931; revolution promotion by, 921; travels of, 901 (map)
Guillotin, Joseph, 661
Guillotine, in Reign of Terror, 661
Guinea, 913, 983
Gunpowder technologies (guns). *See also* Cannon: Ottoman, 502, 517; muskets, 502; of Spanish conquistadors, 452, 460; in China, 595; saltpeter for, 606; Amerindians and, 546; machine guns, 789; Maxim gun, 791
Guomindang (Nationalists, China), 870; army of, 888; Communists and, 826, 865, 866 (map), 903
Gutenberg, Johannes, 449
Gypsies (Roma), 885, 889, 986

Habsburg dynasty, 511; in Austria, 505, 511, 517, 698; Ottoman empire and, 505, 512; failure to hold Europe together, 514; military affairs of, 516–517; women in, 516; in Spain, 533, 555
Haciendas (estates): Latin American, 536–537, 551, 774; Mexican, 765

I-20 Index